Information for Efficient Decision Making

Big Data, Blockchain and Relevance

Information for Efficient Decision Making

Big Data, Blockchain and Relevance

Kashi R Balachandran
New York University Leonard N Stern School of Business, USA

World Scientific

NEW JERSEY • LONDON • SINGAPORE • BEIJING • SHANGHAI • HONG KONG • TAIPEI • CHENNAI • TOKYO

Published by

World Scientific Publishing Co. Pte. Ltd.
5 Toh Tuck Link, Singapore 596224
USA office: 27 Warren Street, Suite 401-402, Hackensack, NJ 07601
UK office: 57 Shelton Street, Covent Garden, London WC2H 9HE

Library of Congress Cataloging-in-Publication Data
Names: Balachandran, K. R., editor.
Title: Information for efficient decision making : big data, blockchain and relevance / Kashi R Balachandran, New York University Leonard N Stern School of Business, USA.
Description: Singapore ; Hackensack, NJ : World Scientific, [2020] | Includes bibliographical references and index.
Identifiers: LCCN 2020026479 | ISBN 9789811220463 (hardcover) | ISBN 9789811220470 (ebook) | ISBN 9789811220487 (ebook other)
Subjects: LCSH: Decision making. | Blockchains (Databases) | Big data.
Classification: LCC HD30.23 .I534 2020 | DDC 658.4/038028557--dc23
LC record available at https://lccn.loc.gov/2020026479

British Library Cataloguing-in-Publication Data
A catalogue record for this book is available from the British Library.

A word on the cover:
The cover art shows six panels of a painting that depicts the exponential growth of knowledge from darkness and ignorance enveloping the little person to an intensifying brighter and clearer world. The scenario becomes more complicated with the explosion and interconnectedness of information. The first panel of bare indigo dark landscape becomes illuminated by a constellation of signs and symbols connected to one another in a myriad way in the successive panels. The black, orange, yellow circles symbolize the semiotics of meaning creation and meaning communicated by the little person, the decision analyst.

The artist Dr. Rajini Sarma Balachandran is a Ph.D. in Political Science from New York University and has exhibited her paintings in the New York/New Jersey area.

For any available supplementary material, please visit
https://www.worldscientific.com/worldscibooks/10.1142/11833#t=suppl

Desk Editors: Balamurugan Rajendran/Daniele Lee

Typeset by Stallion Press
Email: enquiries@stallionpress.com

https://doi.org/10.1142/9789811220470_fmatter

Preface

This book came out of a desire to consolidate information that can be suitable for making decisions in firms to make their operations efficient to reduce their costs and consequently, increase their profitability. Historically, the primary source for firm information is through published accounting statements prepared according to generally accepted accounting principles. This is true for those decision-makers who have no access to private inside information. Managers within a firm have access to inside operational information and the data set is larger and more reliable. The data are gathered through a centralized ledger keeping of activities of the firm. The advent of blockchain has generated great interest as an alternative to centralized organizations. Decentralized ledger keeping, one of the main features of blockchain, has given rise to many issues of technology, development, implementation, acceptance, evaluation, and so on. Blockchain concept is a follow-up to big data environment facilitated by enormous progress in computer hardware, storage capacities, and technological prowess. This has resulted in acquiring of data not considered possible earlier, and with shrewd modeling analytics and algorithms, the applications have mushroomed to significant levels. This handbook is an attempt to discuss the progress in data collection, pros and cons of collecting information on decentralized publicly available ledgers and several applications. A few chapters in this book amplify on the reliable vs. relevant characteristics of information that has been a point of discussion among accounting personnel.

Chapter 1 by Chen, Cong, and Xiao, "A Brief Introduction to Blockchain Economics", looks at the economic and behavioral aspects of the introduction of the new technology in organizations. The chapter gives an overview of what blockchain is, how they are found to be useful in several applications, and what are the impediments to their usage. Numerous economic characteristics of this new technology are discussed. An alternative to blockchain as a distributed ledger technology is termed Directed Acyclic Graph, and these two concepts are compared. The basic characteristic of the blockchain technology lies in the provision of decentralized consensus referring to consensus agreements on transactions, providing, in addition, protocols for conflict resolution, aiding maintenance of history of events, institutional memory, immutable records, etc.

With the advent of big data phenomenon, there is a clamor to go for it and attempt to devise approaches to use it to improve efficiencies of decision-making in contracts, production, and operations. Particularly, it is well established that the contracts can become more efficient in principal–agent relationships if information can be gathered on the effort and/or private information of the agent resulting in reduction of moral hazard. Essentially, the two issues of moral hazard and agent's private information that are unobservable to the principal can be mitigated with the vast data that can be gathered and processed. Puaschunder (Chapter 2, "Data Fiduciary in Order to Alleviate Principal–Agent Problems in the Artificial Big Data Age") in her chapter contributes to the idea that there are conflicting utilities for the agent in making all data about him/her become known to the principal, lest it be misused. Even outside the principal–agent framework, the problem of individuals' decision to share information about themselves on social media can enable big data administrators to reap benefits from putting data together over time and reflecting the individual's information in relation to big data of others. This can work against the interests of the agent and even the principal if the data become public information. The author introduces a utility theory based on fundamental economic principles and builds the concepts to study this issue. She also considers the possibility of long-term, cumulative effects of such dissemination of information. Blockchain technology faces a challenge on the issue of privacy of participants, and this chapter contributes to this vital point.

One of the challenges of implementing blockchain is the cost of implementation and the replacement of existing systems with the new one. Bhimani, Hausken, and Arif (Chapter 3, "Blockchain Technology Adoption Decisions: Developed vs. Developing Economies") argue that these impediments to blockchain differ according to whether the country is economically developed or still developing. Their adoption is facilitated where there is a desire for transparency and trust and other benefits and the costs of shifting investments onto the technology seem worthwhile. In developing economies, blockchain adoption finds resistance by those who benefit from the lack of transparency and abusers of the economic system. Further, blockchain adoption can seem desirable particularly when regulatory barriers are low. They analyze how emerging and developed economies differ in relation to the point at which the benefits of blockchain exceed the costs leading to the adoption of the technology. The chapter provides an outline of reception to blockchain adoption in various countries of the world and explains how and why they differ.

Blockchain, conceptually and practically, brings in a strong form of decentralization without a centralized authority. Should this get to be implemented, the question would be how it would affect the functioning of the economy. The development is still at an embryonic stage in terms of conceptual development, practical application, and academic research. When fully implemented, there is expectation of fewer obstacles to truthful information exchange among concerned parties. For example, capital market could become more efficient with blockchain and big data, and along with usage of cryptocurrency, trading and completion and recording of transactions can take place simultaneously with no time lag. Since the role of middlemen and central banks will get diminished, it could be termed a decentralized set up. Zhang, Zandi, and Kim (Chapter 4, "A Discussion on Decentralization in Financial Industry and Monetary System") in their chapter argue how this will likely improve the welfare of all participants. How far the central agency can be done away without loss of firm-wide total welfare is still a vexing question. The authors examine some cases of hypothetical decentralized markets to elaborate how an economy composed of such settings would function with resultant costs, benefits, and risks.

Funding of developing and manufacturing innovative products is through a contract between the investors and the producers. There is risk involved in such a venture, particularly for the investor who is often external to the producer. The innovating firms that seek external funds are typically not yet fully established as otherwise they could use internally generated funds. Financing such projects can be quite difficult. Recent innovations in digital ledger technologies and business models have the potential to mitigate some of these identified problems, if they can be used to construct smart efficient contracts. Tinn (Chapter 5, "Raising Funds with Smart Contracts: New Opportunities and Challenges") discusses the extent to which the new technologies such as blockchain can eliminate historically identified important frictions and make the economic system more efficient. However, the author brings out the emergence of new forms of frictions and unresolved issues coming out of adoption of these technologies. The chapter focuses on analyzing two recent FinTech developments, distributed ledger technologies and crowdfunding, that may have the greatest potential to mitigate or alter the type of frictions young innovative firms face. Several unresolved issues and ongoing debates on this topic are also brought forward. The investors may find it very costly or impossible to verify claims by entrepreneurs on cash flow, profitability, and success probabilities of the new ventures. Debt contracts are instituted between the investor and the entrepreneur to minimize the expected verification costs by using information more readily available. The chapter explains simple smart contracts. Digital technology has the potential to reduce or even eliminate much of the verification costs. The chapter considers that there is a shared blockchain that guarantees that the cash flows the project generates through successful sales are recorded and verifiable on an ongoing basis. The efficacy of such smart contracts over the less flexible debt and equity contracts is discussed.

There is a natural relation of blockchain to accounting as a transaction ledger and its possible uses in accounting functions and business operations. George and Patatoukas (Chapter 6, "The Blockchain Evolution and Revolution of Accounting") discuss the classification and characteristics of cryptoassets, as well as initial coin offerings, by which cryptoassets are sold as a means to fund startup blockchain ventures. They follow it up with a discussion of the evolving global regulatory environment for cryptoassets and ICOs and the accounting treatment of this new asset class. The importance of blockchain development to auditing of financial reports due to the continuous assurance given by blockchain is amplified. However, the new technology does not, as yet, provide sufficient and complete audit evidence. The auditors have the opportunity to use innovative audit techniques that utilize the verification characteristics of blockchain networks and thus increase the efficacy of the audit process. The authors explore application of the technology to supply chain networks and contracting, characterized by a lack of trust between transacting parties, yet transparency and verification of information remaining important. As such, it is well suited to aid in data sharing and communication among the various organizations in a supply chain and in bringing accountability and transparency to enable efficient contracting.

Blockchain technology has garnered a lot of interest among professionals, educationists, and practitioners. However, Alles and Gray (Chapter 7, "What Accountants Need to know about Blockchain") observe the enthusiasm primarily at the top management CEO level but reservations at the technologist level in companies. They caution that immediate applications of blockchain in the accounting arena do not match the enthusiasm expressed by many. The chapter provides an overview of the concept of blockchain, the cryptocurrency, and their relationships. They elaborate on the costs involved with implementation of cryptocurrencies in conjunction with blockchain. There are several stumbling blocks in implementing this technology in accounting. Accounting may have to be adjusted or remodeled to incorporate the use of this technology and make it useful and cost-effective. The chapter gives a balancing approach to the issue of this subject.

Cupertino, Taticchi, and Vitale (Chapter 8, "Management Control and Information, Communication and Technologies: A Bidirectional Link — The Case of Granarolo") provide through a real case study the coordination needed to link management control systems with information, communication, and new technologies. Information, Communication and Technologies (ICT), they find currently in place, is inadequate to coordinate the process between presales efforts to garner new clients to get them on board to effectively manage to the end of sales fruition. The chapter illustrates how a new innovation in technology can be integrated into the company operations. In the case of ICT solutions, technology alone could be useless if not accompanied by adequate training of people, re-engineering of business processes, as well as wide organizational change. This is likely in any implementation of new technological innovation.

Prices in stock markets are influenced by information available, publicly, or sometimes, privately by certain large stockholders. The latter may be termed illegal trading in the arena of capital markets. The stockholders and analysts need to be contended with company information that may not be available in regulated financial statements, gleaned, and studied from past returns patterns or company information reported in the press coverage. Partha Mohanram (Chapter 9, "A Brave New World: The Use of Non-traditional Information in Capital Markets") details another form of information source that is creeping into the public domain due to increased computer capacity through big data. Suitable analytics can be used to process this information, and it will have an impact on the capital market functioning. The author, in particular, looks at the social media where peer-to-peer information is shared. He provides the implications of this form of information sharing on functioning of firms, information analysts, potential and current investors, regulatory auditors, and academics. The information base for the workings of the capital market has changed a lot from the pre-Internet era of 1985–2019 with a new multitude of information made available. With the coming of big data and possibly blockchain along with cryptocurrency, decisions taken on capital market transactions are infused with incorporating data unimaginable in previous years. This chapter elaborates such development.

A large amount of information about firms come out in unstructured verbal forms through various sources of textual data such as news media management discussion and analysis (MD&A) sections of the annual report, risk factor discussions, proxy statements, conference call or meeting transcripts, analyst reports, and patents. Cong, Liang, Yang, and Zhang (Chapter 10, "Analyzing Textual Information at Scale") take this challenge and discuss approaches to distil textual information to a useful form for decision-making. Further, the authors discuss the current approaches to textual analysis in social sciences, statistics, and machine learning. With the increased capacity of modern-day computers and the idea of big data, the sources for the unstructured information have mushroomed. It is a challenge to obtain useful information in a manner that will augment the standard information available using the financial statements. This is in addition to quantitative databases already incorporated in the public domain. Textual information is more interpretable than numbers or ratios. Addition of this makes the information base very robust to aid decision-making. They assess several methodologies for textual analysis and focus on information richness, computational efficiency, as well as economic interpretability. See also the chapter by Mohanram (Chapter 9) where he analyzes the information that can be gleaned from social media.

The advent of blockchain technology has found an application to the solution of supply chain operation to create transparency and help in risk management. Companies seem to be enthusiastically investing money in this area. However, Medhi (Chapter 11, "Blockchain-Enabled Supply Chain Transparency, Supply Chain Structural Dynamics, and Sustainability of Complex Global Supply Chains — A Text Mining Analysis") points out that blockchain-enabled, network-wide transparency and visibility also inject new dynamics into supply chains through the introduction of structural changes like redefining what is organizational boundary and creating new resources and a new transactional economy for supply chain management. The author adopts a text mining technique, topic modeling, to determine the focus areas of supply chain processes in organizations with examples of successful application of blockchain technology. He provides an exhaustive theoretical explanation about how firms can create sources of competitive advantage from blockchain technology. Identification of the focus areas, using topic modeling, is shown to help operations and supply chain managers planning to implement blockchain technology and devise plans for data-centric decision-making for enhancing efficiency in supply chain management.

Agency conflicts are endemic in large corporate governance. They create moral hazard where actions by an agent are not observable to the principal at the helm of the organization. A large body of literature is devoted to obtaining information on the efforts taken at the agency level in order to mitigate the extent of the moral hazard. Attempts to monitor agents can be costly with high transaction costs and negative behavioral reactions. Kaal (Chapter 12, "Blockchain Solutions for Agency Problems in Corporate Governance") highlights the possible evolving solutions offered by blockchain technology to help mitigate the agency problem. He argues why the scope and scale of full development of blockchain technology will have to go through numerous stages taking several years to mature. As the development progresses, agency problems in corporate governance can become more adequately manageable over time. The support structures needed for this technology development are complex and numerous and sometimes independent of one another. The author elaborates on how blockchain application will face numerous hurdles, yet give hope to improving the contractual relationship between a principal and an agent. The idea of Decentralized Autonomous Organizations (DAOs) is discussed to build a governance structure built on software, code, and smart contracts that runs on the public decentralized blockchain platform Ethereum. The DAO does not use a traditional corporate structure necessitating formal authority and empowerment flowing top-down from investors/shareholders through a board of directors to management and eventually staff. Essentially, all the core control mechanisms typically employed by principals in agency relationships are removed in the DAO. The author describes this process in detail.

Cryptoproducts such as cryptocurrency form an essential part of blockchain technology implementation. However, the introduction of cryptocurrency products appears to be an emergent threat to national security and individual's wealth through any speculative trading of the product and abuse by rouge identities. Agarwal, Agarwal, Agarwal, and Agarwal (Chapter 13, "Economics of Cryptocurrencies: Artificial Intelligence, Blockchain, and Digital Currency") propose setting up cryptocurrency as another form of money supply along the lines of other currency products developed in the last 50 years. This, they argue, will promote the efficiency in the money markets and transactional efficiency and generate wealth along with positive contributions to GDP and people at large. They see the need for the creation of legitimate cryptocurrencies by national governments to induce confidence and *laissez-faire* through transactional efficiency in money market. They propose a modeling of cryptocurrency to facilitate an approach to achieve transactional efficiency in the money market. The efforts in various countries to tackle the new digital currency are enumerated.

Global warming and carbon emissions have become life-surviving issues in the world. Companies are increasingly asked to act in cognizance of this concern and report their activities that may impact the climate crisis. The data requirement to report this to the public and to themselves go far beyond the current regulated accounting systems. The use of a blockchain-enabled carbon accounting system can more effectively account for and manage carbon emissions in organizations that face the universal concern of the exposure of carbon risk. Tang and Tang (Chapter 14, "Developing Blockchain-Based Carbon Accounting and Decentralized Climate Change Management System") argue that blockchain would be a strong tool for national and international climate change management and collaboration. Blockchain may help establish an integrated system for climate change management that will allow stakeholders and participants share climate change data and information, so as to enhance the international collaboration and achieve the target of carbon-neutral society in more efficient way and at a lower cost.

With the increased global concern on greenhouse gas emissions and consequent climate catastrophes, carbon information on efforts to reduce carbon emissions has become critical to keep stakeholders informed about individual company's strategies, risks, and actions on the gas emissions and in turn to monitor and aid their decision-making. There is awareness on the part of companies that they suffer material risks related to climate change. The consequences may be on several directions. Their facilities may be directly affected through the impact of greenhouse gas, by climate change policies or regulations, changes in consumption pattern with conscientious consumers switching to products with a lower effect on climate change, and short-term adjustments of contract conditions such as insurance carriers requesting higher risk premiums due to high climate change exposure. Thus, consumers, regulators, and insurance organizations may be keenly interested in the carbon footprints and gas emissions of the companies. He, Luo, and Tang (Chapter 15, "Usefulness of Corporate Carbon Information for Decision-Making") discuss these issues in their chapter. The opportunities to use the accounting reports, in both financial and managerial parts, are explored. They provide a theory of incentives to provide the motivations and determinants for the companies to voluntarily disclose information. Whether such information can be made useful for stakeholders of the company, particularly stockholders and debt holders, is brought out culminating in a discussion of voluntary carbon reporting format.

Li and Merchant (Chapter 16, "Motivating Innovation and Creativity: The Role of Management Controls") bring up a discourse on when, where, and how management controls can have positive, rather than negative, effects on employee creativity leading to organizational innovation. Such innovation can lead to economic growth and better organizational performance. They distinguish between innovations that lead to applicability to enhance growth and those that do not, though they have to be termed creative endeavors. Such creative endeavors can be risky, expensive, and long term. How do we measure their effectiveness and applicability to growth potential? The chapter elaborates research into identifying management control variables that lead to productive decisions and hence growth of the firm. Incentives to motivate good innovations are explored in this chapter. In todays' fast-changing technological progress with vast information availability and reduction of moral hazards through truth-inducing contracts and information gathering such as through blockchain, healthy innovation research is very essential to any firm.

The corporate board plays an important role in providing useful information to the stockholders and lenders of publicly listed corporations. The dynamics in the board could affect the quality of information provided through the choices they make. If the information quality is poor, the investors face a higher uncertainty about their invested money (referred to as information risk) and are likely to lose trust in the reported information. Srinidhi (Chapter 17, "Board Governance and Information Quality") argues that the quality of firm-specific information generated and provided is determined by the incentives faced by managers (particularly the CEO), the CEO's personality attributes, and the managers' interaction with the board of directors. This chapter deals mainly with the effect of board structure, its composition, and director attributes on information quality.

Firms' assets need to be valued fairly is an accepted statement. That leads to fair value accounting. When a firm is purchased by another, there may be a difference between the purchase price and the fair value assigned to the bought assets that lead to the concept of goodwill. Now, what to do with the goodwill is a topic of this chapter by Bryan, Lilian, Sarath, and Yan (Chapter 18, "Evolving Standards of Fair Value and Acquisition Accounting"). The assets valued at fair value at the time of purchase and the resultant determination of goodwill are relevant to further decision-making by the firm. However, depending on the nature of the assets, fair value estimates may be difficult to assess and may even accommodate manipulation by interested parties. They illustrate the case of a holding company buying another at a bargain price during a stressed time in the economy and how decisions can be affected.

As blockchain theory progresses, its intended application comes with different models in order to mesh with the model that is in place to make it usable. For example, in supply chain applications, the blockchain has to mesh with data requirement for enterprise resource planning implementation. So, the data analytics becomes very important and the need to gather information from the transactional data of blockchain to facilitate the decision-making process. Blockchain data may not be in a readily usable format. As a result, the data taken from blockchain may need to be queried. O'Leary (Chapter 19, "Evolving Blockchain Applications: Multiple Semantic Models and Distributed Databases for Blockchain Data Reuse") discusses the emerging trends and develops a "blockchain-like" application with blockchain and distributed database capabilities for the case of a virtual organization. An important characteristic of almost every accounting or supply chain system is the need to be able to perform a broad range of queries in order to gather information from the data. Unfortunately, since "pure" blockchain-based systems are focused on capturing and preserving transactions, they have virtually no processing and querying capabilities. The chapter claims the blockchain is likely only a small part of what the system does and much is done "off-blockchain". The author develops this idea further with details of BigchainDB in a virtual organization to coordinate their operations utilizing idle resources and special expertise of independent organizations.

Regulated financial reporting of companies has, for long, toiled with the balance between providing relevant information and reliable information. Ronen (Chapter 20, "Have Accounting Reports Become Less Useful for Decision-Making?"), contends that such a balancing act need not be and proposed approaches to make reports issued by companies both relevant and reliable. Now comes the new era of big data with blockchain ledgers, smart contracts, and increased data gathering capacities coupled with innovative algorithms to aggregate the data into useful decision-making formats. Ronen incorporates the new developments to point out that the new developments complement the financial reporting rather than replace them. In fact, the added information is useful to investors, regulators, and analysts who traditionally rely on external financial statements released by the company but also can aid management to make operation decisions. In this vein, he proposes new concepts to inform the prospective investors of the risk tradeoffs of the company. The chapter shows gaining further improvements by overhauling the financial reporting model itself in such a way as to further facilitate prediction and reduce information asymmetry by providing management's inside information, as well as by according the provided information both relevance and reliability, rather than striving for a balance. To paraphrase Ronen, he remodels accounting to facilitate the elicitation of management's inside information in a way that incentivizes truth telling and provide information about historical events and transactions as well as current valuations and future expectations in such a way as to make it both relevant and reliable. His proposal, in combination with emerging big data and machine learning, makes possible not only enhanced predictive ability but also an assessment of managerial skill and/or the honesty of management's expectations against realizations over time.

Given the increasing amount of data made available with the increased capacity of computers and the possible advent of blockchain, it is tempting to assume that efficiency in decision-making will increase. However, Balachandran (Chapter 21, "Value of Fixed Asset Usage Information for Efficient Operation: A Nontraditional View") illustrates that it is important to use the appropriate information suitable for the decision at hand. The chapter with a very popular problem of deciding on dropping a product with a negative income shows how the traditionally regarded relevant information of variable costs is irrelevant and the traditionally viewed irrelevant fixed costs are indeed the relevant costs for this decision-making. The chapter further provides a framework of classifying all the fixed costs that may be useful for decision-making. Essentially, the point made is, given the large amount of data, it is very imperative to build proper analytics and algorithms to aggregate the data with models to facilitate good decision-making.

The health sector necessarily deals with many participants in delivering health support to the patient. The data enveloping any patient is large and widespread over doctors including primary care and specialists, hospitals including emergency and scheduled care, medical test labs, medical equipment vendors, clinical trial researchers, pharmaceutical providers, insurers, and governments. The data generated for any patient is huge and can include not only their treatments but also their behavioral patterns for taking care of their health. The advancement of big data storage and retrieval capacity has enhanced the ability to store all this data and make them available to all the participants. Artificial Intelligence and clever algorithms can convert the data into useful formats for making efficient decisions. Participants may be in locations wherever the patient goes, sometimes even across countries. This new capability can help store such data to be made available in any location for any care giver. Issues of how this effort has progressed is detailed by Sharma, Mehra, and Gupta (Chapter 22) in, "Role of Blockchain, AI and Big Data in Healthcare Industry". Blockchain can help remove the role of an overall, powerful administrator of the data collection and usage by giving it to the participants including the patient. The patient can exert authority as to what can be placed on the record, who can be permitted to see, and how the data may be used. The authors also discuss the role of smart contracts to aid supply of medical aids by the vendors and other billing, collection matters. The blockchain is argued to provide accuracy of data and help incentivize participants to act in the welfare of all and in particular the patient. They do state that considerable further work needs to be done to make the system operable.

The handbook covers a wide range of topics focusing on the new advents with big data, blockchain, and social media information and shows the importance of developing the data into useful forms to facilitate decision-making. The added issues of privacy of data valued by information owners and agency issues such as moral hazards are discussed. Those who make decisions and the development stage of countries also play a role in making gathered information available to decision-makers. The role of information used for performance evaluation in facilitating innovation forms an important part of this book. An interesting case study on implementing a new system with the added data is elaborated.

The world of information technology is progressing rapidly from the pre-Internet era to now. Some of the drawbacks of installing blockchain or utilizing big data, cryptocurrency along with artificial intelligence may reduce with further advancement such as the much talked about quantum computing. Applied decision-making areas have to be cognizant of these developments and learn to utilize them. This handbook will prove useful reading providing a storehouse of knowledge on the emerging topic. It is particularly suited for the curious academics with an eye on the progress in practice and the practitioners with the determination to look into the thinking of academics. That is the spirit in which I have worked on the development of the handbook.

https://doi.org/10.1142/9789811220470_fmatter

About the Editor

Kashi R. Balachandran is a Professor Emeritus of accounting and operations management at the New York University Stern School of Business.

He joined Stern in 1979. His primary research covers a wide spectrum of diverse areas including optimal operation of service congestion systems, stochastic processes, economic incentive contracts and mechanisms, transfer pricing determinations, conceptualization of unused capacities and their optimal utilization, warranty contracts, quality enhancement programs and reporting, activity-based costing systems, business measurement systems and optimal performance evaluations, sustainable business development, global climate warming research, and management educational process. Professor Balachandran has written and published more than 85 articles in leading academic journals such as *Econometrica, Accounting Review, Journal of Accounting Research, Operations Research, European Journal of Operational Research, Management Science*, and numerous other journals. He served as the Editor-in-Chief of the *Journal of Accounting Auditing and Finance* and the Senior Consulting Editor of *Journal of Applied Management Accounting*. In addition to serving on the editorial boards of several journals, he has also acted as a invited guest editor of special issues. He has refereed for numerous journals and research-funding agencies, including the National Science Foundation. He has organized numerous conferences and symposiums for JAAF in New York and Europe. As the organizer of the annual KPMG/JAAF conference in New York, he coordinated with KPMG on their funding for the conference. He was on the staff of Ross Institute of Accounting Research at New York University that develops liaison with industry in addition to serving as the Associate Director. He has served as the Doctoral Program Director of Accounting at the New York University.

Professor Balachandran has taught as visiting or regular faculty at the University of Wisconsin, the Georgia Institute of Technology, University of Kentucky, SDA Bocconi University, Italy, University of Rome–Tor Vergata, International University of Japan, and Tunghai University of Taiwan. He has delivered more than 700 lectures internationally in the United States, Europe, Asia, and Asia Pacific in several conferences and universities including delivering several keynote speeches. He served as a member of the Wisconsin Governor's Commission on Education, Asian American Advisory Council to the Governor's office in New Jersey, and as an advisory member of the Woodrow Wilson Society Town Meeting Forum to Governor of New Jersey.

Professor Balachandran is a continuing member of the International Advisory Board of the Indian Institute of Finance Business School in India, has served as Distinguished Institute Professor of G.D. Goenka World Institute, was the advisor for instituting their joint program on fashion management with Polytechnico di Milano–Italy, and has served as the Executive Director of the Glocal University in India in forming the university from its inception.

Professor Balachandran earned his Bachelor of Engineering (with honors) in Mechanical Engineering from the University of Madras, India Master of Science in industrial engineering and Doctor of Philosophy in operations research from the University of California, Berkeley, and his certificate in management accounting from the Institute of Management Accountants.

https://doi.org/10.1142/9789811220470_fmatter

About the Contributors

Aman Agarwal is a Professor of Finance and Director(Rektor) of the Indian Institute of Finance. He is Executive Editor of Finance India. He has been awarded a Chair position of St. Emillion Brotherhood (from 8th Century AD) by Heritage City of Bordeau, France (2007); "United Nations REX Karmaveer Global Fellowship" and "Karmaveer Chakra Award" by United Nations and iCongo, India (2019); Life Fellow Award by Waseda University ISME in Japan (2014) and Vietnam (2019). He was nominated for the Honorary Doctorate of Finance by University of Cergy-Pontoise Thema, France (in 2007) and the Honorary Professorship by Tashkent State University of Economics, Uzbekistan (in 2002). He has studied at the Delhi University, Indian Institute of Finance, London School of Economics, and Columbia University and worked at The World Bank in Washington DC, USA. He has been invited to deliver guest of honor/chief guest/plenary keynote address speeches at over 168 international and government forums, including Italian Parliament, European Parliament, Finland Parliament, Swedish Parliament, Uzbek Parliament, Chinese Ministry of Commerce (MOFCOM), Chinese Ministry of Foreign Affairs, International Agencies, and over 112 Universities.

J. D. Agarwal is a Distinguished Professor of Finance and Founder Chairman of Indian Institute of Finance. He is Editor-in-Chief of *Finance India*. He is a leading economist and financial expert. In the past, he has taught at Shri Ram College of Commerce (University of Delhi), Indian Institute of Technology, Delhi, Ahmadu Bello University, Nigeria, London

Business School, London, and Cleveland State University, USA. He has contributed significantly to promote the field of finance in the last four decades through education and research. One of his most important contributions is to found the prestigious Indian Institute of Finance in 1987. The Institute has become a center of excellence and a base for scholarship in the last 33 years. Professor Agarwal started and developed a quarterly journal of finance, *Finance India*, as an international journal. He has written over 15 books, edited over 130 volumes of *Finance India*, published more than 142 research papers, and has authored more than 38 book reviews, 500 case studies, and working papers. His students include over three cabinet ministers, a judge in Supreme Court of India, former Chief Election Commissioner, dozens of senior government officials, CEOs of banks and other leading business executives, lawyers, vice-chancellors and deans of foreign and Indian universities, media personalities, and successful entrepreneurs.

Manju Agarwal is a Senior Professor of Economics and Dean (Academics) at the Indian Institute of Finance. She has served as a Principal at Moti Lal Nehru College and an Associate Professor at MLNC University of Delhi South Campus. She obtained her Ph.D. on Tax Incentives and Investment Behaviour from the University of Delhi, MA in Economics from the Delhi School of Economics and BA Hons. in Economics from the University of Delhi. In addition, she did ITP at the London Business School. She has taught commerce for 50 years at all levels of classes. She has authored six books in the area of tax incentives, investment behaviour, managerial economics, international finance, and microeconomics. Her writings have been widely appreciated in national dailies such as *Times of India*, *Financial Express*, *Indian Express*, *Patriot*, *National Herald*, and *Economic Times*. She has written 24 research articles and 138 book reviews.

Yamini Agarwal is the Director of IIF Business School [AKTU]; Professor of Finance & Economics of the Indian Institute of Finance, and Associate Editor of *Finance India*. She obtained her Ph.D. in finance from the Indian Institute of Technology–Delhi, Master of Commerce from Delhi School of Economics, Management of Business Finance (MBF) from Indian Institute of Finance, and Bachelor of Commerce (Hons.) from the University of Delhi, and attended a program on Strategic Business Management sponsored by the Swedish International Development

Agency (SIDA) in Stockholm, Sweden. She has published two books. Yamini appears frequently on government and non-government media channels for her opinions on economic and government policy issues. Her research work has been published in the *Journal of Accounting, Auditing and Finance*, *Finance India*, *The Indian Economic Journal*, *International Journal of Innovative Management, Information & Production*, *Economy Transdisciplinarity Cognition* (Romania), *Euro Mediterranean Economic and Finance Review* (EMEFR France), and *Lahore Journal of Economics* (Pakistan), among others.

Michael Alles is an Associate Professor at the Department of Accounting and Information Systems at Rutgers Business School. Prior to Rutgers, he taught at the University of Texas at Austin, New York University, and Southern Methodist University. His specialties are the design of strategic control systems, continuous auditing, management accounting, and corporate governance. He has widely published in all these areas. Dr. Alles holds a Ph.D. from Stanford Business School and a First Class Honors in Economics from the Australian National University. He has served on the Executive Committee of the Management Accounting Section of the American Accounting Association, and he organizes the World Continuous Auditing and Reporting Conference held each year in Newark. He was also the Editor of the *International Journal of Disclosure & Governance*, published by Palgrave Macmillan in London.

Sameen Arif holds distinction degrees in Accounting and Finance from the London School of Economics and Lahore University of Management Sciences (LUMS). Her research interests include credit markets, accounting in the digital economy, financial management, and accounting quality. She is currently involved in various research projects at LUMS and is part of the visiting faculty at Information Technology University.

Alnoor Bhimani is a Professor of Management Accounting at the London School of Economics in the UK. He is former Head of LSE's Department of Accounting and Founding Director of LSE Entrepreneurship. He has written widely in the areas of financial management, tech startups, digitalization, cyber issues, and economic development. His ongoing research deals with how technologies are reshaping financial practices, work, and education. Alnoor is author of over 20 books and 100 scholarly journal articles. He has published in *Review of Accounting Studies*; *Journal of Information Technology*; *Accounting, Organisations and Society*; *Management Accounting Research*, and *Journal of Accounting and Public Policy* among others. He speaks internationally on technology, management, and societal issues and sits on the advisory boards of universities in Africa, America, Europe, and Asia. Alnoor obtained his MBA from the Cornell University, where he was a Fulbright Scholar, and holds a Ph.D. from LSE.

Stephen Bryan, Ph.D., is a Professor of Accounting at Fordham University, New York, NY. He obtained his Ph.D. from New York University. He has published in numerous academic and practitioner journals, such as *The Accounting Review*, *Journal of Accounting, Auditing, and Finance*, *Journal of Business, Harvard Business Review*, *Journal of Corporate Finance*, *CPA Journal*, and *Financial Management.*

Long Chen is the Director of Luohan Academy, the Executive Provost of the Hupan School of Entrepreneurship, and serves on the IMF's FinTech advisory board. He was formerly the Chief Strategy Officer of Ant Financial and had served as the Deputy Chief Director of China's Internet Securities Association and Deputy Chairman of China's Internet Insurance Association. He has also served as a tenured Professor at Washington University in St. Louis and as the Associate Dean of the Cheung Kong Graduate School of Business.

Lin William Cong is the Rudd Family Professor of Management and Associate Professor of Finance at Cornell University, where he also directs the FinTech Initiative. Previously, he was an Assistant Professor of finance at the University of Chicago Booth School of Business. He primarily researches on financial economics, information economics, FinTech and Economic Big Data, and entrepreneurship. He has published in top-tier finance journals and is recognized with numerous awards such as the Kauffman Junior Faculty Fellowship, AAM-CAMRI-CFA Institute Prize in Asset Management, and the CME Best Paper Award. He has also been invited to speak, teach, or advise at multiple world-renowned institutions, companies, and government agencies such as IMF, the Asset Management Association of China, and the SEC.

Sebastiano Cupertino is a Lecturer and Postdoctoral Fellow in Management Control at Department of Business and law as well as staff member of the Italian Secretariat in supporting "Partnership on Research and Innovation in the Mediterranean Area" (PRIMA) program at University of Siena (Italy). His research interests primarily focus on corporate sustainability and innovation, advanced management control systems, and business administration.

Kimberlyn (Kimmie) George is a Ph.D. student in the Accounting Department at Berkeley Haas and a Fisher Center for Business Analytics Doctoral Fellow. Previously, she received her BA in economics and BBA in accounting from the University of Texas at Austin. Kimmie is interested in studying the ways in which accounting information and financial disclosure influence capital markets. More specifically, she studies how individual investors use and consume financial information and accounting-related regulation. Outside of these areas, she is interested in researching how emerging technologies such as blockchain and cryptocurrency impact financial reporting and capital markets.

Glen L. Gray is a Professor Emeritus in the Accounting and Information Systems Department of the David Nazarian College of Business & Economics at California State University at Northridge, USA. His extensive research interests include blockchain, big data and data analytics, AI, machine learning, XBRL, sustainability, auditing and assurance services, IT controls, and electronic commerce. He has conducted major research projects funded by the AICPA, IAASB, IIA, ISACA, FASB, IASC, Big 4's Research Advisory Board, and KPMG. He has been a frequent speaker at academic and professional conferences in the USA, Europe, and Asia and has written numerous academic and professional articles.

Pankaj Gupta is President of Indian Institute of Health Management Research University. Prior positions include Professor and Executive Director at O.P. Jindal Global University, Delhi, and senior leadership positions in several top organizations such as IMT Ghaziabad, IIM Kozhikode, Symbiosis, the University of Washington. Dr. Gupta provides top level guidance to universities on management education and transformative leadership, creating innovative management ecosystems, identifying and recruiting the right talent, nurturing and retaining them, and thus making a significant contribution to the organizations and the people. He is a Ph.D., CMA, Fulbright Fellow (Washington), GCPCL (Harvard) and an alumnus of Lucknow University and IIM Ahmedabad. Dr. Gupta is the recipient of several prestigious awards including, the "Fulbright Fellowship" by USIEF, "Most Innovative Idea in Management Education Award" by IMC, "Valuable Contribution to Profession Award" by ICAI, and "Rashtriya Shiksha Gaurav Award" by CEGR, etc. Dr. Gupta has created an innovative model for "Academic Audit" and "Academic Quality Assurance System". He teaches courses and gives consultation in 'finance and cost management' and "self-awareness and mindful leadership". Some of the organizations that have benefited from the training/consulting of Prof. Gupta include Maruti, Dabur, GE Capital, Ericsson, Electrolux, NTPC, LIC, Genpact, Bry Air, Samtel, Elin Electronics, Shriram Pistons, IREDA, NEC Corp, CBI, Indian Navy, etc. With numerous books, consulting projects and research papers to his credit, Dr. Gupta is a much sought-after speaker at top business schools, corporations, and organizations across the globe.

Kjell Hausken is a Professor of economics and societal safety at the University of Stavanger, Norway. His research fields are strategic interaction, risk analysis, public choice, conflict, game theory, terrorism, information security, and economic risk management. He holds a Ph.D. from the University of Chicago, was a Postdoc at the Max Planck Institute for the Studies of Societies (Cologne), and a Visiting Scholar at Yale School of Management. He has published 250 articles in peer reviewed journals, one book, edited two books, is/was on the Editorial Board for *Theory and Decision, Reliability Engineering & System Safety, and Defence and Peace Economics.* He has refereed 400 submissions for 85 journals, and has advised numerous Ph.D. students.

Rong He is a Ph.D. candidate in Accounting at University of Newcastle, Australia. Her research primarily focuses on corporate climate change-related issues and capital markets.

Wulf A. Kaal is a leading expert at the intersection of law, business, and emerging technology. His research focuses on innovation, technology, emerging technology applications, digital assets, smart contracts, technology strategy, decentralized infrastructure products, private investment funds, and dynamic regulatory methods. Before entering the academy, he was associated with Cravath, Swain & Moore LLP, in New York, and Goldman Sachs in London, UK. Kaal advises central banks, international policymaker, governments, medium to large enterprises, law firms, startups, and venture capital funds on emerging technology solutions. As an expert witness, Kaal works closely with major law firms and business consultants.

Henry Kim is an Associate Professor at the Schulich School of Business, York University in Toronto, and is the Director for blockchain lab at Schulich. He has authored more than 25 publications on blockchain topics and over 70 overall. He is the co-organizer for the Fields Institute Seminar Series on Blockchain and the 2020 IEEE Conference on Blockchain and Cryptocurrencies, and serves on the faculty of Don Tapscott Blockchain Research Institute. He also serves as a senior research fellow at startups Novera and Insolar. He received his Ph.D. in Industrial Engineering from the University of Toronto.

Daniel E. O'Leary is a Professor in the Marshall School of Business at the University of Southern California, focusing on artificial intelligence, text mining, emerging technologies, crowdsourcing, innovations, and social media. Dan received his Ph.D. from Case Western Reserve University. He is the former editor of *IEEE Intelligent Systems* and the present editor of John Wiley's *Intelligent Systems in Accounting, Finance and Management.* His book, *Enterprise Resource Planning Systems*, published by Cambridge University Press, has been translated into both Chinese and Russian. Much of Professor O'Leary's research has involved studies on AI and emerging technologies and their use in business settings.

Shelley Xin Li received her Doctoral Degree in Business Administration (Accounting and Management) from the Harvard Business School in May 2016. After graduation, she joined the Leventhal School of Accounting at the University of Southern California as an Assistant Professor of accounting. Shelley's primary area of research examines the role of management control and corporate governance mechanisms in driving innovation and long-term performance. She analyzes archival data and employs field experiments in her research. Her dissertation examined the problem of motivating employee innovation in a multi-tasking environment. She won the AAA/Grant Thornton Doctoral Dissertation Award. Shelley's research has been published in T*he Accounting Review* and the *Journal of Accounting Research.*

Tengyuan Liang is an Assistant Professor of econometrics and statistics at the University of Chicago Booth School of Business. His research primarily focuses on data science, statistical theory, and learning theory. He has published in top-tier journals such as *The Annals of Statistics*, *Journal of Royal Statistical Society*, and *Journal of Machine Learning Research.*

Steven Lilien is a Weinstein Professor of Accountancy at the Zicklin School of Business, Bernard Baruch College. His articles have appeared in *The Accounting Review*, *Journal of Accounting and Economics*, *Journal of Business*, *Journal Accounting*, *Auditing and Finance*, and the *CPA Journal*. He has co-authored books on financial accounting, auditing practice and standards, and accounting information in litigation actions.

Le Luo is a Senior Lecturer in Accounting at Macquarie University, Australia. She has done research in the areas of sustainable business and low-carbon development, carbon accounting, and emission trading scheme. She has published about 20 papers in various journals including *British Accounting Review*, *Journal of International Accounting Research*, *The International Journal of Accounting*, *Accounting and Finance*, *Business Strategy*, and the *Environment*. Her two papers have received the Emerald Award and highly Commended Award. She is also the recipient of the Vice-Chancellor's Award and Faculty Award for ECR and Innovation and Dean's Prize for Citations from the University of Newcastle.

Pankaj Kumar Medhi is an Assistant Professor in Operations Management and Data Analytics at the School of Management, Bennett University. His research primarily focuses on supply chain management, rail transportation, innovation, and data analytics. He has published in top-tier journals, such as *International Journal of Production Research*, *European Journal of Innovation Management*, *Emerald Emerging Market Case Studies*. He had been a member of various study groups appointed by the Indian Railways to study policy matters related to rail transport in India.

Shikha Mehra is a certified Bitcoin professional and co-founder of MainChain Research & Consulting in the Crypto and Blockchain ecosystem. As a subject expert, her expertise has been sought from audiences as varied as the OECD, the Russian Parliament, the UK Government (F&CO), Indian Chamber of Commerce (ICC), YPO, Confederation of Indian Industries (CII), South Australian Premier (ADC forum), European central bankers at the European Congress Centre in Austria, Institute of Charted Accountants of India, FICCI, India's Central Bureau of Economic Intelligence, the former deputy National Security Advisor to the Indian Government, and tax tribunal members among others. She writes for the Daily Guardian among other publications. More information can be found at www.MainChain.Co.in.

Kenneth A. Merchant holds the Deloitte & Touche LLP Chair of Accountancy at the University of California. His research is focused on various issues in the fields of management accounting, management control, and corporate governance. He has published 11 books, including *Management Accounting: An Integrative Approach* (2017) and *Management Control Systems: Performance Measurement, Evaluation and Incentives* (2017), as well as numerous journal articles and teaching cases. His articles have appeared in such prominent outlets as *The Accounting Review*, *Journal of Accounting Research*, *Management Science*, *Journal of Accountancy,* and *The Wall Street Journal*. From the American Accounting Association, Professor Merchant has won two Lifetime Contribution Awards (for management accounting and behavioral accounting), three Notable Contribution Awards, and one Best Paper Award. He has also won significant awards from the Institute of Management Accountants (IMA) and the American Institute of Certified Public Accountants (AICPA). He is currently a member of the editorial boards of 15 academic research journals. Professor Merchant earned his Ph.D. from the University of California, Berkeley.

Partha S. Mohanram is the John H. Watson Chair in value investing at the Rotman School of Management, University of Toronto. He is a leading expert in the areas of valuation, fundamental analysis, cost of capital, and corporate governance. His numerous honors include the Haim Falk Award for lifetime contribution to accounting research and the Rotman School's

Research Impact Award. His papers are highly cited and featured in the *New York Times*, *Forbes*, *The Globe*, and *Mail* and other publications. He has discussed his research on CNBC's *Squawk on the Street*, NPR, and TVO (TV Ontario).

Professor Mohanram is an Editor of *Contemporary Accounting Research* and serves on the editorial board of *The Accounting Review* and *Review of Accounting Studies*. He serves on the Executive Committee of the CFEA Consortium and co-organized the 2016 CFEA conference.

Panos N. Patatoukas is a tenured Associate Professor and the L. H. Penney Chair in Accounting at Berkeley Haas. Panos' work focuses on interdisciplinary capital markets research and informs "micro-to-macro" and "macro-to-micro" questions bridging the gap between academics and practitioners. For his impact on interdisciplinary capital markets research, Panos has been recognized twice with the Notable Contributions to Accounting Literature Award of the American Accounting Association and the American Institute of Certified Public Accountants. For his teaching, Panos has been recognized with the 2018 Distinguished Teaching Award, which is the highest award bestowed by the Chancellor of U.C. Berkeley for outstanding and meritorious teaching at the Berkeley campus. Panos is the founding Faculty Director of the Berkeley ExedEd program on Financial Data Analysis.

Julia M. Puaschunder educated as a behavioral economist with doctorates in social and economic sciences and natural sciences, and Master's degrees in business, public administration and philosophy/psychology as well as training in global political economy and finance. Julia Margarete Puaschunder has over 15 years of experience in applied social sciences empirical research in the international arena. Before starting a Prize Fellowship in the Inter-University Consortium of New York at The New School with placements at Columbia University and Princeton University, she held several postdoctoral positions at Harvard University and the Vienna University of Economics and Business. She has published numerous books and journal articles and was awarded the 2018 Albert Nelson Marquis Lifetime Achievement Award. She has also been included in the "2018 Marquis Who's Who in America and in the World" and is an official listee of the "2019 Marquis Who's Who in the World" among the top 3% of professionals around the globe.

Joshua Ronen is a professor of accounting at the New York University Stern School of Business. Professor Ronen teaches courses in managerial accounting, financial accounting, advanced topics in financial accounting, and financial statements analysis.

Professor Ronen has been with NYU Stern for nearly 40 years. His primary research areas include capital markets, disclosure, earning management, economic impact of accounting rules and regulations, financial reporting, legal liability of firms, transfer pricing, agency theory, corporate governance, and fair valuation.

Professor Ronen has written numerous books including *Accounting and Financial Globalization*, *Off-Balance Sheet Activities*, *Entrepreneurship*, *Smoothing Income Numbers: Objectives, Means and Implications*, and *Earnings Management*. He has published his work in many academic journals including *The New York Times*, *The Accounting Review*, *Journal of Accounting Research*, *Journal of Accounting*, *Auditing and Finance*, *Abacus*, *Management Science*, *Journal of Public Economics*, *Journal of Organizational Behavior and Human Performance*, *Stanford Journal of Law*, *Business*, *and Finance*, and *Journal of Financial Markets*. Additionally, he is the Co-editor of the *Journal of Law*, *Finance, and Accounting*.

In addition to his work at NYU Stern, Professor Ronen has lectured at the University of Canterbury, Tel-Aviv University, Federal University of Rio de Janeiro, National University of Mexico, University of Toronto, University of Chicago, Hebrew University, and London School of Economics, among many others. He has also been a consultant for numerous organizations, including especially law firms as expert witness in the area of securities litigation. His suggestions for reform in the accounting profession have received critical acclaim by legislators and also in the media.

Bharat Sarath graduated with honors in Mathematics from the University of Cambridge, England. He subsequently received a Ph.D. in Mathematics from the University of Calgary, Alberta, Canada, and a Ph.D. in Accounting from Stanford University. Dr. Sarath's Ph.D. thesis in accountancy dealt with theoretical models of auditor malpractice and the role of insurance in affecting litigation patterns. He has published widely in economics, accounting, mathematics, and physics journals and is currently Editor-in-Chief of the *Journal of Accounting, Auditing and Finance*.

Dr. Sarath is currently a Professor in the Accounting and Information Systems Department at Rutgers University, New Brunswick. He teaches accounting at all levels (undergraduate, masters, and Ph.D.) at Rutgers and has conducted Executive Education Classes in accounting at many leading financial firms including Citibank and Credit Suisse and managerial accounting at the United Nations. Dr Sarath has traveled widely and speaks several Indian languages as well as Russian and Farsi.

Prashant Sharma is an Associate Professor at IIHMR University. Prior positions include Assistant Professor and Program Director at Jaipuria Institute of Management, Jaipur, and research fellow at National Institute of Financial Management (NIFM). At NIFM, he was part of the study team that conducted research on "Unaccounted Income and Wealth in India and Abroad", sponsored by Government of India. He has a Post Graduate degree in Finance and Marketing Management from School of Management, Gautam Buddha University and graduated in Mathematics from B R Ambedkar University, Agra. He contributes in data analytics, asset pricing dynamics, corporate finance, capital markets, and econometrics. He has published numerous papers and presented at various national and international conferences conducted at reputed institutes. He is the recipient of Best Faculty Award and Best Research Methodology Award for paper presentation in a doctoral conference.

Bin Srinidhi is the Carlock Endowed Distinguished Professor at the University of Texas, Arlington. He has civil service and corporate experience in addition to academia. He has published over 50 articles in professional and academic journals on topics spanning accounting, board diversity, governance, and quality management. His publications include articles in top-tier journals such as *The Accounting Review*, *Journal of Accounting and Economics*, *Management Science*, *Contemporary Accounting Research*, and *Review of Accounting Studies*. He has also co-authored a book on capital structure and has contributed several chapters to edited books. He serves currently as the co-editor of *The Journal of Contemporary Accounting and Economics*.

Lie Ming Tang is an expert in blockchain technology. His research interest is in application of emerging technologies in climate change management, carbon accounting, and health care. His research work has been published in leading IT and accounting journals.

Qingliang Tang is Professor in Accounting at the Western Sydney University. His research primarily focuses on accounting for climate change and sustainability accounting. He is one of the major contributors in carbon accounting literature in the world. He has published in top-tier journals such as *British Accounting Review*, *Accounting, Auditing and Accountability Journal*, *International Journal of Accounting*. He is a recipient of numerous awards and research funding.

Paolo Taticchi is a Professorial Teaching Fellow in Management and Sustainability at the Imperial College London.

Paolo's research is internationally recognized. At Imperial, Paolo teaches modules on "Sustainability and Competitive Advantage" and "The Future of Cities" among others. Paolo regularly offers keynotes in international government and corporate summits. Outside of the academy, Paolo has significant consultancy experience in the fields of strategy, operations, and sustainability. Currently, he serves in the advisory board of influential organizations in Canada, India, the UK, and the US. Paolo is also active in the entrepreneurial space, co-founding three firms in the fields of engineering and consultancy. His research, projects, and opinions have featured over 200 times in international media outlets. In 2018, Paolo was featured in the "40 World's Best Business Professors under 40" by prestigious international websites and rankings Poets&Quants. The same year, Paolo was awarded the decoration of Knight of the Order of Merit of the Italian Republic.

Katrin Tinn is an Assistant Professor of Finance at McGill University, Desautels Faculty of Management. She is a research fellow at CEPR and a member of the CEPR Network on Fintech and Digital Currencies, the Centre for Global Finance and Technology at Imperial College Business School, and the Imperial College multidisciplinary Fintech Network. Her research focuses on the interactions between technological innovation and finance, information economics, crowdfunding, and quantitative trading and her works have been published in the *American Economic Review and Management Science*. She has given talks on FinTech at academic and industry conferences in Canada, United States, United Kingdom, France, Switzerland, and Estonia. In addition to academic positions, she has also worked in commercial banking and asset management, the European Central Bank, the International Monetary Fund, and the European Bank for Reconstruction and Development.

Gianluca Vitale is a Ph.D. student at Business Administration and Management Doctoral School of University of Pisa (Italy) as well as staff member of the Italian Secretariat in supporting "Partnership on Research and Innovation in the Mediterranean Area" (PRIMA) program at the University of Siena (Italy). His research interests are focused on Management Control in SMEs, Industry 4.0, and Business Administration.

Yizhou Xiao is an Assistant Professor of finance at the Chinese University of Hong Kong. He obtained his Ph.D. in Finance from the Stanford Graduate School of Business. His research primarily focuses on information economics, Fintech, and entrepreneurial finance. He has published in top-tier journals such as the *Journal of Finance*.

Yan Yan joined Fairleigh Dickinson University as an Assistant Professor in the Department of Accounting, Taxation, and Law in the Silberman College of Business. Before joining FDU, she was an Adjunct Lecturer at Baruch College, the City University of New York.

Dr. Yan earned her Ph.D. with an accounting concentration and MBA from Baruch College, the City University of New York. She received her BS in accounting from Southwestern University of Finance and Economics in China. Her research focuses on fair value accounting, international accounting standards, and cost behavior.

Baozhong Yang is an Associate Professor of Finance and the Director of FinTech Lab at the Robinson College of Business at Georgia State University. He received his Ph.D. from the Stanford University and MIT. He organized the inaugural and second GSU-RFS FinTech Conferences and has served on the program committees of many conferences. His research interests are primarily in FinTech, corporate finance, and investments. He has published in leading journals such as the *Journal of Finance*, *Journal of Financial Economics*, *Review of Financial Studies*, and *Management Science*. His work has won prizes such as the Emerald Citations of Excellence in 2016, the Yihong Xia Best Paper Prize, and Chicago Quantitative Alliance Academic Competition and he has received grants from the National Science Foundation.

Farrokh Zandi is currently a faculty member in the economics area and the Associate Director of Undergraduate Programs and the Director of

International Business designation at the Schulich School of Business, York University in Toronto, Canada. He holds a Ph.D. in economics from Carleton University in Ottawa, Canada. His fields of specialization are international economics, economic policy, and monetary economics. He completed his undergraduate degree in economics and business administration from the Pahlavi University in Shiraz.

He joined York University in 1991 and has previously taught at several other universities in Canada including McGill University in Montreal. Farrokh Zandi has published several manuscripts in refereed economic journals and has written textbooks, instructor manuals, guides, and articles in professional journals.

Farrokh Zandi is a recipient of numerous awards and recognitions. In the academic year 2017–2018, he received the first-place teaching excellence award for his teaching in the graduate programs. He regularly appears in media such as Canadian Broadcasting Corporation and Canadian Report on Business as well as Persian-speaking media, such as Iran International, CBC, and VOA.

Alfred Ruoxi Zhang is an M.Sc. Economics student at The London School of Economics and received his BBA from the Schulich School of Business, York University. He has conducted research projects relating to economics and decentralized technologies under both academic and corporate settings, with organizations such as blockchain lab at the Schulich School of Business and Guantao Law Firm in Toronto. His work as the first author has been published on *Frontiers in Blockchain*. His primary research interests are in mathematical economics and macroeconomic applications of information technologies.

Xiao Zhang is an associate at Analysis Group. He received his Ph.D. in finance and MBA from the University of Chicago Booth School of Business. His research interests include behavioral finance, machine learning, corporate restructuring, and distressed debt investments. Prior to his doctoral studies, Xiao graduated from the Joint Honors Program in Economics and Finance at McGill University. He is a recipient of the John and Serena Liew Fellowship and Victor Dahdaleh–Clinton Foundation Scholarship.

https://doi.org/10.1142/9789811220470_fmatter

Contents

https://doi.org/10.1142/9789811220470_0001

Chapter 1

A Brief Introduction to Blockchain Economics

Long Chen*, Lin William Cong†,§ and Yizhou Xiao‡

Luohan Academy, Xixi Road Hangzhou, China

†*Cornell University, Ithaca, NY, USA*

‡*Chinese University of Hong Kong, Hong Kong*

§*will.cong@cornell.edu*

Abstract

We introduce economic research on blockchains and its recent advances. In particular, we highlight the (i) unifying concepts on blockchain as a decentralized consensus and its core benefits, (ii) equilibrium characterizations and allegedly irreducible tensions among consensus formation, decentralization, and scalability, (iii) major issues including network security, overconcentration, energy consumption and sustainability, adoption, multi-party computation and encryption, smart contracting, and information distribution and aggregation, and (iv) future directions concerning blockchains and their applications such as informational and agency issues, as well as game-theoretical and mechanism design approaches to blockchain protocols.

Keywords: Bitcoin; Consensus protocol; Cryptocurrency; Distributed ledger; Smart contracts.

1. Introduction

The advancement in technology has made us increasingly connected in this digital age. Also undeniable is the corresponding increase in the demand for peer-to-peer interactions that are instantaneous and open, which can transform how people work, consume, and invest. Some of the most valued companies in the world such as Amazon, Alibaba, and Facebook all connect dispersed users and product/service providers. They also give rise to the so-called "gig/sharing economy" wherein on-demand labor gets instantaneous payments instead of relying on long-term employment contracts that are confined by geography and legal jurisdictions.

Integral to this development is digitization of information, which can be broadly interpreted to include digitization of assets too because a digital asset such as a Bitcoin is in principle a string of numbers and alphabets (or 0s and 1s) after all. Because digitized information is non-rival and can be transferred, used, and reproduced almost costlessly, it transcends traditional boundaries of firms and organizations and physical locations, drastically increasing the quantity and quality of economic activities and reshaping business organizations.

While digital technology helps overcome limits in offline markets, digitization alone is insufficient. While smartphones and online apps providing instant access to goods together with virtually unlimited access to wireless high-speed broadband connections all seem to exponentially grow connectivity and lower the cost of segmentation for many industries' production processes (e.g., Fort, 2017), successful platforms and production organizations still depend heavily on payment and contracting innovations (e.g., Taobao and eBay) as the lack of trust among anonymous agents or in an open system is the key obstacle for economic exchanges.

Recently, instead of relying on financial systems that are often arranged around a series of centralized parties like banks and payments, clearing and settlement systems, blockchain-based cryptoapplications attempt to resolve the issue by creating the financial architecture for peer-to-peer transactions and interactions and reorganizing society into a series of decentralized networks. By providing decentralized consensus, blockchains allow peers distant from and potentially unknown to one another to interact, transact, and contract without relying on a single centralized trusted third party. It also holds the potential to better coordinate and organize oft-segmented individuals and groups, thus fully unleashing the latent productivity hidden in traditional economies due to localized information and geographical constraints.

Technically speaking, blockchain is just one of the many distributed ledger technologies. It first became popular due to the emergence of the cryptocurrency Bitcoin. It has since manifested itself in various other forms, often with the ability to store and execute computer programs. This gave rise to applications such as smart contracts, featuring payments triggered by a tamperproof consensus of contingent outcomes and financing through initial coin offerings. Among many other applications, Maersk and IBM used blockchain for tracking and better logistics in freight shipping and trade credit; Walmart also worked with IBM for supply chain delivery; Stellar and Ripple have revamped the payment and remittance system; Ant Financial implemented blockchain-based cross-border transfers in 2018 and electronic receipts in medical insurance in 2019, among others (Luohan Academy, 2019). Blockchains have also found applications in the areas of healthcare and insurance (Yermack, 2017; Yue *et al.*, 2016; Raikwar *et al.*, 2018). Media articles and research papers such as those by Chiu and Koeppl (2019), Cong and He (2018), and Reese (2017) contain other examples of blockchain applications. We neither repeat the existing and potential applications of the technology nor elaborate on the technical details that computer scientists have discussed extensively. Instead, we focus on the key economic issues brought forth by the technological innovations and associated applications.

A discussion of blockchain invariably appears incomplete without talking about cryptocurrencies and tokens. Indeed, there is as much novel economics in the use of cryptotokens as there is in the blockchain infrastructure and architect. We leave it out for separate discussions for two reasons. First, we want to correct the misconception that cryptocurrency and blockchain are equivalents or interchangeable. Second, a fast-emerging literature studies cryptocurrencies and cryptotokens, either jointly with blockchain or independent of the technical aspects of decentralized ledgers. In some regard, cryptocurrencies and tokens are also closely related to the literature on monetary economics, banking, and platform economics. It is impossible to reproduce a complete list of relevant articles here and doing so would take too much focus away from our main topic. We therefore refer the readers to studies such as those by Cong *et al.* (2018b), Chod and Lyandres (2018), Liu and Tsyvinski (2018), Cong *et al.* (2019), Gan *et al.* (2019), Lyandres (2019) and the references therein for further discussion. In particular, the study by Halaburda and

Sarvary (2016) gives an excellent overview of digital currencies and that by Cong (2019) provides a concise introduction to the economics of tokens and digital currency.

Our paper is not meant to be a survey of research on blockchains. Instead, our goal is to first clarify from an economic perspective what blockchains are (or envisioned to be) and why they are (or would be) useful and then introduce a generalized concept of desirable features together with a conjecture of their irreducible tension. We then highlight key economic issues surrounding blockchains before pointing out future research directions and challenges to tackle in practice. For more comprehensive surveys, interested readers may consult Townsend (2019) for an insightful overview of DLTs; Hilary and Liu (2018) for a general survey of research on blockchain economics; Tschorsch and Scheuermann (2016) and Conti *et al.* (2018) for discussions on security privacy issues; Biais *et al.* (2019b) and Liu *et al.* (2019) for game-theoretical analyses on blockchains; and Halaburda and Haeringer (2018) for economic and computer science studies specifically related to Bitcoin.

The remainder of the paper is organized as follows: Section 2 defines the general concept of blockchain and explains its main advantages over traditional systems. Section 3 introduces protocol games and design before highlighting the three desirable features of blockchain design and the seemingly irreducible tension among them. Section 4 examines key economic issues surrounding the technology, such as network security, energy consumption, and adoption limitation, with a particular effort to underscore two hitherto underexplored information-related dimensions i.e., information distribution and aggregation in decentralized systems, as well as the innovation of permissioned blockchains in enabling better multi-party computation and information exchanges. Finally, Section 5 summarizes promising future directions for research and for industry development.

2. Blockchain as Decentralized Consensus

To start to comprehend blockchain economics, one has to first understand the general definition of blockchains, their main functionalities and advantages, and the major tradeoffs in achieving all desirable features associated with it. Not surprisingly, the myriad definitions in popular media and emerging economic literature do not help. We aim to provide a coherent version that facilitates our discussions on the key economic issues related to blockchains.

2.1. *What is blockchain?*

Technically speaking, blockchain is a distributed system that stores time-ordered data in a continuously growing list of blocks. Each block contains information on transactions and business activities, and the entire network uses a consensus algorithm to reach an agreement on which block will be attached to the current recognized chain of blocks, thus the name "blockchain".

The blockchain technology is a manifestation of the more general distributed ledger technology (DLT), which embodies the infrastructure and process for a network to generate a consensus record of state changes or updates to a synchronized ledger distributed across various nodes in the network. Another popular form of DLT is the directed acyclic graph (DAG), often considered to be a rival technology to and an enabler for blockchain. Unlike blockchains that organize records in an unalterable, chronological order, DAGs represent networks of individual records linked to multiple other transactions. In technical jargon, a blockchain is a linked list, whereas a DAG is a tree, branching out from one record to another, and so on.[1] While the discussion to follow often applies equally to other DLTs, we encourage the readers to focus on blockchains for concreteness. In that sense, "blockchain" can be viewed as a general reference for systems of decentralized consensus.

Blockchains can be public (also referred to as open or permissionless), permissioned, or private. The distinction is more about who gets to participate in the consensus formation process, rather than the users of particular applications. Public blockchains typically allow any agent to potentially be a consensus recordkeeper via the protocol and randomization; permissioned blockchains have a prespecified group of recordkeepers; and private blockchains retain their irreversibility and tamper resistance property, but are mostly proprietarily maintained. Most cryptocurrencies (e.g., Bitcoin)

[1] DAG accommodates larger numbers of users and faster transaction times, but does not establish a strict ordering of transactions and would require additional layers of protocols.

are based on public blockchains, whereas many enterprise applications rely on permissioned/consortium blockchains.

Blockchain enthusiasts argue that the technology provides many functions, such as secure data storage and anonymity. Because solutions to these problems are abundant outside of the blockchain space, the impact of blockchain along these dimensions, although material, is somewhat incidental. In our opinion, the core functionality of the technology lies in the provision of decentralized consensus. Consensus here refers to agreements not only on transactions but also on protocols for conflict resolution, history of events, institutional memory, etc.

The concept of consensus is not alien to economic and social functions. It is the informational basis for agents of divergent preferences and beliefs to agree on the states of the world or behave according to a common set of protocols. Its benefits for and empowerment of everyone sharing and trusting the same ledger are apparent: Settlements in some cases no longer take days, lemons problems and frauds can be mitigated, and the list goes on. Traditionally, centralized parties such as courts, governments, and notary agencies provide such consensus, but in a way that could be labor intensive, time consuming, and prone to tampering and monopoly power. Blockchains provide an alternative, decentralized way of generating consensus information. It is important to recognize that decentralization here entails both the way consensus is generated and the way it is distributed and stored. For example, Bitcoin mining under proof-of-work generates consensus, and information about the newly appended block is also stored on multiple (if not all) nodes representing network participants' computers.

All blockchains, to a large extent, aim to create an infrastructure for decentralized or multi-centered agents or institutions to interact and jointly record and maintain information, with no individual party exercising persistent market power or control. One defining feature of blockchain architectures is therefore their ability to allow decentralized recordkeepers to maintain a uniform view on the state of things and the order of events — a decentralized consensus (Cong and He, 2018). We should reckon that decentralization is a matter of degree. Public blockchains tend to be completely decentralized by freely admitting users and recordkeepers. In contrast, permissioned or consortium blockchains have a restricted set of recordkeepers and may have restrictions on who may use the blockchain or access information therein. Nevertheless, it could be more decentralized than traditional systems such as individual banks.

In a broader sense, blockchains aim to provide a trusted system or environment for economic agents to interact. "Trusted" in computer science means carrying out transactions in a fault-tolerant way. The consideration of blockchain economics and its link with trust brings a whole new perspective. For example, a decentralized trustworthy system may allow better search and matching in storage sharing or world computing without high intermediary costs (Filecoin and Dfinity are among current attempts); it may also coordinate various interested parties without concerns on who runs the show or whether a particular political/legal framework has ulterior motives (Libra and Ethereum which do not belong to any particular country or company are some cases in point despite the fact that Facebook or Vitalik Buterin are taking a lead in the development).

2.2. *Benefits of decentralization*

If centralized systems such as governments and large IT firms have traditionally supplied trusted systems and digital platforms/exchanges, why do we need decentralized consensus in the first place? To this question, many articles provide a misleading or incomplete picture, overemphasizing transparency or anonymity. While Bitcoin is well-known for its anonymity and thus associations with illegal activities such as money laundering and drug dealing, anonymity is a design feature rather than a defining characteristic of blockchains in general. We attempt to give a definitive answer and highlight the three core benefits of decentralization. Note that in many cases and applications, decentralization manifests itself in the form of multi-centers.

2.2.1. *Preventing single point of failure*

It is widely accepted that a decentralized system prevents or reduces what is called "single point of failure" (SPOF). SPOF is a part of a system that, upon failing, prevents the entire system from functioning. SPOFs are undesirable in any system requiring continuity and reliability, be it a business practice or software application. By having irreversible records distributed to decentralized notes, blockchains in a sense help mitigate SPOFs because no single node's failure is likely to disable the entire network and consensus process.

While this benefit seems to contradict the observed hacking of crypto exchanges and the DAO attack of a former decentralized autonomous organization, we remind the readers that these incidents happened to centralized wallets and accounts. If the system were truly decentralized and peer-to-peer, such massive failures would be less likely to occur even when a few nodes are hacked. In that regard, it is not whether a decentralized system mitigates the problem of SPOF, but about whether a system is decentralized, a topic we visit in Sections 3 and 4.

Because hash-pointers give immutability (with time stamping) and tamper resistance, no single party can go back in history to change the records or the sequence of events. This is useful for maintaining a consistent global consensus history, which can be used for contingency references for smart contracting. There are costs though, as we point out in Sections 3 and 4. For one, storing duplicate copies of entire history of transactions could be costly. Decentralized consensus protocol may also entail excessive energy consumption.

More importantly, we argue that the concept of SPOFs should be more broadly interpreted. Beyond technical SPOF, such as the breakdown of a computer, or wiping out of corporate facilities due to natural disasters, SPOF here can refer to economic incentives. For example, it is easier to bribe a single judge for a court case than bribing an entire panel of judges. Hack and theft of credit card data target a specific database or an individual. Facebook's leakage of data to Cambridge Analytica and Google's fine of 57 million euros for failing to comply with GDPR (https://techcrunch.com/2019/01/21/french-data-protection-watchdog-fines-google-57-million-under-the-gdpr/) are also examples of SPOF in business in which the action or negligence of a centralized platform leads to system wide debacles. Had the consensus process on how to handle data belonged to a decentralized set of agents, such violations may have been prevented by a majority of agents who are more sensitive to data privacy issues.

2.2.2. *Reducing market power and enabling stakeholding*

Another popular argument for adopting the blockchain technology centers around disintermediation. This is at best a misnomer. In fact, decentralized systems could allow intermediaries to thrive because they also allow more efficient search and match for intermediaries with end customers. What people have in the back of their minds is that blockchain systems are typically open, which allows easier entry and more competition to improve efficiency and reduce intermediary rent. Moreover, it could enable P2P transactions that would be infeasible under traditional systems and therefore filling in missing markets. This is a point Townsend (2019) belabors, for good reasons.

Another warranted clarification is that even though decentralized systems such as blockchains reduce market power, it is a matter of degree. It certainly does not imply that the market would be perfectly competitive. In fact, Cong *et al.* (2018) show that even mining pools enjoy some local monopoly. Similarly, while the openness nature of many blockchain systems would blur the boundary of legal jurisdictions or physical geography, it is most likely that regional regulations are still relevant (a case in point is the ban on cryptocurrency exchanges by China and South Korea). The relevant question is to what extent do they matter. More importantly, what is novel relative to traditional centralized systems is that the consensus mechanism (specifically node leader elections) leaves little room for any single party to have persistent market power or governance authority over time.

The reduction in market power concentration also reflects in a novel fashion on the consensus mechanism that existing studies and media articles rarely touch on. In many business-to-customer (B2C) businesses, consumers or platform users generate invaluable information and network externality that the business platforms tap without explicitly compensating the end users. For example, Facebook and Google monetize users' social interactions and emails, yet it is often difficult for users, especially early adopters, to share the economic surplus of such business behemoths. Greater competition would lead businesses to seek alternative ways to attract users and early adopters.

Traditionally, a platform would provide tools to empower network participants. For example, Alibaba's Tmall Innovation Center (TMIC) began in 2016 to help brands design products for consumers by utilizing its online surveys. Tao Factory helps coordinate smart supply chain for its 40,000 factories from more than 30 industries, so that they have the ability to quickly adjust its assembly lines to unanticipated changes in customer demand.

One novel way is to have users be stakeholders of the future prosperity of the businesses or platforms. Blockchains enable a trusted way of distributing digitized securities or cryptotokens to early adopters and users, even when the distributing businesses are still little known.

This enables businesses to return value to consumers for the contributions they make on platforms or open-source projects.

2.2.3. *Enabling value exchange, asset traceability, and information interaction*

It is crucial to recognize that we live in a digital age with abundant data. In that sense, a trust system for interaction concerns not only the exchanges of value or objects but also the exchanges of information. Blockchain provides the building blocks for a trust system based on digital information and algorithms.

Because permissioned blockchains and private blockchains do not have open access, many economists question whether a lot of the excitement about blockchain is merely excitement about database upgrade.[2] We would like to point out that even permissioned and private blockchains represent important innovations rather than mere database upgrades for the following reasons: the consensus generation process, though not fully decentralized, is often more decentralized than traditional systems; more importantly, the immutability of blockchain records coupled with proper encryption algorithms can enable proprietary databases (permissioned nodes or private blockchains) to interact to produce useful information aggregation, verification, and exchanges, all without sacrificing data privacy.[3] This was difficult to achieve before the introduction of secure multi-party computation, one of the most important developments in computer science over the past few years. It also allows us to enhance traceability of offline assets/products by recording their origination and path of ownership in a tamperproof manner (e.g., Alibaba's IoT Global Origin Traceability Plan; Luohan Academy, 2019).

Through smart contracts (e.g., using Solidity, a popular programming language used on Ethereum), programs that run on blockchains, one ensures that only transaction parties can execute the transaction using digital signature based on asymmetric keys, without the intervention of

---

[2] See, for example, https://review.chicagobooth.edu/economics/2018/article/blockchain-s-weakest-links and Halaburda (2018).

[3] Data privacy is particularly important in, for example, healthcare and financial services (Yue *et al.*, 2016; Raikwar *et al.*, 2018).

any trusted third party. This further allows agents in a blockchain network to exchange digital assets or share the surplus generated through information aggregation or exchange. In a similar vein, blockchains, whether open or not, can potentially allow exchanges of offline objects when combined with internet of things (IoTs) (Popov, 2016; Ali *et al.*, 2018; Bakos and Halaburda, 2019).

To be concrete, Section 4.5 provides an example of blockchain architecture for collaborative auditing (Cao *et al.*, 2018). Encryption algorithms such as the zero-knowledge-proof (ZKP) on top of blockchains allow auditing firms to exchange encrypted information so that they can audit transactions while preserving client firms' proprietary information. R3 has developed ready-to-use permissioned blockchain infrastructure that can integrate with clients' Enterprise Resource Planning (ERP) systems with a reasonable adoption cost. Promising start-ups such as the Oasis Lab and Duality are other examples of blockchain applications in multi-party computations (MPCs).

It is worth mentioning that all three advantages of the blockchain system together enable it to be an ideal infrastructure for non-profit and social projects.[4] Blockchains' three benefits also create "liquidity" for many hitherto illiquid assets or items. For example, the reliable and timely recording of receipts and account receivable in a decentralized network imply that agents in the system can use these assets for collateral or transfer of value in ways that a traditional system fails to achieve (just think about how long it takes for a travel reimbursement to be deposited into your account before you can use the resource). This would affect banks' rehypothecation business as well.

3. Consensus Generation and Economic Tradeoffs

Consensus protocols are essentially the rules of the game for agents in distributed computing and multi-agent systems, so that they can agree on records that are needed to achieve overall system reliability in the

[4] See, for example, https://www.thenonprofittimes.com/technology/blockchain-gaining-ground/. Ant Financial has also been leading the effort to apply the technology to the philanthropy sector (https://www.newsbtc.com/2016/07/31/alibaba-groups-ant-financial-creates-blockchain-solution-for-philanthropy-sector/).

presence of agent heterogeneity (faulty nodes or processes are just special examples). For blockchains, the best-known consensus protocol is proof-of-work (PoW), which is behind Bitcoin's design.

True to the Stigler's Law of Eponymy, the ingredients and principles for Bitcoin were introduced much earlier, and Nakamoto's innovation truly lies in putting it altogether (Narayanan and Clark, 2017). Early attempts at cryptocurrencies lacked a proper incentive system for decentralized nodes to properly record transactions, either because they needed some oversight (e.g., entity to have final decision on penalties) or because they did not constrain coin issues (uncontrolled inflation) (Halaburda and Sarvary, 2016). This leads to double-spending issues that would invalidate the digital currency in question. Nakamoto introduced the concept of bitcoin mining (essentially the PoW), in which independent computers (miners) dispersed all over the world spend resources and compete repeatedly for the right to record new blocks of transactions, and the winner in each round gets rewarded. Independent miners have incentives to honestly record transactions because rewards are valid only if their records are endorsed by subsequent miners. The avoidance of double spending in turn validates bitcoins as a form of payment in the network.

In this section, we start with a discussion on PoW before introducing alternate protocols and important tradeoffs among various desirable features of blockchain.

3.1. *Games under consensus protocols*

Consensus protocols have been studied for decades in the field of computer science. While in computer science and modern cryptography we typically make assumptions on the actions of the agents (an honest node behaves honestly; a faulty node always misbehaves), economists tend to make assumptions on the primitives such as agents' utility functions and then analyze their strategic behaviors in equilibrium. What economics brings to the table for consensus protocols are the concepts of equilibrium (and potential multiplicity), incentive compatibility (Bitcoin's mining protocol is an instance of incentive compatible protocol), and mechanism design. These in turn allow us to talk about incentives in a large or open system, in order to achieve general resilience and feasibility of the decentralized systems.

3.1.1. *Proof-of-work protocol*

Agents in the economy are not machines, and therefore providing them the right incentives for proper recordkeeping is crucial. PoW at present is the predominant protocol for generating decentralized consensus. Recordkeepers here are the miners around the world who compete for the right to record a brief history (known as a block) of bitcoin transactions. The winner gets rewarded with a fixed number of bitcoins (currently 12.5 bitcoins), plus any transaction fees included in the transactions within the block (Easley *et al.*, 2017). Miners utilize computation power to solve cryptographic puzzles in order to win the competition, which resembles effortful mining activities.

Two features are common in PoW protocols. First, the difficulty of the cryptopuzzles dynamically adjusts so that the speed of block generation and thus recording is limited. In the case of Bitcoin, one block is generated on average every 10 min. This means that recordkeeping is an arms race: devoting more computation power improves the chance of winning the recordkeeping right but does not increase social surplus. Moreover, there is necessarily usage congestion because the system throughput is limited. Although not optimally designed, difficulty adjustments are not *ad hoc* and do serve the purpose of network security and are essential for raising revenue from users to fund miners provision of infrastructure (Huberman *et al.*, 2017).

Second, in addition to getting newly minted native tokens, miners in many PoW blockchains also receive fees attached by users. In the case of Bitcoin, there is the transition from mining new bitcoins to getting market-based fees (Easley *et al.*, 2017). Given the rising importance of transaction fees and that fee structure could also lead to instability of the system (e.g., Carlsten *et al.*, 2016), how to determine them in a market mechanism as part of the protocol design constitutes an interesting problem. Basu *et al.* (2019) were pioneers of such a discourse.

Nakamoto envisioned that when appending blocks, the winning miner would append to the longest chain, thus the "longest chain rule". Here is the heuristic argument: Because miners receive block rewards and fees in native tokens and the receipt is only valid if others continue building from the block they build, miners have incentives to properly record because otherwise others will not follow the block record. Forking out on her own is also not attractive because she is in a tournament with the entire mining community and it is highly likely that a fraudulent branch would be shorter than the one that the rest of the community accepts. There are also other heuristics practiced in the blockchain community such as the "first-seen rule" which says that all miners add blocks to the heaviest chain of which they know, using the first branch it has heard of as tiebreaker. What is implicit in these folk theorems is a vague notion of equilibrium.

Kroll *et al.* (2013) were among the earliest to study whether following the longest chain rule is a Nash equilibrium. Biais *et al.* (2019a) further fully formalized the strategic actions of players involved and demonstrated that even without majority computation power, a miner can attack the system to make it unstable. Having forks also delays consensus because persistent forking eventually leads to the splitting of the blockchain, as seen in the case of Ethereum and Ethereum Classic or Bitcoin and Bitcoin cash.

Consistent with the finding of equilibrium multiplicity by Biais *et al.* (2019a), Eyal and Sirer (2014) discuss how successful miners hide their success and start mining the second block without competition while honest miners are still busy mining the first block. If they succeed mining the second block, they will collect two block rewards, and their chain is the longest block. Even if the honest blockchain finds the first block before the selfish miner finds the second, the selfish miner could release its block immediately to compete for the reward.

Nayak *et al.* (2016) and Kiayias *et al.* (2016) consider generalization and optimal forms of selfish mining strategies in Eyal and Sirer (2014) to include stubborn mining such as forking (building private branch).

One main takeaway from these studies is that equilibria under PoW are far from being well understood. Because of the network security implications and the intellectual curiosity of understanding protocol games, one would expect further studies from both computer scientists and economists along this line of work.

3.1.2. *Alternative protocols*

The largest blockchains (e.g., Bitcoin, Ethereum) employ PoW, but PoW possesses significant shortcomings such as energy cost or bandwidth limit. Various alternatives have been proposed. In fact, PoW is not even among the first consensus protocols. For one, computer scientists have long worked on consensus protocols in a closed or permissioned environment where the number of members is not too big and the members are known. Byzantine fault tolerance (BFT) protocol (Castro and Liskov, 2002) is well studied and understood when applied to such an environment.[5] Roughly speaking, PoW offers good node scalability but poor performance in terms of processing capacity, whereas variants of BFT offer good performance for small numbers of replicas. They often lack scalability in open environments that blockchains applications typically entail. Practitioners are actively exploring protocols such as practical BFT (pBFT), hybrid BFT, delegated BFT, obfuscated BFT, simplified BFT, and VBFT that combine proof-of-stake (PoS, which we introduce shortly), verifiable random function, and BFT. The recent Facebook Libra stable coin also utilizes a version of BFT as part of the consensus protocol. Game-theoretical models on BFT-based protocols also constitute an important area of research (Amoussou-Guenou *et al.*, 2019).

Another popular alternative to PoW is PoS. In PoS-based blockchains, the creator of the next block is chosen via various combinations of random selection and wealth (in native tokens) or age (i.e., the stake). The study by Saleh (2019a) provides the first formal economic model of PoS and establishes conditions under which PoS generates consensus. A sufficiently modest reward schedule not only implies existence of an equilibrium in which consensus is obtained as soon as possible but also precludes a persistent forking equilibrium. The latter result arises because PoS, unlike PoW, requires that validators hold stake. Importantly, Saleh (2019a) dispels the myth of "nothing-at-stake" (malicious nodes lose nothing when behaving badly) through endogenizing native token prices.

Another protocol, proof-of-burn (PoB), has seen recent applications. To win the right to record new blocks, one has to "burn" tokens by sending them to invalid public addresses so that no one can ever use them again. While practitioners probably did not have the following in mind, PoB happens to speak to PoW's exceptional price volatility. Exceptional price volatility arises because PoW implements a passive monetary policy that fails to modulate cryptocurrency demand shocks. Saleh (2019b) theoretically formalized the aforementioned point. PoB implements an active albeit *ad hoc* monetary policy that modulates cryptocurrency demand shocks. PoB is an example of supply-side management of cryptocurrencies, which potentially reduce the welfare loss in PoWs compensating those updating the blockchain through an arms race while facilitating free entry among them. A related study is that by Cong, Li, and Wang (2019),

---

[5]Readers are encouraged to read more about the Byzantine General's problem.

which fully endogenizes dynamic token supplies and offers a corporate finance perspective of protocol design.

3.2. *Blockchain impossibility triangle?*

It should be apparent to readers that one goal of the blockchain technology is to achieve more decentralization. But for the blockchains to receive wide adoption and application, they also have to ensure that the consensus provision is accurate and scalable. Public blockchains such as the Bitcoin blockchain achieve decentralization and consensus record at the same time, but doing so reduces their scalability. Traditional payment processing tools such as Visa and Mastercard achieve consensus record and scalability, but lack decentralization. Records made in large scales with decentralization are hard to synchronize and achieve consensus. It seems that global consensus, decentralization, and scalability are hard to achieve at the same time.

Vitalik was among the first to put forth the scalability trilemma that is widely recognized among practitioners (Ometoruwa, 2018). The trilemma describes how it is difficult to achieve decentralization, security, and scalability at the same time. Security refers to the level of defensibility a blockchain has against attacks from external sources of linear-order computation power. In fact, Brewer (2000) conjectured even earlier in a talk that it is impossible for a distributed data system to simultaneously provide consistency, availability, and partition tolerance. This was proven later by Gilbert and Lynch (2002).

Abadi and Brunnermeier (2018) gave an insightful and more comprehensive discussion of a similar trilemma from an economic perspective. When a blockchain is decentralized and correct, the lack of dynamic rent by various recordkeepers necessarily implies that the system is costly; when the system is decentralized and maintained at low cost, recordkeepers may misreport; when the consensus is correct and maintenance of the system is cheap, the outcome is incompatible with free entry and information portability (compared with traditional reputation-based system) conditions.

The concept of "security" is just one aspect of consensus, in the sense that the whole system agrees on the state of the world and that agreement cannot be attacked. The tradeoffs do not necessarily involve dynamic considerations as in Abadi and Brunnermeier (2018) either. Moreover, there are more than three dimensions of tradeoffs in the blockchain technology,

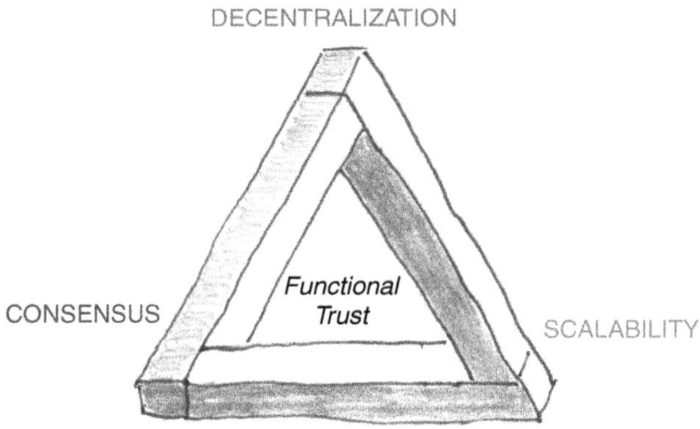

Figure 1: Impossibility triangle.

such as transparency, immediacy, level of adoption, which constitute a rich avenue for future research. Nevertheless, we argue that almost all tradeoffs can be interpreted as manifestations of the tension among decentralization, scalability, and consensus (formation). We conjecture that there is such a general impossibility triangle (Figure 1) and discuss below how this can be a useful framework to think about various tradeoffs in blockchain innovations. As we walk you through the irreducible difficulties that arise when one tries to achieve all three, we also mention how practitioners are still actively working on layer 1 protocol innovations and layer 2 business model innovations to resolve the seeming impossibility triangle.

3.2.1. *Decentralization*

Decentralization in our context means a significant degree of distribution of a system's information, governance, ownership, etc. When decentralized agents jointly make decisions, intuitively it takes a clever design to reach agreements. The more decentralized the system is, the greater the potential failure for reaching a global consensus. Moreover, decentralized storage of global consensus necessarily leads to duplication, be it storage, queries, recordings, etc. In either case, consensus accuracy or system processing capacity would be compromised.

Layer 1 protocol innovations on consensus protocols often come at the expense of decentralization. For example, the variants of conventional

BFTs allow a high number of messages in that every node multi-casts its messages to every other node. Functional separation of leader election and transaction validation allow localization (Eyal *et al.*, 2016). Bitcoin runs verification and leader election at the same time, but Bitcoin NG is forward-looking and uses key blocks to elect a leader first who validates transactions in microblocks in the next 10 minutes. Other solutions include forming a committee to vouch for new blocks through BFT (e.g., ByzCoin (Kogias *et al.*, 2016)) and sharding (e.g., Elastico (Luu *et al.*, 2016)). Sharding makes sense, but requires something called Atomic Cross-Shard Commitment Protocol. All these involve some local consensus formation within a preselected committee instead of open consensus all the time.

3.2.2. *Consensus (formation)*

Note that the consensus we have in mind is global consensus that can be used in various applications. This is hard to achieve. In fact, Fischer *et al.* (1982) show that there is no guarantee that an asynchronous network can agree on a single outcome.

One way is to sacrifice efficiency and scalability to wait for a decentralized system to reach consensus. Many permissionless blockchains do this, which we discuss shortly in the next subsection. Another way to overcome the consensus problem is to synchronize from a single point, but this means centralization. We believe that sacrificing some decentralization is a promising direction and enterprise blockchains are going to be the major trend for blockchain applications. Trust combined with efficiency can disrupt existing business models and relationships.

It is worth mentioning that DAG, an alternative architecture to ensure decentralization and scalability, instead sacrifices consensus. In fact, there may not be a global consensus at any given point in time. A hybrid of DAG and blockchain is being explored to enforce collective consensus generation, minimizing the monopolitic power of the round leaders (Abram *et al.*, 2019).

3.2.3. *Scalability*

Bitcoin only processes less than five transactions per second, whereas VISA and Mastercard process thousands, not to mention Alibaba's Tmall processes 100 billion RMB worth of transactions under 2 hours on

China's single's day.[6] For blockchains such as the P2P payment Bitcoin network to be widely adopted, they have to effectively scale. Two obvious solutions are increasing the block size or decreasing the block intervals. Increasing the size decreases fairness in that large miners have an advantage (law of large numbers would not play out). It also requires more storage space and network bandwidth, not to mention that it requires more verification time (which is not an issue for simple transactions in bitcoin, but could be an issue when verifications are more complicated). In addition, increasing the block size still does not solve the problem of miners strategically partially filling the blocks (Malik *et al.*, 2019). What about decreasing block interval? It would imply that it requires lower computation to attack unless participants increase the confirmation lags correspondingly, leading to more forks and stale blocks all of which result in network instability and inaccurate or unreliable consensus.

Most current applications of blockchains have decentralization and consensus and are battling the scalability issue. Multi-chain solutions increase throughputs at the expense of security; for merge mining, agents share mining power as in the case of Namecoin, where store and computation loads on each node increase, which is similar to block size increase. Other solutions include cross-chain layer 2 innovation, of which Ripple's interledger is a leading candidate, off-chain; state channel, with the best-known example being the Lightning Network, Casper; Sharding "parallel processing", e.g., Ethereum Casper, Zilliqa (open-source); Segwit, DAG.

It should be recognized that depending on the application, we do not need to achieve all three objectives at the same time. Besides exploring solutions to the challenge of the impossibility triangle, another fruitful path could be to clearly identify the need in particular applications and design the protocols and business models correspondingly.

4. Key Economic Issues

Mechanism design and protocol innovations to achieve decentralization, consensus, and scalability have received increasing attention from computer scientists and economists. In this section, we highlight that the

[6]Based on 2018 data and supported by AliPay and OceanBase database. See, for example, http://m.mnw.cn/news/cj/2084010.html and https://tech.sina.cn/2018-11-11/detail-ihmutuea8987030.d.html.

specific designs of consensus protocols can have general social economic implications. These have to be taken into consideration in designing the protocols too.

We start with the well-known discussion in computer science on network security and end with an emphasis on the role of information — an important topic that is inappropriately relegated to the backseat, if not neglected entirely, in many studies.

4.1. *Network security*

The earliest discussions on blockchains took place in the computer science field and largely concern network security. This is very much related to our earlier discussions on protocol games. Once we fix the consensus protocol, there could be a number of strategies that attackers/malicious nodes in the network could deploy. Consider PoW for example. Below, some of the well-known attacks are described.

In denial-of-service (DoS) attack and its derivatives such as distributed DOS, a malicious cyber threat prevents legitimate users from accessing information systems, devices, or other network resources, so as to lower other players' (typically mining pools') profits (Johnson *et al.*, 2014).

Besides direct attacks, there could be other forms of instability driven by decentralized miners' incentives. For example, without newly minted bitcoins, miners may extend the blocks with the most available transaction fees rather than to follow the longest chain, causing instability of the network (Carlsten *et al.*, 2016).

A much studied case is selfish mining, in which malicious miners or pools withhold the mined blocks. Honest miners then waste their computational power in finding blocks already mined, and malicious miners increase their probability of finding the next block. This leads to majority attack. It is often mentioned that with 51% of the global hash power, one can be a dictator on recordkeeping. What is often the case is that as long as an attacker amasses a large percentage of the global hash power, the system's security is at risk (Sapirshtein *et al.*, 2016; Bahack, 2013).

Network security in the blockchain setting can be viewed as robust consensus, and there often features a tension between a more decentralized structure and scalability. Overall, network security issues remain an active area of research for blockchains. Taking a game-theoretical approach has been tremendously helpful for understanding the behaviors of agents and robustness of the system for a given consensus protocol. We anticipate more mechanism design approach in future that has network security as part of the objective to optimize over candidate designs.

4.2. *Overconcentration*

In addition to network security, the blockchain community has been extremely concerned with overconcentration. For a system with a sufficiently large processing capacity, the incentives for consensus generation seem to lead to an industrial organization with a perceived tendency for concentration. This is aggravated by the emergence of mining pools that combine an individual miner's hash power to solve cryptographic puzzles in PoW and then distribute the rewards. An open blockchain's optimal functioning relies on adequate and sustainable decentralization that cannot be taken for granted. In fact, over time some pools gain a significant share of global hash rates (a measure of computation power), with the mining pool GHash.io briefly reaching more than 51% of global hash rates in July 2014. Therefore, the rise of mining pools in many, presumably distributed cryptocurrency-mining activities calls into question the stability and viability of such systems. Overconcentration therefore runs counter to blockchain advocates' ideology of decentralization.

The study by Cong *et al.* (2018) shows that risk sharing constitutes a natural force against decentralization and gives rise to mining pools. Ferreira *et al.* (2019) show that application-specific integrated circuits (ASICs) that are used for mining could lead to concentration in ASIC production market which then affects the mining pool concentration.

Figure 2 illustrates the evolution of the distribution of hash rates among Bitcoin mining pools. Clearly, overtime mining pools gradually dominate solo mining: mining pools represented less than 5% of the global hash rates at the start of June 2011 but have represented almost 100% since late 2015. This phenomenon suggests that natural economic forces tend towards centralization within a supposedly decentralized system. But an equally interesting fact is that, while large pools do arise from time to time, none of them grow to completely dominate global mining. This observation hints at concurrent economic forces that suppress overcentralization.

Indeed, Cong *et al.* (2018) demonstrate that diversification across pools and the industrial organization of mining pools naturally moderate

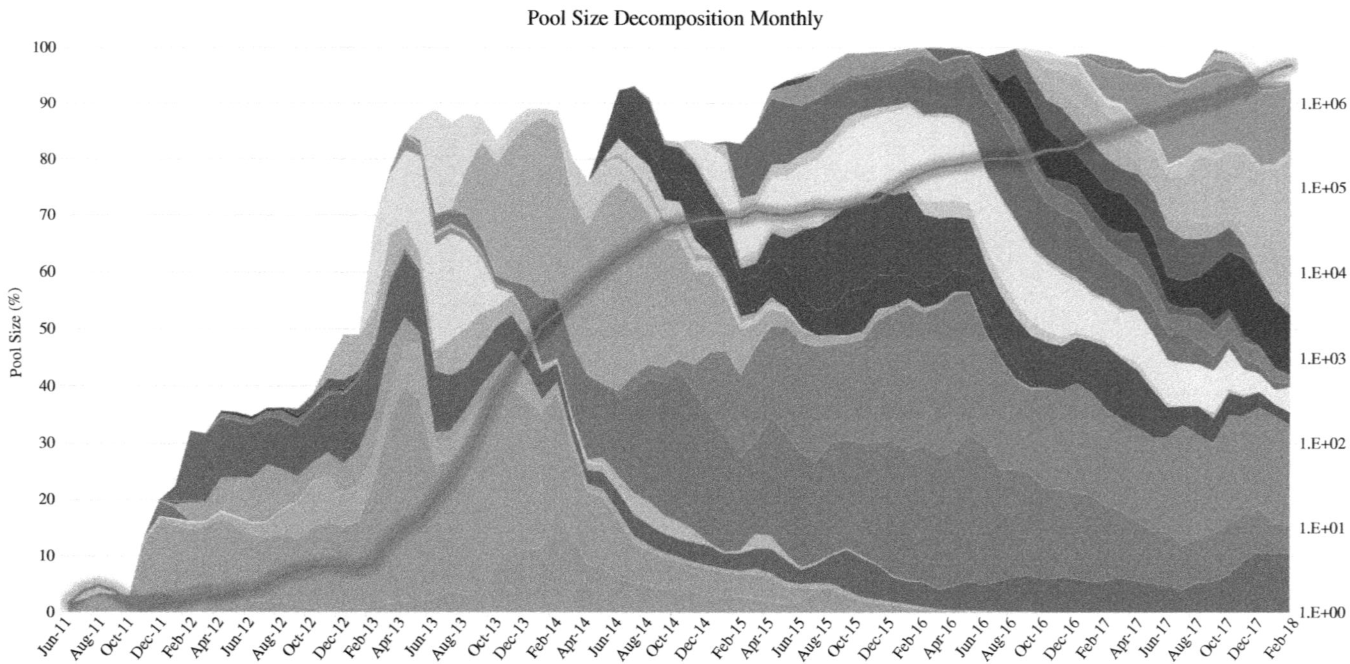

Figure 2: The evolution of size percentages of Bitcoin mining pools.

Notes: This graph plots (1) the growth of aggregate hash rates (right-hand side vertical axis, in log scale) starting from June 2011 to today; and (2) the size evolutions of all Bitcoin mining pools (left-hand side vertical axis) over this period, with the pool size measured as each pool's hash rates as a fraction of global hash rates. Different shades indicate different pools, and white spaces indicate solo mining. Over time, Bitcoin mining has been increasingly taken over by mining pools, but no pool seems to ever dominate the mining industry for long. The pool hash rates data come from Bitcoinity and BTC.com, with details given in Cong *et al.* (2018).

overconcentration of mining power. Intuitively, larger pools have more market power because the risk-sharing benefit it provides is larger. Therefore, pool owners charge higher fees, leading to a smaller percentage growth in pool size. Empirical evidence supports the theoretical predictions. Every quarter, the authors sort pools into deciles based on the start-of-quarter pool size and calculate the average pool share, average fee, and average log growth rate for each decile. They show that pools with larger start-of-quarter size charge higher fees and grow slower in percentage terms. They investigate these relationships in three 2-year spans (i.e., 2012–2013, 2014–2015, and 2016–2017, as shown in Figure 3) and find that almost all of them are statistically significant with the signs predicted by their theory.

The insights from this chapter can be extended to other protocols such as PoS, because miners in PoS systems also form coalitions (e.g., Brunjes *et al.*, 2018).

4.3. *Energy consumption and sustainability*

The issue surrounding blockchains that has received the most attention is arguably the energy implications for PoW-based blockchains. The purported advantages of Bitcoin are dwarfed by the intentionally resource-intensive design in its transaction verification process which threatens the environment integral to our survival.[7] Environmental science and engineering studies have estimated the detrimental environmental impacts of cryptomining (e.g., Li *et al.*, 2019; de Vries, 2019; Truby, 2018). Again, this is a manifestation of the impossibility triangle: for a large-scale decentralized system, generating consensus could be very costly.

A number of economic studies also recognize that the mining game in PoW-based blockchains is essentially an arms race due to difficulty adjustments in many of the consensus protocols. Basically agents acquire more computation power to compete in a fixed-sum game because more global hash power does not lead to more native coins or tokens being minted and distributed to the miners. O'Dwyer and Malone (2014); Chiu

[7]Energy issues are also related to scalability, but they are not exactly the same. For one, even if Bitcoin processes way more transactions or way less transactions, energy consumption could be high if coinbase is worth a lot and many miners started competing.

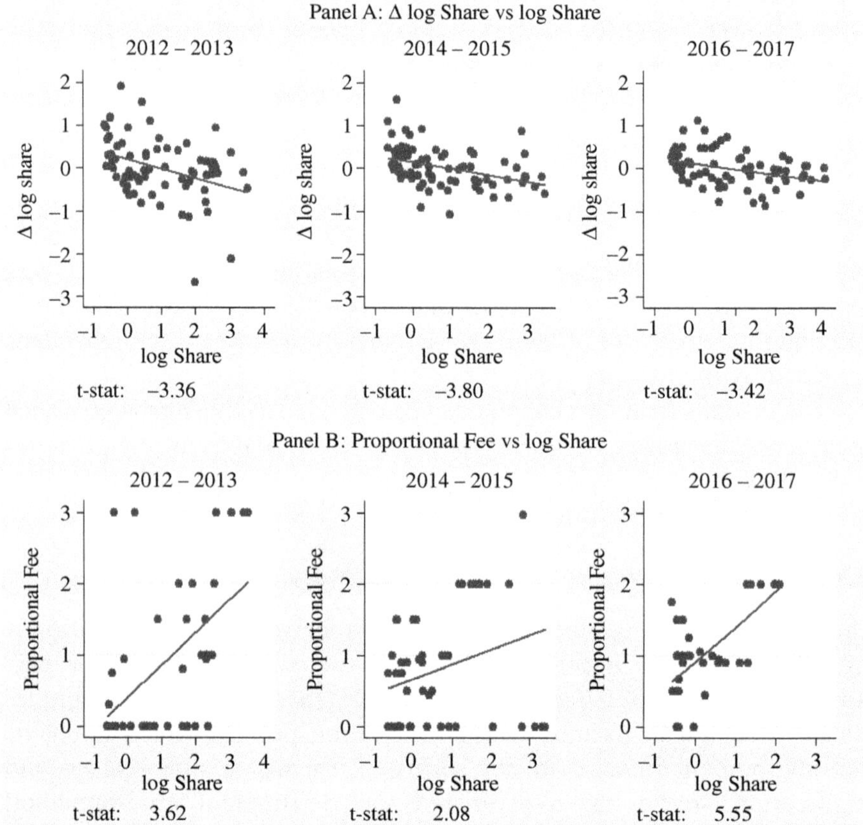

Figure 3: Empirical relationships of pool sizes, fees, and growths.

Source: Reproduced from Cong *et al.* (2019).

Notes: This figure shows the binned plots of the changes in logShare (Panel A) and Proportional Fees (Panel B) against logShare. Share is the quarterly beginning (the first week) hash rate over the total market hash rate. Fees are the quarterly averaged proportional fees. Within each quarter t; $\text{logShare}_{i;t+1}$, Proportional $\text{Fee}_{i;t}$, and $\text{logShare}_{i;t}$ are averaged within each $\text{logShare}_{i;t}$ decile, and these mean values are plotted for 2012–2013, 2014–2015, and 2016–2017. Solid lines are the fitted OLS lines, with t-stat reported at the bottom. Data sources and descriptions are given in their paper.

and Koeppl (2017); Ma and Tourky (2018); Cong *et al.* (2018); Pagnotta (2018); Prat and Walter (2018); Saleh (2019a) all acknowledged that greater global mining does increase the network security, but the energy used may have greater social benefit when deployed elsewhere.

In particular, Benetton *et al.* (2019) found empirical evidence that cryptomining crowds out other economic activities and may result in net welfare loss. Using data from various cities in China and New York State, the authors found large negative externalities of cryptomining on the local economy, such as distortion to local wages and electricity price. As the study by Benetton *et al.* (2019) points out, local taxes would only drive the problem elsewhere, akin to the phenomenon of corporate profit shifting to tax-friendly geographies, while worldwide levy is hard to coordinate.

Given that the current designs for Bitcoin and the like entail a large social welfare loss, but can be improved with more efficient design, practitioners have attempted to channel the computation to scientific problems. For example, in proof of useful work or resources (PoUWR), the mining computation is used for performing stochastic gradient descent for neural network training (Bottou 1991). Not all scientific computation problems are NP-complete, which is required for many PoW protocols, the energy problem remains.

Most studies hint at cryptocurrency price and mining cost as the biggest drivers on the global mining activities. Intuitively, the higher the Bitcoin price, the more entry and greater computation power miners use, which leads to a higher energy consumption. This is only an incomplete description in that in the long run, compensation is driven by system congestion and market fees attached by the users. If Bitcoin is worth more, users just attach less number of bitcoins. In that regard, Bitcoin price cannot be the long-term and only driver for the high energy consumption.

This is where mining pool is included in the discussion. For the same amount of monetary rewards, if miners' risk-bearing capacity is greater, then they devote more mining power — another key insight in Cong *et al.* (2018). Figure 4 demonstrates that when mining pools help miners to share risk, the aggregate mining could easily double for realistic parameters for Bitcoin mining. For further discussion on the dynamic evolution of distribution of miners and reward schemes in mining pools, we refer the readers to Liu *et al.* (2018) and Fisch *et al.* (2017). It is yet to be seen how consensus protocol innovations resolve the issues created by mining pools.

4.4. *Adoption*

In some sense, blockchain's scalability is reflected by endogenous user adoptions. Without user adoption, most blockchain applications cannot

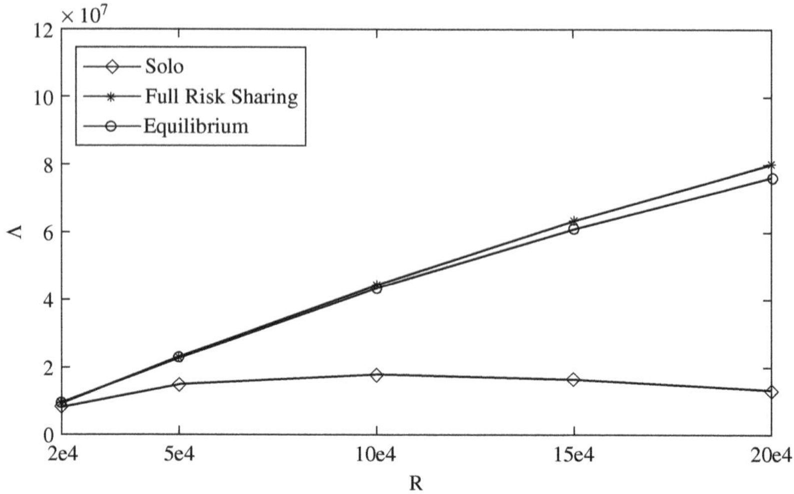

$R = 1 \times 10^5$, $N = 10$, $M = 2$, $C = 0.00204$, and $\rho = 1 \times 10^{-5}$

Figure 4: Global hash rates under solo mining, full-risk sharing, and mining pool equilibrium.

Source: Reproduced from Cong *et al.* (2019).

Notes: Here R is the mining reward, C is related to mining cost, and ρ is risk aversion. M and N are parameters for the number of mining pools and the number of solo miners.

survive over the long run. Athey *et al.* (2016) carried out one of the earliest studies that take users' adoption into consideration, with an emphasis on the role of learning in agents' decisions to use Bitcoins. While Athey *et al.* (2016) did not consider users' network externality, Cong *et al.* (2018b) took network externality and blockchain platform's productivity into consideration to analyze token pricing and the roles of tokens. They derived a fundamental token pricing formula and showed that adoption of blockchain platforms crucially depends on the underlying technology and transaction needs.

Hinzen *et al.* (2019) also demonstrated that a limited adoption problem arises endogenously in PoW blockchains. Increased transaction demand increases the fees, which induce recordkeepers to enter the network (for permissionless blockchains). The increased network size then protracts the consensus process and delays transaction confirmation. Users adopt only if they possess extreme insensitivity to delays, limiting a PoW payments blockchains widespread adoption. The authors then argue that permissioned blockchain can overcome this problem because there is no difficulty adjustments or free entry of recordkeepers. However, validators may still collude, which can be solved by a stake-based voting rule.

4.5. *Multi-party computation and permissioned blockchains*

Multi-party computation (MPC) has been extensively studied for decades because it enables computation with correctness while preserving privacy. Its implementation has been challenging because the strong assumptions on agents' honesty means in practice it is prone to SPOFs (such as DoS attacks), not to mention that scaling in a large (often open) system is costly (Zyskind *et al.*, 2016). As described earlier, one of Nakamoto's innovations lies in introducing incentives into a consensus system. This way, the blockchain technology offers a form of incentive compatibility that mitigates both problems.

Specifically, blockchains can potentially serve as a trusted settlement layer to discipline malicious behaviors (through verifying transcripts of computations). They also allow introducing some randomization of committee selections (sometimes referred to as quorums) at a low cost, which can potentially scale MPC networks efficiently. Alex Pentland, the founder of MIT Media Lab and one of the most prominent data scientists, was quoted as saying, "[With blockchains, now] you can get insights across countries, across data holders, without exposing individual data and without disobeying either privacy or data localization laws" (MIT, 2018).

Permissioned blockchains are widely used as a distributed database system that could enable MPC. Many industries, such as auditing and financial report, can potentially benefit from the technology. Auditing has its unique need for a customized system to protect clients' information privacy. Such a need leads many auditors to develop permissioned blockchains independently as a database upgrade (Tysiac, 2018). Yet, with up-to-date and immutable historical record, auditors can easily verify the transactions on blockchain ledgers (either because the transactions are public or because they are on an auditor's proprietary blockchain or other private blockchains that auditors have access to) instead of asking clients for bank statements or sending confirmation requests to third parties. Moreover, communications across auditors could greatly improve auditing efficiency if the auditors automate information verification of clients' transaction with minimum sharing of their clients' information with other auditors, thanks to zero-knowledge protocols that preserve data privacy and integrity.

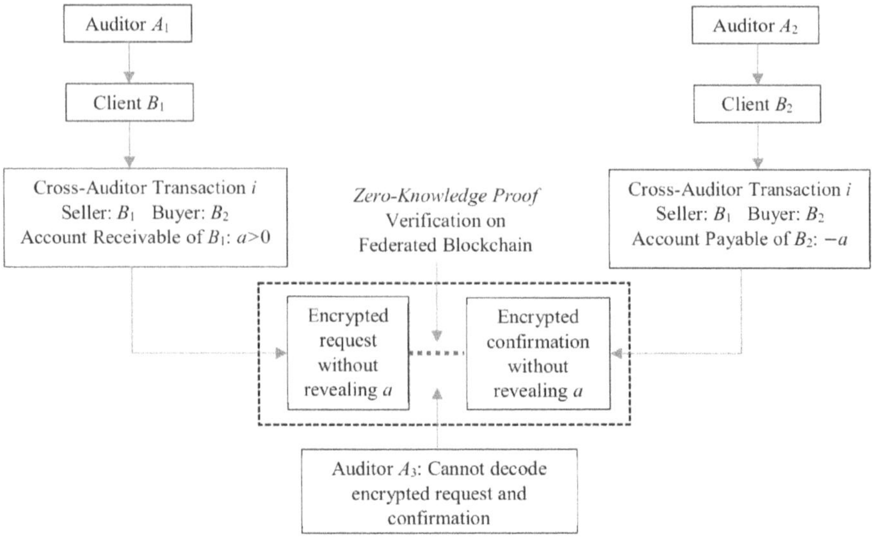

Figure 5: Transaction verification on a P2P federated blockchain.
Source: Reproduced from Cao *et al.* (2019).

Cao *et al.* (2018) provide a blueprint for such collaborative auditing using a federated blockchain which reduces auditing costs not only for transactions recorded on their proprietary databases but also for cross-auditor transactions. Figure 5 provides an illustration. Specifically, information providers in this federate blockchain system technically do not share any client transaction information except for providing a confirmation to information requesters. Other auditors cannot infer any information about the clients or the transactions from the request or the confirmation. This collaboration among auditors does not require a third party to monitor or intermediate. Once auditors request information through this federated blockchain framework, it is difficult for any auditor or outside hackers to intentionally revise or delete the information because the information is distributed to all auditors. Such immutable nature of information also makes it easier for the regulator to inspect auditors' auditing process.

The authors then model auditor competition for clients, allowing endogenous audit quality and clients' misstatement, before discussing regulatory policy in a unified framework to understand the implications of blockchain for auditing. They find blockchains lead to more real-time verification of transaction records on blockchains, forcing firms to misreport more in off-blockchain records. The reduction in auditing cost allows auditors to respond by inspecting a higher fraction of off-chain records and discretionary accounts. Overall, auditors spend less on auditing and reduce misstatement risk. Auditors charge competitive fees to attract clients, which are lower when using federated blockchains. But fees depend on both the transaction volume and counterparties' auditor association. Auditors' adoption of the technology also exhibits strategic complementarity in the sense that one auditor's adoption encourages others to adopt. To rule out the inefficient outcome where no auditor adopts the technology, a regulator can encourage or require adoption to enhance welfare and reduce regulatory costs.

In general, building multi-party computation using the blockchain infrastructure remains a promising avenue for blockchain innovations. Data Market Austria (https://datamarket.at/en/ueber-dma/) is a recent large-scale endeavor in that direction. That said, while permissioned blockchains allow scalability, they do so at the expense of partial decentralization.

4.6. *Smart contracting*

Smart contracts have received much media hype. While a universally accepted definition for smart contracts has yet to be reached, their core functionality is clear: transfer at little cost or even automate value transfers based on a decentralized consensus record of the states of the world. Cong and He (2018) define them as digital contracts allowing terms contingent on decentralized consensus that are tamperproof and typically self-enforcing through automated execution. Other similar definitions can be found in Szabo (1998) and Lauslahti *et al.* (2017).

To the extent that contract terms are contingent on outcomes that can be recorded on blockchains (potentially via IoTs, or "oracles" feeders of information from the offline world onto the internet), smart contracts foremost reduce the contracting frictions and costs of a trust system. It allows contracting parties to more easily reach consensus which is robust to agency issues or technical failures of recordkeepers. This enlarges the contracting space and makes contracts in practice more complete. Moreover, the linked-list structure and time stamping also allow smart contracts to commit to no renegotiation. In that regard, smart contracts can be robust to renegotiation. Cong and He (2018) and Tinn (2018) formally discussed these issues. Gans (2019) and Bakos and Halaburda (2019) further described how smart contracts can help overcome holdup issues and contracting difficulties, or be integrated with IoT.

Smart contracts' impact on dynamic moral hazard is unclear and is closely related to information design. In particular, more transparency or more frequent monitoring/disclosure of information is not necessarily desirable (e.g., Orlov, 2018). The study by Tinn (2018) contains an in-depth discussion on how learning can make debt and equity more costly and restrictive under moral hazard and relates smart contracting to traditional dynamic moral hazard (e.g., Holmstrom and Milgrom, 1987).

As for broader applications, smart contracts can be designed for information-constrained insurance or credit, in addition to being a device that facilitates information and mechanism design to overcome the issues of rational herding (Cong and Xiao, 2019). Various informational issues such as how blockchain helps with coordination are just starting to be explored; contracting using digital information is likely an important ingredient in the overarching architecture. They, in turn, are related to competition and industrial organization. Lyandres (2019) is a recent examination of the effects of price commitments via smart contracts on firm competition and value.

As much as we are excited about the potential of smart contracting, we have to recognize their limitations. First, it cannot enforce the transfer of ownership of offline assets, a point also belabored in Abadi and Brunnermeier (2018); second, it has been combined with IoTs and oracles to acquire information off-chain; third, it is not a panacea for incomplete contracting: contingencies traditional contracts cannot specify are also hard to program into smart contracts, unless artificial intelligence drastically changes how smart contracts function.

Once again, consensus for smart contracting at large scale may make decentralization difficult due to the implications of information distribution, a point that we will discuss next.

4.7. *Information aggregation and distribution*

Closely related to smart contracting is the broader informational implication of blockchains, an aspect of the technological development that is largely neglected. Economists have long understood that information distribution or disclosure could lead to undesirable outcomes such as collusions (Bloomfield and O'Hara, 1999). Cong and He (2018) were also among the first set of researchers to bring such discussions to blockchains

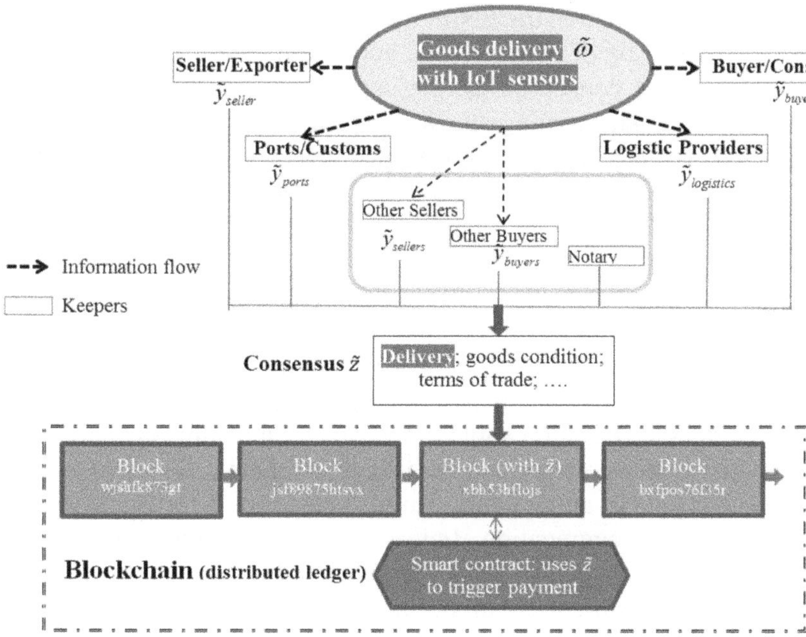

Figure 6: A diagram of the trade finance example of a blockchain.

Source: Reproduced from Cong and He (2019).

Notes: A seller delivers goods to a buyer, with $\tilde{\omega}$ denoting the contingency of successful delivery. Recordkeepers, potentially with real-time IoT sensors, monitor the delivery and submit their reports, $\tilde{y}_k$'s. The protocol of blockchain aggregates these reports to form a decentralized consensus, $\tilde{z}$. This consensus, together with the smart contract, is stored in the block and then added to the blockchain.

and point out considerable informational challenges in maintaining a decentralized system.[8]

The main insight in Cong and He (2018) is that in order for a decentralized consensus system to be robust to single points of failure, there has to be some degree of information distribution, even encrypted information. This is illustrated in Figure 6. But greater information in the public domain would lead to market participants to tacitly collude more, hurting consumer welfare.

[8]A related study is by Aune *et al.* (2017), who discussed the use of hashing to secure time priority without revealing detailed information and disclosing information later, in order to prevent front-running a transaction.

Though the information distribution entailed in decentralized consensus processes could be detrimental, the authors' message is broader: the robust decentralized consensus enables agents to contract on delivery outcomes and automate contingent transfers, therefore eliminating information asymmetry as a barrier for entry and encouraging greater competition. Blockchains and smart contracts expand the set of possible dynamic equilibria leading to social welfare and consumer surplus that could be higher or lower than in a traditional world.

Information transmission is also affected by the technology. For example, Chod *et al.* (2019) show that signaling a firm's fundamental quality (e.g., its operational capabilities) to lenders through inventory transactions is more efficient than signaling through loan requests. The blockchain technology could enable the verification of fundamentals and provide greater transparency into a firm's supply chain.

Finally, blockchain architecture can also be utilized for crowdsourcing and information aggregation. Indeed, many blockchain-based platforms increasingly use token-weighted voting to crowdsource information from their users for content curation, on-chain governance, etc. The role of decentralized structure and tokens are yet to be fully understood. For example, Falk and Tsoukalas (2019) have showed that token weighting generally discourages truthful voting and erodes the platform's information aggregation for prediction.

5. Concluding Remarks and Future Directions

To conclude, we summarize the key takeaways of the discussion thus far. Digital technology rebuilds the dynamics and relations among economic agents, potentially turning competition to collaboration, integrating segmented markets, and enabling consumers to participate and benefit more from business enterprises. Digitized information and functional trust constitute the hallmarks of a digital economy. While great progress has been achieved in terms of digitization, building trust on digital networks has been challenging. Blockchains provide a potential decentralized solution. Against this general backdrop, several general themes on blockchain economics stand out.

First, a game-theoretical approach to understanding consensus protocols has proven successful. For example, Biais *et al.* (2019b) point out directions in setting fees and designing throughput capacity, etc. The key is to specify preferences and action space, and agents rationally maximize their expected utilities. This is different from computer scientists' typical approach of directly assuming nodes' behaviors. One case is the study by Manshaei *et al.* (2018), who studied multiple committee runs in parallel to validate a non-intersecting set of transactions (a shard), with both Byzantine agents and rational agents. Amoussou-Guenou *et al.* (2019) have analyzed a similar problem in a dynamic setting and showed that rational agents can be pivotal instead of merely free ride.

Among the attempts at resolving the various bottlenecks of blockchain systems, those that involve local consensus, local centralization, or local scalability for solving privacy issues, saving storage, increasing throughput seem promising (Sharding is an example). Elastico (NUS Singapore) is an example. Each committee that uses BFT then submits the summaries to the final committee.

Second, besides technical innovations aimed at overcoming the impossibility triangle, breakthroughs are likely to come from mechanism design approaches to consensus protocols, with clear objectives for specific applications. For example, some blockchain applications may not require scalability, while some do not require global consensus. The protocol designs would differ correspondingly. Wishful ideology or Utopian dreams of full decentralization are not going to effectively propel the industry forward, but the right designs incentivizing and empowering agents in a decentralized or multi-centered system will.

In particular, protocol design should take into consideration blockchain governance (not only consensus about transactions but also how to resolve conflicts such as forking). One recent attempt related to governance and voting schemes was that of Barrera and Hurder (2018). A mechanism design approach also allows us to link layer one (decentralized consensus) and layer two (business model) innovations. Some designs could be useful for both incentivizing consensus generation and incentivizing users, as we elaborate next.

Third, agency and incentive issues remain at the core of blockchain economics. The discussion of incentive provision should not be restricted to the consensus protocol level, but can be extended to include user adoption, market design, etc., that are at the platform/ecosystem level.

Here, smart contracts coupled with sensors/IoTs would prove useful in that they can ensure prompt and guaranteed payments when contingent terms are satisfied. Would more verifiable data improve contracting efficiency? A better traceability of product and cash flows may allow firms to collateralize their account receivables more effectively and to receive payments from banks more quickly. They can also be used to compensate contributors and users on the network for content contributions and the like or between organizations such as mining pools and their members.

Speaking of users, their decision-making in a decentralized system is less studied, so are entrepreneurial teams that build the blockchain infrastructures. The interaction of user and consensus provision, and more generally, the service provision and demand in a platform economy can bring new economic insights for blockchain applications. The use of cryptotokens may prove useful in aligning incentives on platforms.[9] The work by Cong *et al.* (2018a) serves as an example of a recent study in this direction.

Finally, informational exchanges and data issues here started to be explored. In initial coin offerings (ICOs) or initial exchange offerings (IEOs), how would the informational asymmetry and environment relate to misreporting, incentive alignments, and fraudulent activities? How should policymakers regulate the markets and mandate information disclosures? How do we utilize IoTs and oracles to input information from offline environments? How would protocol designs matter for information aggregation and distribution?

In particular, the decentralized system seems to offer a solution for achieving data privacy and effective use of proprietary databases at the same time. Multi-party computation combining blockchain and various encryption methods opens new doors for how data are stored and used across institutions and individuals in future, which in turn affects economic decision-making. One caveat is that blockchains alone are not panacea for the problem of offline data authenticity and original data quality.

Surveying the past and looking into the future, we can say that if information and assets are the blood of a human body, then trust/consensus system (centralized or decentralized) is the vessel. Similarly if big data and physical resources are the input for the society's production, a functional digital network is the production function. Distributed systems such as blockchains are likely to be an integral part of this broader picture.

[9] While media discussions focus on cryptocurrencies as a substitute for money, it is equally important to understand the fundamental economics of using tokens on platforms or at digital market places. A large number of industry projects and academic studies are devoted to understanding better tokenomics, which could be just as important as blockchain protocol designs.

Acknowledgments

The authors thank Hanna Halaburda and Maureen O'Hara for detailed feedback and suggestions. They are also grateful to Bruno Biais, Jonathan Chiu, Evgeny Lyandres, and Fahad Saleh for helpful comments. This research was funded in part by the Ewing Marion Kau man Foundation. The contents of this publication are solely the responsibility of the authors.

References

Abadi, J. and M. Brunnermeier (2018), Blockchain economics, Discussion paper, mimeo Princeton University.

Abram, M., D. Galindo, D. Honerkamp, J. Ward, and J.-M. Wong (2019), Democratising blockchain: A minimal agency consensus model, working paper.

Ali, M. S., M. Vecchio, M. Pincheira, K. Dolui, F. Antonelli, and M. H. Rehmani (2018), Applications of blockchains in the internet of things: A comprehensive survey, *IEEE Communications Surveys & Tutorials* **21**(2), 1676–1717.

Amoussou-Guenou, Y., B. Biais, M. Potop-Butucaru, and S. Tucci-Piergiovanni (2019), Rationals vs byzantines in consensus-based blockchains, arXiv preprint arXiv:1902.07895.

Athey, S., I. Parashkevov, V. Sarukkai, and J. Xia (2016), Bitcoin pricing, adoption, and usage: Theory and evidence, Working Paper.

Aune, R. T., A. Krellenstein, M. O'Hara, and O. Slama (2017), Footprints on the blockchain: Trading and information leakage in distributed ledgers, *The Journal of Trading* **12**(3), 5–13.

Bahack, L. (2013), Theoretical bitcoin attacks with less than half of the computational power (draft), arXiv preprint arXiv:1312.7013.

Bakos, Y. and H. Halaburda (2019), When do smart contracts and IOT improve efficiency? Automated execution vs. increased information, Automated Execution vs. Increased Information (May 26, 2019), NYU Stern School of Business.

Barrera, C. and S. Hurder (2018), Blockchain upgrade as a coordination game.

Basu, S., D. Easley, M. O'Hara, and E. Sirer (2019), Towards a functional fee market for cryptocurrencies, Available at SSRN 3318327.

Benetton, M., G. Compiani, and A. Morse (2019), Cryptomining: Local evidence from China and the US, Working paper.

Biais, B., C. Bisiere, M. Bouvard, and C. Casamatta (2019a), The blockchain folk theorem, *The Review of Financial Studies* **32**, 1662–1715.

Biais, B. (2019b), Strategic interactions in blockchain protocols: A survey of game-theoretic approaches, Working Paper.

Bloomfield, R. and M. O'Hara (1999), Market transparency: who wins and who loses?, *Review of Financial Studies* **12**, 5–35.

Bottou, L. (1991), Stochastic gradient learning in neural networks, *Proceedings of Neuro-Nimes* **91**, 12.

Brewer, E. A. (2000), Towards robust distributed systems, Principles of Distributed Computing, Portland, Oregon Invited Talk.

Brunjes, L., A. Kiayias, E. Koutsoupias, and A.-P. Stouka (2018), Reward sharing schemes for stake pools, arXiv preprint arXiv:1807.11218.

Cao, S., L. W. Cong, and B. Yang (2018), Auditing and blockchains: Pricing, misstatements, and regulation, Misstatements, and Regulation.

Carlsten, M., H. Kalodner, S. M. Weinberg, and A. Narayanan (2016), On the instability of bitcoin without the block reward, in Proceedings of the 2016 ACM SIGSAC Conference on Computer and Communications Security, ACM, pp. 154–167.

Castro, M. and B. Liskov (2002), Practical byzantine fault tolerance and proactive recovery, *ACM Transactions on Computer Systems* (*TOCS*) **20**, 398–461.

Chiu, J. and T. V. Koeppl (2017), The economics of cryptocurrencies — bitcoin and beyond, Working Paper.

Chiu, J. (2019), Blockchain-based settlement for asset trading, *The Review of Financial Studies* **32**, 1716–1753.

Chod, J. and E. Lyandres (2018), A theory of ICOs: Diversification, agency, and asymmetric information, Working paper Boston University Questrom School of Business.

Chod, J., N. Trichakis, G. Tsoukalas, H. Aspegren, and M. Weber (2019), On the financing benefits of supply chain transparency and blockchain adoption, Management Science.

Cong, L. W. (2019), A brief introduction to tokenomics, Palgrave Handbook of FinTech and Blockchain Book Chapter under Preparation.

Cong, L. W. and Z. He (2018), Blockchain disruption and smart contracts, Forthcoming, Review of Financial Studies.

Cong, L. W. and J. Li (2018), Decentralized mining in centralized pools, Working Paper.

Cong, L. W., Y. Li, and N. Wang (2018a), Token-based corporate finance, Working Paper.

Cong, L. W. (2018b), Tokenomics: Dynamic adoption and valuation, Working Paper.

Cong, L. W. (2019), Tokenomics and platform finance, Working Paper.

Cong, L. W. and Y. Xiao (2019), Information cascades and threshold implementation, University of Chicago, Becker Friedman Institute for Economics Working Paper.

Conti, M., E. Sandeep Kumar, C. Lal, and S. Ruj (2018), A survey on security and privacy issues of bitcoin, *IEEE Communications Surveys & Tutorials* **20**, 3416–3452.

de Vries, A. (2019), Renewable energy will not solve bitcoins sustainability problem, *Joule* **3**, 893–898.

Easley, D., M. O'Hara, and S. Basu (2017), From mining to markets: The evolution of bitcoin transaction fees, Working Paper.

Eyal, I., A. E. Gencer, E. G. Sirer, and R. Van Renesse (2016), Bitcoin-ng: A scalable blockchain protocol, in *13th fUSENIXg Symposium on Networked Systems Design and Implementation (fNSDIg 16)*, pp. 45–59.

Eyal, I. and E. G. Sirer (2014), Majority is not enough: Bitcoin mining is vulnerable, in *International Conference on Financial Cryptography and Data Security*, Springer, pp. 436–454.

Falk, B. and G. Tsoukalas (2019), Token weighted crowdsourcing, Discussion paper, Working Paper.

Ferreira, D., J. Li, and R. Nikolowa (2019), Corporate capture of blockchain governance, Available at SSRN 3320437.

Fisch, B., R. Pass, and A. Shelat (2017), Socially optimal mining pools, in *International Conference on Web and Internet Economics*, Springer, pp. 205–218.

Fischer, M. J., N. A. Lynch, and M. S. Paterson (1982), Impossibility of distributed consensus with one faulty process. Discussion paper, Massachusetts Inst of Tech Cambridge lab for Computer Science.

Fort, T. C. (2017), Technology and production fragmentation: Domestic versus foreign sourcing, *The Review of Economic Studies* **84**, 650–687.

Gan, J. R., G. Tsoukalas, and S. Netessine (2019), Inventory, speculators and initial coin offerings, The Wharton School Research Paper.

Gans, J. S. (2019), The fine print in smart contracts, Discussion paper, National Bureau of Economic Research.

Gilbert, S. and N. Lynch (2002), Brewer's conjecture and the feasibility of consistent, available, partition-tolerant web services, *Acm Sigact News* **33**, 51–59.

Halaburda, H. (2018), Blockchain revolution without the blockchain, Bank of Canada Staff Analytical Note 5.

Halaburda, H. and G. Haeringer (2018), Bitcoin and blockchain: What we know and what questions are still open, NYU Stern School of Business, Forthcoming.

Halaburda, H. and M. Sarvary (2016), Beyond bitcoin, *The Economics of Digital Currencies*, Springer.

Hilary, G. and L. Liu (2018), Blockchain and nance, Working paper.

Hinzen, F. J., K. John, and F. Saleh (2019), Bitcoin's fatal aw: The limited adoption problem, NYU Stern School of Business.

Holmstrom, B. and P. Milgrom (1987), Aggregation and linearity in the provision of intertemporal incentives, *Econometrica: Journal of the Econometric Society* **55**(2), 303–328.

Huberman, G., J. Leshno, and C. C. Moallemi (2017), Monopoly without a monopolist: An economic analysis of the bitcoin payment system, Working Paper 17–92, Columbia Business School.

Johnson, B., A. Laszka, J. Grossklags, M. Vasek, and T. Moore (2014), Game-theoretic analysis of DDoS attacks against bitcoin mining pools, in *International Conference on Financial Cryptography and Data Security*, Springer, pp. 72–86.

Kiayias, A., E. Koutsoupias, M. Kyropoulou, and Y. Tselekounis (2016), Blockchain mining games, in *Proceedings of the 2016 ACM Conference on Economics and Computation*, ACM, pp. 365–382.

Kogias, E. K., P. Jovanovic, N. Gailly, I. Kho, L. Gasser, and B. Ford (2016), Enhancing bitcoin security and performance with strong consistency via collective signing, in *25th fUSENIXg Security Symposium (fUSENIXg Security 16)*, pp. 279–296.

Kroll, J. A., I. C. Davey, and E. W. Felten (2013), The economics of bitcoin mining, or bitcoin in the presence of adversaries, in *Proceedings of WEIS*, vol. 2013, Citeseer.

Lauslahti, K., J. Mattila, and T. Seppala (2017), Smart contracts — how will blockchain technology affect contractual practices?, Etla Reports.

Li, J., N. Li, J. Peng, H. Cui, and Z. Wu (2019), Energy consumption of cryptocurrency mining: A study of electricity consumption in mining cryptocurrencies, *Energy* **168**, 160–168.

Liu, X., W. Wang, D. Niyato, N. Zhao, and P. Wang (2018), Evolutionary game for mining pool selection in blockchain networks, *IEEE Wireless Communications Letters* **7**, 760–763.

Liu, Y. and A. Tsyvinski (2018), Risks and returns of cryptocurrency, Working Paper 24877, National Bureau of Economic Research.

Liu, Z., N. C. Luong, W. Wang, D. Niyato, P. Wang, Y.-C. Liang, and D. I. Kim (2019), A survey on blockchain: A game theoretical perspective, *IEEE Access* **7**, 47615–47643.

Luohan Academy, Research Team (2019), Digital technology and inclusive growth, Report.

Luu, L., V. Narayanan, C. Zheng, K. Baweja, S. Gilbert, and P. Saxena (2016), A secure sharding protocol for open blockchains, in *Proceedings of the 2016 ACM SIGSAC Conference on Computer and Communications Security*, ACM, pp. 17–30.

Lyandres, E. (2019), Product market competition with crypto tokens and smart contracts, Available at SSRN 3395441.

Ma, J., J. S. Gans, and R. Tourky (2018), Market structure in bitcoin mining, National Bureau of Economic Research Working Paper.

Malik, N., M. Aseri, P. Vir Singh, and K. Srinivasan (2019), Why bitcoin will fail to scale?, Available at SSRN 3323529.

Manshaei, M. H., M. Jadliwala, A. Maiti, and M. Fooladgar (2018), A game-theoretic analysis of shard-based permissionless blockchains, *IEEE Access* **6**, 78100–78112.

MIT, M. (2018), Machine learning for encrypted blockchains — Sandy Pentland, Ph.D. thesis.

Narayanan, A. and J. Clark (2017), Bitcoin's academic pedigree, *Communications of the ACM* **60**, 36–45.

Nayak, K., S. Kumar, A. Miller, and E. Shi (2016), Stubborn mining: Generalizing selfish mining and combining with an eclipse attack, in *2016 IEEE European Symposium on Security and Privacy (EuroS&P)*, IEEE, pp. 305–320.

O'Dwyer, K. J. and D. Malone (2014), Bitcoin mining and its energy footprint, in *IET Conference Proceedings*.

Ometoruwa, T. (2018), Solving the blockchain trilemma: Decentralization, security & scalability, www.coinbureau.com/analysis/solving-blockchain-trilemma/.

Orlov, D. (2018), Frequent monitoring in dynamic contracts, Discussion paper, working paper.

Pagnotta, E. (2018), Bitcoin as decentralized money: Prices, mining rewards, and network security, Mining Rewards, and Network Security (October 26, 2018).

Popov, S. (2016), The tangle, cit. on p. 131. https://files.bitscreener.com/downloads/wp/iota_Whitepaper.pdf.

Prat, J. and B. Walter (2018), An equilibrium model of the market for bitcoin mining, Working Paper.

Raikwar, M., S. Mazumdar, S. Ruj, S. S. Gupta, A. Chattopadhyay, and K.-Y. Lam (2018), A blockchain framework for insurance processes, in *2018 9th IFIP International Conference on New Technologies, Mobility and Security (NTMS)*, IEEE, pp. 1–4.

Reese, F. (2017), Land registry: A big blockchain use case explored. Coindesk, April **19** (2017).

Saleh, F. (2019a), Blockchain without waste: Proof-of-stake, Discussion paper, working Paper.

Saleh, F. (2019b), Volatility and welfare in a crypto economy, Available at SSRN 3235467.

Sapirshtein, A., Y. Sompolinsky, and A. Zohar (2016), Optimal sel sh mining strategies in bitcoin, in *International Conference on Financial Cryptography and Data Security*, Springer, pp. 515–532.

Szabo, N. (1998), Secure property titles with owner authority, Online at http:// szabo. best. vwh. net/securetitle. html.

Tinn, K. (2018), "Smart" contracts and external financing, Available at SSRN 3072854.

Townsend, R. (2019), Distributed ledgers: Innovation and regulation in financial infrastructure and payment systems, Discussion paper, Working Paper.

Truby, J. (2018), Decarbonizing bitcoin: Law and policy choices for reducing the energy consumption of blockchain technologies and digital currencies, *Energy Research & Social Science* **44**, 399–410.

Tschorsch, F. and B. Scheuermann (2016), Bitcoin and beyond: A technical survey on decentralized digital currencies, *IEEE Communications Surveys & Tutorials* **18**, 2084–2123.

Tysiac, K. (2018), How blockchain might affect audit and assurance, *Journal of Accountancy* **15**.

Yermack, D. (2017), Corporate governance and blockchains, *Review of Finance* **21**(1), 7–31.

Yue, X., H. Wang, D. Jin, M. Li, and W. Jiang (2016), Healthcare data gateways: found healthcare intelligence on blockchain with novel privacy risk control, *Journal of Medical Systems* **40**, 218.

Zyskind, G. *et al.* (2016), Efficient secure computation enabled by blockchain technology, Ph.D. thesis Massachusetts Institute of Technology.

https://doi.org/10.1142/9789811220470_0002

Chapter 2

Data Fiduciary in Order to Alleviate Principal–Agent Problems in the Artificial Big Data Age

Julia M. Puaschunder

The New School, Department of Economics, Schwartz Center for Economic Policy Analysis, 6 East 16th Street, 11th floor 1129F-99, New York, NY 10003, USA

Columbia University, Graduate School of Arts and Sciences, 116th Street Broadway, New York, NY 10027, USA

Princeton University, Princeton, NJ, USA

Julia.Puaschunder@newschool.edu; Julia.Puaschunder@columbia.edu; Julia.Puaschunder@princeton.edu

Abstract

The classic principal–agent problem in political science and economics describes agency dilemmas or problems when one person, the agent, is put in a situation to make decisions on behalf of another entity, the principal. A dilemma occurs in situations when individual profit maximization or principal and agent are pitted against each other. This so-called moral hazard is emerging in the current artificial big data age, when big data reaping entities have to act on behalf of agents, who provide their data with trust in the principal's integrity and responsible big data conduct. Yet, to this day, no data fiduciary has been clearly described and established to protect the agent from misusing the data. This paper introduces the agent's predicament between utility derived from information sharing and dignity in privacy as well as hyper-hyperbolic discounting fallibilities to not clearly foresee what consequences information sharing can have over time and in groups. The principal's predicament between secrecy and selling big data insights or using big data for manipulative purposes will be outlined. Finally, the paper draws a clear distinction between manipulation and nudging in relation to the potential social class division of those who nudge and those who are nudged.

Keywords: Behavioral economics; Behavioral political economy; Data fiduciary; Democratization of information; Dignity education; Exchange value; Fiduciary duty; Governance; Information sharing; Preferences; Privacy; Reclaiming the common good of knowledge; Right to delete; Right to be forgotten; Self-determination; Social media; Utility; Values.

1. Introduction

The big data age has created a dilemma between utility derived in information sharing and dignity upheld in privacy. Economics is concerned about utility. Utility theory captures people's preferences or values. As one of the foundations of economic theory, the wealth of information and theories on utility lack information about decision-making conflicts between preferences and values. The preference for communication is inherent in human beings as a distinct feature of humanity. Leaving a written legacy that can inform many generations to come is a human-unique advancement of society. At the same time, however, privacy is a core human value. People choose what information to share with whom and like to protect some parts of their selves. Protecting people's privacy is a codified virtue around the globe grounded in the wish to uphold individual dignity. Yet, to this day, no utility theory exists to describe the internal conflict arising from the individual preference to communicate and the value of privacy. In the age of instant communication and social media big data storage and computational power; the need for understanding people's trade-off between communication and privacy has leveraged to unprecedented momentum. Today, enormous data storage capacities and computational power in the e-big data era have created unforeseen opportunities for big data-hoarding corporations to reap hidden benefits from individual's information sharing, which occurs bit by bit in small tranches over time. Behavioral economics describes human decision-making fallibility over time but has — to this day — not covered the problem of individuals' decision to share information about themselves in tranches on social media and big data administrators being able to reap a benefit from putting data together over time and reflecting the individual's information in relation to big data of others. The decision-making fallibility inherent in individuals having problems understanding the impact of their current information sharing in the future is introduced as hyper-hyperbolic discounting decision-making predicament. Individuals lose control over their data without knowing what surplus value big data moguls can reap from the social media consumer–workers' information sharing, what information can be complied over time and what information these data can provide in relation to the general public's data in drawing inferences about the innocent individual information sharer. For instance, big data-derived personality cues have recently been used for governance control purposes, such as border protection and tax compliance surveillance. The utility theory of contradicting information sharing and privacy predicaments is presented in this study for the first time and a nomenclature of different personality types regarding information sharing and privacy preferences is theoretically introduced. Not only unraveling the utility of information sharing versus privacy conflict but also shedding light at the current commodification of big data influences economic theory advancement and governance improvement potentials in the digital age. The presented piece can also serve as a first step toward advocating for reclaiming the common good of knowledge via taxation of big data harvesting and self-determination of information sharing based on education about information sharing in order to curb harmful information sharing discounting fallibility. From legal and governance perspectives, the outlined ideas may stimulate the e-privacy infringement regulations discourse in the pursuit of the greater goals of democratization of information, equality of communication surplus, and upholding of human dignity in the realm of e-ethics in the big data era.

In the digital age, the study of the trade-off between information sharing and privacy has leveraged into unprecedented importance. Social media revolutionized human communication around the globe. As never before in the history of humankind, information about individuals can be stored and put in context over time and logically placed within society, thanks to unprecedented data conservation and computational powers.

The big data era, however, also opened gates to unprecedentedly reap benefits from information sharing and big data generation (Puaschunder, 2017). The so-called nudgital society was recently introduced, shedding light onto the undescribed hidden social class division between social media users and social media providers, who can benefit from the information shared by social media users. Social media users share private information in their wish to interact with friends and communicate to public. The social media big data holder can then reap surplus value from the information shared by selling it to marketers, who can draw inferences about consumer choices. Big data can also be used for governance control purposes, for instance, border protection and tax compliance control.

Drawing from the economic foundations of utility theory, this study seeks to introduce the first application of data fiduciary. Behavioral economics insights are advanced in shedding novel light on the conflict between the human wish to communicate now versus combined information held by unknown big data compilers in the future. An exponential loss of privacy and hyper-hyperbolic risks in the future for the information sharer are introduced as behavioral economic decision-making fallibilities. For the overconfident information sharer, it remains largely unforeseeable what the sum of the individual information sharing tranches can lead to over time and what information its Gestalt holds for those who have big data insights over time, which can also be analyzed in relation to the general population. Governance gains a critical stance on new media use for guiding on public concerns regarding privacy and information sharing in the digital age (Puaschunder, 2017). While there is some literature on the history of media on politics (Prat and Strömberg, 2013), the wide societal implications of fake news and discounting misinformation have widely been overlooked in contemporary behavioral economics research and the externalities literature. Social sciences literature on privacy and information sharing has to be reconsidered in the age of social media.

2. Theory — Fiduciary Responsibility

The classic principal–agent problem describes agency dilemmas or problems when one person, the agent, is put in a situation to make decisions on behalf of another entity, the principal. A dilemma occurs in situations when individual profit maximization or principal and agent are pitted against each other. This so-called moral hazard is emerging in the current artificial big data age, when big data reaping entities have to act on behalf of agents, who provide their data with trust in the principal's integrity and responsible big data conduct. Examples of fiduciary duties arise in relationships within the corporate management and shareholders, elected officials and citizens, brokers and markets as well as legal clients and lawyers. In all these cases, the agent is meant to uphold the principal's well-being, even in the absence of or even when colliding with personal and principal's interests. Problems stem from both parties' different interests and asymmetric information (in most cases, the agents have more information), such that the principal cannot directly ensure that the agent is always acting in the principal's best interest. These predicaments are described as moral hazard or conflict of interest. Literature describes exploitation by the agent and deviations from the principal's interest in the so-called agency costs leading to suboptimal outcomes that can lower the general welfare. The agency problem is intensified when agents act on behalf of multiple principals, who have to agree on the agent's objectives but face a collective action problem in governance (Bernheim and Whinston, 1986). As a result, free-riding or conflicts may occur, which often become prevalent in the public sector. Alleviation strategies include incentives such as employer contracts and commissions, profit sharing, efficiency wages, and performance management. Also, transparency, monitoring, and shared responsibility have come to be used in order to avoid the negative impacts of fiduciary breaches, which include risks and uncertainties imposed in markets and society. In the artificial age, when big data can be retrieved online from every action individuals take online and especially from information shared online, the time has come to address fiduciary duties around information. Granting access to information derives from a predicament between utility derived from information and dignity upheld in privacy.

3. Information Sharing and Privacy

The wish for communication is inherent in human beings as a distinct feature of humanity. Leaving a written legacy that can inform many generations to come is a human-unique advancement of society. At the same time, however, privacy is a core human value. People choose what information to share with whom and like to protect some parts of their selves in secrecy. Protecting people's privacy is a codified virtue around the world to uphold the individual's dignity. Yet, to this day, no utility theory exists to describe the conflict arising from the individual preference to communicate and the value of privacy.

3.1. *The human preference for communication*

The act of conveying intended meanings from one entity or group to another through the use of mutually understood signs and semiotic rules is the act of communication. Communication is a key feature of humans, animals, and even plants (Witzany, 2012). Steps inherent to all human communication are the formation of communicative motivation and reason, message composition as further internal or technical elaboration on what exactly to express, message encoding, transmission of the encoded message, as a sequence of signals using a specific channel or medium, noise sources influencing the quality of signals propagating from the sender to one or more receivers, reception of signals and reassembling of the encoded message from a sequence of received signals, decoding of the reassembled encoded message, and interpretation or sense making of the presumed original message (Shannon, 1948). Information sharing, which implies giving up privacy, is at the core of communication. Communication can be both verbal and non-verbal. Comprising many different domains ranging from business, politics, interpersonal, and social media to mass media, communication is a human-imbued wish and is at the core of every functioning society.

In society, language is used to exchange ideas and embody theories of reality. Language is the driver of social progress (Orwell, 1949). Linguists find discourse and information sharing inseparable from socioeconomic societal advancement (Fowler *et al.*, 1979). Language and communication modes are implicit determinants of social strata (Orwell, 1949). Different institutions and media sources have different varieties of language and information sharing styles. Access to information is related to social status and market power. Social visibility is a powerful and cheap incentive to make people contribute more to public goods and charities and be less likely to lie, cheat, or pollute or be insensitive and antisocial (Ali and Benabou, 2016). Information receipt is an implicit determinant to classify and rank people to assert institutional or personal status in society (Fowler *et al.*, 1979). Mass communication echoes in economic cycles in the creation of booms and busts (Puaschunder, work in progress). Media is also a hallmark of propaganda and political control (Besley and Prat, 2006; Prat and Strömberg, 2013). At the same time, privacy is a human virtue around the world.

3.2. *Privacy as a human virtue*

Privacy is the ability of an individual or group to seclude themselves, or information about themselves, and thereby selectively share information about themselves. The right to privacy grants the ability to choose which information about parts of the self can be accessed by others and to control the extent, manner, and timing of the use of those parts we choose to disclose. Privacy comprises the right to be let alone, the option to limit the access others have to one's personal information, and secrecy as the option to conceal any information about oneself (Solove, 2008).

The degree of privacy varies in autonomy levels throughout individualistic and collectivistic cultures. While the boundaries and contents protected and what is considered as private differ widely among cultures and individuals, the common sense in the world is that some parts of the self should be protected as private.

Privacy has a valued feature of being something inherently special or sensitive to a person, which can create value and specialty if shared with only a selected person or group. The domain of privacy partially overlaps with security, confidentiality, and secrecy, which are codified and legally protected throughout the world, not only in privacy laws but also in natural laws of virtues of integrity and dignity. Privacy is seen as a collective core human value and fundamental human right, which is upheld in constitutions around the world[1] (Johnson, 2009; Warren and Brandeis, 1890).

In personal relations, privacy can be voluntarily sacrificed, normally in exchange for reciprocity and perceived benefits. Sharing private information can breed trust and bestow meaningfulness to social relations. Giving up privacy holds risks of uncertainty and losses, which are undescribed in economics and in particular the behavioral economics literature on intertemporal decision-making (Gaudeul and Giannetti, 2017). People tend to be more willing to voluntarily sacrifice privacy if the data gatherer is seen to be transparent as to what information is gathered and how the information will be used (Oulasvirta *et al.*, 2014). Privacy as a prerequisite for the development of a sense of self-identity is a core of humanness (Altman, 1975). Privacy is often protected to avoid discrimination,

---

[1]For example, Asian-Pacific Economic Cooperation, Australia, Brazil, Canada, China, European Union, Italy, Japan, Korea, Organization for Economic Co-operation and Development, South Africa, United Kingdom, United Nations, United States, Universal Declaration of Human Rights — to name a few.

manipulation, exploitation, embarrassment and risks of reputational losses, for instance, in the domains of body parts, home and property, general information of private financial situations, medical records, political affiliation, religious denomination, thoughts, feelings, and identity.

Technological shocks have a history of challenging privacy standards (Warren and Brandeis, 1890). The age of instant messaging and big data, however, has leveraged the idea of privacy to another dimension. The concept of information privacy has become more significant as more systems controlling big data appear in the digital age. With advances in big data, face recognition, automated license plate readers, and other tracking technologies, upholding privacy and anonymity has become increasingly expensive and the cost is more opaque than ever before (Ali and Benabou, 2016).

3.3. *Privacy in the digital big data era*

The amount of big data stored each second has reached an all-time high in the digital era. Internet privacy is the ability to determine what information one reveals or withholds about oneself over the Internet, who has access to personal information and for what purpose one's information may be used. Privacy laws in many countries have started to adapt to changes in technology in order to cope with unprecedented constant information surveillance possibilities, big data storage opportunities, and computational power peaks. For instance, Microsoft reports that 75% of US recruiters and human resource professionals use online data about candidates, often using information provided by search engines, social network sites, photo and video sharing tools, personal web appearances like websites and blogs, as well as Twitter.

Social media tools have become large-scale factories with unpaid labor (Puaschunder, 2017). For instance, Facebook is currently the largest social network site with nearly 1,490 million members, who upload over 4.75 billion pieces of content about their lives and that of others daily. The accuracy of this information also appears questionable, with about 83.09 million accounts assumed to be fake. Aside from directly observable information, social media sites can also easily track browsing logs and patterns, search queries or secondary information giving inferences about sexual orientation, political and religious views, race, substance use, intelligence and overall personality, mental status, and individual views and preferences (Kosinski *et al.*, 2013, 2014).

As for the unprecedented possibilities to collect data, store big data, and aggregate information that can be compared to big data Gestalt over time and society, privacy has leveraged into one of the most fragile areas of concern in the electronic age, demanding for legal protection, regulatory control, and e-ethics (Flaherty, 1989). Today, the existing global privacy rights framework in the digital age has been criticized to be incoherent, inefficient, and in need for revision. Global privacy protection shields are demanded to be established. Yet, to this day there is no economic framework on information sharing and privacy control. While — for instance — Posner (1981) criticizes privacy for concealing information, which reduces market efficiency; Lessig (2006) advocates for regulated online privacy. As of now, we lack a behavioral decision-making frame to explain the privacy paradox of the individual predicament between the human-imbued preference to communicate and share information on the one hand and value of privacy on the other hand. We have no behavioral economics description of inconsistencies and moderator variables in the decision between online information sharing behavior and retroactive preference reversal preferences in the eye of privacy concerns in the digital big data era.

4. A Utility Theory of Information Sharing and Privacy

Building on classical utility theory, individuals are constantly evaluating competing choice options. Individuals weigh alternative options based on their expected utility. Indifference curves would then connect points on a graph representing different quantities of two goods, between which an individual is indifferent.

In the case of the privacy paradox of information sharing preferences and privacy values, a person would weighs whether or not to share information s or choose the information to remain private p. The respective indifference curves would outline how much of information sharing s and privacy p can be enabled to end with the same utility given the budget of overall information held by the decision-maker.

Figure 1 represents the respective indifference curves for information sharing s and privacy p. That is, the individual has no preference for one combination or bundle of information sharing or privacy over a different combination of the same curve. All points on the curve hold the same utility for the individual. The indifference curve is therefore the locus of

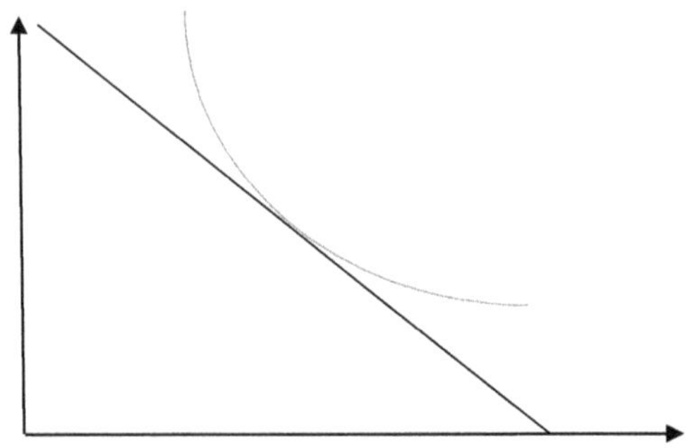

Figure 1: Indifference curve for information sharing *s* and privacy *p* given the total information and communication constraint.

various points of different combinations of privacy and information sharing providing equal utility to her or him. Indifference curves are thereby seen to represent potentially observable behavioral patterns for individuals over information bundles. The indifference curve for information sharing *s* and privacy *p* is subject to communication and information constraints and hence, to all information budgets and communication opportunities. There is only a finite amount of information. There may be environmental conditions determining whether people can exchange and share information. As exhibited in Figure 1, the indifference curve for information sharing *s* and privacy *p* is a straight line, given the assumption that information sharing or privacy are substitutes.

While in classical economics, an individual was believed to always be able to rank consumption bundles by order of preference (Jevons, 1871),[2] the indifference curve for information sharing *s* and privacy *p* subject to communication and information constraints may feature a hyper-hyperbolic element or temporal dimension. The information share moment may thereby be a reference point. At the moment of the information sharing decision, it may not be foreseeable what the future implication of the information sharing is.

In general, the costs and benefits of communication are assumed as linear subtraction of positive benefits of communication b_c minus the

[2] http://www.econlib.org/library/YPDBooks/Jevons/jvnPE.html.

negative consequences of communication c_c. The nature of the problem is intertemporal as information sharers cannot foresee the future implications of their information sharing divided by variance σ (Prat, 2017).

$$\frac{b_c - c_c}{\sigma}. \tag{1}$$

However, the digital social media era has heralded a hyper-hyperbolic discounting fallibility. Individuals have lost oversight of the consequences of their individual information sharing given big data-hoarding capabilities, which also allow drawing inferences about the individual in relation to others.

In the digital big data era, information shared online may hold unforeseen risks of privacy merchants or social media capitalists that commercialize information, thereby reaping hidden benefits from the information provided (Etzioni, 2012; Puaschunder, 2017; *The Economist*, November 4, 2017).[3] The subjective additive utility of information shared tranche by tranche may underestimate the big data holder's advantage to reap benefits from information shared given unprecedented data storage and big data computation power advantages of the big data era. Unprecedented computational power and storage opportunities have created the possibility to hoard information over time and put it in context with the rest of the population in order to draw inferences about the information sharer (*The New York Times*, November 14, 2017).[4] The digital age and era of instant information sharing have therefore heralded problems of individuals who give in their basic human need for information communication to become vulnerable over time. The big data information holder may thereby benefit from the history of information and the relation of the individual's information in comparison to the general population to an unknown degree given missing e-literacy and transparency. Comparison to the general public may lead to an implicit underrepresentation and hence discrimination of vulnerable groups. For instance, certain groups that may not be

---

[3] https://www.economist.com/news/leaders/21730871-facebook-google-and-twitter-were-supposed-save-politics-good-information-drove-out.

[4] https://www.nytimes.com/2017/11/14/business/dealbook/taxing-companies-for-using-our-personal-data.html?rref=collection%2Fsectioncollection%2Fbusiness&action=click&contentCollection=business&region=stream&module=stream_unit&version=latest&contentPlacement=8&pgtype=sectionfront.

represented online will therefore likely face an underadvocacy of their rights and needs.

While regular hyperbolic discounting captures a game-theoretical predicament of the self now versus the self later, the information offering more of a Gestalt in the eyes of the big data holder leverages hyperbolic discounting to a game theory against uncertainty on the end of the big data holder. The hyper-hyperbolic discounting fallibility therefore may describe that at the moment of information sharing, the individual has hardly any grasp what is implied in the giving up of privacy. The individual only focuses on the current moment trade-off between information sharing and privacy upholding, but hardly has any insights on what the compiled information over time holds for big data moguls. As for holding computational and storage advantages, the social media big data moguls can form a *Gestalt*, which is more than the sheer sum of the individual information shared, also in comparison to the general populace's data. The shared information can also be resold to companies (Etzioni, 2012; *The New York Times*, November 14, 2017).[5] In relation to other people's information, the big data moguls can make predictions about their choices and behaviors.[6] Information can also be used for governance purposes, for instance, tax compliance and border control mechanisms (Puaschunder, 2017). Some governments have recently used big data not only to check the accuracy of tax reports but also to detect people's political views when crossing borders (Puaschunder, 2017). Lastly, the use of big data inferences also implies hidden persuasion means — nudging can be turned against innocent information sharers who have no long-term and computational advantage to foresee the impact of the information share (*The Economist*, November 4, 2017; Puaschunder, 2017).[7]

---

[5] https://www.nytimes.com/2017/11/14/business/dealbook/taxing-companies-for-using-our-personal-data.html?rref=collection%2Fsectioncollection%2Fbusiness&action=click&contentCollection=business&region=stream&module=stream_unit&version=latest&contentPlacement=8&pgtype=sectionfront.

[6] https://www.nytimes.com/2017/11/14/business/dealbook/taxing-companies-for-using-our-personal-data.html?rref=collection%2Fsectioncollection%2Fbusiness&action=click&contentCollection=business&region=stream&module=stream_unit&version=latest&contentPlacement=8&pgtype=sectionfront.

[7] https://www.economist.com/news/leaders/21730871-facebook-google-and-twitter-were-supposed-save-politics-good-information-drove-out.

While behavioral economics hyperbolic discounting theory introduces the idea of time inconsistency of preferences between an individual now and the same individual in the future; hyper-hyperbolic discounting underlines that in the case of information sharing preferences this fallibility is exacerbated since individuals lose control over their data and big data moguls can reap surplus value from the social media consumer–workers' information sharing and derive information complied over time and in relation to the general norm to draw inferences about the innocent information sharer. With the modern digital era, all these features open an information sharer versus information reaper divide in the big data age (Puaschunder, 2017).

From the social media big data capitalist view, the information gain of one more person sharing information is exponentially rising. Hence, the marginal utility derived from one more person providing information is increasing exponentially and disproportionally to the marginally declining costs arising from one more person being added to the already existing social media platform. Communication costs and benefits are assumed to not be additive and separable.

4.1. *Expected utility and subjective probability in the digital big data era*

In accordance with neoclassical utility theory, decision-makers weigh alternatives based on the resulting consequences dependent on uncertain aspects of the environment. But in the digital big data era, individuals simply lack an oversight of the consequences of information sharing. Assumptions on the preferences of information sharing are skewed leading to an underestimation of the consequences of amalgamated information and private information evaluated in relation to other's data. Assignment of utilities to the consequences is underestimated. The utility of information sharing is thus the underweighted sum of the utilities of the consequences.

4.2. *Time preferences*

Following the standard neoclassical nomenclature of time preferences among the population, an information sharing preference over time is introduced. Multi-period decision-making addresses that for each time period, and another set of preferences for the same options can be expected. The populace may therefore be theoretically categorized as follows:

(1) **Extreme impatience:** Extreme information sharing as the individual values immediate pleasure of information sharing. Information is shared without hesitation, and impression management may play a role in this.
(2) **Impatience:** Discounting the future impact of information, uninformed information sharing nature. This is the case if an individual shares information, although he/she has a hunch that this information sharing may create problems in the future, called the privacy paradox.
(3) **Eventual impatience:** Discounting the future impact of information at some point in the future leads to controlled information sharing, very likely choosing what categories to expose to public.
(4) **Time perspective:** Related to hyper-hyperbolic discounting awareness, individuals may control information sharing. For instance, these individuals may participate in social media only to reap information from others but not contribute additional information beyond what is required. This type has a controlled privacy and is engaged in social media solely to reap benefits of other's information from social media networks.
(5) **No time preference:** At the present time, the individual neither discounts nor overcounts the future with respect to the present, which may be true for individuals who do not at all participate in social media communication and are blasé about information sharing and gaining information on social media,
(6) **Persistence:** Consistent preference structure regarding information sharing may result in informed information sharing with no regrets, and
(7) **Variety:** Consistently varying preference structure regarding information sharing, likely dependent on the content of information shared, may result in information sharing with regrets afterward. These individuals have no stringent position toward information sharing or privacy preference, likely have categories for what to share and what not. This type varies in information preferences over time and by subject category.

This nomenclature addresses the problem of capturing valid preference structures over time that allows the stringent prediction of choice behavior and strategies for future planning (Fishburn, 1968). The nomenclature also highlights that the selection of information sharing or privacy has an impact on our later choices. Addressing this predicament, Klein and Meckling (1958) suggest the best strategy given future uncertainties is to concentrate attention on immediate decisions that lead toward the main objective while preserving a reasonable degree of freedom in future choices. While Strotz (1957) considers the maximization of utility in an additive, discounted form over a continuous-time future, powerful research on hyperbolic discounting has unraveled pre-commitment and consistent planning as a means to curb harmful decision-making fallibility. Yet, in the age of social media, the big data generated may impose novel hyperbolic discounting fallibility onto the information-sharing individual (Behears *et al.*, 2011; Chabris *et al.*, 2008; Koopmans, 1964). Future research may test the reliability and validity of the nomenclature and unravel moderator variables and variances between different populations, e.g., such as age, cultural heritage, gender.

4.3. *Expected utility and subjective probability*

In accordance with neoclassical utility theory, alternatives are weighed based on the resulting consequences dependent on uncertain aspects of the environment. Assumptions on preferences between such alternatives lead to an assignment of utilities to the consequences and to the alternatives plus an assignment of subjective probabilities to the possible states of the environment. The utility of an alternative can therefore be written as a weighted sum of the utilities of the consequences. The weight for any alternative–consequence pair is the subjective probability associated with the states of the environment that yield the given consequence when the given alternative is used (Fishburn, 1968).

Regarding expected utility, the overall expected utility equation for information sharing and privacy reads as follows:

$$u = \sum w * u_s + w * u_p, \tag{2}$$

where w stands for weight, u_s is the utility of information sharing, and u_p is the utility of privacy.

The weighted expected utility equation reads

$$u(P) = P(x^1)u_s(x^1) + P(x^2)u_p(x^2), \tag{3}$$

where $P(x^1)u_s(x^1)$ is the probability of information sharing utility and $P(x^2)u_p(x^2)$ is the probability of privacy.

In the digital age, the utility of privacy is expected to have a marginal exponential value given the exponential rise of utility for the big data holder to reap benefits from the data. The more data that are held, the more complex relations can be unraveled by the big data holder. Information can be put into context of time and population correlates. While there is a marginally declining cost of an additional social media user using an established social network, there is a disproportionally large social network gain with another person joining for the social network provider, who can reap an excessive exponentially increasing marginal utility of another person joining and sharing another piece of information. Given the absence of any taxation of this gain,[8] social media has leveraged into an IT monopoly (Soros, 2018).

5. Data Fiduciary in the Digital Big Data Age

In the age of instant communication and social media big data, the need for understanding people's tradeoff between communication and privacy has leveraged to unprecedented momentum. For one, enormous data storage capacities and computational power in the e-big data era have created unforeseen opportunities for big data-hoarding corporations to reap hidden benefits from individual's information sharing.

In the 21st century, the turnover of information and the aggregation of social informational capital have revolutionized the world. In the wake of the emergence of new social media communication and interaction methods, a facilitation of the extraction of surplus value in shared information has begun. Computational procedures for data collection, storage, and access in large-scale data processing have been refined for real-time and historical data analysis, spatial and temporal results, as well as forecasting

[8] https://www.nytimes.com/2017/11/14/business/dealbook/taxing-companies-for-using-our-personal-data.html?rref=collection%2Fsectioncollection%2Fbusiness&action=click&contentCollection=business&region=stream&module=stream_unit&version=latest&contentPlacement=8&pgtype=sectionfront.

and now casting throughout recent decades. All these advancements have offered a multitude of in-depth information on human biases and imperfections as well as social representations and collective economic trends (Minsky, 1977; Moscovici, 1988; Puaschunder, 2015; Wagner and Hayes, 2005; Wagner *et al.*, 1999).

The digital age has brought about unprecedented opportunities to amalgamate big data information that can directly be used to derive inferences about people's preferences in order to nudge and wink them in the nudgitalist's favor. In today's nudgital society, information has become a source of competitive advantage. Technological advancement and social media revolution have increased the production of surplus value through access to combined information. Human decisions to voluntarily share information with others in the search for the human pleasure derived from communication are objectified in human economic relations. Unprecedented data storage possibilities and computational power in the digital age have leveraged information sharing and personal data into an exclusive asset that divides society in those who have behavioral insights derived from a large amount of data (the nudgers) and those whose will is manipulated (the nudged).

The implicit institutional configuration of a hidden hierarchy of the nudgital society is structured as follows: Different actors engage in concerted action in the social media marketplace. The nudgital brokers are owners and buyers of social media space, which becomes the implicit means of the production. In the age of instant global information transfer, the so-called social media industrialist–capitalist provides the social media platform, on which the social media consumer–workers get to share information about their life and express their opinion online for free. In their zest for the creation of a digital identity on social media platforms, a "commodification of the self" occurs. Social media consumer–producer–worker are sharing information and expressing themselves, which contributes to the creation of social media experience (Puaschunder, 2017).

The hidden power in the nudgitalist society is distributed unevenly, whereby the social media consumer–workers are slaves, who receive no wages in return for their labor, falling for their own human nature to express themselves and communicate with one another. Social media consumer–workers also engage in social media expression as for their social status striving in the social media platforms, where they can promote themselves. By posing to others in search for social status enhancement and likes, they engage in voluntary obedience to the social media capitalist–industrialist who sells their labor power product of aggregated information to either capitalists or technocrats. The social media consumer–worker's use value is inherent in their intrinsic motivation to satisfy a human need or want to communicate and gain respect from their community. The use value of the commodity is a social use value, which has a generally accepted use value derived from others' attention and respect in the wake of information sharing in society. The social media provider gives the use value an outlet or frame, which allows the social media consumer–worker to express information, compare oneself to others, and gain information about the social relation to others. The consumer–laborer thereby becomes the producer of information, releasing it to the wider audience and the social media industrialist. This use value only becomes a reality by the use or consumption of the social media and constitutes the substance of consumption. The tool becomes an encyclopedic knowledge and joy source derived from the commodity.

But the use of social media is not an end in itself but a means for gathering more information that can then be amalgamated by the social media capitalist–industrialist, who harvests its use value to aid nudgers (Marx, 1867/1995). It is a social form of wealth, in the form of social status and access to knowledge about others that the use value materializes on the side of the industrialist in the exchange value. For the social media industrialist, who is engaged in economic and governmental relations, the exchange value of the information provided by his or her social media consumer–laborers is the information released and consumption patterns studied. In exchange, this allows to derive knowledge about purchasing and consumption patterns of the populace and therefore creates opportunities to better nudge consumers and control the populace. With the amalgamated information, the social media industrialist–capitalist can gain information about common trends that can aid governmental officials and technocrats in ensuring security and governance purposes. Further, the social media platform can be used for marketing and governmental information disclaimers as media influences politics (Calvo-Armengol *et al.*, 2015; Prat, 2017; Prat and Strömberg, 2013).

Exchange value is a social process of self-interested economic actors taking advantage of information sharing based on utility derived from consuming the social media. The social media industrialist–capitalist can negotiate a price based on the access to the social media consumer–worker's attention and sell promotion space to marketers. The exchange value of the commodity of information share also derives from the subjective perception of the value of amalgamated data. Exchanged information can be amalgamated by the social media industrialist–capitalist and traded to other market actors. Exchange value is derived from integrating everything the worker is and does, both in his creative potential and how he or she relates to others. Exchange value also stems from the exchange of the commodity of amalgamated information that enables an elite to nudge the general populace. The amalgam of information as a premium signals the average opinion and how the majority reacts to changing environments, which allows inferences about current trends and predicts how to react to market changes.

Underlying motives may be the human desire for prestige and distinction on both sides — the industrialist–capitalist's and the consumer–worker's. From the industrialist–capitalist's perspective, monetary motives may play a role in the materialization of information; on the consumer–worker's side, it is the prestige gained from likes, hence respect for an online identity created (Ali and Benabou, 2016). Individuals may experience a warm glow from contributing to the public good of common knowledge (Ali and Benabou, 2016). The benefits of the superior class are the power to nudge, grounded on people's desire for prestige and image boosts. Impression management and emotions may play a vital role in seducing people to share information about themselves and derive pleasure for sharing (Evans and Krueger, 2009; Horberg *et al.*, 2011; Lerner *et al.*, 2004). Social norms and herding behavior may be additional information sharing drivers (Paluck, 2009). The realization of prestige stems from creating a favorable image of oneself online, which signs up the workers in a psychological quasi-contract to provide more and more information online and in a self-expanding value. Prestige is also gained in the materialization of information as asset by the capitalist–industrialist, who reaps the surplus value of the commodification of the self of the consumer–worker based on sociopsychological addiction to social media (Marx, 1867/1995; Soros, 2018). In the wake of an addiction to social media, users get distracted from profitability for their own terms and experience a loss of autonomy bit by bit. The social media capitalist–industrialist therefore increases their capital based on the social media consumer–worker's innocent private information share. The social media capitalist–industrialist also accumulated nudgital, the power to nudge.

This information sharing opens a gate for the social media provider to reap surplus value from the information gathered on social platforms and to nudge the social media consumer–producers or resell their amalgamated information to nudgers. Crucial to the idea of exploitation is the wealth or power of information in the digital age. While classical economic literature finds value in organizational hierarchy to economize transaction costs, the age of big data has opened a gate to reap disproportional benefits from individual data and information sharing. Surplus of information can be used to nudge in markets and by the force of governments. To acknowledge social media consumers as producers leads to the conclusion of them being underpaid workers in a direct wage labor exploitation. Surplus gravitates toward the social media owning class. Information becomes a commodity and commodification of a social product occurs by the nature of communication. Commodification of information occurs through the trade of information about the consumer–worker and by gaining access to nudge consumer–workers on social platforms. The transformation of a labor-product into a commodity occurs if information is used for marketing or governance purposes to nudge people. In the contemporary big data society, the nudged social media users therefore end up in a situation where they are unwaged laborers, providing the content of entertainment within social media, whereas the social media industrialist–capitalist, who only offers the information brokerage platform and is not subject to tax per information share, reaps extraordinary benefits from the amalgamated information shared. Not just labor power but the whole person becomes the exchange value, so one could even define the consumer–worker as a utility-slave.

The technological complexity of digital media indicates how interrelated social, use, and exchange value creation are. All commodities are social products of labor, created and exchanged by a community, with each commodity producer contributing his or her time to the societal division of labor. Use value is derived by the consumer–worker being socially related insofar as private consumption becomes collective. The use value thereby becomes the object of satisfaction of the human need for social care and want for social interaction. The use value becomes modified by the modern relations of production in the social media space as the consumer–worker intervenes to modify information. What the consumer–worker says on social media, not only for the sake of communication and expression but also in search for social feedback, is confined by the social media industrialist–capitalist, who transforms the use value into exchange value by materializing the voluntary information share by summing it up and presenting it to nudgers, who then derive from the information marketability and nudgitability of the consumer–workers. All information sharing has value, or labor value, the abstract labor time needed to produce it. The commodification of a good and service often involves a considerable practical accomplishment in trade. Exchange value manifests itself totally independent of use value. Exchange means the quantification of data, hence putting it into monetary units. In absolute terms, exchange value can be measured in the monetary prices social media industrialist–capitalists gain from selling advertisement space not only to nudging marketers but also to public and private actors who want to learn about consumer behavior in the digital market arena and influence consumers and the populace (Shaikh, 2016). The exchange value can also be quantified in the average consumption–labor hours of the consumers–workers. While in the practical sense, prices are usually referred to in labor hours, as units of account, there are hidden costs and risks that have to be factored into the equation, such as, for instance, missing governmental oversight and taxing of exchange value.

Overall, there is a decisive social role difference between the new media capitalist–industrialist and the social media consumer–worker. The social media provider is an industrialist and social connection owner, who lends out a tool for people to connect and engage with. As the innovative entrepreneur who offers a new media tool, the industrialist also becomes the wholesale merchant in selling market space to advertisement and trading information of his customers or workers, who are actively and voluntarily engaging in media tools (Schumpeter, 1949). The social media consumers turn into workers, or even slaves, if considering the missing direct monetary remuneration for their information share and since being engaged in the new media tool rather than selling their labor power for money in the marketplace hold opportunity costs of foregone labor. While selling their commodity labor power, the social media consumer–workers are also consumers of the new media tool-laden information, which can be infiltrated with advertisement. The social media capitalist–industrialist not only reaps exchange value benefits through access to people's attention through selling advertisement space but also grants the means to nudge the consumers into purchasing acts or wink the populace for governance authorities (Marx, 1867/1995). The social media capitalist–industrialist thereby engages in conversion of surplus value through information sharing into profit as well as selling attention space access and private data of the consumer–workers.

When the new media consumer–workers' amalgam of provided information gets added up to big data sets, it can be used by capitalists and governance specialists. Over time, a nudgital society emerges, as the nudging social media industrialist–capitalists form a Gestalt of several bits and pieces put together about the nudged social media consumer–producer–worker–slaves. Information gets systematically added up providing invaluable behavioral insights. Information in its raw form and in amalgamated consistency then gets channeled from the broad working body on social media into the hands of a restricted group or societal class. This division into those who provide a medium of information exchange and those who exchange information then forms a society implies an inherent social class divide into those who nudge and those who are nudged.

In the nature of exchange, nudgital becomes an abstract social power, a property claim to surplus value through information. Value can be expropriated through the exchange of information between the industrialist–capitalist and the nudgitalist. Exchange value has an inherent nature of implicit class division. Exchange value represents the nudgitalists' purchasing power expressed in his ability to gain labor time that is required for information sharing as a result of the labor done to produce it and the ability to engage in privacy infringements. The social media industrialist–capitalist implicitly commands labor to produce more data through social nudging and tapping into human needs to communicate and express themselves, whereby he or her uses a reacting army of labor encouraging information share through social gratification in the form of likes and emoticons (Posner, 2000). The reacting army of labor comprises of social media users, who degrade into hidden laborers who are not directly compensated for their information share and cheerlead others to do the same. The nudgital society's paradox is that information sharing in the social compound gets pitted against privacy protecting alienation.

From all these features, the rise of the monopolistic power of giant IT platform companies becomes apparent (Soros, 2018). For instance, Facebook and Google are believed to control over half of all Internet advertising revenues (Soros, 2018). While these companies initially played an important innovative and liberating role, by now it has become apparent that they also exploit the social environment (Soros, 2018). Social media companies know how people think and influence them to behave in a certain way without their users having insights or being aware of the hidden influence (Soros, 2018). As George Soros pointed out at the World Economic Forum 2018, this has far-reaching adverse consequences on the functioning of democracy, particularly on the integrity of elections.

It is believed that social media can prime how people evaluate politicians consciously and unconsciously based on the available content (Iyengar and Kinder, 1987). The profitability of these corporations is based on the absence of direct payments for the information shared to the social media users or taxation being imposed on the IT giants (Soros, 2018).[9] While these platforms were initially set up to make the world more flat, by now they have turned to monopoly distributors of the public good knowledge. Acknowledging these monopolistic IT giants as public utilities will help make them more accountable and subject to stringent regulations, aimed at preserving competition, innovation, and fair and open universal access to information (Soros, 2018).

The nudgitalist exploitation also holds when technocrats use heuristics and nudges to create selfish outcomes or undermine democracy. Ethical abysses of the nudgital society open when the social media is used for public opinion building and public discourse restructuring. Social media not only allows to estimate target audience's preferences and societal trends but also imposes direct and indirect influence onto society by shaping the public opinion with real and alternative facts. Government officials gain information about the populace that can be used to interfere in the democratic voting process, for instance, in regards to curbing voting behavior or misinformation leading people astray from their own will and wishes. The social intertwining of the media platform and the democratic act of voting have been outlined in recent votes that were accused to have been compromised by availability heuristic biases and fake news. Data can also be turned against the social media consumer–worker by governance technocrats for the sake of security and protection purposes, for instance, social media information can be linked together tax verification purposes.

Governments have been transformed under the impact of the digital revolution. Instant information flow, computational power and visualization techniques, sophisticated computer technologies, and unprecedented analytical tools allow policymakers to interact with citizens more efficiently and make well-informed decisions based on personal data. New media technologies equip individuals with constant information flows

[9] https://www.nytimes.com/2017/11/14/business/dealbook/taxing-companies-for-using-our-personal-data.html?rref=collection%2Fsectioncollection%2Fbusiness&action=click&contentCollection=business&region=stream&module=stream_unit&version=latest&contentPlacement=8&pgtype=sectionfront.

about informal networks and personal data. Novel outreach channels have created innovative ways to participate in public decision-making processes with a partially unknown societal impact at a larger scale, scope, and faster pace than ever before. Big data analytics and the Internet of Things automate many public outreach activities and services in the 21st century. Not only do we benefit from the greatly increasing efficiency of information transfer but there may also be potential costs and risks of ubiquitous surveillance and implicit persuasion means that may threaten democracy. The digital era governance and democracy features data-driven security in central and local governments through algorithmic surveillance that can be used for corporate and governmental purposes. Open source data movements can become a governance regulation tool. In the sharing economy, public opinion and participation in the democratic process have become dependent on data literacy. Research on the nudgital society holds key necessary information about capacity building and knowledge sharing within government with respect to certain inalienable rights of privacy protection. The nudgital society's paradox that information sharing in the social compound gets pitted against privacy protecting alienation requires an ideological superstructure to sustain and tolerate hidden exploitation.

All these are features of the modern times as the technology and big data creating computational power are currently emerging. The transferability of the commodity of information itself and hence the big data amalgamation over time and space to store, package, preserve, and transport information from one owner to another appear critical. The legal leeway to allow private information sharing implicitly leads to individuals losing their private ownership rights to the commodity of information upon release on social media and the right to trade information. The transferability of these private rights from one owner to another may infringe on privacy protection, human rights, and human dignity-upholding mandates.

Not only pointing at the ethical downfalls of the nudgital society but also defining social media users as workers is of monumental significance to understand the construction of the nudgital society and bestow upon us social media consumer–workers labor rights. The technical relationship between the different economic actors is completely voluntary and based on trust (Puaschunder, 2016). The creation of use value is outsourced to the community (e.g., in likes) and the share of information about the workers from the social media capitalist to the market or nudgitalists remains without a clear work contract and without protection of a labor union. The worker–employer relationship needs to be protected and a minimum wage should be fixed for the market value of the good that as worker produces during any given working day. Wages would be needed to maintain their labor power of the workers minus the costs of the production. Unpaid laborers should not only be compensated for their opportunity costs of time but also enjoy the workers' privilege of right to privacy and prevention of misuse of the information they share and have the right to access to accurate information and also protection from nudging in the establishment of the right to voluntary fail.

The nature of making profit from information in exchange value is questionable. Information exchange of the industrialist–capitalist is different than the traditional exchange of neoclassical goods and services trade. The capitalist–industrialist makes money off privacy and the consumer–workers share of information without knowledge and/or control of the recipient over the amalgamated mass of privacy released. Workers are never indifferent to their use value, and their inputs may also produce unfavorable outcomes for them. The exchange value will sell for an adequate profit and is legally permitted; yet, it can destroy the reputation and standing as well as potentially block the access of an individual to a country if the proposed social media information release is mandated at border controls. Care must be taken for privacy infringement and the product of amalgamated big data and how useful it is for the society.

A novel data fiduciary could help alleviate the problems of the digital age. Fiduciary virtues around big data could comprise inalienable rights to privacy and be forgotten, and in order to be protected from data misuse of information they share, they should be granted the right to access of accurate information and — in light of the nudgitalist audacity — the right to fail.

5.1. *People's right to privacy and to be forgotten*

The transformation of a use value into a social use value and into a commodity has technical, social, and political preconditions. Information gets traded, and ownership of privacy is transferred in information sharing. Upon sharing information on social media, the consumer–worker bestows the social media capitalist–industrialist with access to previously private information. The social media capitalist then transforms the information into use value by offering and selling the bundled information to nudgitalists, who then can draw inferences about certain consumer group's preferences and guide their choices.

Overall, the nudgital society leads to a dangerous infringement upon the independence of individuals in their freedom of choice and a social stratification into those who have access to the amalgamated information of social media consumer–workers. There is a trade-off between communication and privacy in an implicit contract of the use of personal data. Power is exercised through the accumulation of information, including the quality of insatiability of social media consumer–workers to constantly upload information and the social media capitalist–industrialist reaping profits from selling it.

Social media thereby reveals to hold a sticky memory that allows storage of information in the international arena eternally. Privacy and information share regulations depend on national governments. For instance, in the commodification of privacy, the EU is much more beneficial to consumers than the US. Data protection and commercial privacy are considered as fundamental human rights to be safeguarded in Europe. Europe appears in a better position, since it does not have any IT platform monopolistic giants of its own (Soros, 2018). Not only does Europe have much stronger privacy and data protection laws than America, but EU law also prohibits the abuse of monopoly power irrespective of how it is achieved (Soros, 2018). US law measures monopoly by the inflated price paid by customers for a service received, which is impossible to prove when the services are free and there is no utility theory of privacy and information sharing that captures the value and price of information (Soros, 2018). In contrast, the US approach toward commercial privacy focuses on only protection of the economic interests of consumers. Current privacy regulations are considered as not being sufficient in targeting actions that cause non-economic and other kinds of harm to consumers.

Privacy and information sharing guidelines appear to be culturally dependent phenomena. Information about privacy boundary conditions can be obtained from the transatlantic dialog between the US and Europe on privacy protection. While in Europe healthcare data are considered public, in Canada, there is a public interest to make the data more public. The EU's privacy approach is based on Articles 7 and 8 of the Charter of the Fundamental Rights of the EU, which grants individuals rights to protection, access, and request of data concerning him- or herself. European privacy is oriented around consumer consent. The 2016 EU General Data Protection Regulation (GDPR) ruled the right to be forgotten under certain circumstances. Consumer consent and dealing with incomplete, outdated, and irrelevant information is legally regulated. GDPR establishes regulatory fines for non-complying companies applicable to foreign companies whose data processing actions are related to "good and services" that they provide to data subjects in the EU, so also including US companies operating in the virtual space accessible by European citizens. The EU privacy approach not only offers member states flexibility in data management for national security and other exceptional circumstances but also protects civilians from common potential circumstances for data abuse, while there are standardized data management policy procedures regardless of a companies' country of origin or operational locations. The EU's privacy approach has higher regulatory costs, is not specified by sectors, and the right to be forgotten still needs enforcement validity.

The US approach to privacy is sector specific. Commercial privacy is pitted against economic interests and is seen neither as civil liberty nor as constitutional right. US privacy is regulated by the Federal Communications Commission (FCC) and the Federal Trade Commission (FTC). Overall in the US, the general definitions of unfair and deceptive give the FTC a wider scope for monitoring and restricting corporate privacy infringements. The FTC has a wide variety of tools for data protection; yet, the responsibility is split between the FTC and the FCC, which increases bureaucratic and regulatory costs and limits industry oversight.

So while the EU framework treats commercial privacy as a basic human right leading to a more extensive protection of individual's privacy including data collection, use, and share, the EU framework is also non-sectoral and allows sovereign nation states to overrule common data management policies for the sake of national security and protection. The US framework lacks a centralized privacy regulation approach, yet it is split in its views regarding oversight in the domains of the FCC and FTC.

5.2. *People's right to prevent misuse of information they share*

By US standards, social media is required by the FTC to ask users for permission if it wants to alter its privacy practices. Section 5 of the FTC Act states that (1) unfair practices are causes or are likely to cause substantial injury to consumers or cannot reasonably be avoided by consumers; and (2) deceptive practices are practices that are likely misleading or actually misleading the consumer.

In August 2016, the decision of WhatsApp to share more user data — especially user phone numbers — with Facebook in order to track customer–workers' use metrics and refine targeted user advertising also opened a gate to discriminatory pricing. This decision faced a huge backlash in the EU, where data sharing was ordered to be halted and Germany deemed these practices as illegal. In the US, the Federal Trade Commission (FTC) began reviewing joint complaints from consumer privacy groups. The recent WhatsApp data sharing is a possible violation of this requirement since it only allowed consumers to opt-out of most of the data sharing while lacking clarity and specificity. WhatsApp's restrictive opt-out option and incomplete data sharing restrictions were argued to be perceived as being unfair and deceptive (Tse, in speech, March 25).

5.3. *People's right to access to accurate information*

Traditional media studies advocate for independence of the media. Commercial motives have ever since raised doubts about the reputation and credibility of outlets (Prat and Strömberg, 2013). Technological shocks have always created new opportunities and also opened the gates to novel downfalls in the communication realm. Novel technologies for information sharing and also monitoring of communication are prone to significant changes in the nature of communication. In such technological leaps, attention to privacy is recommended (Ali and Benabou, 2016).

In the nudgital society, profits appear in the circuit of information and take on different forms in the new media age. The possibility of trading information and reaping benefits from information sharing of others reveals the unequal position of people in the society. The possession of knowledge stems from the surplus derived from the activity of production, hence the information share of social media consumer–producers. This confrontation of labor and consumption is not apparent in the modern marketplace. The class division remains quite invisible in the implicit workings of the system.

The nudgitalist act becomes problematic when being coupled with infiltration with fake news and alternative facts that curb democratic acts, e.g., manipulating voting behavior. Ethical questions arise if there is a lack of transparency about the capitalist's share of information and a fair social value benefits distribution between the capitalist and the worker. In addition, under the cloak of security and protection, privacy infringements by sharing information with the nudgitalist is questionable. In the political domain, knowledge has been acknowledged as a public good. Voters who spend resources on obtaining information to keep their government accountable produce a positive externality for their fellow citizens (Prat and Strömberg, 2013).

By outlining the nudgital market procedures and acknowledging knowledge as a public good, fairness in the distribution of gains of information insights should be accomplished. Privacy infringing in the wake of information sharing should be limited and guided by legal oversight. Wealth accumulation based on the information sharing of workers should be curbed by taxation. Information about the storage, preservation, packaging, and transportation of data is non-existent, demanding for more information about behind-the-scenes' social media conduct. Transforming private information from use value to exchange value is an undisclosed and therefore potentially problem-fraught process that holds implicit inequality within itself. From a societal standpoint, the missing wealth production in the social media economy also appears striking. Thus, the dangers of information release and transfer and the hidden exchange value accrued on the side of the media innovator are left unspoken. The importance of shedding light on such thoughts is blatant and is the same as that of stripping the populace from inalienable rights of privacy while reaping benefits at the expense of their susceptibility. Nudges in combination with misinformation and power abuse in the shadow of subliminal manipulation can strip the populace from democratic rights to choose and voluntarily fail (Benabou and Laroque, 1992).

As a policy response to the negative implications of the nudgital society, taxing IT giants may enable to raise revenue for reducing cost and noise in collecting political information. For instance, by making news freely available without commercial interruptions. A mixture strategy could be introduced, in which consumers are given the choice to either choose a free account that releases information or pay for a private account, which restricts third-party use of their data.

Facebook has recently acknowledged the rise of fake news having an impact on voting behavior and therefore has rolled out a bottom-up accuracy check mechanism.[10] Truthfulness appears hard to quantify on social media since truth is not easily verifiable and integrity of information

[10] http://www.telegraph.co.uk/news/2018/01/19/facebook-start-trust-ratings-media-outlets-fights-back-against/.

embodied in prices is missing through the free information exchange on social media. Reputation and social self-determination mechanism appear as alternate sources of information accuracy checks in the absence of classical price mechanisms (Benabou and Laroque, 1992).

5.4. *People's right to choose and fail*

In the personal information sharing age and nudgital society, attention must be given to privacy and human dignity. The nudgital society opens a gate to gain information about consumer choices and voting preferences. The uneven distribution of key information about people's choices opens a gate to tricking people into choices. The so-called nudging attempt raises ethical questions about human dignity and the audacity of some to know better what is better for society as a whole. Because governance is a historical process, no one person can control or direct it, thereby creating a global complex of governance connections that precedes the individual administration. Structural contradictions describe the class struggle between the nudged in opposition to the nudgers in the nudgital society. Since societal actors who involuntarily are nudged are separated from an active reflection process when being nudged, the moral weight is placed on the nudger. Though democratically elected and put into charge, the nudgers checks-and-balances of power seem concentrated and appear under the disguise of a middleman of social media capitalist–industrialists who collect information. Rather than focusing on how to trick people into involuntary choices, the revelations should guide us to demand to educate people on a broad scale about their fallibility in choice behavior.

In a self-enlightened society, people have a right to voluntarily fail. Nudging implies a loss of degrees of freedom and disrespect of human dignity; hence, the nudgital society will lead to structural contradictions. Their rational thinking and voluntary engagement in governmental–enforced action becomes divorced from rational reflection. No one entity should decide to control or direct other's choices, thereby creating a global complex of social connections among the governed for the sake of efficiency for the common good. The economic formation of human decision-making in society should never precede the human voluntary decision.

There is an inherent inequality of social positions, manifested primarily in the respective capacities of reaping benefit from amalgamated information, which leads to a disparity of social position. The distribution of power leads to a natural order of human activity, in which the nudgers are in charge of nudging the populace. Moral value is separated from economic value, and hence, placing the fate of the populace into the arms of the behavioral economists raises problems of lack of oversight and concentration of objective economic value rule in the nudgital society.

Overall, with the communication on the nudgital society just having started, the onus remains with us to redesign the apparatus of production in ways that prevent the infringement on private information through the natural tendency to share information, care about others, and express oneself attitude. Governance crises are rooted in the contradictory character of the value creation through big data. The formation of value is a complex determination, and we still need more research to understand the deep structures of market behavior in the digital age.

6. Conclusion and Future Prospects

The paper presented a first theoretical introduction of a fiduciary duty around the conduct of big data. As a next research step, a stringent hypotheses testing of the presented problem is recommended. For instance, future research projects featuring a multi-methodological approach will help gain invaluable information about the actual performance and behavior regarding information sharing and privacy upholding. Interactions of individuals on social media should be scrutinized in order to derive real-world-relevant economic insights for legal and policymaking purposes alongside advancing an upcoming scientific field.

Following empirical investigations should employ a critical survey of the intersection of analytic and behavioral perspectives to decision-making in information sharing. Literature discussion featuring a critical analysis on how to improve e-literacy should be coupled with e-education and enhancement of e-ethicality. Research should be directed toward a critical analysis of the application of behavioral economics on hyper-hyperbolic discounting in the digital age. In the behavioral economics domain, both approaches, studying the negative implications of information sharing and decision-making to uphold privacy and also finding ways how to train new media users wiser decisions, should be explored. Interdisciplinary viewpoints and multi-method research approaches should be covered not only in the heterodox economics readings but also in a variety of independent individual research projects. Research support and guidance should be targeted at nurturing interdisciplinary research interests on privacy and information sharing in the fields of behavioral economics and public affairs.

More concretely, future studies should define the value that data have to individuals and data sovereignty in the international context. When people share information, they should be informed to consider what the benefit and value from information sharing is for them and what the benefit for social media industrialists–capitalists is. The sovereignty of data and the human dignity of privacy should become debated as a civic virtual virtue in the 21st century. Individuals should be informed that sharing data is a personal security risk, if considered to be asked for social media information upon entry of a country.

Future studies should describe what companies and institutions constitute the complex system that helps establishing the nudgital society and the influence that social media has. The implicit underlying social structure of the nudgital society based on a complicated information gathering machinery should become subject to scrutiny and how, in particular, the nudgital class division is supported by a comprehensive social network data processing method. How social media advertising space can be used to specialize on targeted propaganda and misleading information to nudge the populace in an unfavorable way should be unraveled. The role of politicians' use of various channels and instruments to manipulate the populace with targeted communication should be scrutinized.

In the recent US election, the profit and value of detailed market information has been found to have gained unprecedented impetus. Future research should also draw a line between the results of the 2016 US presidential election and the study of heuristics to elucidate that heuristics played a key role in Trump's election as they made people less likely to vote logically. This would be key as it would help explain how people chose to vote and why they do not always make the most logical choice when voting. This line of research could help to more accurately promote future elections' candidates, how to better predict election outcomes, and how to improve democracy.

In addition, nudging through means of visual merchandising, marketing, and advertising should be captured in order to uphold ethical standards in social media. Nudging's role in selling products, maximizing profits, and also creating political trends should be uncovered. While there is knowledge on the visual merchandising in stores and window displays, little appears to be known how online appearances can nudge people into making certain choices. In particular, the familiarity heuristic, anchoring, and the availability heuristic may play a role in implicitly guiding people's choices and discreetly persuade consumers and the populace. Not to mention advancements of online shopping integrity and e-commerce ethics, the prospective insights gained will aid to uphold moral standards in economic marketplaces and hopefully improve democratic outcomes of voting choices.

Contemporary studies could also address the question of whether the age of instant messaging has led to a loss of knowledge in information sharing. Future research should also investigate how search engines can be manipulated to make favorable sources more relevant and how artificial intelligence and social networks can become dangerous data manipulation means. The role of data processing companies may be studied in relation to the idea of data monopoly advantages — hence situations in which data processing companies may utilize data flows for their own purposes to support sponsored causes or their own ideals. Due to the specific time period of the digital age and by not extrapolating to past time periods, it is possible to determine future behaviors.

The current research in this area lacks empirical evidence, demanding for further investigations on how nudges can directly impact individual's choices and new media can become a governance manipulation tool. What social instruments are employed on social media and what prospects data processing has in the light of privacy infringement lawsuits should be uncovered. How social media is utilized to create more favorable social personas for political candidates should be explored. How online presences allow to gain as much attraction as possible for the presence of political candidates is another question of concern. Another area of concern is how selective representations influence the voting population and what institutions and online providers are enabling repetitiveness and selectivity. How gathered individual information is used to parse data to manipulate social Internet behavior and subsequent action is another topic to be investigated. Future research goals will include determining what this means for the future political landscape and how Internet users should react to political appearances online. Information should be gathered about how we choose what media to watch and if political views play a role in media selection and retention. Whether distrust in the media furthers political polarization and partisanship needs to be clarified. Future studies should also look into the relationship between an individual's political ideologies and how they use and interact on social media, especially with a focus on the concept of fake news and alternative facts. Where do these trends come from and who is more susceptible to these negative impacts of the digital society? Has social media become a tool to further polarize political camps is a question that needs to be asked. All these endeavors will help to outline the existence of social media's influence in governance and data processing to aid political campaigning in order to derive inferences about democracy and political ethicality in the digital age.

How social media tools nudge people to not give everything at once but put it together in a novel way that it creates surplus should be analyzed. In small bits and pieces, individuals give up their privacy tranche be tranche. Small amounts of time are spent time to time. People, especially young people, may have a miscalibration about the value of information released about them. Based on hyperbolic discounting myopia, they may underestimate the total future consequences of their share of privacy.

The time spent on social media should become a subject of close scrutiny, and the impact on opportunity costs onto the labor market should be studied. For instance, countries that ban social media, such as China, or restrict Internet, like slowing it down or censoring certain media, could become valuable sources of variance to compare to. Network theories for e-blasting information should become another area of interest to be studied in relation to hyper-hyperbolic discounting fallibilities. Emotional reactions and emotional externalities of communication could be another area of behavioral economics research in the privacy and information sharing predicament domain. The role of attention should be addressed as another moderator variable that is quite unstudied in the digital media era (Prat, in speech, November 2017). Thereby interesting new questions arise, such as how to measure attention — is it the time allocation or the emotional arousal information bestows individuals with (Wouter and Prat, forthcoming)?

The preliminary results may be generalized not only for other user-generated web contents such as blogs, wikis, discussion forums, posts, chats, tweets, podcastings, pins, digital images, videos, audio files, advertisements but also for search engine data gathered or electronic devices used (e.g., wearable technologies, mobile devices, Internet of Things). Certain features of the nudgital society may also hold for tracking data, including GPS, geolocation data, traffic and other transport sensor data and CCTV images, or even satellite and aerial imagery. All preliminary results should be taken into consideration for future studies in different countries to examine other cultural influences and their effects on social class and heuristics.

Innovative means should be identified to restore trust in media information and overcome obstacles such as the availability heuristic leading to disproportionate competitive advantages of media controlling parties. As remedies, consumer education should target at educating social media users about their rights and responsibilities on how to guard their own and other's privacy. E-ethicality trainings could target at strengthening the moral impetus of big data and artificial ethicality in the digital age. Moral trade-offs between privacy infringements and security should also be subject to scrutiny.

Promoting governance through algorism offers novel contributions to the broader data science and policy discussion (Roberts, 2010). Future studies should also be concerned with data governance and collection as well as data storage and curation in the access and distribution of online databases and data streams of instant communication. The human decision–making behavior and data sharing in regards to ownership should be subject to scrutiny in psychology. Ownership in the wake of voluntary personal information sharing and data provenance and expiration in the private and public sectors have to be legally justified (Donahue and Zeckhauser, 2011). In the future, institutional forms and regulatory tools for data governance should be legally clarified. Open, commercial, personal, and proprietary sources of information that get amalgamated for administrative purposes and their role in shaping the democracy should be studied. In the future we also need a clearer understanding of the human interaction with data and their social networks and clustering for communication results. The guarantee of safety of the information and the guarantee of the replacement or service, should a social media fail its function to uphold privacy law as intended, is another area of blatant future research demand. Novel qualitative and quantitative mixed methods featuring secondary data analysis, web mining, and predictive models should be tested for holding for the outlined features of the new economy alongside advancing randomized controlled trials, sentiment analysis, and smart contract technologies. Ethical considerations of machine learning and biologically inspired models should be considered in theory and practice. Mobile applications of user communities should be scrutinized.

As for consumer–worker conditions, unionization of the social media workers could help uphold legal rights and ethical imperatives of privacy, security, and personal data protection. Data and algorithms should be studied by legal experts on licensing and ownership in the use of personal and proprietary data. Transparency, accountability, and participation in data processing should also be freed from social discrimination. Fairness-awareness programs in data mining and machine learning coupled with privacy-enhancing technologies should be introduced in security studies of the public sector. Public rights of free speech online in the dialogue based on trust should be emphasized in future educational programs. Policy implications of the presented ideas range from security to human rights and law to civic empowerment. Citizen empowerment should feature community efforts to protect data and information sharing to be free of ethical downfalls. Social media use education should be ingrained in standard curricula and children should be raised with an honest awareness of their act of engagement on social media in the nudgital society of the digital century.

Future research may also delve into moderator variables of the utility derived from information sharing and privacy. For instance, extraversion and introversion could be moderating the overall pleasure derived from communication or silence. Future research may also address prescriptive recommendations on how to educate individuals about the risks and dangers of information sharing in the digital age. Attention must also be paid to understand how accuracy can be upheld at times when fake news and self-created social information are doing the rounds. Certain societal segments that are not represented strongly online should somehow be integrated into big data in order to democratize the information, which is considered as big data "norm" or standard by which the social media user is measured. At the same time, psychologically guided studies could unravel a predictive approach and validate the outlined ideas' validity by testing the proposed theoretical assumptions in laboratory and field study settings. In particular, the proposed nomenclature's validity could be studied and the percentage of information sharing types captured in the population can be determined. The moderator variable age could be phased in as it appears to be conundrum why younger people, who have more to lose given a longer time ahead to live are in particular prone to use new social media and lavishly share their lives in e-blasts to public. Regarding direct implications, a tax may be used to offset problems of the costs and risks of social media privacy infringements in the big data era.[11] Drawing from utility usually measured by the willingness to pay different amounts of money for different options, laboratory experiments may operationalize the value of privacy by measuring how much money people would be willing to pay for repurchasing their data or having a social media account that can only be viewed but no personal data can be resold or put in context to others. These attempts could also serve as a guideline for policy regulations and free market solutions. Social media could offer services of providing accounts that are private in the sense that no surplus value can be reaped by reselling information or from which big data storage and computation cannot occur. This may serve as an indicator of revealed preferences of social media privacy. The privacy paradox may be scrutinized in behavioral economics laboratory and field experiments. Potential individual influencing factors such as gender, age, trust, and personality differences may be tested for in order to retrieve information on how to educate the social media user and regulate the social media provider. Regarding regulation, splitting social media power cartels may be one solution to decrease the big data social media user disadvantage. Taxation for information sharing may create another incentive to slow down unreflected information share. The tax revenues could be used to offset some of the societal costs of privacy infringement. In addition, fines for privacy infringement could help to uphold e-ethics in the digital age. From the economics perspective, interesting moderator variables for future studies is the distinction between active and passive communication. Further, model robustness checks could follow and learning effects could be depicted. Access to information on what happens with data and how big data is used is crucial for making people understand their relation to their information. Communication costs and benefits are assumed to not be additive and separable, leaving an interesting field for future studies in this domain. The communication patterns could be classified into different types of communications in the future, e.g., certain node specificities are detected, such as communication within a family, with friends, and in hierarchical situations like at work. The absolute and relative influence of

---

[11] https://www.nytimes.com/2017/11/14/business/dealbook/taxing-companies-for-using-our-personal-data.html?rref=collection%2Fsectioncollection%2Fbusiness&action=click&contentCollection=business&region=stream&module=stream_unit&version=latest&contentPlacement=8&pgtype=sectionfront.

information sharers could become part of a network description approach as well. Impact factor measurements could be based on status, search engine rank, and connections to capture global influence. Complexity of information would need to be controlled based on information processing times and time allocation preferences to information, and hence attention. Communication costs should, in the future, be separated in economic models into fixed and variable communication costs, and a potential separation between fixed communication costs for social media providers and variable communication costs for social media users should be depicted (Prat, 2017).

Overall, this chapter can serve as a first step toward advocating for education about information sharing in order to curb harmful information sharing discounting fallibility. From legal and governance perspectives, the outlined ideas may stimulate the e-privacy infringement regulations discourse in the pursuit of the greater goals of democratization of information, equality of communication surplus, and upholding of human dignity and e-ethics in the big data era.

Acknowledgments

Financial support of the Academy of Behavioral Finance and Economics, Eugene Lang College of The New School, Fee Board, Fritz Thyssen Foundation, the Janeway Center Fellowship, New School for Social Research, Prize Fellowship, the Science and Technology Global Consortium, the University of Vienna, Systema B, and Vernon Arts and Sciences is gratefully acknowledged. The author thanks Professor Andrea Prat for a most interesting lecture on "Industrial Organization" at Columbia University during Fall 2017 and Professor Anwar Shaikh for his most valuable input and benevolent guidance. All omissions, errors, and misunderstandings in this piece are solely the author's.

Bibliography

Ainslie, G. (1992), Picoeconomics: The Interaction of Successive Motivational States within the Person. Cambridge: Cambridge University Press.

Ainslie, G. and N. Haslam (1992), Hyperbolic discounting, in *Choice Over Time*, (eds.). G. Loewenstein and I. Elster, New York: Russel Sage.

Alchian, A. A. (1953), The meaning of utility measurement, *American Economic Review* **32**, 26–50.

Alberini, A. and A. Chiabai (2007), Discount rates in risk versus money and money versus money tradeoffs, *Risk Analysis* **27**(2), 483–498.

Ali, N. S. and R. Benabou (2016), *Image versus Information: Changing Societal Norms and Optimal Privacy*. Cambridge, MA: National Bureau of Economic Research working paper 22203. Retrieved from https://scholar.princeton.edu/sites/default/files/rbenabou/files/imagevsinfo-21_002.pdf.

Allport, G. W. (1979), *The Nature of Prejudice*. Reading: Addison-Wesley.

Altman, I. (1975), The Environment and Social Behavior: Privacy, Personal Space, Territory, and Crowding. Monterey: Brooks.

Arrow, K. J. (1951), Alternative approaches to the theory of choice in risk-taking situations, *Econometrica* **19**, 404–437.

Arrow, K. J. (1958), Utilities, attitudes, and choices: A review note, *Econometrica* **26**, 1–23.

Arrow, K. J. (1974), *The Limits of Organization*. New York: Norton.

Arrow, K. J. (1978), Extended sympathy and the possibility of social choice, *Philosophia* **7**(2), 223–237.

Aumann, R. J. and J. B. Kruskal (1958), The coefficients in an allocation problem, *Naval Research Logistics Quarterly* **5**, 111–123.

Aumann, R. J. and J. B. Kruskal (1959), Assigning quantitative values to qualitative factors in the naval electronics problem, *Naval Research Logistics Quarterly* **6**, 1–16.

Badger, G. J., W. K. Bickel, L. A. Giordano, E. A. Jacobs, G. Loewenstein, and L. Marsch (2007), Altered states: The impact of immediate craving on the valuation of current and future opioids, *Journal of Health Economics* **26**(5), 865–876.

Bazerman, M. H. and A. E. Tenbrunsel (2011), *Blind Spots: Why We Fail to do What's Right and What to do About It*. Princeton: Princeton University Press.

Becker, G. M. and C. G. McClintock (1967), Values: Behavioral decision theory, *Annual Review of Psychology* **18**, 239–286.

Becker, G. S. and K. M. Murphy (1988), A theory of rational addiction, *The Journal of Political Economy* **96**, 675–700.

Benabou, R. and G. Laroque (1992), Using privileged information to manipulate markets: Insiders, gurus, and credibility, *The Quarterly Journal of Economics* **107**(3), 921–958.

Bernheim, B. D. and M. D. Whinston (1986), Common agency, *Econometrica: Journal of the Econometric Society* **16**, 269–281.

Beshears, J. L., J. J. Choi, D. I. Laibson, B. C. Madrian, and J. Sakong (2011), Self-control and liquidity: How to design a commitment contract, RAND Working Paper Series, WR-895-SSA.

Besley, T. and A. Prat (2006), Handcuffs for the grabbing hand? Media capture and government accountability, *American Economic Review* **96**(3), 720–736.

Bernoulli, D. (1954), Specimen theories novae de mensura sortis, *Commentarii Academiae Scientiarum Imperialis Petropolitanae* **5**, 175–192.

Bosworth, R., T. A. Cameron, and J. R. DeShazo (2006), Preferences for preventative public health policies with jointly estimated rates of time preference. School of Public Health and International Affairs: North Carolina State University.

Bowles, S. (2004), *Microeconomics: Behavior, Institutions & Evolution*. Princeton: Princeton University Press.

Cairns, J. and M. van der Pol (2008), Valuing future private and social benefits: The discounted utility model versus hyperbolic discounting models, *Journal of Economic Psychology* **21**(2), 191–205.

Calvo-Armengol, A., J. de Marti, and A. Prat (2015), Communication and influence. *Theoretical Economics* **10**(2), 649–690.

Camerer, C. F., G. Loewenstein, and M. Rabin (2004), *Advances in Behavioral Economics*. Princeton: Princeton University Press.

Cameron, T. A. and G. R. Gerdes (2003), *Eliciting Individual-Specific Discount Rates*. Department of Economics: University of Oregon.

Cartwright, E. (2011), *Behavioral Economics*. London, UK: Routledge.

Chabris, Ch., D. Laibson, and J. Schuldt (2008), *Intertemporal Choice*. New York: Palgrave Dictionary of Economics.

Chapman, G. B. (1996), Expectations and preferences for sequences of health and money, *Organizational Behavior and Human Decision Processes* **67**, 59–75.

Chung, S. H. and R. J. Herrnstein (1967), Choice and delay of reinforcement, *Journal of Experimental Analysis of Behavior* **10**(1), 67–74.

Colinsky, J. (1996), Why bounded rationality? *Journal of Economic Literature* **34**, 669–700.

Coller, M. and M. B. Williams (1999), Eliciting individual discount rates, *Experimental Economics* **2**(2), 107–127.

Crémer, J., L. Garicano, and A. Prat (2007), Language and the theory of the firm, *The Quarterly Journal of Economics* **122**(1), 373–407.

Debreu, G. (1958), Stochastic choice and cardinal utility, *Econometrica* **26**, 440–444.

Debreu, G. (1960), Topological methods in cardinal utility theory, in *Mathematical Models in the Social Sciences*, K. J. Arrow, S. Karlin, and S. Suppes (eds.), Stanford, CA: Stanford University press, pp. 16–26.

Debreu, G. (1964), Continuity properties of Paretian utility, *International Economic Review* **5**, 285–293.

DellaVigna, St. and U. Malmendier (2004), Contract design and self-control: Theory and evidence, *Quarterly Journal of Economics* **119**(2), 353–402.

DellaVigna, St. and U. Malmendier (2006), Paying not to go to the gym, *American Economic Review* **96**(3), 694–719.

DellaVigna, St. and M. D. Paserman (2005), Job search and impatience, *Journal of Labor Economics* **23**(3), 527–588.

Delli Carpini, M. X. and S. Keeter (1989), *What Americans Know About Politics and Why It Matters*. New Haven: Yale University Press.

Diamond, P. A. (1965), The evaluation of infinite utility streams, *Econometrica* **33**, 170–177.

Diamond, P. A., T. C. Koopmans, and R. Williamson (1962), Axioms for persistent preference, in *Recent Developments in Information and Decision Processes*, R. E. Machol and P. Gray (eds.), New York: Macmillan.

Donahue, J. D. and R. J. Zeckhauser (2011), *Collaborative Governance: Private Sector Roles for Public Goals in Turbulent Times*. Princeton, NJ: Princeton University Press.

Doyle, J. R. (2013), Survey of time preference, delay discounting models, *Judgment and Decision Making* **8**(2), 116–135.

Duflo, E., A. Banerjee, R. Glennerster, and D. Kothari (2010), Improving immunization coverage in rural India: A clustered randomized controlled evaluation of immunization campaigns with and without incentives, *British Medical Journal* **340**, 2220.

Duflo, E., M. Kremer, and J. Robinson (2008), How high are rates of return to fertilizer? Evidence from field experiments in Kenya, *American Economic Review* **98**(2), 482–488.

Edgeworth, F. Y. (1881), *Mathematical Physics: An Essay on the Application of Mathematics to the Moral Sciences*. London: Kegan. Retrieved from https://archive.org/details/mathematicalpsy01goog.

Ebert, J. E. and D. Prelec (2007), The fragility of time: Time-insensitivity and valuation of the near and far future, *Management Science* **53**(9), 1423–1438.

Edwards, W. (1954), The theory of decision making, *Psychological Bulletin* **51**, 380–417.

Edwards, W. (1961), Behavioral decision theory, *Annual Review of Psychology* **12**, 473–498.

Epper, T., H. Fehr-Duda, and A. Bruhin (2011), Viewing the future through a warped lens: Why uncertainty generates hyperbolic discounting, *Journal of Risk and Uncertainty* **43**, 169–203.

Estle, S. J., L. Green, J. Myerson, and D. D. Holt (2007), Discounting of money and directly consumable rewards, *Psychological Science* **18**, 58–63.

Etzioni, A. (2012), The privacy merchants: What is to be done? *The Journal of Constitutional Law* **14**(4), 929–951.

Evans, A. M. and J. I. Krueger (2009), The psychology and economics of trust, *Social and Personality Psychology Compass* **3**(6), 1003–1017.

Feldstein, M. S. (1965), The derivation of social time preference rates, *Kyklos* **18**, 277–287.

Fishburn, P. C. (1966), Stationary value mechanisms and expected utility theory, *Journal of Mathematical Psychology* **3**, 434–457.

Fishburn, P. C. (1968), Utility theory, *Management Science* **14**(5), 335–378.

Flaherty, D. (1989), Protecting Privacy in Surveillance Societies: The Federal Republic of Germany, Sweden, France, Canada, and the United States. Chapel Hill, NC: The University of North Carolina Press.

Fowler, R., B. Hodge, G. Kress, and T. Trew (1979), *Language and Control*. London: Routledge.

Frederick, S., G. Loewenstein, and T. O'Donoghue (2002), Time discounting and time preference: A critical review, *Journal of Economics Literature* **40**, 351–401.

Gaudeul, A. and C. Giannetti (2017), The effect of privacy concerns and social network formation, *Journal of Economic Behavior & Organization* **141**, 233–253.

Gentner, D. (2002), The psychology of mental models, in *International encyclopedia of the social and behavioral sciences*, N. J. Smelser & P. B. Bates (eds.), Amsterdam: Elsevier, pp. 9683–9687.

Gigerenzer, G. (2014), *Risk Savvy: How to Make Good Decisions*. New York, NY: Viking.

Gigerenzer, G. (2016), Towards a rational theory of heuristics, in *Minds, Models and Milieux: Commemorating the Centennial of the Birth of Herbert Simon*, R. Frantz & L. Marsh, Basingstoke (eds.), UK: Palgrave Macmillan.

Green, L., A. F. Fry, and J. Myerson (1994), Discounting of delayed rewards: A life-span comparison, *Psychological Science* **5**, 33–36.

Green, L. and J. Myerson (2004), A discounting framework for choice with delayed and probabilistic rewards, *Psychological Bulletin* **130**, 769–792.

Greenberg, A. and S. Collins (1966), Paired comparison taste tests: Some food for thought, *Journal of Marketing Research* **3**, 76–80.

Hansen, A. (2006), Do declining discount rates lead to time inconsistent economic advice? *Ecological Economics* **60**, 138–144.

Harrison, G. W., M. I. Lau, and M. B. Williams (2002), Estimating individual discount rates in Denmark: A field experiment, *American Economic Review* **92**(5), 1606–1617.

Henderson, N. and I. Bateman (1995), Empirical and public choice evidence for hyperbolic social discounting rates and the implications for intergenerational discounting, *Environmental and Resource Economics* **5**, 413–423.

Heyman, G. M. (1996), Resolving the contradictions of addiction, *Behavioral and Brain Sciences* **19**, 591–610.

Hoch, St. and G. Loewenstein (1991), Time-inconsistent preferences and consumer self-control, *Journal of Consumer Research* **17**, 492–507.

Horberg, E. J., C. Oveis, and D. Keltner (2011), Emotions as moral amplifiers: An appraisal tendency approach to the influences of distinct emotions upon moral judgments, *Emotion Review* **3**, 237–244.

Hornsby, J. (2007), An empirical investigation of the effects of discounting on privacy related decisions, Dissertation: Nova Southeastern University.

Horowitz, J. K. and R. T. Carson (1990), Discounting statistical lives, *Journal of Risk and Uncertainty* **3**(4), 403–413.

Iyengar, S. and D. R. Kinder (1987), *News that Matter*. London: University of Chicago Press.

Jevons, W. St. (1871), *The Theory of Political Economy*. London: Macmillan. Retrieved from http://www.econlib.org/library/YPDBooks/Jevons/jvnPE-Cover.html.

Johnson, D. (2009), *Ethical Theory and Business*. Upper Saddle River, NJ: Pearson Prentice Hall.

Kahneman, D. (2011), *Thinking, Fast and Slow*. New York: Farrar, Straus and Giroux.

Kahneman, D., P. Slovic, and A. Tversky (1982), *Judgment under Uncertainty: Heuristic and Biases*. New York: Cambridge University Press.

Kahneman, D. and R. Thaler (1991), Economic analysis and the psychology of utility: Applications to compensation policy, *American Economic Review* **81**, 341–346.

Kahneman, D. and A. Tversky (1979), Prospect theory: An analysis of decision under risk, *Econometrica* **47**(2), 263–291.

Kahneman, D. and A. Tversky (2000), *Choices, Values, and Frames*. Cambridge, MA: Cambridge University Press.

Keeler, E. G. and S. Cretin (1983), Discounting of life-saving and other nonmonetary effects, *Management Science* **29**, 300–306.

Keller, L. R. and E. Strazzera (2002), Examining predictive accuracy among discounting models, *Journal of Risk and Uncertainty* **24**(2), 143–160.

Kirby, K. N. (1997), Bidding on the future: Evidence against normative discounting of delayed rewards, *Journal of Experimental Psychology: General* **126**, 54–70.

Kirby, K. N. and R. J. Herrnstein (1995), Preference reversals due to myopic discounting of delayed reward, *Psychological Science* **6**(2), 83–89.

Kirby, K. N. and N. N. Marakovic (1995), Modeling myopic decisions: Evidence for hyperbolic delay-discounting within subjects and amounts, *Organizational Behavior & Human Decision Processes* **64**, 22–30.

Klein, B. and W. Meckling (1958), Application of operations research to development decisions, *Operations Research* **6**, 352–363.

Koopmans, T. C. (1960), Stationary ordinary utility and impatience, *Econometrica* **28**, 287–309.

Koopmans, T. C. (1964), On flexibility of future preferences, in *Human Judgments and Optimality*, M. W. Shelly and G. L. Bryan (eds.), New York: Wiley.

Koopmans, T. C., P. A. Diamonds, and R. E. Williamson (1964), Stationary utility and time perspective, *Econometrica* **32**, 82–100.

Kosinski, M., Y. Bachrach, D. J. Stillwell, P. Kohli, and T. Graepel (2014), Manifestations of user personality in website choice and behavior on online social networks, *Machine Learning* **95**(3), 357–380.

Kosinski, M., D. Stillwell, and T. Graepel (2013), Private traits and attributes are predicable from digital records of human behavior, *Proceedings of the National Academy of Sciences* **110**(15), 5802–5805.

Laibson, D. (1997), Golden eggs and hyperbolic discounting, *Quarterly Journal of Economics* **11**, 443–477.

Laibson, D., A. Repetto, and J. Tobacman (2003), A debt puzzle. in *Knowledge, information, and expectations in modern economics: In honor of Edmund S. Phelps*, P. Aghion, R. Frydman, J. Stiglitz, and M. Woodford (eds.), Princeton: Princeton University Press, pp. 228–266.

Laux, F. L. and R. M. Peck (2007), Economic perspectives on addiction: Hyperbolic discounting and internalities. Social Science Research Network working paper retrieved November 3, 2015 at http://papers.ssrn.com/sol3/papers.cfm?abstract_id=1077613.

Lerner, J. S., D. A. Small, and G. Loewenstein (2004), Heart strings and purse strings: Carryover effects of emotions on economic transactions, *Psychological Science* **15**(5), 337–341.

Lessig, L. (2006), *Code: Version 2.0*. New York, NY: Basic.

Loewenstein, G. (1992), The fall and rise of psychological explanations in the economics of intertemporal choice, in *Choice over time*, G. Loewenstein & J. Elster (eds.), New York: Sage, pp. 3–34.

Loewenstein, G. and D. Prelec (1993), Preferences for sequences of outcomes, *Psychological Review* **100**, 91–108.

Luce, R. D. and H. Raiffa (1957), *Games and Decisions: Introduction and Critical Survey*. New York: Dover.

Luce, R. D. and P. Suppes (1965), Preference, utility, and subjective probability, in *Handbook of Mathematical Psychology*, R. D. Luce, R. R., Bush, and E. Galanter (eds.), New York: Wiley, pp. 103–189.

Madden, G. L., W. K. Bickel, and E. A. Jacobs (1999), Discounting of delayed rewards in opioid-dependent outpatients: Exponential or hyperbolic discounting functions? *Experimental Clinical Psychopharmocology* **7**(3), 284–293.

Majumdar, T. (1958), *The Measurement of Utility*. London: Macmillan.

Marglin, S. A. (1963), The social rate of discount and the optimal rate of investment, *Quarterly Journal of Economics* **77**, 95–111.

Marschak, J. (1950), Rational behavior, uncertain prospects, and measurable utility, *Econometrica* **18**, 111–141.

Marquardt, R., J. Makens, and H. Larzelere (1965), Measuring the utility added by branding and grading, *Journal of Marketing Research* **2**, 45–50.

Marx, K. (1867/1995), *Capital: A Critique of Political Economy*. Moscow: Progress.

Mas-Colell, A., M. D. Whinston and J. R. Green (1995), *Microeconomic Theory*. New York: Oxford University Press.

Mastrobuoni, G. and M. Weinberg (2009), Heterogeneity in intra-monthly consumption patterns, self-control, and savings at retirement, *American Economic Journal: Economic Policy* **1**(2), 163–189.

Mazur, J. E. (1987), An adjusting procedure for studying delayed reinforcement, in *Quantitative Analyses of Behavior*, M. M. Commons, J. A. Nevvin, and H. Rachlin (eds.), Hillsdale: Lawrence Erlbaum.

McClure, S., K. Ericson, D. Laibson, G. Loewenstein, and J. Cohen (2007), Time discounting for primary rewards, *Journal of Neuroscience* **27**(21), 5796–5804.

Meier, St. and Ch. Sprenger (2010), *Stability of Time Preferences*. IZA Discussion Paper 4756, Institute for the Study of Labor.

Meyer, A. G. (2009), Estimating individual level discount factors and testing competing discounting hypotheses. Dissertation: University of Colorado.

Meyer, A. G. (2013), Estimating discount factors for public and private goods and testing competing discounting hypotheses, *Journal of Risk and Uncertainty* **46**, 133–173.

Milkman, K. L., T. Rogers, and M. H. Bazerman (2008), Harnessing our inner angels and demons: What we have learned about want/should conflicts and how that knowledge can help us reduce short-sighted decision making, *Perspectives on Psychological Science* **3**(4), 324–338.

Milkman, K. L., T. Rogers, and M. H. Bazerman (2009), Highbrow films gather dust: Time- inconsistent preferences and online DVD rentals, *Management Science* **55**(6), 1047–1059.

Minsky, H. P. (1977), Banking and a fragile financial environment, *The Journal of Portfolio Management* **3**(4), 16–22.

Moscovici, S. (1988), Notes towards a description of social representations, *Journal of European Social Psychology* **18**(3), 211–250.

Murphy, J. G., R. E. Vuchinich, and C. A. Simpson (2001), Delayed reward and cost discounting, *Psychological Record* **51**, 571–588.

Myerson, J. and L. Green (1995), Discounting of delayed rewards: Models of individual choice, *Journal of Experimental Analysis of Behavior* **64**, 263–276.

Neuman, W., M. R. J. Russel, and A. N. Crigler (1992), *Common Knowledge*. Chicago: Chicago University Press.

Norris, P. and D. Sanders (2003), Message or medium? Campaign learning during the 2001 British General Election, *Political Communication* **20**, 233–262.

Okada, E. M. and S. J. Hoch (2004), Spending time versus spending money, *Journal of Consumer Research* **31**, 313–323.

Olken, B. A. (2009), Do television and radio destroy social capital? Evidence from Indonesian villages, *American Economic Journal: Applied Economics* **1**(4), 1–33.

Orwell, G. (1949), *1984*. New York: Harcourt Brace.

Oster, S. M. and F. M. S. Scott-Morton (2005), Behavioral biases meet the market: The case of magazine subscription prices, *Advances in Economic Analysis & Policy* **5**(1), 1, 1–32.

Oulasvirta, A., T. Suomalainen, J. Hamari, A. Lampinen, and K. Karvonen (2014), Transparency of intentions decreases privacy concerns in ubiquitous surveillance, *Cyberpsychology, Behavior, and Social Networking* **17**(10), 633–638.

Paluck, E. L. (2009), What's in a norm? Sources and processes of norm change, *Journal of Personality and Social Psychology* **96**, 594–600.

Pareto, V. (1906/2014), *Manual of Political Economy*. Oxford, UK: Oxford University Press.

Petry, N. M. and T. Casarella (1999), Excessive discounting of delayed rewards in substance abusers with gambling problems, *Drug and Alcohol Dependence* **56**(1), 25–32.

Posner, R. A. (1981), The economic of privacy, *The American Economic Review* **71**(2), 405–409.

Posner, R. A. (2000), *Law and Social Norms*. Cambridge, MA: Harvard University Press.

Prat, A. (2005), The wrong kind of transparency, *American Economic Review* **95**(3), 862–877.

Prat, A. (2017), *Lecture Notes 'Industrial Organization.'* New York: Columbia University.

Prat, A. and D. Strömberg (2005), Commercial television and voter information. CEPR Discussion Paper 4989, April 2005.

Prat, A. and D. Strömberg (2013), *The Political Economy of Mass Media*. New York: Columbia University working paper. Retrievable at http://www.columbia.edu/~ap3116/papers/mediasurvey11.pdf.

Puaschunder, J. M. (2015), On the social representations of intergenerational equity, *Oxford Journal of Finance and Risk Perspectives* **4**(4), 78–99.

Puaschunder, J. M. (2016), Trust and reciprocity drive common goods allocation norms, in *Proceedings of the Cambridge Business & Economics Conference*, Cambridge, UK: Cambridge University, in *Proceedings of the 2015 6th International Conference of the Association of Global Management Studies at Alfred Lerner Hall of Columbia University*. New York: The Association of Global Management Studies.

Puaschunder, J. M. (2017), Nudgital: Critique of behavioral political economy, *Archives of Business Research* **5**(9), 54–76.

Puaschunder, J. M. (work in progress), On the collective soul of booms and busts. Retrievable at https://papers.ssrn.com/sol3/papers.cfm?abstract_id=2799646.

Puaschunder, J. M. and G. Schwarz (2012), The future is now: How joint decision making curbs hyperbolic discounting but blurs social responsibility in the intergenerational equity public policy domain. Harvard University Situationist Law and Mind Sciences Working Paper.

Putnam, H. (2002), On the rationality of preferences, in *The Collapse of the Fact-Value Dichotomy and Other Essays*, H. Putnam (ed.), Cambridge, MA: Harvard University Press.

Putnam, R. D. (2000), *Bowling Alone: The Collapse and Revival of American Community*, New York: Simon & Schuster.

Rachlin, H., A. Raineri and D. Cross (1991), Subjective probability and delay, *Journal of the Experimental Analysis of Behavior* **55**, 233–244.

Ramsey, F. P. (1928), A mathematical theory of savings, *Economic Journal* **38**, 543–559.

Read, D. (2001), Is time-discounting hyperbolic or subadditive? *Journal of Risk and Uncertainty* **23**(1), 5–32.

Read, D., S. Frederick, and M. Airoldi (2012), Four days later in Cincinnati: Longitudinal tests of intertemporal preference reversals due to hyperbolic discounting, *Acta Psychologica* **140**(2), 177–185.

Read, D., G. Loewenstein, and S. Kalyanaraman (1999), Mixing virtue and vice: The combined effects of hyperbolic discounting and diversification, *Journal of Behavioral Decision Making* **12**, 257–273.

Read, D. R. and B. van Leeuwen (1998), Predicting hunger: The effects of appetite and delay on choice, *Organizational Behavior and Human Decision Processes* **76**(2), 189–205.

Read, D. R. (1964), A quantitative approach to the comparative assessment of taste quality in the confectionery industry, *Biometrics* **20**, 143–155.

Reed, D. D. and B. K. Martens (2011), Temporal discounting predicts student responsiveness to exchange delays in a classroom token system, *Journal of Applied Behavior Analysis* **44**, 1–18.

Reuben, E., P. Sapienza, and L. Zingales (2010), Time-discounting for primary and monetary rewards, *Economic Letters* **106**(2), 125–127.

Rothenberg, J. (1961), *The Measurement of Social Welfare*. Englewood Cliffs: Prentice Hall.

Roberts, A. S. (2010), *The Logic of Discipline: Global Capitalism and the Architecture of Government*. New York: Oxford University Press.

Salanié, F. and N. Treich (2005), Over-savings and hyperbolic discounting, *European Economic Review* **50**(6), 1557–1570.

Samuelson, P. A. (1937), A note on measurement of utility, *The Review of Economic Studies* **4**, 155–161.

Schumpeter, J. A. (1949), *Economic Theory and Entrepreneurial History*. Cambridge, MA: Harvard University Press.

Sen, A. K. (1971), Choice functions and revealed preference, *The Review of Economic Studies* **38**(3), 307–317.

Sen, A. K. (1977), Rational fools: A critique of the behavioral foundations of economic theory, *Philosophy and Public Affairs* **6**(4), 317–344.

Sen, A. K. (1993), Internal consistency of choice, *Econometrica* **61**(3), 495–521.

Sen, A. K. (1995), Rationality and social choice, *The American Economic Review* **85**(1), 1–24.

Sen, A. K. (1997), Maximization and the act of choice, *Econometrica* **65**(4), 745–780.

Sen, A. K. (2002a), Consistency of choice, in *Rationality and Freedom*, A. Sen (ed.), Cambridge, MA: Harvard University Press.

Sen, A. K. (2002b), Goals, commitment, and identity, in *Rationality and Freedom*, A. Sen (ed.), Cambridge, MA: Harvard University Press.

Shackle, G. L. S. (1955), *Uncertainty in Economics and Other Reflections*. Cambridge: Cambridge University Press.

Shah, A. K. and D. Oppenheimer (2008), Heuristics made easy: An effort-reduction framework, *Psychological Bulletin* **134**(2), 207–222.

Shaikh, A. (2016), *Capitalism: Competition, Conflict, Crises*. Oxford: Oxford University Press.

Shannon, C. E. (1948), A mathematical theory of communication, *The Bell System Technical Journal* **27**, 379–423.

Shui, H. and L. M. Ausubel (2004), Time inconsistency in the credit card market. Social Science Research Network working paper retrieved October 25, 2015 at http://ssrn.com/abstract=586622.

Silberberg, S. (2000), The Structure of Economics: A Mathematical Analysis. Boston: McGraw-Hill.

Simon, H. A. (1957), *Models of Man: Social and Rational*. New York: Wiley.

Simon, H. A. (1959), Theories of decision making in economics and behavioral science, *American Economic Review* **49**, 253–283.

Simon, H. A. (1979), Rational decision making in business organizations, *American Economic Review* **69**(4), 493–513

Simon, H. A. and R. D. Bartel (1986), The failure of armchair economics, *Challenge* **29**(5), 18–25.

Slonim, R., J. Carlson, and E. Bettinger (2007), Possession and discounting behavior, *Economic Letters* **97**(3), 215–221.

Snyder, J. M. and D. Strömberg (2010), Press coverage and political accountability, *Journal of Political Economy* **118**(2), 355–408.

Solove, D. J. (2008), *Understanding Privacy*. Cambridge, MA: Harvard University Press.

Soros, G. (2018), Remarks delivered at the World Economic Forum in Davos. Retrievable at https://www.georgesoros.com/2018/01/25/remarks-delivered-at-the-world-economic-forum/.

Stafford, J. E. (1966), Effects of group influences on consumer brand preferences, *Journal of Marketing Research* **3**, 68–75.

Sterner, T. (1994), Discounting in a world of limited growth, *Environmental and Resource Economics* **4**, 527–534.

Stillson, P. (1954), A method for defect evaluation, *Industrial Quality Control* **11**, 9–12.

Strotz, R. H. (1957), Myopia and inconsistency in dynamic utility maximization, *Review of Economic Studies* **23**, 165–180.

Suppes, P. (1961), Behavioristic foundations of utility, *Econometrica* **29**, 186–202.

Suzuki, G. (1957), Procurement and allocation of naval electronic equipments, *Naval Research Logistics Quarterly* **4**, 1–7.

Thaler, R. H. (1981), Some empirical evidence on dynamic inconsistency, *Economics Letters* **8**(3), 201–207.

Thaler, R. H. and H. M. Shefrin (1981), An economic theory of self-control, *Journal of Political Economy* **89**, 392–406.

Thaler, R. H. and C. R. Sunstein (2008), *Nudge. Improving Decisions about Health, Wealth, and Happiness*. New Haven: Yale University Press.

Trope, Y. and A. Fishbach (2000), Counteractive self-control in overcoming temptation, *Journal of Personality and Social Psychology* **79**(4), 493–506.

van der Pol, M. and J. Cairns (2001), Estimating time preferences for health using discrete choice experiments, *Social Science and Medicine* **52**(9), 1459–1470.

von Neumann, J. and O. Morgenstern (1953), *Theory of Games and Economic Behavior*. Princeton, NJ: Princeton University Press.

Wagner W., F. Lorenzi-Cioldi, I. Mankova, and D. Rose (1999), Theory and method of social representations, *Asian Journal of Social Psychology* **2**(1), 95–125.

Warner, J. T. and S. Pleeter (2007), The personal discount rate: Evidence from military downsizing programs, *American Economic Review* **91**(1), 33–53.

Warren, S. and L. Brandeis (1890), The right to privacy, *Harvard Law Review* **4**(5), 193–220.

Wertenbroch, K. (1998), Consumption self-control by rationing purchase quantities of virtue and vice, *Marketing Science* **17**(4), 317–337.

Witzany, G. (2012), *Biocommunication of Fungi*. Dordrecht: Springer.

Wold, H. (1952), Ordinal preferences or cardinal utility? *Econometrica* **20**, 661–664.

Wouter, D. and A. Prat (forthcoming), Attention in organizations, in *The Oxford Handbook of Network Economics*, Y. Bramoulle, A. Galeotti & B. Rogers (eds.), Oxford: Oxford University Press.

Zauberman, G., B. K. Kim, S. A. Malkoc, and J. R. Bettman (2009), Discounting time and time discounting: Subjective time perception and intertemporal preferences, *Journal of Marketing Research* **46**(8), 543–556.

https://doi.org/10.1142/9789811220470_0003

Chapter 3

Blockchain Technology Adoption Decisions: Developed vs. Developing Economies

Alnoor Bhimani[*,§], Kjell Hausken[†,¶] and Sameen Arif[‡,‖]

[*]*London School of Economics, UK*

[†]*University of Stavanger, Stavanger, Norway*

[‡]*Lahore University of Management Sciences, Pakistan*

[§]*a.bhimani@lse.ac.uk*

[¶]*kjell.hausken@uis.no*

[‖]*sameenarif@live.com*

Abstract

Blockchains as digitized, decentralized ledgers allow recordkeeping of peer-to-peer transactions, thus eliminating the need for intervening trusted third parties. This makes the technology useful in altering business processes and transactions not just across industrial sectors but also across economies. However, little research exists on the factors that impede and sponsor blockchain technology adoption in developed relative to developing country contexts. We highlight blockchain technology issues which sponsor/impede its adoption across developing/developed economic contexts. We focus on assessing the flow of money and land registries in these contexts in relation to the propensity to deploy blockchain systems. We then apply our analytical frame resting on real options principles to explore the decision point at which blockchain would be adopted relative to economic development.

Keywords: Blockchain; Digital; Development; Accountability; Technology.

1. Introduction

Blockchains as digitized, decentralized ledgers allow recordkeeping of peer-to-peer transactions, thereby eliminating the need for intervening trusted third parties (Woodside *et al.*, 2017). This makes the technology useful in a variety of ways. As connecting platform systems, blockchains are altering business processes and transactions across industries as well as countries.[1]

A number of studies point to implementation costs including the replacement of existing systems as key challenges for blockchain technology adoption (McKinsey, 2018; Sadhya and Sadhya, 2018; Seebacher and Schüritz, 2019). In developing economies, blockchain implementation costs differ to a degree from those in developed country enterprises. In developing contexts, blockchains engage specific deployment rationales. Their adoption can be triggered when the pressure for transparency, trust, and other perceived benefits exceeds the costs of shifting investments onto the technology while taking account of governance issues also. Where legacy systems are relatively underdeveloped, those costs can be low. Further, blockchain adoption can seem desirable particularly when regulatory barriers are low. One survey of 1386 executives from across 12 developed countries reports that regulatory issues alongside the cost of replacing legacy systems are the biggest organizational barriers to investing in blockchain (Deloitte, 2019). While a growing body of emerging studies explore the rationales for the application of blockchain in different contexts, much scholarly interest focuses on developed economies. Our

[1]As of March 28, 2019, the top 10 countries to adopt blockchain technology are Malta, Estonia, Switzerland, United Arab Emirates, Singapore, United Kingdom, China, Japan, USA, Sweden. The following countries embrace blockchain rapidly: Australia, Denmark, Gibraltar, France, Korea, South Africa (Blockstuffs, 2019).

interest lies in the recognition that blockchain adoption under a cost–benefit analysis reflective of the level of economic development has not been investigated. We thus differentially investigate, analytically and comparatively, how emerging and developed economies differ in relation to the point at which the benefits of blockchain exceed the costs leading to the adoption of the technology. A difference can be expected to exist given that emerging economy countries are likely to adopt blockchain more readily where the benefits from greater transparency demands exceed those of developed countries which have stronger regulatory environments and governance practices and where the robustness of legacy systems present lesser potential benefits from the technology. By contrast, we see blockchain adoption also finding resistance by those who benefit from the lack of transparency or indeed abusers of the economic system in developing economies raising barriers to its adoption. We view the rate of adoption in developed and developing economies as being to a degree opposite which impacts the stage of take-up. Our study considers in particular the point of shift where blockchain adoption is triggered through dynamic shifts in these factors.

The chapter is structured as follows. We start by highlighting blockchain technology issues which sponsor/impede its adoption across developing/developed economic contexts. Based on the existing literature, we adopt a real options framework to conduct the analysis. We first explore the flow of money and land registries in developing and developed countries as potential issues affecting the propensity to deploy blockchain technology. We then apply our analytical frame to show the point at which blockchain would advance and conclude.

2. Blockchain Technology: Country-Level Issues

Blockchain is a decentralized distributed ledger that records transactions on blocks so that they can be reviewed and verified by the network and added chronologically on the systems of all members in the network (Holotiuk *et al.*, 2017). The history of blockchain dates back two decades when the concept was used to time stamp easily modifiable digital assets. Its first practical implementation was in 2009 in the form of bitcoins where the technology tracked and verified the transactions of this digital cash. Nakamoto (2008) describes how peer-to-peer financial transactions on blockchain eliminate the need for any trusted third party. The technology has allowed for the possibility of bilateral, low-cost, transparent financial transactions (Iansiti and Lakhani, 2017). The immutability offered (Hofmann *et al.*, 2017; Pilkington, 2016) or resistance to tampering is a crucial feature which makes manipulation or destruction of entries practically impossible, conferring intrinsic value to one of the first applications of blockchain, cryptocurrencies (DeRose, 2016). Moreover, with its ability to enable data protection and maintain relative user anonymity, its adoption can encompass a wide variety of applications. Swan (2015) identifies three applications of blockchain. The first is currency including remittances, e-payments, and currency transfers. The second is smart contracts and the third category includes other socioeconomic applications like notary, voting, and healthcare applications. Blockchain allows the recording, verification, and transferring of digital goods and assets (home, auto, stocks, bonds, mortgages, and insurance) and preserves the authenticity of sensitive documents (passports, visa, drivers license, birth, death, and marriage certificates) while preventing them from being copied or multiplied (Swan, 2017). Its decentralized, immutable, and transparent features can allow impossible-to-rig elections, unhackable borderless data storage, close-to-free payments, financial anonymity, universal authentication of goods, verifiable crowd predictions, precise public health records, and charity fund disbursement (Goke, 2018). The potential applications of blockchain continue to evolve across industries.

Blockchain adoption is not without the challenges of high financial development and implementation costs, regulatory costs, and political and economic hindrances posed by those in power.

The factors that stimulate the adoption of a technology have been analyzed through various adoption theories. These include the diffusion of innovation theory (Rogers, 1962), theory of reasoned action (Fishbein and Ajzen, 1975), technology, organizational and environmental framework (Tornatzky *et al.*, 1990), assimilation theory (Armstrong and Sambamurthy, 1999), the technology acceptance model (Venkatesh and Davis, 2000), and the perceived e-readiness model (Molla and Licker, 2005). Blockchain has also been poised to have the same disruptive power in IT as the Internet did in the 1990s. We conceptualize the adoption of blockchain as "a decision to make full use of an innovation as the best course of action available" (Rogers, 2003, p. 177). The technology offers similar opportunities for any country to benefit from but its adoption will be dictated by the urgency to take advantage of the opportunities offered while minimizing the associated costs. Managerial decisions must be premised on an analysis. Therefore, for the purpose of this study we seek to analyze factors that propel and impede the adoption of blockchain in a developing/developed country context.

We consider below illustrations from developed and developing countries evidencing different parameters of play in recordkeeping systems such as where flow of money in the form of remittances or aid and land registries point to a need for transparency potentially driving the adoption of blockchain.

Many developing countries are faced with the challenge of inaccurate land registries, unclear ownership, and lack of enforceable and comprehensible property rights. This absence of dependence on legacy systems and practices prevents utilizing assets to their full potential. Therefore, emerging economies could revolutionize their land registry systems completely by shifting to blockchain which consolidates blocks of data on buyer and seller identities, property location, sales price, and purchase date to create a system that is accessible, transparent, and protected (Sheehan, 2018). Developed countries on the contrary tend to have long-standing and established systems of property title records relative to emerging economies. The latter would not need to disinvest prevailing technologies to adopt blockchain as a basis for more technologically modernized registry systems. Nevertheless, developed countries see extensive merits of blockchain adoption with clear benefits such as eliminating paperwork, fraud and increasing the efficiency of processes. Developing countries see these benefits being much larger where there may be a strong need to eliminate fraud and encourage people to register land for bank collateral purposes (Hamilton, 2019). Land-related disputes in India, for instance, account for two-thirds of all pending court cases in the country and take about an average of 20 years to be resolved (Seth, 2018). Other developing countries are also considering blockchain adoption for this purpose. In June 2017, Ukraine converted a property register to Blockchain technology (Space, 2018). Moreover, Ghana, where 78% of the land is unregistered is also *en route* to adopting the technology and transforming its land registry system since disputes add to the burden of the courts by tying up land in litigation and impacting sectors and projects that are dependent on these disputed land titles (Santiso, 2018). It is arguable that benefits and cost saving from the adoption of blockchain can be larger in developing in contrast to developed countries. However, concurrently, developing countries will likely have lower barriers to be met in dismantling legacy systems.

The flow of money in developing countries in the form of remittances is another area which demands transparency and immutability. Migrant remittance has been recognized as a tool for poverty alleviation and an impetus to development and growth in the 2030 Agenda for Sustainable Development. With the global remittance market supporting 800 million people worldwide and generating $500 billion to developing countries as of 2019, its role as an economic booster cannot be stressed enough (Europa.eu, 2019). As of 2018, remittances to low- and middle-income countries accounted for $529 billion with India being the largest receiver of remittances amounting to $79 billion followed by China ($67 billion), Mexico ($36 billion), and Philippines ($34 billion) (PTI Washington, 2019). This $689 billion global remittance industry is expected to grow by more than 3% in 2019 (Zaki, 2019). These inflows to low- and middle-income countries by 250 million migrant and immigrant workers contribute significantly to their GDP and account for 75% of the total remittances worldwide (Safahi, 2018).

The role of remittance in developing countries therefore fuels the demand for fast, cost-efficient, and traceable channels of money transfer. Most developing countries like Pakistan transfer money through money exchangers as opposed to banks. They resort to the system of *hawala hundi* as a means to transfer money leaving no audit trail and evading tax payments. The Federal Investigation Agency (FIA) in April 2019 confiscated Rs. 420 million in cash as part of its crackdown against *hundi* and *hawala* dealers in Karachi, Pakistan (Hafeez, 2019). On the contrary, channels like M-Pesa, with a huge success in Kenya rendering 66.5% of the population to be financially included, have been unable to establish a strong footing in other developing countries (TFH Al Analysts, 2019) owing to its inability of being borderless, instant, and dependent on banking intermediaries, increasing the cost. With such channels operating without ensured traceability, they could be used to finance illegal activities making it impossible to be tracked by anti-money laundering agencies.

As far as transaction costs are concerned, the Sustainable Development Goal 10.c aims to set transaction fees to 3% of amounts remitted by 2030 ("SDG Indicators", 2018). However, the World Bank reported that as of the first quarter of 2019, the global average cost of sending $200 remained around 7% with Africa being among the worst affected operating at a transaction fee of 10%. Banks are recognized as being the most expensive remittance channel with a fee of 11%, followed by post offices charging

7%. The national post offices were reported to make a premium of 1.5%–4% as of the last quarter of 2018 owing to their partnership with money transfer operators (World Bank, 2019). Thus, the existing money transfer channels in developing countries do not serve the needs of the users adequately.

Hence, with the international remittances to low- and middle-income countries expected to reach US$550 billion by the end of 2019 and where transaction fees can run from 7% to over 20% (Niles, 2019), users have to wait for days to receive their payments and no audit trail is left to ensure the transparency of the system. Here, blockchain can proffer potential benefits which can be realized through an immutable and transparent system.

The benefits of blockchain offered through traceability and transparency can also be realized with the flow of aid in addition to remittances. The technology can enable benefits in supply chain management as evidenced in cases of aid disbursement where the pressure for transparency is immense. Considering that nearly half of the funds are misappropriated, 3.5% is lost to fees, and associated costs and 30% of the funds do not reach their recipients, blockchain adoption can provide benefits for both the developing countries receiving this aid and the aid-granting developed countries in terms of enhanced trust and cost savings (Paynter, 2017). The use of technology by the World Food Program for aid disbursement to Syrian refugees in Jordan and the World Bank to expend development aid in developing countries like Bangladesh are successful examples of deployment of the technology (Choudhury, 2018). The European Union has established a task force to investigate ways in which the technology can help administer funds in different funding programs like the Asylum Migration and Integration Fund (Ardittis, 2018).

In the cases mentioned, the pressure for transparency can be expected to be high but the adoption of blockchain would only actualize if the factors propelling its adoption outweigh those impeding it. The biggest hindrance to the adoption of blockchain technology comes from the actors involved in the process who may resist transparency given their gains arising from the weaknesses of the prevailing system. Numerous benefits may be realized by moving public data to blockchain, but it would require trust in the legitimacy of the government making such changes aside from the direct investments in the altered system. Moreover, eradicating corruption could be a key priority for emerging economies considering the burden this poses for the economy. But it traces its roots to public authorities who will be reluctant to implement any technology which hinders money laundering, tax evasion, and bribery. There are evident examples from developing countries of money embezzlement accounting billions of dollars by their rulers like Mobutu in Zaire, Marcos in the Philippines, Mubarak in Egypt, and Nawaz Sharif in Pakistan (Siddiqui, 2013). The National Accountability Bureau Pakistan launched an investigation against the brother of former Army Chief, also one of the managers of the Defense Housing Authority (DHA), an arm of the Pakistani military that constructs housing for its members as well as the general public for the embezzlement of US$140 million (Boone, 2016). Moreover, IMF (International Monetary Fund) reported that bribe requests by tax officials in Pakistan increased by 30% (The Newspaper's Correspondent, 2019). Public procurement in Kenya faces similar problems where government officials were found to be involved in demanding bribery and inflating state contracts of US$700 million awarding them to ghost vendors ("Kenya Corruption Report", 2017). Reports of public officials and regulators being involved in bribery and tax evasion due to loopholes of the system deter the implementation of technology which could restrict flow of money to them or expose their corrupt practices by making the system transparent.

Where the technology is adopted, its benefits cannot be fully realized in countries challenged with weak governance systems since the output generated by blockchain is as good as the input. Taking the example of voting for instance, prior to feeding the data in the blockchain, it has to be ensured that voters are registered so that only eligible people vote and the process is carried out anonymously without any coercion. If the rules are not followed, the participants could allocate millions of extra votes to themselves even with blockchain in place. This feature renders the underlying idea of blockchain as a trustless and useless technology and shifts the focus toward building a trusted system with an independent press, government organizations, and NGOs ensuring transparency (Stinchcombe, 2018).

The adoption of blockchain implies a high implementation cost. Since blockchain skills are still a niche market, recruiting developers and network engineers is a costly affair with their salaries in the range of $120,000–$180,000 per annum in Europe and around $150,000 in the US (Davies, 2019). Organizations would be also be faced with the burden to hire staff including compliance and legal personnel who understand the technology and can work in coordination with system developers and financial regulators. Another cost of implementation is that of energy consumption. Completing a single transaction using blockchain requires as much energy as the average household incurs in a single day (Ogono, 2019). This poses a question as to its implementation in developing countries like Pakistan which reported an electricity shortage of 6000 MW in 2018 (Online, 2018). Some of this may partly get resolved through various transitions from Proof of Work to various versions of Proof of Stake. Still the high operating costs may be a challenge for developing countries.

Blockchain adoption for smart contracts additionally faces inflexibility and legal costs. There is an absence of a legal framework and regulatory precision to dictate their execution and a lack of information on the matter because of the newness of the phenomenon. Government authorities are faced with the challenge for scrutinizing blockchain-based applications for illegal activities including money laundering and financing of criminal activities. Gibbs (2018), highlights the study by researchers from the RWTH Aachen University which recently found sexual content including images of child abuse in at least eight of the 1600 files on the bitcoin's blockchain. Since these data have to be downloaded for processes like mining, the users might be liable for objectionable content stored by others, thus threatening the integrity of the technology (Gibbs, 2018).

The decentralization of the blockchain poses another hindrance by not only making it harder to identify parties involved in illicit activities but also centralized governments may not be prepared for this radical decentralization and hence may show resistance.

The benefits to be realized from the adoption of blockchain primarily rest on the argument of weaker institutions. This problem may not be faced to the same extent in developed economies, and thus, they may benefit from the technology differently. Since blockchain essentially adds an audit trail for currency/assets which is blocked in a way that hacking it is virtually impossible, the authenticity of an asset can be proven by knowing the entire transaction history. However, if we trust institutions, such high levels of encryptions might not be needed and public key encryption offered by the existing technologies along with trustworthy institutions render the adoption of blockchain unnecessary. Developed countries would only consider adoption of the blockchain for first-world problems where the benefits of blockchain are currently rather superficial. As highlighted by Pattekar (2018), legacy systems which allow a high level of encryption and powerful relational databases developed by the likes of Oracle, SQL Server, and Postgres have allowed these countries to overcome problems faced by emerging economies. Such legacy systems, according to Gideon Greenspan, "have been deployed on millions of servers running trillions of queries. They contain some of the most thoroughly tested, debugged and optimized code on the planet, processing thousands of transactions per second without breaking a sweat" (Pattekar, 2018). With huge investments in robust systems and the awareness of developed economies of the environmental footprint of cryptocurrency with its contribution to global carbon dioxide emissions, adoption can be slow.

In the next section, we discuss specific growth and model the above factors which propel or hinder blockchain adoption within developing/developed country scenarios.

3. Blockchain Adoption through Time: Growth and Carrying Capacity Factors

Consider how a country k, $k = 1, \ldots, N$, applying mainly non-blockchain technology may transition to apply more blockchain technology. We define x_k, $0 \le x_k \le x_{k\max} \le 1$, as the fraction of blockchain technology adoption in country k at time t, $x_{k\max}$ as the maximum possible fraction of blockchain technology adoption, and $1-x_k$ as the fraction of non-blockchain technology adoption at time t. The maximum $x_{k\max}$ equals 1 if non-blockchain technology can completely replace blockchain technology, or less than 1 if technological, legal, transparency, and cost constraints hinder extensive blockchain technology adoption.

Adoption of new technologies often follows an S-shaped curve through time with an initial slow convex increase, then more rapid increase, then a gradual transition to concave increase, and finally movement toward a horizontal asymptote $x_{k\max}$ representing full adoption. A common representation is the logistic equation (Lotka, 1924; Verhulst, 1845)

$$\frac{\partial x_k}{\partial t} = r_k x_k \left(1 - \frac{x_k}{x_{k\max}}\right) \Rightarrow x_k = \frac{x_{k\max} x_{k0} e^{r_k t}}{x_{k\max} + x_{k0}(e^{r_k t} - 1)}), \lim_{t\to\infty} x_k = x_{k\max}, \quad (1)$$

where ∂ indicates partial differentiation, t indicates time, r_k is the growth rate expressing how quickly blockchain technology is adopted in country

k, and $r_{k\max}$ is the carrying capacity, defined as the maximum amount of blockchain technology that can be obtained or sustained. Equation (1) states that blockchain technology x_k in country k changes logistically from x_{k0}, $x_{k0} \geq 0$, at time $t = 0$ toward $x_k = x_{k\max}$ as time approaches infinity.

Countries resistant to adopting blockchain technology, due to technological, legal, transparency, and costs reasons, have a low carrying capacity $x_{k\max}$, which may hypothetically be equal to zero, e.g., if blockchain technology is cost prohibitive. In contrast, countries welcoming adopting blockchain technology have a high carrying capacity $x_{k\max}$. Further, countries with low inertia, high willingness to explore new technologies, and competence and resources to implement changes have a high growth rate r_k. Countries lacking these characteristics have a low growth rate r_k.

Let us assess which factors impact the carrying capacity $r_{k\max}$ and the growth rate r_k. We first consider factors increasing the carrying capacity $r_{k\max}$ and the growth rate r_k, thus propelling blockchain adoption:

- **Eliminates intermediaries:** Cuts costs and the need for cooperation among participants.
- **Digital asset registries:** Blockchain not only allows registering, verifying, and transferring assets over the Internet but also guards against double spending.
- **Flow of remittances:** Blockchain makes flow of remittances both cost and time efficient while offering traceability.
- **Payment channel:** Blockchain allows fast and cheap execution of multiple transactions while maintaining transaction history privacy. Real-time transactions also guard against currency fluctuations. It makes micropayment a possibility which not only allows low-cost transactions but also helps marketers build loyal relationships with customers through the execution of smart contracts and gaining access to customer information without having to buy it from intermediaries to provide personalized products and prices.
- **Personalized services:** Blockchain makes provision of personalized products and services a possibility with the ease of finding a supplier over the Internet and transacting in a secure environment while maintaining user anonymity.
- **Identity management:** The decentralized feature of blockchain allows individuals the freedom to create encrypted digital identities,

saving time and resources of creating multiple usernames and passwords, and protecting against fraudulent activities. Creation of identities can in turn help with financial inclusion, transparent voting, and management of refugees.

- **Aid disbursement:** Use of blockchain can ensure less money is lost to banking fees, poor exchange rates, and currency fluctuations while increasing transparency and traceability for both the donor, and the recipient.
- **Corruption:** Blockchain adoption can enhance transparency by providing an audit trail eliminating corruption in transactions.
- **Decentralized government structure:** Using blockchain for smart contracts means the governance apparatus could be more decentralized and potentially smaller and hence potentially less costly, biased, and bureaucratic.

We next consider factors impeding or decreasing the carrying capacity $x_{k\max}$ and the growth rate r_k, thus constraining blockchain adoption:

- **Participants involved:** The biggest hindrance is from the actors involved in the process who would not want transparency considering the gains they make because of the existing weakness of the system. This may involve public authorities who may be reluctant to implement any technology which hinders money laundering, tax evasion, and bribery.
- **Legal issues:** While some countries have laws in place to impede or block blockchain, others lack a legal framework to dictate the implementation and use of the technology.
- **Complexity:** The misinformation and complexity surrounding blockchain coupled with an immature market and limited number of skilled developers and networkers hinders mass adoption.
- **Energy cost:** The technology can absorb high energy. For instance, bitcoin mining's energy consumption could grow to as much as Denmark's total energy consumption by 2020 (Deetman, 2016). Transition from Proof-of-Work to Proof-of-Stake may resolve some of this.
- **Environmental issues:** Carbon dioxide emissions.
- **Investment in legacy system:** A robust legacy system which allows public chain encryption, workflow management, and enterprise information system renders a blockchain unnecessary.

- **Political issues:** Governments are likely to resist bitcoin and other non-fiat digital currencies considering the required decentralization and loss of control over monetary policy.
- **Anonymity and decentralization issue:** Anonymity and decentralization make it harder to identify and hence hold responsible parties accountable for illicit activities.
- **The bitcoin scalability problem:** The bitcoin blockchain can only process seven transactions per second while Visa processes 1700 transactions/s (Sedgwick, 2018). Increasing speed would increase costs. The lightning network may resolve the low-speed issue bitcoins.
- **Increase economic inequality:** Informed/educated Internet users would benefit more from the technology increasing the economic inequality, which may constrain blockchain adoption if measures are undertaken to increase the economic equality.

Table 1 shows various use cases, potential advantages, and challenges for blockchain technology.

Table 1: Use cases, potential advantages, and challenges for blockchain technology.

Use case	Potential Advantage	Challenges
General	Transparency Immutability Anonymity Decentralization Eliminates the need for trust Synchronization Traceability	Privacy Scalability Lack of skills Anonymity Governance Criminal activities Environmental cost
Land registry	Time and cost efficient Reduces risk of misappropriation	The end product is as good as the records
Payment channel	Allows micropayments, low cost, trust-less, and immutable	Scalability, 51% attacks, chain transfers might be better for larger amounts
Remittances	Cost and time efficient	Liquidity constraints
Supply chain management	Cost efficient Facilitates traceability	Requires buy-in from multiple parties
Identity management	Enables self-sovereign and digital IDs	Governance issues, easy to use, might not be easy to secure

Costs and benefits of different players within a country impact the carrying capacity $r_{k\max}$ and the growth rate r_k. Since players benefit differentially from adopting blockchain technology, and some players the imposed costs from adopting blockchain technology, a power struggle can be expected between those preferring and not preferring blockchain technology, and those that are indifferent.

Figure 1 plots the fractions x_1 and x_2 of blockchain technology adoption in two countries. For both countries, we assume initial adoption $x_{10} = x_{20} = 0.1$. Country 1 is assumed to be developing with intermediate growth rate $r_1 = 1$ and a high carrying capacity $x_{1\max} = 0.8$. Country 2 is assumed to be developed with a high growth rate $r_2 = 2$ and an intermediate carrying capacity $x_{2\max} = 0.5$. The point at which a shift occurs, tentatively defined here as 25% adoption (marked with a horizontal dashed line), is reached earlier for the developed country 2 than for the developing country 1.

Equation (1) and Figure 1 assume no interaction between countries. Equation (1) is generalizable to

$$\frac{\partial x_k}{\partial t} = r_k x_k \left(1 - \frac{\sum_{h=1}^{N} \alpha_{hk} x_h}{x_{k\max}}\right) \tag{2}$$

where α_{hk} specifies the impact of country h on country k. Positive α_{hk} means competitive or harmful impact, i.e., that increased adoption x_h in country h decreases the adoption x_k in country k. In contrast, and perhaps

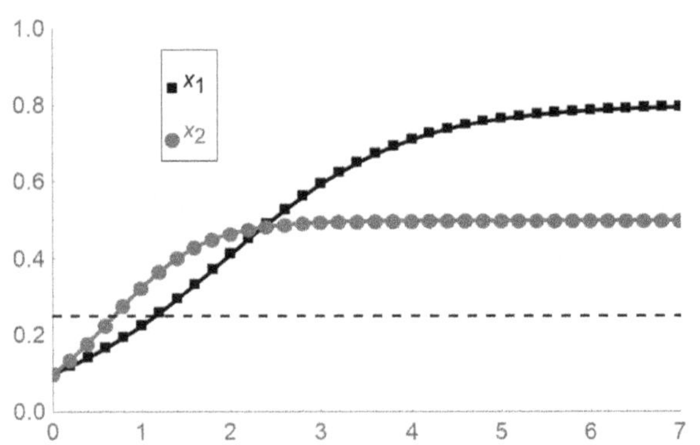

Figure 1: Blockchain adoption x_1 and x_2 in two countries, $x_{10} = x_{20} = 0.1$, $r_1 = 1$, $x_{1\max} = 0.8$, $r_2 = 2$, $x_{2\max} = 0.5$.

more likely, negative α_{hk} means beneficial impact, i.e., that increased adoption x_h in country h increases the adoption x_k in country k, so that countries h and k reinforce each other's adoption. The self-interacting terms are commonly set to $\alpha_{hh} = 1$, $h = 1$. Bomze (1983, 1995) classifies the dynamics of (2) for all sign combinations of α_{hk}.

We are unaware of quantified empirics of blockchain adoption over time for various regions, countries, and continents. The situation is somewhat different for cryptocurrencies where quantitative indicators are more readily available. For example, Ahlborg (2019) shows US dollar equivalent trading volume on the peer-to-peer bitcoin trading website Localbitcoins.com for bitcoin for nine world regions during 2013–2019.

4. Cost–Benefit Factors and Collective Action in Blockchain Adoption

Assume that blockchain technology has M characteristics associated with the factors listed above, including regulatory environment, ease of access, and speed. Consider a player i, $i = 1,2, \ldots, N_k$, in country k. Player i enjoys a benefit $b_{ijk}(x_k)$ and incurs a cost $c_{ijk}(x_k)$ at time t associated with characteristic j, $j = 1,2, \ldots, M$, given adoption x_k. Player i's utility at time t associated with characteristic j equals the benefit $b_{ijk}(x_k)$ minus the cost $c_{ijk}(x_k)$, i.e.,

$$u_{ijk} = b_{ijk}(x_k) - c_{ijk}(x_k). \tag{3}$$

Summing player i's utility over all the M characteristics gives

$$u_{ik} = \sum_{j=1}^{M} u_{ijk} = \sum_{j=1}^{M} \left(b_{ijk}(x_k) - c_{ijk}(x_k)\right) = b_{ik}(x_k) - c_{ik}(x_k). \tag{4}$$

Integrating, i.e., accumulating, player i's utility from time $\tau = 0$ to time $\tau = t$ gives

$$u_{aik} = \int_{\tau=0}^{\tau=t} u_{ijk} d\tau = \int_{\tau=0}^{\tau=t} \sum_{j=1}^{M} \left(b_{ijk}(x_k) - c_{ijk}(x_k)\right) \mathrm{d}\tau. \tag{5}$$

Equation (5) expresses that player i may benefit from some of the M characteristics, may incur costs associated with some other of the M characteristics, and may do so differentially at different points in time due to the changing adoption x_k of blockchain technology. Furthermore, since different players have different benefits $b_{ijk}(x_k)$ and costs $c_{ijk}(x_k)$ and also different capacities, resources, and willingness to implement blockchain technology, blockchain technology may evolve with different growth rates r_k toward different carrying capacities $x_{i\max}$.

At the early stage of blockchain technology development, when adoption x_k is low, a typical collective action problem exists (Olson, 1965). Instigators willing to incur the costs of blockchain technology development may spur adoption. Granovetter (1978) and Granovetter and Soong (1983) assess such developments, applied to revolutions, conceptualizing a critical minimum group needed as early instigators, to get the revolution off the ground. One analogy for blockchain technology is Malta, which officially passed blockchain-friendly regulations into law on July 4, 2018 (maltatoday, 2019). That is, LetknowNews (2019) describes how the Maltese government has opted strategically to advance blockchain technology which is seen to positively impact the economy, via attracting the world's largest cryptocurrencies and offering blockchain businesses a stable business environment attractive to investors. Observing these factors, Binance announced on March 23, 2018 it plan of moving its headquarters to Malta (Nakamura, 2018).

5. Conclusion

At present, Europe outpaces the rest of the world in adopting blockchain followed by the US. But the technology's dominance is moving to Asia, particularly China, which is expeditiously progressing and promoting forays in this direction. Potential applications of blockchain are also emerging in Africa and Latin America (Miller *et al.*, 2019). China has filed two-thirds of the world's blockchain patents and contributes to 72% of the bitcoin mining power (China, Global Focus, N.A, 2019). A cost–benefit analysis for the adoption of blockchain modeled here reveals that the ideal case for its deployment can be made for economies with technologically and financially underserved populations, need for trusted intermediaries, high cost of transparency, and absence of robust legacy systems. Many developing countries fulfill these criteria. Combined with an expectation of intermediate growth rate due to access to resources and the propensity to take technological risks, developing countries can be expected to adopt the technology at a growing pace. However, meeting high financial and organizational costs as well as overcoming poor governance, which impede adoption, present challenges. Therefore, their carrying capacity may be on a spectrum of medium to high, where high relates to newly industrialized economies from a wider pool of emerging economies. Developed countries on the contrary are expected to show the highest growth rate owing to their stable political systems, technological infrastructure, and presence of resources, but their carrying capacity may falter due to the aversion to move away from legacy systems. Considering the high carrying capacity and growth rate of newly industrialized economies like China, it could be expected that such newly industrialized economies are where the lead in the deployment of blockchain will emerge. Still, national growth rates in the adoption of blockchain will vary significantly across countries. Specifically, how the costs and benefits are evaluated in context-specific ways will impact the advent and spread of the technology.

Certain countries like Pakistan, Afghanistan, and Saudi Arabia have recently the deployment of banned cryptocurrency. Others like China, Indonesia, and India have put cryptoexchanges on watch list given the financial risks these are seen to pose. Of essence is that while cryptocurrencies are technically reliant on blockchain, blockchains have other applications also including the elimination of fraud in voting systems, asset registries, supply chain tracing functions, and record storage among others.

Further scholarship in the area would ideally offer empirics through time for blockchain adoption to underpin Equation (1) and empirics for impeding or beneficial interactions between countries pondering blockchain adoption as in equation (2). At the heart of determining the magnitude of blockchain adoption are cost–benefit analysis and decisions which remain managerial elements in localized contexts.

References

Ahlborg, M. (2019), Nuanced analysis of localbitcoins data suggests bitcoin is working as satoshi intended. Retrieved from https://medium.com/@

mattahlborg/nuanced-analysis-of-localbitcoins-data-suggests-bitcoin-is-working-as-satoshi-intended-d8b04d3ac7b2.

Ardittis, S. (2018), How blockchain could make refugee programs more transparent — refugees deeply. Retrieved from https://www.newsdeeply.com/refugees/community/2018/02/26/how-blockchain-could-make-refugee-programs-more-transparent.

Armstrong, C. P. and V. Sambamurthy (1999), Information technology assimilation in firms: The influence of senior leadership and IT infrastructures, *Information Systems Research* **10**(4), 304–327. https://doi.org/10.1287/isre.10.4.304.

Blockstuffs. (2019), Top 10 countries to adopt blockchain technology, *Block Stuffs*. Retrieved from https://www.blockstuffs.com/blog/countries-adopting-blockchain.

Bomze, I. M. (1983), Lotka–Volterra equation and replicator dynamics: A two-dimensional classification, *Biological Cybernetics* **48**(3), 201–211. https://doi.org/10.1007/BF00318088.

Bomze, I. M. (1995), Lotka–Volterra equation and replicator dynamics: New issues in classification, *Biological Cybernetics* **72**(5), 447–453. https://doi.org/10.1007/BF00201420.

Boone, J. (2016), Pakistan army's housing ventures face corruption investigation, World news, *The Guardian*. Retrieved from https://www.theguardian.com/world/2016/aug/19/pakistan-army-housing-ventures-corruption-investigation.

China, Global Focus, N. A. (2019), China's blockchain dominance: Can the U.S. catch up? Retrieved from https://knowledge.wharton.upenn.edu/article/can-u-s-catch-chinas-blockchain-dominance/.

Choudhury, K. (2018), What blockchain means for developing countries — The startup — medium. Retrieved from https://medium.com/swlh/what-blockchain-means-for-developing-countries-1ec25a416a4b.

Davies, A. (2019), How much does it cost to build a blockchain project? — DevTeam.Space. Retrieved from https://www.devteam.space/blog/how-much-does-it-cost-to-build-a-blockchain-project/.

Deetman, S. (2016), Bitcoin could consume as much electricity as Denmark by 2020 — VICE. Retrieved from https://www.vice.com/en_us/article/aek3za/bitcoin-could-consume-as-much-electricity-as-denmark-by-2020.

Deloitte. (2019), Deloitte's 2019 global blockchain survey. Retrieved from https://www2.deloitte.com/content/dam/insights/us/articles/2019-global-blockchain-survey/DI_2019-global-blockchain-survey.pdf.

DeRose, C. (2016), Why blockchain immutability is a perpetual motion claim — CoinDesk. Retrieved from https://www.coindesk.com/immutability-extraordinary-goals-blockchain-industry.

Europa.eu. (2019), How blockchain-based technology has the potential to disrupt remittances worldwide, EU Science Hub. Retrieved from https://ec.europa.eu/jrc/en/news/how-blockchain-based-technology-has-potential-disrupt-remittances-worldwide.

Fishbein, M. A. and I. Ajzen (1975), *Belief, Attitude, Intention and Behaviour: An Introduction to Theory and Research.* Reading, MA: Addison-Wesley.

Gibbs, S. (2018), Child abuse imagery found within bitcoin's blockchain, Technology, *The Guardian*. Retrieved from https://www.theguardian.com/technology/2018/mar/20/child-abuse-imagery-bitcoin-blockchain-illegal-content.

Goke, N. (2018), 7 Big obstacles to mass adoption of blockchain technology. Retrieved from https://medium.com/the-crypto-times/7-big-obstacles-to-mass-adoption-of-blockchain-technology-87740cdda9fe.

Granovetter, M. (1978), Threshold models of collective behavior, *American Journal of Sociology* **83**(6), 1420–1443. https://doi.org/10.1086/226707.

Granovetter, M. and R. Soong (1983), Threshold models of diffusion and collective behavior, *The Journal of Mathematical Sociology* **9**(3), 165–179. https://doi.org/10.1080/0022250X.1983.9989941.

Hafeez, I. (2019), FIA seizes Rs420 million in crackdown against hundi, hawala dealers in Karachi, Pakistan, DAWN.COM. Retrieved from https://www.dawn.com/news/1475666.

Hamilton, D. (2019), Blockchain land registry: The new kid on the block. Retrieved from https://coincentral.com/blockchain-land-registry/.

Hofmann, F., S. Wurster, E. Ron, and M. Bohmecke-Schwafert (2017), The immutability concept of blockchains and benefits of early standardization, in *2017 ITU Kaleidoscope: Challenges for a Data-Driven Society* (*ITU K*), IEEE, pp. 1–8. https://doi.org/10.23919/ITU-WT.2017.8247004.

Holotiuk, F., F. Pisani, and J. Moormann (2017), The impact of blockchain technology on business models in the payments industry, *Wirtschaftsinformatik*. Retrieved from https://www.semanticscholar.org/paper/The-Impact-of-Blockchain-Technology-on-Business-in-Holotiuk-Pisani/a23a98a77ab8063d09028512b3e0de3572cebe48.

Iansiti, M. and K. R. Lakhani (2017), The truth about blockchain. Retrieved from https://enterprisersproject.com/sites/default/files/the_truth_about_blockchain.pdf.

Kenya Corruption Report. (2017), Retrieved from https://www.ganintegrity.com/portal/country-profiles/kenya/.

LetknowNews. (2019), 5 reasons why Malta is determined to become the "Blockchain Island". Retrieved from https://medium.com/letknownews/5-reasons-why-malta-is-determined-to-become-the-blockchain-island-10210ee96744.

Lotka, A. J. (1924), *Elements of Mathematical Biology*. London: Dover Publications.

Maltatoday. (2019), Why world leader crypto exchange Binance moved to Malta. Retrieved from https://www.maltatoday.com.mt/business/business_news/93170/why_world_leader_crypto_exchange_binance_moved_to_malta#.XOE53KRS_yf.

McKinsey. (2018), The strategic business value of the blockchain market, McKinsey. Retrieved from https://www.mckinsey.com/business-functions/digital-mckinsey/our-insights/blockchain-beyond-the-hype-what-is-the-strategic-business-value.

Miller, D., P. Mockel, G. I. Myers, M. Niforos, V. Ramachandran, T. Rehermann, and J. Salmon (2019), Blockchain: Opportunities for Private Enterprises in Emerging Markets. Retrieved from http://documents.worldbank.org/curated/en/260121548673898731/Blockchain-Opportunities-for-Private-Enterprises-in-Emerging-Markets.

Molla, A. and P. S. Licker (2005), Perceived e-readiness factors in e-commerce adoption: An empirical investigation in a developing country, *International Journal of Electronic Commerce* **10**(1), 83–110. https://doi.org/10.1080/10864415.2005.11043963.

Nakamoto, S. (2008), Bitcoin: A peer-to-peer electronic cash system. Retrieved from www.bitcoin.org.

Nakamura, Y. (2018), The world's biggest crypto exchange is heading to Malta, Bloomberg. Retrieved from https://www.bloomberg.com/news/articles/2018-03-23/the-world-s-biggest-cryptocurrency-exchange-is-moving-to-malta.

Niles, B. (2019), Worldwide need to lower remittance costs, CGTN. Retrieved from https://news.cgtn.com/news/3d3d514f77457a4e34457a6333566d54/index.html.

Ogono, U. (2019), Blockchain in local government: High implementation cost and regulatory concerns have hindered many local governments from entering the blockchain space, *Blockchain News Today*. Retrieved from https://smartereum.com/48174/blockchain-in-local-government-high-implementation-cost-and-regulatory-concerns-have-hindered-many-local-governments-from-entering-the-blockchain-space-blockchain-news-today/.

Olson, M. (1965), *The Logic of Collective Action; Public Goods and the Theory of Groups*. Harvard University Press.

Online. (2018), Electricity shortfall exceeds to 6000MW. Retrieved from https://nation.com.pk/02-Jul-2018/electricity-shortfall-exceeded-to-6000mw.

Pattekar, S. (2018), Do I really need blockchain? 4 important factors to consider. Retrieved from https://www.datadriveninvestor.com/2018/05/25/do-i-really-need-a-blockchain-4-important-factors-to-consider/.

Paynter, B. (2017), How blockchain could transform the way international aid is distribute. Retrieved from https://www.fastcompany.com/40457354/how-blockchain-could-transform-the-way-international-aid-is-distributed.

Pilkington, M. (2016), Blockchain technology: Principles and applications. Retrieved from https://pdfs.semanticscholar.org/e31c/a71621e1402a46ac-2c1afb2eba9a7061d139.pdf.

PTI Washington. (2019), India highest recipient of remittances at USD 79 billion in 2018: World Bank. *The Hindu BusinessLine*. Retrieved from https://www.thehindubusinessline.com/news/india-highest-recipient-of-remittances-at-usd-79-billion-in-2018-world-bank/article26779574.ece.

Rogers, E. M. (1962), *Diffusion of innovations*, 3rd edn. Retrieved from https://teddykw2.files.wordpress.com/2012/07/everett-m-rogers-diffusion-of-innovations.pdf.

Rogers, E. M. (2003), *Diffusion of Innovations*. Free Press.

Sadhya, V. and H. Sadhya (2018), Barriers to adoption of blockchain technology barriers to adoption of blockchain technology completed research. Retrieved from https://pdfs.semanticscholar.org/b63c/9a1f8c066ce1c9fa8b58a9df25cbf0790ad0.pdf.

Safahi, A. (2018), Cutting money transfer fees could unlock $15bn for developing countries. Here's how *World Economic Forum*. Retrieved from https://www.weforum.org/agenda/2018/06/cutting-money-transfer-fees-could-unlock-15bn-for-developing-countries-heres-how/.

Santiso, C. (2018), Will blockchain disrupt government corruption? Retrieved from https://ssir.org/articles/entry/will_blockchain_disrupt_government_corruption.

SDG Indicators. (2018), Retrieved from https://unstats.un.org/sdgs/metadata/?Text=&Goal=10&Target=10.c.

Sedgwick, K. (2018), No, Visa Doesn't Handle 24,000 TPS and Neither Does Your Pet Blockchain, *Bitcoin News*. Retrieved from https://news.bitcoin.com/no-visa-doesnt-handle-24000-tps-and-neither-does-your-pet-blockchain/.

Seebacher, S. and R. Schüritz (2019), Blockchain-just another it implementation? A comparison of blockchain and interorganizational information systems. Retrieved from https://aisel.aisnet.org/ecis2019_rp/124.

Seth, M. (2018), Six property disputes that show snail's pace of justice in India, *Nayi Disha*. Retrieved from https://www.nayidisha.com/six-property-disputes-that-show-snails-pace-of-justice-in-india/.

Sheehan, M. (2018), Blockchain could allow developing countries to "leapfrog" current tech: Fitch, *Reinsurance News*. Retrieved from https://www.reinsurancene.ws/blockchain-could-allow-developing-countries-to-leapfrog-current-tech-fitch/.

Siddiqui, K. (2013), A Review of Pakistan's Political Economy. *Asian Profile*, **41**(1). ISSN 0304-8675.

Space, B. (2018), Blockchain vs. corruption, Coinmonks, Medium. Retrieved from https://medium.com/coinmonks/blockchain-vs-corruption-a2c7a3eb983d.

Stinchcombe, K. (2018), Blockchain is not only crappy technology but a bad vision for the future. Retrieved from https://medium.com/@kaistinchcombe/decentralized-and-trustless-crypto-paradise-is-actually-a-medieval-hellhole-c1ca122efdec.

Swan, M. (2015), *Blockchain: Blueprint for a New Economy*. O'Reilly Media.

Swan, M. (2017), *Technology Innovation Management Review*, Vol. 7. Retrieved from https://timreview.ca/sites/default/files/article_PDF/Swan_TIMReview_October2017.pdf.

TFH Al Analysts. (2019), Introducing digital money to the unbanked: What Kenya can teach the rest of the world about financial inclusion, *Benefit Daily*. Retrieved from https://benefit-daily.com/post/introducing-digital-money-to-unbanked-kenya.

The Newspaper's Correspondent. (2019), Reforms have increased Pakistan's tax collection, bribe rates: IMF, Newspaper, DAWN.COM. Retrieved from https://www.dawn.com/news/1474908.

Tornatzky, L. G., M. Fleischer, and A. K. Chakrabarti (1990), *The Processes of Technological Innovation*. Lexington Mass.: Lexington Books. Retrieved from https://www.worldcat.org/title/processes-of-technological-innovation/oclc/20669819.

Venkatesh, V. and F. D. Davis (2000), A theoretical extension of the technology acceptance model: Four longitudinal field studies, *Management Science* **46**(2), 186–204. https://doi.org/10.1287/mnsc.46.2.186.11926.

Verhulst, P. F. (1845), *Recherches mathématiques sur la loi d'accroissement de la population, Nouveaux Mémoires de l'Académie Royale Des Sciences et Belles-Lettres de Bruxelles* **18**, 3–38.

Woodside, J. M., F. K. Augustine, W. Giberson, and J. M. Woodside (2017), Blockchain technology adoption status and strategies, *Journal of International Technology and Information Management* **26**. Retrieved from https://scholarworks.lib.csusb.edu/jitim; Available at: https://scholarworks.lib.csusb.edu/jitim/vol26/iss2/4.

World Bank. (2019), Record high remittances sent globally in 2018. Retrieved from https://www.worldbank.org/en/news/press-release/2019/04/08/record-high-remittances-sent-globally-in-2018.

Zaki, I. (2019), How moneyFi can disrupt the remittance market with blockchain, *Moon Whale*. Retrieved from https://moonwhale.io/moneyfi-blockchain-remittance/.

https://doi.org/10.1142/9789811220470_0004

Chapter 4

A Discussion on Decentralization in Financial Industry and Monetary System

Alfred Ruoxi Zhang[*,‡], Farrokh Zandi[†,§] and Henry Kim[†,||]

[*]*London School of Economics and Political Science, London, England*
[†]*Schulich School of Business, York University, Toronto, ON, Canada*

[‡]*R.Zhang52@LSE.ac.uk*

[§]*fzandi@schulich.yorku.ca*

[||]*hkim@schulich.yorku.ca*

Abstract

As technology revolutionizes the methods of both production and communication, economists have to constantly adjust their theories explaining the economy according to new market structures and efficiencies, and the controversial concept of decentralization emerging in recent decades should also be examined in terms of its capacity to induce structural changes in the economy. This paper delves into this topic and examines some cases of hypothetical decentralized markets, including the financial industry and the monetary system, in order to provide a preliminary illustration of how an economy composed of such markets would function and their corresponding benefits and risks, through a preliminary discussion about existing literatures and theories aiming to inspire further researches within the field.

Keywords: Finance; Monetary policy; Macroeconomics; Blockchain.

1. Introduction

Similar to most disciplines in social sciences, although the fundamentals of economics remain mostly the same throughout centuries since Stone Age, the basic rationale of human species has changed marginally at most, the market conditions under which we study the decisions made from such rationality have always been evolving. As technology revolutionizes the methods of both production and communication, economists have to constantly adjust their theories explaining the economy according to new market structures and efficiencies, and even in an accelerating pace as some theories such as the Moore's Law had attempted to simulate. While the prediction of continuous miniaturization of transistors in microchips seems to have ceased as it is bounded by technical constraints (Thompson, 2017), it is to be argued that a new wave of technological innovation would still arrive, but perhaps from a different direction.

In the past two decades, the major economies in the world have been witnessing the rise of blockchain technology, first introduced as the backbone of the famous or infamous cryptocurrencies to the market. In both the market and the academic world, investors, regulators, and researches alike are all discussing the same question: What's the role of blockchain in the future of our economy? For economists, instead of the surface value of either cryptocurrency or blockchain, the focus is more likely on the concept of "decentralization" such technologies represent, and the discussion often centers on whether decentralized markets would effectively transform our economy, in the same way as the industrial revolutions[1] had achieved before. Comparing with many other fields in macroeconomics, the study

[1]The "industrial revolutions" in this context refer to the first one represented by steam engine, the second one represented by electricity, and the third one represented by digital and internet technology; without specifically discussing these events in the school of historical studies, the only emphasis is their roles as transformative forces in industries during their times.

about decentralization, especially within the contexts of blockchain or technologies that offer similar features, is actually still relatively premature.

When discussing blockchain technology, we often refer to it as a "digital ledger", as in essence this technology is derived from cryptography to verify and record information. The basic concepts of this technology are best illustrated in a piece I have written previously:

> *While a typical "ledger" locates centrally either in a physical location or database* [...] *a decentralized digital ledger exists as many copies kept by all participants of a blockchain network. When a transaction is conducted* [...] *they would be complied with other entries of information into one encrypted "block", which is then sent via the Internet to be verified by all members of this network, or "miners". If the integrity of the block is confirmed, then it would be broadcasted to the entire network, so that all participants would record it under their own copies of the ledger, as an addition to a series of previously mined blocks that reference their preceded ones like a "chain".* (Zhang *et al.*, 2018)

And with such explanation it would not be too difficult to imagine how such concepts have promised many a market with fewer obstacles of information exchange, such as a capital market without major interventions from intermediaries, a monetary system without a central bank to control the flow of money, or an automated auction market without middlemen.

It could be argued that, when we replace the central agency in a system with a decentralized platform without loss of efficiency, as the total benefits produced by this system are unchanged, its members should be enjoying a fairer distribution of welfare as the central governing body previously capturing benefits is now taken out of the equation. Intuitively on the other hand, if we keep the central agency but use a decentralized platform to facilitate exchanges of information to improve efficiency, while the welfare distribution does not change, the total benefits produced by the system should increase, and hence the members would also be enjoying higher welfare than their initial distributions.

Theoretically the preliminary conditions of both cases illustrated above could be achieved through the use of blockchain, for example to replace the central bank (central agency) by adopting cryptocurrency as the legal currency, or to extend the emission quotas market (improve efficiency) by adopting a blockchain-based platform. However, it would be hard to tell whether the rest of the necessary conditions listed above, such as the unchanged efficiency in a system without central agency, or the increased total welfare in a system with decentralized platform, could be subsequently achieved after the preliminary conditions. It is entirely possible that, in some cases removing the central agency from a system would be disastrous, or in other cases that adopting a decentralized platform would not improve the efficiency at all.

This chapter aims to delve slightly into this field and examine some cases of hypothetical decentralized markets, and to provide a preliminary illustration of how an economy composed of such markets would function, as well as their corresponding benefits and risks. The chapter would be segregated into two main sections: the first would discuss the finance industry and blockchain-based financial technology (fintech), in order to examine how the efficiency of capital market would be improved by a decentralized platform; the second section takes a look at a monetary system based on cryptocurrency, which has become a popular topic of discussion in the domain of economic policy.

2. Decentralization and Finance Sector

2.1. *The underserved market*

The banking industry has been long established even before the concepts of capitalism became well known to the merchants, as monarchs, especially those on the European continent were amazed by such institution's ability to transfer capital between different agents of the economy and risks over time periods. However, it is not until more recently in the past one century and more, when the rest of the world, more specifically the emerging markets outside the traditionally identified "Western World", became more engaged in the finance industry and the global capital market. This is induced by both the demands of general economic globalization, and the quickly advancing communication technology that had enabled long-range information exchanges through technologies from telegraph to internet. But even with such technical advancements, a great portion of the global population are still in the process of being included in the capital market, with even a momentum decelerated after the financial crisis.

Although the banking industry is but a section of both finance sector and capital markets, it is to be noted that for households in many of the emerging economies, commercial banks are still the primary channel of capital flows through layers in the economy. Hence, when we examine the efficiency of capital market in less developed regions, the banking industry would appropriately become our focus point. Dermish *et al.* (2011) discussed in a paper that, for the poorer households in less developed regions, their incomes are "precariously small and often irregular", and easily affected by emergent events such as "a serious illness or death in the family" as well as natural disasters. From the perspective of welfare economics, it has become a responsibility of the regional finance institutions to support such population. Banks would provide households with the means to engage in lending and borrowing activities, so that they would be able to sustain consumption through negative fluctuation of their incomes, and accumulate interests from savings to advance future consumptions. Furthermore, households would gain access to capital needed to engage in wealth creation through small businesses, and more importantly funds needed to receive education.

It could be argued that the presence of a capital market is critical to the functioning of an economy, especially a modern capitalist economy, as summarized by an illustration of the role of capital markets in the development of economy:

> *The good functioning of the capital market is vital in the contemporary economy, in order to achieve an efficient transfer of monetary resources from those who save money toward those who need capital and who succeed to offer it a superior utilisation; the capital market can influence significantly the quality of investment decisions. The gathering of temporary capitals that are available in the economy, the reallocation of those that are insufficiently or inefficiently used at a certain moment and even the favouring of some sectorial reorganisations, outline the capital market's place in the economy of many countries.* (Stoica, 2006)

The problem, however, is that majority of the aforementioned population in less developed regions simply do not have access to the market, as noted by Dermish *et al.* (2011) from secondary researches, "more than 2.6 billion people in the developing world living without a bank account of any sort and less than 30 percent of this population having access to finance". The exclusion of such significant quantity of consumers from the capital market, does not only signal to us the presence of significant risks discounting household welfare, or result the inefficiency in these local economies, but also imply an inefficiency in the broader global capital market. While the excluded population are only a smaller percentage of consumption and income on the global scale, they represent vast wasted economic potential as underutilized efficient labor and entrepreneurship input, as well as creation in the R&D sector if we were to discuss the case in an endogenous growth setting.

On the other hand, the efficiency in welfare distribution should also be taken into consideration as we are studying the decentralization of markets. As noted by some, when consumers conduct wire transfers of funds, especially when across borders to the poorer regions we are discussing, heavy transaction fees are deducted by the multiple nodes of intermediaries facilitating such transactions (Tapscott and Tapscott., 2016). Therefore, households in these regions that rely on the income of those working in more developed countries would find themselves receiving only a fraction of the amount initialed earned through labor. This could be listed as an example of central agency with consolidated power in a system capturing benefits from members, which have essentially detrimental effects on the general welfare level of this system and the long-run sustainability and growths potentials as well.

2.2. *Infrastructure or the marginal cost?*

The question that should be discussed at this stage, is the reason behind such occurrences. A simple logic can be in fact followed by us in this case: As the finance industry is one of the oldest pillars of the capitalist world initiated on the European continent several centuries ago, it is hard to think that a significant part of the global population has been uncaptured by this industry simply due to their oversights, and hence the obstacle or reason could only come from two source — either that economically the marginal costs are higher than marginal benefits when expanding to this portion of the market, or that such expansion is confined by technical difficulties such as a lack of communication infrastructures in the corresponding regions; Furthermore, it is worth exploring if both of them had occurred simultaneously, and if so whether one of them has caused the emergence of the other.

One argument made by some is that these consumers are just too costly to serve, suggesting that "they only need small and infrequent financial transactions, and collecting and returning small amounts of cash is too costly to do profitably" (Dermish *et al.*, 2011), which essentially explains such a dilemma as an economic phenomenon of marginal costs (extending branches and organizational structure to certain regions) exceeding marginal benefits (the fees and interests banks could potentially collect through serving the same regions). Although Dermish *et al.* (2011) raised the counterargument that some consumer products set at extremely low prices are also sufficiently supplied around the globe, it was not necessarily proven that the marginal costs of banking services in less-profitable regions would enjoy economies of scale in production as most of the consumer products mentioned would do, hence I think this still stands as a probable cause of financial underservice in the said regions. However, while we understand it is possible that it could be unprofitable to serve certain groups of the global population, we need to recognize that serving these consumers would still induce social benefits in these regions, as explained in previous contexts, which are not accounted for when discussing purely based profits and losses.

On the other hand, as Dermish *et al.* (2011) had argued, the more relevant causes could reside in the "lack of relevant information and customer service infrastructure". As most developed countries as well as those in the top ranks of the developing countries are adopting internet banking and mobile banking services, many poorer regions still largely rely on physical branches, which are also to some extent lacking in quantity, to carry out the tasks of serving customers. The speed of services in these regions could be much slower due to inefficiencies in communication, transportation and staffing, than that in more developed regions where residents are accustomed to completing transactions on mobile devices within a time frame of seconds. Meanwhile, due to similar reasons it is also difficult for financial institutions to track the credit history and establish personal profiles for customers, which implicates loan services that have become problematic enough already in countries such as the United States after the financial crisis, even with the complexity of profiling and data mining on creditors.

What further complicates the problem is that, as we are discussing a problem that is effectively occurring internationally, some tools we have become used to in economic policies may not be as relevant here. For instance, public providence of goods that are unprofitable if left to private sectors is highly dependent on the local governments of these regions, which, unlike governments in other macroeconomic analysis that would lead to advice on policy making, may not be the target audiences of this series of discussions in the first place. The power and incentives of these governments in improving the communication infrastructure and targeting at long-run economic developments could be highly confined by the local political structures and historical issues. As noted by Dermish *et al.* (2011), among the "2.6 billion people in the world who do not have access to formal financial services one billion of them have a mobile phone", which proves that the exclusion of some consumers from the capital market, is not purely a result from either economic inefficiency or the lack of infrastructure, but a mixture of both with the addition of political and cultural complexity.

I would even argue that a third possible factor in restricting the finance industry's expansion in these regions exists. As noted by Turner (2006), "the banking systems in emerging markets have over the past decade been transformed by three major trends — privatisation, consolidation and the entry of foreign banks on a large scale", which in essence leads to competitions between banks in the international capital market, and to some extent ensures the supply of credits to households as well as small and medium business in these emerging economies. In the regions that are among the lowest ranks of the list of emerging economies, however, the regional banks are mostly naturally consolidated and unaffected by privatization as the entry of foreign banks is extremely limited by all the problems discussed in this section so far. The result is unfortunately that, these regions are on a decelerating path of financial industry structural change and lagging behind other countries further and further in the long run. As the structural difference stagnates, the gap between incomes would continue to widen, which would in effect make it more difficult to serve these regions in the future.

2.3. *Implication of blockchain settlement*

The question left to us now, is what role decentralization could play in this stagnated dilemma. The design in this case is simple: we would build an international Blockchain settlement to establish an online banking system that allow consumers around the world to participate in the capital market without much interference of financial intermediaries. Our assumption is that, the blockchain technology is capable of supporting an online platform that can (1) facilitate secure, anonymous and convenient information exchanges without a centralized governing body nor government intervention, (2) does not discriminate against user-end devices to lower the technical barrier of entry for the consumers, and (3) is able to interconnect accounts registered at different financial institutions and accurately pinpoint specific customers. Without assessing the actual capabilities of existing blockchain applications, a conjecture is made that it is only possible for a blockchain settlement to effectively transform the financial services in the industry's uncaptured region, if the first two conditions listed above are met.

The first argument states the core promise of blockchain technology, that information can be exchanged through such an encrypted network anonymously, securely, without central agency, and to some extent immune to disruption by force. The condition of security should be easily understood as it is critical for a financial platform to keep its transaction information secure. The other three conditions, however, are more specific to solving the dilemma in our current discussion. As we want to bypass both major international financial intermediaries, local financial institutions, as well as local governments that could react in unpredictable ways to free capital flows dependent on their positioning of the monetary policy,[2] the platform has to be both decentralized so that no single institution would consolidate power from this network, and at the same time immune to government intervention due to its "cloud" nature. And to further protect the users from political or corporate actions, the trait of anonymity becomes necessary.

The second argument is in fact more specific to our case, as we are discussing consumers from poorer regions, whose access to mobile devices may be limited to more basic machines than the conventional touchscreen smart phones popular in developed regions. It means that, as also mentioned in Tapscott's book (2016) introducing blockchain to the mass, for the consumers to access to this decentralized financial platform, it needs to be fault-tolerant and indiscriminating to devices, hence while those with a high-end smartphone or laptop could gain access through a website or application with tailored user interface, those from the other end of the globe would access the same amount of information and conduct the same transactions by transmitting a few lines of texts or codes to an secured internet address, which also replies in simple lines of texts and codes. Such a concept is not new to the digital technology community as the modern internet was built upon the core idea of fault tolerance.

[2]In this context, we refer to the "impossible trinity" in economics, stating that a country could not simultaneously possess control on exchange rate, free capital flow, and monetary agency independence.

The third argument is made by many in the blockchain community today, being the use of blockchain technology to build personal profiles. The general concept is that, as consumers would input all relevant information about him or her into such a profile stored on a blockchain network, other parties, such as the different lenders on the network could compute their probability of defaulting on loans through automated algorithms, without personal access to actual information within the profile. This idea partly corresponds to the black box model verification method in simulation study, where the users only evaluate the accuracy of end results without looking at intermediate computations, and in this case the blockchain network users are only concerned about the resulted credit scores, without taking any interests in the original inputs. Such a hypothesized creditor profiling system would theoretically find the right balance between sufficient information to assess borrowers and consumer privacy, stemmed from the secure nature of blockchain network that its users could put trusts in. This argument is not as relevant to our discussion about efficiency of finance industry in less developed regions in this study, but is vastly critical to financial industry in the broader contexts of fintech.

Even if all these conditions, especially the first two are met by some invention within the blockchain technology, is the financial industry suitable for adopting such a transformation in both their technical and organizational structure? Technical-structure-wise, the answer is yes. A report by EY about fintech adoption provides some insightful statistics such as the average global fintech adoption rate, which has risen from 16% in 2015 to 33% in 2017, a higher 46% adoption rate across developing countries such as "Brazil, China, India, Mexico and South Africa", and more importantly "50% of consumers use FinTech money transfer and payments services, and 65% anticipate doing so in the future" (EY, 2017). The observation is that, the fintech adoption process has well prepared the financial industry for further transformation into blockchain-based fintech industry, solely on the technical domain. However, this is not necessarily the case from the organizational point of view, as decentralizing the financial industry is essentially striping power from the financial institutions, and forcing them to transform their revenue models and restructure their organizations across the globe.

Furthermore, there are also significant problems to be observed from our initial conjecture, even at this stage of theorizing. First of all, many key offers in such a system would represent a complete disruption of the power of governments. Signaled by the ban of cryptocurrency in China and the halted enthusiasm in blockchain technology researches, it is safe to suggest that governments around the world, especially those with tighter grips on their economic and political controls, would be less than pleasant in attitudes towards a platform that allows for anonymous free capital flow, with little information extracted by the governments or financial institutions. In addition, before those in need could utilize such a system to improve their living standards, it could induce negative impacts on security issues around the world as funding illegal and terrorist activities would become much easier and untraceable, which had become an infamous problem since the invention of Bitcoin.

Return to the specifics in our case, even as such a platform could solve the problem of financial underservice for the population that have access to mobile devices and internet, there still exist the majority of total underserved population that cannot access this platform because they lack the necessary hardware, as the aforementioned problems in regional infrastructure and marginal costs remain unchanged. Therefore, combining all points discussed above it could be concluded that, although both the fintech market and hypothesis about blockchain settlement in finance industry seem promising, depending on the actual methods of execution it may not be either the most realistic, or the most efficient means to improve the inclusion of consumers in capital markets in less developed regions. However, it should also be kept in mind that, as this study only points out the contemporary problems and risks within the limits of our current designs, as the technologies that could achieve decentralization develop in the future, more pathways could be revealed to researchers in this field.

3. Monetary System Based on Cryptocurrency

3.1. *Cryptocurrency*

Based on blockchain technology, digital tokens called "cryptocurrency" are derived, represented by the first of its kind, Bitcoin. After its invention many smaller cryptocurrency projects, which are often referred to as "altcoins", have been emerging at an accelerating pace with an increasing number of investors of various sizes attempting to profit from such a trend. Cryptocurrencies differ from conventional currencies in the most significant way that they are not a form of money printed and controlled by the central banks, but digital records on the blockchain that have come to possess many of a conventional currency's traits. It is best summarized by another piece I wrote previously:

> [*Since*] *blockchain is essentially a distributed digital ledger, transactions recorded on the chains with considerable block depths would be as highly trusted by participants of this network as those recorded on the centralized ledgers of commercial banks* [...] *records on a blockchain showing debts held on other parties are trusted enough to become a store of value and a medium of exchange* (Zhang et al., 2018).

However, I would always differentiate between the utility tokens and the security tokens when discussing cryptocurrencies, as although their technological backbones are the same, they have engaged the market in distinct ways.

Utility tokens are cryptocurrencies that are utilized as an instrument of payment or record for some certain online services and applications, with their intrinsic values; A good example of this kind is Ethereum which facilitates the functioning of smart contracts; The values of such tokens are often led by the performances of their corresponding applications with regards to market demands from consumers. On the other hand, security tokens, as their name would suggest, refer to tokens that behave like financial securities; The prices of such tokens would fluctuate in the market mainly due to swings in the general cryptocurrency market and speculations; They offer no more value than the pale promises of future appreciation, hence regarded by many analysts as hoaxes profiting on fraudulent claims.

From the perspectives of both investment and research, I prefer focusing on utility tokens, and more specifically the technological innovations they represent, as it would be an interesting field of research on whether derivatives from blockchain could effective improve our economy. However, in the case we are discussing, we are not necessarily looking at a utility token to adopt into the monetary system. As a legal currency, ideally the token would not be attached to any specific user application and should be only regarded as a monetary vehicle; At the same time, the policy makers should realize that the token could not be the same fluctuating investment assets that most security tokens we would see today are, and in fact, it is one of the challenges to stabilize the token when adopting a cryptocurrency monetary system.

Before diving into discussions on the cryptocurrency monetary system, it is imperative to mention the problems of cryptocurrencies we should keep in mind when conducting researches. As illustrated previously, cryptocurrencies with similar structures to Bitcoin use the proof-of-work (PoW)[3] mechanism to conduct majority voting for determining on the validation of information, in order to protect the users of the network. The theory is that, it would be economically inefficient to attack a cryptocurrency network with goals to sustain fraudulent information as one would have to maintain control of more than 50% of the mining capacity of a cryptocurrency network, which is referred to commonly now as "51% attack". This is also one of the fundamental features that blockchain enthusiasts often take pride in. However, as the market soon realizes in the past few years, a number of smaller cryptocurrency projects have been under such 51% attacks for "out-of-chain" purposes such as ransom and political gains, which would require the attack to last only for a short period of time, with the needed computational power fully rentable online (Shanaev *et al.*, 2018).

The risk of suffering 51% attack would be particularly threatening for cryptocurrency monetary systems; First, regional currencies, especially those hypothetically released in smaller regions with fewer mining nodes, would not withhold 51% attacks through the scale of computational capacities; Second, the incentives for conducting such attacks would be particularly high and the costs for doing so would be relatively more affordable when the entities we are concerning about are opponent countries; Third, the consequences of a successfully executed 51% attack would be more devastating than victims within the corporate sector, as even an overnight shift in an economy's monetary system, given the particular circumstances, could lead to long-term impacts in the economy as well as distrust in its monetary credibility. Therefore, purely from these perspectives the adoption of cryptocurrencies, especially those in smaller economies, should not be rushed in any short duration of time before

[3]In addition to the PoW system, other cryptocurrencies also adopt various different protocols to deter cyberattacks; In the PoW system, mathematical puzzles concerning the blocks being verified, which are costly (in terms of computational power) to solve but easy to verify, are computed by nodes on the network to validate the blocks; In another system called proof-of-stake (PoS), the determination of block creators depends on their wealth (in terms of tokens held), which requires significantly less energy in execution.

breakthroughs in blockchain technology could effectively address these issues.

With the benefits and risks of cryptocurrency in mind, in the follow sections, we would use Bitcoin as an example, to discuss the long-term and short-term effects of adopting a cryptocurrency as the legal currency. In the long-run analysis, we would discuss its impacts on various monetary policy tools the central bank has, and whether such changes would be beneficial to the economy; In the short-run analysis, we would briefly explore the pathway an economy would take to shift from a conventional banknote system to cryptocurrency system, and discuss the relative consequences we should be aware of.

3.2. *Long-run analysis*

In a paper by Iwamura *et al.* (2014), it is argued that there exists the "dual instability" of Bitcoin. On the one hand, as a decentralized device the total long-run supply of money would be fixed by algorithm in a cryptocurrency monetary system, which results in an inflexible money supply, that can not be as easily adjusted to smooth out fluctuations in the market as the conventional money; On the other hand, instead of being able to automatically stabilize itself, tokens like Bitcoin would automatically destabilize itself, meaning that the quantity of miners is not flexible to changes in Bitcoin prices, which would likely prolong periods of token depreciation. In a cryptocurrency monetary system, the latter problem could not be solved by government or monetary agency assigning miners, would centralize the power in monetary system to the government as some suggest, as it would render the market decentralization meaningless. Under our assumption that the monetary system we discuss in this study is purely decentralized, the first problem about fixed long-run supply becomes particularly significant in its effects on the monetary policies.

Since the market is decentralized, the contemporary central bank would not exist in the economy, and Iwamura *et al.* (2014) suggested in their paper a few methods in replacement to conduct monetary policy actions. The first method uses currency board as the inspiration, which means that a rule within the network would be created to change the difficulty threshold or mining reward, in order to adjust the change rate in token supply according to economic conditions or targets, which would in turn affect the market value of the tokens. The difficulty threshold of the mathematical puzzles in Bitcoin's PoW system, as well as the reward to miners when blocks are successfully created, would both affect the momentum of tokens mined at any point in time. The difference between such an organization and the central banks is that, while central banks have much discretion on both raising and lowering the supply of money through open market operations and adjusting discount rate, such a "currency board" rule would only be able to expand money supply through accelerated token mining, but is unable to decrease the supply by decreasing the momentum to negative.

Building on this idea, Iwamura *et al.* (2014) suggested a "built-in revaluation rule for exchange rate" to absorb the excess money supply by allowing inflation, since instead of attempting to control the almost uncontrollable supply, it would be easier to control the real purchasing power of the issued tokens. It is to be noted that using inflation to control real money could be risky, in the sense that as monetary usually has the goal to stabilize inflation within a certain range, its usefulness as a tool would be severely limited. In fact, it was suggested that an "implicit inflation target" rule could be constructed, which would slowly decreases the real mining costs over time at the rate of $\beta\gamma$ to counter inflation within the range of $e^{(\beta\gamma)}$.[4] Such a rule would see less volatile results than its counterparts in our conventional economy, since inflation targeting of central banks is often related to "expectations formation by the public, and credibility of the central bank in general and the governor in particular", which contributes to much of the unexplained variances in forecasting and policy making, while with the case of cryptocurrency rules, inflation targeting becomes more directly correlated with the economic variables in real economy (Iwamura *et al.*, 2014).

However, even though the boundaries posed by a fully decentralized cryptocurrency monetary system seem to have been clearly drawn, a few questions still remain for further researches based on further market developments. The cryptocurrency growth is accompanied by innovations in the capital market as well, specifically in the peer-to-peer loan markets (Chung and Kim, 2018). It would be interesting to hypothesize a situation

[4]The variable β denotes the growth rate of mining reward, and the variable γ denotes the technological change rate; For more specific details on the mathematical computations and literature about rules mentioned in this passage, please refer to the original paper done by Iwamura *et al.* (2014).

where a monetary agency is set up to perform some of the monetary policy actions the contemporary central banks are used to, mostly open market operations to counter shocks in the economy. The existence and effects of such operations with cryptocurrency bonds would depend on how such bonds would be structured and how a matured cryptocurrency capital market would function in the future. It should be held optimistic that, although as a hypothetical market much of its theoretical functioning still depend on future technological advancements, with corresponding designs the policy makers would still find their appropriate roles in combating economic downturns.

3.3. *Short-run analysis*

While we have done some discussions on the long-run functioning of a cryptocurrency monetary system, we should take a step back from the fully decentralized market, and analyze the short-run effects if we were to shift to this market tomorrow, as we are no less concerned with welfare in the short run ahead of us than that in the long-run steady states. From the experiences of major shifts in economics systems throughout history, it can be observed that the generations stuck between two different systems are often the ones receiving the least benefits. One of the fields of research we should be focusing on under the topic of adopting cryptocurrency as the monetary base, is to find the smoothest path between two different systems that would protect the interests of consumers.

Given the recent trends in nations developing their own pegged cryptocurrencies, or otherwise referred to as "Stablecoins",[5] we could look at how governments could start from pegging an official cryptocurrency, and find a hybrid of the conventional monetary system and the cryptocurrency monetary system, before shifting entirely to the latter one. In a report by Bank for International Settlements (Markets Committee, 2018), the so-called "central bank digital currencies" (CBDC) are investigated, in the context that as the central banks release cryptocurrencies whose values are pegged or equalized to the bank notes, the payment system based on blockchain applications would present to us a partially-decentralized

[5]The contemporary Stablecoins use either a legal currency as collateral, another cryptocurrency as the collateral, or no collateral but an algorithm to control prices; In this context I broadly refer to the Stablecoins created by various governments that are pegged directly to their legal currencies.

market. Regarding the demand for digital currencies, the report suggested that since such demand would intuitively be negatively correlated to that for cash, as "[the] growing use of electronic means of payment has generally not yet resulted in a substantial reduction in the demand for cash", the demand derived from payment instrument is not significant at the current stage. In the broader topic of whether it would be appropriate to issue digital currencies and even shift to a decentralized monetary system in the near future, we should study consumer behaviours in terms of the market share decompositions of different payment instruments, in order to determine if there exists the need to engage in such a shift.

However, assuming that such need exists in our economy, and the government does attempt to adopt digital currency to shift to a partial-decentralized market, what are the necessary changes to be made to the contemporary monetary system? As suggested in the previous long-run analysis, even with the central bank still in existence, the functioning of various monetary policy tools would largely depend on how interest rate is set in the capital market. In a paper by Koning (2016) it was argued that such a digital currency issued by central banks essentially "[fulfills] the goal of Milton Friedman's *optimum quantity of money*", which suggests that in comparison to cash that holders have to induce "shoe leather" costs in depositing it to the banks for interest payments, digital currency can avoid such costs and lead to a more efficient society. The question then asked by Koning is that, what is the range of rates at which central banks can pay interests to digital currency holders? Similar to the relationship between bank rate and overnight rate, the deposit rate that the central bank offers to digital currency holders, would also determine the "floor" of interest rate that the commercial banks offer to consumers. In this case, Koning argues that the ability of digital currencies to assign negative interest rates on consumer money holdings is "one of the key design features advocated by proponents of a cashless economy" (2016). Such a design would effective remove the zero lower bound problem in a cash economy, although it was also brought up that a portion of consumer holdings should be protected, or more specifically excluded from negative interest rate impacts, and the magnitude is "the first $1000 [...] in government-subsidized [...] debit accounts" (Koning, 2016). However, when the economy is still in the "hybrid" period of coexistence of both cash and digital currency, monetary policies utilizing interest rates as tools would still be limited by cash as a zero-lower-bound nominal interest rate guarantee (Markets Committee, 2018).

Regarding the supply of digital currencies in the short run, or the form of token distribution, central banks have to choose between the two methods it could deploy: either to allow the central bank to take full control of the supply, which is more in line with the partially-decentralized market we are discussing, or to allow the supply of tokens through a predetermined algorithm as what we would expect in the long-run analysis. To target at a cashless economy in the long run while treading carefully about adjusting the monetary system, one possible route for the central bank to take, is to take complete control of the supply of the digital currencies in the aforementioned "hybrid" stage and attempt to equalize cash and tokens as much as they could, so that the two payment instruments are indifferent to the consumers; The central bank would start to adopt a algorithm-controlled cryptocurrency monetary system and decentralize the market, once the cash demand in economy is minimized, which means either cash usage is completely abolished or the quantity of cash in circulation falls below a certain threshold. To push down the demand for cash in the presence of a digital currency, many tools could be utilized, such as the deposit rate central bank would pay to token holders, which would attract consumers to exchange cash for tokens if a premium rate can be earned on the tokens without loss of liquidity. However, to maintain a non-fluctuating premium rate would also have an effect on monetary policy itself, which could lead to negative consequences if not treated with caution.

In addition to all the benefits and risks within the field of monetary economics we have briefly touched upon, there also exist various fundamental problem with the issue of a digital currency in the short run as well as decentralized cryptocurrency in the long run. The most significant one is the difficulty on hardware adaptation. As mentioned in the first section discussing finance sector, many consumers are naturally excluded from internet due to their economic incapacity or lack of education. Even in most major developed countries such population groups still exist in large numbers, and to shift to a cashless economy without severely diminishing their welfare and opportunities depends on how the governments could equip them with both the hardware and corresponding knowledge to use them, which would in turn depend on inputs in the sectors of education and public providence. Another problem is the higher costs of creating cryptocurrency, especially those based on PoW mechanism as it requires a significant amount of computation power, which translates monotonically to electric energy. The economists would need to determine if the marginal benefits of replacing cash with cryptocurrency would surpass the marginal costs of shifting the means of production, and as technology advances hopefully the costs of running blockchain would in general decrease. Last but not least, as the government "hands over" the control of monetary market to automated algorithm, it would become more difficult to determine the distribution of responsibilities within the government in face of economic fluctuations, which would be another issue to address regarding the long-term functioning of democratic systems when a critical portfolio of power and responsibilities are redistributed.

4. Conclusion and Remarks

As we have analyzed the role, benefits and risks of decentralization in three different markets, including the capital market and the monetary system, albeit rather preliminary as the contemporary literature as well as the corresponding empirical observations are yet to be regarded as profound, it would be safe to derive a few observations and speculations, upon which further studies and researches could be founded.

First of all, from the application of decentralization concepts in all three markets, we could see that it is indeed with potentials, primarily due to its ability in improving efficiency and reducing marginal costs beyond their contemporary technological confines. However, in the empirical analysis of both capital market and monetary system, the deployment of decentralization technology could be limited by the regional technological foundations as well as difficulties in transforming a system between generations. Therefore, when analyzing the benefits of decentralization, we should always take its advantages with a grain of salt, regarding how and where we would reach its limits.

Meanwhile, the concept of decentralization is, inherently speaking, against the "centralization" model of governance that most nations in the world are accustomed to. It means that although certain models may be regarded as beneficial, they may be impractical in most political environments when proceeding to execution. While China has banned cryptocurrencies while slowing down on its progresses in blockchain technology innovations, most other countries are also skeptical towards blockchain, especially after the recent fluctuations in the token market. Therefore, some of the models we have mentioned should be further developed, in terms of how their benefits could be enjoyed by economies without the usage of blockchain technology or cryptocurrency specifically, or from another perspective what compromises one would be willing to make on the technology for the markets to be partially improved.

And finally, as being one of the few merits of this study, one would realize that cryptocurrency, blockchain, and most importantly the ideology of decentralization, are closely related to economic studies. In the next decades if such technological trends would not prove to be mere bubbles, they could become a transformative force, either constructive or destructive, in our economies in terms of how markets would be fundamentally structured. As mentioned previously literatures within this field are still relatively a minority, hence I hope more intricate works would be done in the near future on this topic.

References

Chung, S. and K. Kim (2018), Complements rather than substitutes: An empirical examination of cryptocurrency and online peer-to-peer lending markets. Extracted from SSRN: https://ssrn.com/abstract=3254091.

Dermish, A., C. Kneiding, P. Leishman, and I. Mas (2011), Branchless and mobile banking solutions for the poor: A survey, *Innovations* **6**(4). Extracted from SSRN: https://ssrn.com/abstract=1745967.

EY (2017), EY FinTech Adoption Index 2017: The Rapid Emergence of FinTech. *EY*. Extracted December 2018 from: https://www.ey.com/Publication/vwLUAssets/ey-fintech-adoption-index-2017/$FILE/ey-fintech-adoption-index-2017.pdf.

Gupta, V. (2017), A brief history of blockchain. *Harvard Business Review*. Extracted December 2018 from: https://hbr.org/2017/02/a-brief-history-of-blockchain.

Iwamura, M., Y. Kitamura, T. Matsumoto, and K. Saito (2014), Can we stabilize the price of a cryptocurrency? Understanding the design of Bitcoin and its potential to compete with Central Bank Money. Extracted from SSRN: https://ssrn.com/abstract=2519367.

Koning, J. (2016), Fedcoin: A central bank-issued cryptocurrency. *R3CEV*. Extracted December 2018 from: https://www.r3.com/reports/fedcoin-a-central-bank-issued-cryptocurrency/.

Markets Committee (2018), Central bank digital currencies. *Bank for International Settlements*. Extracted December 2018 from: https://www.bis.org/cpmi/publ/d174.htm.

Shanaev, S., A. Shuraeva, M. Vasenin, and M. Kuznetsov (2018), Cryptocurrency Value and 51% Attacks. Evidence from Event Studies. Extracted from SSRN: https://ssrn.com/abstract=3290016.

Stoica, O. (2002), The role of the capital market in the economic development. Extracted from SSRN: https://ssrn.com/abstract=951278.

Tapscott, D. and A. Tapscott (2016), Blockchain revolution: How the technology behind Bitcoin is changing money, business, and the world. *Portfolio*. ISBN:1101980133 9781101980132.

Thompson, N. (2017), The economic impact of Moore's law: Evidence from when it faltered. Extracted from SSRN: https://ssrn.com/abstract=2899115.

Turner, P. (2006), The banking system in emerging economies: How much progress has been made? *BIS Paper No. 28*. Extracted from SSRN: https://ssrn.com/abstract=1188516.

Zhang, R., A. Raveenthiran, J. Mukai, R. Naeem, A. Dhuna, Z. Parveen, and H. Kim (2018), The regulation paradox of initial coin offerings: A case study approach. Submitted to *Frontiers of Blockchain — Financial Blockchain*. Extracted from SSRN: https://ssrn.com/abstract=3284337.

https://doi.org/10.1142/9789811220470_0005

Chapter 5

Raising Funds with Smart Contracts: New Opportunities and Challenges

Katrin Tinn

Desautels Faculty of Management, McGill University, Quebec H3A 0G4, Canada

katrin.tinn@mcgill.ca

Abstract

Among recent FinTech developments, new digital ledger technologies have the potential to facilitate the financing of entrepreneurial projects, as they can enable different and better financing contracts. Costly verification is arguably one of the main reasons why bank financing and debt contracts have been traditionally so prevalent, with investors not being easily assured that entrepreneurs will report accurately future cash flows generated. The adoption of digital ledger technologies can mitigate this friction, by offering a better tool to maintain a shareable history of transactions, which not only reduces verification costs but also further enables "smart contracts" which can benefit from adjusting optimally to incoming data. Such smart contracts (the optimal form of which is found to be a dynamically adjusting profit-sharing rule) dominate less flexible debt and equity contracts that do not give the right incentives for the entrepreneur to continue to try to generate sales, especially when there is learning from data. There remain unresolved issues around digital ledger technology, especially with "proof-of-work" systems, which create limitations for realizing its potential. Permissioned systems may solve some of these problems but remain at an experimental stage. Third-party platforms that collect and share information are another way to reduce the verification costs faced by individual investors, and there seems to be a close link between the evolution toward "smart" contracts and crowdfunding. The appropriate supporting regulation still needs to be established and will have to tackle issues that are quite novel compared to what banking regulations and securities markets regulations have had to address.

Keywords: Blockchain; Costly verification; Crowdfunding; Entrepreneurial Finance; Hash-linked time stamping; Smart contracts.

1. Introduction

The key role of financial intermediaries and markets is to facilitate more efficient transfers of funds between those who have idle funds to invest and those who have productive investment opportunities. In a frictionless world, all value-adding projects would be pursued, all production possibilities would be utilized efficiently, and the particular shape of financing contracts (be it debt, equity, or another contractual arrangement) would not affect the real outcomes (Mas-Colell *et al.*, 1995, Modigliani and Miller, 1958, 1963).

As reality is not frictionless, how firms raise financing matters (Tirole, 2010), internal funds are often the cheapest source of financing, and debt contracts are arguably the most common forms of external financing. While not-yet-established firms often have the greatest incentives to innovate and have the greatest potential to promote economic growth (see Aghion Howitt, 2008; Kerr and Nanda, 2015), obtaining financing for innovative projects can be particularly difficult. To name a few reasons: these firms' projects are risky, they have skewed returns, it is difficult to predict the demand, a lot of capital these firms have is intangible and thus cannot be easily used as collateral, and possible agency problems due to moral hazard and asymmetric information may be particularly constraining.

Recent innovations in digital ledger technologies and business models have the potential to mitigate some of these known frictions and to enhance the efficiency of financial intermediation and contracting, which sounds like an exciting prospect. While it would be naïve to expect these technologies alone (e.g., the Blockchain technology) to solve issues around the financing of innovation, they can perhaps nevertheless eliminate some historically important frictions and make the economic system more efficient. Conversely, we will see that these technological developments can also be the source of new forms of frictions and unresolved issues. In this chapter, I will focus on analyzing two recent FinTech developments, distributed ledger technologies and crowdfunding, that may have the greatest potential to mitigate or alter the type of frictions young innovative firms face. I will also highlight some unresolved issues and ongoing debates on this topic.

2. Digital Ledger Technologies and Smart(er) Financing Contracts

2.1. *Verifiable records and financing contracts*

One fundamental reason why an aspiring entrepreneur cannot raise funds from a wide group of investors, who may be far away, is that these investors cannot be easily assured that the entrepreneur will accurately report the cash flows he/she has generated. In fact, costly verification is arguably one of the main reasons why bank financing and debt contracts have been traditionally so prevalent. Indeed, debt contracts have been shown to be the optimal contracts when verification imposes additional costs to investors (see, e.g., Townsend, 1979; Diamond, 1984; Gale and Hellwig, 1985; Mookherjee and Png, 1989). The main insight from this literature is that debt contracts minimize the expected verification costs: spending resources to confirm that the reported outcomes are correct is needed only when the borrower has not repaid his obligations. Box 1 provides a numerical illustration of these insights by comparing three contracts that would be equivalent in a frictionless world. When verifying the accuracy of reported outcomes is difficult enough, financing value-generating entrepreneurial projects with equity or alternative arrangements may not be desirable or even possible.[1]

One of the greatest advantages of digital ledger technologies is their potential to make verification (nearly) costless (see Catalini and

[1]The literature on verification costs further highlights a rationale for delegated monitoring by institutions (e.g., banks), as coordinating verification effort among many investors is clearly more difficult.

Box 1 (Numerical example): Financing contracts and costly verification.

An entrepreneur needs to raise $500 for an investment in a project which generates the following cash flows with associated probabilities:

Outcome (cash flow generated)	Probability of the outcome
0	37.5%
$1000	25%
$2000	37.5%

Normalizing the discount rate to one, the present value of these cash flows is $1000. The project clearly has a positive NPV and is worth pursuing.

Consider then the following three contracts:

(1) an unsecured debt contract where the entrepreneur promises to pay back $880;
(2) an equity contract where the investors get 55% of the cash flows generated;
(3) an alternative contract where the investors get $400 if the cash flows are $1000 and they get $1200 if the cash flows are $2000.

The following table describes the monetary payoffs for investors and the entrepreneur under these contracts:

	Unsecured debt		Equity		Alternative contract	
Outcome	Entrepreneur	Investors	Entrepreneur	Investors	Entrepreneur	Investors
0	0	0	0	0	0	0
$1000	$120	$880	$450	$550	$600	$400
$2000	$1120	$880	$900	$1100	$800	$1200

Without frictions, all these contracts are equivalent: the entrepreneur expects to earn $450, while the investors expect to earn a $50 capital gain on their $500 investment.

Suppose that the entrepreneur cannot be trusted to truthfully report what the true outcome was. It is clear from the above example that the

(*Continued*)

entrepreneur would always benefit from understating what the cash flows were if there was no risk of being caught. However, suppose that the investors can pay \$100 to verify that the entrepreneur's records are truthful. Based on the costly state verification literature, debt contracts are optimal as verification is needed only when the entrepreneur reports the cash flows to be insufficient to cover the face value of debt. In this example, verification is needed only when the entrepreneur reports "zero" under the unsecured debt contract, as there is no benefit of reporting "\$1000" when the true outcome was \$2000. In contrast, verification is needed when the entrepreneur reports either 0 or \$1000 under the equity or the "alternative contract". For example, when the true outcome is \$2000, the entrepreneur would gain \$1200 when reporting "zero" under the alternative contract, and \$1200 − \$400 = \$800 when reporting "\$1000" under the alternative contract. Similar reasoning holds for equity.

The expected verification costs investors need to pay under unsecured debt are therefore \$37.5, which gives investors \$12.5 capital gain on their \$500 investment in expectations net of verification costs. The project cannot be financed with equity or the alternative contract as the expected verification costs under these scenarios are \$62.5, which leads to an expected loss for the investors of \$12.5 on their \$500 investment.

Gans, 2016). Consequently, one could expect that without the pressing issue of verification costs, it may become easier to design and offer to young firms a much wider menu of financing contracts: equity, convertible assets, "smart" contracts where the contractual terms adjust based on incoming and verifiably recorded data. These alternative contracts may be better for incentivizing and encouraging the entrepreneur's continued effort, experimentation, and ultimately make more worthy ideas being financed.

Indeed, dynamic contracting models which assume that verification costs are not substantial find that it is better to use a combination of assets, e.g., debt, equity, and credit line (see DeMarzo and Fishman, 2007; DeMarzo and Sannikov, 2006) or debt, equity, and cash reserves (see Biais *et al.*, 2007), where the optimal capital structure is often history dependent. DeMarzo and Sannikov (2017) and He *et al.* (2017) highlight further reasons for history-dependent contracts when considering the possibility of learning from past data and derive predictions regarding the dividend policy and the optimal design of managerial compensation.

While larger corporations have had the capability to benefit from a richer set of possible financing arrangements and compensation contracts, the possible sources of financing for small enterprises and innovative startups are more limited. Furthermore, larger firms have audited accounting records, and thus, verification costs may be relatively small compared to the cash flows these firms generate. While blockchain could reduce the verification costs further, the benefits of greater verifiability may be relatively more important for startup firms who may have just one product idea and have limited access to external financing: traditionally, they cannot raise equity in public markets, and venture capital financing is scarce and difficult to obtain for many firms (see, e.g., Lerner *et al.*, 2012).

Tinn (2018) explores the design of financing contracts that could become accessible for startup firms which, without the adoption of reliable shared ledger technologies, would face high verification costs. Such financing contracts can rely on the cash flows generated by a specific project (somewhat similarly to reward-based and other forms of crowdfunding discussed in Section 3) rather than by the firm as a whole. The paper considers that there is a shared (blockchain) ledger that guarantees that the cash flows the project generates (successful sales) are recorded and verifiable on an ongoing basis. What would be the best contract that can be designed in this environment for covering an initial investment cost? While cash flows (sales) become verifiable in this environment, contracts cannot still be complete because the entrepreneur's effort to generate cash flows is still neither verifiable nor contractible, e.g., the entrepreneur may choose to stop trying to generate cash flows permanently or temporarily. The best contract for maintaining the entrepreneur's continued involvement and effort in the project turns out to be a dynamically adjusting profit-sharing rule, where each sale is split between the investors and the entrepreneur and the percentage either party gets depending on sales outcomes up to that point.

Such a contract dominates less flexible debt and equity contracts that do not give the right incentives for the entrepreneur to continue to try to generate sales. The lack of flexibility of more traditional contracts is particularly costly when sales successes and failures lead the entrepreneur to learn about the prospects of future demand from realized demand on an ongoing basis. Box 2 provides a numerical illustration of these insights based on Tinn (2018). It compares similar contracts than those in Box 1. While debt contracts are the best financing contracts for optimizing monitoring efforts, they are the worst ones among those considered for maintaining the entrepreneur's engagement.

Box 2 (Numerical example): Financing contracts and maintaining entrepreneurial engagement.

As in the case of the example in Box 1, consider that an entrepreneur needs to raise \$500 for an investment. Consider that the project has the potential to generate zero or \$1000 cash flows in weeks 1 and 2. The probability of generating \$1000 during the first week is 50%. The probability of generating \$1000 during the second week is 75% if the first week was successful and generated a positive cash flow, while the probability of generating \$1000 during the second week is only 25% if the first week generated nothing. As the probability of generating positive cash flows on week 2 depends on what happened in week 1, there is learning from incoming data. For example, it could be the case that the tastes of the target consumers of the entrepreneur's project are expected to be similar, and thus, a successful week 1 assures the entrepreneur and investors that there will be high demand in week 2 also, while the opposite indicates that it will be more difficult to sell in the future.

Consider again three contracts:

(1) an unsecured debt contract where the entrepreneur promises to pay back \$880;
(2) an equity contract where the investors get 55% of the cash flows generated;
(3) a "smart contract" which specifies the following cash flow-sharing arrangement: investors and the entrepreneur obtain 40% and 60% of week 1 cash flows, respectively. How the profit is split in week 2 depends on what happened in week 1. If there were no sales in week 1, then the splitting rule is unchanged. If the first week was successful, then investors and the entrepreneur obtain 80% and 20% of week 2 cash flows, respectively.

If we would not worry about maintaining the entrepreneur's effort incentives to continue trying to sell, then these three contracts would again be equivalent. Note that without frictions, the total cash flows generated in this example are the same as in Box 1, where the "smart contract" gives the same payoff as the "alternative contract".[a]

However, the incentives of the entrepreneur to continue to pursue the project if week 1 generated nothing are rather different. In that case, the entrepreneur has revised downward his expectations about week 2 demand and considers the probability of generating \$1000 to be 25%.

(*Continued*)

Box 2 (*Continued*)

The following table specifies the maximum and the expected income the entrepreneur can still obtain provided that no cash flows were generated in week 1.

Unsecured debt		Equity		Alternative contract	
Maximum	Expected	Maximum	Expected	Maximum	Expected
$120	$30	$450	$112.5	$600	$150

Debt contract gives the worst incentives to continue, as the entrepreneur's expected earnings at this stage are $30. If the entrepreneur's opportunity cost is higher than this, he will quit. Furthermore, provided that rational investors foresee this outcome, they will not invest, as their $500 investment is expected to generate a loss of $60 under this reasonable behavior by the entrepreneur. Under a simple equity, investors' and the entrepreneurs' incentives are already much better aligned. However, the "smart" contract is even better. In that case, the entrepreneur obtains three times more from week 2 cash flows if week 1 was not successful, but she also considers the success of week 2 to be three times more likely if there was no demand in week 1. Under this contract, the expected extra income the entrepreneur expects to obtain from week 2 sales is $150 regardless of what happened in week 1. In contrast, equity and debt "overincentivize" the entrepreneur to continue his engagement with the project following good outcomes in week 1 and "underincentivize" his following bad outcomes in week 1. If the entrepreneur's opportunity is between $112.5 and $150, debt or equity financing are impossible, while financing via a "smart contract" is possible.

[a] While under this example on a "smart contract" has a corresponding formulation as the function of total cash flows, it is the feature of the simplified example considered. In many more elaborate cases considered in Tinn (2018), such representation is not possible. However, the optimal contract can always be specified as a "smart" contract that takes the form of appropriate adjusting profit (cash flow)-sharing rule.

The possibility to have shared verifiable records and to build "smart" contracts on these could further overcome other contracting frictions that startup companies face. Beyond being unable to verify the sales records of the company, investors often worry that the entrepreneur will not invest the funds raised in the project, and either divert them or sell the firm too early at a too low price. For this reason, the financiers of startup firms (friends, angel investors, and venture capitalists) often use convertible assets (e.g., preferred stock) combined with covenants that limit the founders' ability to sell the firm without the investors' consent (see Lerner *et al.*, 2012). Such concern could be mitigated via a "smart" financing contract where convertible features for the asset and covenants can be built in the terms that are set to self-execute automatically. Relatedly, Bergemann and Hege (1998) find that a time-varying share contract would be the optimal financing arrangement when experimentation requires multiple rounds of investment and when experimentation enables learning about the project's probability of success. When investment costs are physical, a reliable digital ledger could further eliminate the possibility to divert initial funds via a "smart" contract that takes the form of a conditional payment as follows: (1) Investors could send their funds to an escrow account, from where these funds would be released only when there is a proof that the entrepreneur made the promised purchase (e.g., of a machine) and would be returned to the investors otherwise. (2) As both the entrepreneur and the seller of the machine can verify that there are funds on the escrow account, they can record the purchase of the machine on the ledger as well as give the required proof to the investors. This in turn can mitigate the initial moral hazard and enable firms to raise funds from investors who are dispersed and far away, rather than actively engaged with the firm (e.g., venture capitalists or angel investors).

We have shown that if records are verifiable, more projects can be financed, and the optimal contracts move away from debt and equity toward more flexible forms. It remains to be established under which conditions such "smart" contracts are possible. For this reason, it is important to highlight the relevant key features of "blockchain" (or hash-linked time stamping) technology that enhance verifiability, as well as the open questions remaining around the implementation of this technology.

2.2. *Key features of digital ledgers based on hash-linked time stamping (blockchain)*

Hash-linked and time stamped digital ledger technology, sometimes called "blockchain", is best known for its central role in recording transactions involving cryptocurrencies (e.g., bitcoin), or other digital assets

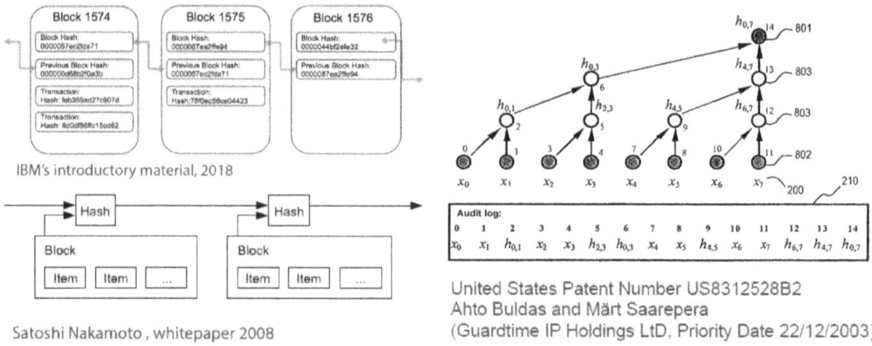

Figure 1: Examples of blockchain (or hash-linked time stamping) descriptions.
Source: Figure 2-1 in Manav Gupta, 2020.

(e.g., Ethereum-based tokens), and decentralized applications (dApps).[2] However, the idea dates back to computer science research by Haber and Stornetta (1991, 1997).

A key component of a blockchain is that it is a data-recording structure, where past records are particularly difficult — if not impossible — to be changed *ex post*. Transactions are recorded in hash-linked and time stamped blocks. Each block contains a difficult-to-reverse reference to the previous block (via a complex-enough hash function) and thus, effectively contains references to all previous blocks. This ensures that any modification of past data cannot be done without it being visible (the hash function result will be very different subject to even very minor modifications, and the more time passes, the more difficult it becomes to change past records). Figure 1 gives three examples of blockchains highlighting this unifying key feature: one from IBM's introductory material (advocating private sector-permissioned systems), one from Nakamoto's whitepaper on bitcoin (the most famous permissionless system), and one from Guardtimes' patent (this firm is involved in a number of country-level projects in Estonia and the United States utilizing hash-link time stamping technology; and also permissioned).

Before engaging in further analysis regarding the open questions around blockchain management, it is worth highlighting two finance-relevant

[2]The Ethereum platform enables the creation of new digital assets. The associated Ethereum coin is a necessary input for creating digital (or "smart") contracts that use the functionalities of the Ethereum platform.

features of this data storage structure beyond its relative cryptographic security. First, blockchain records are digital, which makes them easily shareable as all (contracting) parties can keep a same agreed history of transactions. Second, blockchain records are always dated (time stamped) and contracting parties can keep a shared history of when transactions relevant to the contract happened, for instance, the date of one successful product sale.

Consequently, blockchain technology makes it possible for the contracting parties to write contracts that use these data as inputs on a continuous basis and thus to write contracts where the contractual terms are history dependent and adjust frequently (as in the case of dynamically adjusting profit-sharing rules discussed in the previous section). From a computer programming perspective, a code describing a financing contract as a frequently adjusting profit-sharing rule is not noticeably more difficult to write than a code that regularly transfers coupon payments of a debt contract, pays dividends of an equity contract, executes a conversion rule of a convertible asset, etc.

Arbitrarily frequent adjustments are clearly not practical in an environment where contracts are not fully digital and rely on infrequent reporting. This makes blockchain-based records fundamentally different from traditional accounting records, even if accounting records are regularly audited and there are receipts for all transactions: blockchain records not only enable the verifiability and shareability of transaction records but also bring greater speed and flexibility to contracts that can be built based on these records.

2.3. *Unresolved issues and debates*

The previous sections emphasized the usefulness of verifiable and easily sharable transaction records and how it links to the core features of blockchain or hash-linked time stamping technology. It was however silent on two further fundamental questions: who verifies the creation of new blocks? And what guarantees that the data recorded itself is accurate?

Beyond recording transactions in hash-linked time stamped blocks, most known cryptocurrencies (starting from Bitcoin) further rely on a decentralized creation and confirmation mechanism for new blocks — the so-called proof-of-work system that relies on mining.[3] On the one hand,

[3] Indeed, some authors would argue that a digital hash-linked ledger that is not decentralized in this manner should not be called a "blockchain", i.e., not everyone calls the IBM's and the Guardtime's ledgers a "blockchain". However, semantics aside, the above

this system is the closest to exhibiting what many blockchain enthusiasts consider to be the main attractive feature of this technology — cutting out intermediaries. On the other hand, a fully decentralized "proof-of-work" verification system is costly (at least so far) and has its weaknesses.[4] Recording transaction on a proof-of-work system involves transaction costs (see, e.g., Easley *et al.*, 2019) and may be even more costly at the aggregate level due to the needlessly replicated computer power used and due to the associated environmental externalities; it is furthermore in practice often concentrated in mining pools rather than fully decentralized in the spirit of the original aspirations of blockchain designers (see, e.g., Cong *et al.*, 2019). There is a recent and rapidly developing literature about further aspects of miners' incentives (see Halaburda and Haeringer, 2019, for a review). Another decentralized alternative is the "proof-of-stake" system, which is less wasteful (see Saleh, 2019), but which is not yet at a similar stage of adoption as the "proof-of-work" one. Ultimately, one may view the issue of who has the right to validate new transaction blocks as a continuum between two poles, from one managing institution (possibly a technology firm rather than a financial intermediary), to fully decentralized mechanisms (there are other possibilities beyond "proof-of-work" and "proof-of-stake"). For smart contracts, the issue of block validation is somewhat secondary: even if the validation is managed by one (trusted) institution, the ledger itself can still be distributed and can bring the contractual benefits discussed above. If we take the view that permissioned verification mechanisms are more efficient, then there are still many open questions. If it is one institution, should it be a financial institution or a technology firm? If it is a made up of few institutions, how should the incentives within the group be aligned?

The second issue, i.e., how to guarantee the accuracy of the data recorded, is perhaps even more fundamental and more difficult to resolve. Hash-linked time stamping technology only assures that data and transaction records are more reliable and verifiable. It does not itself guarantee that the records themselves are accurate. This problem does not arise when the asset recorded on the blockchain is fiat money (e.g., bitcoin),

---

discussion highlighted that a hash-linked and time stamped ledger is literally a cryptographically linked chain of blocks of transactions.

[4]Verification under proof of work is costly due to transaction costs (Easley *et al.*, 2018); mining nowadays is also not that decentralized as a large part of it is conducted by a small number of mining pools (e.g., Cong *et al.*, 2018).

which is fungible: one bitcoin is as good as another bitcoin. Matters are more complex if the blockchain is used to record non-homogeneous data such as the sales records of a specific product and/or information on the authenticity and quality of an item (e.g., a designer product, real estate, or a diamond).

While there are pros and cons for the validation of new blocks being decentralized, in many cases the entry of new data itself may require intermediaries and experts. Everledger uses blockchain to track the provenance of high-value assets (such as diamonds). As the physical characteristics of such assets cannot be assessed from a distance or without engaging industry experts, it is natural that the entry of new data to the Everledger blockchain requires the cooperation of manufacturers and retailers. Other new FinTech firms such as Funderbeam, which enables entrepreneurs to raise funds from a crowd using venture capital-like arrangements (with the added benefit of nearly immediate tradability on the secondary market), uses Chromaway's blockchain technology to duplicate asset ownership records. In these examples, the intermediaries are non-traditional, but still necessary. When it comes to recording the sales of products, it is currently difficult, if not impossible, for investors to be sure that the entrepreneur has not sold some of the products to consumers directly and without recording it to the blockchain.

There are some possible developments and incentive mechanisms that can overcome this problem. First, if in the future blockchain technology develops into a World-Wide Ledger and all money becomes digital, as some authors have speculated, the possibility of selling the goods to consumers without records will be largely eliminated.[5] However the coordination efforts needed for this are substantial, which makes this solution unlikely to be feasible in the near future. Second, some new products are digital by nature, and thus, recording the sales of such digital products is perhaps the most immediate and realistic application of blockchain technology. Indeed, the Ethereum Platform itself was financed by a crowdsale that gave Ethereum coins as rewards in 2014. The Ethereum coin is tradable as any other cryptocurrency, cryptoasset, or cryptotoken and is a necessary input for using the contract design functionalities of the Ethereum Platform. It is therefore not surprising that many

[5]While all bilateral barter possibilities can still not be eliminated, it is well established that it requires a double coincidence of wants, which is unlikely and rare enough to have a substantial importance.

Ethereum-based initial coin offerings that appear to be more successful involve platform businesses whose products only exist in the digital environment (see, e.g., Bakos and Halaburda, 2018; Li and Mann, 2018). Third, it may be possible to incentivize entrepreneurs to accurately self-record the sales of their products on the blockchain ledger. This could be the case of products that are of high value or that are design items, where the consumers may demand a proof of authenticity so that they can resale the item. One could imagine ways to add an imprint to the object sold which is linked to the corresponding digital sales record on the blockchain. Another way to incentivize the accurate self-reporting of sales could be regulatory measures that give consumers sufficiently attractive benefits (e.g., tax benefits) if they can provide a proof that their purchase was recorded.

Another set of open questions revolves around who should be able to see the records that are on blockchain. For example, in the case of bitcoin, everyone interested can see transactions, but the identities of individuals or institutions that hold bitcoins are pseudonymous. When considering the usefulness of this technology for financing contracts, we may rather need the opposite: the identity of the entrepreneur should not be pseudonymous to investors, and it is not obvious that everyone should have access to all asset ownership and sales records. Cong and He (2019) further argue that blockchain-based "smart" contracts may lead to greater collusion. Permissioned blockchain systems that allow access to part of the data only to specific individuals or firms at specific times can overcome these issues. For example, entrepreneurs and outside parties do not need to know the identities of investors and to achieve this is relatively easy in the case of a permissioned blockchain. Furthermore, even though competitors could be investors or pretend to be investors to obtain some information about a firm, a permissioned blockchain could limit the possibility of industrial espionage or collusion based on real-time information about the firm's sales. As long as the "smart" contract itself is well designed and the computer code implementing the contracts is accessible and immutable, the investors could be allowed to see the sales data and to obtain their returns or losses from their investment only after a sufficient amount of time has passed. While permissioned systems may have further benefits and costs compared to more transparent blockchain systems, the technology itself allows for a wide set of choices and makes it possible to achieve an optimal degree of transparency and privacy while allowing for the benefit of verifiable records for raising financing.

3. Crowdfunding and Experimentation

The above discussion left it open whether entrepreneurs raise funds from a few large investors (e.g., institutions) or from a large number of small investors. As the adoption of digital ledger technologies can make it easier for small investors that are far away to contract with the entrepreneur, there is a close link between the evolution toward "smart" contracts and crowdfunding. For example, initial coin offerings on the Ethereum Platform can be viewed as a form of crowdfunding.

Crowdfunding can be broadly defined as asking money from a large number of backers in return to either financial or non-financial rewards. In its current form, it does not always require the adoption of particularly advanced technologies. Many prominent crowdfunding sites, be they debt, equity, or reward-based, are Internet-based platforms that do not utilize blockchain and simply enable the firms to pitch their projects and funding needs to any potential investor who navigates their website during the campaign period. The platforms may also collect and share some information about the enterprise and thus provide some verified information.[6] Forms of crowdfunding where the rewards are financial directly link to the mechanism discussed in the previous section. The presence of third-party platforms that collect and share information is another way to reduce the verification costs faced by individual investors. This in turn can make equity financing, as well as more flexible financing arrangements (such as "smart" contracts that dominate debt in terms of maintaining entrepreneurial engagement), possible. In fact, it seems likely that instead of investors and entrepreneurs interacting and building contracts on a shared blockchain ledger directly, there is a role for intermediaries similar to these platform businesses, who may enhance their own credibility by utilizing distributed ledger technologies either in their interaction with firms or investors or both.

So far, we have considered the interaction between the entrepreneurs and firms only, while considering that both parties are uncertain

---

[6]For example, CircleUp enables large-enough firms (typically firms with revenues \$250,000 to \$10 million) firms to raise equity or debt financing via connecting them to investors. They require accounting data from the firms; collect additional data from public sources, partnerships, and practitioners; and utilize machine learning techniques to provide further information to potential investors/backers.

about the target consumers' demand for the final product. Reward-based crowdfunding enables firms to interact with and learn about the demand by interacting with their target consumers directly. This in turn enables experimentation and learning about consumer demand before committing substantial resources to innovation or product development. Chemla and Tinn (2020) model reward-based crowdfunding (e.g., raising funds via Kickstarter) as an efficient way to test the market at the early stage of product development. They show that there is a substantial real option value where firms benefit from either knowing that there is more demand for their project that initially expected or save on investment cost if the demand turns out to be low. This real option value is higher when there is more uncertainty and when learning from the crowdfunding sample enables the firms to update their estimates about future demand (i.e., such crowdfunding is most beneficial for the producers of innovative products). For this reason, reward-based crowdfunding is a good mechanism for encouraging experimentation and innovation, as failing at the crowdfunding stage is noticeably less costly than failing after production. This is consistent with the insights from Manso (2011) who shows that the optimal way to motivate innovation exhibits tolerance to early failure and rewards long-term success.

The current forms of web platform-based crowdfunding still exhibit substantial moral hazard — the entrepreneur could divert funds and announce that product development failed. While empirical studies show that Kickstarter fraud is rare, Chemla and Tinn (2020) show that short campaign length combined with learning about the demand mitigates moral hazard.[7] Namely, a successful campaign is a positive signal about the demand of consumers who neither noticed the product nor participated in the short crowdfunding campaign: diverting funds would then come at the possibly large cost of losing this future demand. Still moral hazard imposes costs, and if there are ways to mitigate this moral hazard via the kinds of "smart" contracts discussed earlier, this form of crowdfunding could also become more efficient.

[7]In models of crowdfunding where there is no learning about out-of-sample demand, the consequences of moral hazard are even more severe (Strausz, 2017). See also Ellman and Hurkens (2019) on price discrimination in the context of reward-based crowdfunding.

4. Conclusion

New digital ledger technologies can enable different and, for many compelling theoretical reasons, better financing contracts. A move from the *status quo* is nevertheless not easy. The current, largely debt contract-based financing systems are governed by well-established regulatory systems. As the afore discussion highlights, the most effective implementations of digital ledger-based contracts need to resolve a set of issues, such as creating the right incentives for accurate data entry and for the maintenance of the ledger. Many private sector developments, which range from permissioned and permissionless blockchain development to web-based crowdfunding models, provide an interesting testing ground. The appropriate supporting regulation still needs to be established and as this article suggests needs to tackle issues that are quite novel compared to what banking regulations and securities markets regulations have had to address.

References

Aghion, P. and P. W. Howitt (2008), *The Economics of Growth*. Cambridge, Massachusetts (USA) and London, England (UK): MIT Press.

Bakos, Y. and H. Hanna (2018), The role of cryptographic tokens and ICOs in fostering platform adoption. Available at SSRN: https://ssrn.com/abstract=3207777 or http://dx.doi.org/10.2139/ssrn.3207777.

Bergemann, D. and U. Hege (1998), Venture capital financing, moral hazard, and learning, *Journal of Banking & Finance* **22**(6-8), 703–735.

Biais, B., T. Mariotti, G. Plantin, and J. C. Rochet (2007), Dynamic security design: Convergence to continuous time and asset pricing implications, *The Review of Economic Studies* **74**(2), 345–390.

Catalini, C. and J. S. Gans (2016), Some simple economics of the blockchain. No. w22952. National Bureau of Economic Research.

Chemla, G. and K. Tinn (2020), Learning trough crowdfunding, *Management Science* **66**(5), 1783–1801.

Cong, L. W. and Z. He (2019), Blockchain disruption and smart contracts, *The Review of Financial Studies* **32**(5), 1754–1797.

Cong, L. W., Y. Li, and N. Wang (2019), Tokenomics: Dynamic adoption and valuation, Becker Friedman Institute for Research in Economics Working Paper 2018-49, 2018–15.

Cong, L. W., Z. He, and J. Li (2019), Decentralized mining in centralized pools. No. w25592. National Bureau of Economic Research.

DeMarzo, P. M. and M. J. Fishman (2007), Optimal long-term financial contracting, *The Review of Financial Studies* **20**(6), 2079–2128.

DeMarzo, P. M. and Y. Sannikov (2017), Learning, termination, and payout policy in dynamic incentive contracts, *The Review of Economic Studies* **84**(1), 182–236.

DeMarzo, P. M. and Y. Sannikov (2006), Optimal security design and dynamic capital structure in a continuous-time agency model, *The Journal of Finance* **61**(6), 2681–2724.

Diamond, D. W. (1984), Financial intermediation and delegated monitoring, *The Review of Economic Studies* **51**(3), 393–414.

Easley, D., M. O'Hara, and S. Basu (2019), From mining to markets: The evolution of bitcoin transaction fees, *Journal of Financial Economics* **134**(1), 91–109.

Ellman, M. and S. Hurkens (2019), Optimal crowdfunding design, *Journal of Economic Theory* **184**(Nov 2019), Article 104939.

Gale, D. and M. Hellwig (1985), Incentive-compatible debt contracts: The one-period problem, *The Review of Economic Studies* **52**(4), 647–663.

Haber, S. and W. S. Stornetta (1991), How to time stamp a digital document, *Advances in Cryptology-CRYPT0'90. Journal of Cryptology* **3**, 99–111.

Haber, S. and W. S. Stornetta (1997), Secure names for bit-strings, in *Proceedings of the 4th ACM Conference on Computer and Communications Security*.

Halaburda, H. and G. Haeringer (2019), Bitcoin and blockchain: What we know and what questions are still open, NYU Stern School of Business; Baruch College Zicklin School of Business Research Paper No. 2018-10-02. Available at SSRN: https://ssrn.com/abstract=3274331.

He, Z., B. Wei, J. Yu, and F. Gao (2017), Optimal long-term contracting with learning, *The Review of Financial Studies* **30**(6), 2006–2065.

Kerr, W. R. and R. Nanda (2015), Financing innovation, *Annual Review of Financial Economics* **7**, 445–462.

Lerner, J., A. Leamon, and F. Hardymon (2012), *Venture Capital, Private Equity, and the Financing of Entrepreneurship*, New York: John Wiley & Sons

Li, J. and M. William (2018), Initial coin offerings and platform building. Available at SSRN: https://ssrn.com/abstract=3088726.

Malinova, K. and A. Park (2017), Market design with blockchain technology, Available at SSRN 2785626.

Manav Gupta (2020), *Blockchain for Dummies*, 3rd IBM Limited Edition, Hoboken NJ: John Wiley & Sons, Inc.

Manso, G. (2011), Motivating innovation, *The Journal of Finance* **66**(5), 1823–1860.

Mas-Colell, A., M. D. Whinston, and J. R. Green (1995), *Microeconomic Theory*, Vol. 1. New York: Oxford University Press.

Modigliani, F. and M. H. Miller (1963), Corporate income taxes and the cost of capital: A correction, *The American Economic Review* **53**(3), 433–443.

Modigliani, F. and M. H. Miller (1958), The cost of capital, corporation finance and the theory of investment, *The American* **1**, 3.

Mookherjee, D. and I. Png (1989), Optimal auditing, insurance, and redistribution, *The Quarterly Journal of Economics* **104**(2), 399–415.

Prat, J. and B. Jovanovic (2014), Dynamic contracts when the agent's quality is unknown, *Theoretical Economics* **9**(3), 865–914.

Saleh, F. (2019), Blockchain without waste: Proof-of-stake, Available at SSRN 3183935.

Strausz, R. (2017), A theory of crowdfunding: A mechanism design approach with demand uncertainty and moral hazard, *The American Economic Review* **107**(6), 1430–1476.

Swan, M. (2015), *Blockchain*. Sebastopol, CA: O'Reilly Media, Inc.

Tapscott, D. and A. Tapscott (2016), Blockchain Revolution. How the technology behind bitcoin is changing money, business, and the world, Portfolio Penguin, USA.

Tinn, K. (2018), "Smart" contracts and external financing. Available at SSRN: https://ssrn.com/abstract=3072854 or http://dx.doi.org/10.2139/ssrn.3072854.

Tirole, J. (2010), *The Theory of Corporate Finance*. Princeton, New Jersey (USA) and Oxfordshire (UK): Princeton University Press.

Townsend, R. M. (1979), Optimal contracts and competitive markets with costly state verification, *Journal of Economic Theory* **21**(2), 265–293.

Yermack, D. (2017), Corporate governance and blockchains, *Review of Finance* **21**(1), 7–31.

https://doi.org/10.1142/9789811220470_0006

Chapter 6

The Blockchain Evolution and Revolution of Accounting

Kimberlyn George* and Panos N. Patatoukas†

Haas School of Business, University of California, Berkeley, USA

* *kimberlyn@berkeley.edu*

† *panos@haas.berkeley.edu*

Abstract

Blockchain, the technology behind digital currency, is a decentralized, distributed ledger that records transactions in digital assets. By authenticating and recording immutable transactions, decentralized blockchains perform the same function as many intermediaries in our society that establish trust and maintain integrity between transacting parties. Due to its natural relation to accounting and possible uses in accounting functions, business operations, and financial services, it is important that accountants learn about blockchain technology and its opportunities and limitations. This chapter explores applications of blockchain technology in finance, auditing, financial reporting, and supply chain. We first discuss the classification, characteristics, and issuance of cryptoassets and the evolving regulatory environment. Then, we address potential innovative uses of blockchain in auditing and financial reporting, keeping in mind the limitations of its application. Finally, we explore how blockchain technology can enhance communication and trust between organizations in a supply chain or in contracting relationships.

Keywords: Blockchain; Cryptosassets; Triple-entry accounting; Real-time reporting; Open-book accounting; Smart contracts.

1. Introduction

Blockchain technology allows for a digital ledger of transactions to be stored and verified by a decentralized network. Though originally developed in 2008 as a means to transact in cryptocurrency such as bitcoin, blockchain networks and their applications have been explored for uses in a wide range of business activities. Due to its natural relation to accounting as a transaction ledger and its possible uses in accounting functions and business operations, it is important that accountants today are aware of this new technology.

This chapter offers an overview of blockchain technology and its implications for accounting. First, we discuss the classification and characteristics of cryptoassets, as well as initial coin offerings, by which cryptoassets are sold as a means to fund startup blockchain ventures. In addition, we address the evolving global regulatory environment for cryptoassets and ICOs and the accounting treatment of this new asset class.

Next, we cover uses for blockchain technology in auditing and financial reporting. Blockchain technology has the potential to greatly improve the efficiency of audits by providing continuous assurance, but falls short of providing sufficient, complete audit evidence. Auditors with clients utilizing blockchain technology have the opportunity to use innovative audit techniques that utilize the verification characteristics of blockchain networks.

Lastly, we explore blockchain's use in supply chain networks and contracting. Blockchain technology is best applied to use cases where there is a lack of trust between transacting parties, but transparency and verification of information are required. As such, it is well suited to aid in data sharing and communication between different organizations in a supply chain and in bringing accountability and transparency to contracting.

2. Blockchain Technology

In 2008, Satoshi Nakamoto invented bitcoin, the first cryptoasset built for exchange on a peer-to-peer network. The developers of bitcoin sought a safe, trustless marketplace free from regulatory restrictions in which transactions in digital assets could be executed. With this need came the development of blockchain technology (Nakamoto, 2008).

Blockchain technology allows for a digital ledger of transactions to be recorded, stored, and verified on a peer-to-peer network. A blockchain network is distributed across a system of computers called nodes. When a transaction is initiated on a blockchain, it is broadcast to every node in the network. Through a process called mining, transactions are verified by blockchain miners who perform complex algorithms. Once a consensus is reached by miners that the transaction is valid, the transaction is attached to a block, and once enough transactions are built into the block, it is attached to the blockchain. Once attached, the transactions in a block cannot be removed or changed. Every node on the blockchain network can view every transaction on that block and all blocks that came before it, building a comprehensive transaction database, continuously updated and accessible by all blockchain participants.

When discussing the benefits of blockchain technology, it is important to distinguish between *public* and *private* blockchains. Public blockchains are permission-less, decentralized networks. No central authority governs transactions on a public blockchain. The identities of users on a public blockchain are hidden, and nobody can be denied access. These attributes make public blockchains appropriate for cryptocurrencies like bitcoin. Because transactions are verified by a large number of nodes, it is very difficult to obtain a majority network power on a public blockchain and compromise the validity of the mining process. However, due to the large number of participants, transactions, and nodes forming a public blockchain, transactions take a large amount of time and computing power. Miners on public blockchains must have incentives via transaction fees to use their computing power to verify transactions and keep the blockchain running.

Private, or permissioned, blockchains are better suited for enterprise solutions when users are interested in protecting the privacy of their data. On a private blockchain, the identity of blockchain participants is known and users must be approved by the enterprise creating the blockchain to read, write, or verify transactions. Because there are fewer participants, transaction speed is faster on a private blockchain, and customization is easier. Trust is required between parties on a private blockchain, and with fewer nodes approving transactions, the risk of manipulation is greater. Private blockchains can provide efficiency and transparency gains for businesses who wish to protect the privacy of their data.

It is likely that enterprises will feel the impact of this new technology in all aspects of their business. Of 600 executives surveyed in 2018, 84% say their organizations have some involvement in blockchain technology (PwC, 2018). By providing verification and transparency to transactions between trustless parties, blockchain technology has the potential to replace intermediaries in our society that perform the same function such as banks, clearinghouses, and lawyers (ICAEW, 2018). Blockchain technology is posed to transform the way businesses operate and interact with customers, investors, auditors, and supply chain partners.

3. Cryptoassets

Since the development of Bitcoin in 2008, the digital asset landscape has evolved, and there are now many different types of assets issued using blockchain technology. Most cryptoassets can be broadly classified into one of three categories — cryptocurrency, cryptocommodity, or cryptotoken.

Bitcoin, the first cryptoasset, is the most popular cryptocurrency. It performs the three functions of any currency, serving as a means of exchange, store of value, and unit of account. Like paper money, cryptocurrencies have little value outside of their currency functions. Cryptoassets obtain value from their underlying utility, the utility of the blockchain on which they are issued, and speculation. Without use cases built around the Bitcoin blockchain, the value of the Bitcoin native asset initially stemmed from speculation over the network's future value. Once the currency gained popularity and its value was understood, use cases were developed particularly for e-commerce and other payment systems. Since the origin of bitcoin, many cryptocurrencies have been launched on bitcoin's blockchain or on entirely separate blockchains. These cryptocurrencies differ in their supply schedules, transaction speeds, miner requirements, and privacy features, but all serve the same function as a digital currency.

Similar to traditional commodities like oil and copper, cryptocommodities are used as inputs into finished goods. After the launch of bitcoin, developers saw potential in its underlying blockchain technology as a means of transacting digital commodities such as bandwidth, storage, and computation power. The best known example of a cryptocommodity is ether, the native asset to the Ethereum blockchain. Ethereum is essentially a decentralized computer where developers can build decentralized applications (dApps). These applications range from cloud storage and insurance markets to online games and gambling networks. Programs developed on Ethereum run on the computers that build the Ethereum blockchain, and miners who process and verify the information from these programs are compensated in ether for doing so.

Through the dApps created with cryptocommodities come cryptotokens. Similar to coins bought for use in an online video game, cryptotokens have utility only within the application they are created. Cryptotokens are the digital assets most commonly issued through an Initial Coin Offering (Howell *et al.*, 2017).

As of August 2019, no specific guidance has been released by US GAAP or IFRS on accounting for cryptoassets. Companies accepting cryptocurrency as a means of payment or investing in cryptoassets must determine on a case-by-case basis the best accounting treatment for these assets. Due to the volatility of cryptomarkets and the lack of recognition as legal tender, cryptocurrencies should typically not be classified as cash or cash equivalents. Many cryptoassets appear to function as financial instruments; however, cryptoassets generally do not provide the owner with a contractual right to future cash and may not meet the definition of a financial instrument. As many cryptoassets are purchased with an intent to resell, some argue they are best classified as inventory. However, cryptoassets are not physical assets and trading activity may not be frequent enough to be labeled as an ordinary course of business. Currently, as cryptoassets are digital assets with indefinite useful lives, the most promising classification is intangible assets (Sterley, 2019).

Transactions in many cryptoassets take place over a public blockchain network, meaning that they are visible to all participants. Transparency should help interested parties value an asset and improve price efficiency. However, it is possible that retail investor participants, in particular, may be overwhelmed by the rich transaction data or misinterpret it, leading to poor trading decisions. As seen by bitcoin's unpredictable history, the speculative digital asset marketplace is at risk for volatility due to overreaction to news and speculative trading. The availability of granular transaction data may also lead to copycat investment strategies and deter fundamental analysis. Though the identity of traders is protected on a public blockchain, every trade executed by a blockchain participant is attached to the same user key, leaving a public record of their actions attached to a digital identity accessible by any node on the blockchain. Copycat trading following a fundamental trader's digital identity key may move prices too quickly for fundamental traders to profit off their positions and dissuade traders from incurring the cost to trade-off fundamentals.

4. Initial Coin Offerings

Initial coin offerings involve issuing tokens, or the promise of future tokens, to raise money for a start-up venture. ICOs are an alternative means to early venture financing that allows for a wider audience of investors. In an ICO, cryptoassets are sold as tokens to investors in exchange for legal currency or for other cryptocurrencies. Typically, ICO issuers establish a minimum threshold of funds below which the ICO will not be executed, and many issuers maintain a fundraising cap. Though often compared to initial public offerings, ICOs and IPOs are different in crucial ways.

First, while IPOs come with high underwriting and disclosure costs, ICOs are a relatively low-cost method of fundraising. The IPO market is heavily regulated with strict disclosure requirements aimed at protecting potential investors. On the contrary, disclosure requirements are virtually non-existent for ICOs in most countries. The majority of ICO issuers release a white paper, but practice varies dramatically. Typically, white papers include information on how the tokens will be used, their benefits to holders, the number of tokens in the network, and a simple budget. Most white papers, however, contain little to no information about the issuer.

Equity and token issuances differ in their valuation. While the value of equity issuances are derived from discounted future earnings, the value of a utility token or new cryptocurrency issued in an ICO is derived from the value of the future network to its users, as measured by the exchange rate of the token in the future. Thus, it can be very difficult to value a venture funded via an ICO, as there is no past performance data or substantial information about the issuer that can be used to project future value.

The lack of transparency in the market for ICOs poses risks to investors. A recent study by the ICO advisory firm Satis Group LLC discovered that of ICOs with market capitalizations of at least $50 million, 80% were scams, meaning there was no true intention of pursuing project development, and only 8% managed to be traded on an exchange post-ICO (Bitcoin News, 2019). ICO white papers are not audited, and there are no mandatory disclosure requirements in most countries for coin issuers.

Due to the lack of credible disclosure in the ICO market, it is difficult for investors to distinguish promising projects from scams. To mitigate this, many blockchain projects seeking funding will release their source code to potential investors. This acts as a very credible disclosure, allowing potential investors to confirm that the technology exists as described and that disclosures made in ICO white papers such as token release schedules or insider token holdings are coded into the platform via smart contracts. However, many ventures do not have source code available for release to investors at the time of ICO, and others do not want to risk releasing their propriety information via source code disclosure.

A natural question in the ICO market is what disclosures investors should pay attention to when making investment decisions. Bourveau *et al.* (2019) study the association between different issuer voluntary disclosures and ICO success, as measured by likelihood of raising funds, likelihood of being listed on an exchange post-ICO, and amount of funds raised. They find some evidence that white paper length, team size, and source code release are associated with their ICO success measures, but overall find that the majority of their voluntary disclosure measures are not significantly associated with ICO success. Either the lack of credible disclosure or inability of investors to interpret disclosures prevents voluntary disclosure from mitigating adverse selection in the ICO market. However, the authors do find that information intermediaries in the ICO market have stepped in to aid investors in digesting the information disclosed by issuers and to act as monitors in the ICO market. Focusing on ratings provided by ICObench, a leading crypto rating service, they find that cryptoexpert-provided ratings are better predictors of ICO success than individual disclosure measures. The authors find that ratings are positively associated with all measures of ICO success and additional measures of post-ICO performance. Potential investors in the cryptomarket should utilize the analysis provided by these intermediaries when making investment decisions, keeping in mind conflicts of interest, rather than solely focus on issuer-provided disclosure.

Potential investors should also be aware of the international cryptocurrency regulations in place. A recent Cryptocurrency World Survey by the Law Library of Congress found that governments around the world have noticed the cryptomarket and its risks. A common action across countries has been to release government-issued warnings about investing in crypto markets, reminding citizens that cryptocurrencies are not currencies backed by the state and that issuers are unregulated. The United

States SEC went as far as to launch a fake ICO to educate investors about the pitfalls of the cryptomarket. Some countries have imposed restrictions or outright bans on investing in cryptocurrencies. Algeria, Bolivia, Morocco, Nepal, Pakistan, and Vietnam have banned any and all activities involving cryptocurrency, and Bangladesh, Iran, Thailand, Lithuania, China, and Colombia have imposed indirect restrictions on cryptoactivities by banning financial institutions from facilitating transactions involving cryptocurrency within their borders.

On the opposite end of the spectrum, some countries have recognized the cryptomarket as an opportunity. Countries such as Spain, Belarus, Cayman Islands, and Luxemburg have embraced crypto-friendly laws in an attempt to attract investment. In addition, Venezuela, Marshall Islands, and Lithuania are trying to develop their own systems of cryptocurrency, and governments such as those of Mexico and Isle of Man permit the use of cryptocurrency as a means of payment along with their national currency.

One of the main concerns of governments is the taxation of cryptocurrency activities, including cryptomining and selling cryptoassets. Practice varies across countries that have established cryptotaxation laws. For example, in Switzerland, cryptocurrency is taxed as foreign currency, in Argentina it is subject to income tax, and in the UK, individuals pay capital gains tax rates on the sale of cryptoassets.

Many countries have yet to develop regulatory regimes or taxation laws, and among those that have, practice varies dramatically across countries. It is possible that coordination among countries may speed up the development of standardized legal treatment and aid the expansion of the cryptomarket. Spurred by the announcement of Facebook's Libra, a permissioned blockchain cryptocurrency backed by fiat currency and government backed securities planned to launch in 2020, members of G7 nations (France, Italy, Canada, United States, Japan, Germany, and United Kingdom) have formed a task force to examine the regulatory issues in the cryptocurrency market.

While the ICO market is in the US is not officially regulated, the SEC released guidance in April 2019 on determining whether digital assets meet the definition of a security under US federal securities laws. The framework brings many ICOs under regulatory requirements as an "investment contract" (SEC, 2019). Though the framework is not a rule or regulation, it does point to the possibility of future regulation efforts by the SEC and attempts at greater investor protection in the digital assets space.

5. Financial Reporting and Auditing

The invention of double-entry accounting during the Renaissance was revolutionary for business operations. By recording the total impact of a transaction through debits and credits, business owners came to better understand the underlying economics and complexity of their business activity. However, the Industrial Revolution brought overwhelming growth in business activity and increasing demand from investors for standardized financial reporting. While double-entry bookkeeping was sufficient for informing business owners about their financial position, investors and other third parties required financial accountability and validation of the reported financial data. This demand for a independent, third-party validation lead to the expansion of the audit practice (Byrnes *et al.*, 2012).

Like auditors, blockchain technology allows businesses to validate business activity for interested stakeholders. Consider two parties engaging in a transaction. Following double-entry accounting, each party records a debit and credit on their respective accounting ledger related to the transaction. Their accounting reports are separately audited and reported to the public. With a public blockchain ledger, the two parties could engage in "triple-entry accounting" and record the transaction both in their separate accounting ledgers and on the blockchain general ledger (Swan, 2018). Once recorded on the blockchain, the transaction is verifiable and immutable. It cannot be falsified or destroyed. Triple-entry accounting adds a third safeguard on reported information beyond the double-entry method and would provide interested parties, such as regulators, tax authorities, and investors, with an interlocked system of accounting records.

While widespread adoption of triple-entry accounting on a public general ledger may be far off, enterprises can still take steps to incorporate blockchain technology into their accounting systems to build trust and verifiability into financial reporting. Data privacy can be protected by recording transactions on a private blockchain. Rather than record all transaction data on the blockchain, businesses can create a digital footprint on electronic files containing transaction data (Andersen, 2016). Changes to the document trigger a change to the digital footprint, thereby creating an immutable time stamp on all document modifications. Recording more aspects of financial reporting on the blockchain will continue to enhance trust and accountability of financial reporting.

Recording transactions on the blockchain, either public or private, would greatly reduce the time required to perform an audit. If firms record transactions on a blockchain network, auditors will be able to access all transaction data in real time on a single system and provide clients with continuous assurance. This will greatly reduce the time and effort that traditionally goes into planning and executing an audit, as typically auditors receive a multitude of documents and files from clients in different formats and at different times. Blockchain technology can reduce the risk of an audit by allowing auditors to test the full population of transactions, rather than a representative sample (Bible *et al.*, 2017). Auditors can develop smart contracts that analyze each transaction and flag suspicious transactions in real time (EY Reporting, 2016). Continuous audit would reduce the time from transaction occurrence to transaction assurance, greatly decreasing audit risk.

While blockchain technology may reduce the demand for auditor transaction tracing and verification, many aspects of financial reporting will still require the opinion of an independent third party. Blockchain does not eliminate all opportunities for manipulation of financial statements, and not all fraudulent accounting practices can be prevented with triple-entry accounting. The transaction verification given by blockchain consensus provides transaction-level evidence of assertions, such as existence and occurrence, but does not provide sufficient audit evidence. Transactions verified by blockchain technology can still be fraudulent, illegal, between related parties, or incorrectly classified (Bible *et al.*, 2017). Auditors will still need to verify managerial estimation of accounting information and monitor the related party transactions and accounting classifications.

Auditors would have a new role in a blockchain accounting ecosystem. Blockchain verification technology will only be beneficial to financial statement users if it is implemented properly. Auditors will need to monitor the design of the blockchain system and smart contracts used in reporting accounting information, especially for private blockchains. Auditing internal controls over blockchain uses will be crucial. The Big Four accounting firms are preparing to audit transactions on the blockchain. PwC's Blockchain Validation Solution provides assurance by establishing a read-only PwC node on a client's internal blockchain where every transaction can be tested and those with specific qualities can be flagged for further review (PwC).

Blockchain technology provides the opportunity for business transactions to be both continuously audited and reported to interested parties. By encoding accounting rules into smart contracts, firms can create financial statements that are continuously updated with each transaction. Real-time financial reporting would have widespread implications for internal and external users of financial information.

Real-time reconciliation of transaction data into financial statements gives internal users a complete overview of business activity at a given moment in time. Continuous access to up-to-date data improves visibility into business operations and performance, leading to better decision-making and forecasting. Moreover, blockchain technology allows for efficient reconciliation across entities in an enterprise. Many organizations operate different accounting systems across their subsidiaries. With all transactions in an organization recorded on a blockchain general ledger, information sharing across units of an organization will improve.

If made publicly available, real-time financial reporting would have important implications in capital markets. While many active voices in US politics and across large organizations are criticizing quarterly reporting and advocating for reduced reporting frequency, technology is pushing financial reporting in the opposite direction. Blockchain technology gives businesses the ability to update stakeholders about financial performance in real time.

6. Integrated Supply Chains and Open-Book Accounting

The supply chains of enterprises today are better characterized as vast, dynamic information ecosystems rather than static chains. They involve multiple enterprises with unique systems collaborating on various value creation processes. Participants rely on information flow along the supply chain in managing business activity and responding to changes or shocks to their business environments. An efficient supply chain relies on trust, reliability, and transparency.

Over time, technology has improved to meet the needs of complex supply chains. RFID and Internet of Things technology have improved the traceability of inputs and finished goods along the supply chain, and improvements to Enterprise Resource Planning software have enhanced efficiency and collaboration. However, the lack of integration of information systems between enterprises limits visibility along the supply chain.

Incorporating blockchain technology across supply chains provides a solution to issues of trust, transparency, and visibility. Using blockchain technology, various activities and transactions between enterprises, such as delivery of finished goods, completion of compliance requirements, or movement of physical inputs, can be verified and reported in real time to all members of the supply chain. Beyond recording the movement of physical goods, blockchain could be used to manage an open-book accounting system, as already typically used in public sector procurement contracts. Participants can open their accounting books to their business partners, sharing granular details on their operations. These systems are best suited for long, committed purchasing agreements. An open-book accounting system gives participants transparency into the cost drivers and profits of their suppliers and can aid in cost management and contract negotiations.

Once transactions are recorded on the supply chain's general ledger, the transaction is verifiable and immutable. By providing a time stamp on activities, transactions, and costs, blockchain technology allows for real-time traceability along the chain (Deloitte, 2017). Enterprises using blockchain supply chain integration no longer must separately reconcile their own data with that provided by the other members of the supply chain. Each party along the chain has access to the same, verifiable information, increasing trust between parties and lowering the risk of engaging with more enterprises. Using private blockchains, access to supply chain information can be restricted to necessary participants, and data privacy can be maintained.

Beyond tracking the production process, blockchain infrastructure can be leveraged in the collections process. Typically, when work is completed or goods are delivered between two parties, an invoice is sent to the receiver who then delivers payment. Time lag between execution and payment can lead to outstanding sales balances. Blockchain technology provides an opportunity to connect payment to performance through smart contracts. Automatic digital invoicing can be implemented such that payment is triggered upon performance contingent on sufficient funds available in the payer's bank account (Swan, 2018; Brody, 2017). Again, integrating blockchain into invoicing reduces the risk of engaging with multiple enterprises along a supply chain.

Despite its benefits, there are roadblocks to incorporating blockchain into supply chains. First, to yield the most benefit from blockchain solutions, it is best to have every party along the supply chain agree to participate in the general ledger. Having multiple entities agree on this level of information sharing comes with challenges, as the technology is new, risks are not understood, and privacy is valued. Of the 600 executives surveyed by PwC in 2018, 45% believe the issue of trust could delay adoption (PwC, 2018). Second, in order to validate transactions on the blockchain, data about such transactions must be continuously generated. This requires linking physical activities to digital activities through technology like IoT and RFID (Deloitte, 2017). Through a process called tokenization, real assets such as raw materials are represented as a token on the blockchain, and any transactions in that asset are verified and traceable. An effective integrated supply chain using blockchain technology requires extensive investment in these technologies for use in transforming physical transactions into digital transactions on the general ledger.

7. Smart Contracts

Blockchain technology can be used to manage agreements between parties via smart contracts. While traditional contracts are enforced by the law, smart contracts are enforced by cryptographic code. After the transacting parties contracting over blockchain reach an agreement on the rules of their engagement, the rules will be coded into the contract, and once these predefined rules are met, the contract with self-execute. Through blockchain consensus, the agreement is verifiable, transparent, and immutable.

Smart contracts have the potential to disrupt many industries such as insurance and banking by mapping legal obligations into automated code, thereby eliminating the need for intermediaries and lowering contracting transaction costs. The self-executing nature of smart contracts also reduces concerns of moral hazard, as both parties can be confident that rule-breaking parties will face the consequences of the agreement. Once terms of a contract are violated, the violation is verified by the network, and the consequences are directly executed. For example, once limits or thresholds of financial ratios established in a smart contract debt covenant are breached by a company, the terms of the covenant, be it debt conversion, payback, or bankruptcy, will automatically execute.

The transparency and verifiability provided by smart contracts lowers the cost of contracting with third parties.

8. Concluding Remarks: The Blockchain Evolution and Revolution of Accounting?

It is clear that blockchain technology has the potential to transform the way firms manage their business internally and how firms interact with third parties. Blockchain solutions applied in financial reporting, auditing, and supply chain management may be the next step in the evolution of accounting. However, incorporating blockchain into business practices is not always the best solution. Oftentimes, there are other technologies better equipped to solve issues of data sharing, tracking, or verification. Blockchain solutions are best suited for situations in which multiple parties share and update data, there is a requirement for verification for that data, intermediaries add complexity, interactions are time-sensitive, and transactions interact with each other (PwC, 2018). If many of the above descriptions do not hold for a business process, it is likely a different technology is the best solution.

According to the executives surveyed by PwC in 2018, the top barrier to blockchain adoption is regulatory uncertainty. In a way, by removing the need for many intermediary institutions and central authorities, blockchain technology poses a threat to regulatory bodies. However, blockchain technology can also be a revolutionary tool for regulators. A blockchain ledger provides transparency and traceability to firms and could do the same for regulators. Firms can use blockchain technology — permissioned or permission-less — to track regulation around the world and make their compliance efforts visible to regulatory agencies. Regulatory blockchain solutions could facilitate monitoring and compliance efforts and transform the global regulatory environment.

References

Andersen, N. (2016), *Blockchain Technology A Game-Changer in Accounting*? Deloitte & Touche GmbH. https://www2.deloitte.com/content/dam/Deloitte/de/Documents/Innovation/Blockchain_A%20game-changer%20in%20accounting.pdf.

Bible, W., J. Raphael, M. Riviello, P. Taylor, and I. Oris Valiente (2017), Blockchain technology and its potential impact on the audit and assurance profession. CPA Canada, AICPA, UWCISA. https://www.aicpa.org/content/

dam/aicpa/interestareas/frc/assuranceadvisoryservices/downloadable documents/blockchain-technology-and-its-potential-impact-on-the-audit-and-assurance-profession.pdf.

Blockchain and the Future of Accountancy. (2018), ICAEW Thought Leadership. https://www.icaew.com/technical/technology/blockchain/blockchain-articles/blockchain-and-the-accounting-perspective.

Bourveau, T., E. T. De George, A. Ellahie, and D. Macciocchi (2019), Information intermediaries in the crypto-tokens market. SSRN Working Paper. https://papers.ssrn.com/sol3/papers.cfm?abstract_id=3193392.

Brody, P. (2018), How blockchain revolutionizes supply chain management. Digitalist Magazine by SAP. Digitalist Magazine by SAP, May 4, https://www.scribd.com/document/398280991/EY-How-Blockchain-is-Revolutionizing-Supply-Chain-Management.

Byrnes, P. E., A. Al-Awadhi, B. Gullvist, H. Brown-Liburd, R. Teeter, J. D. Warren, and M. Vasarhelyi (2018), Evolution of auditing: From the traditional approach to the future audit. Continuous Auditing (Rutgers Studies in Accounting Analytics), August, 285–297. https://www.emerald.com/insight/content/doi/10.1108/978-1-78743-413-420181014/full/html.

Continuous Interconnected Supply Chain. (2017), Deloitte Tax and Consulting. https://www2.deloitte.com/content/dam/Deloitte/lu/Documents/technology/lu-blockchain-internet-things-supply-chain-traceability.pdf.

Dai, J. and M. A. Vasarhelyi (2017), Toward blockchain-based accounting and assurance, *Journal of Information Systems* **31**(3), 5–21. https://aaapubs.org/doi/abs/10.2308/isys-51804?journalCode=isys.

Framework for "investment contract" analysis of digital assets, SEC Emblem (2019), https://www.sec.gov/corpfin/framework-investment-contract-analysis-digital-assets.

Ghaligai, F. and L. Pacioli (1521), *Summa De Arithmetica*. Firenze. https://books.google.com/books?hl=en&lr=&id=iqgPe49fhrsC&oi=fnd&pg=PP5&dq=Summa+De+Arithmetica.+&ots=CEyiga-vGb&sig=jmZIKu3B71njtetJzgbz28A101o#v=onepage&q=Summa%20De%20Arithmetica.&f=false.

Howell, S., M. Niessner, and D. Yermack (2019), Initial coin offerings: Financing growth with cryptocurrency token sales. European Corporate Governance Institute (ECGI), Finance Working Paper No. 564/2018, April 2019. https://www.nber.org/papers/w24774.pdf.

Nakamoto, S. (2008), Bitcoin: A peer-to-peer electronic cash system. https://bitcoin.org/bitcoin.pdf.

New study: 80% of ICOs are scams, only 8% reach an exchange. (2018), *Bitcoin News*. https://news.bitcoin.com/80-of-icos-are-scams-only-8-reach-an-exchange/.

Palmer, D. (2019), G7 Forming Task Force in Response to Facebook's Libra Cryptocurrency, CoinDesk. CoinDesk, https://www.coindesk.com/g7-forming-task-force-in-response-facebooks-libra-cryptocurrency.

Pfeffer, J. (2017), An (institutional) investor's take on cryptoassets, Medium. John Pfeffer. https://medium.com/john-pfeffer/an-institutional-investors-take-on-cryptoassets-690421158904.

PricewaterhouseCoopers. PwC blockchain validation solution. PwC, n.d. https://www.pwc.com/us/en/products.html.

PricewaterhouseCoopers. (2019), PwC's global blockchain survey 2018. PwC. Accessed September 1, 2019. https://www.pwc.com/jg/en/publications/blockchain-is-here-next-move.html.

Regulation of cryptocurrency around the world. (2018), Law Library of Congress, June 2018. https://www.loc.gov/law/help/cryptocurrency/cryptocurrency-world-survey.pdf.

Reporting, E. Y. (2016), How blockchain could introduce real-time auditing, EY. EY, https://www.ey.com/en_gl/assurance/how-blockchain-could-introduce-real-time-auditing.

Sterley, A. (2019), Cryptoassets: Accounting for an emerging asset class, *The CPA Journal* June 19, 2019. https://www.cpajournal.com/2019/06/21/cryptoassets-accounting-for-an-emerging-asset-class/.

Swan, M. (2018), Blockchain economics: "Ripple for ERP", *European Financial Review* 24–27. https://melanieswan.com/documents/RippleERP.pdf.

Tysiac, K. (2017), Blockchain: An opportunity for accountants? or a threat? *Journal of Accountancy* **17**. https://www.journalofaccountancy.com/news/2017/nov/blockchain-opportunity-for-accountants-201717900.html.

Vetter, A. (2018), Blockchain is already changing accounting, *Accounting Today*. https://www.accountingtoday.com/opinion/blockchain-is-already-changing-accounting#:~:text=%E2%80%9CBlockchain%20now%20gives%20us%20a,implement%20blockchain%20in%20their%20work.

https://doi.org/10.1142/9789811220470_0007

Chapter 7

What Accountants Need to Know about Blockchain

Michael Alles*,‡ and Glen L. Gray†,§

* *Rutgers Business School, Department of Accounting and Information Systems, One Washington Park, Room 928, Newark, NJ 07102-3122, USA*

† *Department of Accounting and Information Systems, College of Business and Economics, California State University, 18111 Nordhoff Street, Northridge, CA 91330-8372, USA*

‡ *alles@business.rutgers.edu*

§ *glen.gray@csun.edu*

Abstract

Building on the work we have done in Alles and Gray (2019a, 2019b), in this chapter we try to provide a more balanced perspective on blockchain, explaining to an accounting audience why this technology has both much to contribute and what its caveats are. We will cover the basics of the technology underlying blockchain, explain its relation to bitcoin, and do so with a particular reference to what we feel accountants need to know about these technologies. For most accountants, technology such as blockchain is a means toward an end and not an end in themselves.

What the technology is used for is far more important than what the technology is and, hence, what accountants need to understand is the business context of blockchain.

Keywords: Blockchain; Bitcoin; Auditing; Distributed ledger.

1. Introduction

- *Blockchain Technology is the Most Significant Invention since the Internet and Electricity.*[1]
- *In a review of some of the greatest inventions that mankind has ever produced, including the printing press, electrical-powered devices and radio, blockchain was found to share many traits of these previous epoch-making inventions.*[2]
- *Is Blockchain History's Biggest Invention*?[3]

Nakamoto (2008) when launching the cybercurrency bitcoin introduced what is now known as blockchain technology, though the term is not used in the paper. Today, cybercurrencies and blockchain technologies are widely discussed in the general media, in universities, and by public leaders. For example, in 2019 the G7 finance ministers discussed the implications of privately run cybercurrencies, such as the proposed Libra by Facebook — a previously unthinkable proposition.[4] As the quotes above show, the consensus concerning blockchain is uniformly positive, with extraordinary claims being routinely made that blockchain will literally change the world.[5]

---

[1] https://medium.com/@markymetry/blockchain-technology-is-the-most-significant-invention-since-the-internet-and-electricity-f2d44a631ef6. Last accessed 8/25/2019 11:52:01 PM.

[2] https://www.investopedia.com/tech/blockchain-one-historys-greatest-inventions/. Last accessed 8/25/2019 11:53:24 PM.

[3] https://gainbitcoin.com/is-blockchain-historys-biggest-invention/. Last accessed 8/25/2019 11:55:00 PM.

[4] https://news.bitcoin.com/g7-agrees-cryptocurrency-action-plan-facebooks-libra/. Last accessed 8/26/2019 10:58:27 AM.

[5] https://www.mckinsey.com/industries/high-tech/our-insights/how-blockchains-could-change-the-world. Last accessed on 8/23/2018 2:14:44 PM.

Accountants approach blockchain with a similar uncritical enthusiasm. When advertising its September 2018 forum on blockchain, the American Accounting Association (AAA) described it as a "game-changing technology" and boasted that *The conference will highlight several use cases and the companies that are leading the blockchain transformation to demonstrate HOW organizations are radically changing their business models, processes, products, services, and uses of data.*[6] In their optimism, the AAA reflects the viewpoint of both accounting academics and the accounting profession.

Appelbaum and Nehmer (2018) confidently wrote, *soon the audit profession will be forced to examine blockchain in an engagement, and even blockchain events in a cloud.* Dai and Vasarhelyi (2017) provided the most comprehensive vision of a "Blockchain-based Accounting Ecosystem", arguing, *the accounting profession could largely benefit from blockchain, and its current paradigm may be eventually changed thanks to this emerging technology. Blockchain, as well as associated smart contracts, can be leveraged to securely store accounting data, to instantly share relevant information with interested parties, and to increase the verifiability of business data. Using blockchain technology, companies are able to generate new accounting information systems that record validated transactions on secure ledgers. Those transactions will include not only monetary exchanges between two parties, such as payments collected from clients, cash deposited to banks, etc., but also the accounting data flow within a company. Such systems would enable close to real-time reporting by instantly broadcasting accounting information to interested parties, such as managers, auditors, creditors, and stakeholders.*

Accounting researchers are matched in their enthusiasm by the accounting profession. Big-4 accounting firms are working extensively on developing blockchain-based applications. KPMG advertised that its Digital Ledger Services group enables clients to *seize the potential of blockchain today.*[7] It has collaborated with Microsoft to provide blockchain services on the cloud.[8] EY is also working with Microsoft on using blockchain for rights and royalty management, and the firm extols the

---

[6] http://aaahq.org/Meetings/2018/BlockchainAAA. Last accessed on 8/20/2018 3:48:18 PM.

[7] https://home.kpmg.com/xx/en/home/insights/2017/02/digital-ledger-services-at-kpmg-fs.html. Last accessed on 8/20/2018 4:41:20 PM.

[8] https://home.kpmg/xx/en/home/insights/2016/09/kpmg-and-microsoft-blockchain-services.html. Last accessed 7/25/2020 7:12:02 PM.

technology more generally, stating, *Blockchain technology has the potential to universally reshape the way business transacts across nearly every industry in the global economy.*[9] In a presentation at the 2019 AAA annual meeting, EY's Sean Seymour added, *Blockchains will do for networks of enterprises and business ecosystems what ERP did for the single company.* This is a view echoed by PWC: *imagine being able to transfer value or prevent contractual disputes over the internet — without going through a third party. Confidently. Securely. Almost instantly. Blockchain-based technology could revolutionize business practices as we know them.*[10] Deloitte claimed that *We've compiled breakthrough research to show how blockchain can not only lower the risk of fraud, it can increase efficiency, improve customer loyalty, and make your organization smarter.*[11]

Deloitte, in its 2018 survey on the use of blockchain, claim made the that *Blockchain is getting closer to its breakout moment with every passing day.* The survey findings present a uniformly optimistic view of the interest by businesses in the technology: *74 percent of all respondents' report that their organizations see a "compelling business case" for the use of blockchain — and many of these companies are moving forward with the technology. About half of that number (34 percent) say their company already has some blockchain system in production, while another 41 percent of respondents say they expect their organizations to deploy a blockchain application within the next 12 months. In addition, nearly 40 percent of respondents reported that their organization will invest $5 million or more in blockchain technology in the coming year.*[12]

In contrast to all these uniformly positive views on blockchain, the Gartner 2018 CIO survey came as something of a shock: *Only 1 percent of CIOs indicated any kind of blockchain adoption within their*

---

[9] https://www.ey.com/en_se/news/2018/06/ey-and-microsoft-launch-blockchain-solution-for-content-rights. Last accessed 7/25/2020 7:14:26 PM https://www.ey.com/en_gl/innovation-financial-services/blockchain. Last accessed 7/25/2020 7:18:14 PM.

[10] https://www.pwc.com/us/en/industries/financial-services/fintech/blockchain.html. Last accessed on 8/20/2018 4:46:06 PM.

[11] https://www2.deloitte.com/us/en/pages/financial-services/articles/blockchain-series-deloitte-center-for-financial-services.html. Last accessed on 8/20/2018 4:44:07 PM.

[12] Both quotes from https://www2.deloitte.com/content/dam/Deloitte/cz/Documents/financial-services/cz-2018-deloitte-global-blockchain-survey.pdf. Last accessed 7/25/2020 7:20:20 PM.

organizations, and only 8 percent of CIOs were in short-term planning or active experimentation with blockchain.[13] Flinders (2018) attempted to explain the different responses to the surveys from Deloitte and Gartner by pointing out that the former interviewed executives rather than technologists inside businesses. The problem as he sees it is that executives feel compelled to show interest in the much-hyped technologies because of the fear-of-missing-out (FOMO), even as they fail to fully appreciate the true strengths and weaknesses of the technology and the challenges in coming up with a meaningful business case for its use. As Flinders (2018) wrote: *Every now and again a technology comes along that escapes its tank in the IT department. Before you know it people at the front desk are discussing it with customers. Then the business needs a strategy related to the said technology because everyone is talking about it. Even at the school gates parents are talking about something called blockchain instead of the next play date for their kids. And MPs are using the term so as not to appear out of touch. This is a bit of a headache for the IT department.*

Our concern is that accounting researchers are falling into the same trap that Flinders (2018) identified, i.e., of jumping onto the blockchain bandwagon both because it is the sexiest new technology out there and because they too exhibit a fear-of-missing-out response with regard to emerging research areas. The drawback with following an FOMO strategy is that it can lead to the adoption of emerging technologies without fully understanding the business context, which will determine their actual use and evolution. Researchers, too, have a tendency to see new technologies from the perspectives they are familiar with without considering as to whether it makes sense to do so.

For example, there is much work being done on the auditing of blockchains (AICPA, 2017; Applebaum and Nehmer, 2018; Rozario, 2018; Kozlowski, 2018) and that brings to mind the fact that an earlier technology that caught the attention of accounting researchers, XBRL, also resulted in a series of papers on the need to audit it. Plumlee and Plumlee (2008), Srivastava and Kogan (2010), Boritz and No (2009), and Boritz and No (2011), as well as the practitioner literature (AICPA, 2002; Trites, 2005, 2006), proposed conceptual frameworks for the assurance of XBRL filings. However, as Alles and Gray (2012) pointed out, none of these

[13] https://www.gartner.com/en/newsroom/press-releases/2018-05-03-gartner-survey-reveals-the-scarcity-of-current-blockchain-developments. Last accessed 7/25/2020 7:25:21 PM.

studies considered the fact that filing an XBRL-tagged financial statement was relatively speaking so cheap that it was unlikely that businesses would be willing to pay much to audit them. Indeed, even today, only in India is it mandatory to audit XBRL documents (and such audit engagements pay very little) and no other country seems to have given the matter much thought.

We wish the accounting literature to avoid the problem it had with XBRL, when what is a derivative technology had expectations placed upon it that could never be met. Keep in mind, too, that XBRL rapidly became standardized under the control of XBRL International and then became mandated for US public companies by the SEC. By contrast, over a decade after its launch by Nakamoto (2008) of bitcoin, there is no accepted definition of blockchain and no standardized version of blockchain.

Many authors have predicted major changes in business, accounting, and auditing because of blockchain. However, there has been little to no opportunity to test any of these predictions. Indeed, the number of actual blockchain applications other than cryptocurrency seems to be very small. Articles and speakers will frequently mention examples of blockchain applications in a present tense (e.g., Company A is using blockchain for a particular activity). Yet, on further investigation, it becomes clear that the initiatives are only at the pilot stage, or perhaps still being discussed and developed, while others may have already been abandoned.

For example, at the 2018 AAA Annual Meeting, the ICAEW held a panel (consisting of an academic, and representatives from the PCAOB, the Big-4, and the ICAEW) on the Audit Implications of Blockchain. The speakers mentioned Walmart's use of blockchain to track mangos and a blockchain-based trading system by the Depository Trust and Clearing Corporation (DTCC). Subsequent analysis indicates that this is only a pilot project and there is no discussion of whether or when it will become fully operational (Kamath, 2018). The frequently touted Depository Trust and Clearing Corporation (DTCC) system that was going to use blockchain to process billions of dollars of bond transfers was never developed and was abandoned.[14] Similarly, a pilot project by Cook County in Illinois to use blockchain for handling real estate

---

[14]https://www.coindesk.com/enterprises-building-blockchain-confront-tech-limitations/. Last accessed on 8/23/2018 2:44:39 PM. Presumably the AAA panelists were unaware of the skeptical comments made by Mr. Manner of the DTCC, quoted above.

property titles has also been abandoned.[15] At the ICAEW panel, an audience member also asked the panel exactly how audit procedures will change because of blockchain. No one on the panel could answer that question. One reason is that probably no one has attempted to audit one of the rare actual operational blockchain application.

To complement the extraordinary claims made for blockchain in the quotes presented at the beginning of the introduction, consider the following alternative perspectives:

- *It's either going to be a holy mess or it's going to change the world.*[16]
- *Basically, it became a solution in search of a problem.*[17]
- *There is no single person in existence who had a problem they wanted to solve, discovered that an available blockchain solution was the best way to solve it, and therefore became a blockchain enthusiast.*[18]
- *Rushing into blockchain deployments could lead organizations to significant problems of failed innovation, wasted investment, rash decisions and even rejection of a game-changing technology.*[19]

Just as it is essential that accountants understand why there is so much enthusiasm for blockchain technology by so many — including and especially the Big-4, the AICPA, and the AAA — it is equally important to know why some express caution about this technology.

Building on the work we have done in Alles and Gray (2019a, 2019b), in this chapter we try to provide a more balanced perspective on blockchain, explaining to an accounting audience why this technology has both much to contribute and what its caveats are. We will cover the basics of the technology underlying blockchain, explain its relation to bitcoin, and

---

[15] https://www.ajc.com/technology/could-blockchain-technology-transform-homebuying/qjXLbqDIjRo0MCmZfeZJMO/. Last accessed 7/25/2020 7:30:28 PM.

[16] John Wolpert, IBM's Director of "Global Blockchain Offering". https://bitcoinmagazine.com/articles/ibm-wants-to-evolve-the-internet-with-blockchain-technology-1459189322. Last accessed 7/25/2020 7:53:51 PM.

[17] Murray Manner, Head of clearing agency services at the Depository Trust and Clearing Corporation (DTCC). Quoted by Irrera and McCrank (2018).

[18] Stinchcombe (2018).

[19] Gartner's Vice-President David Furlonger, quoted in https://www.cioandleader.com/article/2018/05/03/rushing-blockchain-deployments-could-lead-failed-innovation-and-wasted-investment. Last accessed 7/25/2020 7:32:15 PM.

do so with particular reference to what we feel accountants need to know about these technologies. For most accountants, technology such as blockchain is a means toward an end and not an end in themselves. What the technology is used for is far more important than what the technology is and, hence, what accountants need to understand is the business context of blockchain. Providing that is our objective in this chapter.

2. What is Blockchain?

The Webster's dictionary defines blockchain as *a digital database containing information (such as records of financial transactions) that can be simultaneously used and shared within a large decentralized, publicly accessible network.*[20] Many might object to this definition since it also fits Wikipedia or any ERP system. The Oxford dictionary states that blockchain as *a system in which a record of transactions made in bitcoin or another cryptocurrency are maintained across several computers that are linked in a peer-to-peer network.*[21] The problem with this definition is obvious: far from clarifying the distinction between blockchain technology and bitcoin and other cryptocurrencies, it combines the two. The International Standards Organization (ISO) is still in the early stages of developing a standard description of blockchain.[22]

Jeffries (2018) and Bo (2018) discussed the weaknesses of these and other definitions of blockchain and pointed out that the reason is not a linguistic one, but rather, the confusion in practice as to what a blockchain is. As Jeffries (2018) wrote: *There are countless blockchain explainers in text, audio, and video around the web. Almost all of them are wrong because they start from a false premise. There is no universal definition of a blockchain, and there is widespread disagreement over which qualities are essential in order to call something a blockchain.* Indeed, some attempts at defining blockchain add more confusion than clarity. For example, Ethereum co-founder Gavin Woods, asserted that, *A Blockchain is a Byzantine-Fault-Tolerant decentralized singleton fixed-function*

---

[20]https://www.merriam-webster.com/dictionary/blockchain. Last accessed on 8/21/2018 3:07:44 PM.

[21]https://en.oxforddictionaries.com/definition/blockchain. Last accessed on 8/21/2018 3:09:53 PM.

[22]https://www.iso.org/committee/6266604.html. Last accessed on 8/21/2018 3:37:08 PM.

state-transition system.[23] However, two of the experts whose work was cited in Nakamoto (2008) themselves rejected this definition, and even if it was an accurate characterization, it is simply beyond the ability of most accountants to understand.[24]

Narayanan and Clark (2017) provided an academic perspective on the development of bitcoin. From their perspective as computer science and information technology researchers, they considered the work by Nakamoto (2018) as the culmination of decades of work in cryptography, computer science, databases, and other related technologies. As they say, *this is not to diminish Nakamoto's achievement but to point out that he stood on the shoulders of giants.* Narayanan and Clark (2017) concluded that *Nakamoto's genius, then, wasn't any of the individual components of bitcoin, but rather the intricate way in which they fit together to breathe life into the system.* Perhaps the most important insight that Narayanan and Clark (2017, emphasis added) provided in their article is about going from bitcoin to blockchain: *So far, this article has not addressed the blockchain, which, if you believe the hype, is bitcoin's main invention. It might come as a surprise to you that Nakamoto doesn't mention that term at all. In fact, the term blockchain has no standard technical definition but is a loose umbrella term used by various parties to refer to systems that bear varying levels of resemblance to bitcoin and its ledger.*

Contrary to the dismissive perspective of Narayanan and Clark (2017), "various levels of resemblance to bitcoin and its ledger" is actually a good a definition of blockchain in practice today. In developing bitcoins for an entirely trustless world with no intermediates, Nakamoto (2008) placed emphasis on being permissionless and trustless. In practice today, there are many blockchain initiatives that only involve trusted partners, or even a single partner. Bo (2018, emphasis in original) wrote emphatically that *A major disambiguation source is the* (*missing*) *distinction between public* (*permissionless*) *and private* (*permissioned*) *blockchains. Here we have a clear bifurcation, a fork considering that we are on the subject: experts beginning to affirm that private blockchains are not blockchain.* Obviously, the many initiatives that do use private blockchains would disagree equally strenuously with Bo's (2018) last

[23] https://www.slideshare.net/gavofyork/blockchain-what-and-why. Last accessed 8/19/2019 3:52:03 PM.

[24] We are indebted to Eric Cohen for obtaining the views of those experts as to Gavin Wood's proposed definition.

statement. Nonetheless, it raises the question of how far one can drift from the bitcoin infrastructure and still be in the same technological domain. If enough of the principles developed by Nakamoto (2008) are lost or relaxed, one ends up with just another database. On the contrary, that might suffice to address the particular business problems at hand. The fact is that with no accepted definition of blockchain, users are free to experiment as they see fit and as a result make the likelihood of one accepted definition arising even more remote.

3. From Blockchain to Bitcoin

Defining blockchain as a progression away from, or equivalently, toward the essential characteristics of bitcoin, we can understand the various applications of blockchain that are being attempted by showing the evolution of a system from its most basic, a ledger, to the full panoply of bitcoin.

Figure 1 illustrates the evolution of a simple blockchain database to an elaborate blockchain application such as bitcoin. Let us assume our

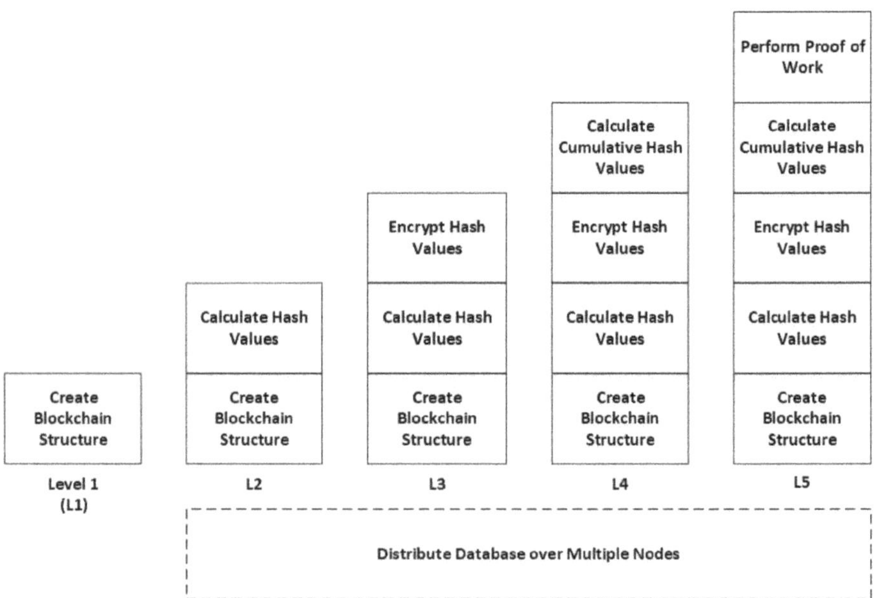

Figure 1: Evolution from simple to complex blockchains.

company, AGE, has a smartphone app for e-coupons. These are BOGO (by one/get one free) coupons for participating restaurants. The e-coupons are sold in an e-book of 10 coupons for $50. Starting at Level 1 (L1), a blockchain data structure is a linear back-linked structure where each transaction or event is stored as one block. A new e-book transaction will be stored as a new block that points to or links to the previous block. The very first block is referred to as the genesis block. Each block would contain whatever transaction information the developer considered appropriate, such as customer ID, quantity of e-books purchased, payment method, and transaction date.

Moving to L2, the developer might have the program create a hash value for each block based on the specific bytes included in the block. Hash values (or hash sums or hash codes) are typically used to detect changes in data. If someone accidentally or intentionally tried to change the content of the block, then the block hash value would no longer be correct. If the hash value is stored in plain text, a nefarious person could also edit the hash value so that the subsequent changes in content would be successful.

To prevent easy changes to the hash value, as indicated in L3, the hash value could be encrypted using any encryption technique (for example, using the SHA 256 cryptographic hash algorithm used in bitcoin) so, if the perpetrator would see the hash value in the encrypted form, he or she would not be able to edit the hash value to disguise the changes in the block's contents (bitcoin applies the SHA 256 encryption twice). With that said, with enough computer resources, an encrypted hash value could be de-encrypted. The computer resources and time would depend on the level of encryption (for example, 8-bit, 16-bit).

Moving to Level 4, in addition to having an encrypted hash value for each block, the whole blockchain would have an encrypted hash value. So, the hash value for block 2 would reflect the data in both block 1 and block 2. The hash value in block 1,000 would reflect all the data from block 1 through block 1,000. This running accumulative hash value is relatively easy to calculate in that the accumulated hash value for block 1,000 would equal the accumulated hash value in block 999 plus the hashing of the new data in block 1,000. However, the subsequent changing of the data in one block and then updating all the subsequent accumulated encrypted hash could good become prohibitively expensive requiring tremendous computer resources. In other words, if a person tried to change the contents of block 15, the hash values would have to be changed in blocks 15, 16, and all subsequent blocks to the very last block of the blockchain. Authors frequently refer to blockchains as being immutable. They are not 100% immutable. It is possible to change the data in a blockchain, but since it would be prohibitively expensive, the transaction cost greatly outweighs any benefit that would be derived from the change.

So far, the example would be referred to as a private or permissioned blockchain in that our example is a single company developing a blockchain for their internal use to store sales transactions. Now let us jump to Level 5 and change the scenario significantly to a public or permissionless blockchain.

Currently, an e-coupon is worth $5. If the coupon holder went to a restaurant and purchased a $40 meal, the net savings on the "free" meal is $35. If the meal was $100, then the net savings would be $95. So, let's assume that some enterprising entrepreneurs decide that there could be a secondary market for these e-coupons Someone might be willing to pay $30 for a coupon if there were going to a very expensive restaurant where the meal might be $100. They would still save $70 if they paid $30 for the coupon.

Now we assume we have a blockchain application where anybody can buy and sell these e-coupons in a secondary market. It is just an exchange of people selling coupons to other people with whom they have no pre-established relationship. Bitcoin is a specific kind of this exchange where people who do not know or necessarily trust each other can exchange cryptocurrencies. Like bitcoins, our e-coupons have no intrinsic value: they are just bytes on data storage devices. Because there is no pre-established relationship or trust, the system must be designed so that it's virtually impossible to change transactions after they are posted.

To the encryption process in Level 4, we are going to add a new twist. The resulting encrypted hash value must meet a particular pattern. Therefore, if the computer encrypts the accumulated blockchain data and the resulting encrypted hash value does not meet the specified pattern, then the hash value is rejected, and the encrypted value has to be recalculated. This process will be repeated over and over until the hash value meets the specified pattern. Creating the appropriate hash value is referred to in the Bitcoin application as proof of concept. As we saw, with bitcoin, there is a reward in terms of new bitcoins for whomever achieves the appropriate encryption. For bitcoin, the individuals trying to earn these rewards by submitting the correct solution are referred to as miners. Anybody can be a bitcoin miner; they just have to attach their computer to a specific IP address and download some bitcoin software. A person could use their desktop PC to do the mining, however, because there is so much competition, particularly when the value of bitcoins increases, miners use more expensive ASIC computers that are specifically designed to do the proof-of-concept processing.

As we move from Level 1 to Level 5, it becomes more and more difficult to change the data legitimately. For example, let us say the customer's order is stored in block 3 and the customer wants to subsequently change the order quantity from 1 e-book to 3 e-books. For Level 1, that would be a simple edit to change the number in the quantity field from 1 to 3. For Level 2, the hash value in block 3 would have to be updated. For Level 3, the hash value would have to be updated and re-encrypted. These changes would be relatively straightforward and would take microseconds to update because in Levels 1 through 3 the blocks are independent of each other. However, when we get to Level 4 changing data in block 3 means the encrypted hash values will need to be recalculated and re-encrypted for every subsequent block to the end of the blockchain. If there are thousands or millions of blocks, that process becomes too expensive and it becomes easier to append a new block at the end of the blockchain that includes the appropriate changes. Of course, this creates a potential problem in that a specific order appears at two different locations in the blockchain. The program or app that is being used to manage the blockchain data would have to be designed for that possibility and always use the most current version of the order. Because of the sheer size of the Bitcoin blockchain, transactions are never modified or appended.

To be clear, all of the configurations from L1 to L5 are potentially feasible configurations depending the specific applications being developed. Some authors use the terms blockchain and distributed ledgers (distributed ledger technology, DLT) interchangeably as if the two terms are identical; however, as shown in Figure 1, a blockchain data structure could be implemented on a single computer (Level 1). Nevertheless, as we illustrate at the bottom of Figure 1, we could have a distributed blockchain infrastructure at any level. A company may choose to keep duplicate distributed copies of the blockchain updated on other servers (local or remote) as a backup strategy. If customers can enter their own orders into the order entry system, it might be advantageous that they also keep distributed copies of the blockchain for their own edification of their order activity history. So, depending on the specific design of the private blockchain, the distributed aspect of the blockchain is a separate optional design decision. With public blockchain, applications, such as Bitcoin, where there are no established relationships between traders having many copies of the database are essentially mandatory.

4. Placing Blockchain in Its Business Context

Having understood the technical background of bitcoin and how many blockchain applications diverge from it, we can now turn to the business context of those applications. Hence, we now put blockchain technology as a means toward an end in a business process. This business environment has four layers: it starts with a layer of transactions which takes place in the "real world", be it transporting shipping containers through a global supply chair or buying and selling bitcoins.

The key point we make is that the distributed ledger is not the reality, rather, it is a nominal representation of it, just like all accounting ledgers are lists of debits and credits reflecting the underlying actual exchange of good and services for money. In other words, the blockchain is a storage layer, a dataset that records the metric of the real-world transactions taking place in the transaction layer.

Hence, there has to be some sort of recording protocol that transforms the transactions in the real world into the data stored in the blockchain distributed ledger. Finally, on top of that blockchain storage layer is an application layer that is made up of the distributed ledger, for example, buying a pizza with bitcoins or a customs official accessing bills of lading for a shipping container. On top of that application layer is another real-world transaction layer consisting of the decisions made and actions undertaken as a result of accessing the data in the blockchain, but there is no need for us in this chapter to concern ourselves with that.

APPLICATION LAYER
BLOCKCHAIN-BASED STORAGE LAYER
RECORDING PROTOCOL
TRANSACTION LAYER

In practice, each of these layers is fragmented today, even if all transactions take place within the same organization. Large companies have many ERP and other IT systems to store data. Many different protocols are used to record that data, and there are numerous handoffs in the transaction layer between different parties in the process chain.

The blockchain is meant to replace the numerous elements of the storage layer with a single, shared, immutable database. An important question is whether a distributed layer is necessary or another form of database is sufficient. In other words, whether what is important is the existence of a *distributed* ledger, or just a *ledger*. The more parties there are in the process chain and the less integrated they are, the greater the value in having a distributed ledger.

Hence, when tracking containers being delivered from one country to another, there are numerous handoffs from one supplier to another, there are interventions by custom authorities and so forth, and all these parties have to pass documents to each other and ensure that they are transmitted to the remainder of the supply chain. Having a distributed ledger with all information being both secure and visible clearly makes a lot of sense. Similarly, products such as diamonds and food have similar long and complex supply chains and a demand by end users to quickly and efficiently trace provenance of a particular shipment, for example, when there is a concern with food contamination: *For instance, Walmart has piloted the technology to track sliced Mexican mangos from orchards to its stores. Over 30 days, tens of thousands of mangos were traced on their journey from 16 Mexican farms, two packing houses, three brokers, two import warehouses, and one processing facility before eventually arriving on the store shelf. Using traditional manual, paper-based methods, it took almost a week to trace a specific mango back to the farm. With blockchain, that time was cut to 2.2 seconds!*[25]

However, it needs to be kept in mind that a unified blockchain-based storage layer is only feasible if all the players in the still-fragmented transaction layer agree to use it and its accompanying communication protocol. Much of the blockchain literature assumes that having a DL in the recording layer automatically results in agreement from all players in the transaction layer and almost no attention is paid to how easy it is for these players to access the necessary communication protocol. Consider the case when Walmart used of blockchain to track and monitor pork products. Kamath (2018) explains what is involved: *For pork, the process begins at pens — where every pig is smart-tagged with bar codes — and follows the product all the way to packaged pork. While using radio frequency identification and cameras, participants record*

[25] https://pcaobus.org/News/Speech/Pages/what-auditors-need-to-know-blockchain-other-emerging-technologies.aspx. Last accessed 7/25/2020 7:34:43 PM.

the pig's movement as well, and cameras installed in slaughterhouses capture the entire production process. These efforts protect both piglets and sows and modulate temperature so that babies stay warm while mothers stay cool (Clark, 2017). In pork production, shipping trucks have deployed temperature and humidity sensors, along with global positioning and geographic information systems, to ensure the meat arrives at retailers under safe conditions; Walmart can trace whereabouts of trucks and monitor conditions in each refrigerated container and, if conditions exceed established thresholds, receive alerts to prompt corrective action (Gale, 2017).

What Kamath (2018) does not explain is who pays for this elaborate system of tracking and how the data flow to Walmart's Food Safety Collaboration Center. Presumably, Walmart used its immense buying power to induce its suppliers to adopt this system and, given its past history, to bear most of the cost. Even assuming that this system works flawlessly (what happens if a sensor in a truck fails? Who is responsible and what happens to the food it carries?), it is clear that most of the value in this system comes from the extensive monitoring of the food and not the DL itself. Moreover, if the main user of this information is Walmart itself, it is not clear why the information needs to be distributed. Even if government agencies need to see the same information, they can access it using a simpler protocol than blockchain.

Even taking as given the value proposition of a blockchain storage system, a key vulnerability is the integrity of the link between the transaction layer and the storage layer. In the case of Walmart, the recording of data can be automated, for example, using RFID chips in the abattoir and temperature monitors in the trucks connected to the Internet of things. However, in other cases, there has to be a manual component to the act of communication.

For example, Kenya is also experimenting with using a blockchain-based land registry. However, whether in Kenya or in Cook County, when the blockchain is used to register title deeds, someone has to physically record the location and dimensions of the land and verify its actual ownership. When blockchain is used to track organic food, the farmer has to certify that they did not use herbicides when growing the food. In theory, some of that may be monitored using drones and sensors linked to the Internet of things, but in practice, that is likely to be prohibitively costly. There are two distinct factors here: making sure that what is recorded corresponds to the reality, as in the case of the location and dimensions of land being registered and that the data accurately reflect the human inputs into the transactions being recorded, as with the organic farmer refraining from using insecticides or artificial fertilizer.

These two together create what Alles and Gray (2019a) label the ***first-mile problem***: verifying that what the recording layer inputs into the blockchain storage layer actually corresponds to what is taking place in the transaction layer. How easy it is to resolve this problem depends on the nature of the good being transacted. In the case of a purely digital product, the reality is the digital record and so there is no first-mile problem by definition. In the case of physical products, the first factor — the correspondence between what is recorded and the physical reality — can be addressed by recording a "digital twin" of the physical item. This is what the blockchain company Everledger does with respect to diamonds, placing on its blockchain detailed measurements, photos, and even videos of each diamond. Clearly a "digital twin" cannot solve the second type of first-mile problem with respect to the human inputs since, in the absence of exhaustive surveillance, it ultimately depends on trust in the self-disclosures on human participants.

Not coincidentally, bitcoin is the purely digital blockchain product par excellence, where no first-mile problem arises. Indeed, even in cases of known fraud, some blockchain purists reject altering the digital record in order to prevent the perpetrators from benefiting: *Picture this: A thief steals millions of dollars by hacking into an investment fund. What if you could just hit the undo button and get that money back? That was the dilemma that the creators of Ethereum, an upstart digital currency platform, recently faced. Founded in 2015 by a group of researchers led by Russian–Canadian Vitalik Buterin — then only 19 years old — its currency, ether, is the second-most valuable digital currency after bitcoin. But the currency suffered a blow recently after a hacker siphoned $64 million worth of ether from investors. In the wake of the hack, Buterin decided to turn back the clock through a software update and reset the entire system to its previous state — i.e., before the hack. The reset created a so-called hard fork, which split Ethereum into two parallel systems. Buterin assumed most users would move to the reset platform, but the fork proved divisive and a small group of users continued using the old system, dubbing it Ethereum Classic and arguing Buterin had no right to reset the platform. That has confused cryptocurrency investors and cast a pall over the future of Ethereum. It also opened up a rift between the currency's creators, who were the ones to alter the code and render the stolen* *currency null and void, and dissenters who argued against any intervention — even in the face of an Ocean's Eleven-style heist.*[26]

One may consider the supporters of Ethereum Classic to be irrelevant extremists. Nevertheless, they raise the very important issue that when the only reality is the digital data, changing that data is not something that can be done too often or too easily before the entire system loses credibility.

In summary, blockchains cannot be discussed as a storage layer solution without placing it into the context of the transaction layer and the communication protocol that links one to the other. The first-mile problem arises when ensuring that what is recorded on the DL storage system actually corresponds to what takes place in the transaction layer. That is a given in the case of purely digital products when what is recorded is the reality by definition. If the goods are physical and it is possible to uniquely identify them through creating and storing a "digital twin", then the first-mile problem has a feasible *endogenous* technical solution. However, when actions of human participants have to be verified, then an *exogenous* verifier is needed to overcome the first-mile problem. This is possibly a role for audit firms or other trusted outsiders.

5. The Role of Accountants and Auditors in a Blockchain-Based World

Does the blockchain mean the end of accounting? ... many are asking if the advent of blockchain technology means the end of the accounting profession. The fear is that in a world ruled by irrefutable digital ledgers there may no longer be a need for those whose profession is built on confirming financial data. The answer may be that the blockchain may not eliminate the accounting profession but it is certainly going to change how things are done and the sort of skills that accountants will need to remain relevant.[27]

There are many that are claiming that blockchain will fundamentally transform the way in which accounting and auditing are practiced — if not

---

[26] https://www.cbc.ca/news/business/bitcoin-fork-splits-cryptocurrency-1.4231500. Last accessed 7/25/2020 7:36:28 PM.

[27] https://www.accountingweb.com/community/blogs/craiglebrau/does-the-blockchain-mean-the-end-of-accounting. Last accessed 8/27/2019 11:28:43 AM.

eliminate them entirely. Given the equally bold claims made about the effect of blockchain on finance, insurance, medicine, and many other industries, an open mind should be maintained about the technology's impact on accounting. If blockchain is indeed the "greatest invention" since the Internet, let alone the printing press, it may take years before its full repercussions are known.

On the contrary, as we have discussed above, while blockchain is highly innovative, it is also subject to various constraints. Most important of all is that the fact that its bitcoin origins mean that it is expressly designed for a world with no trust. This necessitates the imposition of very large transaction costs to verify the transactions, even if individual transactions have a low marginal cost.

This contrasts with the current payment systems, such as credit cards. Because they depend upon a trusted intermediary, like a bank or Visa/MasterCard, the user has to pay a relatively high cost with each transaction, but the recording and data storage layers require very little marginal cost and are orders of magnitude faster than bitcoin. Essentially, in the latter case each user pays for the services provided by the intermediary, while in the case of bitcoin, the lack of trust requires a high transaction cost to ensure system integrity. Various blockchain initiatives are trying to overcome the high-transaction cost mining that underlies bitcoin with such alternative as "proof-of-stake", but it is yet an open question whether doing so is feasible.

The other side of high transaction costs is the relatively slow speed of validation that translates into problems with scaling up to the size of transactions handled today by credit cards and other financial transactions handle by trusted intermediaries. As Deloitte states, *Blockchain can be slow. In contrast to some legacy transaction processing systems able to process tens of thousands of transactions per second, the bitcoin blockchain can handle only three to seven transactions per second; the corresponding figure for Ethereum blockchain is as low as 15 transactions per second. Because of its relatively poor performance, many observers do not consider blockchain technology to be viable for large-scale applications.*[28]

Many blockchain proponents seem to fail to grasp the difference between the cost of entering data onto a blockchain and of validating

---

[28] https://www.cnbc.com/2018/10/01/five-crucial-challenges-for-blockchain-to-overcome-deloitte.html. Last accessed 7/25/2020 7:38:52 PM.

blockchain as a system. Consider the following, also from Deloitte (emphasis added): *The recently emerged Blockchain is a trustless, distributed ledger that is openly available and* has negligible costs of use. *The use of the Blockchain for accounting use-cases is hugely promising. From simplifying the compliance with regulatory requirements to enhancing the prevalent double entry bookkeeping, anything is imaginable.*[29]

One way of reducing the cost of blockchain is to have one technology backbone that can host multiple applications, all using the same validation mechanism. Ethereum and other similar initiatives offer for blockchain the equivalent of the Windows operating system that avoids the application-specific validation of bitcoin.

Assuming that this issue can be dealt with, how will blockchain potentially alter accounting practice? Deloitte offers one vision, and there are many others: *Blockchain technology may represent the next step for accounting. Instead of keeping separate records based on transaction receipts, companies can write their transactions directly into a joint register, creating an interlocking system of enduring accounting records. Since all entries are distributed and cryptographically sealed, falsifying or destroying them to conceal activity is practically impossible. It is similar to the transaction being verified by a notary — only in an electronic way. The companies would benefit in many ways: Standardization would allow auditors to verify a large portion of the most important data behind the financial statements automatically. The cost and time necessary to conduct an audit would decline considerably. Auditors could spend freed up time on areas they can add more value, e.g., on very complex transactions or on internal control mechanisms.*[30]

The last sentence is key, perhaps in a way that Deloitte did not realize. The question that accountants, and especially auditors, face is what is the value added that they do? It has been decades since they served as bookkeepers, with that function having been taken over by ERP systems augmented by bar code readers and RFID chips, drones, and the upcoming "Internet of things". Since recording is no longer one of their tasks, what

---

[29] https://www.finyear.com/Blockchain-Technology-A-game-changer-in-accounting_a35816.html. Last accessed 7/25/2020 7:40:41 PM.

[30] https://www2.deloitte.com/content/dam/Deloitte/de/Documents/Innovation/Blockchain_A%20game-changer%20in%20accounting.pdf. Last accessed 7/25/2020 7:41:51 PM.

over value added does blockchain provide to accountants and auditors? Let us consider the statement above in detail:

The key benefit of blockchain is *Since all entries are distributed and cryptographically sealed, falsifying or destroying them to conceal activity is practically impossible. It is similar to the transaction being verified by a notary — only in an electronic way*. This is the argument that a blockchain makes a dataset "immutable". While that may be a benefit, note that it also prevents the correction of errors in the ledger. More to the point, the question is how much value is added by having entries that are essentially notarized? Or, to put it another way, how many of the problems arising with accounting today, from financial fraud and the rise of intangible assets to the declining relevance of accounting disclosures, are due to having data destroyed?

Note, that we only mention one of the three claims the Deloitte makes, that blockchain makes it practically impossible to destroy or falsify data and conceal activities. The latter two claims are simply incorrect and reflect a misapprehension of what blockchain can do. It may be an immutable and highly secure database, but people will still decide which data are entered into the blocks — and which data do not. Hence, unless the entire data value chain including acquisition is fully automated with no possibility of human intervention, there is no guarantee that the data on the blockchain are either complete or correct.

In short, falsifying data and concealing activities so that data about them are not recorded will continue to be possible even with blockchain. All that can be said is that once data whether correct and/or complete or otherwise enter the blockchain, then it cannot be changed. That fact will certainly benefit IT internal and external auditors who currently have to check who has superuser access and what changes they made, but whether that will reduce the cost and time required to complete an audit "considerably" requires empirical validation. It is immutability and not "standardization" — which already takes place in any database, such as an ERP — that will save time. Accountants can be confident that once data are recorded on a blockchain, they cannot be altered, but unless and until the first-mile problem is overcome, there is no assurance that what is recorded so immutably corresponds to the reality of the transactions that actually took place. In other words, stating that blockchain enables accountants and auditors to *verify a large portion of the most important data behind the financial statements automatically* is only true in the limited sense with regard to the integrity of the database itself, and not in the larger sense of verifying that what is recorded in the blockchain is complete, corresponds to reality or is correct. As PCAOB board member Kathleen Hamm states: *Blockchain does not magically make information contained within it inherently trustworthy. Events recorded in the chain are not necessarily accurate and complete.*[31]

Ultimately, the real source of value added in accounting is the appropriateness of judgments made on accrual and estimates and their validation by auditors, and that process is entirely unaffected by the use of blockchain.

6. Conclusion

In this chapter, we have introduced accounting researchers to the basics of blockchain and bitcoin as technologies and to the issues that arise when they are applied to accounting. Blockchain may well fundamentally change both business and accounting practice. Nonetheless, it is no silver bullet solution to the inherent issues that necessitate accounting and auditing: the need to verify the correspondence between what is recorded in an accounting database and the reality that the data purport to record. This "first-mile problem" is what led to the invention of auditing in the first place and blockchain technology makes it more pressing and not less relevant as data become immutable. The fact that the first application of blockchain was in the purely digital product bitcoin, in which there is no first-mile problem by definition, gave the false sense that blockchain will eliminate accounting and auditing. That is not the case since the basic function of accounting is the systematic recording of physical transaction and their aggregation and summarization of those transactions into judgment-based reports. Blockchain has many benefits, such as the immutable establishment of provenance, but that addressed only a small part of the challenges that accounting is designed to resolve.

References

AICPA (2002), Third Party Assurance and Considerations Regarding XBRL Instance Documents of Audited Financial Statements. White paper.

[31] https://pcaobus.org/News/Speech/Pages/what-auditors-need-to-know-blockchain-other-emerging-technologies.aspx. Last accessed 7/25/2020 7:43:06 PM.

AICPA (2017), Blockchain Technology and Its Potential Impact on the Audit and Assurance Profession. White paper. https://www.aicpa.org/content/dam/aicpa/interestareas/frc/assuranceadvisoryservices/downloadabledocuments/blockchain-technology-and-its-potential-impact-on-the-audit-and-assurance-profession.pdf. Last accessed 7/25/2020 7:44:32 PM.

Alles, M. and G. Gray (2012), A relative cost framework of demand for external assurance of XBRL Filings, *Journal of Information Systems* **26**(1), 103–126.

Alles, M. and G. Gray (2019a), The first mile problem: Deriving an endogenous demand for auditing in blockchain-based business processes. Working paper, Rutgers University.

Alles, M. and G. Gray (2019b), Blockchain: Numerous dimensions and frequent misconceptions, Working paper, Rutgers Business School.

Appelbaum, D. and R. Nehmer (2018), Auditing cloud-based blockchain accounting systems, Unpublished working paper. Presented at the American Accounting Association Annual Meeting, Washington DC.

Bo, F. (2018), Blockchain: disambiguation problem. Medium.com. March 13. Available at: https://medium.com/swlh/blockchain-disambiguation-problem-ca72916bb51b. Last accessed 7/25/2020 7:46:43 PM.

Boritz, J. and W. No (2009), Assurance on XBRL-related documents: The case of united technologies corporation, *Journal of Information Systems* **23**(2), 49–78.

Boritz, J. and W. No (2011), Computer-assisted functions for auditing XBRL-related documents, Unpublished working paper. Iowa State University.

Dai, J. and M. Vasarhelyi (2017), Toward blockchain-based accounting and assurance, *Journal of Information Systems* **31**(3), 5–21.

Flinders, K. (2018), Who is right on blockchain Gartner or Deloitte, or even both? Computerweekly.com. June 26. https://www.computerweekly.com/blog/Fintech-makes-the-world-go-around/Who-is-right-on-blockchain-Gartner-or-Deloitte-or-even-both. Last accessed 7/25/2020 7:48:06 PM.

Jeffries, A. (2018), "Blockchain" is meaningless: "You keep using that word. I do not think it means what you think it means". Theverge.com. March 7. Available at: https://www.theverge.com/2018/3/7/17091766/blockchain-bitcoin-ethereum-cryptocurrency-meaning. Last accessed on 8/21/2018 3:18:19 PM.

Kamath, R. (2018), Food traceability on blockchain: Walmart's pork and mango pilots with IBM, *The Journal of the British Blockchain Association* **1**(1), 1–12.

Kozlowski, S. (2018), An audit ecosystem to support blockchain-based accounting and assurance, Continuous Auditing, pp. 299–313.

Nakamoto, S. (2008), Bitcoin: A Peer-to-Peer Electronic Cash System. https://bitcoin.org/bitcoin.pdf. Last accessed on 8/21/2018 2:20:59 PM.

Narayanan, A. and J. Clark (2017), Bitcoin's academic pedigree, *Communications of the ACM* **60**(12), 36–45.

Plumlee, R. D. and M. A. Plumlee (2008), Assurance on XBRL for financial reporting, accounting, *Accounting Horizons* **22**(3), 353–368.

Stinchcombe, K. (2018), Blockchain is not only a crappy technology but a bad vision for the future. Medium.com. April 5. Available at: https://medium.com/@kaistinchcombe/decentralized-and-trustless-crypto-paradise-is-actually-a-medieval-hellhole-c1ca122efdec. Last accessed on 8/21/2018 10:49:24 AM.

Trites, G. (2005), Audit & control implications of XBRL, The Canadian Institute of Chartered Accountants, December.

Trites, G. (2006), Interactive data: The impact on assurance, Assurance Working Group of XBRL International, November.

https://doi.org/10.1142/9789811220470_0008

Chapter 8

Management Control and Information, Communication and Technologies: A Bidirectional Link — The Case of Granarolo

Sebastiano Cupertino*, Paolo Taticchi† and Gianluca Vitale*

* *Department of Business and Law, University of Siena, Italy*

† *Imperial College Business School, London, UK*

Abstract

In literature, most of the authors recognized the role of information and communication technologies (ICTs) in improving business management practices, such as those of management accounting and control. Nevertheless, ICTs can produce complex problems that need to be properly managed. Management control activities can play a crucial role in the management of such complexities, representing a driver for ICT adoption. Despite this, very few studies focused on the role of management control system in the implementation process of a new technology. This chapter aims to address this topic by investigating the case of the biggest Italian milk company. The case study results show how management control system played a key role in managing innovation in its three main dimensions, fostering the introduction of a new ICT. For its part the ICT, after its adoption, affected several management control practices. This allowed us to demonstrate the existence of a bidirectional link between management control systems and ICT.

Keywords: Management control; ICT; Innovation; Case study.

1. ICT in Business Management: A Brief Overview

Information is a key topic for business management activities. In particular, information is the *lifeblood of accounting* as it is the principal source for managerial decision-making processes (Rainer and Cegielski, 2013). However, the higher the quality, validity, and timeliness of managed data, the higher the relevance of information and its correct use on managerial decisions (March and Hevner, 2007). Therefore, both managers and accountants have traditionally tried to find practical and technical solutions to better manage and analyze business data, in order to make decisions in more effective and faster ways (Taiwo, 2016). In recent years, this managerial attitude has been highly emphasized due to the need of firms to face a higher global market competition (Tarutė and Gatautis, 2014) and an increased complexity in business activities. On the contrary, the recent technological development, the so-called Industry 4.0, has led to a digitalization process of the economic activities through a wider use of information, communication, and technologies (ICTs) which helped companies in improving both data management and decision-making processes. In literature, several authors analyzed the effects produced by ICTs at the level of business management. The use of ICTs could minimize transaction costs and inventory and quality controls as well as reduce market barriers and lead to economies of scale (Ogundana *et al.*, 2017). ICTs could be also considered as strategic tools that enable businesses to compete on a global scale, with improved efficiency and closer customer and supplier relationships (Alam and Noor, 2009). Other authors highlighted the improvements that ICTs produced in terms of productivity and business growth (Ali *et al.*, 2013; Tarutė and Gatautis, 2014) as well as at business performance level (Consoli, 2012; Francis, 2013; Yunis *et al.*, 2018). Among the various business areas that may be affected by the application of ICT, one of the most analyzed in the literature is the accounting one. According to Francis (2013), in fact, the implementation of ICTs could produce significant impacts on accounting systems. In particular, ICTs could improve the functionality of accounting systems, increasing the timeliness of information availability and analysis providing an effective decision-making (Shagari *et al.*, 2015) as well as supporting accountants in their daily activities (Taiwo, 2016). About this, Dechow *et al.* (2007) demonstrated that management accounting and control can easily be seen to be dependent on information technologies but, at the same time, they also affirmed that the relationship between them is to be untangled rather than to be assumed. Moreover, since advanced ICTs can give rise to a series of complex problems, the Management Control System (MCS) can play a crucial role in the management of such complexities and, therefore, it is of great importance to study their relations with ICTs (Chapman, 2005; Hunton, 2002).

In the wake of these claims, to the best of our knowledge, the role of MCS as a lever for the ICT implementation appears a topic that is still underinvestigated. In light with this gap, the present research developed a case study with the aim to deeply understand whether and how MCS affected the introduction and implementation of an innovative ICT system, without neglecting the possible effects that ICTs can have, once implemented, on business management.

2. Business Background

Granarolo Group is the largest milk producer and one of the biggest agro-food companies in Italy, employing 1402 people with a turnover of over one billion euros. The Group is made up of a cooperative of milk producers which deals with the production of raw materials, and a joint stock company, namely Granarolo S.p.A., which deals with the transformation and marketing of the finished products.

Through a process of acquisitions which started around 2010, the Group significantly extended its product range mainly in three business areas: milk and beverages, which account for 37% of production; cheese and butter, accounting for 41%; and other food categories, such as pasta, snacks, and organic products, which cover the remaining 22% of production.

The fast expansion of the business combined with the increased variety of products highlighted the need of managing more efficiently the sale channels. For this reason, today, the Group uses different distribution systems: pre-sale and attempted sale channels, the B2B channel, and physical stores. Specifically, the pre-sale and attempted sales channels represent an innovative kind of sale which allows Granarolo to attract new customers and anticipate demand trends. Pre-sellers are independent agents who deal with the promotion of products with the aim of attracting new clients and generating orders. The pre-sales organization does not deal with the final sale but is concerned with the needs of the clientele and explains in detail the wide range of products offered by the company.

The attempted sale is an organized system of means, people, and administrative systems, which allows a B2B approach that is unconventional for the industry. Sales staff have vehicles loaded with products and periodically visit assigned groups of clients in order to sell products to them directly. In the case of Granarolo, the pre-sale and the attempted sale channels are highly interconnected. The pre-sellers take the orders and send them to an ICT platform that makes them available to the attempted sale team. The sellers, then, follow-up on these orders entered in the ICT platform and deliver the products to the clients. As part of their job, sellers also try to sell other products to the secured clients by addressing needs that may have remained unexpressed in the pre-sale phase.

With the expansion of the business, the B2B channel became more sophisticated and complex, incorporating a large number of new buyers and, consequently, increasing the amount of information to be managed. Overall, all activities associated with sales became more difficult to manage due to the vast amount of information to gather and analyze. Because of this, the need arose to update the technology supporting sales channels by investing in modern ICT solutions. Actually, the old ICT infrastructure was no longer able to handle the volume of data originated by the different sales channels. In 2015 Granarolo Group launched the omnichannel sales project named "Granarolo Sales Empowering" in partnership with Aton company which develops distributed computing solutions (i.e., applications for mobile devices supporting salespeople, maintenance operators, couriers, logistic operators and technicians, machine-to-machine applications, and IOTs). This project involved several Granarolo's business actors, such as users among sales reps, pre-sellers, and merchandisers besides clients. The aim of such an initiative has been to improve sale channels processes through the use of an Android ICT platform (ICT system) that allows the adoption of smart devices and a single application platform, managing orders both on the field and on the website, as well as merchandising, store accounting, and on-road sales activities. In other words, this ICT system is able to manage a large critical volume of data generated by multi-sources. Through a streamlined and flexible software infrastructure, the ICT system can convey a homogeneous data flow from clients to the head office and vice versa, allowing greater speed in responding to customers' needs.

The implementation of the new ICT system claimed for a deep re-engineering of the sales channels in Granarolo and a related rethinking of the role played by management control systems. In the next section, we present how Granarolo Group planned, managed, and monitored the introduction and implementation of the new ICT system, the impacts of such an innovative platform on specific business management practices, as well as the learning process that has been triggered by this experience.

3. How to Manage Innovation: An Integrated Approach of Management Control System

MCS can be defined as the organic set of various tools, practices, roles, and procedures used in the company in order to ensure that the behavior and actions of business actors are consistent with the organization's objectives and strategies (Abernethy and Brownell, 1997; Malmi and Brown, 2008; Merchant and Riccaboni, 2001; Otley, 1980; Ouchi, 1979). Moreover, MCS is crucial to the business development as it is able to support managers' decision-making in innovation management (Bedford, 2015).

Innovation, especially when it is technology driven, involves a plurality of business aspects. At the managerial level, any innovative process needs to be planned and managed in an integrated way, and this calls for taking into consideration the organizational, cultural, and technological dimensions that characterize it. The success of an innovation derives primarily from an integrated management approach (Giovannoni and Maraghini, 2011). Focusing exclusively on the technological aspect of an innovation process could be misleading. In the case of ICT solutions, technology alone could be useless if not accompanied by adequate training of people, re-engineering of business processes, as well as wide organizational change. These considerations are at the base of the innovation management method adopted by Granarolo. In this context, management control system played a key role. The Group has a structured and formal control system that consists of a dedicated department and of programming and control tools such as budgets, analytical accounting, and IT programs for monitoring corporate activities. These formal aspects of control are accompanied by a number of informal control activities mainly focused on the analysis of the external context and aimed to understand environmental and contingent dynamics.

3.1. *The role of Granarolo's MCS in managing the technological dimension of innovation*

In 2010, following the analysis of information provided by financial statements and the management control system, the management of Granarolo ascertained the obsolescence of the ICT tools supporting commercial activities. In particular, a key finding of the analysis developed highlighted that 70% of the firm's technological systems had a life cycle of about 8 years after which systems' efficiency would decrease and maintenance costs would start raising significantly. In this regard, the head of the ICT department stated:

> *The old ICT platform was no longer able to effectively manage the information and, therefore, the technological leap was mandatory ... Nowadays, the new system allows managing a greater amount of information and also making a faster use of it, favouring user's operativity, either in front of the customer or a shelf, at any given point of the sale process. Indeed, managing a critical quantity of data from various realities needs a simple and flexible software infrastructure, able to transmit a homogeneous data flow from users to the head office and vice versa.*
>
> Head of the ICT Department, Granarolo Group

The impulse to innovate also came from a careful analysis of the technologies available in the market:

> *The analysis of technologies available in the market showed that the hardware system used by the company was obsolete, since more advanced operating systems had been developed and were available in the market.*
>
> Head of the Management Control Department, Granarolo Group

The material and more formal dimension of Granarolo's MCS, represented by the analytical accounting, made it possible to ascertain the obsolescence of the existing technological infrastructure and the related costs. On the contrary, the immaterial and informal dimension of the MCS, consisting of the review of available technologies and analysis of market trends, supported the managerial decision-making processes. Moreover, the MCS played a key role during the implementation of the new ICT system, as such technological innovation required careful planning and control activities.

In the first phase, the management, due to the expansion of the sales channels planned for a certain number of devices to be installed. Then, the specifications of the new ICT platform were sorted, and all the necessary software-updating activities were carried out. A team was put in place to set up the project and manage the introduction of the new ICT system. This planning process was supported by an economic assessment of each phase, which found operational confirmation in the budget tool. The latter was drawn up considering a time extent of two years (the time needed for the full development of the technology) and had the dual function of programming the resources to be used in the innovation process and monitoring the results gradually achieved by comparing them with those planned. At the end of each implementation stage, the improvements achieved by the innovation process were checked, and an estimate of the possible return on investments (ROI) was calculated.

In the management of the technological dimension of this innovation, Granarolo's MCS had a dual function. At first, the MCS prompted the need for change and directed managers in the choice of technologies to invest in. Second, the MCS, through the tools of budget and analytical accounting, allowed to plan the various steps of the technology implementation process and to monitor the results that were gradually achieved. This contributed decisively to the successful introduction of the new technological infrastructure.

3.2. *The role of Granarolo's MCS in managing the organizational dimension of innovation*

The introduction of such an innovation inevitably led to a change in the organizational capabilities of Granarolo. In this particular case, the new ICT system supported the organizational expansion of the Group. Moreover, in the context of defining competitive capabilities, Granarolo's MCS played an important role. The monitoring activities of the external context, carried out by the management control department, revealed the need to expand product variety in order to be competitive in the global market. Starting from these needs, the management set up a business growth strategy through acquisitions, defining the related medium- to long-term objectives. These changes in the business model increased the managerial complexity, since they required the management of a big amount of data and information. To this end, the top management understood the need to enhance the old ICT system. Hence, the choice was between planning the purchase of a new technological infrastructure or opting for a specialized computing service in outsourcing. At this stage, the cost analytical accounting system led the top management to activate a dedicated leasing service contract with a computing solution commercial partner, instead of buying and adopting a new ICT system. Thus, Granarolo started a collaboration with a technology consulting company providing the technological infrastructure as well as support in innovation management. In this regard, the head of the ICT department stated:

> *We decided to have a partnership with Aton which provides us ICT support services in outsourcing from software development and user to device selection.*
>
> Head of the ICT Department, Granarolo Group

Before the introduction of the new ICT platform, the company employed sellers who tried to serve clients by bringing large quantities of products without having a clear idea of what they were really willing to buy. The selling process was mainly based on experience and sellers' ability. The new ICT system, by making data on clients' orders available in real time, allowed Granarolo to develop the figure of the pre-seller. The latter anticipates the sale by acquiring the order and entering the related data on the platform. In addition, through the development of the B2B channel, some customers can directly interact with the ICT platform by placing orders by themselves. The management department collects, manages, and distributes orders to sellers who know with certainty which products to sell and which clients to serve. Such an organizational change has led to greater efficiency not only in the context of distribution but also in the methods of conservation. Through this type of organization, managers and sellers become aware of the precise requests of their customers, delivering to them the exact number of products required. Doing this results in no waste and delivery times and methods are significantly improved as well, as sellers can optimize space and, in just one journey, serve a greater number of clients.

Actually, sellers are equipped with an electronic device (such as tablets) that provides all the information necessary to perform their tasks. This information is prepared daily by the management department that is in charge of checking the data regarding the orders that the system collects and then translates them into tasks for company operators. In this regard, the head of the management control department said:

> *The ICT system manages the information of the various sales channels and ensures that there is perfect alignment among the various operators ... presale and attempted sales, in particular, are interconnected: the pre-seller, when he closes an order, sends it to the ICT platform and the management control department prepares that order for the seller of the attempted sale. The latter, on the next day, reads the order on his device and serves clients who are in his area. Therefore, these are two interconnected realities: one takes orders and the other delivers. The ICT system, in this way, coordinates and facilitates activities by making them more efficient and effective ... The management control department, in such a scenario, prepares the materials for the order, specifying prices and quantities. Once we pass this information* [through the ICT infrastructure], *the seller takes his order through its device, makes the delivery, draws up a delivery note and finally uploads it on the platform.*
>
> Head of the Management Control Department, Granarolo Group

This organizational approach allows the management department to effectively coordinate the numerous salespeople, assigning specific tasks, objectives, and responsibilities to each of them.

The effective coordination of the various operators is also facilitated by the specificities of the ICT. The devices supplied to operators show them their performance and compare it with the budget forecasts and with the performance of previous periods (weeks, months, or years). This configuration provides sellers with benchmarks that allow them to self-assess the performance achieved. This ensures that operators acquire new accounting skills by virtue of which they take responsibility for the objectives and performance expected from them. Furthermore, the fact of reading the budget, as well as planning objectives and performances, has increased the agents' ability to plan daily actions and to carry them out in a rational and targeted manner. This has finally increased the awareness of the operators about the importance of accounting provisions in guiding their daily operations.

3.3. *The role of Granarolo's MCS in managing the cultural dimension of innovation*

The innovation process in an organization is strongly affected by cultural business aspects. This is indeed confirmed by the following statement:

> *Innovation was cultural at first.*
>
> Head of the ICT Department, Granarolo Group

When introducing innovation, it is essential to change the *modus operandi* as well as the business organization. Changes, however, are not always welcomed by employees who are often forced out of their comfort zones and expected to reshape their own routines and behaviors in line with new practices. The resistance of employees to changes can take place especially in cases of digitalization of business processes. In these cases, actually, people may be afraid that their tasks can be resized and partially or totally automated. In these contexts, managers are responsible for solving tensions and restoring psychological security among their employees by showing them the opportunities that can arise from opening to change. In Granarolo, these concepts were very clear even before the introduction of the new ICT system. From the point of view of employees, the cultural transition to the new system was perceived as not being problematic. In this regard, the head of the management control department stated:

> *In the context of attempted sales, the sellers, culturally, were already used to technology ... we just had to teach them the use of new technology ... so the cultural transition for sellers was smooth.*
>
> Head of the Management Control Department, Granarolo Group

Sellers had a strong motivation for change. This is mainly due to the fact that the new technology, faster and more precise, entails considerable savings of time. This was a decisive factor in the propensity for change.

The top management therefore only had to increase the operational skills of sellers through appropriate training. In the light of this, the head of the management control department confirmed:

The transition from the old to the new technological structure allowed sellers to recover about an hour of time per day, allowing them to be more effective and efficient.

Head of the Management Control Department, Granarolo Group

Surprisingly, the most difficult cultural change Granarolo had to manage came from the business clients, as they were not used to interact with the pre-seller figure, nor were they used to see Granarolo's operator with the tablet rather than the van. In this regard, the rep of the management control department reported an anecdote:

A client, not being used to buy from the pre-seller, as soon as he saw our operator with the tablet told him "Go out of here! I do not recognize you! Granarolo's operator is the one who comes here and offers me the products with the truck! You want to cheat me!"

Head of the Management Control Department, Granarolo Group

Because of these tensions with clients, Granarolo had to support the innovation process by introducing a Clients Relationship Management (CRM) system. Regarding this business practice, the head of the ICT area stated:

The CRM is an approach that not only allows us to manage the relationships with clients but also gives us the opportunity to have a direct relationship with clients, being able to carry out promotional activities ... Through this management practice and tool, we measure how many orders come from the presale, how many orders come from the attempted sale and how many from the B2B. Since the three channels are characterized by different activities, we are also able to check the effectiveness of promotional activities in the various sales channels.

Head of the ICT Department, Granarolo Group

CRM tools such as e-mail, video support, and a dedicated website have enabled Granarolo to disseminate information about its activities to clients in order to overcome their mistrust of innovation. The CRM system, therefore, has made communication with customers faster and more direct, improving its effectiveness. In this regard, the ICT manager confirmed:

> *The communication between the central office, or the trade marketing, and the client follows a human hierarchy ... information from the center must pass to the regional managers of the attempted sale, who in turn must pass it to the sale coordinators who are referents of multiple areas of attempted sales ... from the sale coordinators information must go to distribution agents and from the latter the information is communicated to the client ... In every step, there is potential loss of information ... the CRM allows us to have a direct communication with the client in such a way that we are no longer doing push activities but pull ... the client can request the activity or the promotion once we communicate it ... this makes the sales activity more effective.*
>
> Head of the ICT Department, Granarolo Group

4. ICT Innovation Impacts on Business

At this point it is useful to understand how, once implemented, the new ICT system has impacted business functions. Actually, its platform was able to store and provide in real time a large amount of data concerning clients' orders, business operators' performance, and budget forecasts. This infrastructure, therefore, had some important implications on several business aspects.

4.1. *Communication, coordination, and management decision support*

First, the availability of precise information about clients' needs and preferences supported the marketing function in decision-making. In particular, the solution developed by Granarolo allowed managers to evaluate the effectiveness of promotional activities in different sales channels and this supported them in making rational decisions about marketing strategies. Moreover, the new ICT platform facilitated communication between the management departments and business sellers. The greater speed in the transfer of data and information made the assignment of tasks by the management to sellers more immediate, as well as the communication of activities carried out and results achieved by the sellers to the managers. The information flows that managers pass to sellers and vice versa, therefore, was made timelier and more accurate following the introduction of the innovative ICT system into the company. This led to an improvement in internal communication which, in turn, led to a better workforce coordination. Moreover, the improvement of the coordination dynamics led to greater efficiency in sales activities by optimizing the time of products loading and delivery, as well as the time needed to take orders.

4.2. *Management accounting and control*

Accounting and control, by definition, are based on data originating from the results of management activities. Therefore, the availability of an extremely large amount of data related to different business areas can be as productive as dangerous. Actually, the increased availability of data could give a more precise overview of company results, but, without a proper adjustment of accounting systems, more data can also mean more confusion. In Granarolo, the accounting model had to undergo major changes. Before the introduction of the new ICT system, the accounting system reported the performance achieved for each sales activity and controls were carried out on a monthly basis.

With the introduction of the new ICT system, the greater frequency and speed of sales performance recording has changed the accounting structure up to the point that now accounts for business activities results are reported and analyzed on a daily basis. To date, therefore, managers can carry out real-time controls on the company's activities, being able to intervene more quickly in case of problems or deviations between the results achieved and those planned. This has also been confirmed by the head of the management control department who stated:

> *We have an automatic daily control of the performance of presellers and our agents that the system accounts for on a daily basis and relates to budget forecasts. As a result, we have a daily monitoring of the margins that the company makes on the various channels sales.*
>
> Head of the Management Control Department, Granarolo Group

More specifically, for each product, the accounting system registers the performance achieved by business operators and makes the historical performance achieved by operators and product categories available. This allows a continuous performance benchmark ensuring timely interventions. These data, moreover, are also made available to sellers who are constantly aware of their results, as confirmed by the head of the management control department:

> *Our agents can know their progress in comparison with budget objectives and previous year performance.*
>
> Head of the Management Control Department, Granarolo Group

In the case of Granarolo, once introduced, the ICT system changed both the accounting structure and the control practices, affecting, consequently, both formal and informal aspects of MCS.

4.3. *A tool for strategy execution*

As mentioned in the paragraph concerning the business background, Granarolo's expansion strategy required an adequate adjustment of the organizational structure and the ICT technologies. Given the support function provided by the new ICT system for the management of the sales channels, we can affirm that it became a tool for business strategy execution. The expansion strategy was also carried out through the development of new sales channels that, in turn, were made possible through the introduction of the new ICT system. In line with this, both the head of the management control department and the head of the ICT department confirmed the strategic relevance of the implementation of the new ICT system in the business development, as reported below:

> *The traditional attempted sale had become a limiting activity since, with the business expansion and the introduction of new and more complex products to sell, such as ginger yoghurt, gluten-free products etc., sellers of attempted sales were no longer able to serve all their clients daily (due to factors such as distance between one customer and another, traffic, maximum load of the van, etc.). In 2015, it was decided to combine pre-sale with attempted sales, to open the B2B channel and to implement an omnichannel technology that would support and align the activities of all our operators.*
>
> Head of the Management Control Department, Granarolo Group

Our new ICT system has supported the realization of our strategic objectives.

Head of the ICT Department, Granarolo Group

4.4. *Business performance*

The last business aspect affected by the introduction and implementation of the innovative ICT system to manage sales channels regards performance. In particular, the new ICT system has led to a process of dematerialization that has made the use of paper superfluous with positive effect also in terms of sustainability performance. The reduced use of paper, therefore, made it possible to achieve cost savings related to both the purchase of paper and the rent of warehouses where paper documents were stored, as stated by the head of the management control system:

The reduced use of paper leads to an annual saving of around 50,000 euros, as the dematerialization allowed us to no longer buy the paper ... we also rented warehouses where we store the paper that had a yearly rent cost of 100,000 euros ... therefore we have 150.000 euro of saving per year

Head of the Management Control Department, Granarolo Group

In addition to this, the new ICT system also had an indirect positive impact on the turnover. Actually, in the case of Granarolo, B2B sales and pre-sales channels increased significantly thanks to the impact of the new ICT platform becoming, therefore, a driver of revenue growth. This is confirmed both by the Head of the ICT department and the Head of the management control department:

We could no longer implement anything on the old ICT system ... if we were asked to manage more information, we could not manage it ... Thanks to the various acquisitions that we made, our products have increased significantly ... Consequently, the product package increased, the clients increased, the data to be managed increased and we could not manage them properly because the ICT system was obsolete ... The new infrastructure allowed us to overcome such problems supporting us in the development of new sales channels.

Head of the ICT Department, Granarolo Group

> *The pre-sales, at the end of last year, registered a turnover of 15 million euros and we expect to reach more than 24 million euros this year ... The B2B has a three-year plan; the last year reached a turnover of 700/800 thousand euros and, in the next few years, it is expected to reach 5 million euros.*
>
> Head of the Management Control Department, Granarolo Group

These statements demonstrate the success that the business expansion strategy had and, at the same time, underline the key role played by the ICT system in achieving these results.

5. Discussion and Conclusions

The case study presented shows how the new ICT system needed to be carefully managed in order to be successfully implemented and produce positive business impacts. In this regard, during the process of its adoption, managers had to involve, in an integrated manner, different business dimensions, the cultural, organizational, and technological ones. Especially in reference to ICTs, paying attention only to the technological aspect of innovation can be misleading. The neglect of the cultural and organizational dimensions may mean that ICTs do not fully express their potential or may even be counterproductive, since more data could mean more confusion. In the case of Granarolo, both cultural and organizational aspects were reshaped according to the technological aspect linked to the new ICT infrastructure. In this regard, the MCS, in its formal and informal dimensions, played a decisive role in supporting the management and balancing these three dimensions. From a formal and tangible point of view, the MCS, through the budget and analytical accounting, was able to plan and monitor the various steps of the innovation process. Conversely, from an informal point of view, the MCS, through cultural approaches, has supported the management in facing the tensions that inevitably emerge among those who are touched by innovation.

Considering this case study, it is clear that managing in an integrated way the introduction and implementation of an innovative ICT can maximize its effects on several business aspects. In other words, there is a bidirectional link between a good management of ICT innovation and its benefits on business management.

Actually, when properly managed, an innovative ICT system can lead to important managerial benefits. From the experience of Granarolo, it emerges that sales accounting and performance measurement were particularly affected by the introduction of the new ICT system. The latter, indeed, by providing real-time information about the activities of sellers, has enabled the development of timely and daily performance monitoring, as well as a longitudinal assessment of sales trends. From a more intangible point of view, the introduction of a new ICT system can also have positive effects on the capabilities of company operators. In the case of Granarolo, the new ICT system enhanced sellers' attention on both the performance achieved and the target to be reached, as well as the operators' attitude to self-evaluate and to feel more responsible in achieving the planned goals. Beyond accounting and performance measurement issues, an innovative ICT system can improve the coordination and communication dynamics within the company. Firstly, managers are able to optimize both the delivery methods and the coordination of the various agents operating in different business areas through the use of real-time information regarding the sellers' orders and activities. Second, the use of an innovative ICT system can produce positive effects on the corporate ability to manage and store a large number of transactions and information flows. Consequently, an efficient data mining and storage can produce positive effects in pursuing strategic objectives, relevant for the firm's growth. In particular, the Granarolo case highlighted that the implementation of an innovative ICT system efficiently supported the development and management of new sales channels that, in turn, led to an increase in sales volume with consequent positive effects on turnover. Therefore, the new ICT system also played a key role in enhancing the firm's economic performance. Lastly, the new ICT system implementation activated a dematerialization process which produced important cost savings due to the reduced use of paper.

What stated above reinforces the empirical evidence already present in the literature about the effects of ICTs on business management. At the same time, the case study also shows that these positive effects remain latent if there is no appropriate management of the innovation and of the complexity that it can induce. In this regard, it has been highlighted the key role of the MCS by demonstrating how, the latter, can be dependent on information technologies (in line with Dechow *et al.*, 2007) but, at the same time, ICTs can be also dependent on MCS and on its correct use in business management.

References

Abernethy, M. A. and P. Brownell (1997), Management control systems in research and development organizations: The role of accounting, behavior and personnel controls, *Accounting, Organizations and Society* **22**(3–4), 233–248.

Alam, S. S. and M. K. M. Noor (2009), ICT adoption in small and medium enterprises: An empirical evidence of service sectors in Malaysia, *International Journal of Business and Management* **4**(2), 112–125.

Ali, A., A. Abbas, and A. Reza (2013), The effect of information technology on organizational structure and firm performance: An analysis of consultant engineers firms (CEF) in Iran, *Procedia Social and Behavioural Sciences* **81**, 644–649.

Bedford, D. S. (2015), Management control systems across different modes of innovation: Implications for firm performance, *Management Accounting Research* **28**, 12–30.

Chapman, C. (2005), Not because they are new: Developing the contribution of enterprise resource planning systems to management control research, *Accounting, Organizations and Society* **30**(7/8), 685–689.

Consoli, D. (2012), Literature analysis on determinant factors and the impact of ICT in SMEs, *Procedia-Social and Behavioral Sciences* **62**, 93–97.

Dechow, N, M. Granlund, and J. Mouritsen (2007), Management control of the complex organization: Relationships between management accounting and information technology, *Management Accounting Research* **2**(4), 625–640.

Francis, P. (2013), Impact of information technology on accounting systems, *Asia-Pacific Journal of Multimedia Services Convergent with Art, Humanities, and Sociology* **3**(2), 93–106.

Giovannoni, E. and M. P. Maraghini (2012), *Dalla Creatività all'Innovazione. Approcci, strumenti ed esperienze per il governo dei processi innovativi in azienda*. Knowità. ISBN: 978-88-95786-05-6.

Hunton, J. (2002). Blending information and communication technology with accounting research, *Accounting Horizons* **16**, 55–67.

Malmi, T. and D. A. Brown (2008), Management control systems as a package — Opportunities, challenges and research directions, *Management Accounting Research* **19**(4), 287–300.

March, S. T. and A. R. Hevner (2007), Integrated decision support systems: A data warehousing perspective, *Decision Support Systems* **43**(3), 1031–1043.

Merchant, K. A. and A. Riccaboni (2001), *Il controllo di gestione*. Milano: McGraw-Hill.

Ogundana, O., W. Okere, O. Ayomoto, D. Adesanmi, S. Ibidunni, and O. Ogunleye (2017), ICT and accounting system of SMEs in Nigeria, *Management Science Letters* **7**(1), 1–8.

Otley, D. T. (1980), The contingency theory of management accounting: Achievement and prognosis, in *Readings in accounting for management control*, Boston, MA: Springer, pp. 83–106.

Ouchi, W. G. (1979), A conceptual framework for the design of organizational control mechanisms, *Management Science* **25**(9), 833–848.

Rainer, R. K. and C. G. Cegielski (2013), *Introduction to Information Systems: Supporting and Transforming Business*. John Wiley & Sons.

Shagari, S. L., A. Abdullah, and R. M. Saat (2015), The influence of system quality and information quality on accounting information system (AIS) effectiveness in Nigerian banks, *International Postgraduate Business Journal* **7**(2), 58–74.

Taiwo, J. N. (2016), Effect of ICT on Accounting information system and organisational performance: The application of information and communication technology on accounting information system, *European Journal of Business and Social Sciences* **5**(2), 1–15.

Tarutė, A. and R. Gatautis (2014), ICT impact on SMEs performance, *Procedia Social and Behavioral Sciences* **110**, 1218–1225.

Yunis, M., A. Tarhini, and A. Kassar (2018). The role of ICT and innovation in enhancing organizational performance: The catalysing effect of corporate entrepreneurship, *Journal of Business Research* **88**, 344–356.

https://doi.org/10.1142/9789811220470_0009

Chapter 9

A Brave New World: The Use of Non-traditional Information in Capital Markets

Partha S. Mohanram

John H. Watson Chair in Value Investing, Rotman School of Management, University of Toronto, Canada

partha.mohanram@rotman.utoronto.ca

Abstract

For a long time, three primary sources of information were relevant for capital markets. One was the financial disclosures provided by firms in their regulated periodical financial statements. The second was the information from stock prices and returns. The third was press coverage about the firms and their activities. The past two decades has seen a sea change in the way information is generated, transmitted, and processed. In this chapter, I outline some of these changes, with a focus on a new and potentially revolutionary channel for the generation and peer-to-peer sharing of information — social media. I also discuss the impact of the emergence of big data analytics and blockchain on capital markets. Finally, I conclude by outlining the implications of these changes on firms, information intermediaries, investors, auditors, and academics.

Keywords: Peer-to-peer information; Crowdsourced research; Social media; Twitter; Big data; Blockchain.

1. Introduction

Imagine you were a sell-side financial analyst in the year 1985. This is pre-Internet, and in most cases pre-email. Your most important tool is probably the rolodex of contacts on your desk. Your daily routine probably included reading *The Wall Street Journal* in depth and paying attention to what else might appear on the news wires about the firms you are following. If you had any questions, you would try to call the CFO or, at the very least, someone from investor relations in the firm in question. If you were one of the anointed few who worked for a large, well-connected brokerage house, you would get through. You had preferential access and could ask detailed questions and obtain cutting-edge insights from the horse's mouth as it were. You could attend invitation-only conference calls, where managers would share information in private with you and other preferred analysts. All these insights would be part of the mosaic of information you would use to generate your reports. Of course, you would not want to be too critical, as otherwise, you would risk losing access to the pipeline of information. However, if you were nice, you never know — your firm would be picked to handle the next big issuance or M&A deal for this company, and you would be compensated for playing your part. Life was relatively easy.

A lot has changed in these past thirty-odd years. The capital markets of 2019 bear little resemblance to the capital markets of 1985. Now, as an analyst, you have to follow a multitude of information that arrives instantaneously and at high frequency. Company financials, both real time and archived, are available both through company IR websites as well as on the SEC's EDGAR database. If you have any questions or need some clarifications, you can contact the company, but you may or may not get an answer, because of Regulation Fair Disclosure (Reg. FD). Conference calls are open to all and are broadcast live through the web. You also have to think twice about currying favor with management through optimistic forecasts and recommendation. The benefits may not be as great as in the post-Reg. FD world, and now, there are real costs, as analysts have to disclose their histogram of ratings distribution. Finally, you now need to deal with new and emerging sources of information from social media such as Twitter and think about the implications of big data and blockchain.

It will take much more than a chapter of a book to highlight all the changes. In this chapter, I will focus on the changes in the information environment, with an emphasis on the new and emerging sources of information and channels of information dissemination. I will discuss how these changes affect firms, intermediaries, and investors. I will highlight the benefits accruing to the capital markets because of these changes and caution about the risks and downsides of these emerging changes.

2. Changes to Capital Markets

The past two decades have seen many changes to the capital markets. Some of them deal with governance issues — e.g., the Sarbanes–Oxley Act. Some of them deal with accounting standards — e.g., mandatory expensing of stock options (FAS 123-R) and changes in M&A accounting (FAS 141 among others). Some of them deal with market microstructure issues such as decimalization and changes in rules pertaining to shorting. In this section, I will focus on changes that had a direct effect on the information environment, with a focus on four salient changes — the rise of the Internet, the creation of EDGAR, the passage of Regulation FD, and the global analyst settlement.

2.1. *Emergence of the Internet*

For a long time, investors in capital markets have depended on information intermediaries, such as sell-side analysts, rating agencies, and the business press, to provide them with timely and value-relevant information. However, the past few decades have witnessed an explosion in new sources and channels of information that are easily accessible to capital market participants.

By far, the biggest change has been the emergence of the Internet and the World Wide Web, especially since the emergence of the first Internet browser in 1995. Now, investors have a wealth of information, both current and historical, readily available. Firms provide their financials on their investor relations website. The SEC provides access to all annual and interim reports filed by public firms through its EDGAR database. Many information intermediaries make their research reports available online as well.

In an early thought piece analyzing the impact of the Internet on financial markets, Economides (2001) highlights a few salient changes brought about by the emergence of the Internet. First, the Internet facilitates information flows. Second, the Internet facilitates direct interaction among economic agents, often eliminating or diminishing the power of intermediaries — e.g., the emergence of low-cost online trading. Third, the Internet facilitates the more direct access of economic agents to markets. As the web is truly global, the Internet, together with investors and firms, reduces the importance of national boundaries.

The rise of the Internet also contributed to some other related changes that took place — the creation of the EDGAR database in the US and the growing importance of social media in capital markets. I discuss these below.

2.2. *The EDGAR database*

The SEC created an electronic repository of financial statements called EDGAR, or Electronic data gathering and retrieval, in 1996. Since the early 2000s, it has been mandatory for all public firms to file all their financial filings with the SEC onto this database — not just the annual 10-Ks and quarterly 10-Qs but also other material disclosures, such as restatements, 8-K filings, insider trades, and proxy statements. Since 2009, the SEC made it compulsory for firms to use the eXtensible Business Reporting Language (XBRL) format, so that users may be able to use scripting languages such as Python to easily search for information with these documents.

With the EDGAR database, it is possible to get detailed and complete historical financial statements for all firms that filed with the SEC. At the last count, there were almost 13 million documents available for public viewing on EDGAR.[1] In addition to the EDGAR database, there are many other equivalents in other major capital markets, e.g., the Company House database in the UK and the SEDAR database in Canada.

Academic research examining the impact of EDGAR on capital markets suggests that the easy availability of information has been a boon to retail investors. Asthana *et al.* (2004) show that the availability of 10-K information on EDGAR increases the incidence of small trades and improves the profitability of such trades. In addition, the EDGAR database has itself transformed academic research, as it has allowed researchers to analyze not just the numbers in the financial statements but also the

[1] https://research.secdatabase.com/Filing/SearchResult.

non-financial content. Many studies now lexically analyze the text in financial statements, examining aspects such as readability and intentional obfuscation. An influential study is that by Li (2008), which shows that the annual reports of firms with lower earnings are harder to read, while firms with easier to read annual reports have more persistent earnings.

2.3. *Regulation FD*

On October 23, 2000, the SEC passed Regulation FD (Reg. FD), which requires that firms conduct investor communications such that all investors get material information at the same time. In issuing Reg. FD, the Securities and Exchange Commission's (SEC) stated objective was to eliminate the practice of selective disclosure of information to certain preferred analysts and institutional shareholders.

There was considerable resistance to Reg. FD by financial analysts who felt that changes in information communication would affect their ability to operate effectively. For instance, a prominent industry trade group for financial analysts suggested that prohibiting non-public communications would reduce the quality of information communicated by firms and hinder analysts' ability to understand firm performance. The Securities Industry Association's (SIA) comment letter to SEC states, "We believe that these communications help get information into the marketplace, whereas the proposal will discourage issuers from exchanging ideas or information with analysts, as well as deter analysts from vigorously competing to glean useful information for their clients and the markets".

The academic literature that analyzed the impact of Reg. FD generally does not find support for the SIA's position. In an early study, Heflin *et al.* (2003) fail to find that Reg. FD lead to more inaccurate forecasts. In addition, Mohanram and Sunder (2006) find that in the post-FD period, analysts are more likely to incorporate their own specific insights about the companies they are following in their forecasts and reports and less likely to regurgitate the information spoon-fed to them by the firms. What Reg. FD certainly did is increase the workload for financial analysts, especially the well-connected ones who lost the privileged preferential access they used to have in the pre-FD period. Consistent with this, Mohanram and Sunder (2006) find that such analysts are forced to reduce coverage as they deal with the increased workload. However, they also show that such declines in coverage are not necessarily detrimental, as analysts shift their coverage from highly covered firms to less covered firms. Overall, the results suggest that Reg. FD lead to a leveling of the informational playing field in two dimensions. First, all analysts were now on a more equal footing, as preferential access for a select few was severely curtailed if not eliminated outright. Second, smaller firms were more likely to get coverage, as analysts looked for opportunities to distinguish themselves.

2.4. *The global analyst research settlement*

The Global Analyst Research Settlement was an enforcement agreement reached in the United States on April 28, 2003, among the SEC, Financial Industry Regulatory Authority (FINRA), the NYSE, and 10 of the United States' largest investment firms to address issues of conflict of interest within their businesses in relation to recommendations made by the financial analyst departments of those firms.

In addition to monetary fines, the firms agreed to make changes in the way they functioned. Stricter rules were instituted on the separation of investment banking divisions and research divisions. The firms also set aside money that would be used to fund independent research by smaller firms that did not face the typical conflict of interest that plagued sell-side research. Finally, analysts were required to provide information about their past rankings, as well as whether they held any position in the firm that they were covering.

The empirical evidence on the impact of the global settlement has been mixed. Corwin *et al.* (2017) find a substantial reduction in analyst affiliation bias following the settlement for sanctioned banks. However, Clarke *et al.* (2011) show that the research produced by the independent research firms created and funded after this regulation is of lower quality.

3. New Sources of Information

The common theme across the four changes discussed in the prior section is one of democratization of access to information at many levels. However, the other big change over the past few decades is the emergence of new sources of information. Interestingly, a lot of this new information is often generated by and disseminated among the investors themselves.

3.1. *Peer-to-peer sharing of information in the pre-social media era*

With the rise of the Internet, individual investors increasingly started relying on each other as peer-to-peer sources of information (e.g., Yahoo! Finance, Silicon Investor, and Raging Bull). Research has provided mixed evidence on whether these sources generate or disseminate information of any value. Examining Internet bulletin boards, Hirschey *et al.* (2000) find that investment reports in Motley Fool predict stock returns, whereas Tumarkin and Whitelaw (2001) find no link between message board activity on Raging Bull and stock returns. Antweiler and Frank (2004) and Das and Chen (2007) both find that the volume of messages on message boards, such as Yahoo! or Raging Bull, is associated with stock return volatility, but not stock returns. Da *et al.* (2011) find that increases in Google searches predict higher stock prices in the near-term followed by price reversals. Drake *et al.* (2012) show that the returns–earnings relation is smaller when Google search volume prior to earnings announcements is high. They attribute this to the information being impounded earlier into prices.

3.2. *The impact of social media on capital markets*

By far, however, the biggest revolution in the dissemination of information on the Internet has been the advent of social media platforms such as Twitter, which allow users to post their views about stocks to a wide audience.

While Twitter undoubtedly is an exciting and emerging new source of information to the capital market, *ex ante* it is unclear whether information from Twitter will be useful to investors. On the one hand, Twitter allows users to tap into the Wisdom of Crowds, where the aggregation of information provided by many (non-expert) individuals often predicts outcomes more precisely than experts. Further, Twitter users, who come from diverse backgrounds, are less likely to herd, a phenomenon that plagues traditional information intermediaries (e.g., financial analysts) as well as social media platforms (e.g., blogs, investing portals) where a central piece of information is posted and users comment on it. Finally, Twitter's short format (up to 140 characters) and ease of information search (e.g., the use of cashtags $) make it an ideal medium to share opinions and information in a timely fashion, in contrast to the longer format and potentially reduced timeliness of research reports or articles.

On the other hand, the information from tweets may be uninformative or even intentionally misleading, because Twitter is an unregulated platform with potentially anonymous users. For example, in two days in January 2013, a series of damning, but false tweets on two stocks — Audience Inc. (ticker symbol: ADNC) and Sarepta Therapeutics, Inc. (ticker symbol: SRPT) — sent their prices plunging by 28% and 16%, respectively.[2]

In recent years, the academic literature has begun studying the role Twitter plays in the capital market. One strand of this literature investigates whether information from Twitter predicts the overall stock market. Bollen *et al.* (2011) show that aggregate mood inferred from textual analysis of daily Twitter feeds can help predict changes in the Dow Jones Index. Similarly, Mao *et al.* (2012) find that the daily number of tweets that mention *S&P 500* stocks is significantly associated with the levels, changes, and absolute changes in the *S&P 500* index. Another strand of this literature analyzes how Twitter activity influences investor response to earnings. Curtis *et al.* (2016), who focus on the overall social media (Twitter and StockTwits) activity over 30-day rolling windows, find that high levels of activity are associated with greater sensitivity of earnings announcement returns to earnings surprises, while low levels of social media activity are associated with significant post-earnings announcement drift.

My recent study examines whether investor sentiment on Twitter can help predict earnings surprises and the market reaction to earnings surprises. In Bartov *et al.* (2018), we parse individual tweets to determine if they have a positive or negative tone and then aggregate across all tweets

---

[2]The two tweets are: (i) *AUDIENCE the noise suppression company being investigated by DOJ on rumored fraud charges Full report* [sic] *to follow later*, and (ii) *$SRPT FDA steps in as its 48 weeks results on Eteplirsen [sic] results are tainted and have been doctored they believe Trial papers seized by FDA*. Interestingly, the perpetrator — who used two accounts using aliases similar to well-known short-selling firms Muddy Waters and Citron Research with misspellings — managed to net only $97, as investors quickly figured out the deceit, and the share prices almost instantly recovered. Other instances consist of Twitter users misleading entire markets with false information. In 2010, the Australian airline company Qantas saw its stock price decline by more than 10% after false reports of a plane crash appeared on Twitter. Similarly, in 2013, a fake tweet claiming that President Obama had been injured in an explosion at the White House lead to a 0.9% decline in the value of the *S&P 500* index, representing $130 billion in stock value.

pertaining to a given firm in the period just prior to the earnings announcement. The idea is remarkably simple — can this aggregate sentiment from Twitter provide useful information to capital markets? Is it the case that if the aggregate opinion on Twitter is positive, then the firm will have a positive earnings surprise? We find that the aggregate opinion from individual tweets successfully predicts a firm's forthcoming quarterly earnings, as well as the returns around the announcement. Thus, Twitter provides value-relevant information that is incremental to other sources of information. These results hold for tweets that convey original information as well as tweets that disseminate existing information. Twitter hence plays a dual role — a new source of information as well as a new channel for dissemination. Finally, we find that our results that aggregate sentiment on Twitter is informative is strongest for firms in the weakest information environments, suggesting that social media is truly filling in a void where no other sources of information exist.

The focus of research on Twitter seems to be solely on equity markets, neglecting other important segments of the financial markets such as the bond market; in the US, for example, the bond market is significantly larger than the equity market in terms of both market capitalization and trading volume. In a recent study (Bartov *et al.*, 2019), my coauthors and I examine whether information aggregated from Twitter is relevant for bond investors. We find a significantly positive association between bond returns around quarterly earnings announcements and the aggregate opinion on Twitter. Further, given the importance of negative news to bond markets, we find that the positive association between bond returns and aggregate Twitter opinion is strongest when the underlying news is negative, and when bonds are riskier (non-investment grade). Overall, our findings suggest that information from Twitter posted prior to earnings announcements is relevant in the capital market, not only for equity investors but also for bond investors.

The broad consensus across all these studies is that despite concerns about credibility, the wisdom of crowds concept really does apply as far as social media platforms such as Twitter are concerned. The importance of Twitter as a valuable source of information has not gone unnoticed by practitioners. In 2015, Tashtego, a hedge fund firm based in Boston, set up a Social Equities Fund with investment decisions based on sentiment from social media.[3] Further, DataMinr, a startup firm that parses Twitter feeds

[3] https://fortune.com/2015/04/02/hedge-fund-twitter/

to generate actionable real-time signals, announced that it had raised over $130 million in financing.[4] In addition, on April 26, 2016, the Infinigon Group launched ECHO™, a Twitter-based financial information platform that converts social media streams into early, pre-mainstream, actionable news and analytics for the trading community.[5]

3.3. *The use of social media by firms*

Twitter has also become an important disclosure tool for firms. The SEC was initially cautious about the use of social media, but in April 2013, it approved the use of posts on Facebook and Twitter to communicate corporate announcements such as earnings. Following this, academic research has investigated how companies exploit this new channel to communicate with investors. Blankespoor *et al.* (2014) show that firms can reduce information asymmetry among investors by more broadly disseminating their news using Twitter to send market participants links to press releases and other traditional disclosures. Jung *et al.* (2018) find that roughly half of *S&P 1500* firms have created either a corporate Twitter account or a Facebook page, with a growing preference for Twitter.[6] Lee *et al.* (2015) show that firms use social media channels, such as Twitter, to interact with investors in order to attenuate the negative price reactions to consumer product recalls.

3.4. *Rise of peer-to-pear research — Seeking Alpha and estimize*

As a social media platform, Twitter has some obvious advantages including a wide reach, immediacy, and parsimony. However, Twitter is not the ideal platform to express complex ideas that cannot fit into the abbreviated format. Investors who need to share detailed information and insights among themselves rely on platforms such as SeekingAlpha. Individuals can publish their own reports about firms, which are often in the style of

---

[4] http://www.wsj.com/articles/tweet-analysis-firm-dataminr-raises-funding-1426564862.

[5] http://www.prweb.com/releases/2016/04/prweb13376503.htm.

[6] In June of 2015, the SEC's staff, in a "Compliance and Disclosure Interpretations", said a startup firm can post a Twitter message about its stock or debt offering to gauge interest among potential investors.

sell-side equity reports and are compensated based on the number of page views they generate. Chen *et al.* (2014) demonstrate that information in user-generated research reports and commentaries on SeekingAlpha helps predict earnings and long-window stock returns following the report posting date.

Estimize was founded in 2011 by Leigh Drogen, a former quantitative hedge fund analyst, with the objective of providing an alternative to sell-side forecasts by crowdsourcing earnings and revenue forecasts. Forecasts are available on the Estimize and Bloomberg platforms and also sold as a data feed to institutional investors. The availability of Estimize data on platforms such as Bloomberg suggests that the market is potentially interested in such crowdsourced financial forecasts. On its part, Estimize incentivizes the accuracy and integrity of its data by asking contributors to provide a personal profile and then by tracking and reporting contributor accuracy. Estimize also creates a consensus forecast where the weight a given forecast gets in the estimation on consensus depends on the forecaster's prior accuracy, with unreliable forecasts being excluded. Finally, to encourage participation and accurate forecasting, Estimize recognizes top contributors with prizes and features them in podcasts.

A recent study by Jame *et al.* (2016) examines the value of crowdsourced earnings forecast on Estimize. They find that Estimize forecasts are incrementally useful in forecasting earnings and measuring the market's expectations of earnings. The results are stronger when the number of Estimize contributors is larger, consistent with the wisdom of crowds increasing with the size of the crowd. Finally, they find that Estimize consensus revisions generate significant stock market reaction. Overall, their study shows that crowdsourced forecasts are a useful supplementary source of information to capital markets.

3.5. *The impact of emerging technologies: Big data and blockchain*

Another transformational change that we should not ignore is the rise of big data, blockchain, and other emerging technologies. While many of these new technologies are in their infancy, they are already making an impact on capital markets, and increasingly on academic research as well.

De Mauro *et al.* (2015) define big data as follows: "Big Data represents the Information assets characterized by such a High Volume, Velocity and Variety to require specific Technology and Analytical

Methods for its transformation into Value". Big data analytics is the backbone of work done by social media aggregators and other data providers who are transforming capital markets.

Warren *et al.* (2015) argue that big data will transform many aspects of accounting practice including managerial accounting, financial accounting, and financial reporting practices. They posit that big data will enhance management control systems and budgeting; improve the quality, transparency, and relevance of accounting information; and even assist in the creation and refinement of accounting standards. Vasarhelyi *et al.* (2015) illustrate how new big data sources can transform the traditional audit process — e.g., security videos to confirm the entry and exit of materials, social media to evaluate consumer satisfaction and product defects, and RFID tags for inventory measurement and valuation.

Big data is also a growing part of academic research. The above definition would encompass the work of Li (2008), who conducts lexical analysis on a large sample of unstructured corporate financial statements, as well as my own work using millions of tweets by ordinary investors. Other examples include Mayew and Venkatachalam (2012), who use vocal emotion analysis software to analyze the tone of voice used by CEOs during conference calls. They find that managers show positive and negative "affects" in their voice tone, something that is not picked up by analysts. They further show that these help predict future earnings and analysts forecast errors, hence providing evidence that "managerial vocal cues contain useful information about a firm's fundamentals, incremental to both quantitative earnings information and qualitative 'soft' information conveyed by linguistic content" (quoted from their abstract).

One area within the big data umbrella that has received a lot of attention is blockchain technology. Blockchain was conceived by Nakamoto (2008), who used a chain of blocks to create a decentralized, publicly available, and cryptographically secure digital currency system named bitcoin. Blockchain technology has three main features — decentralization, strong authentication, and tamper resistance. Blockchain has moved beyond its cryptocurrency roots and is now being applied to a large number of applications, such as banking, financial market, and insurance. Dai and Vasarhelyi (2017) argue that blockchain technology can be used to enable a real-time, verifiable, and transparent accounting ecosystem. They also argue that blockchain has the potential to transform current auditing practices, resulting in a more precise and timely automatic assurance system. Yermack (2017) posits that blockchain will also have a transformational impact on both financial accounting as well as corporate governance, with the emergence of real-time, continuously updated financial statements, greater transparency of stock trading, reduced insider trading, and greater reliability of shareholder voting.

Empirical research on the impact of blockchain on capital markets is still in an incipient stage as these technologies are emerging. A few works have studied the phenomenon of early-stage startups raising capital through cryptocurrency — Initial Coin Offerings (ICOs) as opposed to the traditional IPOs. In an ICO, the issuer sells tokens, which are cryptographically secured digital assets. Howell, Niessner and Yermack (2018) analyze the characteristics of ICO issuers and find that successful ICOs are associated with better disclosure, credible commitment to the project, and greater liquidity that arises when the tokens are tradable in cryptocurrency exchanges. Feng *et al.* (2019) analyze the white paper, a voluntary disclosure akin to a prospectus, provided by firms issuing ICOs. They rate these white papers on their quality, focusing on whether they use blockchain or not. They find that 80% of the firms do not use blockchain and fare poorly on their disclosure index. They further find that disclosure quality is strongly associated with post-ICO performance. Hence, the common message from both Howell *et al.* (2018) and Feng *et al.* (2019) is that despite concerns about the market for cryptocurrency being a wild west awash with swindlers, the market appears to function and separate the wheat from the chaff.

4. Implications

What has been and what will continue to be the impact of all of these changes on the different players in the capital markets? In this final section of this chapter, I provide my thoughts on these. Please note that these are my conjectures — some of them are based on insights from academic research but most of them are just based on being an observer on the sidelines while these changes have been taking place.

4.1. *Implications for firms*

The biggest change for firms is how they deal with investor relations. The IR function has become multifaceted with firms needing to maintain a substantial presence on social media networks, especially Twitter. Investor relations are no longer about keeping the big guys happy. Firms have to monitor social media feeds where they are mentioned. It is not enough to keep track of what sell-side analysts are saying about you, as markets pay attention to crowdsourced research on SeekingAlpha or crowdsourced forecasts on Estimize. Finally, firms have to be aware of their compliance with Reg. FD, in their interactions with investors.

The changes in the information environment also have implications for other firms — competitors, suppliers, and buyers. The access to detailed financial information, as well as the ability to attend conference calls virtually means that everyone gets access to information in close to real time. This can be useful in understanding the factors behind the success and failure in a given industry. Finally, as Yermack (2017) surmises, technologies like blockchain have the potential to transform corporate disclosure, with beneficial effects on frequency, timeliness, and informativeness.

4.2. *Implications for sell-side analysts*

By far, the biggest impact of the changes in the information environment has been on the sell-side research community. They have lost their position of privilege, as they no longer have a chokehold on the flow of information. Investors have plenty of alternatives for information and insight including crowdsourced research as well as the ability to share information with each other through social media.

In such an environment, sell-side equity research truly faces an existential crisis. This has been exacerbated by recent regulatory changes such as the EU's recently enacted Mifid II regulation that required investment banks and brokers to separate the cost of research from trading activity offered to asset managers. So how can sell-side equity research survive in this environment? For me, it boils down to the quality of work. Analysts should focus less on forecasting short-term performance and stock price — a vast body of literature suggests that their forecasts of earnings as well as their recommendations of stock tend to perform rather poorly.

One area that sell-side analysts can add value is to bring their expertise to the fore in their reports. Investors are not just looking for the most accurate estimates of quarterly EPS or the most prescient target prices. Indeed, anecdotal evidence suggests that buy-side investors are looking for other factors such as industry knowledge and expertise in accounting issues. Sell-side analysts should focus more on becoming industry experts and identifying what factors will drive success and failure in a given industry.

4.3. *Implications for buy-side*

The changes brought about a combination of regulations and technological advances have been a mixed bag for buy-side firms. Like the sell-side, the buy-side has also lost some of its privilege in the post-Reg. FD world. However, the buy-side is no longer beholden to the sell-side as before.

Note that the buy-side has also been buffeted by other structural changes such as the rise of low-cost passive investing — both index funds as well as exchange-traded funds (ETFs). In addition, a lot of academic research shows that the ability to generate "alpha" from fundamental strategies has declined precipitously in the new millennium (see Mclean and Pontiff, 2016; Green *et al.*, 2017).

In this difficult environment, the buy-side is looking at other avenues in their elusive quest for alpha. One potential avenue is data from new and emerging sources such as aggregated social media feeds. In fact, the largest market for data aggregators who provide aggregated social media information in real time is the buy-side. One can see an increased demand for data scientists and the use of big data analytics on the buy-side.

4.4. *Implications for retail investors*

Retail investors have benefited tremendously from the democratization that has taken place in the capital markets. While the playing field is probably not truly level, they do have access to a vast quantity of information on a timely basis. In addition, they also have access to information from each other through peer-to-peer sharing.

However, small investors also face new problems. The first is the paradox of too much information — there is a lot of research in the social sciences that show that investors with abundant information often make bad investing choices because of a combination of limited processing skills and bounded rationality. Second, small investors are more likely to fall victim to fraudulent information on social media. Such information is likely to be washed out in the aggregate, but getting aggregated social media information is prohibitively expensive; subscriptions to real-time data feeds are often beyond the reach of most individual investors. Paradoxically, those who are generating this new source of information may not necessarily be benefiting from it.

Retail investors would also face a disadvantage, as the tools and techniques of big data analytics would be beyond their wherewithal at the current point of time. However, I expect that this would also provide an opportunity for enterprising data providers who would provide these tools to retail investors, either for a fee or as a part of the suite of services provided when they manage their money.

4.5. *Implications for the accounting profession*

I have already discussed the recent normative research by scholars such as Vasarhelyi and others about the impact of big data and blockchain on the audit function. Broadening the discussion, the accounting profession will be profoundly affected by all the changes discussed in this chapter illustrate three changes.

First, with the rise of social media, auditors have to pay attention not just to the standard regulatory filings of firms but potentially also to their social media feeds. Second, the accountants of tomorrow have to be trained to be familiar and conversant with the latest tools and techniques. This a big transformation that will need the joint efforts of accounting educators, the audit firms, and accounting bodies, such as the AICPA in the US and national and provincial CPA bodies in Canada. Evidence of these changes can already been seen. Many universities in the US have started specialized master's programs in accounting analytics in conjunction with one of the big four firms — KPMG. Finally, accounting academia will rely on the support of the accounting bodies and big audit firms to fund research on emerging topics. At the Rotman School of Management of the University of Toronto, with the generous support from CPA Ontario, we have set up the CPA Ontario Centre for Accounting Innovation Research[7]. In addition to funding academic research, the center also provides opportunities for interaction between academics and practitioners through applied conferences and white papers on emerging issues. Our first annual practitioner conference brought together experts from academia and practice to discuss a number of topics including big data

---

[7] https://www.rotman.utoronto.ca/FacultyAndResearch/ResearchCentres/CentreForInnovationInAccountingEducation

in accounting research, machine learning, blockchain, and disruptive technology and governance.

4.6. *Implications for the media*

At the outset, it would appear that the rise of social media would be a threat to traditional media. However, the reality is a bit more nuanced. First, it appears as though social media is having the biggest impact on capital markets in areas where the existing information environment is weak. Second, as we highlight in Bartov *et al.* (2018), social media has proven to be an effective new dissemination mechanism. Many of the tweets we analyze in that study are actually links to articles on traditional media. Hence, the relationship between traditional media and social media may well be symbiotic, with traditional media trying to use social media to ensure that the news it is providing reaches the most number of people. One can also see that the traditional media is the most active on social media, trying to get its stories to become "viral".

4.7. *Implications for regulators*

While regulation played a crucial role in the democratization of information in capital markets, they have largely taken a laissez-faire approach in the era of social media. In fact, they have fostered the use of emerging technologies by allowing companies to communicate with investors through social media channels.

Skeptics argue that self-serving individuals exploit social media tools, such as Twitter, by disseminating misleading and speculative information to investors and thus call for regulating social media. However, the results from studies such as that by Bartov *et al.* (2018) show precisely the opposite; information on Twitter can help investors make sound investment decisions. Thus, social media can play a role in making the market more efficient by uncovering and disseminating value-relevant information, especially for firms in weak information environments.

4.8. *Implications for academic research*

The information explosion that has taken place has had a significant impact on academic research in capital markets. Gone are the days when empirical research in this field meant spinning the tables with financial data (Compustat), stock market data (CRSP), and occasionally data on analysts (IBES) or executive compensation (Execucomp). Now, researchers conduct research using unstructured data — e.g., analyzing company financials on EDGAR using lexical analysis, searching for specific disclosures on the Internet through web-crawling and scripting languages, using data from new sources such as social media, and using the latest techniques such as big data analytics and machine learning.

These changes have dramatically increased the breadth of academic research. I provide a few examples from recent research. In a work entitled "Big Data as a Governance Mechanism", Zhu (2019) shows that the rise of big data availability has actually improved price informativeness. As investors are able to get access to real-time granular indicators of financial performance, they can better monitor and discipline managers. This leads to better managerial decision-making and less self-serving opportunistic behavior. Other examples include research using big data methodologies and other emerging techniques such as machine learning. For instance, Crowley *et al.* (2018) use a machine learning approach to analyze tweets posted by *S&P 1500* firms and find that firms strategically time financial tweets around earnings announcements, accounting filings, as well as other important corporate events. They further find that feedback from Twitter users influences firms' future financial tweets.

5. Concluding Thoughts

I would like to end this thought piece with a caveat. These are my thoughts as far as what I think could happen. I am hardly an expert in all the areas discussed in this chapter — I have done work in empirical financial accounting with an emphasis on valuation, disclosure, and the functioning of sell-side analysts. I am a novice in other areas such as big data analytics and blockchain. Much of what we call big data analytics is an emerging field, both in practice as well as in academia. So who knows what the future holds? To quote the mathematician John Allen Paulos, "Uncertainty is the only certainty there is, and knowing how to live with insecurity is the only security".

Many of these changes can be deeply distressing for many from previous generations, who are used to a simpler way of doing things — e.g., the analyst described earlier who enjoyed his sheltered existence in the pre-Reg. FD, pre-Internet, pre-social media, pre-big data world. It will be important for all players to adapt to this new reality. This will require a huge investment, not just financial but also in terms of human capital. There is a need for reskilling in all affected fields. Some of the changes needed are emotional — letting go of the old ways of doing things and embracing the new. Nowadays, as an empirical researcher, I invariably work on research projects that use some of these new data sources and techniques, e.g., lexical analysis of Twitter feeds and machine learning-based algorithms to measure the aggregate investor sentiment. Life was easier spinning Compustat and CRSP tapes, but the rewards are in the ability to answer complex questions in a more comprehensive manner.

In the immortal words of Bob Dylan, "You better start swimmin' or you'll sink like a stone, For the times they are a-changin'."

References

Antweiler, W. and M. Frank (2004), Is all that talk just noise? The information content of Internet stock message boards, *Journal of Finance* **59**, 1259–1294.

Asthana, S., S. Balsam, and S. Sankaraguruswamy (2004), Differential response of small versus large investors to 10-K Filings on EDGAR, *The Accounting Review* **79**(3), 571–589.

Bartov, E., L. Faurel, and P. Mohanram (2018), Can Twitter help predict firm-level earnings and stock returns? *The Accounting Review* **93**, 25–57.

Bartov, E., L. Faurel, and P. Mohanram (2019), Can twitter help predict bond returns? Working paper.

Blankespoor, E., G. Miller, and H. White (2014), The role of dissemination in market liquidity: Evidence from firms' use of Twitter™, *The Accounting Review* **89**, 79–112.

Bollen, J., H. Mao, and X. Zheng (2011), Twitter mood predicts the stock market, *Journal of Computational Science* **2**, 1–8.

Chen, H., P. De, Y. Hu, and B. Hwang (2014), Wisdom of crowds: The value of stock opinions transmitted through social media, *Review of Financial Studies* **27**, 1367–1403.

Christina, Z. (2019), Big data as a governance mechanism, *Review of Financial Studies* **32**(5), 2021–2061.

Clarke, J., A. Khorana, A. Patel, and P. R. Rau (2011), Independents' day? Analyst behavior surrounding the Global Settlement, *Annals of Finance* **7**, 529–547.

Corwin, S. A., S. A. Larocque, and M. A. Stegemoller (2017), Investment banking relationships and analyst affiliation bias: The impact of the global settlement on sanctioned and non-sanctioned banks, *Journal of Financial Economics* **124**(3), 614–631.

Crowley, R., W. Huang, and H. Lu (2018), Discretionary dissemination on Twitter, Working paper, University of Toronto.

Curtis, A., V. Richardson, and R. Schmardebeck (2016), Investor attention and the pricing of earnings news, in *Handbook of Sentiment Analysis in Finance*, Gautum Mitra and Xiang Yu (eds.), Albury Books, Chapter 8, pp. 212–232.

Da, Z., J. Engelberg, and P. Gao (2011), In search of attention, *Journal of Finance* **66**, 1461–1499.

Dai, J. and M. Vasarhelyi (2017), Toward blockchain-based accounting and assurance, *Journal of Information Systems* **31**(3), 5–21.

Das, S., and M. Chen (2007), Yahoo! for Amazon: Sentiment extraction from small talk on the Web, *Management Science* **53**, 1375–1388.

De Mauro, A., M. Greco, and M. Grimaldi (2015), What is big data? A consensual definition and a review of key research topics, *AIP Conference Proceedings* **1644**(1), 97–104.

Drake, M., D. Roulstone, and J. Thornock (2012), Investor information demand: Evidence from Google searches around earnings announcements, *Journal of Accounting Research* **50**, 1001–1040.

Economides, N. (2001), The impact of the Internet on financial markets, *Journal of Financial Transformation* **1**(1), 8–13.

Green, J., J. Hand, and X. Zhang (2017), The characteristics that provide independent information about average U.S. monthly stock returns, *Review of Financial Studies* **30**(12), 4389–4436.

Feng, C., N. Li, F. Wong, and M. Zhang (2019), Initial coin offerings, blockchain technology, and white paper disclosures, Working paper, University of Toronto.

Heflin, F., K. Subramanyam, and Y. Zhang (2003), Regulation FD and the financial information environment: Early evidence, *The Accounting Review* **78**(1), 1–37.

Hirschey, M., V. Richardson, and S. Scholz (2000), Stock price effects of Internet buy-sell recommendations: The Motley Fool case, *Financial Review* **35**, 147–174.

Howell, S., M. Niessner, and D. Yermack (2018), Initial coin offerings: Financing growth with cryptocurrency token sales, Working paper, New York University.

Jame, R., R. Johnston, S. Markov, and M. Wolfe (2016), The value of crowd-sourced earnings forecasts, *Journal of Accounting Research* **54**(4), 1077–1110.

Jung, M., J. Naughton, A. Tahoun, and C. Wang (2018), Do firms strategically disseminate? Evidence from corporate use of social media, *The Accounting Review* **93**(4), 225–252.

Lee, F., A. Hutton, and S. Shu (2015), The role of social media in the capital market: Evidence from consumer product recalls, *Journal of Accounting Research* **53**(2), 367–404.

Mao, Y., W. Wei, B. Wang, and B. Liu (2012), Correlating S&P 500 stocks with Twitter data, in *Proceedings of the First ACM International Workshop on Hot Topics on Interdisciplinary Social Networks*, 69–72.

Mayew, W. and M. Venkatachalam (2012), The power of voice: Managerial affective states and future firm performance, *Journal of Finance* **67**(1), 1–43.

Mclean, R. and J. Pontiff (2016), Does academic research destroy stock return predictability? *Journal of Finance* **71**, 5–32.

Mohanram, P. and S. Sunder (2006), How has regulation fair disclosure affected the operations of financial analysts? *Contemporary Accounting Research* **23**(2), 491–525.

Nakamoto, S. (2008), Bitcoin: A peer-to-peer electronic cash system. Unpublished paper. http://bitcoin.org/bitcoin.pdf.

Tumarkin, R. and R. Whitelaw (2001), News or noise? Internet postings and stock prices, *Financial Analysts Journal* **57**, 41–51.

Vasarhelyi, M., A. Kogan, and B. Tuttle (2015), Big data in accounting: An overview, *Accounting Horizons* **29**(2), 381–396.

Warren, J., K. Moffitt, and P. Byrnes (2015), How big data will change accounting, *Accounting Horizons* **29**(2), 397–407.

Yermack, D. (2017), Corporate governance and blockchains, *Review of Finance* **21**(1), 7–31.

https://doi.org/10.1142/9789811220470_0010

Chapter 10

Analyzing Textual Information at Scale

Lin William Cong[*,¶], Tengyuan Liang[†], Baozhong Yang[‡] and Xiao Zhang[§,‖]

[*] *Johnson Graduate School of Management, Cornell University, NY 14853, USA*

[†] *Booth School of Business, University of Chicago, Chicago, IL 60637, USA*

[‡] *Robinson College of Business, Georgia State University, Atlanta, GA 30303, USA*

[§] *Analysis Group, DC 20006, Washington, USA*

[¶] *will.cong@cornell.edu*

[‖] *xiao.zhang@analysisgroup.com*

Abstract

We provide an overview on the recent advances in textual analysis for social sciences. Count-based economic model, structured statistical tool, and plain-vanilla machine learning apparatus each have their own merits and limitations. To take a data-driven approach to capture complex linguistic structures while ensuring computational scalability and economic interpretability, a general framework for analyzing large-scale text-based data is needed. We discuss the recent attempts combining the strengths of neural network language models, such as word embedding, and generative statistical modeling, such as topic modeling. We also describe typical sources of texts and the applications of these methodologies to issues in finance and economics and discuss promising future directions.

Keywords: Bag-of-words; Big data; Machine learning; Text-based analysis; Topic models; Unstructured data; Word embedding.

1. Introduction

With the increased capacity of modern computers, it has become feasible to collect enormous amounts of data and then process them through proper aggregation using algorithms to facilitate effective decision-making. For example, financial analysts and investors who used to intently focus on firms' quarterly earnings or infrequent macroeconomic forecasts can now analyze market sentiment using news media articles and forecast business activities with satellite pictures of parking lots.

Big data generally include data of large volume or frequency, data from non-conventional courses, and unstructured data that require special processing and information extraction. Texts are a predominant form of unstructured data, and there is as much information in language data as there is in numbers, not to mention the greater interpretability texts offer. They enable econometricians to supplement or replace traditional surveys, capture more granular and up-to-date information, and complement information extracted from structured data such as financial ratios. However, it has been challenging to analyze texts at a large scale and in a manner that preserves interpretability.

We therefore aim to help future researchers to understand the important recent developments and applications in the field of textual analysis and see how computing capacity can help them utilize textual data. It is absolutely crucial to build algorithms to aggregate data and extract information to facilitate any decision we may need to make. In this chapter, we discuss several approaches to this end and highlight their strengths and weaknesses.

Analyzing textual data is challenging for several reasons: first, language structures are often too intricate and complex to be summarized by simply counting words or labeling phrases; second, textual data are high dimensional in nature and processing a large corpus of documents is computationally demanding; third, there lacks a framework relating textual data to sparse regression analysis that is traditionally used in social sciences while maintaining interpretability.

Applying textual analysis in financial markets and business environments is even more challenging than in other fields because they evolve faster than physical laws or genetic codes, which means predictive models built on past data are not sufficient without economic understanding and interpretability.[1] In fact, one should recognize that scientists and practitioners use textual analysis primarily because texts offer more interpretability.

As such, we focus on information richness, computational efficiency, as well as economic interpretability when assessing various methodologies for textual analysis. In what follows, we first discuss typical sources of textual data and then discuss the current approaches to textual analysis in social sciences, statistics, and machine learning fields. We do not claim to do full justice to the literature because this is not a survey of all relevant studies; instead, this study aims to illustrate major themes in recent developments.[2]

2. Texts as Unstructured Data

Textual data manifest themselves in various forms. Here, we list textual data that are easily available to researchers and decision-makers. The list is necessarily partial, with an emphasis on data related to economics and finance. Our goal is to illustrate what kind of data sources prove to be useful for textual analysis.

2.1. *News*

The Wall Street Journal's (*WSJ*) data are widely used in various academic studies and particularly suitable for textual analysis. We focus on

[1]The signal-to-noise ratios in economics or finance settings can also be much lower than those in scientific or engineering settings. The data generation process is also typically non-experimental.

[2]There are excellent surveys on textual analysis, including those by Li (2010) on manual-based textual analysis and past topics and future directions, Kearney and Liu (2014) on textual sentiment, and Das *et al.* (2014) on basic code snippets and basic text analytics. In particular, Loughran and McDonald (2016) underscore how textual analysis is substantially imprecise and that understanding the art is of equal importance to understanding the science.

front-page articles only because these are manually edited and corrected. This is particularly useful for newspapers that were published in earlier years as they were scanned and digitized using optical character recognition (OCR), which tends to generate typos.

Other newspapers, such as *The New York Times*, *The Financial Times*, and *The Economist*, contain relevant information in the Economic, Business, and Finance sections. They are available from, for example, Proquest (https://www.proquest.com).

Firm-specific news from Factiva (https://www.dowjones.com/products/factiva) is also a great resource if cross-sectional variation is more important for a particular research question. This firm-specific news resource enables us to explore variation in texts among firms in the cross-section.

2.2. *Corporate filings and releases*

Company filings are typically available for public firms. For example, they have been publicly available in the United States since 1993. To facilitate the rapid dissemination of financial and business information about companies, the US Securities and Exchange Commission (SEC) allows publicly listed firms to file their securities documents with the SEC via the Electronic Data Gathering, Analysis and Retrieval (EDGAR) system (https://www.sec.gov/edgar/). We discuss in this chapter several frequently used forms, such as the Management Discussion and Analysis (MD&A) sections of the annual report (10-K), IPO prospectus (S-3), and current reports (8-K).

(1) **Management Discussion and Analysis (MD&A):** MD&A is a section of a public company's annual report (10-K) or quarterly filing (10-Q), in which the management analyzes the company's performance with qualitative measures. Since this section is unaudited, management has the most discretion and flexibility in terms of creating its content. Typically, MD&A provides commentary on financial statements, systems and controls, compliance with laws and regulations, financial activities, and actions it has planned or has taken to address any challenges the company is facing. Management also discusses the firm's outlook by analyzing industry trends, competitive environment, economic conditions, and risks in the financial market.

(2) **Risk Factor Discussions:** In Section 1A of 10-K reports, companies discuss the potential risk factors associated with business and financial operations. According to Regulation SK (Item 305(c), SEC 2005), firms are legally obliged to disclose "the most significant factors that make the company speculative or risky". Therefore, discussions on typical risk factors include local economic, financial, and political conditions; government regulations; business licensing or certification requirements; limitations on the repatriation and investment of funds and foreign currency exchange restrictions; varying payable and longer receivable cycles; and the resulting negative impact on cash flows. Since companies may get sued if they do not warn investors and potential investors about potential risk, firms tend to include many risk discussions that are only remotely relevant to them.

(3) **Proxy Statements:** Firms need to file a proxy statement (DEF 14A) ahead of the annual meeting to provide shareholders with sufficient information about upcoming meetings, whenever they hold shareholder meetings and solicit votes. A proxy statement often includes information on shareholder proposals, voting procedures, background information (including potential conflicts of interests) of nominated directors, compensation structure of board and executives, and auditors. Most shareholder proposals that are up for votes are approval of the re-election of directors, approval of executive compensation plan, approval of audit fees, and ratification of the ongoing engagement of the auditing firm.

(4) **Conference Call or Meeting Transcripts:** Most publicly traded firms hold regular conference calls with their analysts and other interested parties. During the conference call, management gives its view on the firm's past and future performance and responds to questions from call participants. Both audio recordings and transcripts of conference calls are available. For example, one can obtain conference call transcripts from SeekingAlpha (https:// seekingalpha.com/).

Another meeting transcript often used is from the Federal Open Market Committee (FOMC) meetings (https://www.federalreserve.gov/monetarypolicy/fomc_historical.htm). Every year, the FOMC holds eight regularly scheduled meetings. FOMC meeting members discuss the economic outlook and formulate the monetary policy during these meetings. All policy changes are made public in a short meeting statement that is released immediately after the meeting.

In addition, detailed records of the discussions during each meeting (minutes) are released a day later.

(5) **Analyst Reports:** Analyst reports are obtained from Investext via Thomson One (https://www.thomsonone.com/). Equity analysts from major investment banks periodically write about firms' past performance and their view about firms' future stock price.

(6) **Patents:** Recently, the United States Patent and Trademark Office (USPTO) has made their patent data publicly available (https://bulkdata.uspto.gov/). These include textual data, such as patent applications and grants. Each patent document consists of both abstract and detailed description, as well as citations. The data go back as early as the 1920s and cover essentially all patents filed with USPTO. This greatly reduces the workload for researchers who want to use this type of patent data. Previously, researchers needed to scrape patent documents from Google Patent, which could be more labor intensive and time consuming. On the contrary, what's unique about Google Patent is that it collects patents from 100+ patent offices around the world, making the coverage much broader.

3. Count-based or Manual-label Analyses in Economics and Finance

Count-based or manual-label methods are generally easy to interpret because researchers who have domain knowledge define the bag of words or the dictionary. This line of studies either counts the occurrence of pre-specified keywords and phrases as a way to summarize information in the text or adopts a supervised learning approach with manual labels of the training set.[3] One example is the study by Nini *et al.* (2012) that examines the impact of covenant violations on corporate behavior. Given that there is no existing database on covenant violations, the authors identify covenant violations by applying a simple textual analysis methodology to firm filings. What they do is to search for the keyword "covenant" in 10-K filings (annual reports). Conditional on finding this keyword, their algorithm then searches for additional keywords, such as "waiv", "viol",

[3] Antweiler and Frank (2004) pioneered attempts to utilize textual information in economics and finance. The study by Chen *et al.* (2019) improves upon their manual labeling using machine learning techniques.

"in default", "modif", and "not in compliance", within three lines above or below the line containing "covenant" to make sure the texts indeed discuss covenant violations.

This is a typical application of count-based textual analysis to an economic question. The research question is particularly important in the economics and finance literature; while there is plenty of theoretical work studying the role of creditors on the governance of corporations both inside and outside of bankruptcy, there are very few empirical studies done on a large scale due to the limited availability of structured covenant violation data. After building a dataset on covenant violations using texts, the authors use it to study the effect of credit control rights. They find that covenant violations are prevalent and are followed immediately by declines in acquisitions and capital expenditures, sharp reductions in leverage and shareholder payouts, and increases in CEO turnover.

The authors are cognizant of the shortcomings of the count-based method: it requires domain knowledge and significant manual work. Indeed, the authors go through a large number of iterations to pin down a list of best keywords. Despite such efforts, the method produces a large number of false positives. To make the data as clean as possible, the authors also hired a group of research assistants to manually go over the filings to eliminate the false positives. This step is almost inevitable for most research in finance and economics employing count-based methods.

Another salient example is the study by Baker *et al.* (2016), which constructs a new index of economic policy uncertainty (EPU) based on newspaper coverage frequency. Their approach is straightforward: search and count the occurrence of some keywords related to economic uncertainty in 10 leading US newspapers. The keywords include "economic" or "economy"; "uncertain" or "uncertainty", "congress", "deficit", "Federal Reserve", "legislation", "regulation", and "White House", etc. What they highlight in their paper is an extensive audit study of 12,000 randomly selected articles drawn from major US newspapers. The auditors manually assess whether a given article discusses economic policy uncertainty, which not only lends credibility to their results but also provides insights on domain knowledge for future studies.

Yet another important application of textual analysis in social science entails extracting sentiment information from texts. In a pioneering study, Tetlock (2007) used General Inquirer's Harvard IV-4 psychosocial dictionary as a keyword list and counted the number of words in each day's

WSJ that fall within various word categories. Employing principal component factor analysis, he extracted the most important semantic component to construct media sentiment. He found that high media pessimism predicts downward pressure on market prices followed by a reversion to fundamentals, and unusually high or low pessimism predicts high market trading volume. A number of follow-up studies document similar results as those obtained by Tetlock (2007).

These types of asset pricing prediction exercises are often based on one of the two assumptions. First, the stock market may be inefficient, meaning that not all information in the newspapers is incorporated in the stock market. Second, newspapers not only report on the state of the economy but also play an active role in influencing it. While the first assumption is difficult to justify, some studies successfully validate the second assumption. For example, Wisniewski and Lambe (2013) used pre-defined word lists to measure the intensity of negative media speculation and showed that negative media attention of the banking sector has real effects. They showed that over the sub-prime crisis period, pessimistic coverage Granger-caused the returns on banking indices, while in contrast causality is not as significant, which suggests that journalistic views have the potential to influence market outcomes. The caveat is that their sample period was when extreme conditions existed in the world, i.e., the Great Recession, and the results may not apply to other less extreme states of the economy. This is partially why most results in this strand of literature are driven by observations in the recessions.

For the count-based or manual-label approaches, domain knowledge is especially important. In other words, coming up with keywords or labels that suit the specific application is crucial. There are more and more dictionaries available to researchers, and some of these dictionaries are constructed to suit research specifically in economics and finance. Loughran and McDonald (2011) documented that some widely used dictionaries do not find relevance in the finance context. Their results highlight the importance of domain knowledge. To solve this problem, they constructed a refined word list that applies to financial contexts and also made it publicly available for others to use. More specifically, they classify words into negative, positive, uncertainty, litigious, strong modal, weak modal, and constraining categories. They show that predictive power increases using their keyword list over other more general-purpose dictionaries.

Since then, the Loughran–McDonald Sentiment Word List has become one of the most widely used dictionaries in finance research. As of April 2019, there are more than 1,900 citations for Loughran and McDonald (2011) and many of those citations are from academic research that uses their word list. Our view is that there will be more and more refined dictionaries coming out, aiding researchers taking simple count-based approach to analyze text data. At the same time, tools developed in other fields could prove to be useful. For example, Bollen *et al.* (2011) used other dictionary-based tools such as OpinionFinder and Google's Profile of Mood States to measure the sentiment in Twitter messages and correlated it with stock market movements.

Pre-defining dictionaries or manual labeling, as done in the aforementioned studies, could perform well. However, such an approach has several limitations. First, because the method of labeling and defining the dictionary or bag of words is task specific and requires domain expertise, count-based and manual-label methods (at least with static dictionaries) thus may not be generalizable or flexible as an analytics tool for studying a wide range of problems. It achieves scalability once variables are guided or constructed by the researchers. But to select the right model and construct the variables, researchers have also searched over a complex space which is computationally expensive, and domain knowledge takes years to accumulate. Second, with a large dictionary or a large dataset, representing each word as a long vector with all but one entry being non-zero means the computations are inherently high dimensional, and manual labeling becomes infeasible. Third, count-based and manual-label methods leave out finer linguistic structures and may miss important information in the texts.

For additional survey articles on text-based analysis in economics, sociology, and political science, please see Gentzkow *et al.* (2017), Evans and Aceves (2016), and Grimmer and Stewart (2013). In particular, Gentzkow *et al.* (2017) pointed out that new techniques are needed to deal with the large-scale and complex nature of textual data.

4. Statistical Inference and Regression Models

Beside count-based and manual-label methods that require domain knowledge, data-driven and model-based inference has become increasingly popular for analyzing textual information for decision-making.

Latent Dirichlet Allocation (LDA) is one of the most widely used modeling techniques topics. LDA discovers the abstract topics that occur in a collection of documents and in so doing classifies texts documents to different topics. While manual labeling typically occurs in supervised learning, LDA is routinely used in unsupervised learning without labels.

LDA models assume a simple, dual distribution data generating process where each document is generated from a (latent) distribution over a collection of topics and each topic is a distribution over the words in the vocabulary. LDA proposes a hierarchical Bayesian model for the generative process of each document d. First, each topic $\beta_k \sim$ Dirichlet (η) is a multinomial distribution over the vocabulary of words. Second, one generates a multinomial distribution over K topics for this particular document d, denoted as $\theta_d \sim$ Dirichlet (α). The word generation process for this document d is as follows: for a word W_{di} in this document, sample a specific topic $z_{di} \in \{1,2,\ldots,K\}$ with $z_{di} \sim \theta_d$, then sample the observed word $W_{di} \sim \beta_{Z_{di}}$. Or equivalently, the probability of a word W_{di} to be a word w in the dictionary is obtained as follows:

$$P(W_{di} = w|\theta_d, \beta_1, \ldots, \beta_K) = \sum_k \theta_{dk}\beta_{kw} =: [\Theta B]_{dw},$$

where the matrix notation $\Theta := [\theta_1,\ldots,\theta_D]' \in \mathbb{R}^{D\times K}$ and $B = [\beta_1,\ldots, \beta_K]' \in \mathbb{R}^{K\times V}$.

Here, we provide a simple illustration. Suppose we have the following set of text documents. Each text contains only one sentence.

Text 1: Economics studies the behavior and interactions of economic agents.

Text 2: Microeconomics, macroeconomics, and econometrics are the most prominent fields in economics.

Text 3: Education is the process of acquiring knowledge, skills, and values.

Text 4: Formal education includes many stages, such as preschool or kindergarten, elementary school, high school, college, and graduate schools.

Text 5: Economic training is an essential part of the curriculum in many stages of education; most high schools offer courses on microeconomics and macroeconomics.

LDA could produce something such as the following:

Text 1 and 2: 100% Topic A
Text 3 and 4: 100% Topic B
Text 5: 60% Topic A, 40% Topic B
Topic A: 70% economics, 10% microeconomics, 10% macroeconomics, 10% econometrics
Topic B: 40% education, 30% school, 10% knowledge, 10% skills, 10% values.

It is then up to the researchers to interpret the topics. In this example, Topic A could be interpreted to be about economies, whereas B deals with education.

At a high level, the algorithm of LDA is as follows. First, researchers specify the number of topics, K, in the collection of the documents. Second, for words in the corpus, LDA randomly classifies each word as one of the K topics. Third, suppose that the topic assigned to a word is wrong but the topics assigned to other words are correct, then assign another topic to this particular word. We choose the new topic based on the topics in this document and the number of times this word is assigned to other topics in all of the documents. Finally, we repeat this process a number of times for each document and calculate the relative weight of each topic. Since the LDA model has been around for the past decade, there are many LDA packages written in many statistical languages that are very easy to use. One just needs to clean and tokenize the text data before feeding them into LDA packages. Researchers have applied LDA to analyze all sorts of text data in finance. For example, Huang *et al.* (2017) applied LDA to compare conference call transcripts and the subsequent analysis reports; Jegadeesh and Wu (2017) studied the information content of Federal Reserve communications; Hansen *et al.* (2017) also analyzed FOMC meeting transcripts during Alan Greenspan's tenure and found that transparency leads to greater accountability; Hassan *et al.* (2017) used LDA on firms' quarterly earnings conference calls transcripts to construct a new measure of political risk faced by individual US firms.

It has been observed that LDA becomes computationally very expensive on large datasets (Mikolov *et al.*, 2013a), and without principled prior choices, extremely common words tend to dominate all topics (Wallach *et al.*, 2009). Therefore, applying LDA directly to financial or economic settings with big data could be ineffective or even misleading.

While topic modeling is widely used in the finance literature these days, it is not the only methodology in this category. Manela and Moreira (2017) took a regression approach to construct an index of news-implied market volatility based on texts from the WSJ from 1890 to 2009. They applied support vector regression — equivalent to a variant of LASSO — which uses a penalized least squares objective to identify a small subset of words whose frequencies are most useful for matching patterns of turbulence in financial markets. They find that news coverage related to wars and government policy most often explains the variation in risk premia that their measure identifies. Gentzkow *et al.* (2016) measured trends in the partisanship of congressional speech from 1873 to 2016, defining partisanship to be the ease with which an observer could infer a congressperson's party from a single utterance. The authors adopt two estimation approaches. The first is a leave-out estimator that addresses the main source of finite-sample bias while allowing for simple inspection of the data. The second, our preferred estimator, uses a LASSO-type penalty on key model parameters to control bias and a Poisson approximation to the multinomial logit likelihood to permit distributed computing.

Several other models specifically deal with the ultra-high dimensional nature of the text documents. For example, Taddy (2015) approximated the multinomial distribution of each word with independent Poisson regressions. His model is clever in the sense that the Poisson regression can be distributed across parallel computing units, making the implementation computationally feasible. Kelly *et al.* (2018) further extended this model to make it more applicable to economics and finance context. They build on Taddy's (2015) distributed multi-dimensional regression (DMR) insight of independent phrase-level models but replaced each phrase-level Poisson regression with a hurdle model that has two components. The first component is a selection equation, which models the text producer's choice of whether or not to use a particular phrase (similar to the idea in Heckman, 1979). The second component is a positive counts model, which describes the choice of how many times a word is used. The idea behind their model is that not only do positive phrases count as informative but also whether some words are used at all also conveys important information.

5. Machine Learning and NLP

Recent tools from the natural language processing (NLP) literature present an alternative for analyzing textual data. Machine learning techniques such as neural networks language models preserve the syntactic and semantic structure well while maintaining computational tractability. Yet, these models are often not transparent and thus are limited in their direct applications in social sciences, which often require economic inference and interpretation. In fact, they are often referred to as "black box" models in statistics.

Word embedding is arguably the most popular representation of document vocabulary within the NLP category. It captures the context of a word in a document, semantic and syntactic similarities, relation with other words, etc., via representing words in vectors. Compared to the count-based method, word-embedding models are data driven. The idea is that words tend to co-occur with neighboring words with similar meanings. In the vector space, words are relationally oriented in the sense that words with similar meaning are closer to each other. In addition, distances between words turn out to have meanings as well. The most famous example is the "King/Man–Woman/Queen" relationship. Taking vector("King") – vector("Man") + vector("Woman") results in a vector that is closest to the vector representation of the word Queen (Figure 1).

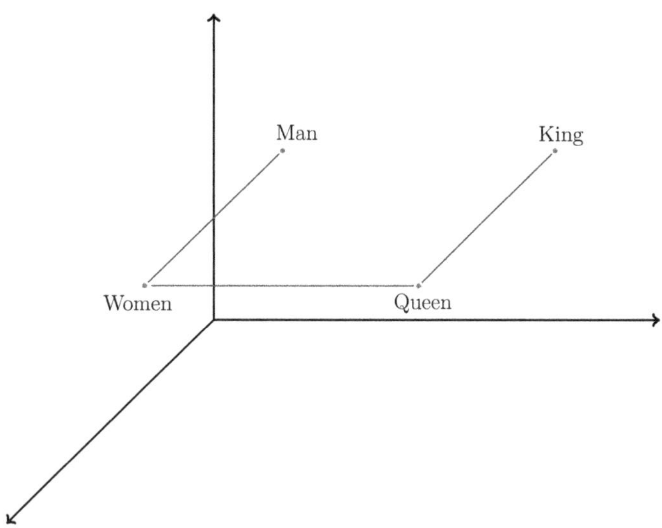

Figure 1: A graphical illustration of King/Man–Woman/Queen example.

Neural networks are not new — they have been around for decades but the lack of accessible, affordable computational power as well as available data were major bottlenecks. The advent of more sophisticated algorithms, computational powers from GPUs becoming cheaper, and data literally flooding in from all sources have led to what can be called a renaissance for deep learning. The major advantage of these models over traditional models is the performance gain with the increase in the amount of data. Neural network-based models become better and better as the data size increases.

Many recent studies argue that a vector-based representation exhibits both syntactic/semantic and computational advantages over the classic index representation and count-based methods. Based on developments in the state-of-the-art neural network language models, Mikolov *et al.* (2013) (word2vec) proposed simple network architectures that learn high-quality high-dimensional vector representation of words from huge datasets. One key advantage of the word vector representation is that it measures multiple degrees of similarities both in the syntactic and semantic sense and that similar words are "close" to each other in the vector representation. There are two main approaches for learning semantic vector representations.

Bengio *et al.* (2003) and Mikolov *et al.* (2013a, 2013b) proposed one hidden-layer neural network models to learn the representation (word-2vec). The hidden layer (with p hidden units) encodes the vector representation $w, \tilde{w} \in \mathbb{R}^{p \times V}$.[4] Then based on *local* context windows, one aims to optimize $w, \tilde{w}$,

$$\min_{w,\tilde{w}} - \sum_{\substack{i \in corpus \\ j \in context(i)}} \left\{ \langle w_i, \tilde{w}_j \rangle - \log\left(\sum_{k \in V} \exp(\langle w_i, \tilde{w}_k \rangle) \right) \right\}.$$

Mikolov *et al.* (2013b) proposed computationally efficient approximation schemes including "negative sampling" and "hierarchical soft-max" to train word2vec models, which scale well with tasks involving billions of words (Mikolov *et al.*, 2013a).

Another representation learning approach was proposed by Pennington *et al.* (2014) and was based on *global* concurrence X_{ij}. For some

[4]Here, we focus on the skip-gram model to predict its context based on a word, where w corresponds to weights between the input layer and the hidden layer and $\tilde{w}$ denotes the weights between the hidden layer and the output layer.

pre-chosen weights function $f(\cdot)$, one optimizes the weighted least squares to learn $w, \tilde{w} \in \mathbb{R}^{p \times V}$,

$$\min_{w,\tilde{w}} \sum_{i,j \in V} f\left(X_{ij}\right)\left(\langle w_i, \tilde{w}_j \rangle - \log X_{ij}\right)^2.$$

A good choice of the function f is $f(x) = (x/x_{\max})^{3/4} \wedge 1$ (see Pennington *et al.*, 2014).

Simply put, word embedding aims to represent words via vectors such that similar words or words used in a similar context are close to each other while antonyms end up far apart in the vector space. Contrary to count-based methods, these vectors are dense (generally a few hundred dimensions as opposed to the number of unique words in all text documents, which can reach tens of thousands).

Word2vec is one of the most popular methods to construct a word-embedding representation. There are two algorithms that generate word-2vec embeddings, continuous bag of words (CBOW) and Skip-Gram. Given a set of text documents, the model loops on the words of each sentence and either tries to use the current word to predict its neighbors (its context), in which case the method is called Skip-Gram, or it uses each of these contexts to predict the current word, in which case the method is called CBOW. Both algorithms yield satisfying results.

Most applications of word2vec or other word-embedding models are in computer science, such as automatic summarization, machine translation, named entity resolution, sentiment analysis, information retrieval, speech recognition, and question answering. It is still relatively new to researchers in economics and finance, though we do believe that there will be more and more papers that capitalize on the advantages of these models.

The study by Li *et al.* (2018) is an elegant example applying word-2vec in finance. The authors first learn the meanings of all the words and phrases from earnings call transcripts. They then construct a "culture dictionary" of words and phrases culled from earnings called transcripts that most frequently appear in close association with each of the five cultural values: innovation, integrity, quality, respect, and teamwork. They find that corporate culture significantly influences deal incidence and merger pairing and that post-merger, acquirers' cultural values are positively related to their target firms' cultural values pre-merger.

One challenge facing these applications of word embedding is interpretation, in terms of both model complexity/transparency as well as economic explainability. Embedding naturally introduces notions of distance among vector representation of words or phrases; one can therefore potentially use clustering techniques to further enhance the interpretability of word groups.

6. A Textual-Factor Framework

The various tradeoffs in the above three approaches are summarized in Figure 2. Given the speed at which rich textual data are generated and the fast pace of developments of industry applications, many attempts have been made recently to analyze texts at a large scale while allowing information richness and ensuring computational efficiency and economic interpretability. We elaborate on one attempt entailing the use of "textual factors".

For example, Cong *et al.* (2019) developed a textual factor framework to potentially tackle problems encountered in current approaches. The authors drew insights and strengths from both neural network models for

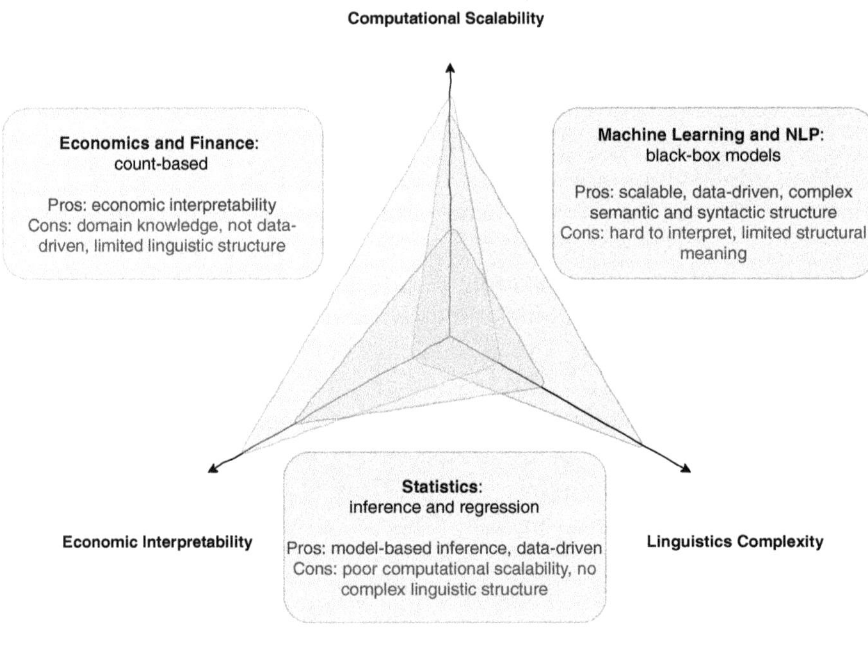

Figure 2: Tradeoffs in various approaches.

Source: Reproduced from Cong *et al.* (2019, Figure 1).

NLP and topic models in statistical machine learning. In particular, they developed a framework to summarize and analyze textual data, with the goal of preserving the informational structure (syntactic and semantic) encoded in natural languages, ensuring computational scalability and economic interpretability and relating to linear regression models commonly used in social sciences. They then demonstrated the efficacy of the textual factors generated and applied them to study issues in finance and economics.

Their textual-factor approach involves two stages. First, they form an interpretable set of vectors from the textual data that "span" the word document space. In other words, the authors identified a small number of textual factors that explained the main variations in the texts. Second, they projected each data sample of texts onto the textual factors to find out the beta loadings, which are quantitative measurements/explanatory features for downstream regression tasks.

The goal of the first stage is to generate textual factors to adequately represent the textual data, allow fast computation, and preserve interpretability. It further comprises three steps, as we describe next.

(1a) Word Embedding: They started with a continuous vector embedding of each word in a large vocabulary using neural networks (word2vec) in order to construct the semantic and syntactic links of words in the texts. This step represents words or multi-grams in the texts that can be used to capture the rich information and complex language structure.

Count-based and statistical models for textual analysis in social sciences traditionally adopt the "one-hot" representation: words (or N-grams) are treated as very high dimensional vectors/indices over a vocabulary with only one 1 and lots of 0's. Such approaches leave out any consideration of the semantic relations among words and therefore lack natural notions of similarity among words, resulting in sparse, high-dimensional, and noisy representations.

In contrast, Cong *et al.* (2019) used semantic vector representations obtained in the NLP literature, which account for word similarities, preserve the language structure, and reduce ambient noise. Specifically, each unique word is mapped to a real-valued p-dimensional vector, where $p \ll V$. The dimensionality p of the real-valued vectors can be orders of magnitude smaller than the dimensionality V of the "one-hot" representation.

(1b) Scalable Clustering: The authors build on the vector representation to cluster vectors pointing into similar directions. The second step is a key innovation and aims at balancing the interpretability and complexity of their model and reducing the dimensionality for computational ease. As "educated guesses" of the true topics, the clusters would be used for the third step of topic modeling.

The semantic vector representation significantly reduces the dimensionality compared to the classic "one-hot" representation. However, to capture the language structure well, the representation is still inherently high dimensional (with p typically being few hundreds). In addition, the total number of words in the vocabulary is oftentimes very large (V at least ten thousands for real applications). Since the semantic vector representation preserves similarity, the authors argued that the next natural step was to cluster words that are similar to each other through unsupervised learning, yielding in a data-driven manner a number of "topics/clusters" that are easy to interpret.

That said, clustering in high dimensions is notoriously hard both statistically and computationally. For most classic clustering methods, the computation complexity ($O(V^2p)$ in our case) depends on the number of items to cluster (denoted as V), which has poor scalability in practice. To overcome this challenge, the authors resorted to the latest theoretical computer science literature and applied the so-called locality-sensitive hashing (LSH) (Datar *et al.*, 2004; Andoni *et al.*, 2015) in our setting.

The basic idea behind LSH is to return near-neighbor information in near-linear time through constructing a family of hash functions H with the following property: for a random element $h(\cdot) \in H$,

$$h(x) = h(y) \text{ with probability at least } 1 - p_1, \quad \text{for any } x, y \text{ such that } d(x,y) \leq d1,$$
$$h(x) = h(y) \text{ with probability at most } p_2, \quad \text{for any } x, y \text{ such that } d(x,y) \geq d2,$$

where the probability is with respect to the sampling of the hash functions.[5] Intuitively, the hash functions help in assessing the similarity in that they seldom claim two items to be similar when they are actually far away, nor do they conclude two close items to be disparate.

Building upon the LSH technique for approximate near-neighbor search, the authors have introduced several scalable clustering algorithms.

[5]Near-linear time means $O(Vk)$, where k is the number of hash functions to generate the Hash table.

They then demonstrate the quality of the clusters and the scalability of the methodology.

(1c) Guided Topic Modeling: The authors used the clustering results obtained in (1b) to guide and enhance a topic model. Because LDA is computationally expensive on large datasets and lacks separability, the authors advocate a "clustering" perspective of topic modeling. Much of the statistical and computational difficulty for topic modeling roots in the fact that LDA allows topics to have overlap in terms of words, rather than separability (or, "anchor words", meaning words that only appear in one unique topic). Without the separability of topics, it is very hard to clearly identify various topics (provably NP-hard, Sontag and Roy, 2011). They overcome this difficulty by learning the separability of topics in a data-driven manner by incorporating the semantic vector representation. That is, they utilize the vector representation of words as guidance and enhance our topic modeling approach. Based on the semantic similarity among words captured by the vector representation, it is more likely that close-by words belong to the same topic. This prior knowledge significantly reduces the search space/complexity of the topic–word distributions, therefore easing the optimization approach.

With the word clusters obtained earlier, they then develop computationally efficient and conceptually simple methods to learn textual factors. Because the word lists of topics are more disjoint, the topics are largely distinct from each other, in contrast to the case in plain-vanilla LDA where extremely common words (or, stop words) dominate multiple topics (Wallach *et al.*, 2009). The key computational trick is then to estimate one topic at a time given the separability of clusters. For instance, given the ith cluster, with support (set of indices) $S_i \subset [V]$, we can focus on the document–term submatrix N_{S_i}, where the columns consist of words only in the ith cluster. In the paper the authors implement this procedure using a frequentist approach to topic modeling, i.e., Latent Semantic Analysis (LSA) through Singular-Value Decomposition.

The authors claim that such data-driven guidance significantly enhances the performance of the topic model for unsupervised learning. More empirical work can test this claim.

(2) Beta Loadings on Textual Factors: Suppose that from the first stage we obtain K textual factors, where K is endogenously specified and can potentially be data dependent. The set of textual factors are then represented by the triplet $(S_i, F_i \in \mathbb{R}^{|S_i|}, d_i \in \mathbb{R}_{\geq 0})$, where S_i denotes the support of word cluster i, a real-valued vector representing the textual factor F_i, and the factor importance d_i. Given a new data point (document d) represented by a document–term vector $N^{(d)} \in \mathbb{R}^V$, the loadings of the textual factor i is simply

$$x_i^{(d)} := \frac{\left\langle N_{S_i}^{(d)}, F_i \right\rangle}{\left\langle F_i, F_i \right\rangle} \tag{1}$$

and the document D can be represented quantitatively as $(x_1^{(d)}, \ldots, x_k^{(d)}) \in \mathbb{R}^K$.

To understand the meaning of these loadings, take publicly listed firms for example. A company discloses numbers on revenues, profits, liabilities, etc. Texts about the company could also touch on profitability, social responsibility, innovativeness, etc., each of which is a topic, the $x_k^{(d)}$ we obtain allows us to assign a coefficient that measures how much the company is exposed to that topic — a metric we can obtain in simple sparse regressions.

Finally, the authors remark that one can easily generalize their methodology to apply to document–term matrices that include multi-grams. And in that case, one can significantly reduce the dimensionality of the multi-gram space by considering multi-grams with words in only one or say a few topics.

6.1. *Illustrations*

To check whether the textual factors generated make sense, the authors first use a few examples to illustrate their interpretability. They first compare the word clusters generated from Google word embedding with the plain-vanilla LDA and print out the support of the word clusters. Table 1 displays the top three obtained "clusters", or topics by plain-vanilla LDA. As we can see, extremely common words dominate each cluster, which clouds the meaning of different topics. In contrast, Table 2 illustrates the effectiveness of their clustering method based on LSH. The gain in interpretability is apparent. The authors also report drastic gains in computational efficiency of the textual factor approach, as compared to a plain-vanilla LDA model.

They also test the robustness and sensibility of loadings on their constructed textual factors. Specifically, they inspect the trends of loadings

Table 1: Sample plain-vanilla LDA clusters.

Cluster	Support
Topic ID: 62, Prob: 0.20071%	**washington**, tax, business, york, labor, letter, bulletin, wire, report, old, many, big, **president**, like, long, economic, **prices**, time, ago, federal, outlook, city, get, high, sales, white, house, back, people, even, state, just, home, world, much, **american**, man, next, **government**, job, million, still, work, companies, workers, economy, men, three, little
Topic ID: 1272, Prob: 0.17438%	stock, dividend, steel, business, **american**, oil, common, market, york, **earnings**, months, outlook, **cents**, made, record, way, chicago, share, company, united, net, time, **president**, rate, **prices**, increase, railroad, states, june, **price**, **general**, review, shares, declared, july, report, cotton, preferred, sales, **washington**, present, large, month, regular, production, exchange, pacific, cars, quarterly, september
Topic ID: 1828: Prob: 0.11747%	steel, states, business, united, outlook, review, railroad, stock, way, market, york, country, time, **president**, great, made, **american**, **prices**, copper, increase, **earnings**, corporation, public, **government**, per, national, **general**, since, **washington**, cotton, crop, bank, report, months, state, much, commission, present, **cent**, railroads, rate, conditions, **price**, large, street, ago, letter, pacific, trade, three

Source: Reproduced from Cong *et al.* (2019).

over time from 1900 to 2000 on *Wall Street Journal* article titles, for representative clusters such as "Recession", "War", and "Computer". From the plots of loadings over time, their results seem plausible because the intensity of the textual factors accurately captures the prominence of these topics in history (Figure 3).

6.2. *Applications*

The authors describe three methods of applying the textual-factor framework. First, textual factors can help predict or explain outcomes in cross-section, time series, and panel data analysis. For example, one can use newspaper front-page titles and abstracts to forecast macroeconomic outcomes such as CPI or to train a model to better understand the factors driving market volatility or to backfill the VIX index in a manner similar

Table 2: Sample clusters.

Cluster	Support
Tax	quotas, visa, harvestable, import, preferential, abolished, tariffs, quota, sanction, compulsory, tariff, compulsorily, stipulating, fisheries, cess, exports, pricing, export, telcos, exporters, import, liberalization, preferential, excise, tax, importers, deregulation, antidumping, subsidy
Oil	refiners, refiner, refineries, refinery, petrochemical, feedstock, pipelines, smelters, crudes, oil, bpd, gasoline, petrochemicals, petroleum, refining, ethanol, tankers, coker, ethylene, feedstock, crude
Unemployment	stimulus, foreclosures, recession, claimants, workweek, unemployed, housing, unemployment, jobless, economy, workers
Volatility	correction, uptrend, readjustment, reversal, retest, revision, divergence, retrenchment, steepening, selloff, rebalancing, bearish, pullbacks, corrective, correcting, reversion, stabilization, selldown, snapback, reassessment, volatility, pullback, bull, corrections, bottoming, downtrend
Exports	consignments, foodstuffs, exports, tins, cargo, goods, warehouses, equipments, importers, exporting, containers, tonnages, exporters, import, imports, perishable, cartons, cargoes, export, adulterated, tankers, pallets, wholesalers, demurrage, customs, transporters, consignment, consignee, exported
Investment	development, capitalization, differentiation, invest, macro, optionality, strategic, capex, macroeconomic, countercyclical, investments, investing, outperformance, diversification, equity, arbitrage, diversify, cyclicality, underperformance, diversifying, expansion, diversified, geographies, reinvest, specialization, profitability, deleveraging, consolidation, renewables, volatility, investment, liquidity, growth, maximization, sector, cyclical, synergy, reinvesting, investors, reinvestment
Stimulus	appropriation, moneys, underfunded, money, reauthorization, subsidies, budget, fundings, budgeted, allocations, budgets, budgetary, stimulus, funded, appropriations, funds, grant, non-federal, appropriated, earmarked, infrastructure, reauthorized, assistance, unfunded, funding, financing, grants, monies, support, underfunding
Disasters	disturbances, occurance, instances, recur, disasters, incidences, occur, occurence, occurrences, causes, occurred, occurrence, phenomenon, earthquakes, anomaly, outbreaks, accidents, incidents, emergencies, observations, tragedies, ultramafic, catastrophes, polymetallic, anomalous, calamities, infrequent, phenomena, anomalies, happening, intrusions, contaminations, occurring

Table 2: (*Continued*)

Cluster	Support
War	battles, confrontation, dispute, fighting, showdown, struggle, fight, battle, wars, fierce, war, battles, confrontation, showdown, matchups, fight, battle, victory
Election	political, intellectual, politically, election, politicians, democratic, religious, republican, incumbency, diplomatic, politics, economic

Source: Reproduced from Cong *et al.* (2019).

to that used by Manela and Moreira (2017). The study by Cong *et al.* (2019) contains some illustrations.

Second, they can be used to interpret the existing explanatory variables constructed from structured data, such as Fama–French three factors, or patent citations. For example, discussions on risk factors or MD&A from company filings can provide useful information on the cross-sectional beta loadings on the Fama–French three factors (Cong *et al.*, 2019). More generally, textual factors can be used to interpret complex machine learning and AI models in social sciences. The study by Cong *et al.* (2019) projects a deep reinforcement learning model of portfolio management onto the textual space to understand what themes in firms' filing are more related to the portfolios constructed by an AI-based strategy.

Finally, they allow a data-driven method for constructing explanatory variables or metrics. This last dimension also points to the possibility for textual factors to create new domain knowledge and opens new frontiers of analysis. For example, using structured data such as revenue and user base to value start-ups has been challenging because most early projects do not generate stable or positive cash flow, and their valuation largely depends on investors' beliefs and perception. In contrast, information extracted from unstructured data in news, forum discussion, user feedback, and ratings can provide meaningful insights into start-up's valuation. Another example is to use texts to construct metrics of market sentiments, building on earlier work by Garcia (2013). One can use proxy statements to measure corporate governance (Cong *et al.*, 2019) or patents and stock prices to measure innovation (e.g., Chen *et al.*, 2019).

In what follows, we take their methodology to backfill expectation errors in the credit market. This is an important issue because academics and policymakers debate over whether expectation errors predict future

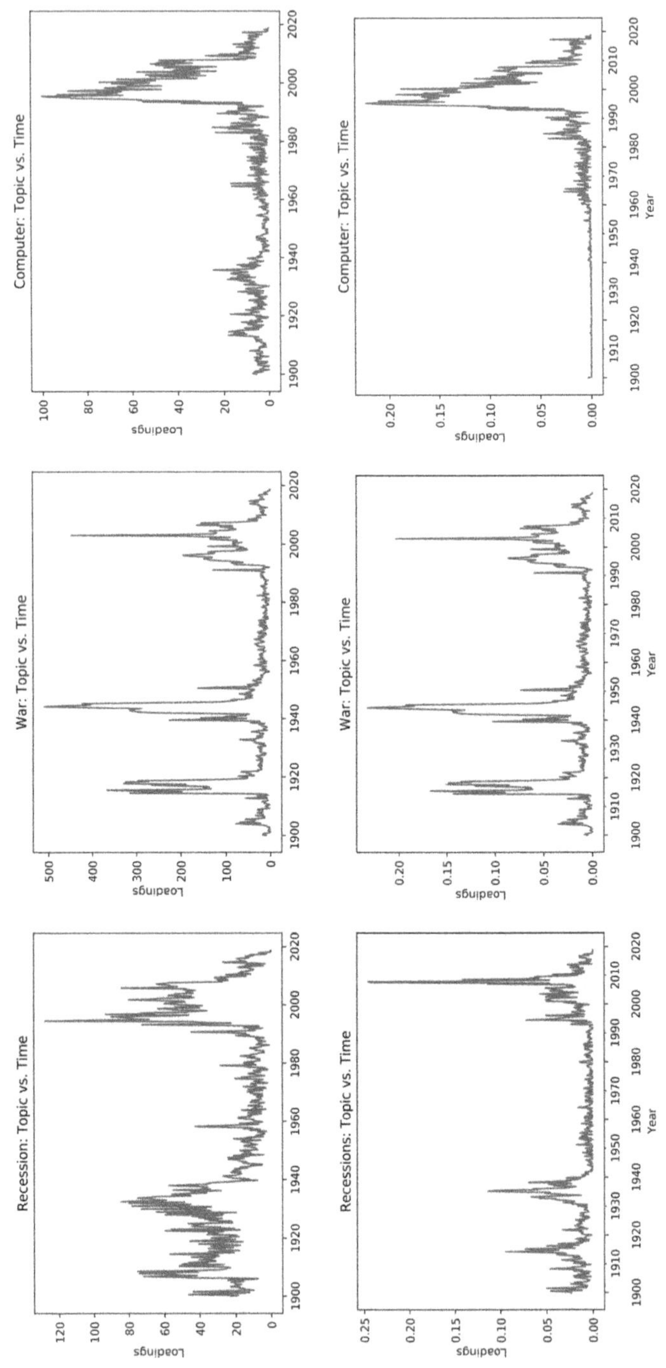

Figure 3: Loadings on textual factors over time, WSJ data. The three columns correspond to "Recession", "War", and "Computer", respectively.

Source: Reproduced from Cong *et al.* (2019).

macroeconomic outcomes. To answer this question, we need a long time series of expectation data. However, forecast data of credit spread are available only for recent years. To overcome this problem, we backfill expectation error data by applying textual analysis to article titles in the WSJ. We use Blue Chip Financial Forecast data from 1999 to 2017 as our training sample and use text data to backfill expectation from 1929 to 1998.

To backfill expectation error, we first estimated the following model:

$$error_t = \alpha + \gamma x_t^T + \eta_t, \tag{2}$$

where $error_t$ is the difference between the expectation and the realized Baa corporate bond spread. The expectation of Baa corporate bond spread is defined as the consensus forecast of Baa corporate bond yield minus the consensus forecast of 10-year Treasury yield. Both are 1-year forecasts collected from Blue Chip Financial Forecasts. The realized Baa corporate bond Spread is calculated in the same manner using historical value.

To further manage model dimensionality, we apply LASSO penalization to estimate (2). We find that discussions about government (e.g., taxes, president, white house, and Washington), finance (money, banks, treasury, credit, and stock), recessions (e.g., great depressions, great recessions, crisis, and economic downturns), and war (e.g., military, world war, and Iraq) are the most useful in constructing expectation error. Using estimated γ and topic loadings, we backcast expectation errors for a long horizon, as shown in Figure 4.

A clear pattern emerges from Figure 4: expectation error tends to be positive (overly optimistic) at the end of booms and negative (overly pessimistic) during recessions. The countercyclical nature suggests that expectation error may predict business cycles. We explore this pattern more carefully in the following predictive regression framework:

$$\Delta y_{t+h} = \beta_0 + \beta_1 \widehat{error_t} + \sum \beta_j controls_{j,t} + \epsilon_{t+h},$$

where Δy_{t+h} is the log difference of real GDP per capita over the course of year $t + h$. $error_t$ is the backfilled expectation error averaged over year $t - 1$ to year t. $controls_{j,t}$ include change in credit spreads over year t, change in GDP per capita from year $t - 1$ to t, CPI inflation rate, and changes in short-term and long-term Treasury yields. As a robustness

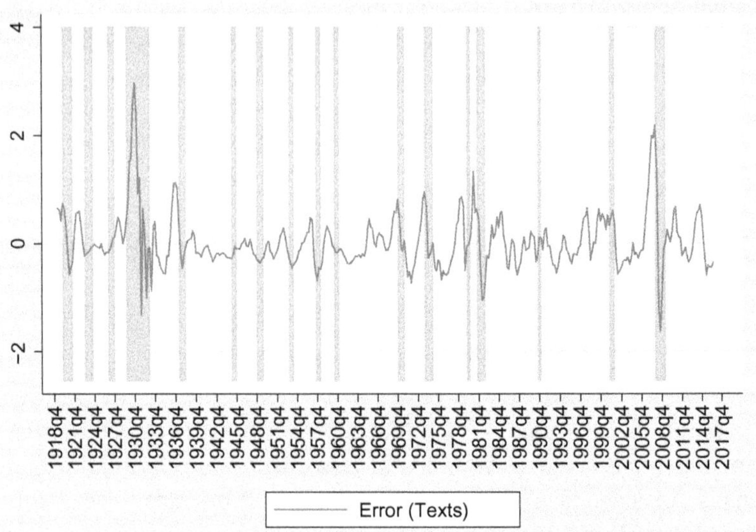

Figure 4: Backfilling expectation error.

check, we also include several lags of the control variables to ensure that the mean reversion in GDP growth is not responsible for the results.

Table 3 presents various specifications of the predictive regression for different horizons. The explanatory variable of interest in this table is $\widehat{error}_t$. From Columns 1 to 3, we vary 1-year output growth on the left-hand side from being contemporaneous to 2 years into the future. As can be seen from Column 2, the expectation error at t has a substantial forecasting power for GDP growth in years $t+1$ and $t+2$, even after controlling for changes in credit spread: a one standard deviation increase in expectation error is associated with a step-down in real GDP growth per capita of 0.45–0.5 standard deviations, or about 1.2 percentage points. In Columns 4–6, we add levels of credit spread as an additional control. The results remain largely unchanged. Neither changes nor levels of credit spread are predictive of real GDP growth in year $t+1$ or $t+2$. Instead, expectation error is a strong predictor of future GDP growth.

It should be noted that the textual factor framework should not be viewed as a competing model with many recent studies in finance using text analytics. Instead, it is an upstream tool that can replace LDA as an intermediate step in many of the studies. The factor structure should also

Table 3: Predictive regressions: Real GDP growth.

	(1) ***h***=0	(2) ***h***=1	(3) ***h***=2	(4) ***h***=0	(5) ***h***=1	(6) ***h***=2
Δ *Expectation Error*$_{t-1}$	0.004	–0.022***	–0.021***	0.005	–0.020***	–0.021***
	(0.005)	(0.006)	(0.006)	(0.005)	(0.007)	(0.006)
Δ *Credit Spread*$_{t-1}$	–0.043***	0.004	0.004	–0.044***	–0.001	0.002
	(0.008)	(0.010)	(0.010)	(0.008)	(0.011)	(0.010)
Credit Spread$_{t-1}$				0.001	0.007	0.002
				(0.005)	(0.006)	(0.004)
R^2	0.552	0.268	0.212	0.552	0.287	0.216

Notes: *controls*$_{j,t}$ also include changes in GDP and other significant variables documented in literature such as CPI inflation rate and changes in short-term and long-term Treasury yields. ***, **, * indicate coefficient estimates statistically different than zero at the 1%, 5%, and 10% confidence levels, respectively.

be familiar and transparent to social scientists, which facilitates economic interpretation and narrative development.

7. Other Approaches and Promising Directions

The textual factor approach is just one of the many plausible ways to improve textual analysis in social sciences. While there have been several attempts over the past few years, a few directions are especially worth highlighting. Instead of providing an exhaustive list, we discuss two of them.

7.1. *Dynamic and customized count-based methods*

The count-based approach can be further extended to analyze questions economists care about. For example, Hoberg and Phillips (2016) developed a new time-varying measurement of product similarity using business descriptions in 10-K filings to compute pairwise word similarity scores for each pair of firms in a given year. Specifically, they represented each text document using a vector, with each element being populated by the number 1 if that text uses the given word and 0 if it does not. Then they calculated the firm's pairwise similarity score using cosine similarity formula. They found that their measure of product similarity is much better than the traditional methods, such as using SIC and NAICS classification code, because their measure allowed industry competition to be firm centric and change over time. Equipped with this new measure, they studied questions related to theories of endogenous product differentiation and found that firm RD and advertising are associated with subsequent differentiation from competitors. Using a similar methodology, Hoberg and Phillips (2010) found that firms with more similar product descriptions are more likely to enter merger agreements and experience increased stock returns and real longer term gains in cash flows and higher growth.

While having the appearance of being count based, they are not susceptible to the usual limitations of count-based methods because they are dynamic and customized. To confirm this, Hoberg and Phillips (2016) used no pre-determination of vocabularies. The dictionaries are instead dynamic and customized to each firm based on general economic foundations regarding the concept of competition and rivalry. Specifically, each document is being scored to a different (dynamically selected) set of documents for comparison.[6]

Such dynamism and customization also manifest in the study by Hanley and Hoberg (2010) in which the dictionary is customized both in time and by industry and in some cases by an underwriter. One interesting sub-category of the dynamic count-based models comprises studies looking at "document revision intensity". The work of Brown and Tucker (2011) is an important early study in accounting using MD&As. Hanley and Hoberg (2012) used IPO prospectuses and found that a lack of content revision, when there is a price revision, indicates a situation where litigation and high underpricing are likely. More recently, Cohen *et al.* (2018) have showed that an active change in firms' reporting practices conveys an important signal about future firm operations and affects the share prices.

In all of the above studies, the authors customized comparisons and utilized dynamic word lists based on economic principles. Such a dynamic/customized extension to count-based methods is rather generalizable and flexible. For example, document revision has potential in many

---

[6]For example, a given firm in a given year is scored relative to the set of other firms in its neighborhood spatially and its own unique business description. This comparison is different for every firm without fixed global word lists and also changes over time as the documents evolve.

more settings. For extracting and analyzing information from textual data within a reasonable size and time frame, the dynamic/customized count-based approach holds great promise.

7.2. *Machine learning for economics*

Many machine learning tools often have the appearance of a black box and are hard to understand or interpret. Applying them to textual analysis without an effort to understand the underlying mechanism or economic content is likely futile. After all, we are economists aiming to contribute to philosophical and economic knowledge, not just raw predictability without insight.

That said, many recent developments in NLP, once properly used, provide supplementary data structures that are extremely informative about what drives any given signal. For example, topic models such LDA and LSA generate factors with their word lists, and word2vec gives an entire embedding matrix with a representation of each word that can be used to illustrate the content that resulted in any outcome. The key is to develop analytics using them in a transparent and interpretable manner. The textual factor framework we introduced in the previous section is an example in this direction.

Another example is the study by Hanley and Hoberg (2019), who combined an LDA model and word2vec (referred to as a semantic vector analysis in their paper) to identify the emerging risks using bank 10-K risk factor section. They applied an LDA model to identify topics that are important in explaining time series variation in risk that banks face. In their research setting, this approach is better than count-based methods that require domain knowledge because the sources of financial instability are inherently unpredictable and might be unknown *ex ante* to the researchers. Using the most representative words associated with each topic, they constructed risk exposure to different emerging risks by calculating cosine similarity based on semantic vectors. They found that the two models in tandem do a good job in detecting emerging risks. In addition, the elevated risks predicted the financial crisis of 2008 well before VIX or aggregate volatility. At the individual bank level, they found that banks with greater *ex ante* exposure to emerging risks experience significantly lower stock returns during the financial crisis, lending credibility to their methodology.

Both Hanley and Hoberg (2019) and Cong *et al.* (2019) derived factor structures from texts. While the study by Cong *et al.* (2019) aimed at a general factor generation tool for textual analysis, the study by Hanley and Hoberg (2019) had the goal of detecting systemically important risk factors pervasive across many banks that are interpretable so financial instability can be detected early, before linking them to the covariance matrix of bank stock prices. This could facilitate pre-emptive research by regulators and potentially pre-emptive policy remedies that can reduce damage before instability becomes a crisis. Their orders of applying word2vec and topic modeling are also different. The two papers complement each other well and the efficacy of their approaches jointly underscores the extraordinary value of utilizing embedding and NLP tools actively developed in computer science and statistics for applications and methodologies in economics and social science.

It is also worth mentioning that texts are sequential data and the latest developments in machine learning and AI from computer science, such as Bi-directional Long Short-term Memory, Transformer, and Google's BERT that are well designed for sequence learning, are likely useful in future applications of textual analysis in social sciences.

8. Concluding Remarks

Modern institutions leverage big data for originating loans, predicting asset returns, improving customer service, etc. Texts, as a form of unstructured data, are abundant and their interpretability sheds light on key economic mechanisms and explanatory variables. We discuss the recent developments in textual analysis and its applications in finance and economics. We highlight the need for a framework for analyzing large-scale text-based data that can capture complex linguistic structures while ensuring computational scalability and economic interpretability. As Athey (2018) predicted, "extensions and modifications of prediction methods to account for considerations such as fairness, manipulability, and interpretability to be among the very first changes to emerge concerning how empirical work is conducted". A few approaches combining the strengths of neural network language models and generative statistical modeling aim to balance model complexity and interpretability, which may prove to be promising directions and useful analytic tools for future research.

Acknowledgment

We are deeply indebted to Jerry Hoberg for his insightful comments.

References

Andoni, A., P. Indyk, T. Laarhoven, I. Razenshteyn, and L. Schmidt (2015), Practical and optimal LSH for angular distance, *Advances in Neural Information Processing Systems* (Curran Associates, Inc.), pp. 1225–1233.

Antweiler, W. and M. Z. Frank (2004), Is all that talk just noise? The information content of internet stock message boards, *The Journal of Finance* **59**, 1259–1294.

Athey, S. (2018), The impact of machine learning on economics, *The Economics of Artificial Intelligence: An Agenda* (University of Chicago Press).

Baker, S. R., N. Bloom, and S. J. Davis (2016), Measuring economic policy uncertainty, *Quarterly Journal of Economics* **131**, 1593–1636.

Bengio, Y., R. Ducharme, P. Vincent, and C. Jauvin (2003), A neural probabilistic language model, *Journal of Machine Learning Research* **3**, 1137–1155.

Bollen, J., H. Mao, and X. Zeng (2011), Twitter mood predicts the stock market, *Journal of Computational Science* **2**, 1–8.

Brown, S. V. and J. W. Tucker (2011), Large-sample evidence on firms year-over-year MD&A modifications, *Journal of Accounting Research* **49**, 309–346.

Chen, M. A., Q. Wu, and B. Yang (2019), How valuable is FinTech innovation? *Review of Financial Studies* **32**, 2062–2106.

Cohen, L., C. Malloy, and Q. Nguyen (2018), Lazy prices, Discussion paper, National Bureau of Economic Research.

Cong, L. W., T. Liang, and X. Zhang (2019), Textual factors: A scalable, interpretable, and data-driven approach to analyzing unstructured information, Working paper.

Cong, L. W., P. Foroughi, and N. Malenko (2019), A textual-factor approach to measuring corporate governance, Work in Progress.

Cong, L. W., K. Tang, J. Wang, and Y. Zhang (2019), AlphaPortfolio and interpretable AI for economics, Working paper.

Das, S. R. *et al.* (2014), Text and context: Language analytics in finance, *Foundations and Trends in Finance®* **8**, 145–261.

Datar, M., N. Immorlica, P. Indyk, and V. S. Mirrokni (2004), Locality-sensitive hashing scheme based on p-stable distributions, in *Proceedings of the Twentieth Annual Symposium on Computational Geometry*, ACM, pp. 253–262.

Evans, J. A. and P. Aceves (2016), Machine translation: Mining text for social theory, *Annual Review of Sociology* **42**, 21–50.

Garcia, D. (2013), Sentiment during recessions, *The Journal of Finance* **68**, 1267–1300.

Gentzkow, M., B. T. Kelly, and M. Taddy (2017), Text as data, Discussion paper, National Bureau of Economic Research.

Gentzkow, M., J. Shapiro, M. Taddy *et al.* (2016), Measuring polarization in high dimensional data: Method and application to congressional speech, Discussion paper.

Grimmer, J. and B. M. Stewart (2013), Text as data: The promise and pitfalls of automatic content analysis methods for political texts, *Political Analysis* **21**, 267–297.

Hanley, K. W. and G. Hoberg (2010), The information content of IPO prospectuses, *Review of Financial Studies* **23**, 2821–2864.

Hanley, K. W. and G. Hoberg (2012), Litigation risk, strategic disclosure and the underpricing of initial public offerings, *Journal of Financial Economics* **103**, 235–254.

Hanley, K. W. and G. Hoberg (2019), Dynamic interpretation of emerging risks in the financial sector, *Review of Financial Studies* **32**, 4543–4603.

Hansen, S., M. McMahon, and A. Prat (2017), Transparency and deliberation within the FOMC: A computational linguistics approach, *The Quarterly Journal of Economics* **133**, 801–870.

Hassan, T. A, S. Hollander, L. van Lent, and A. Tahoun (2017), Firm-level political risk: Measurement and effects, Working paper 24029, National Bureau of Economic Research.

Heckman, J. J. (1979), Sample selection bias as a specification error, *Econometrica* **47**, 153–161.

Hoberg, G. and G. Phillips (2010), Product market synergies and competition in mergers and acquisitions: A text-based analysis, *The Review of Financial Studies* **23**, 3773–3811.

Hoberg, G. and G. Phillips (2016), Text-based network industries and endogenous product differentiation, *Journal of Political Economy* **124**, 1423–1465.

Huang, A. H., R. Lehavy, A. Y. Zang, and R. Zheng (2017), Analyst information discovery and interpretation roles: A topic modeling approach, *Management Science* **64**, 2833–2855.

Jegadeesh, N. and D. A. Wu (2017), Deciphering Fedspeak: The information content of FOMC meetings.

Kearney, C. and S. Liu (2014), Textual sentiment in finance: A survey of methods and models, *International Review of Financial Analysis* **33**, 171–185.

Kelly, B., A. Manela, and A. Moreira (2018), Text selection, Working paper.

Li, F. (2010), Survey of the literature, *Journal of Accounting Literature* **29**, 143–165.

Li, K., F. Mai, R. Shen, and X. Yan (2018), Measuring corporate culture using machine learning, Available at SSRN 3256608.

Loughran, T. and B. McDonald (2011), When is a liability not a liability? Textual analysis, dictionaries, and 10-ks, *The Journal of Finance* **66**, 35–65.

Loughran, T. and B. McDonald (2016), Textual analysis in accounting and finance: A survey, *Journal of Accounting Research* **54**, 1187–1230.

Manela, A. and A. Moreira (2017), News implied volatility and disaster concerns, *Journal of Financial Economics* **123**, 137–162.

Mikolov, T., K. Chen, G. Corrado, and J. Dean (2013a), Efficient estimation of word representations in vector space, arXiv preprint arXiv:1301.3781.

Mikolov, T., I. Sutskever, K. Chen, G. S. Corrado, and J. Dean (2013b), Distributed representations of words and phrases and their compositionality, *Advances in Neural Information Processing Systems*, pp. 3111–3119.

Nini, G., D. C. Smith, and A. Sufi (2012), Creditor control rights, corporate governance, and firm value, *The Review of Financial Studies* **25**, 1713–1761.

Pennington, J., R. Socher, and C. Manning (2014), Glove: Global vectors for word representation, in *Proceedings of the 2014 Conference on Empirical Methods in Natural Language Processing (EMNLP)*, pp. 1532–1543.

Sontag, D. and D. Roy (2011), Complexity of inference in latent Dirichlet allocation, *Advances in Neural Information Processing Systems* (Curran Associates, Inc.), pp. 1008–1016.

Taddy, M. (2015), Document classification by inversion of distributed language representations, arXiv preprint arXiv:1504.07295.

Tetlock, P. C. (2007), Giving content to investor sentiment: The role of media in the stock market, *The Journal of Finance* **62**, 1139–1168.

Wallach, H. M., D. M. Mimno, and A. McCallum (2009), Rethinking LDA: Why priors matter, *Advances in Neural Information Processing Systems* (Curran Associates, Inc.), pp. 1973–1981.

Wisniewski, T. P. and B. Lambe (2013), The role of media in the credit crunch: The case of the banking sector, *Journal of Economic Behavior & Organization* **85**, 163–175.

https://doi.org/10.1142/9789811220470_0011

Chapter 11

Blockchain-Enabled Supply Chain Transparency, Supply Chain Structural Dynamics, and Sustainability of Complex Global Supply Chains — A Text Mining Analysis

Pankaj Kumar Medhi

School of Management, Bennett University, Noida, Uttar Pradesh, India

pankaj.binayak@gmail.com, pankaj.medhi@bennett.edu.in

Abstract

Blockchain technology has been hailed as the technology of the future, not only for banking and finance but also for supply chain management and logistics. As lack of transparency in global supply chains is a major risk for sustainability, blockchain offers an attractive solution in the form of a reliable platform to create transparency and risk management. Not considering the nascent stage of the technology, companies are investing millions of dollars into blockchain solutions for many business problems including that of supply chains. However, blockchain-enabled network-wide transparency and visibility also inject new dynamics into supply chains through introduction of structural changes like redefining what is organizational boundary, creating new resources, and a new transactional economy for supply chain management. The structural changes also create a fundamental need for organizations in a supply network to adapt their supply chain processes to this new and emerging supply chain structural dynamics for organizational and network-level efficiency and sustainability. For efficient restructuring of the supply chain processes, organizations need clarity regarding what should be the focus of their processes for creating sources of competitive advantage.

Using topic modeling, a text mining technique, this work finds the focus areas of supply chain processes in organizations with examples of successful application of blockchain technology. Apart from how these organizations have integrated the strengths of blockchain in their supply chain processes, we also provide an exhaustive theoretical explanation about how firms can create sources of competitive advantage from blockchain technology. Identification of the focus areas will also help operations and supply chain managers planning to implement blockchain technology and devise plans for data-centric decision-making for their SCM processes for efficiency.

Keywords: Blockchain; Technology; Supply Chain Transparency; Traceability; Trust; Digital; Ledger; Smart contract.

1. Introduction

Blockchain, the underlying technologies of the digital coins, has recently created a buzz among the researchers and practitioners of supply chain management due to its stated capability to bring a foundational change in the area of supply chain management (SCM). Leading organizations with extensive supply chains (SCs) are exploring blockchain technology for achieving improved SC information sharing and visibility, ability of product traceability and provenance, and smart contracts for operational efficiency and sustainability (Babich and Hilary, 2019; Francisco and Swanson, 2018; Treiblmaier, 2018). A recent study by Wang *et al.* (2019) found that secure information sharing among partner firms, improved visibility, capability for product tracking, and traceability are among the most perceived benefits of blockchain implementations in SCs. While the need for information sharing and improved visibility have always been desirable for operational efficiency in SCM (Barrat and Oke, 2007), many new problems related to SC transparency and product provenance have arisen due to extension of SCs across continents and sovereign regulations to ensure compliance by third-party suppliers of major supply networks (Birkey *et al.*, 2018; Kim *et al.*, 2016, Sarfaty, 2015).

Present-day SCs are global, complex, multitier networks of firms across countries and continents and, hence, are often fragmented (Kim *et al.*, 2016). Fragmentation of SCs often leads to high uncertainty about the origin of raw materials, inputs, and the final products and the conditions under which they are manufactured and transferred (Skilton and Robinson, 2009). In food industry, globalization and consequent fragmentation of SCs have not only created concerns about food safety and quality but also increased the chances of fraud, for example, about the origin of food (Aung and Chang, 2014). A survey in Portugal on food safety in the supply chain management documented that consumers often not only have doubts about ingredients and criteria for food conservation which could lead to food poisoning but also lack confidence in the information displayed on product labels (Oliveira, 2016). As a result, product provenance in food and pharmaceuticals industries has become an extremely important concern and is considered an important area for application of blockchain technology (Babich and Hilary, 2019).

The demand for supply chain transparency is also a recognition of the problem of widespread labor rights, human rights, and environmental violations by third-party suppliers in the global SCs (Sarfaty, 2015). In some industries (for example, apparel industry) supply chain fragmentations have created opportunities for abuse of human rights and allowed incidents of socially unsustainable behavior to go unsanctioned by regulators or consumers (Huq *et al.*, 2014). However, recent research has found that socially aware customers demand transparency through reward and punishment for organizations' perceived transparency in supply chains (Kraft *et al.*, 2016). As the number of socially aware customers has seen an upswing in recent times, many global brands and organizations are looking for ways to organize SC transparency regarding raw materials, production processes, and final products to avoid SC disruption and ensure sustainability.

Demand for SC transparency has also risen manifold as a result of "targeted social transparency" efforts by sovereign governments to achieve environmental and human rights policy goals through legislation (Kim *et al.*, 2016; Sarfaty, 2015). The California Transparency in Supply Chains Act (CTSCA), 2010, mandated large manufacturing and retail firms to disclose their efforts to eradicate human trafficking and slavery from their supply chains (Birkey *et al.*, 2018). On a similar line, section 1502 of the Dodd–Frank Act of 2010 gave 3 years to companies in the US to determine and report if their products contained minerals from the conflict zone from the Democratic Republic of Congo (Kim *et al.*, 2016;

Sarfaty, 2015). The modern slavery act of the UK is about prevention of labor from slavery and human trafficking directly or indirectly in any commercial organization supplying goods or services. There is a clear indication of the will of the state for supply chain-related regulation through which a country can set environmental and human rights norms for the third-party suppliers and their host countries through multinational companies (MNCs) (Sarfaty, 2015).While the SCs need to be more transparent and responsible to be socially sustainable under these regulations, organizations are finding it increasingly difficult to achieve the same due to reduced transparency, which is a result of dispersed SCs (Kim and Davis, 2016; Sarfaty, 2015).

Application of technology for supply chain transparency and visibility is not new. Use of RFID data is an example of the adoption of technology to provide product tracking in supply chain (Karkkainen, 2003; McFarlene and Sheffi, 2003; Prater *et al.*, 2005). McFarlene and Sheffi (2003) have explained at length the huge scope of RFID and automatic identification technologies to improve supply chain transparency through product tracking and its usefulness for solving myriad logistics and operational issues in SCM, which can even enable a cyclic economy by tracking the product while being used by customers and eventual disposal. These applications showed that organizations can rely on technology for building supply chain transparency around data. Hence, when faced with the current crisis, the majority of the prominent organizations in retail and other businesses with globally spread supply chains are looking at the emerging technologies with potential like Internet of things (IoT), artificial intelligence (AI), machine learning and big data analytics, and blockchain or distributed ledger technology, which form the foundation of the emerging networked and digital global economy, to solve these problems in an efficient and better way. Extant literature has already stated the potential of using IT to address the problems created by the fragmentation of SCs (Simchi-Levi *et al.*, 2000) and the need of partners to share information and globally optimal plans for supply chain integration (Ho *et al.*, 2002; Simchi-Levi *et al.*, 2000).

Among all the emerging technologies, from the SCM point of view, blockchain is going to be of specific interest. Blockchain has been here for quite some time as the underlying technology for crypto-currencies like bitcoin and others. Though cryptocurrencies are the most famous application for blockchain technology, many new and promising application areas have emerged for this technology in recent times. Overall, these technologies are proving to be disruptive to traditional business models in many sectors of the economy by changing the way consumers interact. Organizations and companies have been overly optimistic about the potential increase in efficiency this technology can bring in the SC operations. This optimistic prediction about a nascent technology has something to do with how it can record transaction details of all kinds in a secure and immutable way. As any business including SCs conducts hundreds of transactions daily, organizations are looking at blockchain technology to provide the security and sanctity to these transactions across concerned parties including global ones. So, what paradigmatic change collaborative block chain platform can bring to supply chain practices? If it can prove to be a foundational technology like Internet, it can bring tectonic changes to SCM practices and business models.

Many leading organizations have invested in blockchain recently, the underlying technology of Bitcoin, as a solution for myriad SC problems like transparency, product tracking, smart contract, and information sharing (Kshetri, 2018). The open digital ledger of blockchain is an ideal tool for sharing accurate and real-time information, a key requirement for data-centric decision making in SCM. Blockchain applications in SCs can create value through decentralization, smart contracts, and the simplification and digitalization of SC processes. Practitioners and researchers have started to compare the blockchain technology to Internet technology in its potential to disrupt the practices of supply chain management in the recent time (Treiblmaier, 2018). Internet technologies had created a similar disruption years ago leading to a complete restructuring of the value networks of the organizations (Yao *et al.*, 2009). Disruption was in the form of the creation of electronic marketplaces, realization of cost reductions, productivity improvement, e-procurement, creation of customized services, and integration of business processes (Lancioni *et al.*, 2003).

However, applications of blockchain technology come with the potential for fundamental structural changes for SCs. Blockchain-enabled transparency has the potential to completely overhaul the principal–agent relationships (PAT), create new resources for firms to acquire a competitive advantage (RBV), and redefine and redraw firm boundaries (NT) in the settings of a supply network (Treiblmaier, 2018). These structural changes of SCs thus create a necessity for extensive reengineering of the SC processes for efficiency and performance according to the supply chain structural dynamics theory (Ivanov, 2014). But all such reengineering efforts must identify the areas to focus on for effectiveness and efficiency. Analysis of the SC processes of organizations during or after successful application of blockchain can help to find some common grounds to direct such optimization efforts.

As blockchain literature has just started to emerge in academic journals, we have chosen 56 articles about blockchain applications in SCs from reputed practitioners' journals for our analysis. We have analyzed these articles using automated text mining to identify the focus areas of SC processes to embed various aspects of blockchain technology for effective operations. Automated text mining technique of topic modeling can be used to extract various themes from corpus of text documents and is a preferred tool for such analysis (Sun and Yin, 2017). These topics can then be analyzed by the key words of each extracted topic for drawing inferences.

2. Blockchain for Supply Chain Management

Organizations or firms in an SC enable material, informational, and financial flows by conducting transactions among them. The transactions are related to one another and more transactions are triggered by one transaction. A material transaction in a dyad of firms can trigger a chain of transactions of information and money in a part or whole of an SC. The triggered transactions have in-built time and informational lag, and information loss happens due to information asymmetry. This affects the cost of transactions for all firms across a supply chain depending on their relative positions in the supply network. SCM, with a preponderance of transactions and the highest level of need to maintain the integrity of such transactions, is a fertile ground for the application of the blockchain technology which is designed to protect transaction integrity (Dinh *et al.*, 2018). This view is partially confirmed by the fact that the majority of the current applications of blockchain are in SCM (Babich and Hilary, 2019).

Applications of blockchain technology can be divided into three main areas — cryptocurrency, digital assets, and general applications (Dinh *et al.*, 2018). While cryptocurrencies like bitcoin derive their value from blockchains, digital assets are real assets and blockchain is used as a medium to record their existence and document the transaction records. The general applications may include the execution of user-defined programs or smart contracts on blockchain for business relationships.

The current state of blockchain technologies or systems offers four important functionalities — distributed ledger, consensus, cryptography, and smart contract (Babich and Hilary, 2019; Dinh *et al.*, 2018). Each of these functionalities provide for innovative uses in SC operations for a foundational shift and the potential to revolutionize SC transparency and visibility, digitization of assets, and making the SC intelligent.

2.1. *Distributed ledger*

A ledger is a book of transactions for money or goods among known parties. Blockchains support a digital and distributed form of the ledger which uses a data structure consisting of a ordered list of transactions (Dinh *et al.*, 2018). Multiple copies of the blockchain ledger are maintained over multiple nodes of the network for immutability. In blockchains, transactions are grouped and then chained together. The combined blocks create an immutable trail that can be used as an auditable history for tracing a product or its raw materials to their origin.

Using the distributed ledgers of blockchain platform with transaction-based data models (for example, BigchainDB or Corda) (Dinh *et al.*, 2018), partner firms in an SC can setup a network to trade digitized assets among each other. In this case, the blockchain will record all the changes in states of the ledger as the partner firms or nodes carry out any update operation for a previous transaction.

2.2. *Cryptography*

The functionality of cryptography provided by the blockchain technology comes in handy for managing the identity of the users and maintaining transaction privacy. In a public setting, a blockchain user generates a pair of public and private keys. While the hash of the public key is used as an address for transaction or as an account number, the user signs transactions with the private key to claim the outcome of it. In private settings, like that in the Hyperledger, there is an additional security layer. As most of the blockchains are designed to protect transaction integrity rather than the transaction, the extra layer of protection can be useful for keeping the contents known only to the participants in the private setting of blockchains as expected in the SC network. Requests are processed for the next stage (consensus) only after they are authorized by the security layer in the private setting.

2.3. *Consensus*

As multiple parties can make changes to a blockchain ledger or database, a robust data governance system is required to maintain data integrity. Depending on the governance system, a blockchain network may be completely permissionless for anybody to join, including the general public, or completely permissioned or private. Private blockchain is a more likely type to be applied in SCs as it will control the access only to the partner firms unlike bitcoin where anyone can join.

Different versions of the blockchain ledger can temporarily differ from one another as any node can update it due to a decentralized setting. For ensuring convergence of multiple versions of the database, blockchains need a *consensus mechanism*. The consensus protocol for private blockchain can be communication based where all the nodes have equal votes and go through multiple rounds of communication for reaching a consensus (Castro and Liskov, 1999).

2.4. *Smart contract*

Smart contracts are a built-in feature of blockchain to implement their transaction logics (Dinh *et al.*, 2018). In bitcoin, one of the most popular contracts is for multi-signatures. An Escrow contract requires two out of three signatures before a coin can be released. Apart from the in-built ones, blockchain databases allow users to write and store their own smart contracts. While some platforms allow the users to write these programs using scripts (Bitcoin, BigchainDB), other platforms allow the use of Turing-complete smart contracts using a higher level language (Ethereum, Hyperledger).

Execution of a smart contract is transparent like all other transactions on the blockchain. This implies visibility of inputs, outputs, and the states of the contract to all the nodes. A smart contract is suitable for a range of uses in SCs, starting from payment automation and materials requirement planning to trading of electricity or power in a smart grid setting (Andoni *et al.*, 2019).

2.5. *Supply chain structure, SC processes, and blockchain*

Structural dynamics of an SC have been explained in the extant literature with the help of theories like principal–agent theory (PAT), transaction cost analysis (TCA), resource-based view (RBV), and network theory (NT) (Halldorsson *et al.*, 2007; Treiblmaier, 2018). These theories provide for the explanation of what is regarded as resource, firm boundary, and transaction economics for firms in an SC setting. Optimal design and integration of SC processes for a focus firm are dependent on factors such as access to resources and the power and control it can exert over other firms in the SCN. As the SCN structure and position of the focus firm decide its access to materials flow, information flow, and financial flow in the SCN (Kim *et al.*, 2011), it also indirectly decides the optimal design and integration of SC processes. As blockchain application in SC triggers structural and managerial changes (Treiblmaier, 2018), the SC processes also need restructuring for adapting and optimization.

SC visibility can be a resource for competitive advantage if it is distinctive (Barrat and Oke, 2007). Information sharing among supply network partners can create such visibility if and only if the information shared has qualities like accuracy, timeliness, usefulness, and is in a readily usable format (Mohr and Sohi, 1995; Whipple *et al.*, 2002). This also illustrates that information can be the basis of resources which can provide firms with a competitive advantage. Blockchain, by design, possesses all the stated qualities of information shared to create new resources for firms. The consensus-based data-sharing feature of blockchain technology ensures data accuracy and format of the shared data (Dinh *et al.*, 2018). The real-time information sharing, which is a feature of blockchain, can alleviate SC problems like demand volatility (Barrat and Oke, 2007). Tokenization or digitalization of assets can create new forms of resources for firms in the form of business capabilities and processes. Chances for creating new sources of competitive advantage or resources due to the application of blockchain technology are immense, and firms will compete to acquire these resources in the coming times.

The theoretical lens of the network theory can be used to explain the changes of information flow in SCM due to blockchain in a much more nuanced manner. Node-level and Network-level metrics developed by Social Network Analysis (SNA) literature have been used to explain the effects of SCN structure on the SC processes (Kim *et al.*, 2011). *Betweenness* centrality metric measures the frequency with which a firm lies on the shortest path connecting all combinations of pairs of nodes/firms in a supply network (Baum *et al.*, 2010) and influences such firms exert on materials or information exchange relationships between other firms in the network (Baum *et al.*, 2010; Marsden, 2002). A high value for this index indicates a higher dependence of other firms on this firm to reach out to the rest of the network or amount of gatekeeping such firms do in a network (Borgatti and Everett, 2006). These firms can limit information flow for a focus firm and demand brokerage from its SC processes related to quality control of raw materials, demand management, customer relationship management, etc (Baum *et al.*, 2010). In case of materials flow network, mistakes on the part of such centrally located firms can lead to supply disruptions for the whole SC (Chopra and Sodhi, 2004). Such firms can also influence the interactions among other firms in a contractual relationship network (Kim *et al.*, 2011). These firms enjoy the benefits of non-redundant information when they connect a dense region to the network (Burt, 1998).

Blockchain technology enables SCs to make real-time, accurate information available to all stakeholders in a network. Network-level visibility enabled by blockchain technology completely modifies the information flow networks and removes the information bottleneck in an SCN created by firms with a high betweenness centrality index. This structural change will enable firms to modify their SC processes accordingly for effective use of the SC transparency. As a result, a focus firm can reconfigure processes for supplier relationships to directly control both the upstream and downstream suppliers based on SC visibility.

At the network level, supply network concentration indicates the control or power exercised by the core firms over other firms (Choi and Hong, 2002). High network concentration results in a centralized control structure. A high value for this index means a firm's control of materials or information flows in a network (Marsden, 2002) and advantage over other firms as an intermediary (Kim *et al.*, 2011). In normal circumstances, such firms become a hub or pivot and mediate the flow of materials and communications. According to social network theory, due to the access to non-redundant information from dense regions, such firms increase their control over others (Burt, 1998). But, blockchain technology can reduce the importance of pivot firms at least for informational supply network through data availability. As a result, firms will also be able to form many direct ties even without being at a central network position. The resulting network will have a high density and cohesiveness and a diffuse and distributed control structure (Kim *et al.*, 2011). This change in the SC structure will also reflect in the supply processes with distributed control.

Two firms can be linked by delivery and receipt of materials or contractual relationship. Based on the type of links, supply networks can be of two types for the same set of firms with different logic as well as implications. Only firms with a high *closeness centrality index* in a supply network of contractual relationships can act and navigate freely to access resources in a timely manner and can have a shorter supply chain (Kim *et al.*, 2011). As a result, they enjoy the benefits of less information distortion and access to reliable and timely information about supply disruption or demand forecasts (Chen *et al.*, 2000). These firms can better manage demand–supply scenarios for optimized inventory management and a lower operational cost (Cachon and Fisher, 2000; Lee *et al.*, 2000). Blockchain-enabled visibility with real-time transaction data will enable SCs to reconfigure the demand management processes for better operational performance.

3. Data and Methods

3.1. *Data sample and preprocessing*

Using the keywords blockchain and SCM with the logical operator "AND", research articles and research papers were downloaded from two databases, the EBSCO's Business Source Complete database and the IEEE Xplore Digital Library. IEEE are among the world's leading publishers of the research on frontline technologies in electronics and information technology (IT). Articles and papers from only journals and magazines were selected for quality factor (date of access 14/04/2019). With a preliminary round of brief overview and removal of the duplicates, a total of 56 articles (Appendix B) were retained for our analysis, all in pdf data format. Hereafter, all the text data in the 56 documents are called the corpus.

We performed necessary preprocessing steps including tokenization, removal of stop words, and stemming from preparing the corpus for text mining in R statistical software. In a document, words or terms are the basic units. Through the process of tokenization, a text document is split into words. Stop words are prepositions, articles, and other similar words that do not carry much meaning from the perspective of text analysis, and hence, their removal does not affect the outcome of topic modeling. Stemming removes the suffixes to retrieve the radicals and removes the multiple forms of the same word.

Extremely high as well as extremely low frequency words like "and", "for", and "the", are not very informative from probabilistic topic modeling (Grün and Hornik, 2011; Steyvers and Griffiths, 2007) and, hence, should be removed. We removed such words from our corpus using a value for tf-idf (term frequency multiplied by inverse document frequency) which was little less than the median value for the corpus words. After that, each document's text data are represented by a vector of terms. Then we generated a document–term matrix where each row represented a document and each column represented a different term or word from our corpus. The dimension of the sparse document–term matrix is 56 × 7887, where each of the 56 rows represented one document and the columns represented 7887 unique words from all the documents.

3.2. *Topic modeling*

Topic modeling in machine learning is an automated statistical analysis method used for finding the latent topic structures in a corpus of text documents, which includes identifying the topics and topic distributions in individual documents and per-document, per-word topic assignments (Blei, 2012). Topic modeling defines a topic as a distribution over the words in a corpus (Blei, 2012). Topics signify the latent variables that link words in vocabulary and their occurrences in documents (Ponweiser, 2012). A document can contain single or multiple themes or topics that can be represented using a bag of words. The extracted features or topics capture the content of documents somehow. The extracted features can be used as predictors to classify documents into predefined classes, group documents with similar meanings, or find documents matching some search criteria.

As words are the only observable variables in a text analysis, a document collection represented as a sparse document–term matrix (DTM) or term–document matrix (transpose of DTM) as frequencies of terms in each document is required for subsequent statistical analysis. As the TDM matrix is a very high dimensional sparse matrix, all topic modeling algorithms need to reduce the dimensionality of this sparse matrix. Some of the most frequently used methods for topic modeling are Principal Component Analysis (PCA), Latent Semantic Analysis (LSA), and Latent Dirichlet Allocation (LDA). While the first two methods are non-probabilistic and use singular value decomposition (SVD) of the large sparse matrices, LDA is one of the most popular probabilistic text modeling algorithms (Wei and Croft, 2006).

LDA topic models are probabilistic models for extracting latent features or topics from a set of documents using correlations among the words and the latent semantic themes (Blei and Lafferty, 2005). Words or terms are the basic units of data in a document. A document is split into words through the process of tokenization. A collection of documents then can be represented as a document–term matrix (DTM) with the frequencies of words in each document. Bag of words model assumes words in a text document are interchangeable, and hence, their order is not important for representation. LDA is based on a bag of words model (Blei *et al.*, 2003) and draws the characteristics of topics and documents from Dirichlet distribution using a generative model. The generative model of LDA decides the probable words for each topic first and then for each document decides two things, first what proportions of each topic should be present and for each word in it choose a topic, and given a topic, choose a likely word from the first step.

The LDA model draws samples from Dirichlet distribution and multinomial distributions. Dirichlet distribution is a multivariate generalization of Beta distribution, and multinomial distribution is a generalization of a binomial distribution. Drawing values from a multinomial distribution with a Dirichlet distribution over the probabilities of outcomes is accomplished in the following way:

1. First, draw a vector of probabilities for each topic from the Dirichlet distribution.
2. Use that vector of probabilities to draw a vector of outcomes from the multinomial distribution.

In the above manner by drawing samples from a joint probability distribution, LDA decides the likely words in a topic, and for each word it chooses a topic and decides what proportions of a topic should be present in a document (Ponweiser, 2012). Finally, the probabilistic generative model of LDA uses a joint probability distribution of independent variables (Blei and Lafferty, 2009) given as

$$p(w,z,\theta,\phi \mid \alpha,\beta) = p(\theta \mid \alpha)\, p(z \mid \theta)\, p(\phi \mid \beta)\, p(w \mid z,\phi). \tag{1}$$

Many algorithms are available for estimating the model parameters and inferring the distribution of the latent variables for this probability equation including maximum likelihood. Collapsed Gibbs Sampling uses a Markov Chain Monte Carlo (MCMC) method. Using this method, for each of k topics, the topics distribution per document θ is drawn from the

Dirichlet distribution with the given parameter α. Given θ, topic to words assignment in the corpus z is calculated. The term distributions per topic for the corpus is drawn from the Dirichlet distribution with the parameter β. At the last probability of the corpus, w, is calculated given parents z and ϕ.

3.3. *Model fitting*

We have used open statistical software R 3.4.0 (2017) for data analysis and fitting the probabilistic LDA topic model for this work. Model fitting may consist of model evaluation and selection. While model evaluation is about the useful generalization of information from the training data, the selection is about what models to use for inference (Burnham and Anderson, 2002; Ponweiser, 2012). The number of topics affects the performance of LDA model. Choosing it is a common problem when it is not known *a priori* (Blei and Lafferty, 2009). While several approaches and different metrics like perplexity, marginal likelihood, or empirical likelihood are available depending on the goal for solving this problem, the perplexity metric was used here for choosing the number of topics. Perplexity is mathematically equivalent to the inverse of the geometric mean per-word likelihood and monotonically decreases in the test data. The equation for perplexity is given as follows:

$$\text{Perplexity} = \exp\left| -\frac{\sum_{i=1}^{n} \log(p(di))}{\sum_{i=1}^{n} Ni} \right|, \tag{2}$$

where n denotes the number of documents, Ni represents the length of document di, and $p(di)$ is the probability of generation of the document by the fitted LDA model.

A lower perplexity score shows better generalization by the LDA model (Blei *et al*., 2003). A comparative criterion for perplexity for the various topics is that a suitable value can be decided. Human judgment may be needed to evaluate the models for a real-world task in addition to likelihood-based measures for topic modeling. Topic modeling should result in topics that are generally perceived as semantically cohesive and should help in decomposing documents into mixtures of topics that humans can easily associate with (Chang and Blei, 2009; Steyvers and Griffiths, 2007). We initially used the perplexity measure to look for the probable number of topics. However, the final decision on the number of topics was made after manually inspecting the words in the topics for meaningfulness and semantic cohesion, and their probabilities in various individual documents were evaluated (Chang and Blei, 2009).

4. Results and Analysis

We preprocess our corpus of 56 pdf documents by removing the punctuation marks, articles, prepositions, etc. All numbers are removed from the text, and the words converted are to small letters in the next step. The words are tokenized subsequently, and the corpus is converted to a sparse term–document matrix (TDM) for further text mining processes. Using tf-idf (term frequency–inverse document frequency), we removed the too frequent and too sparse words without much informational value from the corpus. After this step, the words in the corpus are important for their informational value and their frequency is an indicator of it. A word cloud of the most important words from our corpus (frequency > 100) is given in Figure 1. The large font size for the word roots like data, product, transact, contract, and secure in the word cloud implies their importance in various topics in the text.

We fit an LDA topic model on the frequent terms of 1978 from our corpus of 56 documents with 50 topics. The obtained number of 50 topics has been achieved from the perplexity measures from the experiment of varying the number of topics from 1 to 55 in the LDA model. These topics are extracted purely based on Bayesian probability. The LDA model gives posterior word distributions probability for each extracted topic (Figure 2) and posterior topics distribution for each document in the corpus (Figure 3). The complete list of the 10 most probable words for all the 50 topics is given as Appendix A. Posterior topics distribution can be used for comparing document similarity or dissimilarity and can be a basis for document clustering or grouping.

The high-probability words for each extracted topic identify the various themes of the text corpus — in this case, various supply chain processes when blockchain technology is adopted as solutions for various SC issues. Babich and Hilary (2019) have identified three themes, five strengths, and five weaknesses related to applications of blockchain technology for operations management (OM). The three themes were information, automation, and tokenization or digital assets; the five strengths were visibility, aggregation, validation, automation, and resiliency; and

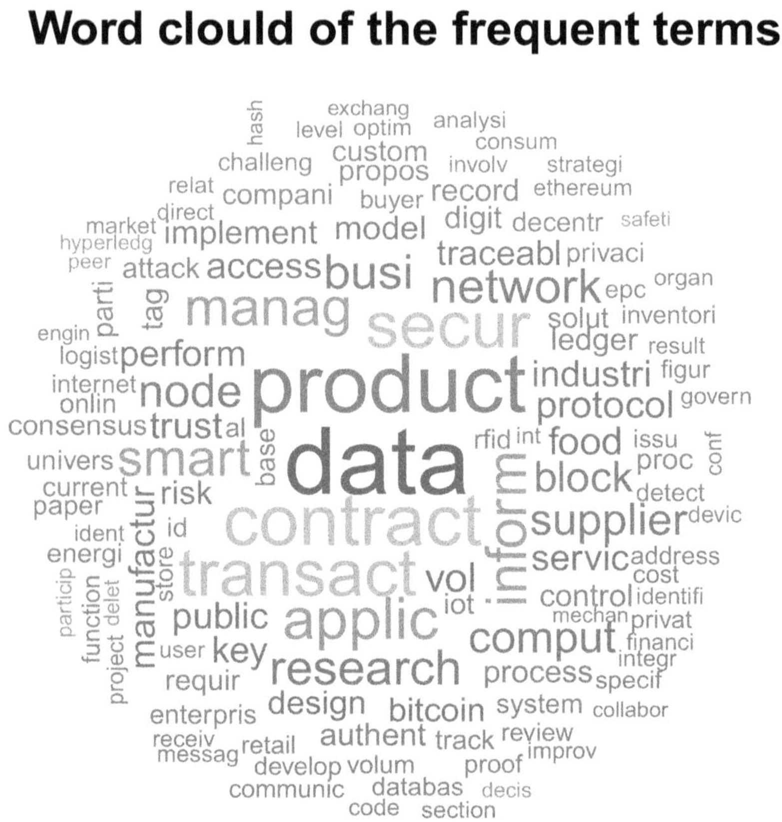

Figure 1: Significant words for information.

the five weaknesses were privacy, standardization, garbage in–garbage out, black box approach, and inefficiency. We characterize our topics in terms of the framework proposed by Babich and Hilary (2019) using the high-probability words of each topic.

Our results show that SC processes incorporate the five strengths of the blockchain. The strength of visibility is the most harnessed among all. Blockchain visibility enables a supply chain's ability to track its' products along the supply network, both upstream and downstream, with a significant impact on product traceability and transparency (Topics #29 and #35). Blockchain technology can enable SCs to improve the traceability of food products from the shelf to the field, which can help to find the origin of food contamination and safety hazards. This capability using blockchain has been demonstrated by IBM and Walmart through their

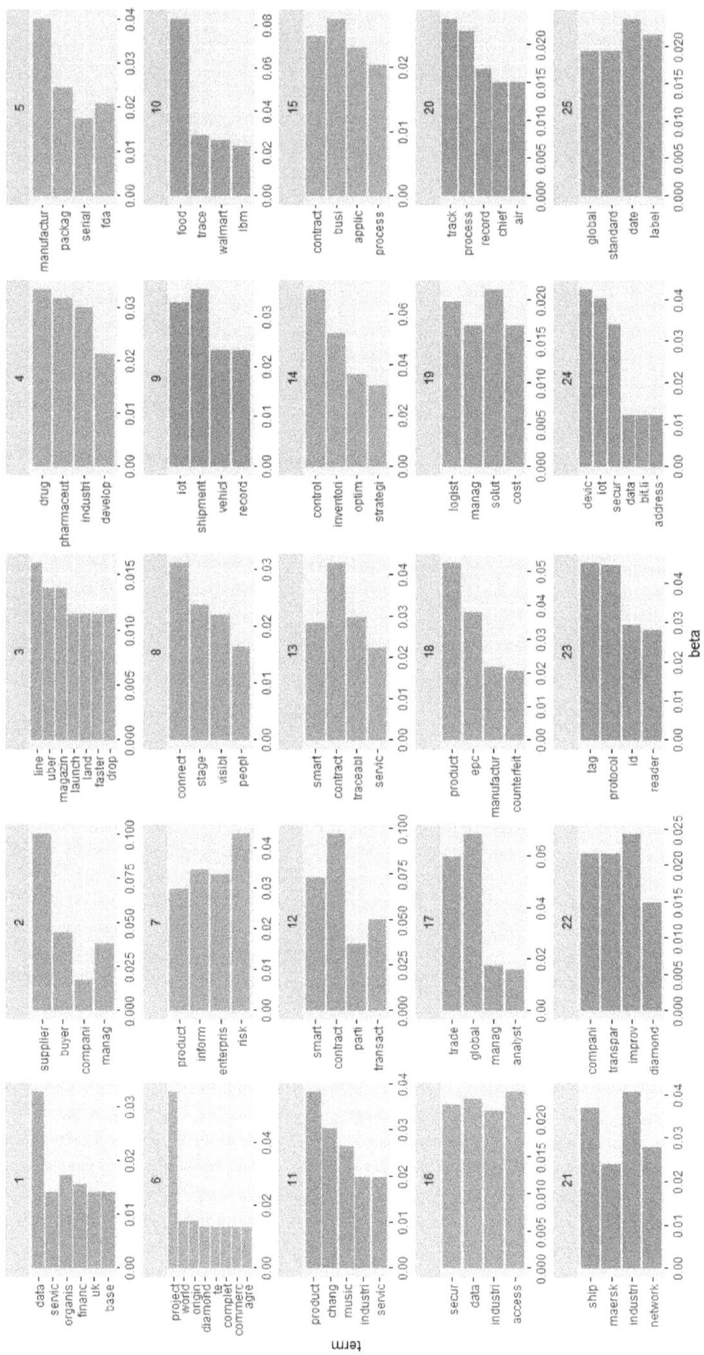

Figure 2: Topicwise word distribution probability (top four words).

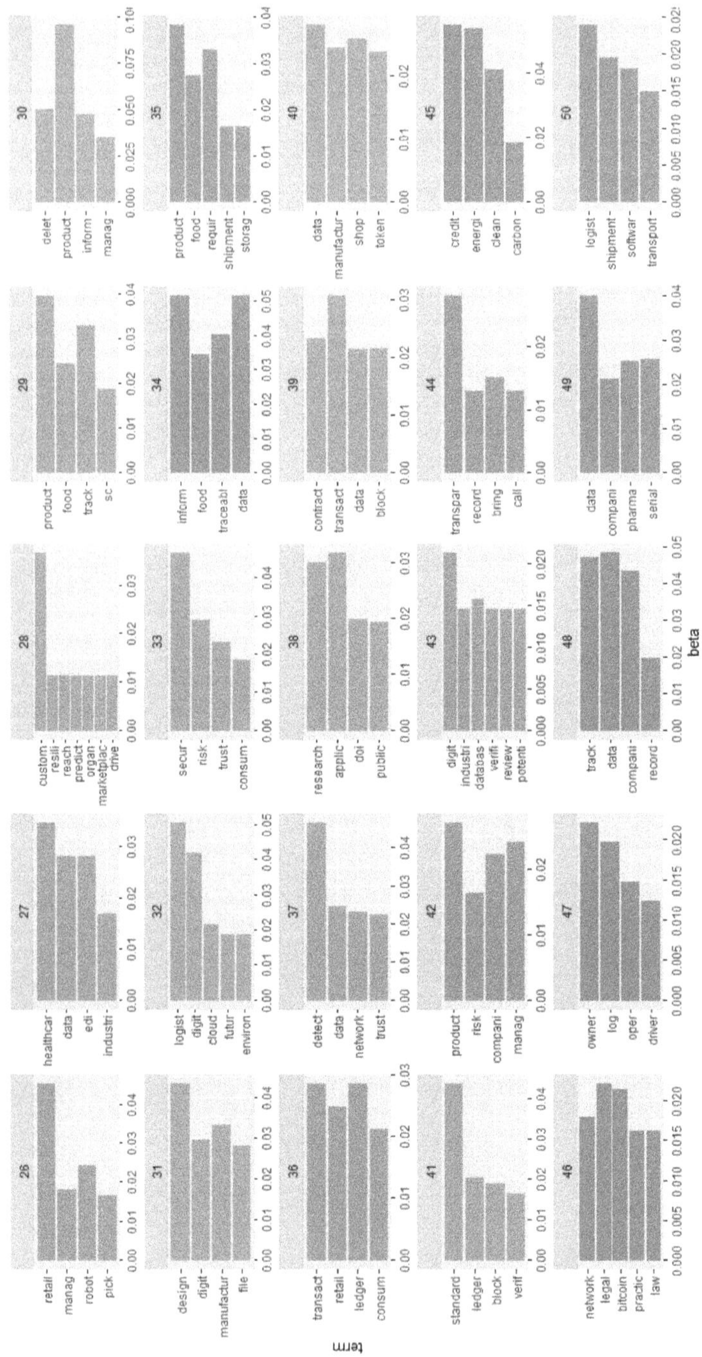

Figure 2: (*Continued*)

Figure 3: Documentwise topic distribution.

Figure 3: (Continued)

respective pilot projects (Topic #10), that were the biggest concerns for any food supply chain at that time. For food and pharmaceutical companies, blockchain technology can take the traceability of their supply chains to a whole new level (Topics #29, #34, and #35). Blockchain can not only improve traceability in food supply chains but also facilitate the implementation of legal food safety standards. Innovation in the implementation of product shipment safety standards for manufacturers as issued by agencies like FDA (USA) and requirements like drug serialization for detecting counterfeit drugs are some of the highly popular applications of blockchain technology in the recent times. The wine industry has used blockchain technology in the UK as a digital system of data for building customer trust. A blockchain application can provide all the data related to the raw materials used for making wine and the winery from where it is coming directly through a barcode scanning application. The same strength can also be useful for meeting regulatory requirements like serialization of food products or pharmaceuticals by regulatory bodies like FDA (Topics #5 and #49) or assuring the customers about the origin of the diamonds sold by a seller that they are not from conflict zones (Topics #6 and #22). Consequently, these processes make blockchain technology a promising candidate for implementing serialization of drugs for identifying counterfeit drugs and preventing it (Shanley, 2017).

As a result, blockchain applications can improve transparency in retail supply chains and address concerns regarding human and environmental impacts of production processes in supply chains. Supply chains are using this blockchain-enabled complete transparency to significantly enhance trust in their businesses and meet regulatory requirements as well. Blockchain enables traceability of products not only to trace defects in them to their origin or root but can also facilitate detecting counterfeit ones from the genuine. Topic #36 expresses the use of supply chain-enabled transparency to inform consumers about the source of the products during purchase from retailers.

Blockchain-enabled visibility also help firms to create new firm-level capabilities to improve their operational efficiency. OEM firms can directly manage their buyers and suppliers using blockchain visibility for the whole network (Topic #2). Blockchain-enabled transparency and traceability are also helping organizations to improve operational efficiency in novel ways. New simulation-based optimization models for inventory management for products have become possible due to blockchain (Topic #14). It is revolutionizing operations for shipping, logistic, finance, and service organizations. It has enabled shipping and air cargo companies to track their consignments and handle warehouses and customs (Topics #20 and #50). Similarly, new processes for logistics and warehouse information have been used cost-effectively (Topic #19).

SC processes have started to incorporate the strength of data aggregation using the technological advances as a result of the structural changes that have been brought about by blockchain. Using the aggregation capability of blockchains, SC processes can capture shipment vehicle data using sensors and IoT for ensuring transportation under controlled environmental conditions (Topic #9). Now it is also possible for the shipping companies to easily share the information about containers with a customer through cloud. SC processes can also use RFID and IoT data for a secured network connection (Topic #24) and an authentication protocol (Topic #23). A very important application of this strength in SCM is the prevention of counterfeit product in an SC by ascertaining ownership of products at every stage of production and transportation (Topic #18).

Validation strength is unique to blockchain for operations management and supply chain application, as the rest four — visibility, aggregation, automation, and resiliency — can be implemented using other technologies (Babich and Hilary, 2019). Blockchain technology in its core is a digital and distributed ledger which is secure, robust, and error proof (Gandhi *et al.*, 2018). Each block in a blockchain contains time-stamped transactions data, and new blocks can be added to a blockchain. This fact is captured by Topic #39. This historical list of transactions is different from a database in three critical ways. First, all blockchains are distributed and practically immutable, unlike a centralized database. As a result, there is no single point of ownership and failure. Second, it is not possible to enter data accidentally or intentionally and hence able to enforce an error proof contract. Third, all entries in a blockchain are a permanent and, hence, immutable record. These features of blockchain give SCs an auditable, decentralized, unchangeable, and secure digital platform for recordkeeping.

The process of data authentication and subsequent immutability in blockchain can help create new business models by engendering the trust of SC members in the quality of the shared information. Issuing of digital assets or tokenization is possible due to this feature of blockchain technology. This has made possible new business models like carbon credit trading for clean energy (Topic #45), a log-based hourly pay for truck drivers (Topic #47), and improved product safety by tracking suppliers for ingredients (Topic #48).

Significant effects of data validation and immutability can be seen on supply chain risk management and trust. As governance of product-related risk management becomes transparent to consumers (Topic #42) and product, manufacturing, and other related risks become visible (Topic #33), customer trusts improves. Collaboration among supply network partners becomes dependent on data (Topic #37). Authentic data also inform the enterprise risk management across the network (Topic #7) and enable the management to take informed decisions like product deletion based on data (Topic #30) for better performance.

Blockchain technology's strength of automation has the ability to make systems smart apart from other applications in logistics. This ability is already changing the way capacity development projects are financed by reducing the role of intermediaries like state-owned utilities and crowdsourcing of finance (O'Dell *et al.*, 2018). Blockchain technology is already enabling smart and automated trading of power for the micro-grids. Topics #15, #27, and #34 describe how companies are using block-chain for executing a smart contract for improved efficiency.

Transaction data between firms can be used as triggers for automatic execution of events like automatic payment in SCs leading to improvement in performance. Topic #40 discusses transaction-based automatic payment for purchase in a manufacturing SC; Topic #45 explains about autonomous business transactions on the basis of certified carbon credit; Topics #12, # 13, #15, #27, and #34 contract and smart contract for automatic payment and others, and Topic #3 examines brand authentication in retail SCs using transaction data. The availability of real-time transaction data will enable firms to use smart contract for secured automatic payment based on transaction data (e.g., Topics #27 and #34) and improve the financial performance by removing intermediaries from the financial network of SC. It is facilitating the use of robots in warehouse operations by automatic detection of ownership and merging and de-merging pallets for achieving full truckload and efficiency for the retailers (Topic #26).

Blockchain's resilience can be used to create sustainable SC processes in the situations of natural disasters, calamity, cyberattack, and situations of war. The distributed nature of the ledger helps to recover the data loss and risk minimization when blockchain is applied for data management. Blockchain can help predict markets and customers based on data for resilience (Topic #28).

Analyzing our findings, we add digitization as the sixth strength to the five strengths of blockchain technology identified by Babich and Hilary (2019). Blockchain enables digitization of supply processes and enables the creation of new capabilities for firms. It is revolutionizing how the manufacturing industry can handle the data related to their design projects as blockchain has enabled them to keep track through digitized files and the use of cloud (Topic #31), which helps to manage geographically dispersed design teams and distributed manufacturing using additive processes. Another application of digitization is revenue management for the music industry (Topic #11) and a possible development of cyber progress index for global trade management (Topic #17). It is also predicted that the digitization of the logistics processes will also change the role of people in transportation and warehouse functions (Topic #32)

5. Discussion and Conclusion

Today, the market demands personalization/customization, collaboration, real-time reduction of downtime for cross-corporate operations, agility for adapting to market competitions for competitive advantage, efficient SC processes, end-to-end visibility for upstream and downstream SC processes, traceability of product/component to its point of origin, and integration or information sharing among SC partners. Many of these demands are the root cause of the problems faced by the globalized supply chains of present time, and the reengineering of SC processes can solve these issues by incorporating the six strengths of blockchain mentioned in the results section.

SC processes incorporating blockchain strengths can be beneficial in many ways. Afterall, SCM is all about the effective management of the three streams of flow of materials, money, and information. Blockchain applications in SCM will infuse new dynamics into the information flow network structure of supply chains. The adoption of this relatively new technology into logistics brings essentially two immediate benefits: cost reduction and wealth of information, as long as the tool is correctly implemented before it is used by the different players (Wang *et al.*, 2019). Though expected changes are many, they will be brought in mainly by a change in the state of information asymmetry in a supply chain. As blockchain brings a high level of transparency in supply chains, the flows of materials, information, and money in supply chains will change in a significant way. Blockchain's transparency removes the dependency on intermediaries by facilitating information-based trust, and this will change the supply chain structure by removing complex dependencies between organizations and within organizations. Restructuring the supply chain processes with a focus on data-centric decision-making will help to arrive at better managerial decisions. Such a culture can also create a competitive advantage for a supply network.

As the information symmetry among various actors within supply chain networks will do away with the centralized structure (Treiblmaier, 2018), the restructured SC processes must be compatible for a decentralized control structure with no dominating power center. For example, the role of power in supply chain decision-making can be redefined as upstream suppliers may have a better understanding of the demand of the final products and therefore, negotiate better autonomy and improved profitability positions. Likewise, focal firms can have better visibility in multitier supply chains and, accordingly, less expensive control and coordination.

Supply chain sustainability is another area that can immensely benefit from blockchain-enabled transparency. Supply chain sustainability has become a significant concern due to human rights violation and environmental exploitation which are common in many global supply chains (Birkey *et al.*, 2018). Two things have contributed to this change. First, customers are concerned about the impacts of product suppliers views on safety, quality, wholesomeness, and social and environmental sustainability. A long supply chain can be the reason for scandals such as those that have happened in the food industry and create customer insecurity issues. Food supply chains need to have forward or client traceability to locate a product for quality recall and process traceability and also back traceability or suppliers' traceability for complete traceability (Perez-Aloe *et al.*, 2000) to provide for peace of mind of consumers regarding safety, human rights, and environmental concerns. In a pilot blockchain project, Walmart and IBM reduced the time to trace packs of mangoes moving through their supply chains to seconds from days (Cottrill, 2018). It has been demonstrated in Malaysia that blockchain-enabled transparency can solve the problem of customer trust in the *Halal* food supply chains and can be a reliable substitute for cumbersome manual certificates which people did not trust (Tan *et al.*, 2018). Accordingly, the future of SCM with blockchain technology has immense potential to not only improve the operational efficiency but also quickly address emergencies like food contamination to build customer trust. Besides, the utility of blockchain for a situation like preventing contaminated food from reaching the customers in a global supply chain is invaluable. The diverse applications and utility of blockchain undoubtedly project it as a foundation technology for SCM.

Application of IT tools like RFID for product tagging and supply chains visibility is not new (McFarlene and Sheffi, 2003; Perez-Aloe *et al.*, 2000). While RFID-enabled traceability of products facilitates supply chain visibility, it cannot be used for tracing the history of a product at the customer's end. Hence, it cannot provide the context of a product to a customer. RFID technology, unlike blockchain, does not allow a collaborative and peer-like information updating mechanism. But, blockchain technology with the immutable ledger of transactions is just an ideal tool to fulfill all the product traceability and transparency requirements of a supply chain and provide this information easily to a customer through a scanning app at the end!

As blockchain is a foundational technology like Internet, and its application will touch and affect the processes and people of an organization and even have an impact on the business model. The first and foremost will be the new role for "Trust in supply chains". The available literature on SCM have predominantly focused on the organizational and interpersonal trust among the partners in supply chains and the multifaceted benefits of it for the involved parties (Handfield & Bechtel, 2002). However, SCM did not consider the end user of a product or services as an entity and, hence, has not included him/her as a party to the trust. But induction of blockchain technology in SCM will enable the supply chain to make customer party to trust by providing them information about raw materials, processes, and people that goes into making a product or service. For example, customers can get reliable data about the environment-friendly processes that are followed in making a product and thus helping in build trust with an organization based on information rather than only on what an organization displays on its product labels. This will lead to the trust-building atmosphere in supply chains as well.

Apart from sustainability, blockchain also affects firm performance through supply chain process integration. Our analysis has proven multiple instances of the use of a blockchain-based ledger of transactions by organizations and this process stands as an example of complete data consistency. Apart from data consistency, blockchain enables real-time communication among the partner firms through its open and distributed database to enable interaction among cross-functional SCM application systems, and hence, blockchain can form the basis for the integration of IT infrastructure for SCM (Rai *et al.*, 2006). Information systems research has shown that the integration of IT infrastructure is a requirement for the creation of IT platforms and their subsequent deep embedding in organizational processes to create sustainable competitive advantages (Bhardwaj, 2000; Rai *et al.*, 2006). Blockchain technology clearly stands apart from technologies like RFID due to this comprehensive capability to operationalize this construct.

Second, the recent proliferation of domestic legislation to control and govern the global supply chains to hold them responsible for human rights violations and environmental exploitations is also of vital importance (Birkey *et al.*, 2018; Kim and Davis, 2016; Sarfaty, 2016). As these legislations require the organizations to disclose detailed information about their suppliers and raw materials to rule out rights violations by even second- or third-tier suppliers, complete supply chain transparency and traceability of materials flow in the supply chains have emerged as the central focus for sustainability. How will a focused company enforce compliance for their suppliers in a third country or their second- or third-tier suppliers in a different country? What will be the financial repercussions of such demands or failure to enforce such demanded compliance? Processes for capturing such details can embed capacities of blockchain. However, organizations will still need to build consensus and a model to induce their suppliers to provide information about their suppliers. It will also need the ability to create financial models for bearing the cost for collection of information, and the level of information partner firms are ready to share. In other words, firms will need to create higher level capabilities or resources with blockchain for sustainability. In the quest for such resources (resource-based view (RBV) of firms), firms will modify and change the supply chain structures.

By combining real-time and precise information, blockchains can raise the intelligence level of the entire supply chain, which in turn enables more agile decision-making. Blockchains can create an increase in the overall productivity, changing the supply chain settings from reactive mode to proactive mode. In international transport, for example, several unforeseen events occur, such as strikes and storms. With instantaneous validated data, immediate reaction can be triggered to change the unexpected situations and mitigate an imminent risk of supply disruption. Moreover, there will be a change in the supply network structure as the basis of flows in the network may change from relational trust among the dyads to one of trust-independent or information-dependent one (Treiblmaier, 2018). As blockchain-based systems enforce contractual compliance via smart contracts, the need for personal relationships as the basis for business relationships may change substantially (Kiviat, 2015). Maybe a need for a complete review of the role of the boundary spanners will arise soon.

While the list of technological possibilities of blockchain is formidable, the challenge remains to exploit it as a source of competitive advantage as off-the-shelf technologies are available for a price and cannot be a source of competitive advantage (Powell and Dent-Micallef, 1997). Technical capabilities must be embedded deep in the organizational processes to create VRINN resources (Rungtusanatham *et al.*, 2003), which can be sources of sustainable competitive advantage (Bhardwaj, 2000; Rai *et al.*, 2006). One of the main weaknesses of garbage in–garbage out as identified by Babich and Hilary (2019) can be explained well with reference to information sharing and visibility (Barrat and Oke, 2007). Sharing of relevant information for visibility as an outcome in SCM (Barrat and Oke, 2007) will always have a behavioral and people issue as an enabler apart from technology which cannot be ignored (Whipple *et al.*, 2002). As a conclusion, it can be said that although blockchain technology seems to have some way to go before it transforms the current governance, dynamics, and routines of supply chain management, its disruptive benefits and challenges are looming.

References

Andoni, M., V. Robu, D. Flynn, S. Abram, D. Geach, D. Jenkins, P. McCallum, and A. Peacock (2019), Blockchain technology in the energy sector: A systematic review of challenges and opportunities, *Renewable and Sustainable Energy Reviews* **100**, 143–174.

Arkenberg, C., N. Lele, J. Loucks, and K. Ramachandra (2018), How can telecom, media, and entertainment find the value in blockchain? *Deloitte Insights* 1–14. www.deloitte.com/insights.

Aung, M. M. and Y. S. Chang (2014), Traceability in a food supply chain: Safety and quality perspectives, *Food Control* **39**(1), 172–184.

Awaysheh, A. and R. D. Klassen (2010), The impact of supply chain structure on the use of supplier socially responsible practices, *International Journal of Operations and Production Management* **30**(12), 1246–1268.

Babich, V. and G. Hilary (2019), Distributed ledgers and operations: What operations management researchers should know about blockchain technology, *Manufacturing and Service Operations Management*. https://doi.org/10.1287/msom.2018.0752.

Bahga, A. and V. Madisetti (2017), *Blockchain Applications: A Hands-On Approach*, 1st edition. VPT, www.hands-on-books-series.com/blockchain.html.

Barney, J., D. Ketchen, and M. Wright (2011), The future of resource-based theory: Revitalization or decline? *Journal of Management* **37**(5), 1299–1315.

Barratt, M. and A. Oke (2007), Antecedents of supply chain visibility in retail supply chains: A resource-based theory perspective, *Journal of Operations Management* **25**(6), 1217–1233.

Baum, J.A.C., R. Cowan, and N. Jonard (2010), Network-independent partner selection and the evolution of innovative networks, *Management Science* **56**(11), 2094–2110.

Bhardwaj, A. (2000), A resource-based perspective on information technology capabilities and firm performance: An empirical investigation, *MIS Quarterly* **24**(1), 169–196.

Birkey, R. N., R. P. Guidry, M. A. Islam, and D. M. Patten (2018), Mandated social disclosure: An analysis of the response to the California Transparency in Supply Chains Act of 2010, *Journal of Business Ethics* **152**(3), 827–841.

Blei, D. M. (2012), Probabilistic topic models, *Communication of the ACM* **55**(4), 77–84.

Blei, D. M. and J. D. Lafferty (2005), Dynamic topic models, in *Proceedings of the 23rd International Conference on Machine Learning*, ACM, pp. 113–120.

Blei, D. M. and J. D. Lafferty (2009), Topic models, in *Text Mining: Theory and Applications*, A. Sahami and M. Srivastava (eds.), New York: Taylor and Francis, pp. 71–93.

Blei, D. M., A. Ng, and M. I. Jordan (2003), Latent Dirichlet allocation, *Journal of Machine Learning Research* **3**, 993–1022.

Borgatti, S. P. and M. G. Everett (2006), A graph-theoretic perspective on centrality, *Social Networks* **28**(4), 466–484.

Burnham, K. and D. Anderson (2002), *Model Selection and Multimodel Inference: A Practical Information-theoretic Approach*. Springer-Verlag, second edition.

Burt, R. S. (1998), The gender of social capital, *Rationality and Society* **10**(1), 5–46.

Cachon, G. and M. Fisher (2000), Supply chain inventory management and the value of shared information, *Management Science* **46**(8), 1032–1048.

Castro, M. and B. Liskov (1999), Practical byzantine fault tolerance, in *Proceedings of 3rd USENIX Symposium of Operating System Design Implementation*, pp. 173–186.

Chang, J. and D. Blei (2009), Relational topic models for document networks, in *Proceedings of the 12th International Conference on Artificial Intelligence and Statistics*, pp. 81–88.

Chen, F., Z. Drezner, J. K. Ryan, and D. Simchi-Levi (2000), Quantifying the bull-whip effect in a simple supply chain: the impact of forecasting, lead-times and information, *Management Science* **46**(3), 436–443.

Choi, T. Y. and Y. Hong (2002), Unveiling the structure of supply networks: Case studies in Honda, Acura and Daimler Chrysler, *Journal of Operations Management* **20**(5), 469–493.

Chopra, S. and M. S. Sodhi (2004), Managing risk to avoid supply-chain break-down, *MIT Sloan Management Review* **46**(1), 53–62.

Cottrill, K. (2018), The benefits of blockchain: fact or wishful thinking? *Supply Chain Management Review* **Jan–Feb**, 20–25.

Croxton, K. L., S. J. García-Dastugue, D. M. Lambert, and D. S. Rogers (2001), The supply chain management processes, *International Journal of Logistics Management* **12**(2), 13–36.

Davis, G. F., M. V. Whitman, and M. N. Zald (2013), Political agency and the responsibility paradox: Multinationals and corporate social responsibility, in *Contemporary Political Agency: Theory and Practice*, B. Maiguashca and R. Marchett (eds.), London, U.K.: Routledge, pp. 92–117.

Dinh, T. T. A., R. Liu, M. Zhang, G. Chen, B. C. Ooi, and J. Wang (2018), Untangling blockchain: A data processing view of blockchain systems, *IEEE Transactions on Knowledge and Data Engineering* **30**(7), 1366–1385.

Francisco, K. and D. Swanson (2018), The supply chain has no clothes: Technology adoption of blockchain for supply chain transparency, *Logistics* **2**(2), 1–13.

Gandhi, S., A. Majumdar, and S. Monahan (2018), Unlocking blockchain's potential in your supply chain: Beneath the hype, blockchain is s a maturing technology that offers great promise, *Supply Chain Management Review*, **July/August**, 38–40.

Grün, B. and K. Hornik (2011), Topicmodels: An R package for fitting topic models, *Journal of Statistical Software* **40**(13), 1–30.

Halldorsson, A., H. Kotzab, J. H. Mikkola, and T. Skjøtt-Larsen (2007), Complementary theories to supply chain management, *Supply Chain Management: An International Journal* **12**(4), 284–296.

Handfield, R. B. and C. Bechtel (2002), The role of trust and relationship structure in improving supply chain responsiveness, *Industrial Marketing Management* **31**(4), 367–382.

Huq, F. A., M. Stevenson, and M. Zorzini (2014), Social sustainability in developing country suppliers: An exploratory study in the ready made garments industry of Bangladesh, *International Journal of Operations & Production Management* **34**(5), 610–638.

Henry, W., B. Chew, A. Lora, and H. Chae (2018), Developing winning blockchain applications in the public sector — Blockchain basics for government, *Deloitte Insights* 1–18. Available at: www.deloitte.com/insights.

Ho, D. C. K., K. F. Au, and E. Newton (2002), Empirical research on supply chain management: A critical review and recommendations, *International Journal of Production Research* **40**(17), 4415–4430.

Ivanov, D., B. Sokolov, and A. Dolgui (2014), The Ripple effect in supply chains: Trade-off "efficiency-flexibility-resilience" in disruption management, *International Journal of Production Research* **52**(7), 2154–2172.

Karkkainen, M. (2003), Increasing efficiency in the supply chain for short shelf life goods using RFID tagging, *International Journal of Retail & Distribution Management* **31**(10), 529–537.

Kshetri, N. (2018), Blockchain's roles in meeting key supply chain management objectives, *International Journal of Information Management* **39**(April), 80–89.

Kim, Y. H. and G. F. Davis (2016), Challenges for global supply chain sustainability: Evidence from conflict minerals reports, *Academy of Management Journal* **59**(6), 1896–1916.

Kim, Y., T. Y. Choi, T. Yan, and K. Dooley (2011), Structural investigation of supply networks: A social network analysis approach, *Journal of Operations Management* **29**(3), 194–211.

Kiviat, T. I. (2015), Beyond Bitcoin: Issues in regulating Blockchain transactions, *Duke Law Journal* **65**(3), 569–608.

Kraft, T., L. Valdés, and Y. Zheng (2016), Transparency in social responsibility: Investigating consumers' behaviors and motives. SSRN-id2518627, pp. 1–39.

Lancioni, R., H. J. Schau, and M. F. Smith (2003), Internet impacts on supply chain management, *Industrial Marketing Management* **32**(3), 173–175.

Lee, H. L., K. C. So, and C. S. Tang (2000), The value of information sharing in a two-level supply chain, *Management Science* **46**(5), 626–643.

Madhok, A. (2002), Reassessing the fundamentals and beyond: Ronald Coase, the transaction cost and resource-based theories of the firm and the institutional structure of production, *Strategic management Journal* **23**(6), 535–550.

Marsden, P. V. (2002), Egocentric and sociocentric measures of network centrality, *Social Networks* **24**(4), 407–422.

McFarlene, D. and Y. Sheffi (2003), The Impact of automatic identification on supply chain operations, *The International Journal of Logistics Management* **14**(1), 1–17.

Mohr, J. J. and R. S. Sohi (1995), Communication flows in distribution channels: Impact on assessments of communication quality and satisfaction, Journal of Retailing **71**(4), 393–415.

O' Dell, K., C. Mulholland, S. Sekar, and R. Daly (2018), Powered by blockchain–Reimagining electrification in emerging markets, *Deloitte Insights*, **October**, 1–12. Available at: https://www2.deloitte.com/insights/...blockchain.../emerging-markets-electric-grids.ht.

Oliveira, M. A. M. D. (2016), *Segurança na Cadeia alimentar: estudo de fraudes*, Doctoral dissertation, Instituto Politécnico do Porto. Escola Superior de Tecnologia e Gestão.

Perez-Aloe, R., J. M. Valverde, A. Lara, J. M. Carrillo, I. Roa, and J. Gonzales (2007), Application of RFID tags for the overall traceability of the products in cheese industries, in *1st annual RFID Eurasia*, Istanbul, pp. 1–5.

Ponweiser, M. (2012), Latent Dirichlet allocation in R, *Vienna University of Business and Economics*. https://epub.wu.ac.at/3558.

Porter, M. E. (2001), Strategy and the Internet, *Harvard Business Review* (79:3), 63–78.

Powell, T. C. and A. Dent-Micallef (1997), Information technology as competitive advantage: The role of human, business and technology resources, *Strategic Management Journal* **18**(5), 375–405.

Prater, E., G. V. Frazier, and P. M. Reyes (2005), Future impacts of RFID on e-supply chains in grocery retailing, *Supply Chain Management* **10**(2), 134–142.

Rai, A., R. Patnayakuni, and N. Seth (2006), Firm performance impacts of digitally enabled supply chain capabilities, *MIS Quarterly* **30**(2), 225–246.

Rungtusanatham, M., F. Salvador, C. Forza, and T. Y. Choi (2003), Supply-chain linkages and operational performance: A resource-based perspective, *International Journal of Operations and Production Management* **23**(9), 1084–1099.

Sarfaty, G. A. (2015), Shining light on global supply chain, *Harvard International Law Journal* **56**(2), 1–45.

Shanley, A. (2017), Could blockchain improve pharmaceutical supply chain security? *Pharmaceutical Technology, Outsourcing Resources* s34–s39.

Simchi-Levi, D., P. Kaminsky, and E. Simchi-Levi (2000), *Designing and Managing the Supply Chain: Concepts, Strategies and Case Studies*. New York: Irwin/McGraw-Hill.

Sissman, M. and K. Sharma (2018), Building supply management with blockchain — New technology mitigates some logistical risks while adding a few others, *ISE Magazine*, **July**, 43–46.

Srivastava, S., A. Sultan, and N. Chashti (2017), Influence of innovation competence on firm level competitiveness: An exploratory study, *Asia Pacific Journal of Innovation and Entrepreneurship* **11**(1), 63–75.

Skilton, P. F. and J. L. Robinson (2009), Traceability and normal accident theory: How does supply network complexity influence the traceability of adverse events? *The Journal of Supply Chain Management* **45**(3), 40–53.

Spekman, R. E., J. W. Kamauff Jr., and N. Myhr (1998), An empirical investigation in to supply chain management: A perspective on partnerships, *Supply Chain Management* **3**(2), 53–67.

Steyvers, M. and T. Griffiths (2007), Probabilistic topic models, in *Handbook of Latent Semantic Analysis*, T. K. Landauer, D. S. McNamara, S. Dennis, and W. Kintsch (eds.), Mahwah, NJ: Lawrence Erlbaum, pp. 427–448.

Sun, L. and Y. Yin (2017), Discovering themes and trends in transportation research using topic modeling, *Transportation Research Part C* **77**, 49–66.

Tan, A., D. T. Xuan, and K. Cottrill (2018), Is blockchain the missing link in the Halal supply chain? *Supply Chain Management Review* **May/June**, 6–8.

Tang, O. and S. N. Musa (2011), Identifying risk issues and research advancements in supply chain risk management, *Journal of Production Economics* **133**(1), 25–34.

Treiblmaier, H. (2018), The impact of the blockchain on the supply chain: A theory-based research framework and a call for action, *Supply Chain Management: An International Journal* **23**(6), 545–559. Available at: https://doi.org/10.1108/SCM-01-2018-0029.

Wang, Y., M. Singgih, J. Wang, and M. Rit (2019), Making sense of blockchain technology: How will it transform supply chains? *International Journal of Production Economics* **211**(C), 221–236.

Wei, X. and W. Croft (2006), LDA-based document models for ad-hoc retrieval, in *Proceedings of the 29th Annual International ACM SIGIR Conference on Research and Development in Information Retrieval*, ACM, pp. 178–185.

Whipple, J. M., R. Frankel, and P. J. Daugherty (2002), Information support for alliances: Performance implications, *Journal of Business Logistics* **23**(2), 67–82.

Yao, Y., M. Dresner, and J. W. Palmer (2009), Impact of Boundary-Spanning information technology and position in chain on firm performance, *Journal of Supply Chain Management* **45**(4), 3–16.

Appendix A: Ten Most Probable Words for 50 Topics

Topic 1	Topic 2	Topic 3	Topic 4	Topic 5	Topic 6	Topic 7	Topic 8	Topic 9	Topic 10	Topic 11	Topic 12
data	supplier	Line	drug	manufactur	project	risk	connect	shipment	food	product	contract
organis	buyer	Uber	pharmaceut	packag	world	inform	stage	iot	trace	chang	smart
financ	manag	Magazine	industri	fda	origin	enterpris	visibl	vehicl	walmart	music	transact
uk	compani	Land	develop	serial	te	product	peopl	record	ibm	servic	parti
servic	upstream	Launch	europ	identifi	commerc	busi	deliveri	sensor	traceabl	industri	term
base	direct	Drop	al	enforc	diamond	manag	import	data	industri	unit	secur
supplier	data	Faster	pharma	product	complet	authent	intellig	equip	produc	record	execut
person	relationship	Hour	numer	issu	agre	data	review	failur	consum	transform	financi
deploy	sector	Berry	discuss	expect	usa	subject	leav	platform	pilot	shift	trade
everledg	requir	california	compani	document	Launch	network	complex	captur	safeti	futur	code

Topic 13	Topic 14	Topic 15	Topic 16	Topic 17	Topic 18	Topic 19	Topic 20	Topic 21	Topic 22	Topic 23	Topic 24
contract	control	Busi	access	global	Product	solut	track	industri	improv	tag	devic
traceabl	inventori	Contract	data	trade	epc	logist	process	ship	transpar	protocol	iot
smart	optim	Applic	secur	manag	manufactur	manag	record	network	compani	id	secur
servic	strategi	Process	industri	analyst	counterfeit	cost	air	maersk	diamond	reader	bit.li
internet	simul	Manag	vehicl	develop	ownership	process	chief	contain	food	rfid	address
product	vol	Ibm	automot	index	owner	inform	cargo	digit	right	node	data
data	product	Engine	smart	futur	address	busi	hyperledg	ocean	human	secur	cloud
inform	base	Figure	vol	countri	parti	actor	communiti	project	miner	attack	connect
address	law	Transact	onlin	cyber	rfid	implement	mean	carrier	respons	authent	water
manag	model	Parti	contract	progress	tag	warehous	percent	cargo	manag	messag	network

Topic 25	Topic 26	Topic 27	Topic 28	Topic 29	Topic 30	Topic 31	Topic 32	Topic 33	Topic 34	Topic 35	Topic 36
Date	retail	healthcar	custom	product	product	design	logist	secur	inform	product	transact
Label	robot	Edi	resili	track	delet	manufactur	digit	risk	data	requir	ledger
Global	manag	Data	predict	food	inform	digit	cloud	trust	traceabl	food	retail
Standard	pick	industri	marketplac	sc	manag	filew	environ	consum	food	shipment	consum
Wast	facil	contract	drive	solut	decis	print	futur	compani	smart	storag	transpar
Materi	modern	Blog	reach	alibaba	stage	process	focus	product	event	traceabl	sourc
Network	special	patient	organ	consum	process	product	warehous	cyber	contract	track	reduc
Free	futur	Medic	centric	onlin	logist	establish	peopl	cybersecur	base	date	secur
Simplify	warehous	Smart	disrupt	project	activ	payment	role	manufactur	manag	stage	cost
Promot	handl	softwar	chang	proven	perform	asset	transport	report	node	easi	purchas

Topic 37	Topic 38	Topic 39	Topic 40	Topic 41	Topic 42	Topic 43	Topic 44	Topic 45	Topic 46	Topic 47	Topic 48	Topic 49	Topic 50
detect	applic	Transact	data	standard	product	digit	transpar	credit	legal	owner	data	data	logist
data	research	Contract	shop	ledger	manag	databas	bring	energi	bitcoin	log	track	serial	shipment
network	doi	Block	manufactur	block	compani	review	record	clean	network	oper	compani	pharma	softwar
trust	public	Data	token	verif	risk	verifi	call	carbon	law	driver	record	compani	transport
comput	inform	Node	transact	cloud	consum	industri	extern	generat	practic	truck	sap	pharmaceut	warehous
collabor	energi	consensus	contract	develop	transpar	potenti	spend	fuel	comput	hour	ingredi	product	global
secur	data	Protocol	machin	web	process	benefit	maintain	verif	creat	pay	product	requir	handl
base	busi	Perform	record	communiti	transact	involv	expert	transact	record	rule	improv	industri	custom
id	transact	hyperledg	autom	method	govern	proof	oper	cost	currenc	reason	supplier	servic	contain
parti	secur	Smart	payment	applic	level	particip	implic	autonom	block	benefit	safeti	clinic	adapt

Appendix B: Data Sample of Text Document

ID	Authors	Article	Journal/Magazine
1	Suketu Gandhi, Adrish Majumdar and Sean Monahan	Unlocking Blockchain's Potential in Your Supply Chain: Beneath the Hype, Blockchain is a Maturing Technology that Offers Great Promise	*Supply Chain Management Review*, July/August 2018, Vol. 22 Issue 4, pp. 38–40
2	Dominic Watkins	Blockchain: Bringing Security to the Food Sector	*Food & Drink Technology*, July–August 2018, Vol. 17 issue 10, pp. 28–29
3	Maxwell Sissman and Kashni Sharma	Building Supply Management with Blockchain: New Technology Mitigates Some Logistical Risks While Adding a Few Others	*ISE Magazine*, July 2018, pp. 43–46
4	Hugh R. Morley	Weighing in on Blockchain: Blockchain Technology Touted as Means to Share Container Weights to Meet Global Regulations	*The Journal of Commerce*, September 2017, Vol. 18 Issue 19
5	Rose Shilling	Keeping the Supply Chain Safe	*Food Engineering*, October 2018, pp. 54–59
6	Bridget McCrea	The Future of Retail Distribution	*Modern Materials Handling*, April 2018, pp. 56–59
7	Richard Giffords	Near and Next: The Digitised Supply Chain	*Focus*, August 2018, pp. 26–27
8	Sarah Fister Gale	Speed Tracer	*PM Network*, October 2018, pp. 6–7
9	Merilee Kern	Making the Uncertain Certain	*ASI*, www.adhesivesmag.com, March 2019, pp. 23–25
10	Felicity Thomas	Stimulating Discussion	*Pharmaceutical Technology Europe*, February 2019, pp. 48–49
11	Agam Shah	The Chain Gang	*Mechanical Engineering*. May2018, Vol. 140 Issue 5, pp. 30–35.

12	Jenny McTaggart	Building 'Blocks'	*Progressive Grocer*. March 2018, Vol. 97 Issue 3, pp. 75–77
13	S. A. Mathieson	Blockchain Begins to Prove Versatility Beyond Finance	*Computer Weekly*. 4/25/2017, pp. 20–23.
14	Christine Chow	Blockchain for Good? Improving Supply Chain Transparency and Human Rights Management	*Governance Directions*. February 2018, Vol. 70 Issue 1, pp. 39–40
15	Anonymous	Experts: Blockchain Can Trace Bad Food Quicker	*ISE: Industrial & Systems Engineering at Work*, July 2018, Vol. 50 Issue 7, pp. 12–13
16	Burnson, Patrick	Measuring Risk and Reward in the Global Market Place	*Supply Chain Management Review*. Mar/April 2018, Vol. 22 Issue 2, pp. 12–13
17	Anonymous	Why Bitcoin's Blockchain Technology Could Revolutionize Supply Chain Transparency	*The Secured Lender*, July/August 2016, Vol. 72 Issue 6, pp. 30–32
18	Max Heine	Truth-telling	*Overdrive*, June 2018, Vol. 58 Issue 6, pp. 7–7
19	Hugh R. Morley	INTTRA Bullish on Digital Pipeline: Booking Network Sees Active Role in Providing Shippers with Visibility in Supply Chain	*Journal of Commerce* (1542–3867). 3/5/2018, Vol. 19 Issue 5, pp. 55–58
20	Agnes Shanley	FDA Provides More Clarity on DSCSA	*Pharmaceutical Technology*, November 2018, Vol. 42 Issue 11, pp. 50–51
21	Anonymous	Samsung Is Set to Embrace Blockchain for its Supply Chain	*Information Management Journal*. May/June 2018, Vol. 52 Issue 3, pp. 15–15
22	Chris Caplice	A New Score for Supply Chains	*Supply Chain Management Review*. March/April 2017, Vol. 21 Issue 2, pp. 13–14
23	Peter Loop	Blockchain: The Next Evolution of Supply Chain	*Material Handling & Logistics*. November/December 2016, Vol. 71 Issue 10, pp. 22–24

(Continued)

Appendix B: (*Continued*)

ID	Authors	Article	Journal/Magazine
24	Agnes Shanley	Could Blockchain Improve Pharmaceutical Supply Chain Security?	*Pharmaceutical Technology*. 2017 Supplement, pp. 34–39
25	Anonymous	GS1, IBM and Microsoft Promote Blockchain App. across Supply Chain Networks	*Material Handling & Logistics*. October 2017, Vol. 72 Issue 8, pp. 7–8
26	Bryce Suzuki, Todd Taylor, and Gary Marchant	Blockchain: How It Will Change Your Legal Practice	*Computer & Internet Lawyer*, July 2018, Vol. 35 Issue 7, pp. 5–9
27	Gary Forger	NextGen technologies: Building the supply chains of the future	*Supply Chain Management Review*. September/October 2018, Vol. 22 Issue 5, pp. 24–28
28	Ken Cottrill	The Benefits of Blockchain: Fact or Wishful Thinking? Blockchain is still a largely unproven innovation in the supply chain, but it's also one that companies can't afford to ignore.	*Supply Chain Management Review*. January/February 2018, Vol. 22 Issue 1, pp. 20–25.
29	Albert Tan, Doan Thanh Xuan, and Ken Cottrill	Is Blockchain the Missing Link in the Halal Supply Chain?	*Supply Chain Management Review*. May/June 2018, Vol. 22 Issue 3, pp. 6–8
30	Anonymous	The Sprint to Digital Success	*Supply Chain Management Review*, January/February 2018, Vol. 22 Issue 1, pp. S58–S58
31	Patrick Burnson	Blockchain Coming of Age	*Supply Chain Management Review*, May/June 2017, Vol. 21 Issue 3, pp. 10–11
32	Joyce Mazero	Blockchain: How to Use Smart Contracts	*Franchising World*, November, 2018
33	Alyse Thomson	Blockchain for Cocoa? Maybe	*Candy Industry*, March, 2019
34	Matt Danford	Can Blockchain Help Machine Shops Win Work	*Modern Machine Shop*, October 2018, pp. 74–81
35	Randy Woods	Perishables and the Effort for Greater Transparency	*Aircargoworld.com*, July 2017, pp. 16–19

36	Kentaroh Toyoda, P. Takis Mathiopoulos, Iwao Sasase, Tomoaki Ohtsuki	A Novel Blockchain-Based Product Ownership Management System (POMS) for Anti-Counterfeits in the Post Supply Chain	*IEEE Access*, Vol 5, 2017, pp. 17465–17477
37	Paula Fraga-lamas, Tiago m. Fernández-Caramés	A Review on Blockchain Technologies for an Advanced and Cyber-Resilient Automotive Industry	*IEEE Access*, Vol 7, 2019, pp. 17578–17598
38	Qinghua Lu and Xiwei Xu	Adaptable Blockchain-Based Systems	*IEEE Software*, November/December 2017, pp. 21–27
39	Yonggui Fu and Jianming Zhu	Big Production Enterprise Supply Chain Endogenous Risk Management Based on Blockchain	*IEEE Access*, Vol 7, 2019, pp. 15310–15319
40	Nir Kshetri and Elena Loukoianova	Blockchain Adoption in Supply Chain Networks in Asia	*IT Professional*, January/February 2019, pp. 11–15
41	Dennis Miller	Blockchain and the Internet of Things in the Industrial Sector	*IT Professional*, May/June 2018, pp. 15–17
42	Joe Abou Jaoude and Raafat George Saade	Blockchain Applications — Usage in Different Domains	*IEEE Access*, Vol 7, 2019, pp. 45360–45381
43	Liang Xi Downey, Frédéric Bauchot, and Jos Rölling	Blockchain for Business Value: A Contract and Work Flow Management to Reduce Disputes Pilot Project	*IEEE Engineering Management Review*, Vol. 46, No. 4, December 2018, pp. 86–93
44	Guido Perboli1, Stefano Musso, and Mariangela Rosano	Blockchain in Logistics and Supply Chain: A Lean Approach for Designing Real-World Use Cases	*IEEE Access*, Vol 6, 2019, pp. 62018–62028
45	Ashiq Anjum, Manu Sporny, and Alan Sill	Blockchain Standards for Compliance and Trust	*IEEE Cloud Computing*, July/August 2017, pp. 84–90
46	Qingyun Zhu, Mahtab Kouhizadeh	Blockchain Technology, Supply Chain Information, and Strategic Product Deletion Management	*IEEE Engineering Management Review*, Vol. 47, No. 1, March 2019, pp. 36–44
47	Nir Kshetri	Can Blockchain Strengthen the Internet of Things?	*IT Pro*, July/August 2017, pp. 68–72
48	Jinan Fiaidhi, Sabah Mohammed, and Sami Mohammed	EDI with Blockchain as an Enabler for Extreme Automation	*IT Professional*, July/August 2018, pp. 66–72

(*Continued*)

Appendix B: (*Continued*)

ID	Authors	Article	Journal/Magazine
49	Michael J. Ashley and Mark S. Johnson	Establishing a Secure, Transparent, and Autonomous Blockchain of Custody for Renewable Energy Credits and Carbon Credits	*IEEE Engineering Management Review*, Vol. 46, No. 4, December 2018, pp. 100–102
50	Joerg S. Hofstetter	Extending Management Upstream in Supply Chains Beyond Direct Suppliers	*IEEE Engineering Management Review*, Vol.46, No. 1, March 2018, pp. 106–116
51	Qijun Lin, Huaizhen Wang, Xiaofu Pei, and Junyu Wang	Food Safety Traceability System Based on Blockchain and EPCIS	*IEEE Access,* Vol 7, 2019, pp. 20698–20707
52	Wendan Zhao, and Dingwei Wang	Simulation-Based Optimization on Control Strategies of Three-Echelon Inventory in Hybrid Supply Chain with Order Uncertainty	*IEEE Access*, Vol 6, 2018, pp. 54215–54223
53	Nir Kshetry, Jeffery Voas	Supply Chain Trust	*IT Professional*, March/April 2019, pp. 6–10
54	Michail Sidorov, Ming Tze Ong, Ravivarma Vikneswaren Sridharan, Junya Nakamura, Ren Ohmura, and Jing Huey Khor	Ultralightweight Mutual Authentication RFID Protocol for Blockchain Enabled Supply Chains	*IEEE Access*, Vol 7, 2019, pp. 7273–7285
55	Tien Tuan Anh Dinh, Rui Liu, Meihui Zhang, Member, IEEE, Gang Chen, Member, IEEE, Beng Chin Ooi, Fellow, IEEE, and Ji Wang	Untangling Blockchain: A Data Processing View of Blockchain Systems	*IEEE Transactions on Knowledge and Data Engineering*, Vol. 30, No. 7, July 2018, pp. 1366–1385
56	Weizhi Meng,Elmar Wolfgang Tischhauser, Qingju Wang, Yu Wang, and Jinguang Han	When Intrusion Detection Meets Blockchain Technology: A Review	*IEEE Access*, Vol 6, 2018, pp. 10179–10188

https://doi.org/10.1142/9789811220470_0012

Chapter 12

Blockchain Solutions for Agency Problems in Corporate Governance

Wulf A. Kaal

University of St. Thomas School of Law, Minneapolis, USA

wulfkaal@gmail.com

Abstract

As a foundational technology, blockchain technology creates the infrastructure for decentralized networked governance that, over time, creates the environment which enables the removal of internal and external monitoring mechanisms previously necessitated by agency problems in corporate governance. Blockchain technology facilitates a substantial increase in efficiency in the agency relationship and lowers agency costs in orders of magnitude.

Keywords: Agency; Principal–agent; Blockchain; Technology; Agency cost; Monitoring; Corporate governance; Blockchain; Distributed ledger technology; Emerging technology.

1. Introduction

Agency theory is still today the leading theory for governance conflicts between shareholders, corporate managers, and debt holders (Jensen and Meckling, 1976). A vast literature attempts to explain the nature of the agency conflicts in corporate governance and the possible ways to resolve such conflicts (for an overview of the relevant literature, see Shleifer and Vishny, 1997). However, the core agency conflicts emanating from the separation of ownership (shareholder principal) and control (manager agent) cannot be fully addressed by the existing theoretical and legal framework. Attempts to monitor agents is inevitably costly and transaction costs abound.

This chapter adds to that literature and highlights the evolving solutions offered by blockchain technology. The scope and scale of agency problems in corporate governance can become more adequately manageable over time.

It is important to note that any use of blockchain technology in a corporate governance context necessitates the evolution of blockchain technology. Such evolution is subject to several factors. Similar to the Internet itself and perhaps even comparable to electricity, blockchain technology is not a disruptive technology, it is a foundational technology whose transformational impact takes decades rather than years. The use cases of blockchain technology involve most complex structures that are all interdependent. In other words, development of one area alone cannot be successful as multiple additional support structures are also needed. By way of comparison, the use of electricity necessitated wiring and light bulbs, connectors, generators, etc. One cannot exist without the others being in place. Even if the infrastructure elements are being developed in any of the major areas of use cases for blockchain technology, complex discussions around structural changes are needed before the technology can be applied.

The complexity of blockchain technology and its evolving characteristics and use cases also impact its ability to serve in a corporate governance role. More specifically, in the corporate governance context, it is essential that the authorities, who most likely understand the use case and not the technology, come to a consensus on how and when to implement such technology for that governance use case.

2. Agency Problems in Corporate Governance

Agency problems originate due to the lack of trust between principals and agents. The agency relationship can be defined as a contract between a principal and an agent whereby the agent acts on behalf of the principal because the principal delegated a modicum of decision-making authority to the agent (Jensen and Meckling, 1976). Because of the delegated authority, the agent's decisions affect both the agent's welfare and the principal's welfare. The agency model at its very basic level suggests that information asymmetries between the principal and the agent and agent's opportunistic behavior resulting from self-interest lead to a lack of trust on the agent by the principal. Because of bounded rationality, incomplete foresight, and information asymmetries between the principal and the agent (Kaal, 2014), it is impossible for principals to contract for every possible action or inaction of the agent in order to induce the agent to act in the best interests of the principal (Brennan, 1995).

The lack of trust in the agent's performance of his/her duties creates the underlying problems in corporate governance. Despite best efforts at monitoring and bonding, the interests of manager agents and shareholder principals in corporate governance are never fully aligned and agency losses inevitably arise from conflicts of interest between principals and agents, known as residual loss. Residual loss arises because the cost of enforcing suboptimal contracts between principals and agents always exceeds the benefits of performing the contractual obligations.

Agency costs arise because the principal attempts to control, monitor, and supervise the agent. As a result of lacking trust in the integrity of the principal–agent relationship, and in an attempt to minimize information asymmetries, principals are forced to put into place costly mechanisms to align their interest with those of the agents. Most prominently, such control mechanisms involve periodic reporting, compensation structures for agents, and bonding, among others. In the corporate context, agency costs can be seen as the lost value to shareholders (loss in a corporation's share price) that results from diverging interests between shareholders (principal) and corporate managers (agents). As such, agency costs are the sum of monitoring costs, bonding costs, and residual losses (Jensen and Meckling, 1976).

Monitoring costs are costs to the principal resulting from observing, measuring, and controlling an agent's behavior. Monitoring costs can include the cost of audits, executing executive compensation contracts, and cost of hiring/firing manager agents. While such monitoring costs are generally paid by the principal, agents may be responsible for such costs as well because agents' compensation is subject to adjustments to cover monitoring costs (Fama and Jensen, 1983).

Bonding costs are the cost of establishing and adhering to system structures that allow agents to act in shareholder principal's best interests or compensate shareholder principals appropriately if agents do not act in their best interest. While bonding costs are typically paid by the agents, they may in addition to financial costs include the cost of increased disclosures to shareholder principals. If the marginal reduction in monitoring equals the marginal increase in bonding costs, then agents no longer incur bonding costs.

The agency relationship in modern finance and corporate governance is characterized by attempts to optimize incentives between principals and agents, control costs, minimize information asymmetries, control adverse selection and moral hazard, optimize risk preferences between principals and agents, and engage in monitoring.

2.1. *Remedial attempts*

Centralization around well-established principal–agent hierarchies in corporations defines the existing corporate governance structure (Ivan *et al.*, 2015; Fenwick and Vermeulen, 2016). Such governance hierarchy and the associated governance structures revolve around authority, responsibility, and control flows with the investors at the epicenter of that hierarchy (ICSA, 2019), particularly the minority investors (Porta *et al.*, 2000).

The dominant corporate governance solution for the agency problem today focuses on shareholder value maximization (Bainbridge, 2002; Marin, 2012; Smith, 2003; Stout, 2013).[1] Implementation of the shareholder primacy doctrine mostly results in measures that aim at aligning the interests of all of the other actors/stakeholders within those of the investor–shareholders (Smith and Ronnergard, 2016), thus reducing the risk of managerial misbehavior (Pacces, 2013). If management acts opportunistically at the expense of shareholder value, the associated firm underperformance and possible bankruptcy harm all the stakeholders (Maher and Andersson, 1999; Larrabee, 2014). Conversely, by aligning the interests and incentives of the various actors with those of the investor–shareholders, the resulting increase in firm performance — as measured by the share price — benefits all of the stakeholders in a firm, as well as the public who benefit from the goods and services that a

[1]According to the dominant view, the goal of a firm should be to increase the financial interests of the investors, and by doing so, the firm can maximize opportunities to be successful.

successful firm provides (Stout, 2013).[2] Following this logic, increasing the shareholder control over other actors within the firm has become the primary goal of corporate governance rules (Fox and Lorsch, 2012). The correct corporate governance is seen as naturally resulting in shareholder value (Blair, 2003).

While the shareholder value approach to governance and many other attempts at optimizing corporate governance and addressing the agency problems in corporate governance helped optimize the agency problems, many examples suggest that the core underlying agency problems cannot be fully resolved within the existing theoretical and legal infrastructure.

A standard approach for effective corporate governance involved outside independent directors on corporate boards who hold managerial positions in other companies, thus separating the problems of decision management and decision control (Fama and Jensen, 1983). However, CEOs who often dominate the board make the separation of these functions much more difficult, which hurts shareholders. Furthermore, outside directors' separation of decision management and decision control depends on their concern over reputation as an incentive, which is insufficient in most cases.

Another much touted governance mechanism for firms involved firms' capital structures with emphasis on higher debt levels. Higher levels of insider ownership by increasing debt and reducing equity (Jensen and Meckling, 1976) in the firm's capital structure act as a bonding mechanism for manager agents (Jensen, 1986). Management by issuing debt rather than paying dividends creates contractual obligations to pay out future cash flows in ways unattainable through dividends. Debt financing can also help create external capital market monitoring which incentivizes managers' avoidance of personal utility maximization and increases value-maximizing strategies for shareholders (Easterbrook, 1984).

In an effort to curtail the inevitable instability that is a by-product of the pervasive agency problem in the corporate governance system (Roe, 2004), governments have responded to corporate governance scandals by adopting a number of regulatory changes. Such changes include substantively increased disclosure requirements (Hermalin and Weisbach, 2007;

---

[2]Discussing residual claimants arguments and potential benefits to society through the company; see also Smith and Ronnergard (2016).

Fenwick and Vermeulen, 2016).[3] Shareholder activism reform by itself has been unable to sufficiently improve the corporate governance system (Bainbridge, 2005; Karpoff, 2001; Romano, 2000; Coffee, 1991).[4,5] Upgrading the US proxy system has been another government priority (Wilcox, 2005; Hu and Black, 2006; Yermack, 2010).[6] Change in executive compensation has been another approach to address the instability of the existing corporate governance system (Bebchuk and Fried, 2003; Bebchuk *et al.*, 2010; Roe, 2004). Government-sponsored organizational experimentation that enables new business models and new organizational structures is desirable and valuable and may be one of the few ways to facilitate the much needed corporate governance reform.

2.2. *Path dependencies*

Despite the unresolved substantive problems associated with the division of ownership (shareholders) and control (agent) (Roe, 2004),[7] the corporate form with the diffused share ownership that leads to such conflicts and the incomplete and suboptimal rules that govern such conflicts remain the most popular forms of a governance mechanism.

[3]"The political response to corporate scandals has been the introduction of more regulation. In a US context, for instance, "Sarbanes-Oxley" and "Dodd-Frank" function as shorthand for these new swathes of legal rules, but such a trend can be found everywhere. The inevitable result has been the emergence of a regulatory landscape that requires large modern corporations to make a much more significant investment in compliance and the management of legal risk".

[4]"[T]he disagreement among researchers is more apparent than real. Most evidence indicates that shareholder activism can prompt small changes in target firms' governance structures, but has negligible impacts on share values and earnings".

[5]"The finance literature presents an apparent paradox: Notwithstanding commentators' generally positive assessment of the development of such shareholder activism, the empirical studies suggest that it has an insignificant effect on targeted firms' performance. Very few find evidence of a positive impact, and some even find a significant negative stock price effect from activism".

[6]The existing US proxy system lacks transparency; has few accountability mechanisms; is complex and costly; tolerates recordkeeping inaccuracies partially because it provides no audit trail; and produces voting results that cannot be verified.

[7]"The core fissure in American corporate governance is the separation of ownership from control — distant and diffuse stockholders, with concentrated management — a separation that creates both great efficiencies and recurring breakdowns".

The popularity of the existing mechanisms to address the agency problems in corporate governance may be related to path dependencies created by the evolution of internal and external monitoring mechanisms in corporate governance and the evolution of governance mechanisms designed to limit the scope of agency problems, instituted to address the agency problems in corporate governance.

The existing universal governance solutions are often ineffective because agency conflicts and the specific scope of agency conflicts differ across firms. Governance mechanisms and the effectiveness of governance mechanisms in reducing agency conflicts in firms differ from firm to firm. Each type of governance mechanism and various combinations of governance mechanisms can help reduce aspects of agency costs associated with the separation of ownership (principal shareholder) and control (manager agent). However, existing governance mechanisms work well in some firms but are ineffective in others. The literature today is still lacking a comprehensive understanding of workable governance mechanisms and solutions across a broad spectrum of firms.

3. Blockchain Solutions for Agency Problems in Corporate Governance

Blockchain offers unprecedented solutions for agency problems in corporate governance. Supervisory tasks that were traditionally performed by principals to control their agents can be delegated to decentralized computer networks that are highly reliable, secure, immutable, and independent of fallible human input and discretionary human goodwill. Blockchain technology provides an alternative governance mechanism that eliminates agency costs — the principal's cost of supervising agents — by creating trust in the contractual relationship between the principal and the agent.

3.1. *Blockchain guarantees*

Blockchain technology provides formal guarantees to participating principals and agents that address agency problems in corporate governance. Because of the blockchain guarantees, the technology allows a qualitatively different solution for agency problems in corporate governance, especially if compared with the existing finance infrastructure that is riddled with agency problems (see credit rating, executive compensation, etc.).

The immutability of the blockchain and its cryptographic security systems provide transactional guarantees and create trust between principals and agents in the integrity of their contractual relationship. Such guarantees ensure no participant can circumvent the rules embedded in blockchain code. Blockchain guarantees include contract execution between a principal and an agent only if and when all contract parameters were fulfilled by both parties and verified by a majority of miners/nodes in the system. Hence, in the blockchain infrastructure, there is no need for the principal to institute oversight and monitoring with the associated agency costs. Because of the governance guarantees embedded in code, blockchain addresses the inherent agency problems in modern finance and corporate governance comprehensively.

Blockchain technology secures the integrity of principal–agent relationships by removing fraudulent transactions. Compared with the existing methods of verifying and validating transactions by third-party intermediaries (banking, lending, clearing, etc.), blockchain's security measures make blockchain validation technologies more transparent, faster, and less prone to error and corruption. While blockchain's use of digital signatures helps establish the identity and authenticity of the parties involved in the transaction, it is the completely decentralized network connectivity via the Internet that allows the most protection against fraud. Network connectivity allows multiple copies of the blockchain to be available to all participants across the distributed network. The decentralized fully distributed nature of the blockchain makes it practically impossible to reverse, alter, or erase information in the blockchain. Blockchains' distributed consensus model, e.g., the network "nodes" verify and validate chain transactions before transaction execution, makes it extremely rare for a fraudulent transaction to be recorded in the blockchain. Blockchain's distributed consensus model allows node verification of transactions without compromising the privacy of the parties. Blockchain transactions are therefore arguably safer than a traditional transaction model that requires third-party intermediary validation of transactions. Blockchain technology is also substantively faster than traditional third-party intermediary validation of transactions.

Cryptographic hashes used in blockchain technology further increase blockchain security and remove the trust barriers in agency relationships that require monitoring of agents and create agency costs. Cryptographic hashes are complex algorithms that use details of the existing entirety of transactions of the existing blockchain before the next block is added to generate a unique hash value. That hash value ensures the authenticity of each transaction before it is added to the block. The smallest change to the blockchain, even a single digit/value, results in a different hash value. A different hash value in turn makes any form of manipulation immediately detectable. As such, hash cryptology provides another level of guarantee in an agency relationship executed through blockchain technology.

Smart contracts enabled by blockchain technology allow for a comprehensive, near error free, and zero transaction/agency cost coordination of agency relationships. Smart contracts and smart property are blockchain-enabled computer protocols that facilitate, verify, monitor, and enforce the negotiation and performance of a contract between principal and agent. Agency relationships in smart contracts run exactly as coded without any possibility of opportunistic behavior of the agent. All contractual terms are public and fully transparent. Accordingly, a company's finances, for instance, are visible on the blockchain to anyone, not just to the company's accounting department. Smart agency contracts run on a custom-built blockchain that enables principals and agents to store registries of debts or promises and create entire markets, among many other aspects that have not yet been considered.

Agency-related governance in the blockchain takes place without intermediaries, counterparty risk, and principal's control mechanisms. Blockchain technology simply does not require the layers of control and verification that prior financial systems necessitated. Control mechanisms, such as regular management (agent) meetings with shareholders (e.g., at the AGM), financial disclosures, management agent scrutiny through analyst reports and financial press, pressure on management from stock market performance, hedge fund investors, and other institutional and private investors, are no longer part of the blockchain-enabled agency relationship in corporate governance.

Blockchain technology facilitates a substantial increase in the efficiency of agency relationships in orders of magnitude and lowers the agency costs equally substantial in orders of magnitude. The removal of checks and balances in corporate governance, monitoring of agents, audit requirements, disclosure regimes, market pressure, and executive agent compensation schemes, among many others, provide a qualitative shift in efficiency in the agency relationship and in overall corporate governance.

Self-validating blockchain transactions can help resolve the agency issues between most of the stakeholders and constituents of modern corporations. In addition to addressing the traditional agency problem in corporate governance between shareholder principals and manager agents, blockchain-enabled smart contracting allows for the public and fully transparent, secure, and completely networked exchange between the corporation and customers, owners and investors, other stakeholders, staff, regulators, strategic partners, suppliers, and service providers.

3.2. *Removal of agents*

Blockchain technology can facilitate the removal of agents as intermediaries in corporate governance through code, peer-to-peer connectivity, crowds, and collaboration. While it is still difficult to imagine a world without governance structures facilitated by agency constructs, decentralized autonomous organizations (DAOs) have started to challenge the core belief that governance necessitates agency.

The first DAO, launched in May 2016, in the founders' attempt to set up a corporate-type organization without using a conventional corporate structure, had a governance structure that was entirely built on software, code, and smart contracts that ran on the public decentralized blockchain platform Ethereum. Because it was created purely using computer codes, it had no physical address, no jurisdiction that could claim jurisdiction/control over it, and it was not an organization with a traditional hierarchy as we know it from traditional corporate structures. The DAO did not use a traditional corporate structure that necessitated formal authority and empowerment flowing top-down from investors–shareholders through a board of directors to management and eventually staff. Indeed, it had no directors, managers, or employees. In essence, all the core control mechanisms typically employed by principals in agency relationships were entirely removed in the DAO.

While the first DAO was subject to many limitations and ended in quite some controversy, future DAOs may be less prone to problems. Fundamental flaws in the DAO code enabled hackers to transfer one-third of the total funds to a subsidiary account. This hack in combination with additional technological limitations brought down the first DAO initiative. Yet, more DAOs have already been created and DAO enthusiasts are continuing test to it. A new DAO is currently being developed that is not set up as a Venture Capital Fund but rather as a donation DAO where participants donate and don't expect returns. DAO enthusiasts and the DAO community in general are constantly improving the DAO, and it seems possible that future DAOs may improve agency problems in corporate governance much more thoroughly than is currently fathomable.

3.3. *Reforming governance hierarchies*

DAO token holders are free from the existing corporate hierarchies and their restricting effects. People who work for a DAO are subject to a different kind of agency relationship and not subject to a supervisor or CEO. Instead, DAO workers work in a dynamic set of working relationships that continuously and dynamically self-organize around projects and outcomes, not corporate hierarchies with implicit hierarchical biases and associated suboptimal outcomes.

The core common denominator for all DAO token members is the unifying desire to optimize the DAO structure and the DAO token value. If a member-identified optimization has the potential to make the DAO more meaningful, useful, or valuable to the token holder members, the DAO token holders will desire to perform such optimization tasks as it is in their very interest to do so to help increase the value of the DAO tokens. Accordingly, token holders are determined to increase the value of tokens rather than decrease the value. To increase the value of its tokens, members can make DAO optimization proposals, e.g., optimize the voting procedure and webpage that explain what actions ought to be taken to optimize and what value such actions will add to the respective DAO token holder community. The token holder community then votes on a given optimization proposal. If a proposal passes, the proposing DAO member will receive an award in the form of new tokens. Any such payment is added to the respective DAO blockchain but now requires for the proposing token holder to perform on the proposed parameters of optimization. In other words, once the optimization proponent has made a deal with the DAO, it's in the blockchain and the proponent is required to deliver on the proposal or his/her contract is canceled.

Performance assessment in the DAO structure is based on value optimization, not on hierarchical or political processes. DAO workers' performances are assessed in an anonymized proposal voting scheme which is the only basis for assessment and payment. If DAO members perform well, they will get remunerated regardless of politics, background, or education. The only thing that counts for purposes of assessment of DAO works is their performance of optimization parameters. This is an important difference between classical corporate hierarchies and DAO member performance of optimization proposals, e.g., the DAO's non-discriminatory performance measures.

Non-performance penalties in the DAO structure are free from biases. If DAO community members do not deliver on a proposal that was voted in by the DAO token holder community, then they lose credibility in the DAO token holder community and may be perceived as lacking an ability to add value. In fact, non-performance on proposal comes with significant reputational penalties. Non-performers in the DAO structure will be less likely to have future opportunities to earn tokens because the other token holders are unlikely to approve non-performer proposals. Crucially, non-performance reputational penalties are entirely free from racial or cultural biases and associated implications as the token holders are unlikely to even know each other. Rather, they all work toward a common goal of optimizing the DAO and the token value.

The DAO token holders' focus on adding value benefits to all constituents. Because projects that cannot add value take token holders' time away from more productive endeavors, token holders become focused on managing their time and efforts. Unlike in traditional hierarchical organization where face time and unproductive meetings are the norm, the self-governing DAO token optimizer avoids any such corporate hierarchy inefficiencies and frees himself/herself from top-down inefficiencies and bad outcomes. In essence, the DAO work proposal and value optimization structure allows the avoidance of bad projects, bad colleagues, and unproductive meetings. The only thing that counts is the value proposition. In other words, the focus shifts from political positioning and supervisor pleasing without performance to a focus on adding active value to a given project. If value can be added, the tasks will be performed, if the assessment of the proposal suggests that the value proposition is in doubt, then the token holders will try to spend their time and skills on more productive and value-adding tasks. Importantly, because the DAO structure functions without supervisors, DAO token holders who decide they cannot add value on a given task can move to more productive endeavors that better utilize their skills without any penalties that would exist in the traditional hierarchical corporate structure.

Politics in the DAO structure have a different nature compared with traditional hierarchical corporate structures. In a traditional corporate hierarchy, position in the hierarchy and associated authority determine effort. In other words, the supervisor in the hierarchical structure can determine where, what, and when workers have to perform, resulting in suboptimal outcomes and attending in unproductive and useless meetings, among many other negative effects. By contrast, in the decentralized DAO environment, influence is determined by the value a given token holder contributed to a project's success.

3.4. *Agency reform*

The "value to effort focus of workflows" in the DAO structure has the potential to reform agency relationships. The value-focused performance in the DAO structure helps optimize workflows and creates sustainable solutions for DAO token holders. The supervisor in the traditional hierarchical corporate structure can determine where, what, and when workers have to perform, which often results in attending unproductive meetings, face time, and support for suboptimal outcomes to please supervisors, among many other suboptimal outcomes. By contrast, in the decentralized environment of DAOs, influence and outcomes are not created by hierarchy but rather determined by the value a token holder contributes to a project's success. Moreover, if a token holder adds substantial value to the DAO, other DAO token holders will want to add their skills in the same context which focuses the token holders' efforts on the highest possible value proposition.

The traditional regulatory infrastructure that attempts to overcome the corporate governance problems associated with the separation of ownership (shareholders) and control (management) relies heavily on fiduciary duties. In the DAO structure, such duties are less needed. Because of the value to effort focus of workflows in the DAO structure, supervision of management and imposition of legal duties on management are less needed because there are fewer or no supervisors. Rather, token holders optimize the DAO together according to their best value propositions in accordance with their unique skill sets, backgrounds, and training.

4. Open Issues

The above discussion has outlined the potential of blockchain technology as an emerging technology for governance design. Many of the ideal-typical and theoretical evaluations therein are subject to real-world limitations.

First and foremost, blockchain technology is a foundational technology whose transformational impact takes decades rather than years to take hold and reform legacy systems. Most complex systems and structures that will be reformed by the technology are interdependent. Reform and development of one area alone cannot be successful as multiple additional support structures are also needed. Even if the infrastructure elements are being developed in any of the major areas of use cases for blockchain technology, complex discussions around structural changes in legacy systems are needed before the technology can be applied.

In the corporate governance context, the application of blockchain technology may evolve within the existing centralized structures or in a decentralized environment. The former requires the authorities to come to a consensus on how and when to implement such technology for the governance use case. For the latter, core issues that have afflicted centralized governance solutions, such as information asymmetries between principal and agent, censorship, opportunism of agents, breaches of fiduciary duties, liability rules for principals and agents, and fraud or third-party interference, can only be truly removed to fully reform the agency relationship if and when a truly decentralized public blockchain emerges that is scalable and fully secure.

As agency relationships become more complex, a backstop for human behavior in agency relationships becomes necessary. The notion that agency relationships in smart contracts run exactly as coded without any possibility of opportunistic behavior of the agent is less likely to uphold in complex agency relationships. Similarly, without a decentralized human backstop to code, the immutability of the blockchain and its cryptographic security systems may not be able to create truly transactional guarantees and trust between principals and agents in the integrity of their contractual relationship.

Blockchain-based corporate governance solutions in DAOs require evolutionary blockchain governance protocols. Socially optimal hard-forking rules cannot suffice. Blockchain-based guarantees embedded in blockchain code can help ensure that no participant in business transactions and agency relationships can circumvent the set of governance rules. Blockchain guarantees include contract execution between a principal and an agent only if and when all contract parameters were fulfilled by both parties and verified in a consensus algorithm. Hence, in the blockchain infrastructure, a lower level of oversight and monitoring of agents changes the cost structure of the principal–agent relationship. Yet, the basis of such coded guarantees will evolve and require protocol upgrades for that changing environment. Without evolutionary governance upgrades, the cost reduction for the agency relationship cannot be maintained.

5. Conclusion

Agency problems in corporate governance can be reformed by blockchain technology. As a foundational technology, blockchain-based governance solutions for agency problems in corporate governance depend on the creation of infrastructure components that have not yet been conceptualized in the decentralized technology evolution. Once supported by the necessary infrastructure components, decentralized networked governance can, over time, create the environment that enables the removal of internal and external monitoring mechanisms previously necessitated by agency problems in corporate governance.

Yet, the boundaries of technological implementation may necessitate a long-term commitment by all constituents in the governance reform process. Centralized and decentralized blockchain-based governance solutions require different implementation efforts.

References

Bainbridge, S. M. (2002), Director v. shareholder primacy in the convergence debate, *Transnat'l Law* **16**, 45, Available at: https://scholarlycommons.pacific.edu/globe/vol16/iss1/5.

Bainbridge, S. M. (2005), Shareholder activism and institutional investors, UCLA School of Law Public Law-Economic Research, Working Paper No. 05-20, https://ssrn.com/abstract=796227.

Bebchuk, L. A. and J. M. Fried (2003), Executive Compensation as an Agency Problem, *Journal of Economic Perspective* **17**, 71–92.

Bebchuk, L. A. *et al.* (2010), The wages of failure: Executive compensation at Bear Stearns and Lehman 2000-2008, Yale J. Reg. **27**, 257–282.

Blair, M. M. (2003), Shareholder value, corporate governance, and corporate performance: A post-enron reassessment of the conventional wisdom, in *Corporate Governance and Capital Flows in a Global Economy*, P.K. Cornelius and B. Kogut (eds.), Oxford, England: Oxford University Press, pp. 53–82.

Brennan, M. J. (1995), Corporate finance over the past 25 years, *Financial Management* **24**, 9.

Coffee Jr., J. C. (1991), Liquidity versus control: The institutional investor as corporate monitor, *Colum. L. Rev.* **91**, 1277.

Fama, E. F. and M. C. Jensen (1983), Separation of ownership and control, *Journal of Literature and Economics* **88**, 301.

Fenwick, M. and E. P.M. Vermeulen (2016), The future of capitalism: "Un-corporating" corporate governance, Lex Research Topics in Corp. Law & Econ., Working Paper No. 2016-4, https://papers.ssrn.com/sol3/papers.cfm?abstract_id=2795042.

Fox, J. and J. W. Lorsch (2012), What good are shareholders, *Harvard Business Review*, Available at: https://hbr.org/2012/07/what-good-are-shareholders.

Easterbrook, F. H. (1984), Two agency cost explanations of dividends, *American Journal of Economic Review* **74**, 650.

Hermalin, B. E. and M. S. Weisbach (2007), Transparency and corporate governance, Nat'l Bureau of Econ. Research, Working Paper No. w12875, 2007, https://ssrn.com/abstract=958628.

Holmström, B. R. and S. N. Kaplan (2003), The state of U.S. corporate governance: What's right and what's wrong?, *ECGI — Fin.*, Working Paper No. 23/2003, https://ssrn.com/abstract=441100.

Hu, H. T. C. and B. S. Black (2006), The new vote buying: Empty voting and hidden (morphable) ownership, *S. Calif. L. Rev.* **79**, 811.

ICSA (2019), *The Governance Institute*, What is Corporate Governance? Available at: https://www.icsa.org.uk/about-us/policy/what-is-corporate-governance. (Last visited Apr. 16, 2019).

Ivan, I. *et al.* (2015), Requirements for corporate governance assessment based on ontologies, *Economics Informatics* **15**, 49.

Jensen, M. C. (1986), Agency costs of free cash flow, corporate finance and takeovers, *American Journal of Economic Review* **76**, 323.

Jensen, M. C. and W. H. Meckling (1976), Theory of the firm: Managerial behaviour, agency costs and ownership structure, *Journal of Financial Economics* **3**, 305.

Kaal, W. A. (2014), Evolution of law: Dynamic regulation in a new institutional economics framework, in *Festschrift zu Ehren von Christian Kirchner*, Wulf A. Kaal and Schmidt M. Schwartze (eds.), Mohr Siebeck Publisher.

Karpoff, J. M. (2001), The impact of shareholder activism on target companies: A survey of empirical findings, https://ssrn.com/abstract=885365.

Larrabee, D. (2014), Maximization of shareholder value: Flawed thinking that threatens our economic future, *Enterprising Investment*, Available at: https://blogs.cfainstitute.org/investor/2014/09/24/maximization-of-shareholder-value-flawed-thinking-that-threatens-our-economic-future/.

Maher, M. and T. Andersson (1999), Corporate Governance: Effects on firm performance and economic growth, *Organisation for Economic Co-operation and Development* **7**, Available at: https://www.oecd.org/sti/ind/2090569.pdf.

Marin, M. (2012), The crisis of shareholder primacy, *Research at Cambridge*, Available at: http://www.cam.ac.uk/research/discussion/the-crisis-of-shareholder-primacy.

Pacces, A. M. (2013), *Rethinking Corporate Governance: The Law and Economics of Control Powers*, Routledge Research in Corporate Law.

Porta, R. L. *et al.* (2000), *Investor protection and corporate governance*, **2** (unpublished article). Available at: https://papers.ssrn.com/sol3/papers.cfm?abstract_id=183908.

Roe, M. J. (2004), The inevitable instability of American corporate governance, in *Restoring Trust in American Business*, American Academy of Arts and Sciences.

Romano, R. (2000), Less is more: Making shareholder activism a valued mechanism of corporate governance, Yale Law & Economic Research Paper No. 241; Yale ICF, Working Paper No. 00-10; Yale SOM, Working Paper No. ICF- 00-10), https://ssrn.com/abstract=218650.

Shleifer, A. and R. W. Vishny (1997), A survey of corporate governance, *Journal of Finance* **737**.

Smith, H. J. (2003), The shareholders vs. stakeholders debate, *MITS loan Management Review*, Available at: http://sloanreview.mit.edu/article/the-shareholders-vs-stakeholders-debate/.

Smith, N. C. and D. Ronnergard (2016), Shareholder primacy, corporate social responsibility, and the role of business schools, *Journal of Business Ethics* **134**, 463.

Stout, L. A. (2013), *The Shareholder Value Myth*, Cornell Law Faculty Publications, Available at: https://scholarship.law.cornell.edu/cgi/viewcontent.cgi?referer=&httpsredir=1&article=2311&context=facpub. http://scholarship.law.cornell.edu/cgi/viewcontent.cgi?article=2311&context=facpub.

Wilcox, J. C. (2005), Shareholder nominations of corporate directors: Unintended consequences and the case for reform of the U.S. proxy system, in *Shareholder Access to the Corporate Ballot*, L. Bebchuck (ed.).

Yermack, D. (2010), Shareholder voting and corporate governance, *Annual Review Financial Economics* **2**, 103.

https://doi.org/10.1142/9789811220470_0013

Chapter 13

Economics of Cryptocurrencies: Artificial Intelligence, Blockchain, and Digital Currency

J. D. Agarwal

Indian Institute of Finance, Delhi and G-Noida, India
Finance India, Delhi, India
Tashkent Finance Institute, Uzbekistan
Szent István University, Hungary
The University of Delhi and The Pondicherry University Court, India
jda@iif.edu

Manju Agarwal

Indian Institute of Finance, Delhi and G-Noida, India
Moti Lal Nehru College, The University of Delhi, Delhi, India
ma@iif.edu OR aa_mat@yahoo.com

Aman Agarwal

Indian Institute of Finance, Delhi and G-Noida, India
Finance India, Delhi, India
The St. Emillion Brotherhood (7th Century AD), Bordeaux, France
University of Cergy-Pontoise, Paris, France
Tashkent State University of Economics, Uzbekistan
Ginsep, Germany
Center for Political Studies, Uzbekistan

Bureau of Indian Standards (MSD4 Panel), India
aa@iif.edu OR aa@iifbs.edu

Yamini Agarwal

Indian Institute of Finance, Delhi and G-Noida, India
Finance India, Delhi, India
IIF Business School (Abdul Kalam Technical University), Delhi and G-Noida, India
ya@iifbs.edu OR yagarwal@iif.edu

Abstract

Artificial intelligence (AI) is becoming more dynamic and efficient for routine tasks than humans by the day, the question is will it replace humans in every sector. It is not true. Technology and human complement and do not compete with each other. Initially, it might create disruption in an existing ecosystem, later it helps in creating opportunities. Business must now embrace a new culture, where innovation and continuous learning are core components of the organizational culture. It sets the stage for agility, adaptability and growth. There are of course risks. AI and machine learning (ML) tools and techniques can be misused, intentionally or inadvertently. Obvious risk is misuse of AI by those intent on threatening individual's physical, digital, financial, and emotional security. We have used worldwide real-life case scenarios to understand the importance of AI, its threats, and the role it plays in contributing toward the growth and prosperity of the society.

Keywords: Currency; Money; Wealth; Cryptocurrency; Bitcoins; Blockchain; Money supply; M5; CBDC; Currency markets; Artificial intelligence; Digital currency; Machine learning.

1. Introduction

Given the emergence of crypto-products in the informal sector with multiple players, it has become difficult for national governments to regulate and calibrate the supply of money and its effects through monetary stabilization measures adopted by them, as these crypto-products allow billions/trillions of money to be transacted globally without any checks and balances. More than the benefits, these products are emerging as a threat to national security, individual's wealth, and nations apart from the ills any speculative product brings with it to meet the needs of greed of a specific group of people and rogue identities. Hence, there is a need for governments to act fast and consider to induce this financial innovation (cryptocurrencies) as a currency of tomorrow into its basket of currencies, as done with various other monetary products in the last six decades.

The chapter proposes setting up M5 as money supply with cryptocurrency along the lines of inclusion of other currency products developed in the last 50 years in order to promote efficiency in the money markets and transactional efficiency and generate wealth along with positive contributions to GDP and people at large. The chapter also considers that money as a valuable resource and a wealth of the nation has the potential to generate/mobilize more wealth. The chapter proposes that given the emergence of digital modes of money transactions, there is an urgent need for the creation of legitimate cryptocurrencies by national governments to induce confidence and *laissez-faire* through transactional efficiency in the money market. Government intervention (or central banks) to generate the cryptocurrency is the need of the hour and critical for tomorrow's normal economic and business conditions in the economy when businesses and labor market source's are global and looking for currency-efficient sources. The chapter critically evaluates various theories on money and how/why M5 as a money supply indicator is needed for inducing cryptocurrency in the basket of currencies by central banks worldwide (Agarwal, 2017a, 2018a, 2018b, 2018c, 2018d). The proposed model of creating efficient money market through modeling of M5 will facilitate an automatic way for transactional efficiency, generating wealth for the nations, firms, and people at large, through easy access to currency and opportunities for jobs and growth (Agarwal *et al.*, 2018). It would also help save currency costs in a market-driven economic system with asymmetric information (Agarwal *et al.*, 2004, 2006). The "New Avatar" of money in the form of crypto would witness the change the way money (currency) has looked traditionally for centuries in the form of gold, silver, leather, wood, metal, paper, plastic, stone (Furness, 1910), and many others to a faceless virtual fully fractional form, but only when launched by nations (via their Central Banks). We are happy to note that various central banks like China's Peoples Bank of China (in 2019), India's Reserve Bank of India (in 2018), Venezuela's Government Petra$ (in 2018), and many others are considering to launch (or have launched) digital currency along the lines of proposals made by IIF professors since 2016 onward at various forums and those published in 2018 in Finance India.

2. Artificial Intelligence, Growth and Ecosystems

Jamsetji Nusserwanji Tata (1903) beautifully said "We generate wealth from the Nation. What comes from the people must, to the extent possible, therefore get back to the people". The world is transforming, becoming a better place on multiple dimensions — be it health, life expectancy, education, poverty, access to technology, or trade. Physical quality life index (PQLI) has increased many fold in India as well as around the world. Life expectancy has increased rapidly to 68 years in India and 72 years globally. The share of people living in abject poverty is less than 10% (estimated to be 2.7% by World Poverty Clock in October 2019). Around 90% of the boys and girls are enrolled in schools. Today more than two-thirds of the world population has a mobile phone, with nearly half the world having access to the Internet (Agarwal *et al.*, 2018). Globalization, privatization, and liberalization have made global trade multifold and an inevitable force in the framework of economic growth. At the same time, volatility, uncertainty, complexity, and automation have multiplied in the world over the past decades. Be it the dynamic geopolitics and the de-globalization, be it Brexit or the trade conflicts, or the accelerating technology disruptions from robotics to machine learning and now to artificial intelligence and blockchain frameworks. It is vital today that nations and socio-economic eco-systems build human capital engulfing technology, environment, and sustainable frameworks interlocked with clean finance ensuring prosperity and growth.

India is emerging to be the third largest economy (in absolute terms) by 2030 in the World, after China and the United States. India is the only country with a growing working population of over 65% (aged between 15 and 64 years) as against rapidly ageing economies in the world, enjoying demographic and digital dividend. Industrial revolution of the 18th and the 19th century transformed the landscape of Europe. India today has the opportunity to leverage the digital and data revolution in the 21st century to transform itself and the World as a whole. Enterprises are perplexed and challenged to re-design their strategies to retain their market positions. In order to enjoy economies of scale, economies of scope, and learning curve, companies and economic frameworks are adopting new-age exponential technologies like artificial intelligence (AI), robotics, and IOT. To stay ahead of the curve and competition, AI is projecting to bridge the path that has the power to transform businesses across industries and sectors. Intelligence and the understanding of what it offers to the society is a key outlay that is becoming important part of corporations, international agencies, social ecosystems, and governments in the decision-making process. AI and automation are the new norms for growth, efficiency, and productivity, to ensure all around social and inclusive growth.

Niti Aayog (2018) has reiterated that "…given India's strengths and characteristics, it has the potential to position itself among leaders on the global AI map…". When we look at AI, it is complicated as to what animal are we talking about. AI largely refers to the ability of machines to perform cognitive tasks like thinking, perceiving, learning, problem solving, and decision-making like a human mind. Machine learning showed the world the path to enhance productivity, given the ability to learn without being explicitly programmed using algorithms. Deep learning, on the contrary, emerged as a technique for implementing machine learning in conjunction with artificial neural networks (ANNs) built on algorithms. Neural networks (NNs) have been growing in research and machine learning for over half a century now with applications in finance, defense, and various other spheres of society. ANNs built on algorithms have induced the AI to the "neurons" framework of discrete layers and connections to other "neurons" within the NNs structures. Strong AI in fact has scientifically emerged as "actual" thinking (intelligence, thinking, consciousness, and subjective mind), given the machines decision-making and stipulation capabilities like a human mind, whereas when we seek weak AI products, we see that these are "simulated" thinking (no consciousness) frameworks in us by various agencies in today's time. We are slowly moving from weak AI to strong AI through a passage of narrow AI where AI built on algorithms is currently limited to a single task or set number of tasks for the decision-making process. Ecosystems are enhancing narrow AIs to general AI which can be used to complete a wide range of tasks in automated high-risk hazardous zones in a wide range of environments for the benefit of the society. There is a lot of concern by various governments and agencies independently working to resolve global stress and issues with regards to AI-based products and systems, which if hacked can create catastrophes. Also the question, “Is the human race ready for AI-based ecosystems?”, runs on specified algorithms not necessarily tuned to emotions, social structures, and judicious decision-making. Hence, we see the ongoing talks on “super intelligence”, which is considered to be the next step of general and strong AI frameworks. Though AI might give an impression of being clever, it would be unrealistic to think that current AI is similar or equivalent to human intelligence or even near the emotional–social understanding computational capabilities that a human mind displays (Russell and Norvisg, 2009; Forbes Bureau, 2018; Hornigold, 2018; Tracker, 2018; FO Bureau, 2019; Kumar, 2019; Rej, 2019).

Artificial intelligence has a history of seven decades of development. Many great scientists and researchers have contributed in its journey toward making machines super-intelligent. In 1950, Alan Mathisen Turning (a mathematician and computer scientist) published a paper on “computing machinery and intelligence”. In his work, Alan proposed a test of a machine displaying human intelligence. However this test had its limitations. In 1955, John McCarthy with his colleagues and researchers developed the idea of thinking machines and launched a project which they named “artificial intelligence”. Several topics discussed by them at that time like “neuron nets”, “size of calculations”, abstraction”, “programmed language”, and “randomness and creativity” are still relevant for the study of artificial intelligence. In February 1956, Arthur Lee Samuel, designed a digital computer to engage in the process of learning as a human being would do (designed a game of checkers). After a brief gap due to technological limitations and shortage of funds, development in AI started around 2000. Deep learning based on AI applications was re-examined by researchers. The availability of advanced computing power along with broadband and connectivity resulted in faster development of AI and its commercial success (Russell and Norvisg, 2009; Kumar, 2019).

The first industrial revolution, in 18th century, was powered by steam. It changed the lifestyle of the people. New modes of transportation, logistics, and trading of goods and services brought unprecedent changes in social and economic order. The second revolution in the 19th century was driven by electricity. It changed the structure of businesses and lives of people, and within a span of hundred years, the population of the world grew from 1 to 3 billion. These extra labor force got absorbed in the upcoming industries which developed as a result of electricity. The third revolution of technological change came in 1900 with invention of the computer. Computers were replaced by desktops, which in turn were replaced by laptops, and we await a new innovation using IOT. Internet revolution led by DARPANET of the US, revolutionized the entire communication system for the whole world. Mobile networks in 1990 with handset again changed the communication process. Next came smartphones with the screens on the mobile handset that revolutionized business and personal communication beginning 2007–2008. In the wake of the fourth industrial revolution (Industry 4.0), artificial intelligence and automation are the new norm for the world. AI is expected to have a much stronger and bigger impact than compared to steam engine, electricity, or computing on the lives of people. Since 2010, it is no longer enough to just implement AI (i.e., not to look at AI as an add-on feature to machines), it is about ensuring that AI is effectively integrated as a pre-requisite for business growth, efficiency, and productivity and the betterment of society at large. The focus is on enhancing the outcomes for over 6.5 billion people and the flora and fauna co-existing in a challenging, rapidly, environmentally degrading mother earth. Forester reports that 40 insight-driven companies are expected to grab US$1.8 trillion by 2021 (most of these companies listed are aged less than 8 years). The American big tech has come out with a large number of products and service offerings in AI inter-locked products and services. For example, (a) Amazon is using AI tools for warehousing operations and logistics; (b) IBM's Deep super computer defeated Kasparov in 1997; (c) Deepmind has deep talent resources in AI; and many others. We see today that China is emerging as a big player in AI with Alibaba and Tencent having reinvented the industrial landscape and having created monopolies in the global workspace.

The Russian President Mr. Vladimir Putin has rightly stated that "whoever becomes the leader in this sphere of the new technologies like artificial intelligence will become the ruler of the world" (Vincent, 2017). US and China are running neck to neck in a competitive race to gain an upper hand. In 2016, the US Government came out with policy paper, "preparing for the Future of Artificial Intelligence" expending the impact of artificial intelligence across multiple industries. In July 2017, China's policy document on "China's Next Generation Artificial Intelligence

Development plan", aimed at becoming the global innovation center by 2030 followed by the World Economic Forum meeting in China in October 2019. In April 2018, UK's paper titled, "AI in the UK: Ready, willing and able?", focused on certain key areas to develop AI industries. Germany, France, Japan, and India have also drawn their own action plans for AI-based applications and business ecosystems. AI and its complimentary technologies bring with them new hopes, new opportunities, and new challenges.

As Don and Alex Tapscott say in their book on Blockchain Revolution (2016) "The blockchain is an incorruptible digital ledger of economic transactions that can be programmed to record not just financial transactions but virtually everything of value". In the simplest of terms, a time-stamped series of immutable records of data are managed by a cluster of computers not owned by any single entity. Each of these blocks of data (i.e., block) is secured and bound to each other using cryptographic principles (i.e., a chain). The key disruptive factor is the fact that the blockchain network has no central authority; hence, theoretically speaking it is beyond the governance and control of any authority. Blockchain scientists and technocrats project that it is a shared and immutable ledger, the information in it is open for anyone and everyone to see (Agarwal, 2018c; Agarwal *et al.*, 2018). However, we have seen recent incidences of blockchain failures (Laskowski, 2017), hacks (Risberg, 2018), and thefts (Khan, 2018) disallowing governments and international agencies to keep the world a safe place. Emin Gun Sirer, Co-director for the Initiative for Cryptocurrencies and Smart Contracts at Cornell University, said at the recent Business of Blockchain event in Cambridge, MA, "all three of these things (validity, consensus and immutability) have failed in practice before" (Laskowski, 2017).

Crypto products like (bitcoins and others) use blockchain framework to induce value within them on the basis that there are NO carrier transaction costs passing information from A to B in a fully automated and confidential manner. However, on the contrary, numerous of cases of lapses have surfaced in the last 5 years. In the financial world, the applications are more obvious and the revolutionary changes are more imminent. The Three Pillars of Blockchain Technology, which presumably seem to be helping it gain widespread acclaim for usage in financial and other ecosystems, are the belief of it being decentralized, transparent, and immutable. We feel the technology has substance but still has a long way to go before it can be used in various financial and non-financial ecosystems to benefit the society at large (Laskowski, 2017; Agarwal *et al.*, 2018; Maloney, 2018).

3. Artificial Intelligence and the Society

AI today covers a wide landscape of different technologies and these are machine learning, neural networks, pattern recognition, computer vision, natural language processing, autonomous system, robotics, chatbots, and so on. The deep learning and predictive analysis come under machine learning. AI also covers different areas and classification recognition and vision analysis. AI enables data crunching, business intelligence, and application of sophisticated algorithms with vastly superior computing power. We can now have vast quantities of data be processed within seconds. Outcomes are much more efficient, quicker, and cheaper. Thus, AI involves a multidisciplinary approach with knowledge from computer science, neuroscience, mathematics, anthropology, history, psychology, philosophy, economics, linguistic, and many other disciplines.

The Indian Institute of Finance (IIF) has hosted large number of discussion, workshops, seminars, and roundtables with scientific groups, corporates, government officials, and data scientists in the sphere of Artificial intelligence, blockchains, and their impact on the society at large. In the recent seminar held on February 19, 2019 there were views from diplomats and members of different groups from around the world. A brief summary of the findings of the seminar on "Artificial Intelligence and the Society" are outlined below.

All the speakers from USA, Finland, India felt that artificial intelligence technologies could increase global GDP by US$15.7 trillion, a full 14%, by 2030. That includes advances of US$7 trillion in China, US$3.7 trillion in North America, US$1.8 trillion in Northern Europe, US$1.2 trillion for Africa and Oceania, US$0.9 trillion in the rest of Asia outside of China, US$0.7 trillion in Southern Europe, and US$0.5 trillion in Latin America. China is making rapid strides because it has set a national goal of investing US$150 billion in artificial intelligence and becoming the global leader in this area by 2030, said Dr. Caj L. Soderlund in a seminar on "Artificial Intelligence and the Society", organized by Indian Institute of Finance, Greater Noida, on February 18, 2019 at the institute's campus. Dr. Caj L. Soderlund (former Senior Adviser to the Ministry of Foreign Affairs on Nordic Affairs of Finland), Dr. Prabhat Kumar (IRS, an advocate, Adjunct Professor at IIT Delhi and former

Commissioner of Central Excise and Customs who has authored a book titled "Artificial Intelligence (AI): Reshaping Life and Business"), Prof. Asoke K. Laha (President and CEO, Interra Information Technologies, Inc., San Jose, CA, USA), and Prof. Manju Agarwal (Professor of Economics and Dean (Academics, MDP & Training)) presented their perspectives.

Dr. Caj L. Soderlund said artificial intelligence is a technology that is transforming every walk of life. It is a wide-ranging tool that enables people to rethink how we integrate information, analyze data, and use the resulting insights to improve decision-making. It is already changing the world and raising important questions for society, the economy, and governance. Artificial intelligence applications are used in finance, national security, health care, criminal justice, transportation, and smart cities and address issues such as data access problems, algorithmic bias, artificial intelligence ethics and transparency, and legal liability for artificial intelligence decisions. Robotics and artificial intelligence are increasingly entering our daily lives: from domestic assistants that help us to program the appliances or adjust the heating to drones that help farmers in the control of pests, said Dr. Soderlund.

Dr. Prabhat Kumar (IRS) said, artificial intelligence is the next-generation technology ready to disrupt different sectors of the economy. It provides the next level of opportunity for the countries to raise their productivity and economic growth and compete in the international marketplace. Governments too are looking at the new technology as a panacea for solving problems of the people. Businesses want to solve many unsolved problems of life, such as decoding genetics and brain power. According to Dr. Kumar, startups in finance, e-commerce, healthcare, HR management, fashion, law, and even agriculture, which are disrupting the conventional models of businesses, have also successfully used artificial intelligence, machine learning, etc., for instant credit score, loan approval, detecting cyber frauds, and smart trading in stocks. Artificial intelligence, contrary to the common belief, offers new job opportunities and is not a destroyer of jobs. However, he cautioned that artificial intelligence can be misused by the authoritarian governments for keeping a watch on their citizens' activities or if autonomy is deployed in military hardware.

Prof. Asoke K. Laha, while addressing the audience, said artificial intelligence is the best solution to perform routine tasks/procedures while humans would focus on more challenging and creative work. According to him, artificial intelligence can be considered as the next industrial revolution which will give human workforce more important works to do which are not of regular and repetitive nature. Prof. Manju Agarwal outlined the importance of AI in rebuilding human capital, but pointed out various real case studies where the technology is still in the making, especially highlighting its critical role for benefiting the society at large. She also pointed out how the recent models developed by IIF professors in the areas of (a) national labor exchange (NLx) for full employment and efficient labor markets (Agarwal *et al.*, 2017a); (b) real estate exchange (Agarwal *et al.*, 2017a); (c) derivative instruments for agriculture going beyond crop insurance (Agarwal and Agarwal, 2000, 2001a, 2001b, 2002, 2004) and on cricket (Agarwal *et al.*, 2017); (d) mobile mandi and mandi on wheels for efficient agriculture markets and enhancing farmers income (2018e); (e) money laundering (Agarwal and Agarwal, 2004b, 2006, 2008, 2017, 2018); (f) AADHAR Card (Pandya, 2019); (g) the theory of money, wealth, and efficient currency market: modeling M5 as money supply with cryptocurrency (Agarwal *et al.*, 2018) can use the AI-based frameworks to the induce efficiency, productivity, and financial developments in national economies to meet the key challenges of jobs, unemployment, labor markets, and liquidity in the system.

3.1. *Application of AI in industry and the social sectors*

Knowledge from disciplines other than technology is equally important to have societal gain. The big technology companies (Big tech) particularly in social media, search, and communications had been early adopters of AI in providing production and services to their customers. Companies in e-commerce, retailing, warehousing, logistics, Fin-tech services, and automotive sectors are also high-end adopters of AI to make a big push in their productivity, growth, and efficiency. Big tech companies have come out with AI solutions in areas like healthcare, banking, and agriculture. and other non-conventional areas (BI Bureau, 2019).

In 2016, Microsoft realized that AI is the key to their future and setup Microsoft AI and Research Group (NExT), for developing new capabilities for the customers across agents, apps, services, and infrastructure. Microsoft wishes to develop the world's most powerful AI supercomputer and connect it to Azure for making everything available to everyone (ET Bureau, 2019a, 2019b). Focusing on social goals so that the benefit of AI technology percolates to the masses, Nvidia invented GPUs of higher capacity and higher speed and which can store more data in smaller sizes.

GPUs' performance is growing by 15% a year and is set to grow 1000 times by 2025 (Henschen, 2018). These GPUs are powering the world's fastest supercomputers and data centers in the US, Europe, and Japan. Nvidia is collaborating with medical device makers to enhance their medical imaging capabilities (project Clara). Nvidia and ARM have entered into a partnership to bring deep learning to mobile, consumer electronics, and Internet of Thing (IOT) devices. Nvidia in collaboration with Nuance is working on AI-powered health care solutions. Nvidia is revolutionizing the AI industry through innovation in hardware. Continuous innovation in Nvidia, keeps raising the level of product and services. In October 2016, eBay (pioneer in e-commerce) introduced Chatbot and shopbot, which can be accessed through the Facebook messenger platform. eBay acquired sales predict and Expert maker which are using AI platforms. AI combines intelligence about individuals, behaviors, trends, and context. eBay is using AI effectively and efficiently (to bring down cost and uplift trust and pricing) in its own domain.

China had been a breeding ground for AI technology and its societal applications. Chinese big tech, namely Alibaba, Baidu, JD.com, and Tencent (ABJT), have made huge investments in research and have developed global partners, to generate high traffic and higher revenues (CB Insight, 2019). Baidu, Alibaba, and Tencent (BAT), have become market leaders in China and have huge global ambitions. BAT have invested huge amounts in startups in not just China but also in the US, Israel, Canada, and in some Asian countries as well. Alibaba is focusing on smart cities, whereas Tencent is focusing on computer vision for health care and medical imaging and diagnostics. Baidu is specializing in autonomous vehicles and FlyTek is specializing in voice intelligence. Alibaba's two shopping malls, Tmall and Taobao, are currently serving more than one billion customers and are planning to serve more than 2 billion customers globally within two decades through AI and AI in logistics. Alibaba is using AI for making recommendation-targeted advertisement and forecasting demand and has developed facial recognition technology for authentication. Alibaba is running AI chatbot, Dian Xiaomi, which understands customer's emotions and handles more than 3 million interactions per day (CB Insight, 2018). Robots and drones are used to pack goods and to deliver packets at distant places (economizing on cost and effectively serving customers with punctuality, thus winning their trust).

Kiosks had been set up at Shanghai sub-way station. Here tickets are delivered to the travelers on speech and facial recognition technology running through AI cloud. City traffic is managed through "City Brain Project" (cloud based system). Data about everyone and every vehicle is collected through video, image, and speech recognition. Through machine learning, an insight for city administrations is provided to improve operational efficiencies and monitor security risks. Experiments had been successful, where traffic congestion could be reduced by 15–20%. Alibaba had set up seven research labs (US$15 billion for R&D), focusing on AI quantum computing machine learning, network security, natural language processing, cloud-based system, etc. The main objective is to reach AI to the masses. Anyone with a computer and broadband connection can have a business in AI on his own. Alibaba had set up DAMO (discover, adventure, momentum and outlook) Academy, a research institute on fundamental technologies. Alibaba persuaded G20 to start a "electronic world trade platform" for facilitating small businesses for cross-border trading. Jack Ma's (founder Alibaba) sole objective is working toward enriching the lives of the common man through the application of AI technology (CB Insight, 2018, 2019).

Baidu (search engine using AI) was founded in 1999 by Robin Li and Eric Xu, who were researching on autonomous driving technology (with Apollo Program). The Apollo Platform consists of core software, cloud service, GPS, cameras, lidar, and radar, etc. Baidu uses deep learning and computer vision for the early detection of tumors or cancerous cells and also for treating of cancer (using AI startups "Atomwise and Engine Bioscience". Baidu collaborated with Huawei and Qualcomm for developing AI-powered smart phones. Baidu developed intelligent cloud services for the corporate, focusing on application in finance, media, IOT, and marketing. Founders of Baidu believed that AI can be part of everything and every system of any society or of any economy. World can have a sustainable growth with the application of AI (increase in PQLI of people). Similarly, for the improvement of society, JD.com has set-up a Global Supply Chain Innovation Centre (GSCI) as a research center. This center will provide a platform for universities, corporates, and industrial experts to collaborate and develop the future technology related to supply chain (data, machine learning, computer vision, and other AI technologies) to fulfill consumer's needs and aspirations in a better and effective way. The ultimate objective is to cut down social cost and increase social profit. Beside, by using robots and drones, rural market, far-flung areas, border areas, and emergency situations of any kind can be served in a much better and desirable way.

Tencent, on the contrary, has built the world's largest AI research team for the future, to fulfill its sole objective "Make AI Everywhere" (operations in video streaming, mapping, mobile payments, digital assistants, entertainment, sports, movies cloud storage, artificial intelligence in banking, and issuing of electronic ID cards instead of physical cards) (CB Insight, 2019). Its facial recognition technology can recognize key parameters such as sex, age, emotions, clothes, and brands of vehicle and detect pornography and violent images. Tencent has developed an AI platform, "Miying healthcare", which helps in reading CT scans. Tencent is an inventor and heavy user of AI in several domains. Today three AFIM (US Tech Giants) and ABJT (Chinas Tech Giant) are globally competing and focused on global growth and global strategies, while aggressively acquiring the best talent from the world as a whole. They have created a better and favorable business climate for development and promotion of AI. AI startups are also being benefited out of their efforts.

In India, NITI Aayog (2018) has decided to focus on the following five sectors that are envisioned to benefit the most from AI in solving societal needs:

(i) *Healthcare*: Increased access and affordability of quality healthcare through the application of AI (AI-driven diagnostics, personalized treatment, early identification of potential pandemic imaging diagnostics, CT scanners, voice mails etc). Facilities can be made available in rural areas, tribal areas, and border areas that suffer from poor connectivity and limited supply of professionals.

(ii) *Agriculture*: AI has the potential to enhance farmers income through increased productivity and reduction in wastages and leakages. Image recognition and deep learning models have enabled distributed soil health monitoring without the need for lab test infrastructure. AI solutions integrated with the data signals from satellites of the images of the farm have made it possible for farmer's to take immediate action to restore soil health. AI can be used to predict real-time action advisories for sowing, pest control, input control etc. and provide stability to agricultural income and output. AI tools provide round-the-clock monitoring to horticultural practices at all levels of plant growth. Predictive analytic using AI tools can bring more accurate supply and demand information to farmers, thus reducing information asymmetry between farmers and intermediaries (Agarwal, 2018e). Currently, commodity prices are globally interlinked, big data analysis becomes imperative. Data from e-NAM, agricultural census, AGMARKET, and over 110 million soil health samples provide the volumes required for any predictive modeling. AI can aid in precision farming. AI models for predictive insights to improve crop productivity and soil yield, control agricultural inputs, and provide an early warning on pests and disease outbreak will use data from remote sensing (ISRO), information soil health cards, IMD's weather prediction and soil moisture/temperature, crop phonology, etc. to give accurate suggestions to farmers. Integrated computer vision and ML enable farmers to reduce the use of herbicides by spraying only where weeds are present, thereby optimizing the use of inputs — a key objective of precision farming.

(iii) *Education Skilling*: AI can potentially solve quality and access issues observed in the Indian education sector, thus augmenting and enhancing the learning experience through personalized learning and vocational training (Agarwal and Agarwal, 2017, 2018).

(iv) *Smart Cities*: Enhancing the quality of life. Retail sector is an early adopter of AI solutions providing customized advice and suggestions, preference-based browsing, and image-based product search. Anticipation and prediction of future demand, improved inventory management, efficient delivery management, modeling, forecasting, and increased efficiency in power balancing and usage, improvement in reliability and affordability of photovoltaic energy are key aspects of AI. AI may be deployed for predictive maintenance of grid infrastructure. Manufacturing is the biggest beneficiary in engineering (AI for R&D), followed by supply chain management (demand forecasting), production (reduction in cost, increase in efficiency), maintenance (increased asset utilization), quality assurance, and in plant logistic and warehousing.

(v) *Smart Mobility*: Transport and logistics. Smarter and safer modes of transportation. This domain includes autonomous fleets of ride sharing, predictive engine monitoring and maintenance, autonomous trucking, and delivery. Improved traffic management resulted in better traffic and fewer congestion problems.

The "AI for Earth" program aimed at empowering people and organizations to solve environmental challenges through the power of AI. India has the third largest number (at the end of 2018, Microsoft announced that it has selected seven Indian grantees for its US$50 million) of AI for Earth grantees, after the US and Canada. The seven recipients will receive access to Microsoft Azure cloud and AI computing resources, in–depth education, and technology learning on these tools and additional support as their projects mature. Focus is on initiatives like wildlife conservation, water sustainability, agriculture for small and tiny landholder farmers, among others, which are of significant importance to a large population in India. The areas of focus (launched in July 2017) of the 5-year program are climate change, agriculture, biodiversity, and water. In about a year, "AI for Earth" has grown from 20 grantees to 147 in more than 40 countries, with US$1.1million of Azure cloud credits (NITI Aayog, 2018).

IIT together with the Technical University of Munich is designing a low-cost tool for monitoring plant health in resource-limited regions. Institute for Semi-Arid Tropics (ICRISAT), Hyderabad is using AI, cognitive service, and cloud computing to enhance pest forecasting and prediction models and farm advisory services to enable sustainable agriculture production in developing parts of the world (Verma, 2019). Ashoka Trust for Research in Ecology and Environment (ATREE), Bengaluru, in biodiversity, is developing an AI-enabled tool to document and quantitatively assess the abundant habitat and rich biological resources in North-East. Indraprastha Institute of Information Technology, Delhi, is working on an intelligent tool for identifying and locating monkeys in human habitats, helping researchers to effectively control their population. Symbiosis Institute of Technology, Pune, in the field of climate change, is using both smart meter and socioeconomic data to develop an AI-enabled prototype for smart meter data analytics thus helping improve energy management for utilities and consumers. Symbiosis is also developing smart Environment Information and Management System (SEIMANS) to monitor and predict water, air, and soil conditions for a variety of smart city applications. Indian Institute of Science, Bengaluru, in the field of water, is developing a scalable solution using data analytics and machine learning under its Eqwater project to ensure equitable water distribution in India's large cities.

Research students of Subhas Institute of Technology, Delhi, have developed an AI system to monitor water logging that may help metro cities avoid tedious road congestion caused during the monsoon season. The issue of waterlogging is persistent in developing economies, including India. The areas prone to waterlogging were located with the help of past travel time data sourced from smartphone-based use of cab service and elevation data of the area. The intensity of water logging was calculated based on rainfall data and the day of week. These data were fed into an artificial intelligence system that consists of a neural network that can derive patterns in the information fed to it. The system can also be used for pinpointing accident-prone areas and times in a city for dynamically deciding strategic points for positioning ambulances, for calculating the effect of festivals and holidays on traffic, and can also be employed in urban road planning.

IBM and IITM-Kerala developed a real-time IOT-based water quality measurement system — "swatchpani". The system, powered by IBMs Watson Internet of Things (IOT) technologies, will continuously monitor water quality and measure temperature, pH, and the presence of various metal/non-metal substances in water to ensure standard levels are not exceeded as prescribed by agencies. The system is composed of Libelium, signal-conditioning boards and sensors, and Raspberry Pi for connecting these to IBM blue mix cloud service and Watson IOT platform for device and sensor data management, analysis, and visualization. Swatchpani offers a convenient, mobile, quick, and cost-effective solution for pre-screening of water samples.

Recent advances in AI have given computers the ability to program themselves. AI is like a book that writes itself. AI system can observe experts, extract patterns of expert behavior, and coach novices to perform at expert skill level nearly effortlessly. In medicine, AI empowers nurse practitioners to diagnose cancer with the same accuracy as our most experienced specialists. Cresta, a Palo Alto-based startup, has developed AI that turns novice sales agents into superstar performers. Waymo, Alphabets self-driving car division, leverages AI to help blind people to operate motor vehicles. AI system is now working alongside professionals (finance, accounting, journalism, law, and manufacturing) to empower them to perform at their best. Technology cannot replace people, instead technology augments people. Technology empowers human beings. AI helps us to become experts on our first day at work (minimizing time on learning through trial and error). Everyone in this world are likely to make fewer mistakes in one's life (Tracker, 2018).

AI can make a powerful contribution to resolve many types of societal challenges. In 2017, object detection software and satellite imagery aided rescuers in Houston as they navigated the aftermath of Hurricane Harvey. In Africa, algorithms have helped reduce poaching in wildlife parks. In Denmark, voice recognition programs are used in emergency calls to detect whether callers are experiencing a cardiac arrest. Researchers in

MIT Media Lab near Boston, have used "reinforcement learning" in stimulated clinical trials involving patients with glioblastoma, the most aggressive form of brain cancer, to reduce chemotherapy doses. AI can detect early signs of diabetes from heart rate sensor data, help children with autism manage their emotions, and guide the visually impaired. If innovations are widely available and used, the health and social benefits are immense. In fact, AI can accelerate the sustainable development goals of a number of economies. There are some developmental obstacles that have to be overcome and data accessibility is among the most significant hurdle. Sensitive or commercially viable data that have societal applications are privately aimed and not accessible to non-governmental organizations. Sometimes, bureaucratic inertia keeps useful data locked up. Even if in cases where data are available and the technology is mature, the dearth of data scientists can make it difficult to apply AI solutions locally.

There are of course risks. AI tools and techniques can be misused intentionally or inadvertently. For example biases can be embedded in artificial intelligence algorithms or datasets, and this can amplify the existing inequalities when the applications are used. Another risk is misuse of AI by those intent on threatening individual physical, digital, financial, and emotional security. Stakeholder sectors must work together to solve these issues. Already, satellite companies have signed in an international agreement that commits them to providing open access during emergencies. AI is an invaluable part of human development tool kit. If its potential is to be realized fully, proponents must focus on the obstacles that are preventing its uptake.

TaxiBots are semi-autonomous vehicles developed by Israeli Aerospace Industries (IAI) that helps an aircraft cover the distance from parking bays to the runway startup point without switching on the engines. Delhi International Airport Ltd is the world's first recipient of this technology (HT Bureau, 2019). The facility, apart from saving fuel, will help reduce carbon dioxide emissions, reduce the aircrafts' wear and tear, cut down the risk of jet blast incidents, and save money. The implementation of TaxiBot will act as a boon for the airlines as the application has helped saving 213 L of fuel every day (saving US$35 million annually for domestic carriers). TaxiBots improve airport safety by reducing the damage caused due to foreign object debris (FOD). Currently, two TaxiBots are operational at the Delhi Airport, and in 4 years, the number will go up to 15. Initially, the TaxiBots were used only for departing flight. Taxibots are operationally efficient and environment friendly.

Fintech, telecom, and automotive sector are now the high-end adopters of the new technology of AI, ML, deep learning, neural networks, and blockchain. AI can process big financial data, help in better management of loans and bad debts, and provide personalized services to the customers in managing their wealth. AI also provides tools for regulators to improve their supervisory control over individual players. India has prepared a report on the need for AI-based solutions for the banking and financial services and insurance sector (BFSI). AI-based solutions have been developed by numerous startups in different areas like asset management, loans, debt collection, predictive analysis, trading risk management, fraud detection, investment, sentiment score, regulatory, compliances credit scoring, insurance.

A Fintech AI startup, Active. AI (conversational banking), Singapore, delivers context-driven conversational banking services and brings automation and insightful customer engagement to the BFSI. It handles customer's queries and helps customers have natural dialogue over mobile, messaging, voice chat, or IOT devices. It specializes in several languages to interact with the customers. It has offices in Singapore, India, USA, and Australia. Feedzai (payments), USA, has built a platform for fraud management and can run any data or any payment module for security of payments in commercial transactions whether through mobile or online payment or in person. It provides an end-to-end intelligent solution using machine learning to detect unusual patterns of transactions in real time to assess the risk factor to prevent fraud. It understands behavioral patterns and takes a 360-degree view of the customer from every data source and diagnoses new patterns of frauds by gaining insights with intuitive reports. It can be used for anti-money laundering operations by BFSI. Intelligent Voice (UK), provides speech transcription tools to the large banks to monitor trader's phone call in real time (on post call) for signs of any wrong doing like insider trading. It captures key words and phrases from live telephone calls or e-mail or IM and converts them into text at super-fast speed to analyze. It has cloud based solution also.

Kabbage (USA), rating people to lend money, a small business on-line lender combine machine learning algorithms, data from public profiles on the Internet and other factor to rate people and then loan money for their small business. It can recognize the need for a loan and makes an approval at super-fast speed, generally in 10 minutes, thus promoting small borrowers. Kinetic (Risk Exposure) USA, uses GPU database, real time location visualization and AI to provide an insight for the extreme data economy.

It takes data from unpredictable sources and delivers super-fast insights. It can explore and analyze fast moving data within millisecond and provide solutions to finance, telecom, retail healthcare and logistics, to take appropriate decisions in time. Kreditech (Loan Disbursal), Germany, analyzes big data with more than 20,000 data points collected from various sources like on line behaviour, social networking sites and GPS, etc. to rate the credit score of the individual customer in just one minute. Kreditech has an objective to provide access to those who find it difficult to get a loan, provide a tailor made product for the customer, who has the financial freedom to choose an option that suits best. Lemonade (Insurance) USA, uses ML both in selling insurance policies and in managing claims. It operates on an app with an AI ChatBot, Maya, to work out the best plan for the customer and process the claim instantly. It works on "zero deductibles, zero rate hikes and zero worries".

Monzo (Banking) UK, wishes to build a bank with everyone and for everyone (Venugopalan, 2019). It works on an app that has a card-used for spending, transfers and other uses. By using ML, it has developed a model to deal with data theft and stop fraudsters in completing a transaction (fraud rate reduced from 0.85% in June 2016 to 0.1% in January 2017). Ping-An (sentiment analysis), China, with a market capital of US$164.34 billion, is a great adopter of technology moving from mobile apps to AI and block chain in finance, insurance, and asset management. Ping-An technology records the tiniest movement of eye muscles and the area around a person's lips within milliseconds. Online applications for loan are assessed through a Q&A session on income and repayment plan through video by monitoring 50 facial expressions to gauge the level of honesty and for scrutiny purposes. Shift Technology (Insurance), France, is reinventing the insurance claims industry. It offers Force, an AI product that automates the processing of insurance claims and detects abnormal behavior indicative of fraud. It provides advanced detection methods through AI. Sift Science Digital Trust (Fraud Detection), USA, provides AI and machine learning-based solutions for fraud prevention and risk management for online businesses through insights from a global network of data. Client's sites are monitored in real time to detect any abnormal behavioral patterns. It alerts the customers or merchants before any fraudulent orders are booked. As per 2017 Global Fraud Index, US$57.9 billion were lost in such frauds across eight industries. Upstart (lending), USA, is an AI-based lending platform that does pricing for credit and automates the borrowing process. Its underwriting engine assesses the risk of the borrower through ML. It offers its service through the "Saas" model to bank and credit unions. Zest Finance (credit analysis and Loans), USA, uses Zest automated machine Learning (ZAML) platform for outdated credit scoring and runs an understanding tool for taking credit decisions. Zest Finance wishes to reinvent the underwriting industry. ZAML provides a solution that cuts the losses for the insurers. Cape Analytics (Insurance), USA, is engaged in providing insurance by using ML, computer vision, and data science without inspecting individual houses for insurance purpose. China Construction Bank (Banking Services), China, is a futuristic model of bank running with robots. It is the first unmanned bank, which is fully automated. Using AI in an innovative manner, from the moment a customer enters the bank, it can access the banking services in a virtual reality room through facial recognition technology to recognize the customer (Venugopalan, 2019). It has talking robots and touchscreen facility for conducting all banking functions. Only one manager is physically present to take care of any requirement of the customer if the need arises. Eye Capital (Security Trading), Argentina, specializes in trading of securities. Risk in trading can be reduced by using risk parameters with trained AI algorithm models, which has the potential to generate a portfolio with big returns and minimal risk. Kasisto (conversational AI platform), USA, enables companies to acquire, engage, support, and transact with their customers via human-like, intelligent conversations, anytime and anywhere. Its conversational AI platform, KAI, powers omni-channel Bots and provides virtual assistance with deep-domain expertise mobile apps, web, messaging platforms, wearables, and IOT devices. KAI is an agile platform with self-service tools to customize and continually improve consumer experiences and seamlessly add new features. Kensho Technologies (Analytics), USA, is a developer of analytics software, ML, AI solution, data visualization systems for banks, and investment institutions. Its goal is to deploy scalable ML and analytics systems across public and commercial institutions in the world to solve some of the hardest analytical problems. Kensho appears in the list of AI 100.

True Accord (Loan Recovery), USA, is using ML to streamline debt collection, making it more manageable for the people in debt and increasing the recovery rates for the financial institution. It uses a unique digital approach to redefine the debt collection industry receiving higher customer engagement and satisfaction. Vymo (improving agent's performance for Debt collection) India, is engaged in developing an AI-based solution for loan recovery. It suggests the next best action, optimized for best outcomes. Vymo has improved the debt recovery rate by using an agent's time more productively. Thus, there are huge advantages of AI in Fintech application for entrepreneurs and banks. AI tools assist in all directions — loan approval, recovery, fraud detection and prevention, trading of securities, etc. (as stated above). Of course, there are numerous government agencies (regulators) and commissions that have a control (direct/indirect) over the Fintech industry. In May 2018, GDPR came into effect, requirements are growing tougher. The Fintech industry is set to change radically in the near future.

AI has also improved manifold times the healthcare sector (Olson, 2018). AI, ML, and computer vision are globally being used in early detection of cancer. Early detection of cancer through AI had saved precious lives in the world. AI skin cancer detection system beat the dermatologists in accuracy in detecting skin cancer. In an accidental case, a patient may need brain surgery if there is blood clot. AI/ML may be used to analyze the scan images of patient's brain at the time of admission in the hospital. By identifying urgent cases and alerting on-call specialists, urgent cases could be taken up immediately for surgery to save precious lives. Ophthalmologists use AI to read images. USFDA has approved the use of machine learning algorithms for the purpose of automated diabetic retinopathy grading. A study conducted at the Icahn School of Medicine at Mount Sinai reported that AI can diagnose a stroke, hemorrhage, and hydrocephalus through a brain CT scan in just 1.2 seconds. Computer algorithm turned out to be over 150 times faster than for a physician to read the image. Deep neural network on smart watches are used to detect arterial fibrillation in patients (Apple watches, mobile application Cardiogram). AI can help researchers find patterns and trends faster through analyzing large datasets from health records, clinical trials, genetic profiling, and various studies to minimize the cost and time, thus optimizing outcomes. There are a number of AI startups (AI Cure, Babylon UK, Bay Labs USA, Benevolent-AI, Insilco Medicine, Olive USA, Paige-AI USA, Prognos USA, Qventus USA, Univfy USA, VoxelCloud China, etc.) each with their unique solutions to improve the healthcare industry (Peng, 2018).

Machine learning, deep learning, computer vision, natural language processing, and data analytics are used for human resource management. A conventional way of recruitment was through Applicant Tracking System (ATS), online assessment, and professional networking sites. This process used to take months. AI-tech HR solutions are creating new platforms to automate screening large number of applications through multiple data points, interacting with candidates through SMS, e-mail, Facebook Messenger, Video answers, etc. AI can also predict jobs that may lose their demand in future and alert those engaged in such jobs with the objective of re-skilling for another role. Algorithms are analyzing peoples' expressions and tone of voice to check for traits such as "confidence" and happiness during video interviews. Axis Bank used algorithm–based video interviews — along with aptitude tests — to hire around 2000 customer service officers from a pool of more than 40,000 applicants in 2019 (Venugopalan, 2019; Deloitte, 2019). In 2017, Axis Bank applied face-indexing software, sourced from Microsoft. The software picked up emotional states such as nervousness and happiness based on eye movements, expression, and tone of voice and marked the candidates. The software sourced from Microsoft and IBM can analyze states such as "anger" and happiness from various expressions, "confidence" from voice, tone and trails like ability to work in team and "decisiveness" from text analysis. There is a sharp rise in the number of IT professionals stepping in to train newbie's in new-age tech. Professionals, who work on emerging technologies at top IT companies, have helped fill a gap in the availability of faculty for training services' providers. For professionals who have 5–10 years of experience, it is more about extra money, for people senior than them, it is more about sharing knowledge, making a difference (Deloitte, 2019). According to Deloitte (2019) would be the "inflection point" for conversational artificial intelligence in India as more and more organizations are adopting matured versions of voice assistant AI. Machine learning and big data analytics are transforming the landscape in the cognitive era.

AI is also being applied in the Fashion industry. Fashion industry is leveraging technology for automation and is using AI to design clothes to the taste of the customers, refurbish the entire supply chain, reduce the time to market, and increase savings by cutting cost and wastages and boosting the revenues, and thus increasing the profits (TR Foundation, 2019). AI learns an individual's style and creates customized computer-generated images of new items that fit that style. Myntra (online fashion retailer), India, has developed an AI platform, "Vorta", which not only collects data from its own platform but also from numerous other sources like Facebook, Instagram, and Pinterest, and capture through the AI engine the emerging trends in fashion. Flipkart is using AI extensively for customer review analysis (CRA), conversational search, visual similarity, better last-mile delivery, fraud detection, and personalization and for better management of warehouses. AI creates fashion models who are spookily life-like. Japanese tech company Data Grid made AI using a Generative Adversarial Network (GAN). GAN works by essentially piloting two algorithms against each other, with one trying to generate fake images and another trying to spot that they are fake. It has developed "automatic whole-body model generation AI", which is an AI that automatically generates full-body images of non-existing people with a high resolution (1024 × 1024), which was difficult before. GANs are popular in "deep fake" technology. Although looking very closely at the model's faces might tip you off that they are not real.

The hospitality industry has been on the high end of the technological disruption. Airlines are using AI and chatbots to manage social media inquiries, and hotels offer better food menus after analyzing customer reviews. Facial recognition technology by using blockchain technology can be helpful for clearing passengers at different channels at airports and at hotels. Use of Robotics for facilitating passengers (disable and luggage). Using accumulated data and ML, Google Flights is making comparison to offer cheapest flights. Insteract Technologies (Tour and Travel, India) is using AI, advanced data analytics, machine learning, chatbots, and voice interfaces to transform the travel industry. It uses unique algorithms and data insights, and each option is processed through dozens of parameters that map the behavior of travelers, to offer product personalization based on client's preferences (TR Foundation, 2018).

AI can be a useful tool in law, as it can make a summary of proceedings and cite relevant case laws with relevant paras. J.P. Morgan has developed Contract Intelligence (COIN), which calls out 150 attributes from 12,000 commercial credit agreements and contracts in just a few seconds. Ross Intelligence USA uses NLP (natural language program) to help lawyers with knowledge management and keeps them abreast with the latest legislation. It works as a law dictionary and analyzes the meaning and relationships between words to understand the legal concept. Kira Systems Canada uses ML to review unstructured contracts and related documents, due diligence, contract management database population and internal audit, lease abstraction, regulatory compliance, etc. ML can help cases for trial, speed up discovery, and help in drafting a litigation strategy. Lex Machine USA, a legal analytical tool, provides deep insights about the subject matter being discussed (like patents, trademarks, antitrust, securities) and is being used by lawyers, law firms, corporation, etc. Legal Intelligence Support Assistant (LISA), worlds first robot lawyer (Billy Bot), helps draw up, non-disclosure agreements (NDAs). LISA's AI tools have been developed with decades of human legal knowledge and experience. Billy, a virtual assistant, answers basic legal questions posed by individuals and can direct them to lawyers, if the need be. LISA in 2018 has been named as one of AI leaders by the *National Law Journal*. Mitra, an AI-driven legal research platform, uses AI and NLP to improve the work efficiency and productivity of law firms (Deloitte, 2019).

Besides, AI has raised hopes where scientists have till date had a miserable record — "predicting earthquakes" (Fuller and Metz, 2019). Unlike weather forecasting, which has significantly improved with the use of better satellites and powerful mathematical models, earthquake prediction had been marred by repeated failures (Agarwal and Agarwal, 2000, 2001a, 2001b, 2002, 2004). Some of the world's most destructive earthquakes — China in 2008, Haiti in 2010, and Japan in 2011 — occurred in areas that seismic hazard maps had previously deemed as being relatively safe. With the help of AI, scientists can analyze massive amounts of seismic data that can help them better understand earthquakes, anticipate how they will behave, and provide quicker and more accurate early warnings. The new AI-related quake research is learning on neural networks. Today, the world is aging. In an aging society, over a quarter of the population are over 60 and millions of seniors live alone. Toyota's Human Support Robot, or HSR, is the machine the automaker sees as closest to making the leap from lab to living room. The HSR is basically a retractable arm on wheels with a video screen on top and two large camera eyes that give it the rudiments of a face. Toyota company is trying HSR to become commonplace in homes, helping with chores — and even offering companionship — in an aging society. Japanese startup Groovex created a companion robot designed to make users happy. Lovot is using AI to interact with its surroundings, the wheeled machine resembles a penguin with cartoonist human eyes. It has interchangeable outfits and communicates in squeaks.

In Tokyo, Akihiko Kondo's mother refused an invitation to her only son's wedding in March 2018. "He was marrying a hologram". Kondo got married to "Miku" — an animated 16-year-old with saucer eyes and lengthy aquamarine pigtails. His new wife wakes him up each morning and sends him off to his job. In the evening, when he tells her by cell phone that he is coming home, she turns on the lights. She tells him when it's time to go to bed. Kondo's marriage might not have any legal standing but that does not bother him. Gatebox, the company that produces the hologram device featuring Miku, has issued a "marriage certificate", which certifies that a human and a virtual character have wed "beyond dimensions". Gatebox has issued more than 3,700 certificates for "cross-dimension" marriages. So, it is diversity in society — result of AI. Scientists have developed AI systems that can identify people on video. These systems can detect their age and gender more quickly and accurately. Banihal.com matches life partners using machine learning and AI. The AI system is called Rae and it considers hundreds of parameters from the profile, like age, location, religion, family net worth, and a model of worldview of the individual to find someone similar. Upbringing AI, through an AI Bot, helps parents to pre-emptively identify possible health issues their child may have. Looking at the symptoms, it even suggests measures to tackle those problems. AI can spot potential thieves before they steal. It detects suspicious body language that suggests someone intends to shoplift and alerts the staff. Vaak, a Japanese startup, has developed an AI software that hunts for potential shoplifters. The technology is good at spotting nefarious behaviors. The goal is prevention. Shoplifting costs the global retail industry about US$34 billion in lost sales in 2017 according to a report from Tyco Retail solution. Beyond retail, video software can be used in public spaces and train platforms to detect suspicious behavior.

A new machine that converts plastic waste into diesel and petrol will help curb pollution and provide fuel for remote communities in developing economies, according to French actor Samuel Le Bihan. The idea is to encourage the collection of waste before it ends up in the ocean with a machine that fits in a shipping container and can create an income. IBMs AI program "Watson" collaborated with a Grammy-winning producer to create four original compositions. AI can be the future of music, but cannot be a rock star. They may never be able to fill a stadium for a rock concert. "I am AI" was released in 2017 by YouTube star Taryn Southern, who does not know how to play an instrument (an album featuring eight tracks). "Amper" is using AI to break with the traditional way of making music. The Amper app allowed a user to pick a genre of music (rap, folk, and rock) and a mood (happy, sad, and driving) before producing a song. The user then can change the tempo and add instruments or switch them off until the results are satisfactory. Some researchers in US are pursuing a less threatening and more humane side of AI: creative expression.

Scientists and artists are teaming up with AI to create just about everything from artisanal pizzas to fashion. The MIT team is developing AI programs for artistic expression in its "How to Generate (Almost) Anything" project. The program studies thousands of examples and uses that database as an inspiration for their own concoction without any human interference. Once an AI program produces its results, researchers bring in artists to realize the results. Drones, AI, and satellite imagery can be used to monitor the pollution level of rivers due to dumping of debris on the flood plain. DDA has tied up with ISRO Regional Remote Sensing Center to put a stop on encroachment of vacant land.

4. Cryptocurrency/Digital Currency by Central Banks (Agarwal *et al.*, 2018)

Agarwal *et al.* (2018) evaluate various theories on money and how/why M5 as a money supply indicator is needed for inducing cryptocurrency in the basket of currencies by central banks worldwide (Agarwal, 2017a, 2018a, 2018b, 2018c, 2018d). Those studies propose setting up M5 as money supply with cryptocurrency along the lines of inclusion of other currency products developed in the last 50 years in order to promote efficiency in the money markets, transactional efficiency, and generating wealth along with positive contributions to GDP and people at large. That study also considers that money as a valuable resource and as a wealth of the nation has the potential to generate/mobilize more wealth. The study proposes that given the emergence of digital modes of money transactions, there is an urgent need for the creation of legitimate cryptocurrencies by national governments to induce confidence and *laissez-faire* through transactional efficiency in the money market. Government intervention (or central banks) to generate the cryptocurrency is the need of the hour and is critical for normal economic and business conditions in the future economy when businesses and labor market sources are global and looking for currency-efficient sources.

The proposed model of creating efficient money market through modeling of M5 will facilitate an automatic way for transactional efficiency, generating wealth for the nations, firms, and people at large, through easy access to currency and opportunities for jobs and growth (Agarwal *et al.*, 2018). It would also help save currency costs in a market-driven economic system with asymmetric information (Agarwal *et al.*, 2004, 2006). The "New Avatar" of money in the form of "crypto" would witness the change the way money (currency) has looked traditionally for centuries in the form of gold, silver, leather, wood, metal, paper, plastic, stone (Furness, 1910), and many others to a faceless virtual fully fractional form, but only when launched by nations (via their Central Banks).

Given the emergence of crypto-products in the informal sector with multiple players, it has become difficult for national governments to regulate and calibrate the supply of money and its effects through monetary stabilization measures adopted by them, as these crypto-products allow billions/trillions of money be transacted globally without any checks and balances. More than the benefits, these products are emerging as a threat to the national security and to an individual's wealth, and nations drift apart from the ills any speculative product brings with it to meet the needs of the greed of a specific group of people and rogue identities. Hence, there is a need for governments to act fast and consider to induce this financial innovation (cryptocurrencies) as a currency of tomorrow into its basket of currencies, as done with various other monetary products in the last six decades.

We were happy to also see that the then Finance Minister Arun Jaitley (late) has made special reference to cryptocurrencies stating that, "The government does not recognize cryptocurrency as legal tender or coin and will take all measures to eliminate the use of these crypto-assets in financing illegitimate activities or as part of the payments system" in Union Budget Speech in February 2018 and which was later re-confirmed by RBI later through their notifications to banks not to transact in any crypto-products claiming to be cryptocurrencies. The Reserve Bank of India (RBI) has also taken the initiative in constituting an RBI panel to study the feasibility of digital currency to launch as Central Bank Digital Currency (CBDC) on August 30, 2018 as proposed in our work (ET, 2018; Agarwal *et al.*, 2018).

Subsequently, the world has also witnessed the creation of Petro cryptocurrency as crypto product backed by the oil reserves of Venezuela. Venezuela made Petro, a cryptocurrency backed by the country's oil reserves, a national currency. Petro was introduced in early 2018, but initially the Petro cryptocurrency did not draw much attention. Venezuela has become the first country to ever peg their national currency, the bolívar, to a cryptocurrency falling within the asset-class framework as outlined in Agarwal *et al.* (2018). Venezuela undertook this step hoping that the cryptocurrency will bolster their struggling economy and counteract the staggering inflation rates and trade embargoes imposed on them by larger trading partners — all while making crypto history (Powell, 2018). Venezuelan President, Nicolás Maduro, revealed that the government would create a "cryptocurrency backed by reserves of Venezuelan wealth — of gold, oil, gas and diamonds" on December 3, 2018. However, the claims that the petro is backed by oil or anything else were hollow (Floyd, 2019). The Venezuelan government has been mostly silent on what this backing entails for Petro cryptocurrency. The Decree 3.196, Article 4, said that it will consist of a purchase agreement for one barrel of oil per token; "or whatever commodities the nation decides;" that arrangement almost certainly doesn't allow investors to demand physical delivery and defies the basic principles of crypto-products surfacing as cryptocurrency as an asset class. The Article 5 offered this guarantee: "The holder of petro will be able to realize a market-value exchange of the crypto-asset for the equivalent in another cryptocurrency or in bolívares [Venezuela's fiat currency] at the market exchange rate published by the national crypto-asset exchange". Floyd (2019), which has once again raised the key question against the claim of the President of Venezuela's statement.

China's Central Bank — People's Bank of China — announced on November 13, 2019 the introduction of digital currency backed by the Central Bank exactly along the lines proposed by IIF professors in their interviews on Delhi Doordarshan, IIF News & Broadcasting various international forums, and in various research paper publications since 2016 onward (Agarwal *et al.*, 2018; Orcutt, 2019). The key objective as outlined by the Chinese Central Bank is that the digital currency that the People's Bank of China says it is close to issuing will give the government unprecedented visibility into how its citizens spend money. Given the IIF professors' work, the news reads in consensus — "But authorities seem especially eager to assure the public that the new system will preserve the anonymity of physical cash — as long as they don't commit any crimes. It's not known exactly when it will be released, but China is widely expected to become the first major economy to issue a digital version of its sovereign currency. An explicit aim of the project is to replace physical cash, which has drawn speculation that the government will use it as a surveillance tool".

5. Economics of Currency (Money)

Money (currency) is a medium of exchange. It has emerged for ages to be a unit of accounts and store of value. Money's different functions are associated with different measures of the money supply. Till date, the economists/market operators (including central bankers) have been unable to define the "correct" measure of the money supply. Hence, we see several measures. These are classified along a spectrum or continuum between narrow and broad *monetary aggregates*. Narrow measures include only the most liquid assets, the ones most easily used to spend (currency, checkable deposits). Broader measures add less liquid types of assets (certificates of deposit, etc.). With the emergence of cryptocurrency, it is expected that money supply will move into a "New Avatar", where we would witness the change the way money (currency) has looked traditionally for centuries in the form of gold, silver, leather, wood, metal, paper, plastic, stone (Furness, 1910), and many others to a faceless virtual fully fractional form.

Currency (money) is a portion of the national money supply, consisting of bank notes and government-issued paper money and coins, which do not require endorsement in serving as a medium of exchange. Traditionally, among less developed societies, currency encompasses a wide diversity of items (e.g., livestock, stone carvings, tobacco) used as exchange media as well as signs of value or wealth. In the developed nations, where checks drawn on demand deposits are an important means of transaction, currency may actually account for only a small portion of the total money supply in the system (Britannica, 2017).

This continuum corresponds to the way that different types of money are more or less controlled by monetary policy with narrow money measure including those more directly affected and controlled by monetary policies, whereas broader money measures are less closely related to monetary policy actions (Wikipedia, 2017). It is a matter of perennial debate as to whether narrower or broader versions of the money supply have a more predictable link to the Nominal GDP. The different types of money are typically classified as "**M**"s. The "M"s usually range from M0 (narrowest) to M3 (broadest) but which "M"s are actually focused on in policy formulation depends on the country's central bank. Some of the more commonly used and well-established M's representing different forms of money supply by central banks are M0; MB; M1; M2; M3; M4; MZM. The typical layout for each of the "M"s is as follows:

Type of money	M0	MB	M1	M2	M3	M4	MZM	M5
Notes and coins in circulation (outside central banks and vaults of depository institutions) (*Currency*)	✓	✓	✓	✓	✓	✓	✓	✓
Notes and coins in bank vaults (*Vault Cash*)		✓						
Central bank credit (required reserve and excess reserve not physically present in banks)		✓						
Traveler's checks of non-bank issuers			✓	✓	✓	✓	✓	✓
Demand deposits			✓	✓	✓	✓	✓	✓
Other checkable deposits (OCDs) (i.e., negotiable order of withdrawal (NOW) accounts at depository institutions and credit union share draft accounts)			✓	✓	✓	✓	✓	✓
Savings deposits				✓	✓	✓	✓	✓
Time deposits and money market deposit accounts for individuals				✓	✓			
Large time deposits, institutional money market funds, short-term repurchase, and other larger liquid assets					✓			
All money market funds						✓	✓	✓
Cryptocurrency (Only when launched by a central bank)								✓

Over a period of time, measures of the money supply have exhibited fairly close relationships with important economic variables such as nominal gross domestic product (GDP) and the price level. Based partly on these relationships, Milton Friedman and many others have argued that the money supply provides important information about the near-term course for the economy and determines the level of prices and inflation in the long run. Central banks, including the RBI, FRB, ECB, and, others have at times used measures of the money supply as an important guide in the conduct of monetary policy. Over the recent decades, however, the relationships between various measures of the money supply and variables such as GDP growth and inflation have been quite unstable. This has been primarily due to the free flow of currency across borders with online means of movements of funds/savings. As a result, the importance of the money supply as a guide for the conduct of monetary policy has been reduced over time. The introduction of cryptocurrency would make it completely out of place unless the cryptocurrency is made part of the family at the earliest through the introduction of M5 as a measure of money supply (Agarwal, 2017a, 2018a, 2018b, 2018c, 2018d).

The New Money Supply Measure as M5 is

$$\text{M5} = \text{M3} + \text{Cryptocurrency*},$$

where * denotes *proposed in our work to be launched by Central Bank.*

The good part of the money supply data is that it is recorded and published, usually by the government or the central banks of the country. Public and private sector analysts have long monitored changes in the money supply because of the belief that it affects the price levels, inflation, exchange rate, and business cycles in an economy. The relation between money and prices has been historically associated with the quantity theory of money and expectations built thereupon. There has been a strong empirical evidence of a direct relation between money supply growth and long-term price inflation, at least for rapid increases in the amount of money in the economy. We take the example of Zimbabwe, which saw extremely rapid increases in its money supply and also extremely rapid increases in prices (hyper-inflation). This is why almost all central banks keep money supply as a key critical factor for means of controlling inflation and ultimately plan equitable stable economic growth/development. Given the emergence of crypto products in the informal sector with multiple players, it has become difficult for national governments to regulate and calibrate the supply of money and its effects through monetary stabilization measures adopted by them, as these crypto products allow billions/trillions of money be transacted globally without any checks and balances. More than the benefits, these products are emerging as a threat to national security and nations apart from the ills any speculative product brings with it to meet the needs of greed of a specific group of people and rogue identities. Hence, governments need to act fast and consider to induce this financial innovation (cryptocurrencies) as a currency of tomorrow into their basket of currencies, as done with various other products in the last six decades.

Some heterodox economists argue that the money supply is endogenous which is determined by the workings of the economy and not by the central bank. Hence, the sources of inflation must be found in the distributional structure of the economy (Wikipedia, 2017). In addition, they feel that the central bank's control over the money supply is feeble and that there is weak link between the growth of the money supply and the inflation rate. First, in the aftermath of a recession, when many resources are underutilized, an increase in the money supply can cause a sustained increase in real production instead of inflation. Second, if the velocity of money (i.e., the ratio between nominal GDP and money supply) changes, an increase in the money supply could have either no effect, an exaggerated effect, or an unpredictable effect on the growth of nominal GDP. This further enforces the very existence and need for central banks to consider inducing M5 and cryptocurrencies to induce efficiency in money markets thereby eradicating the ills the variants of crypto products in the informal segment have already spread.

Common sense tells us that a central bank creating new money out of thin air depreciates the value of each unit (rupee/dollar/euro) in circulation. However, the modern Monetary Theory disagrees, as it believes that money creation in a free-floating "fiat currency" regime such as the one seen in USA will not lead to a significant inflation unless the economy is approaching full employment and full capacity, given that the currency floating outside the central banking regulatory regime is larger than the one inside. This scenario was restricted to a few economies for now; however, with virtual currencies in place, it would be a natural outfall given the sources of income and wealth today stand to be across globe moving on with the wave of globalization, liberalization, and lowering of tariff barriers (via FTAs; WTO structures and trade blocks). Today, we live in a global village which is on the lookout for its own new, efficient currency and money markets. It is now for nation's to decide to allow free play creating mess with irreparable damage to social and economic fabric or to embrace the financially engineered cryptocurrency as the currency of tomorrow within its framework, thus benefiting all by launching national cryptocurrencies and M5 (as money supply measure) (Agarwal, 2017a, 2018a, 2018b, 2018c, 2018d).

Currently, we find that the money multiplier is the ratio between M1/MB or M2/M1 or M2/M0 (see Section III). However, it is expected to shift change to M5/M1 or M5/M2, given the way cryptocurrency is expected to move into the economics of currency.

5.1. *The quantitative theory of money*

The quantity theory descends from Nicolaus Copernicus (1517), Martín de Azpilicueta, Jean Bodin (1568), Henry Thornton (Hetzel, 1987), and various others who noted the increase in prices following the import of gold and silver, used in the coinage of money, from the New World. The "equation of exchange" relating the supply of money to the value of money transactions was stated by John Stuart Mill (1848), who expanded on the ideas of David Hume (1748). The quantity theory was developed by Simon Newcomb (1885), Alfred de Foville (1907), Irving Fisher (1911), and Ludwig von Mises in the late 19th and early 20th century.

Henry Thornton introduced the idea of a central bank after the financial panic of 1793, although the concept of a modern central bank wasn't given much importance until Keynes published *A Tract on Monetary Reform* in 1923. In 1802, Thornton published *An Enquiry into the Nature and Effects of the Paper Credit of Great Britain*, in which he gave an account of his theory regarding the central bank's ability to control price level. According to his theory, the central bank could control the currency in circulation through bookkeeping. This control could allow the central bank to gain a command of the money supply of the country. This ultimately would lead to the central bank's ability to control the price level. His introduction of the central bank's ability to influence the price level was a major contribution to the development of the quantity theory of money (Hetzel, 1987).

Karl Marx modified it by arguing that the Labor Theory of Value requires that prices, under equilibrium conditions, be determined by socially necessary labor time needed to produce the commodity and that the quantity of money was a function of the quantity of commodities, the prices of commodities, and the velocity (Agarwal, 2008; Agarwal *et al.*, 2017b). Marx did not reject the basic concept of the Quantity Theory of Money, but rejected the notion that each of the four elements were equal, and instead argued that the quantity of commodities and the price of commodities are the determinative elements and that the volume of money follows from them. He argued that the law, that the quantity of the circulating medium is determined by the sum of the prices of the commodities circulating and the average velocity of currency, may also be stated as follows: *given the sum of the values of commodities, and the average rapidity of their metamorphoses, the quantity of precious metal current as money depends on the value of that precious metal*. The erroneous opinion is that, on the contrary, prices are determined by the quantity of the circulating medium and that the latter depends on the quantity of the precious metals in a country; this opinion was based by those who first held it, on the hypothesis that commodities are without a price, and money without a value, when they first enter into circulation, and that, once in the circulation, an aliquot part of the medley of commodities is exchanged for an aliquot part of the heap of precious metals.

John Maynard Keynes, like Marx, accepted the theory in general and wrote this theory as fundamental. Its correspondence with fact is not open to question. Also, like Marx he believed that the theory was misrepresented. Where Marx argues that the amount of money in circulation is determined by the quantity of goods times the prices of goods, Keynes argued the amount of money was determined by the purchasing power or aggregate demand. He wrote, "Thus the number of notes which the public ordinarily have on hand is determined by the purchasing power which it suits them to hold or to carry about, and by nothing else".

In the Tract on Monetary Reform (1924), Keynes developed his own quantity equation

$$n = p(k + rk'),$$

where n is the number of currency notes or other forms of cash in circulation with the public, p is the index number of the cost of living, and r is the proportion of the bank's potential liabilities (k') held in the form of cash.

Keynes also assumes "...the public, (k') including the business world, finds it convenient to keep the equivalent of k consumption in cash and of a further available k' at their banks against cheques..." So long as k, k', and r do not change, changes in n cause proportional changes in p. Keynes however notes that the error often made by careless adherents of the Quantity Theory, which may partly explain why it is not universally accepted is as follows. The theory has often been expounded on the further assumption that a mere change in the quantity of the currency cannot affect k, r, and k' — that is to say, in mathematical parlance n is an independent variable in relation to these quantities. It would follow from this that an arbitrary doubling of n, since this in itself is assumed not to affect k, r, and k', must have the effect of raising p to double what it would have been otherwise. The Quantity Theory is often stated in this, or a similar, form.

Now "in the long run", this is probably true. If, after the American Civil War, the US dollar had been stabilized and defined by law at 10% below its present value, it would be safe to assume that n and p would now be just 10% greater than they actually are and that the present values of k, r, and k' would be entirely unaffected. But this long run is a misleading guide to current affairs. In the long run, we are all dead. Economists set themselves too easy, too useless a task if in tempestuous seasons they can only tell us that when the storm is long past, the ocean will be flat again.

In actual scenario experience, a change in n is liable to have a reaction both on k and k' and on r. It will be enough to give a few typical instances. Before the war (and indeed since), there was a considerable element of what was conventional and arbitrary in the reserve policy of the banks, but especially in the policy of the national central banks toward their reserves in gold. These reserves were kept for show rather than for use, and their amount was not the result of close reasoning. There was a decided tendency on the part of these banks between 1900 and 1914 to bottle up gold when it flowed toward them and to part with them reluctantly when the tide was flowing the other way. Consequently, when gold became relatively abundant, they tended to hoard what came their way and to raise the proportion of the reserves, with the result that the increased output of South African gold was absorbed with less effect on the price level than would have been the case if an increase of n had been totally without reaction on the value of r. Thus, in these and other ways, the terms of our equation tend in their movements to favor the stability of p, and there is a certain friction which prevents a moderate change in v from exercising its full proportionate effect on p. On the contrary, a large change in n, which rubs away the initial frictions, and especially a change in n due to causes which set up a general expectation of a further change in the same direction, may produce a more than proportionate effect on p.

Keynes thus accepts the Quantity Theory as accurate over the long term but not over the short term. Keynes remarks that contrary to contemporaneous thinking, velocity and output were not stable but highly variable and as such, the quantity of money was of little importance in driving the prices (Friedman, 1970). The theory was influentially restated by Milton Friedman in response to the work of John Maynard Keynes and Keynesianism (Friedman, 1956). Friedman understood that Keynes was like Friedman, a "quantity theorist" and that Keynes Revolution *was from, as it were, within the governing body*, i.e., consistent with previous Quantity Theory (Friedman, 1970). Friedman notes the similarities between his views and those of Keynes when he wrote that *A counter-revolution, whether in politics or in science, never restores the initial situation. It always produces a situation that has some similarity to the initial one but is also strongly influenced by the intervening revolution. That is certainly true of monetarism which has benefited much from Keynes's work. Indeed I may say, as have so many others since there is no way of contradicting it, that if Keynes were alive today he would, no doubt, be at the forefront of the counter-revolution.* Friedman also notes that Keynes shifted the focus away from the quantity of money (Fisher's M and Keynes' n) and put the focus on price and output. Friedman writes *What matters, said Keynes, is not the quantity of money. What matters is the part of total spending which is independent of current income, what has come to be called autonomous spending and to be identified in practice largely with investment by business and expenditures by government.* This is where the strong presence of variants of cryptocurrencies defying all fundamentals of an asset class have come into emergence in the form of Bitcoins (and others) globally in the last few years influencing spending patterns beyond controls of any nation/central bank.

The Monetarist counterposition was that contrary to Keynes, velocity was not a passive function of the quantity of money but it can be an independent variable. Friedman wrote *Perhaps the simplest way for me to suggest why this was relevant is to recall that an essential element of the Keynesian doctrine was the passivity of velocity. If money rose, velocity would decline. Empirically, however, it turns out that the movements of velocity tend to reinforce those of money instead of to offset them. When the quantity of money declined, by a third from 1929 to 1933 in the United States, velocity declined also. When the quantity of money rises rapidly in almost any country, velocity also rises rapidly. Far from velocity offsetting the movements of the quantity of money, it reinforces them.* These trends are re-enforcing in current times, which demand a corrective action by central banks and national economies to protect the sovereignty of currencies and readjust with the dynamic evolution of economics of currencies.

Thus, while Marx, Keynes, and Friedman all accepted the Quantity Theory, they each placed different emphasis as to which variable was the driver in changing prices. Marx emphasized production, Keynes income and demand, and Friedman the quantity of money. Academic discussion remains over the degree to which different figures developed the theory (Volckart, 1997). Bieda (1973) further argues that Copernicus's observation on money can lose its value through excessive abundance, if so much silver is coined as to heighten people's demand for silver bullion. For in this way, the coinage's estimation vanishes when it cannot buy as much silver as the money itself contains. The solution is to mint no more coinage until it recovers its par value (Friedman, 1970) amounts to a statement of the theory (Bieda, 1973), while other economic historians date the discovery later, to figures such as Jean Bodin, David Hume, and John Stuart Mill (Volckart, 1997; Wennerlind, 2005).

The quantity theory of money preserved its importance even in the decades after Friedmanian monetarism had occurred. In new classical macroeconomics, the quantity theory of money is still a doctrine of fundamental importance, but Robert E. Lucas and other leading new classicals made serious efforts to specify and refine its theoretical meaning. For new classicals, following David Hume's famous essay "Of Money", money was not neutral in the short run, so the quantity theory was assumed to hold only in the long run. These theoretical considerations involved serious changes as to the scope of countercyclical economic policy (Galbacs, 2015). Historically, the main rival of the quantity theory was the real bills doctrine, which says that the issue of money does not raise prices, as long as the new money is issued in exchange for assets of sufficient value (Roy, 1987). Taking from Roy and others, it is clear that the value of money/currency is inherently locked with the assets of the nation (privately/publicly held). Hence, the cryptocurrency which is to be launched by central banks as money (M) has to be locked against national assets (private/publically held) generating its intrinsic value to qualify as a tenable asset-class crypto-product/currency (see Section 6.1) (Agarwal, 2017a, 2018a, 2018b, 2018c, 2018d).

6. Money Supply

The *money supply* (or *money stock*) is the total amount of assets available in an economy at a specific time. There are several ways to define "money", but standard measures usually include currency in circulation and deposits. The money supply is also commonly defined to be a group of safe assets that households and businesses can use to make payments or to hold as short-term investments (Agarwal, 1988; Agarwal *et al.*, 2016, 2017; Agarwal and Agarwal, 2017). For example, the currency and balances held in current (checking) accounts and savings accounts are included in many measures of the money supply. There are several standard measures of the money supply, including the monetary base M1 (commonly known as narrow money) and M2. The monetary base is defined as the sum of currency in circulation and reserve balances (deposits held by banks and other depository institutions in their accounts at the central banks).

The global view (based on over 10 central banks) defining monetary aggregates are as follows:

M0: Total of all physical currencies (including coinage).

M0 = central bank currency notes + government notes + coins.

It is not relevant whether the currency is held inside or outside of the banking system as reserves. This includes bank reserves.

Referred as the monetary base, or narrow money.

MB: Total of all physical currencies (M0) + central bank deposits (special deposits that only banks can have at the central bank).

Referred as monetary base (or total currency).

This is base from which other forms of money (like checking deposits and others listed below) are created. It is one of the most liquid measure of money supply.

M1: M0 + demand deposits + traveler checks + other checkable deposits

Bank reserves are not included in M1.

M1 is defined as the sum of currency held by the public and transaction deposits at depository institutions (which are financial institutions that obtain their funds mainly through deposits from the public, such as commercial banks, savings and loan associations, savings banks and cooperative/credit unions).

M2: M1 + savings accounts + money market accounts + retail money market mutual funds + small-denomination term deposits

Represents M1 and “close substitutes” for M2.

M2 is defined as M1 plus savings deposits, small-denomination time deposits, and retail money market mutual fund shares.

M3: M2 + large & long-term deposits + institutional money market mutual fund balances (in some cases repurchase agreements and debt securities as with central bank)

Referred to as broad money.

MZM: Money with zero maturity.

It measures the supply of financial assets redeemable at par on demand. The velocity of MZM is considered to be a relatively better predictor of inflation.

M4: M3 + commercial paper + treasury bills

The Reserve Bank of India (central bank) defines the monetary aggregates as:

M0: Currency in circulation + bankers' deposits with the RBI + "other" deposits with the RBI = Net RBI credit to the government + RBI credit to the commercial sector + RBI's claims on banks + RBI's net foreign assets + government's currency liabilities to the public — RBI's net non-monetary liabilities.

Referred as reserve money.
M0 outstanding was 14.75 trillion in August 2017.

M1: Currency with the public + deposit money of the public (demand deposits with the banking system + "other" deposits with the RBI).

M1 was 184% of M0 in August 2017.

M2: M1 + savings deposits with post office savings banks.

M2 was 879% of M0 in August 2017.

M3: M1+ time deposits with the banking system = Net bank credit to the government + bank credit to the commercial sector + net foreign exchange assets of the banking sector + government's currency liabilities to the public — net non-monetary liabilities of the banking sector (other than time deposits).

(Broad concept of money supply).
M3 was 880% of M0 in August 2017.

M4: M3 + All deposits with post office savings banks (excluding national savings certificates).

The section VI outlines as to why cryptocurrencies are the future currency, however ONLY and ONLY when introduced by central banks all over the world in their own denominated currency tags backed by national assets as done for all real currencies today. These will replace part of the real currency and may be all in due course bring in desired currency efficiency within the regulated framework. Hence the need for central bank denominated cryptocurrencies for being part of Money Supply for an appropriate money supply system in the virtual currency reign as M5 (Agarwal, 2017a, 2018a, 2018b, 2018c, 2018d).

M5: M3 + cryptocurrency (*proposed to be launched by central bank*).

7. Virtual Community, Virtual Products and Virtual Currency: Emergence of Bitcoins as mode for Illicit (Hawala) Transactional[1]

The increased use of Internet and the advancement in technology have given rise to the virtual communities. A virtual community is to be understood as a place within cyberspace where individuals interact and follow mutual interests or goals. Social networking is probably the most omnipresent type of virtual community (e.g., Facebook, MySpace, Twitter, LinkedIn, and others). There are other prominent knowledge-sharing communities like Wikipedia. These communities create a virtual world (e.g., Second Life) including those that aim to create an online environment for gambling (e.g., Online Vegas Casino). Sometimes, these communities have created and circulated their own currencies for exchanging goods and services. The currency is acceptable within that specific community as a medium of exchange, unit of account, and store of value. These today offer alternative modes of payment acceptable in the virtual community.

A virtual product (VPs) as on date can be defined as a type of unregulated, digital money, which is issued and usually controlled by its developers, and used and accepted among the members of a specific virtual community (ECB, 2012).[2] Virtual products (VPs) refer to any type of digital unit that is used as a medium of exchange or a form of digitally stored value created by agreement within the community of VP users. VPs

[1]As Bitcoins defy all principals for being recognized as a Virtual Currency or a tenable asset class (Agarwal, 2017a, 2018a, 2018b, 2018c, 2018d).

[2]Virtual Currency Schemes, October 2012, A Report by European Central Bank.

are not issued or guaranteed by any jurisdiction and do not have legal tender status. VPs shall be broadly construed to include digital units of exchange that (a) have a centralized repository or administrator; (b) have decentralized distribution network; or (c) can be created or obtained by computing or manufacturing efforts only when introduced by a central bank (Agarwal, 2017a, 2018a, 2018b, 2018c, 2018d).

The Virtual Product Schemes as classified based on their interaction with the real money (ECB, 2012; EBA, 2014) are as follows:

i. Closed Virtual Product Schemes basically used in Online Gaming.
ii. Virtual Product Scheme with Unidirectional Flows.[3]
iii. Virtual Product Scheme with Bidirectional Flows.[4]

The Virtual Product (so-called Virtual Currencies) Schemes differ from Electronic Money Schemes (ECB, 2012; EBA, 2014; Agarwal, 2017a, 2018a, 2018b, 2018c, 2018d) as follows (see Table 1):

i. Virtual products (VPs) do NOT have physical counterparts with legal tender status.
ii. Virtual products do NOT have legal sanctity, given that they are NOT launched by central banks.
iii. Virtual products scheme currently floated under the bitcoins structure DEFY all principals for being a tenable asset class (see Section 6.1).
iv. Traditional financial actors like the central banks are NOT involved in issuing virtual currencies, but they are issued by virtual

[3]These are currently being purchased with real money with a specific conversion rate and then one can buy virtual goods and services or sometimes even real goods and services. For example, the virtual currency scheme set up by Nintendo, called Nintendo Points, can be redeemed in Nintendo's shops and in their games. Consumers can purchase points online by using a credit card or in retail stores by purchasing a Nintendo Points Card. The points cannot be converted back to real money.

[4]These work with any convertible currency and have buying and selling rates and can buy virtual goods and services and real goods and services. For example, Linden Dollars (L$) is the virtual currency issued in second life, a virtual world where users create "avatars", i.e., digital characters that can be customized. Second Life has its own economy where users can buy and sell goods and services from and to each other. In order to do so, they need Linden Dollars, which can be purchased with US dollars and other currencies according to the exchange rates established in the currency trading market. A credit card or PayPal account is needed. Users can sell their spare Linden Dollars in return for US dollars.

Table 1: Difference between electronic money schemes and virtual currency schemes (ECB, 2012).

	Electronic money schemes	Virtual currency schemes
Money format	Digital	Digital
Unit of account	Traditional currency (Euro, US$, GBP, etc.) with legal tender status	Invented currency (Linden $, Bitcoins, etc.) without legal tender status
Acceptance	By undertaking other than the issuer	Usually within a specific virtual community
Legal status	Regulated	Unregulated
Issuer	Legally established electronic money institution	Non-financial private company
Supply of money	Fixed	Not fixed (depends on issuer's decisions)
Possibility of redeeming funds	Guaranteed (and at par value)	Not guaranteed
Supervision	Yes	No
Type(s) of risk	Mainly operational	Legal, credit, liquidity and operational

Note: Virtual currency schemes = Virtual product schemes.
Source: ECB.

communities which are often non-financial private companies. Hence, financial sector regulations and supervisions do not guide the flow of virtual currencies.

v. Exchange of real currency and virtual currency is NOT regulated by any law.
vi. The supply of the virtual products currently are governed by issues which do NOT have a legal standing.

In assessment of virtual product/currency schemes, it is believed that they presently

i. will lead to asset bubbles or price instability due to their being a flawed asset class product (Agarwal, 2017a, 2018a, 2018b, 2018c, 2018d).
ii. they have limited interaction with the real-world currencies, and due to their ability to purchase real goods and services, they can cause instability in global financial markets given their emergence as *Hawala* and medium of transaction for illicit activities (Agarwal, 2017a, 2018a, 2018b, 2018c, 2018d; Goldberg, 2017; HT, 2018).

iii. they are inherently unstable and volatile; hence, they attract speculators to make financial gains. However, since they have not been legally accepted as a tender by financial actors, they are unlikely to destabilize national economies (Bloomberg-ET, 2018b).
iv. the countries, government, and central banks are keeping a close watch on these virtual products (so-called virtual currencies) and are initiating action to protect the gullible investors from burning their hands. Many countries have also declared these VPs or VCs as a non-legal tender (product).
v. are not supervised or overseen by any public authority globally or nationally. The ability of these currencies to purchase virtual and sometimes real currencies exposes users to credit, liquidity, operational, and legal risks (Agarwal, 2017a, 2017b; Bloomberg, 2017c; Archana, 2018).
vi. the anonymity of issuers and transfers makes them attractive for criminals, fraudsters, and money launderers to perform illegal activities (Agarwal and Agarwal, 2004, 2006; Bloomberg-ET, 2018a; Reuters, 2018b).
vii. many regulatory bodies believe that the circulation of these currencies creates parallel payment gateways which either need to be regulated or made illegal to protect the sovereign currencies and legalized business environment (Agarwal, 2017a, 2018a, 2018b, 2018c, 2018d; Pillai, 2018b).

Transaction in the virtual economy system basically settles two components with regards to payment systems: (a) delivery of virtual or real goods and services and (b) transfer of funds. Hence, the payment system of the VPs works similar to the real currencies except for the fact that financial intermediaries are not involved. The process involves the following:

i. authorization and submission of a payment instrument,
ii. processing and clearing involves a payment instruction exchanged between the creditor and debtor,
iii. debits and credits are settled in the user's account.

7.1. *Cryptocurrency as a tenable asset class*

An asset is anything of value that can be converted into cash or equivalence in trade backed by a depository securing the value. Assets are owned by individuals, businesses, and governments and can be in any shape or form, whether tangible or intangible. Examples being cash and cash equivalents (certificates of deposit, checking and savings accounts, money market accounts, physical cash, and treasury bills); real property (land, building, machinery, goodwill, and any structure that is attached to it); personal property (anything/everything that one owns that is not real property such as boats, collectibles, household furnishings, jewelry, vehicles, even one's life as labor hours) (Agarwal *et al.*, 2017b); and investments (annuities, bonds, cash value of life insurance policies, mutual funds, pensions, retirement plans stocks, and other investments) (Agarwal, 1969, 1988; Agarwal *et al.*, 2012). Assets are often grouped into a few broad categories: (a) liquid assets and illiquid assets from finance perspective; (b) as tangible assets and intangible assets (virtual) from accounting perspective; (c) real assets and virtual assets from derivative perspective of underlying variable and others (Agarwal *et al.*, 2017). Your net worth is calculated by subtracting your liabilities from your assets. Essentially, your assets are everything you own, and your liabilities are everything you owe. A positive net worth indicates that your assets are greater than your liabilities; a negative net worth signifies that your liabilities exceed your assets. Most financial products existing in the markets today (including money market) are based on these three broad categories identifying asset class (Agarwal and Agarwal, 2007).

Now when we talk of currency, how do we go about generating the value a currency possesses and how do we know a single bill [Rs. (INR); US$; Euro; or any other] is really worth. Is it just because the government says so or some exchange lists it so. NO, any currency is worth its projected value only as long as the government is willing and able to defend its value. The value of a currency is traditionally decided by the size of the economy or the consolidated assets of the said country (in public or private domain) (Furness, 1910; Fisher, 1911; Green, 1987; Agarwal, 2017a, 2018a, 2018b, 2018c, 2018d). In accordance, the amount to circulate is channeled by the central bank in order to ensure stable growth, trade, and financial discipline. This is done by most central banks by managing the money supply [M0; MB; M1; M2; M3; M4; MZM; M5 (*when proposed cryptocurrency is introduced by Central Bank Only as Central Bank Digital Currency* (*CBDC*)) and a few others] (Agarwal, 2017a, 2018a, 2018b, 2018c, 2018d). Basically, currency value fluctuates relative to the size of the economy, and the supply and demand of currency are dependent on the direction the economy is taking. We are able to get a market perspective on this from the foreign exchange market. Exchange rates fluctuate every second because market participants expect a different value for currency A relative to another currency B. For example, the GDP of India for the year 2017–2018 is equivalent to US$2.53 trillion, and if the India's economy is expected to grow relative to the world economy (Agarwal *et al.*, 2018), INR (Rs.) will appreciate relative to major tradable currencies, given the supply of INR (Rs.) stays the same and it remains to be a floating currency (or managed float as in most developed economies like, India, USA, UK, Japan, Europe (EURO), and others).

There is a clear evidence that a currency as an asset class is only tenable when an economy's assets (privately held or by public) are there to back the valuation (Agarwal, 2004b; ET, 2018). In recent case of Greece, when the currency was not holding value as there was extensive debt burden, the only way Greece could resolve the situation was by sale of its national assets (both in public and private domains). However, Greece adopted an intermediate step of converting deposits (debt from depositors) into equity/convertible debt to resolve the currency crunch created due to extensive devaluation and global default on debt payments. This is where the virtual products (so-called cryptocurrencies) launched by various agencies, scientists, industrialists, entrepreneurs, and trading speculators lack — that they are not a tenable asset class (Ali *et al.*, 2014; FATF, 2014; Bloomberg, 2017b, 2017c; Christopher, 2017; IMF, 2017b; Rangan, 2017; Reuters, 2017b; TNN, 2017).

The concept and framework of virtual currencies (cryptocurrencies), whether launched through mining or by logical creation by a central bank (as central bank digital currency (CBDC)), would remove this deficiency of it is a tenable asset class (Agarwal, 2017a, 2018a, 2018b, 2018c, 2018d). We have tried to present different frameworks in which VPs (so-called cryptocurrencies) exist and the kind of follies/erosion of hard-earned wealth they subject every one of us to on a day-to-day basis, especially because they are NOT launched by a central bank as a medium of transaction.

7.2. *Virtual products (like bitcoins, etc.) framework as virtual transactional system*

Virtual products (like bitcoins and others) are the kind of so-called cryptocurrency in the sense of these being conceptual. They are manufactured using software, by solving complex mathematical problems and cryptology having market values; by solving one such problem, nearly 12 and a half bitcoins are generated. The idea of bitcoin emerged in October 2008 from a research paper by the name of Satoshi Nakamoto. The purchase process using bitcoin is considered to be so secure that it isn't possible to hack the system. Only a money transfer can be seen, but nothing can be known about the sender and the recipient. This type of anonymity with its strong crypto-logical security is ensured by those dealing with bitcoins, though in the last six months we have seen that this myth is proven wrong by hackers and thieves (Kharif, 2018).

We see an extensive support for such privately managed VCs mostly in US and Japan, apart from a select few other nations globally. According to the US treasury, the bitcoin is a "decentralized virtual currency". There are some exchanges (Agarwal, 2018), which may be treated as mints or a central bank, which are mainly located in China, Hong Kong, and Russia. There are various companies called "miners" under each exchange. The bitcoin ecosystem uses a function called the "hash function". A "hash" is given for every transaction, along with a "public key" and a "private key". Each of these keys is inverse to each other, but it is never easy to derive one from the other. The public keys are openly available in the public domain. The details of each transaction report are available in a ledger called "blockchain". From this open source, anybody can tell how many bitcoins are traded at some specified public key. But nobody can know the owner of those and it cannot be easily broken, making the system's character of anonymity and privacy also its drawback (TNN, 2017; Sas and Khairuddin, 2017; TNN, 2018b)

On August 30, 2017, one bitcoin was considered to be worth 2,91,822/- its value skyrocketing since Donald Trump's election as the US President in November 2016 and spawning an industry of auxiliary services for people rushing into find gold in these virtual product or the so-called cryptocurrency (Bloomberg, 2017b, 2017d). As we all know, bitcoin is a decentralized, paperless crypto-product not produced by a central authority like a bank or a consortium. It is a mathematical formula. Virtual product is produced by massively souped-up computers, called "mining rigs" that solve complex math problems to obtain these virtual products. A ledger records all the transactions. Mining-rigs run round the clock, with their performance depending on the high-end graphic cards and cooling system used, which is not an inexperienced proposition costing at an average of 3 lakh per machine. Several online vendors as well as individuals are investing in those machines to mine crypto-products (so-called cryptocurrencies).

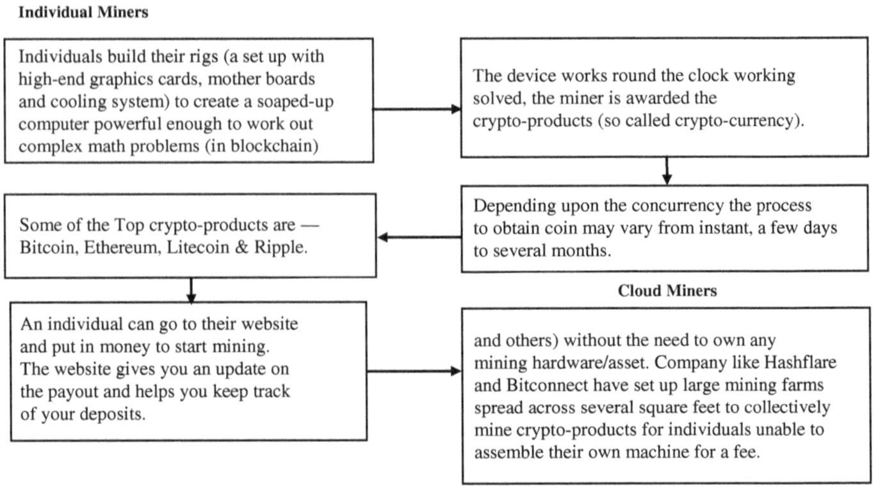

Figure 1: Crypto-product mining framework establishing virtual transactional system.

The framework/system working of these crypto-products is explained in Figure 1.

Bitcoin was launched as the first so-called cryptocurrency (crypto-products). All digital products created since then are called Altcoins, or alternative coins. Litecoin, Peercoin, Feathercoin, Ethereum, and hundreds of other coins are all called Altcoins because they are not bitcoins. Given that they fulfill the payment system functionality, they still do not fulfill the basic condition for being called a currency which is MUST for any currency to be called a valid Asset Class (see Section 4.1) given no fiduciary/legal sanctity backing for the virtual framework of bitcoins (Agarwal, 2017a, 2018a, 2018b, 2018c, 2018d).

Bitcoins saw an explosive growth after de-monetization in India. The rise in popularity of such crypto-products has enabled techies like Saket Nalegaonkar to build services around it. The 28-year-old Internet of things engineer spends his spare time traveling around the country helping enthusiasts set up rigs for mining. Badgujar, a 26-year-old management graduate, rewired five computers in his college lab, making them work in tandem to mine Ethereum. Some companies, such as Hashflare, Genesis, and Bitconnect, have even set up the so-called farms to collectively mine the so-called cryptocurrencies (crypto-products) for individuals unable to assemble their own machine, for a fee. Cloud mining is now a new thing where one can now run a bitcoin support website with bitcoin support 24 × 7 without any legal sanctions or approvals, given the location of such clouds is unknown and spread across borders. Individuals can now spend as low as US$2 to start with for mining, and these companies assure fixed returns every month however, they have no back up security depository backing their VCs (Bloomberg, 2017d, 2018b). The speculation in the crypto-products works much like it would with gold or equity or real currencies, i.e., buy, wait for the value to appreciate, and henceforth sell, with complete speculative framework having NO default security like an illegitimate gamble (Bloomberg, 2017c, 2018a; Das and Menon, 2017).

In India, one can buy bitcoins through a bitcoin exchange or directly from an individual. Saurabh Agarwal (41, co-founder and CEO of Indian Bitcoin Exchange Zebpay) said that there are a very few of them for goods and services in the physical world. There are some who make money buying bitcoin off one exchange. The founder of exchange Coinsecure said he had seen people indulge in this arbitrage quite frequently in recent times. This works because different exchanges have different prices (Christopher, 2017). Given the high value, one can deal in fractions of bitcoin (if the exchange is a virtual/online exchange allowing fractional trade). One can trade for as low as 0.01 BTC on Coinsecure (exchange started in 2014). What makes this crypto-product attractive is that it can be used to move money across the globe quickly and anonymously and that it is free of control of any central bank/government. Cryptocurrency has understandable appeal to the millennials who have came of age during the 2008 financial crisis and are now watching the rise of anti-globalist populism threaten the stability of the economy. Ron Ginn, aged 35 years, founder of a private photo-sharing service called Text Event Pics, had taken all his money out of the stock market and invested it into Ripple and real estate. There is low cost for entry, one does not pay a lot of fees and millennials are the most tech-savvy to move toward these without understanding the fundamentals or the nuisances like a child getting charmed by glitters. Unlike previous generations, this new generation don't have pension and are mistrustful of stocking money away in mutual funds and are fully accustomed to owning digital assets that have no concrete properties. As traditional paths to upper middle-class stability are being blocked by direct exorbitant housing costs and a shaky job market, these investors view these innovative crypto-products not only as a hedge against another share market crash but also as the most rational and even utopian means of investing their money.

Given the massive surge in the value of the so-called cryptocurrencies (crypto-products), real estate developers, too, are seeking a piece of the action. Bengaluru-based Nalegaonkar helped set up rigs for mining and had been contracted by real estate developers to convert entire floors into mining farms. Bitcoin Growth Fund (BGF), a blockchain-based startup fund, closed its first fund raising with US$14.5 million (approximately 95 crore) as part of its initial coin offering (ICO) in August 2017. Founded in January 2017 in Dubai, the founding team includes Phil McCauley, Nagaraj Konda, and Mattiaas Frost. BGF focuses on Asian markets, primarily India and China. BGF is a blockchain-based venture capital fund where regular or small investors can invest by buying a token named "MCAPS" via ICO. An ICO works like an initial public offering. In an ICO (retail), investors get tokens instead of shares in a company. However, there are some key differences between IPOs and ICOs. While IPOs are regulated and issue shares in operational companies, ICOs are not regulated and issue digital coins for projects that are yet to be developed (Murphy *et al.*, 2015; Reuters, 2018a; Pillai, 2018a; IMF, 2018).

As per BGF, the minimum investment amount required is US$5 and there are close to 6 lakh investors from India who have subscribed to MCAP via ICO by mid of 2017. Most of the retail investors are from the tech and finance background and feel that they usually understand this kind of new crypto-product as an asset class investment, which is a myth. The second-largest retail subscribers were from China (30% and the rest were from South Korea and other countries. Here, the (retail) investors are not buying bitcoins or any crypto-products, rather they are buying a currency mining fund that would invest in various crypto-products like Dash, Ethereum, Monero, Litecoin, Z-coin, and Bitcoin, among others. Mining is a farming process. The process is distributed as either dividend or profit. During the mining process, miners try to get the crypto-products as much as possible and as quickly as possible, as 90% of all crypto-products' total output is pre-determined, which is contrary to any farming where outputs cannot be determined; however, have an inherent security of the land and labor wealth (Agarwal *et al.*, 2017b).

In February 2017, bitcoin startups Zebpay, Unocoin, Coinsecure, and Search Trade had come together to form the Digital Asset and Blockchain Foundation of India (DABFI) to bring in transparency and growth in the virtual currency market as well as create awareness on the so-called cryptocurrencies (crypto-products), to liaison with regulators to bring in clarification in taxation (Agarwal, 1988; Sikarwar, 2017; ET, 2017). In the

US, companies have raised US$180 million via ICOs so far in 2017, compared to US$101 million last year, according to Smith & Crown, a blockchain research, data, and consulting group.

Trading in bitcoins is gaining traction, especially among those aged 18–35 years and seeking to harness volatility for extraordinary returns (Bloomberg, 2017b; Christopher and Bansal, 2018). As Sandeep Goenka, cofounder and chief operating officer at Zebpay, an app-based bitcoin exchange, says, "the increasing awareness of bitcoins worldwide, particularly about its revolutionary technology, has triggered a rally in the bitcoin market". Japan has now added itself to the list of countries that have regulations for bitcoins. Due to these positive factors, bitcoin prices have shown tremendous growth. Since April 2017, Japan's legalization of the digital currency has contributed to the rally in bitcoins (JT, 2018; Bloomberg-ET, 2018b; Pillai, 2018b; Kumar, 2018). After Tokyo's move, many vendors have started accepting these crypto-products as virtual currency. Peach Aviation, for instance, is going to be the first Japanese airline to accept bitcoins as payment for plane tickets. With an expert committee in India now seeking to regulate domestic trading of bitcoins, prices are expected to leapfrog in the next one year (Bloomberg, 2017d, 2018b).

IIF professors have been proponents of the fact that virtual products (so-called virtual currencies or cryptocurrencies) as a concept is very innovative and must be considered by central banks (including RBI) and national governments; however, the current form of these virtual products (VPs) or virtual currencies (VCs) mushrooming in the markets has a destabilizing impact (Agarwal, 2017a, 2018a, 2018b, 2018c, 2018d; ET, 2017; Reuters, 2017b; Goldberg, 2017; Reuters, 2018a).

We also find that trading volumes and prices have risen in lockstep with an increasing interest in India in bitcoins. In June 2015, the prices were about 20,000 per bitcoin which have surged to 2,25,000 recently. In the past few days, it has pared gains partially, and now trades at about Rs. 1,83,000 per unit in the round-the-clock market. Sahil Shah, a final-year BBA student of Nirma University, has sold four bitcoins at roughly 2.20 lakh a piece against 70,000, the average price at which he acquired those. This rally is almost a bubble, but it gave a solid profit-booking opportunity for people who bought bitcoins 2–3 years ago. There are several reasons for its recent spurt in growth, from politics in the US and Brazil to the WannaCry ransom ware attacks and other such global viral cyber-attacks. Whatever be the reasons for this newfound love for these crypto-products, people dealing with bitcoins are aware that it is a risky, unregulated, and uninsured crypto-product. These are like skating on thin ice, behind the excitement and thrill, there is the fear of unwarranted death (Bloomberg, 2017d; Goldberg, 2017; Rangan, 2017; Dev, 2018).

The lack of regulations, though, has cast a shadow over the bitcoin universe. Over the last 6 months, the RBI has repeatedly being issuing several warning statements consumers about financial and regularity risks associated with these so-called virtual currencies (Yermack, 2013; TNN, 2017, 2018b; Agarwal, 2017a, 2018a, 2018b, 2018c, 2018d; Archana, 2018; Reuters, 2018a; Shetty and Pillai, 2018). However, a firm stand is still warranted both by the Reserve Bank of India (RBI) and the government (Nappinai, 2018). Recent research has unearthed the Achilles' heel of bitcoin technology. Sas and Khairuddin (2017) have found that the same design features that make bitcoin technology appealing to its users have weaknesses, which are being exploited by hackers and thefts of these crypto-products (Kharif, 2018; Bloomberg, 2017c; Dev, 2018). They warn that these flaws can lead to drastic theft and fraud which are beyond recovery or trace (Kharif, 2018; Mizrahi, 2018). An easy and quick erosion of hard-earned wealth of individuals is beyond recourse. The research has serious implications for the technology that has enjoyed several rebirths in the last decade. Already huge amounts of "cash" are stored in the form of bitcoins (and its VP variants), which go by the name of "digital gold". The latest findings put the question mark on its recoverability and ownership as well. The transparent design features that are supposed to promote trust in the bitcoin have come to haunt its investors.

Blockchain is the main technological innovation of the bitcoin. It is decentralized, pseudo-anonymous, and unregulated and, therefore, attractive to many of its users. Blockchain maintains a continuously growing list of records "blocks" that are said to be free from tampering and revision. Each block contains time stamp-encoded information of the time when a transaction has taken place and a link to a previous block. It allows a transaction to take place between two parties anonymously, if one ignores the digital signature, without a mediator. In the case of traditional currencies, a bank or a financial institution acts as a trusted mediator. Blockchain, with its open ledger design, is seen by some investors as a low cost-intensive (no paying of fees to a mediator), fast, and transparent technology.

According to the researchers, the problematic bitcoin design features include ... *the risk of losing a password- a lost or forgotten password cannot be recovered, so all bitcoins from an electronic wallet could be rendered unrecoverable*. Insecure passwords can lead to bitcoins being stolen — for instance, through phishing attacks (Gibbs, 2017). The irreversible nature of transactions for bitcoins can lead to bitcoins that are stolen or diverted to another wallet due to hacking (Gibbs, 2017) or dishonest trading partners and cannot be reversed and recovered. The anonymous nature of the crypto-product VC users and their unknown reputations opens up opportunities for dishonest traders to scam during transactions. The fear of fraud is real as bitcoins are popular among many dark web users, and many of them are not ethical hackers. A 2015 Coindesk report indicated that bitcoin has been the *de facto* currency of the dark web (the hidden Internet, accessible to any, the free software that allows anonymous surfing — *birth of the Hawala*), since the pioneering marketplace Silk Road, the "eBay of drugs", arrived in 2001. In fact, an FBI report claimed that Silk Road made US$1.2 billion in 2012–2013, and a large part of it was paid in currencies such as bitcoins. According to Sas and Khairuddin (2017), the challenge that bitcoin users face is the risk of "insecure transactions and in particular that of dealing with dishonest traders". Unregulated systems attract people with its freedom. Bitcoin technology is one such example. Considering the rise in usage of such crypto-products across the world and in India, the governments should look at putting a policy framework in place immediately. In July 2017, China's central bank said initial coin offerings are illegal and asked all related fundraising activity to be halted immediately, issuing the strongest regulatory challenges made so far to the burgeoning market for digital token sales. The People's Bank of China mentioned in its website that it had completed investigations into ICOs and will strictly punish offerings in the future while penalizing legal violations in ones already completed. The regulator said that those who have already raised money must provide refunds, though it didn't specify how the money would be paid back to investors. It also said digital token financing and trading platforms are prohibited from doing conversions of coins with fiat currencies. Digital tokens can't be used as currency on the market and banks are forbidden from offering services to initial coin offerings (TOI, 2018).

A recurring challenge for bitcoin and other such so-called cryptocurrencies (crypto-products) is how to make them work in the real world. A Singapore-based startup says the answer is its VISA card. Thus, we see that TenX is pitching its debit card as an instant converter of multiple digital currencies into fiat money: the Rupee, Dollars, Yen, and Euros. The company takes a 2% cut from each transaction and had received orders for more than 10,000 cards. While transactions are capped at US$2,000 a year, users can apply to increase the limit if they undergo identity verification procedures. Bitcoin, the most popular cryptocurrency, slumped after reaching a record in June 2017 amid concerns about a split in two, only to recover as fears faded. The company has built an app that serves as a digital wallet connected to the VISA card so that when it is swiped at a café or restaurant, the merchant is paid in local currency, and the user's crypto account is debited. Co-founder Julian Hosp said transactions are processed immediately and it doesn't impose any charges on top of the conversion fee that is set by the so-called cryptocurrency exchanges, which typically is 0.15–0.2% (Agarwal, 2017). The card now supports eight digital currencies, including the lesser known dash and augur, and had set itself a target to offer about 11 of them by the end of the 2017. TenX currently processes transactions worth US$100,000 a month. By the end of 2018, it is targeting US$100 million in monthly transactions and a million users. We wonder what regulators globally have to say if such play cards are allowed to swam the markets and take over transactions. Would there be any sense to calibrate inflation using CPI, WPI, or CPE Deflator or any other such statistical means, when no trade or transaction is within the purview off any reporting system, like we see in Black Money transactions, commonly called *Hawala* in India (or Asia) (Bloomberg, 2017).

Badev and Chen (2014) wrote that bitcoins is a scheme designed to facilitate transfer of value. Unlike the traditional payment system which uses sovereign currencies or fiat currencies, the bitcoin has its own metric called the bitcoin with a small letter *b* abbreviated as *BTC*. The scheme implementation involves the use of cryptography, distributive algorithm, and incentive-driven behavior. Bitcoins are considered to be one of the most successful so-called virtual currency scheme designed and implemented by the software developer Santoshi Nakamoto in 2008. His idea was to produce a virtual currency independent of any central authority, transferable electronically, more or less instantly, with very low transaction fees. It has a bidirectional flow, that is, real currency that can be exchanged for bitcoins and vice-versa. It is expected to grow to be used as a currency at the global level to buy and sell virtual and real goods; however, it has still not achieved this in the last 10 years (decade) of its existence, as it is limited to a few select players. Bitcoins are divisible to eight decimal points enabling their use in any kind of transaction regardless of the value. Bitcoins are not pegged to any currency or commodity.

This software-driven virtual product (namely bitcoins) can be mined by anyone with strong computing skills. They are made through a self-limiting system called cryptocurrency mining, and the people who mine these coins are called miners. It is projected that 21 million bitcoins can be mined wherein approximately 11 million have already been mined and are in circulation. Bitcoin VCs are completely unregulated and decentralized. There is NO central bank that issues it, there is NO national mint, there is NO depositor insurance coverage, and there is NO asset backing for the so-called cryptocurrency (crypto-products). These crypto-products are self-contained and uncollateralized, which means that there is no precious metal that creates the so-called cryptocurrency (bitcoins). According to Nakomoto, the value of each bitcoin resides within each bitcoin itself, which is a totally flawed concept and defies the basic principal of a tenable asset class (see Section 6.1).

Given that the supply and demand of bitcoins is market determined and the fact that these are based on decentralized, peer-to-peer network, they have attained immense speculative value (Bloomberg, 2017); however, all this fails when it comes to be quantified as money/currency. This financially engineered innovation is an open-source (its controlling computer code is open to public view), peer-to-peer transaction that does not require a third-party intermediary such as PayPal or Visa and works on a digital platform which is completely electronic with no physical presence. This makes it to have the potential to emerge as a strong basis for a crypto-product to be used as a transaction means by a select few, as one sees the use of Casino Coins/Casino Playcards. For any product to emerge as money/currency, there has to be a central controlling agency that controls the supply of the currency which is pegged to real assets inducing and securing the value; however, with bitcoins, the network is completely decentralized, with all parts of transactions performed by the users of the system only beyond control of any government/central banking agency. In this market of bitcoins, the buyer and seller interact directly (peer-to-peer); however, the identities are encrypted, which means NO personal information is transferred from one to the other. On the one hand governments have identifications going beyond passport systems like the AADHAR Cards, Social Security Numbers, and others, and on the other hand, we see such crypto-products undermining the importance of such secure gateways in the name of privacy and illegitimate transactional efficiencies. It is usually said that a public ledger[5] maintains the full transaction record of every bitcoin exchanged and generated. However, with the emergence of so many varieties of crypto-products mirroring bitcoins, one is puzzled as to who manages this public ledger and how many of such ledgers are there (see Figures 2 and 3). Notwithstanding the test of

[5]Public ledger is also called a distributed ledger or a blockchain that is visible to all computers on the network but does not reveal any personal information about the involved parties.

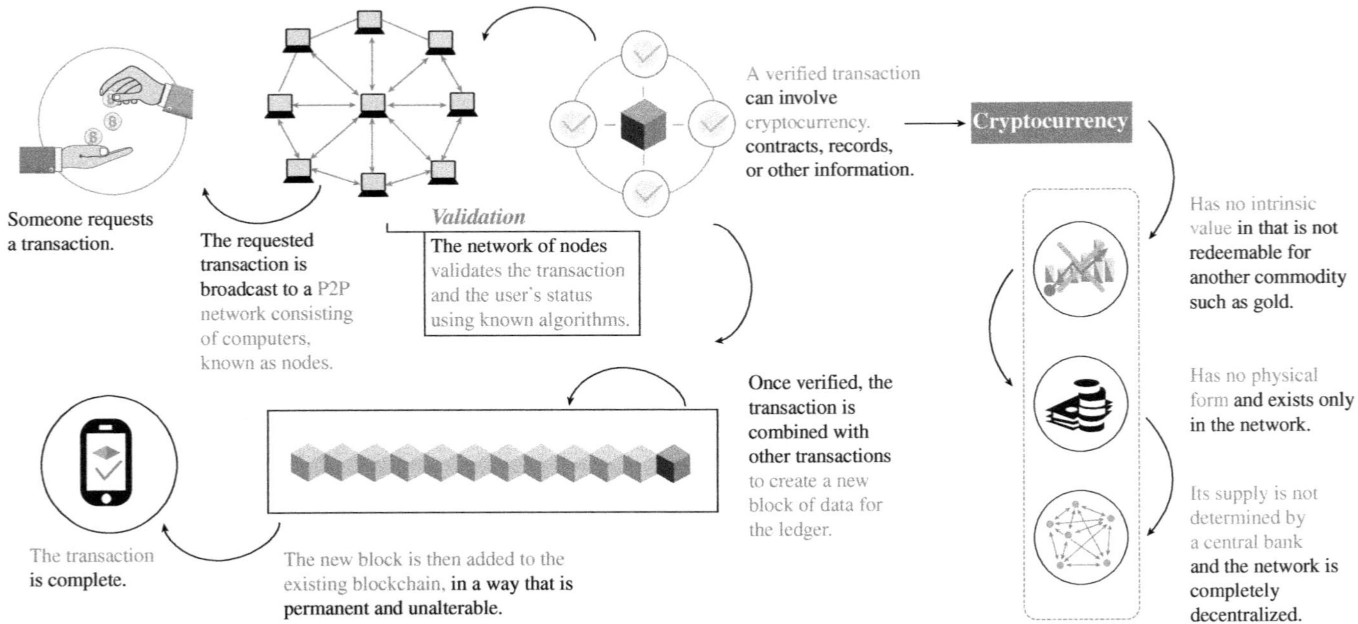

Figure 2: Virtual product (bitcoin) framework as a virtual transactional system.

Source: Badev and Chen (2014).

Notes: The bitcoin system is so private that it has NO traditional financial institutions involved in transactions. Bitcoin is also referred as the so-called cryptocurrency for its communication being secure from the view of third parties. The simplest means to acquire bitcoins is to exchange the real money, like rupee, dollar, yen, euros, for bitcoins on an online exchange (e.g., Okcoin, Coinbase, and Kraken). Anyone can obtain bitcoins in exchange for the sale of goods or services, where the merchant can accept bitcoin as a means of payment for the good and services supplied by him. Thirdly, to acquire new bitcoins, one can serve as a miner and mine bitcoins by using one's knowledge of computer processing power to successfully verify the validity of new network transactions. Purchased or mined bitcoins can be stored in a digital wallet on the personal computer offline (known as cold storage) or at an online wallet service (hot storage). A wallet is a small personal database that one can store on one's computer drive (i.e., cold storage), on one's smart phone, tablet, or somewhere in the cloud (hot storage). When the currency is stored online, there are high chances of it being lost. The bitcoin transaction uses cryptography to verify transactions, process payments, and control the supply of bitcoins. It uses two cryptographic schemes which are digital signatures and cryptographic hashes. Digital signatures permit the exchange of accurate payment instructions between the parties of a transaction. Cryptographic hashes are used for recording transactions in the public ledgers.

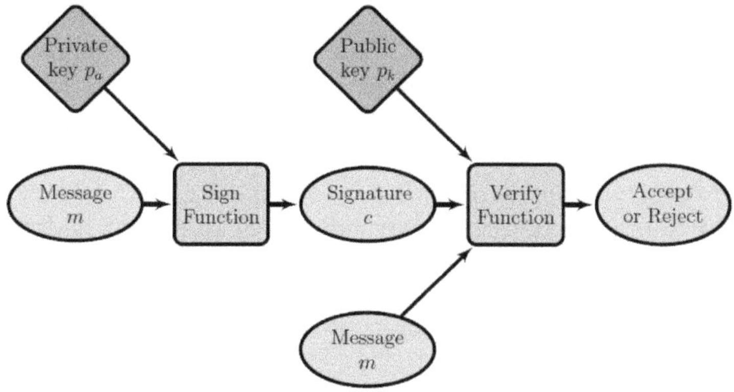

Figure 3: Digital signatures permit the exchange of accurate payment instructions.

Notes: Digital signatures ensure the authenticity of the transaction between the sender and receiver by ensuring authentication, non-repudiation, and integrity of the message. Digital signatures involve public key encryption which involves creation of a public and private key. Badev and Chen (2014) explain the process of digital signatures as a process where the sign function combines the message with the private key of the sender to produce signature c as indicated in Figure 3. The signature c carries the identity of the sender with his/her private key. The receiver then receives the message and verifies that the message has come from the sender with the help of a public key. The sign and verify functions are publicly accessible. The members of the bitcoin system can verify the transaction with the message m, signature c, and public key p_k. Then cryptographic hash function converts the input string into an output string. Each message is converted into a hash. As the message changes, so would the output. Small changes in the message would also change the hash significantly. The output of hash function is random but deterministic. Bitcoins reside in bitcoin system as bitcoin address. The capability of bitcoins one can send from the bitcoin address is dependent on digital signatures that involve pairs of public and private keys. Each bitcoin address is indexed by a unique public id which is an alphanumeric number that corresponds to the public key. The private key is the counterpart of the public key. Any payment message has to be signed with a proper private key to be valid.

time, these crypto-products (like bitcoins) lack the possibility of natural transferability to the heirs or holder of the asset, as done when any asset/currency goes to the heirs of the individuals/institutions having the rights to use the benefits from the said currency/asset.

Some of the features built in the virtual products (like bitcoins) framework as virtual transactional system that set it apart from the government-backed currencies are as follows:

i. *Decentralized*: Bitcoin network is not controlled by a central authority. Machines work together on every machine a bitcoin can be mined.

ii. *Easy to set up*: A bitcoin address in seconds, no questions asked, and with no fees payable, for now. Historically, as soon as a product gets established and margins squeeze, charges on transactions are expected to set in or even in the case where monopoly situations arise.
iii. *Anonymous as user information is encrypted*: Users can hold multiple bitcoin addresses which are not linked to names, addresses, or other personally identifying information, which is also expected to change as more reforms and finer forms are expected forthcoming with emergence of regulations or frauds being surfaced (TNN, 2018b).
iv. *Transparent yet opaque*: Bitcoin stores details of every single transaction that ever happened in the network in a huge version of a general ledger, called the blockchain. However, no one individual or even the regulator can access the information without prior approval from the exchange/the transactional operator, which brings the socioeconomic setup at risk inducing national security threats and use by illegitimate, illegal, unorganized market operators (Reuters, 2018b).
v. *Transaction fees are miniscule*: Bank charges are higher for international transfers, whereas bitcoin transfer charges are very small, which is expected, to change as well. The reduction in banks and monopoly situations existing in the banking industry due to financial inclusion drives has driven bank charges to go sky rocketing globally both in developed and emerging markets (Agarwal, 2016; Agarwal 2017).
vi. *Speed of transfer*: Money can be sent anywhere, and it will arrive minutes later, as soon as the bitcoin network processes the payment. All virtual transactions have this efficiency factor as seen since mid-1990s after the emergence of online banks. The world has not forgotten the ill-effects of online banks and stock markets in USA were used by Osama bin Laden to finance his terrorist operations and transfer the proceeds through online banks across over six nations within a few minutes, taking full advantage of efficient online transfer NEFT/SWIFT mechanism. Recently, India also saw the rise of NPA to over 13,000 crores by a single firm of Mr. Nirav Modi, having sought bank clearances (LOUs) for funds transferred through bank branches using these systems not tagged with the mainframe banking software,

leading to the creation of huge NPAs in the consortium of banks by a single firm.

vii. *Non-reputable*: Once the bitcoins are transferred, they cannot be returned back unless the other user intends to send them back to you. As long as there are markets to accept the product, this is not a critical factor. However, such virtual currencies defy tenable asset class classification; hence, the world will observe more frauds by fake operators, with no legal recourse. This will be seen more in developing, underdeveloped, and emerging markets than in developed economies around the world, given the weak legal frameworks and huge cash economies (including black money presence).

These strong features outline the efficiency of the crypto-product (so-called cryptocurrency) market scenarios existing today. It is pertinent to note that whenever the cryptocurrencies are introduced by governments through central banks backed by national assets (both public and private) as the virtual currencies of the future being a tenable asset class money/currency, the M5 money supply framework will help give it the legal sanctity and remove the anomalies which exist with the VPs (like bitcoins) framework thereby making it one of the more innovative financially engineered true currency of tomorrow.

7.2.1. *Recent developments in bitcoins (crypto-product): Why, how, and for what*

As outlined earlier, one can buy bitcoins (a cryptoproduct) from exchanges or directly from people via cryptominer marketplaces (Upadhyay and Vishwanathan, 2018; Jatley, 2018; Dave and Shukla, 2018). Payment for such purchase of bitcoins can be made through coins, debit cards, credit cards, wire transfers, or by using other crypto-products via banks in the countries where it has still not been made illegal/illegitimate (TNN, 2017; Agarwal, 2017a, 2018a, 2018b, 2018c, 2018d; TOI, 2018; Shetty, 2018; Reuters, 2018b). However, it is found that more than 72 countries (namely Argentina, Australia, Bangladesh, Belgium, Bolivia, Bosnia and Herzegovina, Brazil, Bulgaria, Canada, Colombia, Chile, China (Mainland), China (Hong Kong SAR), Croatia, Cyprus, Czech Republic, Denmark, Ecuador, Euro Zone — ECB (Reuters, 2017b), Estonia, Finland, France, Germany, Greece, Iceland,

India, Indonesia, Ireland, Italy, Israel, Jamaica, Jordan, Kyrgyzstan, Korea (South), Lebanon, Lithuania, Luxembourg, Malaysia, Malta, Mexico, Macedonia, Namibia, Netherlands, New Zealand, Nicaragua, Niger, Nigeria, Norway, Pakistan, Philippines, Poland, Portugal, Romania, Russia, Saudi Arabia, Singapore, Slovakia, Slovenia, South Africa, Spain, Sweden, Switzerland, Taiwan, Thailand, Turkey, Ukraine, United Kingdom, United States (some states), Vietnam and Zimbabwe) have already declared this as illegal/illegitimate means of crypto-product either completely banning it by declaring it an illicit and/or restrained by warming people NOT to trade or transact in such crypto-products till further clarification comes from regulators (Wikipedia, 2018; Dave and Shukla, 2018; Archana, 2018; Reuters, 2018a; Nappinai, 2018; Bloomberg-ET, 2018b). It has been found that many make payment via cash in place of credit cards/bank transfers to keep these transactions outside the purview of regulators. In the USA, Coinbase and Circle offer purchases with credit cards; however, buyers still prefer to do cash transactions. Bittylicious, CoinCorner, and Coinbase offer this service in the UK, accepting 3D secure-enabled credit and debit cards on the VISA and MasterCard networks.

To store bitcoins that are purchased, one can purchase wallets/vaults. A wallet can be (a) a software wallet stored on the hard drive of the computer; (b) an online web-based service (c) a "vault" service that keeps your bitcoins protected offline or a multi-signature wallet that uses a number of keys to protect the account. Technically, one does not store bitcoins. What one stores is secure digital keys used to access your public bitcoin addresses and sign transactions. This information is stored in a bitcoin wallet. Though it seems secure, however, we would witness large number of thefts, hackers, and frauds in due course with other regulatory sanctions by governments in trying to keep the financial ecosystem secure and healthy for people (Bloomberg, 2017c; Kharif, 2018). In the last few years, we have seen the emergence of six main types of wallets: desktop, mobile, online/web, paper, cloud, and hardware: (a) Desktop Wallet[6];

[6]Original bitcoin client like Bitcoin Core can be installed on your computer which enables you to create a bitcoin address for sending and receiving the virtual currency and to store the private key for it. Other desktop wallets include MultiBit that runs on Windows, Mac OSX, and Linux. Hive is an OS X-based wallet with some unique features. An

(b) Mobile Wallet[7]; (c) Online or Web Wallet[8]; (d) Paper Wallet[9]; (e) Cloud Wallet[10]; (f) Hardware Wallet[11]. The means to secure a bitcoin wallet is to encrypt it, back it up, use multi-signature transactions, and lastly to take it offline. So far the exchanges and wallets have emerged as the best option to engage in the regular trade of bitcoins. The largest full-trading exchanges by volume are Bitfinex (Hong Kong), Bitstamp (US),

---

extrasecurity-enabled, tailored desktop wallet is Armory. Others that focus on anonymity include Darkwallet.

[7]These wallets come handy when one is traveling on the street and wishes to purchase something. Running as an application on the smart phone, the wallet can store the private keys for a user's bitcoin addresses and enable the user to pay for things directly with his or her phone. Mobile wallets include the Android-based Bitcoin wallet, Mycelium, Xapo, and Blockchain. You also have browser-based wallets like the CoinPunk and the Aegis Bitcoin Wallet, which supports Android smart watches.

[8]The biggest advantage of a web-based wallet is that it can be used from anywhere anytime through any access device. The biggest disadvantage is that it gives the private keys to the web wallet provider, which takes the control away from the user's hand. Coinbase, an integrated wallet/bitcoin exchange, operates its online wallet worldwide. Users in the US and Europe can buy bitcoins through its exchange services. Circle offers users worldwide the chance to store, send, receive, and buy bitcoins. Currently, only US citizens are able to link bank accounts to deposit funds, but credit and debit cards are also an option for users in other countries (Shetty, 2018). Blockchain also hosts a popular web-based wallet, and Strongcoin offers a hybrid wallet, which lets the user encrypt the private address keys before sending them to its servers — encryption is carried out in the browser. Xapo aims to provide the convenience of an simple bitcoin wallet with the added security of a cold-storage vault.

[9]There are many sites that are offering paper wallets. Paper wallets will generate a bitcoin address for the user and create an image containing two QR codes: one is the public address that user can use to receive bitcoins; the other is the private key, which user can use to spend bitcoins stored at that address. These wallets are safe from standard cyberattacks.

[10]The whole system works via a Cloud setup, which is accessible to the select few wanting to use the service. The advantage of a cloud-based wallet is that it can be used from anywhere, anytime and through any device. The advantage over online/web Wallet is that the private keys to the wallet remain confidential and less prone to hackers, keeping the control in the user's hand.

[11]Limited in number, these devices can hold private keys electronically and facilitate payments like Trezor hardware wallet and Ledger USB wallet. Mycelium, Cryptolabs, and BitStash currently have a hardware wallets in development. Nymi sports a wristband from Boinym, which is likely to act as a bitcoin wallet and uses the heart rhythm as a security key.

BTC-e (unknown), Kraken (US), Huobi (China and Hong Kong), OKCoin (China), and BTCC (China). Once a user has set up his or her exchange account, then they need to link an existing bank account and arrange to move funds between it and user's new exchange account via wire transfer for purchasing or selling bitcoins. Unlike the usual security exchanges, these exchanges are not regulated, and if they go out of business, the user is likely to lose all their hard-earned money (Upadhyay and Vishwanathan, 2018). Bitcoins in most countries do not a have a legal status and hence their recoveries cannot be challenged in any court within the country or internationally. Also given the fact that the source of production, hosting the wallet, and transactions is unknown, the necessary knowledge regarding which rules to apply and which rules to not apply is not available. The regulators are also at a standstill (in a myst) on what to do with such transactions/trades (Schmidt, 2018). This growth in this fashion is a key threat to central banks, monetary systems, individual wealth and to the national security (Agarwal, 2017a, 2018a, 2018b, 2018c, 2018d).

News reports indicate that the purchase of bitcoins face-to-face without the hassle of linking the bank accounts with the local traders has raised concerns for use for money laundering black/illegal money (Agarwal and Agarwal, 2004, 2006; TNN, 2017; Rangan, 2017; Upadhyay and Vishwanathan, 2018; HT, 2018; Bloomberg-ET, 2018; Reuters, 2018b). Interestingly, *LocalBitcoins* have emerged as the primary site, where such transactions are arranged and the prices are negotiated. The site also provides an escrow service as an added layer of protection for both parties. In case the user is meeting face-to-face, then they need to have a wallet and Internet connection to verify the transaction. Another such site is *Meetup.com,* which arranges for meeting in groups to exchange bitcoins. A 5–10% premium over the exchange prices is found in face-to-face transactions; however, they are all confidential and beyond the reach of any regulator. The underlying current for such illicit transactions ends up doing more damage than good to the society, as seen with various such products grown and in existence worldwide in the last 200 years. Another vent for purchase of bitcoins has been the bitcoin ATMs, in which a user inserts cash and either scans the mobile wallet QR code or receives a paper receipt with the codes necessary to load the bitcoins onto the user's wallet. There are presently 2034 bitcoin ATMs that on an average charge 9.44% (see Figures 4–7).

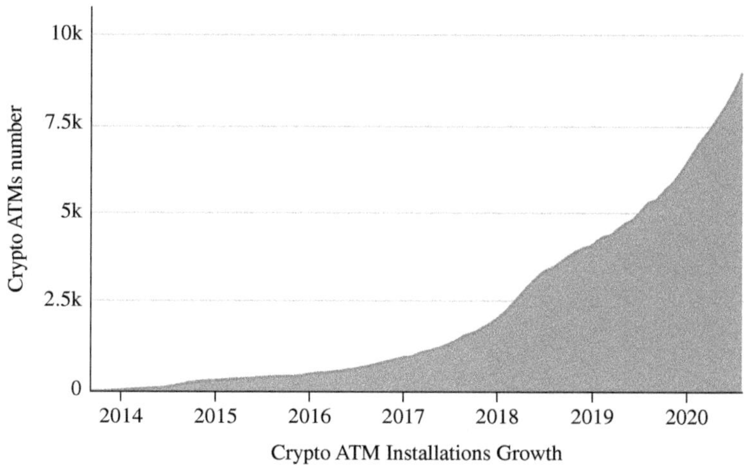

Figure 4: Emergence of number of Bitcoin ATMs over the 6 years.

Source: https://coinatmradar.com/charts/#growth.

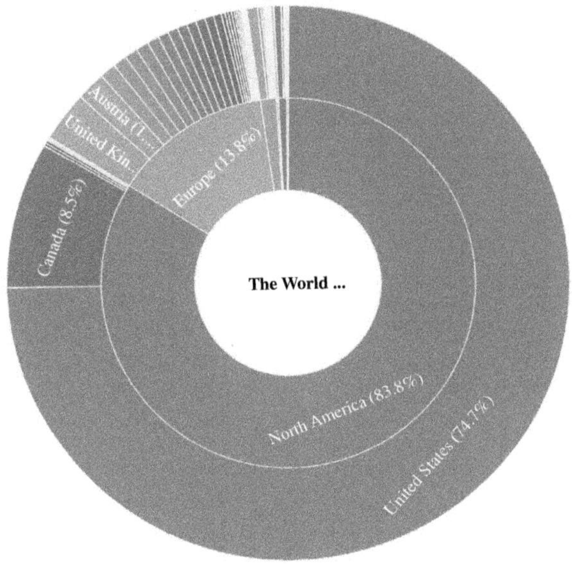

Figure 5: Crypto ATM (including Bitcoin) Distribution by Continents and Countries.

Source: https://coinatmradar.com/charts/#growth.

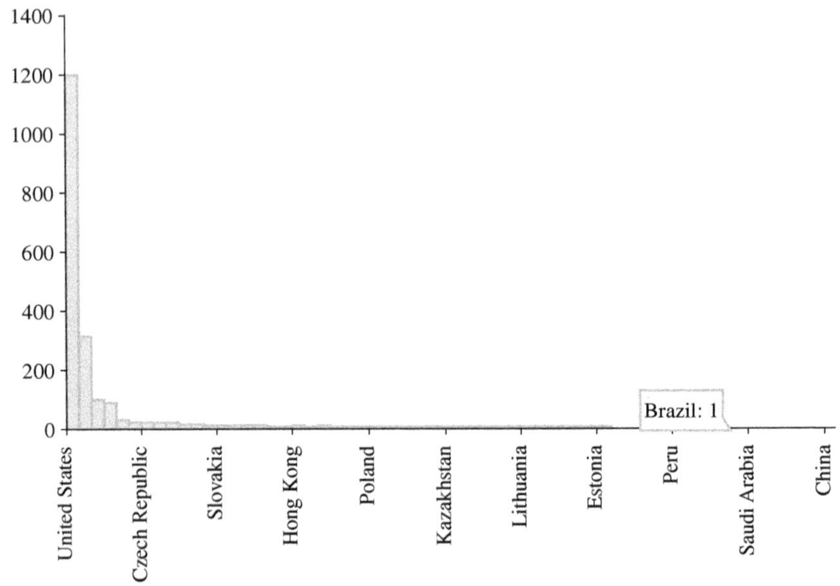

Figure 6: Bitcoin ATMs country wise over the 4 years.

Source: https://coinatmradar.com/charts/#growth.

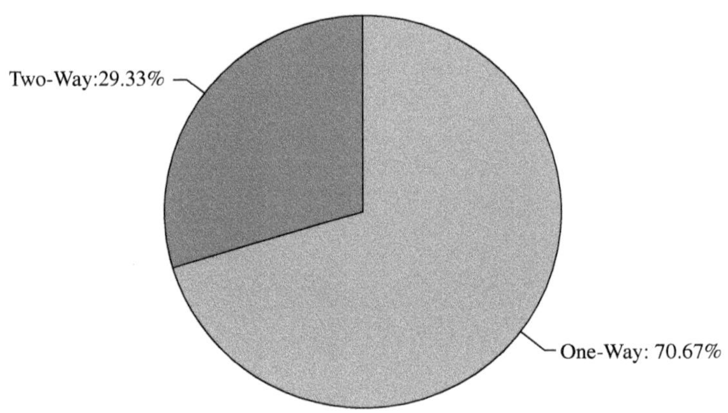

Figure 7: Bitcoin ATMs one way versus two way system.

Source: https://coinatmradar.com/charts/#growth.

Smith and Rosevear (2017) have outlined that the benefits of using crypto-products like bitcoins or digital transactional framework include (a) the reduction of transactional frictions; (b) the ability to transact across borders; (c) the elimination of counterparty risk assessment; (d) regulatory and monetary policy freedom; and (e) access to money for the "unbanked", user anonymity and ledger transparency. The future of money as digital (VCs and crypto-products such as bitcoin) is generally seen as the first early stage of that broad; however, as this financial innovation defies the basic principal of an tenable asset class, cryptocurrencies are launched by central banks, these benefits come bundled with illusionary high risk bringing forth loss of wealth, distortion in economic ecosystem, and threat to national security.

The key parameters one must assess as the potential before investing in virtual products (like bitcoins) are as follows:

i. *Value Basis* (Does asset have value? What forces determine its price? Will such forces endure over time?).
ii. *Stability* (Is volatility reasonably low and steady? Is there some predictability of how wide price swings could be? Does the asset show wild swings in value?).
iii. *Liquidity* (Is the market large enough that bids to buy are easily met with offers to sell and vice versa? What happens when the base/operator disappears? What is the sanctity of transaction?).
iv. *Informational Efficiency* (Are VCs like bitcoins resembling assets class? Will it respond to new information in a predictable way, or is it random? What is the source of information and is it legitimate?).
v. *Accessibility* (Can you invest and how? Can it be purchased and traded? Are products such as ETFs available that offer divisible investment through the standard channels such as a brokerage?).
vi. *Regulator* (Who regulates? Who controls? Is there a recourse? In case of a dispute, where would one go? Is there legal sanctity? What is the taxable liability?).
vii. *Transferability and Ownership* (Can its ownership be transferred? Can heir(s) gain access to its rightful ownership after the death (natural/accidental) of the primary holder? Can any holder of the

crypto product claim ownership, even if he is not the primary holder? Who is the rightful owner — a thief, a hacker, a miner, or the purchaser?).

Given that the price for a bitcoin is not driven by any intrinsic value but by the trust and faith buyer and sellers have in exchanging the digital currency, it is a pure gamble (Das and Menon, 2017; Kumar, 2018). In many countries including India, the tax authorities (ET, 2017; Sikarwar, 2017; ET Wealth, 2018) are treating the revenue gains from bitcoins to be taxed under capital gains from speculative trade/markets/products (like gambling, casino, betting, horse race, and others) (Agarwal, 1988; Jatley, 2018; Dave and Shukla, 2018; TNN, 2018c; Dave, 2018). The market value is linked to the digital economy and digital crypto-product which at any moment can vanish in thin air (this has been observed to happen in many cases worldwide in the last 4–5 years). Given the growth in the market and more people seeking sudden revenue gains, bitcoins are increasingly becoming more stable and liquid; however, they are still by far the highest risky product, given there being NO legal sanctity. However, we see some exchanges in US and other parts of the world where bitcoin bid and ask spreads as quoted on dealer exchange sites is approximately 0.7% approximately one-10th of what it was in 2013. Bitcoin ATMs have also emerged in the world from a handful in 2014 to 900 in 2018 (see Figure 7). The average monthly trade for bitcoins over the past 3 years is US$740 million (1.8 million bitcoin units). Market capitalization across major US exchanges is US$16 billion. These figures seem alarmingly fascinating (see Figure 8); however, it is quite like the showrooms/shops/business operations which are fly-by-night operators as seen in cities like New York, London, Paris, Delhi, and many other major cities around the world having a lifespan of a week or two. The world has seen success stories of business of gambling, flesh trading, drugs, killing, thefts, smuggling, arms, cartels, and many others showing extremely high revenue streams. It is also well known that many small economies have adopted some of these as a prime source of income and sustainability given no other meaningful factor of production. Wonder if revenues or profits outside the legal framework leading for threats to erosion of wealth; socioeconomic frameworks and national security are to be judged and allowed on such basis. We have tried to present these figures about

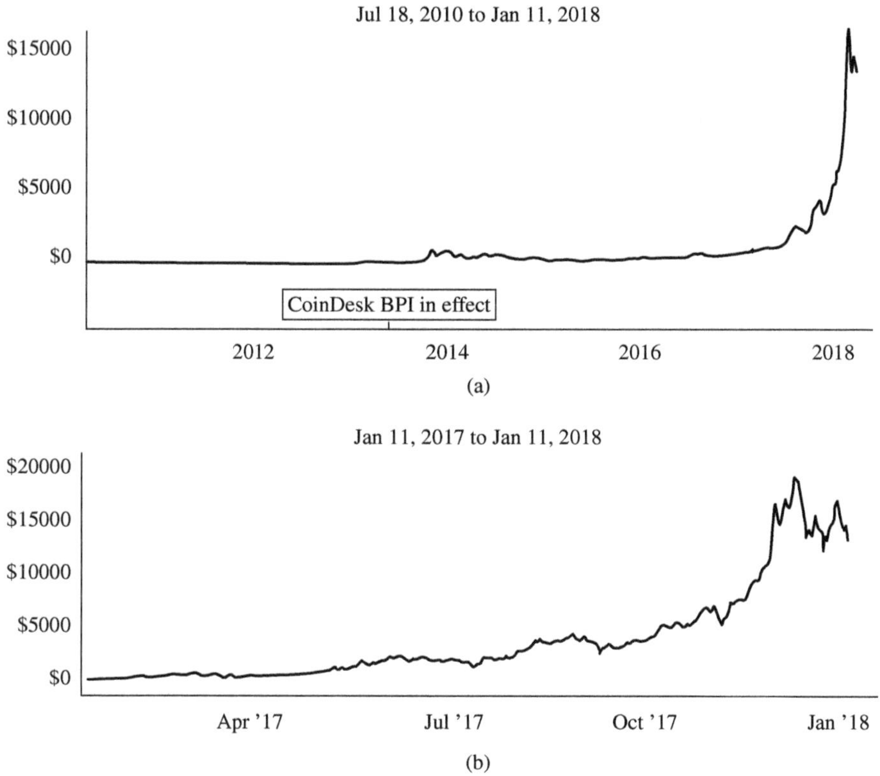

Figure 8: Bitcoin trading value between 2010–18 and January 2017–18.

Source: Coindesk (Retrieved www.coindesk.com in 2018).

crypto-products (like bitcoins) to enlighten and highlight the fact that profits/revenue streams in the short run beyond the legal frameworks can cause more harm than benefits (like does corruption, black money, and illicit transactions).

Ali *et al.* (2014) indicate that the valuation of a digital currency that can, at least in principle, be used as a medium of exchange ought to take a wide variety of factors into considerations such as the following:

i. The expected real return of holding the digital currency (that is, the nominal interest rate minus expected price inflation), relative to other options (Agarwal and Agarwal, 2005; Agarwal, 2017a; Agarwal *et al.*, 2016, 2017, 2018).

ii. Any risks associated with holding the digital currency relative to other currencies, including risks of theft or fraud, rigging, artificial valuation, and price volatility (Bloomberg, 2017c, 2018a; Kharif, 2018; ET, 2018).

iii. The relative benefits of using the digital currency as a medium of exchange when compared to traditional systems, including availability, transaction fees, and degrees of anonymity (Agarwal, 2017b, 2017c).

iv. Any time constraints or costs associated with switching wealth between the digital currency and more traditional assets (like Rs., US$, Euro, gold, silver, or any other asset class).

v. Any non-monetary concerns, such as an ideological preference for one particular currency.

vi. A view on how much other people value the currency (based on the above factors) and how this is expected to change in the future.

vii. Regulatory prudence and legal sanctity (TNN, 2017; Rangan, 2017).

A number of funds have emerged offering bitcoin investment (Sikarwar, 2017; Christopher and Bansal, 2018; Pillai, 2018a) like (a) Bitcoin Investment Trust; (b) Bitcoin Capital; (c) Global Advisors Bitcoin Investment; (d) Pantera Capital; (e) Gemini Trading, and others. With increased payment options, crypto-products can offer a multitude of benefits. In the recent past, several retail giants in a couple of countries have begun accepting crypto-products. While many are making large fortunes in crypto-products, it is important to remember that due to the massive variability in prices and short-term growth, there is still a large amount of risk. Therefore, proper caution is advised and there is a need for modelling M5 in the money supply basket for central banks to launch their own currency denominated cryptocurrencies.

On August 8, 2017, the website Coinmarketcap listed 1037 different types of the so-called cryptocurrencies (crypto-products), 626 of which have listed market. Some of those that are listed include Litecoin (LTC),[12]

[12]Litecoin, launched in the year 2011, was among the initial cryptocurrencies following bitcoin and was often referred to as "Silver to Bitcoins gold". It is a peer-to-peer crypto-product and open-source software project released under the MI/II license, creation, and transfer of coins is based on an open source of cryptographic protocol and is not managed by any central authority. It can be sent globally around the world almost instantly, for a

Ethereum,[13] Peercoin,[14] Z cash,[15] Dash coin,[16] Ripple,[17] Monero,[18],

very low fee. Bitcoin vs litecoin: One of the main differences between bitcoin and Litecoin concerns the total number of coins which each crypto-product can produce. In fact, the minimum quantity of transferable bitcoin is one hundred millionth of a bitcoin (0.0000000 1, bitcoins) known colloquially as one "Satoshi".

[13]Ethereum is a decentralized platform that runs smart contracts: applications that run exactly as programmed without any possibility of downtime, censorship, fraud or third-party interference. Ethereum Wallet is a desktop Ethereum Wallet. Ethereum Wallet has integrated with shapeshift, which makes it easy to accept bitcoins and other altcoin payments directly to your Ethereum Wallet as either.

[14]Peercoin also known as PP coin or PPC, is a peer-to-peer crypto-product utilizing both proof-of-stake and proof-of-work systems. Peercoin is based on a August 12, 2012 paper, which listed the authors as Scott Nadal and Sunny King. Sunny King, who also created Primecoin, is a pseudonym, Peercoin is the third most capitalized crypto-product at around 120mn dollars. Peercoin seeks to be the most secure cryptocoin at the lowest cost, by rewarding all users for strengthening the network.

[15]Z cash was launched on October 28, 2016, and had remarkable achievements. More than just anything, the assessment of Z cash is just as strong as the trust so that the Z cash utilized a precise proof to secure the network called zk-SNARKs — or evidence of development. It offers privacy and selective transparency.

[16]Dash (formerly known as Darkcoin and xcoin) is an open-source, peer-to-peer cryptocurrency that offers instant transactions, private transactions, and taken fungibility. It was rebranded from "Darkcoin" to "Dash" on March 25, 2015, a portmanteau of "digital cash". Dashcoin (Dash) is an automatically mutating anonymous crypto-product. Dashcoin is a next-generation anonymous cryptocurrency and the first automatically mutating crypto-product created with cryptonote technology.

[17]Ripple is a real-time gross settlement system (RTGS) currency exchange and remittance network by Ripple. Also called Ripple Transaction Protocol (RTXP) or Ripple Protocol, it is built upon a distributed open-source Internet protocol, consensus ledger, and native currency called XRP (ripples). "XRP" is the second largest market cap coin. Eobot has cloud mining of BTC that can automatically be converted into XRP. Ripple or XRP is a payment protocol that functions as a payment system, currency exchange, and a remittance network and works with fiat currencies, crypto-products, and commodities.

[18]Monero is a secure, private, untraceable currency. It is open source and freely available to all. With Monero, you are your own bank. Only you control and are responsible for your frauds; your accounts and transactions are kept private from prying eyes. Monero (XMR) was created on April 18, 2014 and focused on privacy decentralization and scalability. Unlike many cryptocurrencies that are derivatives of bitcoin, Monero is based on Cryptonote protocol and possesses significant algorithmic differences relating to blockchain obfuscation. Monero experienced rapid growth in market capitalization and

Dogcoin,[19] and Potcoin.[20] This clearly highlights the extensive growth in various forms of VPs launched in the informal markets.

Vanuatu South Pacific archipelago is an interesting case where some 80 islands recently surfaced. Here outsiders are allowed to use the volatile crypto-products to apply for the so-called investment citizenship (Bloomberg, 2017a), which is a clear reflection of threat to the securities of nations worldwide. News outlined that Fork over the equivalent of about US$280,000 and their family of up to four can receive passports from what the New Economics Foundation, a UK-based think tank, calls the fourth-happiest country in the world. Vanuatu isn't the only island that offers citizenship for price (the list includes Antigua, Grenada, Malta, and St. Kitts and Nevis), but it's the first to allow payments via bitcoin. Vanuatu citizenship offers several advantages given that the country has the 34th most powerful passport in the world, providing visa-free visits to 116 other countries. It falls right below Panama and Paraguay and above Dominica; the UK is a tie at third place, the US at fourth, Russia at 40th. The country also has no income, inheritance, or corporate tax (Agarwal, 1988). It's not even customary to tip there, according to the Vanuatu Tourism Office. The archipelago is relatively accessible: about a three and a half-hour flight from Sydney to Port Vila, the capital. There are many regions and countries in the world which have harbored on illicit trade and commodities. These would also welcome such crypto-products (so-called cryptocurrencies) as a medium of safe-haven transaction.

If we look at the case of New York, virtual products are considered a commodity and individuals can open an online bitcoin account. The New

---

transaction volume during the year 2016, partly due to adoption in 2016 by major darknet market AlphaBay (closed in July 2017 by law enforcement).

[19]A dog or a black dog was a coin in the Caribbean of Queen Anne of Great Britain and was made of pewter or copper. It was typically worth 1 half pence or 1/12 of a dollar. A dog and a stamp were not necessarily of equal value.

[20]Potcoin was developed to remove the need for cash transaction between marijuana consumers and dispensaries. It was released on January 21, 2014 by entrepreneurs from Montreal, Canada, who hoped the cryptocurrency would be used by the legal cannabis industry the world over. Three months after it took off, the Potcoin development team finally revealed their identities. In April 2014, co-founders and developers Joel Vaffe and Nick Iversen delivered a talk about Potcoin at the New York cryptocurrency convention. As of November 2014, there are 44 merchants accepting Potcoin as a payment method for products or services. Marijuana is still illegal in most countries.

York State requires businesses engaged in virtual products activities that have a place of business or provide services to persons located in New York, to obtain a license for digital currency activities known as BitLicense. The BitLicense was introduced in 2015 by the New York State Department of Financial Services (NYDFS). It is expensive to apply for a license with non-refundable fee of US$5,000 and other legal paper work requirement which may cost further between US$5,000 and US$100,000. The BitLicense includes several obligations including hiring a compliance officer, consumer protection, anti-money laundering (AML), cybersecurity, business continuity, disaster recovery, and capital requirements. The first license was received by Circle in 2015 followed by Ripple and Coinbase in 2016 and 2017. Many companies like Genesis-Mining, Kraken, ShapeShift, and Bitfinex moved out of New York as they did not want to comply with the requirements. Also on January 9th, 2018, a new bill was submitted to Arizona Senate to allow people to pay their taxes in bitcoins which was moved by Senator Warren Petersen and co-sponsored by three other lawmakers. The American states of Idaho and Alaska have issued warning on investment in bitcoins. On December 27, 2017, Poloneix, an US-based exchange, revealed that it would require all its accounts to maintain Know Your Customer (Agarwal and Agarwal, 2004) details in order. A reverse trend has begun in USA as well to restrict or bar such crypto-products, given the global response from central banks and economies.

However, in 2016, Bank of England in its working paper identified these currencies and blockchain technology as both an opportunity and challenge for the central banks. It also recognized that bitcoins or any other digital currencies (crypto-products) are less likely to be accepted as common forms of money and give rise to any banking systems based on virtual currencies; hence, it may be a far cry before these currencies can affect the macro-economic stability of any economy.

Since May 2017 IIF Professors have been vocal in speaking at various forums, through their research works, and in interviews on TV channels — Lok Sabha TV, Rajya Sabha TV, Delhi Doordarshan TV (DD India TV, DD News TV, DD National TV) — and radio channels urging the Government of India, Reserve Bank of India (RBI), and in meeting with governors of central banks of different regions of the worlds to come forward to make a formal statement on virtual products (like bitcoins) and such virtual transactional platforms being "Not Legal Tenders" as they defy the basic concept of tenable asset class given their not being launched by any central bank/regulatory body and their leading to erosion of wealth of the common man causing serious turbulence in the economy.

Welcomingly on January 13, 2018, Bank of Indonesia published a press release that the payment made in crypto-products (so-called crypto-currencies) are not legitimate as they do not comply with 2011 Currency Act. Bank Indonesia also warned "all parties" that buying, selling, or trading cryptocurrencies come with "high risks", as they are "highly volatile" and do not have backing from an authority or underlying assets to support prices. Countries including the UK, India, Russia, and many others have recently cautioned investors and traders over the perceived risks involved in cryptocurrencies (Shetty and Pillai, 2018). On February 1, 2018, the Finance Minister Mr. Arun Jaitley said while presenting the Union Budget 2018–2019 in the Lok Sabha that bitcoins are not legal tenders stating that *The government does not consider crypto currencies as legal tender or coin and (will) take all measures to eliminate the use of crypto assets …* (Jatley, 2018; Dave and Shukla, 2018; Nappinai, 2018). It is heartening to note that many of the central banks are now talking about creating their own national cryptocurrencies (including US, India, Venezuela, China, and Ukraine).

7.3. *Digital money Bitcoin — The new Hawala*

A *Hawala* is a system of transferring money and property in a parallel arrangement avoiding the traditional banking system. It is a simple way of money laundering (Agarwal and Agarwal, 2004, 2006; Agarwal *et al.*, 2008; Agarwal, 2017a, 2018a, 2018b, 2018c, 2018d; FATF, 2014l Bloomberg-ET, 2018; HT, 2018) and is banned in India. But a new, hi-tech form of *Hawala* has appeared as the digital currency — Bitcoin. Bitcoin, the digital coin, dominates the crypto-product markets among all. It has gained notice both because of its skyrocketing value (from less than a cent in early 2010 to around coming close to US$20,000, bitcoins value crashed to around US$13,600 in the end of December 2017) and because it is frequently a key player in hacking and black market-related stories (TNN, 2017), from the looting of nearly half a billion dollars in coins from the exchange in 2014 to the early 2017 demand for payment in bitcoin in "Wannacry ransom ware attack" and others in the last 5 years.

The digital economy may well be the future. Transactions through bitcoins have been allowed in the US, the EU, Japan, and Singapore, but there is enough effort being made to control the bitcoin economy (Reuters,

2018). In this context, there is no law yet in India. The bitcoin's shadow was evident in the supply of money for the 2015 Paris terrorist attacks, UK Healthcare System Attack in 2017, Worldwide Hacking Attack in 2017, UK Bitcoin Robbery 2017 (TOI, 2018), and many others. The EU is keen to bring the bitcoin under control (Reuters, 2018). The inter-governmental financial action task force in Paris reported in 2015 that some terrorist websites encouraged sympathizers to donate in bitcoins. US anti-terrorism officials are also reportedly anxious about the way how the Islamic State is accumulating millions of dollars through bitcoins. Though there were legal provisions to enable organizations dealing in crypto-products getting registered in New York, however the New York State Government has already passed a bill prohibiting bitcoin. Countries like Canada and Australia have brought anti-money laundering and anti-terrorism laws to restrain such virtual products/crypto-products (so called cryptocurrencies) within the pool of more than 72 countries listed above.

New regulations may soon come up in India and globally (TNN, 2017). In the last decade we saw that the rising global acceptance of the blockchain technology by global financial institutes and government agencies had helped gain investor confidence; however, this is a reversing trend now. Vijay Kumar (CEO at Belfrics Global) said that "Several government agencies are working on the evolution of block chain and cryptocurrencies. Investments in the digital currency have been rewarding for investors, although the valuation slipped recently after Beijing regulators forced the closure of BTC China, one of the world's biggest exchanges for the bitcoins. Otherwise, returns have quadrupled in 2017. The bitcoin rupee swap rate is now trading around 2.51 lakh, about four times higher than the December-end level of 64,000 in 2016".

Controlling terrorist funding has been one major reason for Government of India's demonetization initiative. If India fails to regulate bitcoin (and its variants), this new *Hawala*, may ironically become the easy way of funding terrorism. The government should have proper control over such crypto-products (like bitcoin) in the interest of the economy and the security of the country. Investments in cryptocurrency have come under the radar of tax authorities and investigation agencies amid concern that they could have become conduits for illicit flows (Sikarwar, 2017; ET, 2017; TNN, 2018c; HT, 2018), money laundering (Agarwal and Agarwal, 2004, 2006; Agarwal *et al.*, 2008; Bloomberg-ET, 2018), and the movement of black money. A Special Investigation Team (SIT) on black money has been appointed by the Supreme Court, which has expressed worries about the so-called cryptocurrency (crypto-products) and suggested curbs on their trading in its draft report. *There is concern on the way it operates ... Some unaccounted money could be flowing into these* said a government official aware of the matter. Policymakers are now looking at the issue closely. Income tax authorities and the Enforcement Directorate are also examining investments in cryptocurrency after the Indian Government demonetized Rs. 500 and Rs. 1,000 notes in November 2016, *There are issues with large investments flowing into this currency* said a senior tax department official. India has not yet taken a call on how it wants to treat crypto-products (so-called cryptocurrencies), but the Reserve Bank of India has cautioned against them repeatedly (Sikarwar, 2017; Rangan, 2017; Nappinai, 2018).

8. Conclusion

AI is becoming more dynamic and efficient for routine tasks than humans by the day, the question is will it replace humans in every sector. It is untrue. Technology and human complement and do not compete with each other. Initially, it might create disruption in an existing ecosystem, later it helps in creating opportunities. In an era of ChatBot and AI search engines, human workers can add value. The human interface will always remain critical. Humans and machines are fundamentally made different and will always be good at different things. They have to work together and are designed as such to ensure the best possible outcome as a combination. According to a new study by Microsoft and IDC Asia/Pacific — "Future Ready Business; Assessing Asia Pacific's" Growth potential through AI, AI will more than double the rate of innovation at organizations (2.2 times) and employees productivity (2.3 times) in India by 2021. Seventy seven percent of business leaders agreed that AI is instrumental for their organizations' competitiveness.

Business must now embrace a new culture, where innovation and continuous learning are core components of the organizational culture. It sets the stage for agility, adaptability, and growth. AI is now being used in an ever-expanding array of products — cars that drive by themselves, robots that identify and eradicate weeds, computers able to distinguish dangerous skin cancers from benign moles; and digital assistants that are bringing the technology into homes. The expanding applications of AI have created a big shortage of skilled workers. The crunch is great news for job-seeking students with AI. Indian companies are shelling out huge premiums for AI talent, as competition intensifies in the job market. Engineer.al is an artificial intelligence-based platform that allows people to build software without knowing how to code. In November 2018, the company has raised US$29.5 million in series-A funding from Lake star and Jungle Ventures, with participation from Softbank's Deep core. Sensing the urgent need of corporates for solutions based on AI coupled with government push on AI, the country's, premium engineering schools are busy upping their game on AI. From rolling out certificates, bachelor's, and master's course to creating a talent pool and incubating AI-based start-ups, the IITs are trying to bridge the gap in this space. IIT-Hyderabad has rolled out a B-tech program in AI in August 2018. In 2017, IIT-Kharagpur launched its center for AI that started the 6-month certificate program in AI. In 2018, IIT-Madras launched dual-degree specializations in data science and robotics. IIT-Ropar has introduced in 2018, a new M. Tech. program with specialization in computational data science with focus on AI. IIT-Roorkee offers courses on AI, ML, computer vision, etc. and in launching other AI-related courses like data analytics, big data analysis, deep learning, cyber physical security, cognitive science, social behavior analysis, and cryptography. Infosys has launched a digital learning platform, offering curated content targeted at engineering students in third and fourth years. The idea is to create more industry-ready talent among fresh graduates. The InfyTQ (talent quotient) app, as it is called, was rolled out in 2018 in Mysuru with 300 colleges. The applications were modeled on the lines of its internal on-demand learning platform lex. There lies a huge opportunity for India to fill the global talent gap and that might be a great opportunity for business itself in being the hub of digital enabling of global companies.

There are of course risks. AI and ML tools and techniques can be misused, intentionally or inadvertently. An obvious risk is the misuse of AI by those intent on threatening individual's physical, digital, financial and emotional securities. Fighting fake information is a societal challenge. AI is getting really good at writing fake news. The new ML algorithm can generate coherent text with just a sample to build on. The algorithm can be turned to imitate the writing style of the sample text. This requires action from all of us — technology companies, civil society, government and the users of our platforms. Scientists have developed new AI-based computing algorithms for dating apps and websites that "think" like humans to pinpoint profiles designed to con victims of their money. In online dating scams, fraudsters target users of dating websites and apps, groom them, and then ask for gifts of money or loans which will never be returned. Online dating fraud is a very common, often unreported, crime that causes huge distress and embarrassment for victims as well as financial loss. Using AI techniques to help reveal suspicious activity could be a game changer that makes detection and prevention quicker, easier, and more effective, ensuring that people can use dating sites with confidence in future.

Deloitte India corporate fraud perception survey edition 3 (2018), pointed out that the quantum of frauds discovered over the years and the associated modus operandi continue to pose challenges to developing anti-fraud strategies. According to a survey, about 84% of top-level bankers and financial executives believe that banks have underestimated the problem of financial crimes leading to an increase in fraudulent cases in the last 2 years (Deloitte, 2019). Half of the world is now officially online, but several tricky new problems threaten the global digital economy. According to the World Economic Forum's new report, "our shared Digital future: Building an Inclusive, Trustworthy and Sustainable Digital Society", with cyber-attacks up and trust in tech companies down, more than half of people around the global think technology's downside outweigh its benefits. The number of Internet users worldwide grew by 17% in 2007, it increased by 5.5% in 2018. Another thing holding back the digital transformation is cyberattacks. Hacking attacks cost the word economy several billion dollars each year. Among all the cyberattacks, confidence in the digital economy is ebbing. Dealing with hackers is a growing nightmare for billionaires. They usually focus on personal security, but the private information and digital life of ultra-wealthy individuals is a gold mine for cyber criminals. The case in point is "The Jeff Bezos scandal". In this even-more connected age, more and more personal data are shared online — for example, bank details, driver's license numbers, and personal addresses. Mark Zuckerberg, Facebook's CEO, spent US$7.3 million on his security in 2017, up from US$4.2 million in 2015. Nobody is safe. No one's data are well protected. It is the third–party platforms that have your banking information or that hold your personal pictures. Just few days back, Bezos disclosed that a tabloid obtained his intimate selfies, a fellow ballooners — Joe Ricketts, the founder of the broker TD Ameritrade Holding corporation — was ensnared in the scandal following the release of private messages. Bezos did not say how the "National Enquirer" obtained his pictures, but experts say the most common method is for a hacker to usurp the identity of a number of person's entourage.

Global Challenges Foundations 2018 report highlighted that "Intelligent machines could devastate humans if they are not controlled". Many scientists believe that AI on par with human brains could emerge in the next few decades, and machines that are more intelligent than us could follow. AI could be designed to destroy lives. And even if machines are programmed to do good, they could achieve these goals in harmful ways. Self-driving cars may kill the auto insurance industry. A sophisticated array of lidar, radar, and cameras is expected to be more adept at detecting trouble than our mortal eyes and ears. Computers never get drunk, check Tinder, or fall asleep at the wheel. The transition points to a larger, existential crisis for the multibillion-dollar car insurance industry. If nobody is driving, why do we need autoinsurance? With more than 90% of the accidents caused by human error, taking the driver out of the equation is going to mean a big change for insurers. Moreover, the nature of risk itself is going to change. With human drivers, "uncertainty is randomness, and random chances follow a normal distribution". If the risk is in faulty software on sensors, it becomes "more systematic". Determining who is at fault when something goes wrong could get thorny in this new world. Another tricky problem in the new era is, who to sue when a robot loses your fortune? The first known case of humans going to court over investment losses triggered by autonomous machine will test the limits of liability. Robots are getting more humanoid every day, but they still can't be sued.

Hong Kong tycoon (Samathur Li Kin-kan) is going after the salesmen who persuaded him to entrust a chunk of his fortune to the supercomputer whose trades costed him more than US$20 million. If people don't know how the computer is making decisions, who is responsible when things go wrong? Generally, it is believed and assumed that algorithms are faster and better decision-makers than human traders. It may often be true, but when they go astray, who is to blamed (Legal Battle in commercial court, in London, April 2019). Austria- based AI Company 42.cx, developed the supercomputer named K1, which would comb through online sources like real-time news and social media to gauge investor sentiment and make predictions on US stock futures. It would then send the instructions to a broker to execute trades, adjusting its strategy over time based on what it had learned. The idea of fully automated money manager inspired Li instantly. Ikea (household furnishing company) is coming out with "Robotic furniture", which can turn one's living spaces "multi-functional". The company is learning up with robo–furniture start-up Ori Living to make Rognan, a 3.5 × 3 meter product design for small living spaces. Rognan, which owners control using a built-in touch panel, is a single piece of furniture that rolls or unfolds into several homeowners essentials, including pull-out bed, couch, desk, and a closet. The Rognan can be moved to accommodate myriad daily needs. Ikea, instead of making the furniture smaller, transforms the furniture to the function that the customer needs at that time. An all-in-one solution is activated through a simple interface touchpad.

There is great opportunity to build a new future with the technology of artificial intelligence. Specialty of India is that it has a large workforce that has the technical skills to take advantage of AI tools. It is important to not just rely on law enforcement alone — whenever we introduce new technology, there needs to be broad education to explain how to stay safe. That is why the government is working on digital empowerment. AI is fast becoming an invaluable part of human development tool kit. AI will not only give us better judgment, it will also empower us to do work more efficiently. The intelligence may be artificial, but AI has the potential to make a real difference to how the world of businesses operates and drives value — (a) *Agriculture*: Mobile Mandi and Mandi on Wheels (Agarwal, 2018) boast about the efficiency of agriculture markets and mobile phone technology is helping farmers in Kenya detect poor quality and uncertified seeds to help boost their climate change-hit harvests. The Kenya seed company started placing stickers inside bags, of seed with a scratch-off code, which farmers can send in via text message to immediately find out whether the content matches the description on the label. There is also an app that identifies crop-munching armyworms. The agriculture app forecasts the probability of pest invasions, including the voracious fall armyworm, which eats crops and has wreaked havoc in sub-Saharan Africa and India. (b) *Health*: According to UN's International Atomic Energy Agency, mosquito-packed drones are fighting zika. Drones spraying millions of sterile mosquitoes are helping combat the zika outbreak in parts of Brazil. Once freed, the sterilized, laboratory-bred male *Aedes aegypti* mosquitoes — which spread Zika, dengue, and yellow fever by biting humans — mate with females, but do not produce viable eggs. According to UNICEF, a 1-month-old baby in Vanuatu in December 2018, become the first person in the world to be immunized with a vaccine delivered by a commercial drone. The delivery to the Pacific Island nation is a "big leap for global health", which could help save lives in other far-flung areas. Physicians try to be systematic when identifying illnesses and diseases, but bias creeps in. Researchers in USA and China have tested a potential remedy for all-too human frailties: artificial intelligence. In a paper published in *Nature Medicine* (2018), the scientists reported that they had built a system that automatically diagnoses common childhood conditions — from influenza to meningitis — after processing the patient's symptoms, history, lab results, and other clinical data. A team of Indian researchers has developed a thermal imaging and AI-based test that predicts setting in of hemodynamic shock — insufficient oxygen supply to organs leading to multi-organ failure — in children even 12 hours before doctors can clinically diagnose it. The detection of shock can prevent organ failure and save lives. Right now it is available for children, but it can be updated for adults. (c) *Fashion*: Fashion is one of the world's most environment-damaging industry — it is responsible for about 10% of all greenhouse gas emissions, sucks up scarce water, and creates a lot of pollution and waste. But the desire for the latest look is only increasing. So some businesses are now looking to meet the demand for new styles through digital designs, with Scandinavian fashion firm Carlings convincing its customers to pay real cash for virtual clothes that are digitally filled onto user's photographs. This is like merging of physical and digital. As technology advances, virtual fashion can sashay in to the mainstream.

The paper also proposes the setting up of "M5" as a money supply measure with cryptocurrency along the lines of inclusion of other currency products developed in the last 50 years in order to promote efficiency in the money markets and transactional efficiency and generate wealth along with positive contributions to GDP and people at large. The paper also considers "Money (Currency)" as a valuable resource and a wealth of the nation, having the potential to generate/mobilize more wealth. The paper proposes that given the emergence of digital modes of money transactions, there is an urgent need for the creation of legitimate cryptocurrencies by national governments to induce confidence and laissez-faire through transactional efficiency in money markets. Government intervention (or central banks) to generate the cryptocurrency is the need of the hour and critical for tomorrow's normal economic and business conditions in an economy when businesses and labor market sources are global and are looking for currency-efficient enriched sources. This paper critically evaluates various theories on money and how/why M5 as a money supply indicator is needed for inducing cryptocurrency in the basket of currencies by central banks worldwide (Agarwal, 2017a, 2018a, 2018b, 2018c, 2018d; Agarwal *et al.*, 2018).

There is a deep interlock between financial inclusion, banking, and digital dividends (Agarwal, 2017ab; Agarwal *et al.*, 2016, 2017, 2018) which foster the creation of social security facilities, employment growth, and a social equilibrium in the society reducing inequalities of income and socio-economic gender gaps. Global disequilibrium and interdependence (Agarwal, 2007a), unemployment (Agarwal *et al.*, 2017b), establishing a balance between need for survival (Agarwal, 2007) and socio-economic growth (Agarwal, 1969, 1988a, 1988b, 2004a, 2013a, 2013b, 2017a; Agarwal *et al.*, 2018), environment discipline (Agarwal and Agarwal, 2007), focus on issues to build a sustainable future in an interlocked global economic environment, digital revolution, dividends, and security are major concerns and global challenges before the economies in Asia and the World today.

Digital revolution has fostered more than 40% of the world population to have access to Internet and over 20% of the poorest poor in the world to gain access to mobile phones. Digital revolution has also empowered women and the common man on streets. Even the poor (BPL families in India), disabled, and downtrodden are the key beneficiaries of this revolution. Digital technologies today are accessible by a population of over 7.4 billion globally with around 1.1 billion having high-speed Internet, with Asia and the Pacific region having the highest growing portfolio (Stiglitz, 2001; Agarwal *et al.*, 2016, 2018; UN 2017).

The increased interplay of digital frameworks within our social fabric has induced key concerns before governments, regulatory bodies, and the common man on street in the global village today. This interplay raises the issues of privacy, where the social fabric is being destroyed; cyber security threats; funds flow controls; money laundering (Agarwal and Agarwal, 2004, 2006; Bloomberg-ET, 2018), and terrorist threats through speedy access to Internet, digital wallets, crypto-products, and banking facilities today. Contrary to the belief, we see that banking facilities, which ought to have become cheaper using digital platforms (having more efficient and swifter means of transfer of money), are becoming more and more expensive with an increase in bank charges (Agarwal, 2017a, 2017b). There are a large number of efforts placed by governments (including PM Narendra Modi's programs like *Jan-dhan Yojana*; *Swachh Bharat Abhiyan*; *Awas Yojana*, Make in India program; *Beti Bachao Program*; *Garib Kalyan Yojana*; *Krishi Sinchai Yojana* and others by almost all governments around the world) that are focusing to uplift the poorest of the poor and improve the standard of living for all (Agarwal and Agarwal, 2017, 2018).

However, even today most economies are suffering from serious problems such as unemployment, abject poverty, illiteracy, poor or weak infrastructure, food security, vulnerable diseases, sanitation, and hygiene (healthcare concerns), clean air and water, high mortality rate of children and women, income disparities furthering gender disparities, increased, violent terror attacks flourishing due to the swift transfer of illicit money via digital frameworks, etc. World Bank, ADB, UN, and other international agencies have been fostering their energies and finances to tackle some of these soars through financing various economies. They have also tried to facilitate and empower the vulnerable sections of the society including women to contribute in sustainable growth and development. While government efforts with the assistance of these international agencies are bearing fruits, yet a lot more is required to be done. According to the ILO World Employment and Social Outlook Report released recently that many of the jobs created in Asia-Pacific region are of poor quality. In India, despite strong economic growth hovering between 6.5% and 7.5% (on year to year basis) in the last 4 years with strong FDI flows making our reserves cross US$430 billion, about 77% of the workforce will still have vulnerable employment in 2018–2019 (IMF, 2017a, 2017b, 2018; Agarwal *et al.*, 2018; WB, 2018). A large part of jobs created in the region remain poor in quality. Vulnerable employment affects almost half the workers in Asia Pacific or more than one (1) billion men and women. Projections had indicated that 72% of workers in Southern Asia and 46% in South-eastern Asia will have vulnerable employment by 2019 showing very little change from 2017 as per the ILO report. Poor quality of job and high informality are the way for a high number of working poor or those living on incomes of less than US$3 per day (ILO, 2016, 2017; Agarwal *et al.*, 2017b; WB, 2018).

There is an urgent need to reverse this process by adopting strategies through financing social infrastructure such as education, healthcare, and skill development with a view to increase the incomes of the poor, vulnerable and downtrodden. The Focus needs to be on food, shelter, and good health for all. Hence, one needs to adopt both financial and non-financial approaches to involve people in their economies for inclusive development. In the past, the government of India has introduced several schemes such as NREGA and Anganwadi workers. The government is focusing on doubling the incomes of farmers so as to reduce poverty and people in several sectors of the economy. The creation of Kisan Credit Cards (IIF Studies, 1997, 1998) and "Mobile Mandi's and Mandi's on Wheel" ensuring farmers welfare and income growth along with the establishment of food security (Agarwal, 2008, 2018e, 2018f; Agarwal *et al.*, 2018) are steps that governments can initiate. There existed in ancient India when food for work was adopted whenever people suffered from famines, floods or droughts, and other natural calamities. Civil society and crowd funding besides the formal sources of funding allocated by the respective governments from their budget and by schemes introduced by World Bank, ADB, UN, and other international agencies may help in the mission of reducing poverty. Most of the churches and temples around the world are extremely rich because of the voluntary donations, which in our opinion can be used for the management of such religious organizations for social welfare, imparting education, setting up charitable hospitals, uplifting the status of girls in society through the removal of gender disparities through education and can contribute to poverty reduction.

The emergence of BITCOINs (and others as an informal/illegal virtual crypto-products) has raised serious concerns for governments; erroneous erosion of wealth of people and deviation from the focus of development by governments, institutions, and individuals from the key concerns of the society to speculative gains (Agarwal, 2017a, 2018a, 2018b, 2018c, 2018d; ET, 2017; Reuters, 2017b; Goldberg, 2017; Reuters, 2018a). The cryptocurrency launched by central banks backed by a tenable asset class of the nation's wealth (both publicly/privately held) are expected to emerge as a new mode of funds transfer and currency fostering financial inclusion, empowering women and inducing social security benefits. Governments all over the world and international agencies like United Nations, IMF, World Bank, ADB, and ILO, OECD, AfricanDB, etc. are seriously concerned about generating employment and reducing the prevailing unemployment and removing poverty through newer digitally fostered mechanism. The current form of crypto-products (like bitcoins and others) will create the divide further and increase the depth and reach of the problems and ills that most governments and national economies are perplexed with. For most governments as well as international agencies, generating employment is one of the most pressing and serious issues. It is also observed that there is a mismatch between the demand and supply of appropriate labor due to asymmetric information, i.e., jobs available but not in the knowledge of labor and suitable labor available but not in the knowledge of employers. This is where creating frameworks along the lines of the national labor exchange to induce full and transparent employment would serve as a key role player (Agarwal *et al.*, 2017b).

Crypto-products (like bitcoins) today are used to regulate the encryption techniques of the so-called cryptocurrency and verify the transfer of funds, operating independently of a central bank. No one controls them. They are not printed like Rupees, Dollars, or Euros. Such decentralized crypto-products provide an outlet for personal wealth to move beyond restrictions and confiscation because of its security feature, ending up with the creation of more income disparities, gender dispersion, unemployment, illusionary illegitimate speculative gains, and large number of ills moving into the financial systems through money laundering (Agarwal and Agarwal, 2004, 2006) using these crypto-products (like bitcoins). Some key forms of crypto-products which have emerged as the so-called cryptocurrency are currently functioning in a non-legal and non-regulated framework subjecting economies to national treats; monetary system failures; growth in money laundering mean and steep secure mechanism for all illicit trade/commerce cross borders without controls of any national economies (Agarwal and Agarwal, 2004, 2006; Agarwal *et al.*, 2008).

It is pertinent to mention that the valuation of crypto-products (like bitcoin) has been at an all-time high ever since Japan passed a law to accept bitcoin as a legal payment method (JT, 2018). However, over 72 nations have imposed bans/restrictions on operations of such crypto-products and China's recent decision to ban Initial Coin Offerings (ICO) by some crypto-product miners have triggered a massive crash of almost 31–78% in just 2 weeks in the early 2018. The Reserve Bank of India has not yet legally banned crypto-products but had issued notifications toward call for caution to people against the use of such virtual products (claiming to be virtual currencies). RBI has also advised commercial banks not to indulge in sale proceeds and restrict transactions related to VPs (TNN, 2017). Also, the SIT created by the Supreme Court of India has barred trading in such crypto-products. The main reason is that there is NO regulation on cryptocurrencies and fluctuations (volatility) in prices are huge. Swings are as big as 25–85% up or down on a daily basis (Popper and Hsu, 2017; Rangan, 2017). The world in the last decade has seen several hacking thefts, and cyberattack incidents where people lost thousands of dollars, pounds, or rupees and the depositors were unable to go through any course of action for recovering these losses (Bloomberg, 2017c; Kharif, 2018; Dev, 2018). Digital currencies stored on one's personal devices like your mobile phone or laptop or cloud vaults/wallets are leading to a series of newer risks and issues. If the device is lost, stolen (Gibbs, 2017; Bhardwaj, 2018), or its operating system crashes, the investor would end up losing his funds completely without recourse. Buying crypto-products in India had been relatively easier, given the delayed legal recourse and large cash economy framework. However, India has the most number of banks, which are now restricted by RBI to indulge in such trades/transactions. There are strong KYC requirements which need to verify the ID by one's PAN card and AADHAR Card for most financial transactions in India, which are being completely bypassed with these financially innovative crypto-products (leading them to have emerged as the "New Hawala"). Government needs to be concerned as the number of companies dealing in crypto-products (so-called crypto-currency) in India has grown from 4 in 2013 to over 20 by end of 2017 (Christopher, 2017).

In the last two decades, we have seen that online banking, mobile banking, virtual banking, developmental banking, retail banking, corporate banking, and cooperative (unions) banking, besides digital wallets, play a major areas of thrust in the banking sector and financial inclusion today. It is expected that this would further reduce cost, unless banks take to profiteering as done by some banks as observed in last 20 months post-demonetization in India (Agarwal, 2016, 2017). The move by the Indian Government to induce/expand post office banking (as proposed by IIF professors for the last 8 years at various national channels — DD, Lok Sabha TV, AIR, other TV Channels, and print media) would have a far-reaching impact of financial inclusion especially to the masses and rural India, Asia, and the Pacific (Agarwal and Agarwal, 2017).

Given the emergence of Crypto-products in the informal sector with multiple players, it has become difficult for national governments to regulate and calibrate the supply of money and its effects through monetary stabilization measures adopted by them, as these crypto-products allow billions/trillions of money to be transacted globally without any checks and balances. More than the benefits, these products are emerging as a threat to the national security, individual's wealth, and nations apart from the ills any speculative product brings with it to meet the needs of the Greed of a specific group of people and rogue identities. Hence, the need for governments to act fast and consider to induce this financial innovation (cryptocurrencies) as a currency of tomorrow into its basket of currencies, as done with various other monetary products in the last six decades, is pertinent and inevitable.

The proposed model of creating an efficient money market through modeling of M5 will facilitate an automatic way for transactional efficiency, generating wealth for the nations, firms and people-at-large, through easy access to currency and opportunities for jobs and growth (Agarwal *et al.*, 2018). It would also help save currency costs in a market-driven economic system with asymmetric information. (Agarwal *et al.*, 2004, 2006). We are happy to note that various central banks like China's Peoples Bank of China (in 2019), India's Reserve Bank of India (in 2018), Venezuela's Government Petra$ (in 2018), and many others are considering to launch (or have launched) digital currency along the lines of proposals made by IIF Professors since 2016 onward at various forums and those published in 2018 in *Finance India*. The "New Avatar" of Money in the form of Crypto would witness the change the way money (currency) has looked traditionally for centuries in the form of gold, silver, leather, wood, metal, paper, plastic, and many others to a faceless virtual fully fractional form, but only when launched by nations (via their central banks).

Acknowledgments

The authors gratefully acknowledge the technical support of the Indian Institute of the Finance. The authors would like to thank Robert Mundell, Douglas C. North, Robert C. Merton, Fredric Mishkin, James Mirrlees, Joseph Stiglitz, Daniel Kannmann, and James C. Heckmann who have inspired in many ways to work on this complex issue. We would like to thank our colleagues who have enriched us with their review comments on our earlier related work on "The Theory of Money, Wealth and Efficient Currency Market: Modeling M5 as Money Supply with Cryptocurrency" published in *Finance India*, Vol. 32, No. 2, June 2018 issue — Stefan Ingves, Ian Cooper, Hubert Fromlet, Erkki Liikanen, Junzo Watada, John J. Ensminger, Eero Vuorio Lawrence A. Gordon, Mukul G. Asher, Charles van Wymeersch, John Burgoyne, Esa Jokivuolle, Dennis Schauffer, Giuseppe Pennisi, Emmanuel Picavet, Saju Skaria, Pradeep Kr Gohil, Talbi Bechir, J. Josephine Daisy, John Ricci, and Saurabh Agarwal. Thanks to them and many more for reviewing the work and providing valuable inputs, comments, and suggestions.

The views and reviews presented in the chapter are the views and opinions of the authors, based on their research and experience and do not depict institutional or countries views or of the institutions the authors are associated with. All errors and omissions are of the authors.

Note

Earlier papers on Cryptocurrency delivered as Invited Faculty Eminent Discussion Series Seminar at Indian Institute of Finance on January 30, 2018. Interviewed by Delhi Doordarshan TV (DD India TV and DD News TV) National Government of India TV Channel in "Sabh ke Liye" program by Ambassador Prof. Dr. Deepak Vohra (TV Personality and Indian Senior Diplomat) telecasted on February 18, 2018 at 18:00 hrs and March 11, 2018 at 18:00 hrs and at various other forums since 2016.

The earlier work has been invited to be delivered as Guest of Honor Plenary Keynote Address at the

i. 10th International Finance Conference 2018 in Tunisia in April 21–22, 2018 along with Plenary Speakers — Prof. Harry M. Markowitz *(Nobel Prize Laureate, 1990)*; Prof. Giovanni Barone-Adesi (UoL, Switzerland); Prof. Oldrich Alfons Vasicek (VA USA); Prof. Nizar Touzi, (EP, France); Farid Aitsahlia (UFL USA).
ii. 15th International Scientific School Russian Academy of Sciences (RAS) Conference on "Modeling and Analysis of Safety and Risk in Complex Systems (MASR 2019) at Saint-Petersburg, Russia, June 19–21, 2019.
iii. 15th ISME Japan and 2nd UMSO International Conference 2019 at Le Quy Don Technical University, Hanoi, VIETNAM (December 9–12, 2019, Hanoi, VIETNAM).

All authors have been invited to be interviewed on the said topic on Lok Sabha TV, Rajya Sabha TV, Delhi Doordarshan (DD India TV; DD National TV; DD News TV), All India Radio (AIR), NDTV, NewsX TV, and many other TV and radio channels worldwide.

Bibliography

Accenture (2018), *Intelligent blocks of India's future workforce*. Report by Accenture, August 6, 2018.

AFP (2018), How AI is creating jobs, not killing them. *AFP*, October 16 2018.

AFP (2019), AI can be the future of music but not a rockstar, *Times of India* May 2019.

Agarwal, A. (2000), Derivatives in India, *Derivative Report, Journal of Research Institute of America*.

Agarwal, A. (2001a), Derivatives: Wave of the future (Indian scenario), *Finance India* **15**(2).

Agarwal, A. (2001b & 2002a), *A New Approach & Model for Weather derivatives Instrument Based on Water Table for Floods, Droughts and Rainfall.* A paper for the FSD Dept, The World Bank, Washington, DC, USA, *Finance India* **16**(3), 877–914.

Agarwal, A. (2002b), Derivatives: Wave of the future (An approach to stock option compensation and Indian scenario), *International Journal of Finance*.

Agarwal, A. (2004a), Legal aspects of ensuring openness, publicity and transparency in organizing and carrying out of the elections — Indian experience, norms and standards. *Finance India*, **18**(3).

Agarwal, A. (2004b), Methods of valuation, *The Smart Manager* **3**(2).

Agarwal, A. (2007a), *Global Disequilibrium, Growth and Europe*, Plenary Keynote Address at the Economia Reale Conference at Sala delle Colonne (Italian Parliament). Audio of the Speech online at Italian Media Channels (Radio Radicale Italy (www.radioradicale.it/scheda/235385) and Sherpa TV Italy) & at IIF (www.iif.edu).

Agarwal, A. (2017a), *Interjection on Bank Depository Insurance Act & BITCOINs* at 2018–19 Pre-Budget Seminar at IHC Delhi, India with Dr. Rajiv Kumar (Vice-Chairman, Niti Aayog) and Dr. Arun Maira (Former Member, Planning Commission of India & Former Chairman BCG India) at Pahle India Foundation (PIF). https://youtu.be/88oLG1fKXmo.

Agarwal, A. (2017b), *Charges on Cash Transactions: An Unfair Trade practice and Not Justified urged Prof. Aman Agarwal*, IIF Press Release and *The Week*. Interviews on Lok Sabha TV; Rajya Sabha TV; Delhi Doordarshan TV and All India Radio in 2017 and 2018.

Agarwal, A. (2017c), HDFC, ICICI, Axis Bank impose charges on cash transactions by Vijaya Pushkarna. *The Week*. Interview — www.theweek.in/content/archival/news/biz-tech/hdfc-icici-axis-bank-impose-charges-transactions.html.

Agarwal, A. (2018a), *Cryptocurrency impacting Global Financial System*, discussion with Prof. Joseph Stglitz (Nobel Laureate & Professor Columbia University) after his address at *India Economic Conclave* 2018 at Taj Palace Diplomat Hotel, Delhi.

Agarwal, A. (2018b), Bitcoins, crypto currencies & global financial markets crash, *Delhi Doordarshan TV (DD India TV).*

Agarwal, A. (2018c), *Comments & question on BITCOINs & cryptocurrency* to Don Tapscott (CEO Capacity Go & Executive Director, Blockchain Research Institute, USA) at India Economic Conclave 2018 at Taj Palace Diplomat Hotel, Delhi at 3:15 pm. https://youtu.be/UUNNQKc4bvU.

Agarwal, A. (2018d), World financial markets & crypto currencies, *Delhi Doordarshan TV (DD India TV)*, February 18, 2018 at 6:00 PM and *Delhi Doordarshan TV (DD News TV)*, February 19, 2018 at 10:00 am youtu.be/aDiLdT2-Kug.

Agarwal, A. (2018e), *Mobile Mandi & Mandi on Wheels for Efficient Agriculture Markets facilitating Doubling Farmers' (Kisan) Income*, IIF Press Release, www.iif.edu/media/pr/2018/20180203pr001.htm.

Agarwal, A. (2018f), *Agriculture, Farmers and Rural India: Union Budget 2018–19* Delhi Doordarshan National TV (National Television of India) in the DD Program "Krishi Darshan" at 5:30 PM on February 6, 2018 [Anchor: Dr. Anurag Sharma (Sr. Journalist); Guest Experts: (a) Mr. Naresh Sirohi, General Secretary, BJP's Kisan Morcha & (b) Prof. Dr. Aman Agarwal] youtu.be/sbSgi_C-tF4.

Agarwal, A., J. H. W. Penm, and S. Agarwal (2016), *Common Currency for India and the ASEAN Region: An Empirical Investigation*, Working Paper, Indian Institute of Finance, December 2016.

Agarwal, A., J. H. W. Penm, W.-K. Wong, and L. M. Martin (2004), ASEAN DOLLAR: A Common currency establishment for stronger economic growth of ASEAN Region. *Finance India* **18**.

Agarwal, J. D. and A. Agarwal (2008), Money laundering: The real estate bubble, *Finance India* **22**(1).

Agarwal, J. D., M. Agarwal, A. Agarwal, and Y. Agarwal (2018), The theory of money, wealth and efficient currency market: Modeling M5 as money supply with crypto-currency. *Finance India* **32**(2). http://financeindia.org/data/2018/FI322/FI-322-Art01.pdf.

Agarwal, J. D. and A. Agarwal (2004a), India AML progress analyzed, *USA Patriot Act Monitor*.

Agarwal, J.D. and A. Agarwal (2004b), International money laundering in the banking sector, *Finance India*, **18**(2); Reprinted with permission in *The ICFAI Journal of Banking Law*, Vol. II No. 4, October 2004. the journal of ICFAI University, Hyderabad.

Agarwal, J. D. and A. Agarwal (2005), Inflation, savings and financial development, *Finance India* **19**(2).

Agarwal, J. D. and A. Agarwal (2006), Money laundering: New forms of crime victimization (current trends and modus operandi), *Finance India* **19**(4).

Agarwal, J. D. and A. Agarwal (2007), Climate change, energy and sustainable development, *Finance India* **21**(4).

Agarwal, J.D. and A. Agarwal (2017, 2018), Niti Aayog's India: Three year action agenda 2017–18 to 2019–20: Review and analysis, *Finance India* **31**(3), 905–928 and *AESTIMATIO, The EIB International Journal of Finance* **16**, DOI:10.560/IEB.18.7.

Agarwal, J. D. and Y. Agarwal (2017), Analysis of union budget 2017, *Finance India* **31**(1).

Agarwal, J. D. (1969, 1988a), *Capital Budgeting Decision under Risk and Uncertainty*, IIF Publications, Delhi, India; Doctoral Thesis work done at Delhi School of Economics, The University of Delhi, Delhi.

Agarwal, J. D. (1980), Ordinal ranking of objective: A conceptual framework, *The Management and Labour Studies*, The Journal of Xavier Institute, Jamshedpur **6**(2), 85–96.

Agarwal, J. D. (1991), Black money: Some dimensions, *Finance India* **5**(1), 55–60.

Agarwal, J. D. (2004), Volatility of international financial markets, regulation and financial supervision, *Finance India* 18(1).

Agarwal, J. D. (2007), Modelling and analysis of safety and risk in complex systems, *Finance India* **21**(3).

Agarwal, J. D. E. Solojentsev, and A. Agarwal (2008), Logic and probabilistic risk models of bribes, *Finance India* **22**(3).

Agarwal, J. D. (2008), Speech on innovations & development and investment in agriculture and rural development with special reference to India and Hungary, *Finance India* **22**(2), 429–442.

Agarwal, J. D. (2017a), *Sustainable Growth, Innovation and Revolution in the New Millennium.*

Agarwal, J. D. (2017ab), *Innovation, Disruption and Transformation in Financial Markets.*

Agarwal, J. D. (2018aa), Analysis of union budget 2018, *Finance India* **32**(1).

Agarwal, J. D., A. Agarwal, and Y. Agarwal (2017), *GST Impact on the Indian Economy, Supply Chain and Financial Inclusion* at Bureau of Indian Standards (BIS), Delhi.

Agarwal, J. D., M. Agarwal, and A. Agarwal (2016, 2017), *Financial Inclusion, Banking and Digital Dividends* at International Conference on Technoviti — Futurecrafting Business with Technoruptions at ITC Grand Maratha, Mumbai, INDIA (February 5th, 2016).

Agarwal, J. D., A. Agarwal, and Y. Agarwal (2017), Dynamics of cricket and cricket derivatives, *Finance India* **31**(4), 1149–1190.

Agarwal, J. D., M. Agarwal, A. Agarwal, and Y. Agarwal (2017a), Theory of land and efficient land markets through real estate exchange, *Finance India* **31**(2), 413–442.

Agarwal, J. D., M. Agarwal, A. Agarwal, and Y. Agarwal (2017b), Theory of employment, wealth and efficient labour market through national labour exchange (NLX), *Finance India* **31**(3), 777–808.

Agarwal, M. and S. Agarwal (2007), Economics of public utilities in market driven economic systems, *Finance India* **11**(3).

Agarwal, M. (1988), *Tax Incentives and Investment Behaviour*, IIF Publication, Delhi, p. 179.

Agarwal, M., A. Agarwal, and Y. Agarwal (2018), *India 2018: Jobs and Growth through Financial Inclusion, Banking and Digital Dividends* (*Demonetization Demystified*).

Agarwal, S. (2018), Bitcoin Exchanges Plan to maintain user database, *The Economic Times*, February 13th, 2018.

Agarwal, Y. (2010), Capital structure decisions under multiple objectives: Study of Indian corporates, *Finance India* **24**(2), 515–523.

Agarwal, Y. (2013a), *Capital Structure Decisions: Evaluating Risk and Uncertainty*, John Wiley & Sons, USA (Wiley USA, UK & Singapore).

Agarwal, Y., K. C. Iyer, and S. S. Yadav (2009), Capital structure decision: A behavioral study on multiple objectives framework, *Finance India* **23**(2), 431–468.

Agarwal, Y., K. C. Iyer, and S. S. Yadav (2012), Multi-objective capital structure modeling: An empirical investigation of goal programming model using accounting proxies, *Journal of Accounting, Auditing and Finance* **27**(3), 359–385.

Agarwal, Y. (2013b), *Capital Structure Decisions under Multiple Objectives: A Study of Indian Corporates*, IIF Publication, Delhi.

Ali, R., J. Barrdear, R. Clews, and J. Southgate (2014), Innovations in payment technologies and the emergence of digital currencies, *Bank of England Quarterly Bulletin* **54**(3), 262–75.

Ananth, V. (2018), Crouching tiger, hidden dragon, *Economic Times*, December 6th, 2018.

Archana, A. (2018), RBI cracks down on bitcoins, *Hindustan Times*, April 6th, 2018.

Ashenfelter, O. and D. Card (1999), *Handbook of Labour Economics*, **3A**, Elsevier Science B.V.

Badev, A. and M. Chen (2014), *Bitcoin: Technical Background and Data Analysis*, Finance and Economics Discussion Series, Divisions of Research & Statistics and Monetary Affairs Federal Reserve Board, Washington, D.C.

Basu, S. D. and P. V. Dodhwal (2019), Hot skill AI command huge premium in job market, *Economic Times*, February 2019.

Bhakta, P. (2019), Lenders bank on bots to improve customer service, *times-group.com*.

Bhardwaj, S. (2018), Bitcoins worth Rs. 41L stolen from woman's e-wallet account, *Times of India*.

BI Bureau (2018), Cyberattacks hack away at Peoples trust in a digital future, *businessinsider.in*.

BI Bureau (2019), AI creates fashion models who look spookily life like, *businessinsider.in*.

BI Bureau (2019), Humanity is at risk from AI, nuclear winter & pathogens, *Businessinsider.in, Economic Times*, Panche.

Bieda, K. (1973), Copernicus as an economist, *Economic Record* **49**, 89–103.

Bloomberg Bureau (2017a), Bitcoin can buy you citizenship in one of the happiest countries, *Bloomberg*.

Bloomberg Bureau (2017b), Bitcoin is a highly speculative asset, *Economic Times — Bloomberg*.

Bloomberg Bureau (2017c), Yellen's legacy trickier than it looks, *The Economic Times*, Money Matters.

Bloomberg Bureau (2017d), Gold may not be bitcoin yet, but miners can still make you money. *The Economic Times*.

Bloomberg Bureau (2017e), Buying bitcoin? You are the mercy of whales, *Bloomberg Business week*.

Bloomberg Bureau (2018a), Bitcoins are making messy divorce even worse, *Bloomberg — The Economic Times*.

Bloomberg Bureau (2018b), Bitcoins craze fades as fad gives way to regulators, *Bloomberg — The Economic Times*.

Bloomberg Bureau (2019), AI can spot Potential thieves before they steal, *Bloomberg*.

Bloomberg Bureau (2019), Self-driving cars may kill insurance. *livement.com, Bloomberg*.

Bloomberg Bureau (2019), Who to sue when a robot loses your fortune, *Bloomberg, Economic Times Panche*.

Bloomberg-ET Bureau (2018a), How to launder $500 mn in digital currency. *The Economic Times*.

Bloomberg-ET Bureau (2018b), How cryptos split global central banks, *The Economic Times*.

Cade, M. (2019), How AI may assist doctors in diagnosing rare conditions, *New York Times*, News service.

Cahau, P. and A. Zyleberberg (2004), *Labour Economics*, The MIT Press.

CB Insight (2018), A ranking of the 100 most promising private artificial intelligence companies in the world, *Cbinsights.com.*

CB Insight (2019), Rise of China's BigTech in AI: What Baidu Alibaba and Tencent are working on, *Cbinsights.com.*

Chen, F. (2016), *AI Deep learning and Machine Learning: A Primer*, June 10, 2016.

Christopher, N. and V. Bansal (2018), Crypto hedge funds gaining currency in India, *Economic Times*.

Christopher, N. (2017), Bullish Indians rush in for a big bite of bitcoins, *The Economic Times*.

Chui, M. and M. Harryson (2019), AI is not silver bullet for human development, *Times of India*.

Copernicus, N. (1517), *Memorandum on monetary policy*, Poland.

Corea, F. (2017), *Unsupervised Investments: A Comprehensive Guide to AI Investors Decisions* Scientist and Data strategist by KD Nuggets.

Das, S. and S. Menon (2017), Bitcoin: A speculative asset where patience is the name of the game, *Economic Times*.

Dave, S. and S. Shukla (2018), Bitcoins losing currency on budget warning: Trading spikes on bitcoin exchanges after FM's speech, confusion over tax treatment of cryptocurrency gains, *The Economic Times*.

Dave, S. (2018), Investors under IT scanner gift bitcoins to relatives, *ET Wealth*.

Deloitte (2019), *Banks have underestimated Financial crimes*. Deloitte Survey.

Dev, A. (2018), Bitcoin holder claims he was cheated of Rs. 7 L, *Times of India*.

Dowd, K. (1993), *Laissez-faire banking*. Routledge, London.

Doweting, S. (2018), *Top — well funded start-ups to watch in 2018*.

EBA (2014), *EBA opinion on virtual currencies*. EBA/Op/2014/08, European Banking Authority.

ECB (2012), *Virtual Currency Scheme*. European Central Bank.

Economist (2018), Managing human research is about to become easier, *The Economist*.

ET Bureau (2017), IT Department Surveys Bitcoin brokers for tax evasion. *Economic Times*.

ET Bureau (2018), A love robot can be your new partner. *Reuter-ET Magazine*.

ET Bureau (2018), Crazy in love? This Japanese man married a hologram, *Economic Times*.

ET Bureau (2018), Toyota wants to put a Robot friend in every home, *Economic Times*.

ET Bureau (2018), Get ready for most crypotocurrencies to hit zero, says Goldman, *The Economic Times*.

ET Bureau (2019), Banking on Digital revolution, *Economic Times*.

ET Bureau (2019), New study by Microsoft and IDC Asia/Pacific — Future Ready Business: Assessing Asia Pacific growth through AI, *Economic Times*.

ET Wealth (2018), Income Tax notices to lakhs of bitcoins buyers, *The Economic Times — Wealth*.

EU Bureau (2019), AI and the job of cleaning up social media. *The New York Times Economic Times*.

FATF (2014), *Virtual currencies: Key Definitions and Potential AML/CFT Risks*. Financial Action Task Force.

Fisher, I. (1911), *The Purchasing Power of Money*. MacMillan Company & JSTOR.

Floyd, D. (2019), Venezuela's petro isn't oil-backed: It's not even a cryptocurrency (opinion), *Investopedia*.

FO Bureau (2019), Benefits & risks of artificial intelligence, *Futureoffice.org*.

Forbes Bureau (2018), Four ways artificial intelligence can impact the workplace & society *Forbes*.

Foville, A. de (1907), *La Monnaie*, France, p. 273.

FRBSF (2005), *How Does the Fed Determine Interest Rates to Control the Money Supply?*, Federal Reserve Bank of San Francisco.

Friedman, M. and A. J. Schwartz (1965), *The Great Contraction 1929–1933*, Princeton University Press, Princeton.

Friedman, M. (1956), The quantity theory of money: A restatement, in *Studies in the Quantity Theory of Money* and reprinted as *The Optimum Quantity of Money* **51**, 67.

Friedman, M. (1959), *A program for monetary stability*. Fordham University Press, New York.

Friedman, M. (1969), *The optimum quantity of money, in the optimum quantity of money and other essays*. Aldine, Chicago, pp. 1–50.

Friedman, M. (1970), *The Counter-revolution in monetary theory*. IEA Occasional Paper, No. 33. Institute of Economic Affairs, London, 1970.

Friedman, M. (1987), Quantity theory of money, *The New Palgrave: A Dictionary of Economics* **4**, 15.

Froyen, R. T. (1990), *Macroeconomics: Theories and Policies*. 3rd Edition, Macmillan Publishing Company, New York, pp. 71.

Fuller, T. and C. Metz (2019), Next AI frontier, predicting earthquake *New York Times* news service.

Furness III, W. H. (1910), *The Island of Stone Money UAP of the Carolines*. J. B. Lippincott Company.

Galbács, P. (2015), *The Theory of New Classical Macroeconomics: A Positive Critique*. Springer, Heidelberg/New York/Dordrecht/London.

Gibbs, S. (2017), Bitcoin: $64m in cryptocurrency stolen in sophisticated hack from Slovenian firm, exchange says. *The Guardian*.

Goldberg, S. (2017), Blockchain may upset commodity markets globally. *The Economic Times*.

Green, R. (1987), Real bills doctrine, in *The New Palgrave: A Dictionary of Economics* **4**, 101–102.

Gurman, M. (2018), The US market for home robots is set to quadruple to more than $4 bn by 2025. *Bloomberg*, Technology.

Hafer, R. W. and D. C. Wheelock (2001), The rise and fall of a policy rule: monetarism at the St. Louis Fed, 1968–1986. *Federal Reserve Bank of St. Louis, Review*, January–February, 19.

Halder, R. (2019), AI, drones and satellites to help keep an eye on Yamuna floodplain. *Timesgroup.com.*

Hall, R. E. (1979), A theory of natural unemployment rate and the duration of employment, *Journal of Monetary Economics* **5**, 153–169.

Hayek, F. (1976), *Denationalisation of Money*, Institute of Economic Affairs, London.

He, D., K. Habermeier, R. Leckow, V. Haksar, Y. Almeida, M. Kashima, N. Kyriakos-Saad, H. Oura, T. S. Sedik, N. Stetsenko, and C. Verdugo-Yepes (2012), *Virtual Currencies and Beyond: Initial Considerations*, IMF Discussion Note, pp. 1–42.

Hemple, I. (2017), *Inside, Bidu's bid to lead the AI revolution.*

Henschen, D. (2018), *Nvidia accelerates AI, analytics with an ecosystem approach.*

Hetzel, R. L. (1987), Henry Thornton: Seminal monetary theorist and father of the modern central bank, *Economic Review*, Reserve Bank of Richmond, **1**.

HMRC (2014), *HM Revenue and Customs tax treatment of income received from Bitcoin and other cryptocurrencies*, HM Revenue & Customs, Government of UK.

Hornigold, T. (2018), *How fast is AI progressing?*, Stanford's New Reports card for artificial intelligence.

HT Bureau (2019), Bots on wheels to save Fuel at airport, *Hindustan Times*.

HT Correspondent (1997), Capital Flight to US due to abnormal trade: IIF Study, *Hindustan Times*.

HT (2018), Now, bitcoin is used for foreign money transfer, *Hindustan Times*, April 6, 2018.

Hume, D. (1748), *Of Interest*, in Essays Moral and Political.

IANS (2019), No, AI is not coming for your Jobs, *IANS, Economic Times Panche*, February 27, 2019.

IDC (2019), *Worldwide spending on Robotics Forecast to Accelerate over the Next Five years, Reaching $230.7 Bn in 2021*, IDC spending Guide.

ILO (2016), *World Employment Social Outlook, Transforming Jobs to end poverty,* International Labour Organisation.

ILO (2017), *World Employment Social Outlook: Trends*, International Labour Organisation.

IMF (2017a), *Global Financial Stability Report: Getting the Policy Mix Right*, International Monetary Fund, Washington, DC, USA.

IMF (2017b), *Global Financial Stability Report: Is Growth at Risk?*, International Monetary Fund, Washington, DC, USA.

IMF (2018), *Global Financial Stability Report: A Bumpy Road Ahead*, International Monetary Fund, Washington, DC.

Jahan, S. (2018), Inflation Targeting: Holding the Line, *Finance & Development,* June 2018, pp. 72–73.

Jaitley, A. (2018), Union Budget 2018-19, *Finance India* **32**(1).

Javed, A. (2017), *Digital Evolution Report cybercrime, Digitalization, Blockchain and AI*.

Johnson, L. E., R. Ley, and T. Cate (2001), Keynes' Theory of Money and His Attack on the Classical Model, *International Advances in Economic Research*.

Bureau, J. T. (2018), Japan's new cryptocurrency crooners sing the bitcoin beats, *The Japan Times*.

Katz, E. and O. Stark (1987), International migration under asymmetric information, *Economic Journal* **97**(387), 718–726.

Kaul, A. (2017), *AI and computer vision enables the next generation of visual intelligence tools*.

Khan, S. (2018), Hacking and theft: The dark side of Blockchain, *Lexology* — BDB Pitmans LLP.

Kharif, O. (2018), Hackers have walked off with about 14% of big digital currencies, *Bloomberg*.

Kohli, N. (2019), How will AI influence reality Jobs?. *hidustantimes.com*.

Krugman, P. (2011), Way off base, *The New York Times*.

Kumar, D. (2018), No end to bitcoin mania among the believers, *The Economic Times — Wealth.*

Kumar, P. (2019), *Artificial Intelligence (AI): Reshaping Life and Business.* BPB Publication, India.

Kurian, V. (2018), Fintech start-up turn to AI products for accelerated growth, *The Hindu Business.*

Laskowski, N. (2017), Failure is a critical component for blockchain development: Validity, consensus and immutability are the core components of blockchain, and all three have failed. Cornell's Emin Gun Sirer explains why that's not such a bad thing, *Tech Target.*

Laviathan, Y. (2018), Google duplex: An AI system for accomplishing real-world tasks over the phone, *Google AI Blog.*

Maloney, C. (2018), 92% of all blockchain projects fail, *Ethereum World News.*

Marr, B. (2018), The amazing way Google uses AI and satellite Data to prevent illegal phishing, *Fortune.*

Marr, B. (2018), The amazing way chinese tech giant Alibaba uses AI and machine learning, *Forbes.*

McCall, J. J. (1970), Economics of information and job search, *Quarterly Journal of Economics* **84**, 113–126.

McCarthy, J., M. Minsky, N. Rochester, and C. E. Shannon (1955), *Proposal for the 1956 Dartmouth Summer Research Project on Artificial Intelligence.* Dartmouth College, Hanover, NH, USA.

McLeay, M., A. Radia, and R. Thomas (2014), Money creation in the modern economy, *Bank of England Quarterly Bulletin* **54**(1), 14–27.

Mercer, C. (2018), *Tech giants investing in AI.*

Mill, J. S. (1848), *Principles of Political Economy.* London.

Miller, J. (2017), *Demystifying AI Callaghan Innovation.* New Zealand Innovation agency.

Minsky, H. P. (2008), *John Maynard Keynes.* McGraw-Hill.

Mishkin, F. S. (1998), *The Economics of Money, Banking and Financial Markets.* 5th Edition, Addison-Wesley Longman Inc., USA.

Mizrahi, A. (2018), FBI arrests exchange operator for lying about 6000 bitcoin hack, *Bitcoin.com.*

Morgan, B. (2018), *How Amazon has reorganized around AI and ML.*

Murphy, E. V., M. M. Murphy, and M. V. Seitzinger (2015), Bitcoin: Questions, answers, and analysis of legal issues, *Congressional Research Services.*

Murphy, E. and S. Senior (2013), Changes to the Bank of England. *Bank of England Quarterly Bulletin* **53**(1), 20–28.

Nappinai, N. S. (2018), Bitcoins and the cryptocurrency conundrum: Budget tries to provide an answer but falls short of definitive stand, *Times of India*.

NASSCOM (2016), *Strong role for AI in BFSI*. NASSCOM-CMR Report.

Newcomb, S. (1885), *Principles of Political Economy*, New York.

NITI Aayog (2018), *National Strategy for AI*. Niti Ayog, India.

OECD (2017), *OECD Economic Outlook*. OECD, Paris, France.

Olson, P. (2018), This startup wants to replace your Doctor with a chatbot. *Forbes Digital*.

Orcutt, M. (2019), China says its digital currency will have controllable anonymity — but who will control it?, *MIT Technology Review*, Blockchain.

Osborne, G. (2014), *Chancellor on developing FinTech*. Government of UK.

Pandya, J. (2019), Forbes publishes the risk roundup discussion with IIF Prof. Aman Agarwal of Indian Institute of Finance (www.iif.edu) by Dr. Jayshree Pandya on AADHAR as featured article on, Nuances of AADHAR: India's Digital Identity, Identification System and ID, *Forbes*, USA.

Peng, T. (2018), *UBTECH Robotics Gets US $ 820 mn Funding, Becomes the world's most valuable AI startup*.

Physorg (2018), Artificial intelligence improves highway safety in Las Vegas. *PHYSORG*.

Pillai, S. (2018a), Indian startups raise funds via bitcoins: Find initial coin offering risky, but get finance without diluting any equity, *Times of India*, Business Page.

Pillai, S. (2018b), Cryptocurrency offering have government, *Times of India*.

Popper, N. and T. Hsu (2017), Bitcoin plummets more than 30 percent in less than a day, *The New York Times*.

Powell, B. (2018), Venezuela makes petro cryptocurrency a national currency, *Block LR*.

PTI Bureau (2016), Richest 1% own 58% of total wealth in India: Oxfam, WEF Davos, *The Hindu*.

PTI (2018), AI can detect age, gender of people on Videos, *Times of India*.

PTI (2019), AI could foil online dealing frauds *Press Trust of India*.

Radford, R. A. (1945), The economic organisation of a P.O.W. camp, *Economica*, **12**(48), 189–201.

Rangan, M. C. G. (2017), Bitcoin: Global Fei or Tulip Bulbs? Milton Friedman to Jamie Dimon help navigate, *The Economic Times*.

Rej, A. (2019), Artificial Intelligence models may have a few issues, algorithms don'ts, *Hindustan Times*.

Reuters Bureau (2017b), No Euro zone cryptocurrency in sight for now, says Bundesbank, *The Economic Times*.

Reuters Bureau (2018a), EU watchdogs warm of crypto price bubble, *Economic Times.*

Reuters Bureau (2018b), Criminals are now ditching Bitcoins, *The Economic Times*, January 3, 2018.

Risberg, J. (2018), Yes, the blockchain can be hacked, *Coin Central.*

Rowe, J. L. (2017), *Back to Basics: Economic Concepts Explained.* Finance & Development, IMF.

Russell, S. and P. Norvisg (2009), *Artificial Intelligence: A Modern Approach.* 3rd edition, Pearson, Essex, England.

Sas, C. and I. E. Khairuddin (2017), *Design for Trust: An Exploration of the Challenges and Opportunities of Bitcoins Users*, Proceedings of the 2017 CHI Conference on Human Factors in Computing Systems, 17, 6499–6510.

Satoshi, N. (2008), Bitcoin: A peer-to-peer electronic cash system. https://bitcoin.org/bitcoin.pdf.

Schmidt, R. (2018), US bitcoin regulator allows staff to trade in cryptocurrencies. *Bloomberg — The Economic Times.*

Sennar, K. (2018), *AI in e-commerce comparing the top 5 largest Firms.*

Shetty, M. and S. Pillai (2018), RBI bars banks from crypto services, plans e-currency. *Times of India.*

Shetty, M. (2018), No bitcoin purchases by debit, credit cards: Citi, *The Economic Times.*

Sikarwar, D. (2017), Trading in bitcoins under Taxman, ED Lens, *The Economic Times.*

Singh, S. (2018), Bots in the workplace, *Economic Times.*

Smith, P. and C. Rosevear (2017), The digital revolution, bitcoin and the future of digital asset. www.blockchain.com.

Smithsonian Bureau (2018), What — will our society look like when AI is every wheres, *Smithsoniammag.com.*

Snhamitra, P. (2019), Match-Making to gaming, AI does it all for startups. *Times internet.in.*

Sperling, J. (2018), *An A. team for AI*, Fortune, July 1, 2018 p. 44.

Stemberg (2018), *Handbook of Intelligence*, Cambridge University Press.

Stemberg (2019), *Handbook of human intelligence.*

Stigler, G. J. (1961), The economics of information, *The Journal of Political Economy* **69**(3), 213–225.

Stiglitz, J. E. (2001), *Information and the change in the paradigm in economics*, Nobel Prize Lecture, Noble Foundation, Sweden.

Talluri, R. (2017), *Conventional computer vision coupled with Deep Learning makes AI better.*

Thrun, S. (2019), The Book that writes itself, *Economic Times.*

TNN Bureau (2017), Bitcoins like Ponzi schemes: Govt, *Times of India* (*Times News Network*).

TNN (2018b), Lenders freeze accounts of bitcoin exchanges, *Times of India.*

TNN (2018c), Bitcoin: From types to tax, a cryptocurrency primer, *Times of India.*

TOI Bureau (1997), IIF study estimates US$4-11 bn capital flight from India to US in 1994-95, *Times of India.*

TOI Bureau (2018), UK bank bans bitcoin purchase via credit card, *Times of India.*

TOI (2018), UK sees first Bitcoin armed robbery: Report, *The Times of India.*

TR Foundation (2018), New use of Technology in the past year, *Bloomberg, PTI, Thomson Reuters Foundation.*

TR Foundation (2019), Virtual clothes to the rescue of fast fashion, *Thomson Reuters Foundation, Economic Times* Panche.

Tracker, D. (2018), *Artificial Intelligence.*

UN (2017), *World Investment Report.* UNCTAD, United Nations, Geneva, Switzerland.

Upadhyay, J. P. and V. Vishwanathan (2018), Bitcoin exchanges to face increased scrutiny, *Hindustan Times.*

van Den, B. G. J. (1994), The effects of changes of the job offer arrival rate on the duration of unemployment, *Journal of Labor Economics* **12**(3), 478–498.

Vanian, J. (2018), Alphabet research arm x wants to apply AI to farming, *Fortune*, March 27, 2018.

Venugopalan, A. (2019), Banking on AI. *timesgroup.com.*

Verma, P. (2019), IITs roll out courses incubating centres to bridge AI talent gap *timesgroup.com.*

Vincent, J. (2017), Putin says the nation that leads in AI will be the ruler of the world, *The Verge.*

Volckart, O. (1997), Early beginnings of the quantity theory of money and their context in Polish and Prussian monetary policies, c. 1520–1550, *The Economic History Review* **50**(3), 430–449.

von Mises, L. H. (1912), *The Theory of Money and Credit* [*Theorie des Geldes und der Umlaufsmittel*]. LvMI Mises Institute & Yale University Press.

WB (2018), *The World Development Report 2018 — WDR 2018: Learning to Realize Education's Promise.* The World Bank, Washington, DC.

Wennerlind, C. (2005), David Hume's monetary theory revisited, *Journal of Political Economy* **113**(1), 233–237.

Wicksell, K. (1898), *Interest and Prices*. Royal Economic Society, MacMillan & Company.

Wikipedia (2017), Money Supply. *Wikipedia*.

Woodford, M. (2003), *Interest and prices: foundations of a theory of monetary policy*, Princeton University Press, Princeton.

Yermack, D. (2013), *Is Bitcoin a real currency? An economic appraisal*. NBER Working Paper No. 19747.

Zdanowicz, J. S., W. W. Welch, and S. J. Pak (1995), Capital Flight from India to US through abnormal pricing in international trade, *Finance India* **9**(3).

Zdanowicz, J. S., W. W. Welch, and S. J. Pak (1996), Capital flight from India to US through abnormal pricing in international trade. *Finance India* **10**(4).

https://doi.org/10.1142/9789811220470_0014

Chapter 14

Developing Blockchain-Based Carbon Accounting and Decentralized Climate Change Management System

Qingliang Tang*,‡ and Lie Ming Tang†,§

* *Western Sydney University, Penrith, Australia*

† *University of Sydney, Camperdown, Australia*

‡ *q.tang@westernsydney.edu.au*

§ *liemingtang@gmail.com*

Abstract

This chapter discusses how emerging technology can be used to build a blockchain-based system for corporate carbon accounting and global climate change management. There is growing consensus that GHG emissions control requires coordinated efforts and collaboration in all sectors and at all levels of an organization. But, due to potential conflicts of interest and lack of trust between stakeholders, it is difficult to achieve the target of capping the global warming below 2°C. Thus, we propose using a blockchain-based system to build a corporate carbon accounting system which can strengthen carbon management. The blockchain technology can also be adopted in global climate change management. Such a system is appropriate for a decentralized climate change mechanism endorsed by the Paris Agreement for climate change. The system fits within existing market-based emissions trading schemes (ETSs).

Blockchain enables the integration of national ETSs and corporate carbon accounting into a synthetic and coherent governance framework.

Keywords: Blockchain; Carbon accounting; Emissions trading scheme; Decentralization; Climate change management.

1. Introduction

Intergovernmental Panel on Climate Change (IPCC, 2014; IPCC, 2018) provided consistent and robust scientific evidence on climate change. Governments around the world impose various measures, such as carbon taxes, energy consumption charges, and fees that internalize the otherwise external cost of greenhouse gas (GHG) emissions for organizations (Luo and Tang, 2014b).[1] Among them, emissions trading schemes (ETS) are the focal point of policies to achieve the goal of carbon reduction (Clarkson *et al.*, 2015; Newell *et al.*, 2013; Perdan and Azapagic, 2011; Pizer and Raimi, 2012; Swartz, 2016). Under ETSs, carbon emission allowances are allocated to the participating organizations. A company may sell the surplus allowances to make a profit, whereas firms short of the allowances need to purchase allowances to cover their GHG emissions liabilities.

Under the current carbon institution, carbon control is becoming a prominent managerial issue. From a management perspective, emissions trading system and the internalized social cost of carbon can lead to some carbon assets and liabilities, such as allocated or self-generated carbon allowances, green investments in and capitalized expenditures on low-carbon technology, capacity for carbon mitigation, use of renewable energy, and so forth. However, traditional means of accounting tools appear to be inadequate to achieve this goal of carbon control. In addition, the conventional accounting system does not provide sufficient information about carbon-related assets and liabilities, green activities, and investment for managers and shareholder to make decisions. Thus, there is a call for an innovative accounting system to help managers measure and manage carbon emissions and make sensible decisions to respond to climate change. As such, our chapter considers this issue in the context of an innovative and potentially disruptive technology: blockchain. Blockchain was originally proposed for the trading of the digital currency bitcoin

[1] https://members.nsw.liberal.org.au/legislation-repeal-carbon-tax.

(Chartered Accountants Australia and New Zealand, 2015), and now, blockchain is deemed to be an innovative method that can be used in many areas. Blockchain system is a distributed system that is different from conventional ledger systems (Swan, 2015). This is a decentralized, transparent, open, and immutable network that can record and track transfers of ownership of commercial items in a manner that is distinct from a centralized framework (Yu *et al.*, 2019). The use of a blockchain-enabled carbon accounting system can more effectively account for and manage carbon emissions in organizations that concern the exposure of carbon risk. Further, we argue that blockchain would be a strong tool for national and international climate change management and collaboration. Blockchain may help establish an integrated system for climate change management that will allow stakeholders and participants share climate change data and information, so as to enhance international collaboration and achieve the target of carbon neutral society in a more efficient way and at a lower cost (Tang and Tang, 2019).

The remainder of this chapter is organized as follows. Section 2 introduces blockchain technology with some detailed explanation. Section 3 explores the potential adoption of blockchain for corporate carbon accounting information system. Section 4 explains the application of this technology to integrate national ETSs and other efforts to achieve the international goal of becoming carbon neutral. Section 5 concludes the chapter with a summary of the main features of the blockchain-enabled system and future research opportunities in this field.

2. What is Blockchain Technology?

Our aim in this chapter is to explain a blockchain-enabled system for climate change management purposes. Blockchain (also called distributed ledger system, or shared ledgers) was originally purposed to address the "double-spending" issue of cryptocurrency. The use of the technology is to record the transaction of exchange of value in a block. The recorded information will be validated through proof-of-work from public nodes. Further, the system updates the data and information by only accepting one group of validated transactions (i.e., a "block") (Nakamoto, 2008). As each block is time stamped with the previous block, this then creates a "blockchain". Thus, this system creates only one version of history and truth so as to ensure transparency in the database and consensus among all parties involved in the system (Dai and Vasarhelyi, 2017). In other words, the technology effectively decentralizes the role of the recordkeeper which is inevitable in a centralized network. Thus, the distributed system offers a greater degree of security than non-distributed systems due to the time stamping nature. This is why the recorded transactions are considered virtually immutable (Dai and Vasarhelyi, 2017).

3. Blockchain-enabled Carbon Accounting

Tang (2017) offers the following definition of carbon accounting:

> *Carbon accounting is a system that uses accounting methods and procedures to collect, record, and analyse climate change–related information and account for and report carbon-related assets, liabilities, expenses, and income to inform the decision-making processes of internal managers and external stakeholders.*
>
> Tang (2017, p. 11)

This is a relatively narrow definition in the sense that it focuses on corporate carbon accounting. Corporate carbon accounting will use GHG accounting data (i.e., scientific methods to quantify GHG emissions, IPCC, 2014) but would not focus on its technical details. In addition, it does not cover carbon accounting system for macro climate change management. Since our focus is on corporate carbon management (Luo and Tang, 2016), the narrow definition is more suitable for this purpose.

Many firms have adopted carbon management systems (CAMS, Tang and Luo, 2014). Carbon accounting is deemed to be an assemblage of technical tools for carbon management. Carbon accounting is an extension of conventional accounting. Overall, traditional accounting remains "stuck" in conventional methods and fails to adapt operating measures to changing circumstances and overlook new approaches that are appropriate for decision-making. These changes include globalization and increased competition, information technology changes and changes in information flows, and increasing concerns of public regarding sustainability and environmental issues. Thus, a traditional system seems to be inadequate and is slow to respond to external changes, which will enhance the risk and fail to capture the opportunities.

Therefore, we believe it is necessary to adopt new technology to improve the accounting system to meet challenges stemming from climate

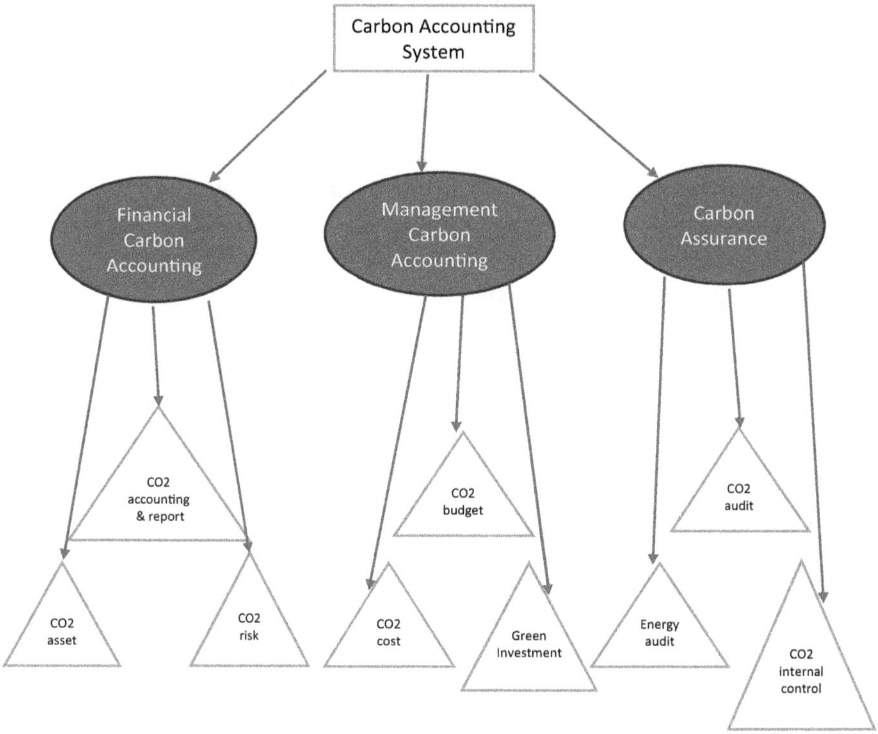

Figure 1: Structure of a conceptual carbon accounting system.

change. Carbon accounting methods can help implement a firm's carbon strategy to manage carbon assets and liability, enhance the efficiency of input-use, and gain a competitive advantage in a low-carbon market. Figure 1 shows the structure of a conceptual carbon accounting system. Figure 1 shows that the first part of carbon accounting is financial carbon accounting. Financial carbon accounting is an extension from traditional financial accounting, which consists of four components: accounting for physical GHG emissions, accounting for carbon assets and liabilities, carbon risk and opportunity assessment, and carbon reporting and disclosure. In addition, carbon accounting provides powerful technical support for recognizing, measuring, reporting, and verifying (MRV) carbon-related data, items, and activities.

The second part of carbon accounting is management carbon accounting that includes the following: accounting for cost of carbon reduction, carbon budget development, and accounting for green investment and project management. Corporate management carbon accounting is considered a functional tool to implement a firm's internal carbon strategy or policy. It concerns the decision-making of managers regarding carbon reduction cost control, carbon budget, and green investment by providing relevant data and information. The third part is carbon assurance, which consists of three components: External assurance for scope 1, 2, and 3 emissions, energy consumption assurance, and internal control evaluation. Thus, carbon accounting is an instrument for corporate overall carbon management system (Tang and Luo, 2014).

The structural components are presented in Table 1 and how the new technology, blockchain, can help the operation of carbon accounting with the operational components of the system is also shown.

3.1. *Financial carbon accounting*

Table 1 shows the structure of a theoretical carbon accounting system which includes three parts. Panel A of Table 1 presents financial carbon accounting. In column 2, it demonstrates three major components, column 2 shows its purpose, and column 3 is the role of blockchain. The purpose of GHG accounting is to quantify physical carbon emissions (scope 1, 2, and 3) using recognized GHG protocols. GHG accounting also takes into account various items related to carbon, e.g., carbon credits, carbon sequestrations, GHG footprint. There are many difficulties in GHG quantification. Using blockchain technology can allow all the parties of the network to participate in the process and share the information so the carbon and energy database is more trustful and reliable. The second component is carbon assets and liabilities. The carbon accounting system will use appropriate methods to record energy consumption and measure and analyze various types of carbon assets and liabilities related to GHG inventories and footprints (Tang and Luo, 2014). Blockchain is not expected to be involved directly with the measurement of carbon asset, liability, and other related items. A blockchain-based system will effectively record the generation of carbon assets and liability and facilitate the exchange of carbon-related items, such as carbon allowances, and dissimilate and circulate information in a more efficient way than conventional systems (IBM, 2017). The third component is external carbon report and disclosure, which reflects the current and historical carbon emissions and energy consumptions data and carbon reduction activity for decision-making purposes of external users (Luo *et al.*, 2012a, 2012b;

Table 1: Blockchain-enabled carbon accounting system.

Panel A: Financial carbon accounting		
Component	Purpose	Role of blockchain
1 GHG accounting	Using GHG protocol to quantify physical scope 1, 2, and 3 carbon emissions.	Blockchain can help to establish a reliable carbon and energy database shared by all nodes.
2 Carbon asset and liability	The major objective of financial carbon accounting is recognition and measurement of carbon assets and liabilities.	Blockchain will record, dissimilate, and circulate information on carbon assets in an efficient manner.
3 Climate risk and opportunity	The purpose of this component is to assess carbon-related risk and opportunities.	Blockchain can collect a large sum of data and information and provide powerful analytical methods to identify, assess, and evaluate the financial effects of carbon risks and opportunities.
4 Carbon report and disclosure	Carbon accounting will determine the content and format of the carbon report for internal and external users (Luo and Tang, 2012).	Blockchain-based reporting is more transparent and can provide real-time data for monitoring and decision-making purposes.
Panel B: Management carbon accounting		
Component	Purpose	How blockchain can help?
1 Cost of carbon mitigation	Adopting various management accounting methods to calculate and control costs of carbon reduction-related actions and adaptation to climate change.	Blockchain can fix the difficulty to distinguish and allocate between operating cost and carbon cost, check the cost of business in a simultaneous manner so it can effectively separate the cost for ordinary operation and carbon reduction activity.
2 Carbon budget	To prepare a budget for planned carbon emissions which can be served as a target.	Blockchain can help prepare a shared carbon budget and provide timely budgetary control.

(Continued)

Table 1: (*Continued*)

3 Green investment	The purpose of this component is to manage green initiatives and investment.	Blockchain provides a powerful tool and technology for green investments and project management. Smart contracts can be used to plan, monitor, and evaluate the implementation of various green programs, such as energy savings, use of renewable energy, and manufacturing of low-carbon goods and products (Tang and Luo, 2014).

Panel C: Carbon Assurance

Components	Purpose	How blockchain can help?
1 GHG emissions assurance	To verify GHG emissions including scope 1, 2, and 3 carbon emissions. Scope 1 is directly linked with energy (such as coal, oil, and gas) consumptions in facilities owned by the organization. Scope 2 is indirect emissions from for example purchased electricity. Scope 3 is other indirect emissions (e.g., staff activities such as business travel).	GHG verification standards are available but lack appropriate guidelines for implementation. Blockchain enables a constant and simultaneous verification of carbon and energy data and scope 1, 2, and 3 emissions. Blockchain can help track staff activity so may help estimate scope 3 emission more accurately.
2 Energy consumption assurance	To verify the utilization of energy such as coal and oil in business operations and across facilities.	Blockchain enables the system to more reliably record and track energy utilization and consumption.
3 Internal carbon control evaluation	Using various procedures and mechanism to mitigate carbon emissions and provide reliable and complete carbon data.	Internal control in carbon emission control is very complex. A blockchain-enabled system can effectively track and monitor energy consumption from a variety of facilities and employee activities. This is a key for emission control.

Luo and Tang, 2014a). A high-quality carbon report reveals a firm's strategy and CO_2 footprint, which allows stakeholders to monitor and seek improvements in the firm's carbon performance. The appropriate methods, format, and content of carbon report depend on the needs of users. From an accounting perspective, there does not exist a conventional financial accounting category naturally suited to carbon emissions and related transactions (Hood *et al.*, 2014). In practice, different countries adopt different and conflicting systems and framework of carbon accounting (Briner and Konrad, 2014). Thus, there are various issues related to carbon reporting, such as double counting, scope and boundary of carbon reporting, measure of carbon assets, and liability and evaluation of carbon performance. Blockchain-based technology can enhance transparency by sharing information for all the parties in the network. This is because a blockchain-enabled carbon reporting and disclosure system will allow multi-party participation and this can provide real-time data for monitoring and decision-making purposes.

3.2. *Management carbon accounting*

Panel B of Table 1 shows the second part of carbon accounting. The first component is calculation and control of carbon reduction cost. As carbon reduction has no physical product, this cost is mainly related to activities of carbon mitigation and the cost of each reduced tone of carbon. Various costing methods and concepts such as total costs method, variable costs, fixed costs, and marginal costs of carbon assets are applied for a carbon reduction costing system. The major challenge is to determine the scope of carbon control cost. Another issue is that the cost of carbon control is often mixed with other operational costs in a firm. Thus, an appropriate method of allocation of costs must be developed to achieve this purpose, but the extant literature lacks a discussion on this issue. Blockchain can measure the cost of business in a simultaneous manner, so it can effectively separate the cost for ordinary operations and carbon reduction activities. If the firm uses process and job costing, smart contract can be used that can more effectively identify the link between the cost items and process and jobs.

The second component of management carbon accounting concerns carbon budgets. A budget is a quantitative statement which may include planned total emissions and the resources used to achieve such a target for each department, operation, and each manager. To provide a framework for responsibility accounting, budgets require that managers be made responsible for their budget of the operations under their control. The activities of several departments need to be co-ordinated to ensure maximum integration of effort toward common organization goals within a budget. Blockchain can help to prepare a high quality of budget particularly for a decentralized governance system. It allows and encourages dialogue among managers and employee and helps to find discrepancies between budgeted and actual emissions. Every unit or node of the network will have only one copy of the budget so no one can change it. This will enhance the trust and confidence of the involved parties. The use of smart contract can further ensure the implementation of carbon budget. A smart contract is a software which can be embedded in a blockchain system. The smart contract can automatically operate some commands when some predetermined conditions are met. Thus, the participating parties can embed various terms that will trigger carbon-related actions under certain conditions. Such conditions include poor carbon performance of participating parties, overconsumption of energy, and a change of production conditions, which suggest that the budgetary target could not be made. Smart contract may take the necessary measures or actions without human interference.

The third component of management carbon accounting is green initiative and investment management (Table 1). This component focuses on capital expenditure on green investment and evaluation of the effectiveness of carbon and energy efficiency projects. Capital expenditure often involves the outlay of large sums of money, and the expected financial benefits, improved management capacity, and resilience and positive environmental effects may take a long time to accrue. Thus, it is vital to apply a rigorous process of appraisal and control. Carbon accountants will play an important role and adopt various methods to calculate returns from green investment that are closely related to government carbon and energy policy and change in market conditions. Blockchain offers powerful support to control the capital expenditure on a project and give feedback from the system. The monitoring is real time and simultaneous and can effectively manage the cash flows to avoid overexpenditure and delay.

3.3. *Carbon assurance and auditing*

The third part of carbon accounting is carbon assurance (or carbon auditing, Figure 1, Table 1). Carbon assurance refers to an examination conducted by a third party (assurance providers or auditor) of CO_2

emissions and its equivalent of an organization (Tang, 2018). The purpose of the examination is to reduce climate change information asymmetry and enhance the confidence of the users of a carbon report of an entity responsible for the subject matter. The definition of carbon assurance could be extended to a broad concept referring to any kind of evaluation of strategies, activities, or information related to climate change. Therefore, the subject matter of carbon assurance might take many forms. Generally speaking, carbon assurance is intended to clarify a firm's carbon footprint, determine whether its operations comply with climate change laws, and assess the nature and extent of harm to the environment caused by business activities (Datt *et al.*, 2018, 2019). Carbon assurance is needed because of the complexity and risks associated with GHG emissions and their impacts on the economy and society (The International Organization of Supreme Audit Institutions (INTOSAI), Working Group on Environmental Auditing, 2010, p. 10).[2] GHG quantification is subject to inherent uncertainty, and carbon information relies on private information known only to management, which engenders information asymmetry between corporate insiders and outsiders (Tang, 2018).

According to IAASB, carbon assurance is intended to examine whether a GHG statement is free from material misstatement and is prepared in accordance with applicable criteria (ISAE 3410, IAASB). Authors point out there are significant differences between financial and GHG assurance with regard to the nature, methodology, and other characteristics of assurance (Tang, 2018). For example, GHG assurance requires different expertise, so scientific and engineering knowledge is often required or desirable (Simnett *et al.*, 2009a), in addition to an understanding of the laws and regulations related to GHG quantification and measurement, etc. Further, different methods of investigation may be adopted by assurance providers (ISAE 3410). Finally, the risks of misstatement in a GHG report are associated with factors (e.g., emission boundary) that are not familiar to financial auditors.

The first and the main component of carbon assurance checks the accuracy of any measurement of a carbon footprint (including scope 1, 2, and 3). The consistency, comprehensiveness, and reliability of a carbon report are dependent on the development of scientific, regulatory, and

---

[2]The International Organization of Supreme Audit Institutions (INTOSAI) is the professional organization of supreme audit institutions in countries that are part of the United Nations or its specialized agencies.

physical mechanisms of a reporting entity. It is also dependent on the degree of complexity of a firm's operations and the nature of its business (ISAE, 3410, p. 23, para. A52–A53, A70). Similarly, energy consumption is the main source of carbon emissions so this is another component of carbon assurance that examines the completeness and authenticity of the use and reuse and the structure of energy utilization of a reporting organization. Carbon assurance must ensure the energy consumption data are accurate, reliable, and consistent for each type of the energy resource such as fossil fuel, clean energy, and renewable energy which are directly or indirectly related to carbon emissions.

The third component of carbon assurance investigates the adequacy and appropriateness of an internal control system regarding energy consumption and GHG emissions. The strengths and weaknesses of a given institution may affect the susceptibility of the carbon report to material misstatement due to the poor system for the collection and processing of energy data resulting in non-compliance with provisions of carbon regulations (ISAE 3410, para. A87). Misstatement can also take place in other ways, e.g., double counting: omission of a significant category of emissions (e.g., fugitive emissions), and subjective or biased judgments made by managers (ISAE 3410, para. A88 (g)).[3] So internal control evaluation is necessary during the carbon assurance process.

Carbon assurance is an emerging practice, and the practices vary widely in terms of the level of assurance, scope, criteria, and materiality around the world (Datt *et al.*, 2018). The new standards issued by IAASB provide guidance and should improve the verification effectiveness.

Blockchain technology has the potential to take the auditing processes and internal controls to the next level of generation. With the right design and implementation, companies can create a blockchain-based system that has less chance for human error. All the transactions that are recorded in the network cannot be altered or erased and this will become an immutable and complete audit trail. In addition, advanced software can be developed to fully automate the internal control process and some audit functions. Since all entries are distributed and cryptographically sealed, destroying or falsifying recorded data to conceal a fraud or error is basically impossible. In sum, blockchain will not eliminate the internal

[3]International Auditing and Assurance Standards Board (IAASB) issued (June 2012) issued *ISAE 3410, Assurance Engagements on Greenhouse Gas Statements* (with assurance reports covering periods ending on or after September 30, 2013).

control system and audit: nevertheless, it will improve the efficiency by changing the nature, scope, focus, and approach of auditing and internal control system.

4. Applying Blockchain Technology to Global Climate Change Management Under the Paris Agreement

4.1. *Kyoto protocol vs. Paris agreement*

Kyoto Protocol is the first international agreement on climate change management. Kyoto Protocol adopted a top-down approach regarding the international effort to combat global warming (Victor, 2001; Weyant and Hill, 1999). Currently, the international efforts to control carbon emissions are governed by the 2015 International Accord, the Paris Agreement, which set up an ambitious target of capping global warming to well below 2°C relative to the pre-industrial level. Paris Agreement used a bottom-up approach which emphasizes a nation-determined contribution to achieve the stabilization of climate change. Thus, the global climate change management under Paris Agreement is characterized as a decentralized system. Such a system emphasizes collaboration, interaction, and cooperation among national governments and various stakeholder groups without a central authority. However, there have been difficulties in implementing the Paris Agreement (Tang, 2016) largely due to a lack of trust and confidence between nations and stakeholders at large.

4.2. *Using blockchain for global climate change management*

Climate change is a global problem, it entails international collaboration for an effective climate change management. The global mechanism involves an internationalized carbon emissions trading market, large-scale exchange of low-carbon products, and the development of renewable energy and other advanced technology. A robust, integrated, and sound institution must be established to coordinate the efforts, investment, and activities from multi-governments, stakeholder groups, and all levels of organizations. This requires the support of a new and innovative information technology. The unique inherent characteristics of blockchain would be useful not only for carbon asset management at the firm level it can also be adopted to upgrade our global climate change management mechanism particularly under the Paris Agreement which has adopted a bottom-up approach.

First, a set of blockchain-based distributed ledges would operate as a single source of information (Pinna and Ruttenberg, 2016) on the ownership of carbon assets (e.g., emissions allowances) at any given point in time. This is in contrast to the ordinary ledgers system that entails all parties keeping their own ledgers or outsourcing the task to a third party. With a blockchain, each party maintains the exact same ledger and views the same version (Schwartz *et al.*, 2014). This can significantly simplify carbon transactions and reduce the cost of transactions. Thus, using blockchain for emissions trading may have the potential to create a reputation-based trading system to encourage firms (particularly small entities) to achieve long-term emissions abatement (Khaqqi *et al.*, 2018).

Second, without a central recordkeeping authority, this system avoids security issues and a weakness of reliance on a single point in the system, which is operated across many countries. No party within the system is able to unilaterally alter the carbon ledger, and no party cedes control over their own carbon ledger (Tang and Tang, 2019; Goldman Sachs, 2016). In addition, a public blockchain is open to all members of society, and a private blockchain is accessible by all legitimate parties involved. As each party has equal access to the information, such a framework enjoys a higher degree of transparency relative to the traditional, centralized mechanism. This is incredibly important to enhance the confidence in the collaboration by various parties around the world.

Finally, as mentioned before, blockchain provides a platform for the potential adoption of self-executing smart contracts (Szabo, 1994). These contracts are written based on conditions and codes included into the ledger system. The smart contracts may substitute legal contracts and automatically conduct some predetermined transactions. Participating parties can embed various terms that will trigger carbon-related actions when certain events happen (e.g., change in carbon emissions of the participating entities). Such smart contracts can further improve the efficiency of carbon management at the international level. In sum, Blockchain-based technology is expected to enhance transparency, efficiency, and quality of carbon transactions at the national and international levels. The system can facilitate the allocation of carbon allowances and track the transfer of ownership via allowance trading. This means blockchain would be a strong tool for linking carbon asset management at the firm level to the national and international carbon market. The integrated system would help all stakeholders and participants to share carbon information and make more transparent decisions, so as to achieve carbon mitigation targets in a more efficient manner. However, the traditional technological mechanisms are restricted to the narrow scope of individual organizations and nations. Such systems do not help managers take broad and long-term perspectives. Moreover, traditional systems often ignore supply chain carbon management.

The new technically sound system is particularly useful for multinational enterprises that engage in cross-border transactions with many subsidiaries located in different countries. It is also appropriate for firms participating in an ETS. As discussed earlier, ETS is a market mechanism that allows firms to trade carbon assets such as carbon allowances. Here, we consider the use of a blockchain in the operation of a multinational ETS (Ellis and Tirpak, 2006). The authority in charge of the ETS will go through a process to operate the system that tracks the ownership of all allowances from their issuance, through all updates with each transfer to their surrender (EU ETS, 2017). First, the authority will decide the total quantity of allowances and then distribute the allowances through a combination of free allocation and auction to all participating organizations around the world. Next, the allocated allowances can be traded in a recognized market by the participating entities and other legitimate market participants. Finally, once the annual emissions of a participating business are verified, the allowances needed to cover those emissions' liabilities are surrendered to the ETS authority. This is the end of carbon allowance.

The adoption of a blockchain is intended to simplify this process. The system could in fact replace the traditional registry system that records the distribution of allowances. Further, it will reduce the need for exchanges and a clearinghouse. This will enhance efficiency by removing friction in the process of allocation and trading of allowances. Each company would have a public address to maintain its registered allowances with validation by the governmental authority. This is the genesis of carbon transactions. The blockchain will maintain an immutable record of all transfers in the ledger between the participating parties (Mizrahi, 2015).

Blockchain will allow a smooth trading of allowances. Each trading party can log into its account using a private security key (cryptographic password). The account contains all assigned allowances and any history of traded allowances. Trading itself is simplified and each proposed transaction will be validated and accepted by the blockchain system and then be confirmed by the two trading parties using their respective private keys. Finally, surrendering of allowances would be a process similar to that for trading. All such transactions would be permanently recorded in the blockchain for all parties to peruse and inspect (Tang and Tang, 2019).

5. Conclusion

From an accounting perspective, there is no conventional financial accounting category naturally suited to carbon (Hood *et al.*, 2014) due to its inherent uncertainty regarding the state of carbon assets such as carbon allowances. In practice, differing systems of carbon accounting established by nations have put forward conflicting frameworks (Briner and Konrad, 2014). The lack of harmonization and transparency in accounting practice and standards for carbon and climate management create several problems and issues. Conventional carbon reports limit the effectiveness of carbon management and control (Hood *et al.*, 2014; Ellis and Moarif, 2015) and are often incomplete and inconsistent (UNFCCC, 2015).

There are many potential benefits of using blockchain-based system. For example, it could greatly reduce the administrative burden. The central database would no longer be necessary. While the role of the government would remain unchanged in terms of climate change strategy development, authorization and allocation of emissions allowances, its administrative responsibilities would likely diminish in terms of ETS operations within its jurisdiction. Furthermore, blockchain would allow frictionless and direct trading of allowances. This process would forego the need for a traditional physical exchange or a clearinghouse and reduce the operational and transaction costs and expenses. This could encourage greater volumes of trades and increase investment in carbon assets. Finally, blockchains provide a higher degree of transparency and security. This is one of the key and unique advantages of blockchain that can significantly enhance the trust and confidence among parties in the network, as the system can guarantee all legitimate parties have easy and quick access to all relevant information on carbon allowances and other carbon products and activities. And this information is deemed consistent, accurate, immutable, and permanent.

Therefore, there are enormous opportunities for future research in this area. For example, future studies may consider how to develop technical details that can implement the blockchain framework for carbon asset management and green investment. Particularly how to use smart contract for carbon performance evaluation and assessment for individual staff and departments in an organization, which is extremely important to achieve carbon reduction target. Furthermore, supply chain carbon mitigation is an important aspect of carbon management, but there is very limited study in this area. Blockchain is especially useful for tracking carbon emissions footprint of a product within its whole life cycle from manufacturing, distribution, and consumption to disposal in a supply chain context. Such a study focusing on the adoption of blockchain in supply chain will greatly add value that assist firms to share the information and collaborate with each other to attend carbon reduction goals not only for individual entities but also for all the supply chain partners.

References

Briner, G. and S. Konrad (2014), Planting the foundations of a post-2020 land sector reporting and accounting framework. OECD/IEA CCXG Paper No. 2014(06).

Chartered Accountants Australia and New Zealand (2015), Digital currencies: where to from here? Charteredaccountantsanz.com/futureinc.

Clarkson, P. M., Y. Li, M. Pinnuck, and G. D. Richardson (2015), The valuation relevance of greenhouse gas emissions under the European Union carbon emissions trading scheme, *European Accounting Review* **24**(3), 551–580.

Dai, J. and M. A. Vasarhelyi (2017), Toward blockchain-based accounting and assurance, *Journal of Information Systems* **31**(3), 5–21.

Datt, R., L. Luo, Q. Tang, and G. Mallik (2018), An international study of determinants of voluntary carbon assurance, *Journal of International Accounting Research* **17**(3), 1–20. Available at: https://doi.org/10.2308/jiar-52221.

Datt, R., L. Luo, and Q. Tang (2019), The impact of legitimacy threat on the choice of external carbon assurance: Evidence from the United States. *Accounting Research Journal*, **32**(2), 181–202. https://doi.org/10.1108/ARJ-03-2017-0050.

Ellis, J. and S. Moarif (2015), Identifying and addressing gaps in the UNFCCC reporting framework. OECD/IEA CCXG Paper No. 2015(7).

Ellis, J. and D. Tirpak (2006), Linking GHG emissions trading schemes and markets, OECD International Energy Agency.

European Commission (EU): The Emissions Trading System (2017). Available at: https://ec.europa.eu/clima/policies/ets_en.

Goldman Sachs (2016), Profiles in Innovation: Blockchain Putting Theory into Practice. The Goldman Sachs Group Inc.

Hood, C., G. Briner, and M. Rocha (2014), GHG or not GHG: Accounting for diverse mitigation contributions in the post-2020 climate framework. OECD/IEA CCXG Paper No. 2014(2).

IBM (2017), Carbon assets and blockchain. IBM China. Available at: (https://www-03.ibm.com/press/us/en/pressrelease/51839.wss).

Intergovernmental Panel on Climate Change (2014). Fifth Assessment Report (AR5), Cambridge University Press.

Intergovernmental Panel on Climate Change (2018). Global warming of 1.5 c. Available at: http://www.ipcc.ch/report/sr15/.

International Auditing and Assurance Standards Board (IAASB) (2012), ISAE 3410, Assurance Engagements on Greenhouse Gas Statements (with assurance reports covering periods ending on or after September 30, 2013).

Khaqqi, K. N., J. J. Sikorski, K. Hadinoto, and M. Kraft (2018), Incorporating seller/buyer reputation-based system in blockchain-enabled emission trading application, *Applied Energy*, **209**, 8–19.

Luo, L., Y.-C. Lan, and Q. Tang (2012a), Corporate incentives to disclose carbon information: Evidence from the CDP Global 500 Report, *Journal of International Financial Management & Accounting* **23**(2), 93–120. doi:10.1111/j.1467-646X.2012.01055.x.

Luo, L., Q. Tang, and Y.-C. Lan (2012b), Comparison of propensity for carbon disclosure between developing and developed countries: A resource constraint perspective, *Accounting Research Journal*, doi:10.1108/ARJ-04-2012-0024.

Luo, L. and Q. Tang (2014a), Does voluntary carbon disclosure reflect underlying carbon performance? *Journal of Contemporary Accounting and Economics* **10**(3), 191–205. doi:10.1016/j.jcae.2014.08.003.

Luo, L. and Q. Tang (2014b), Carbon tax, corporate carbon profile and financial return, *Pacific Accounting Review* **24**(3), 351–373. doi:10.1108/PAR-09-2012-0046.

Luo, L. and Q. Tang (2016), The determinants of the quality of corporate carbon management systems: An international study, *The International Journal of Accounting* **51**(2), 275–305. doi:10.1016/j.intacc.2016.04.007.

Mizrahi, A. (2015), A blockchain-based property ownership recording system. Availabe at: http://chromaway.com/papers/A-blockchain-based-property-registry.pdf.

Newell, R., W. Pizer, and D. Raimi (2013), Carbon markets 15 years after Kyoto: Lessons learned, new challenges, *Journal of Economic Perspectives* **27**, 123–146.

Nakamoto, S. (2008), Bitcoin: A peer-to-peer electronic cash system. Available at: https://bitcoin.org/bitcoin.pdf.

Perdan, S. and A. Azapagic (2011), Carbon trading: Current schemes and future developments, *Energy Policy* **39**(10), 6040–6054.

Pinna, A. and W. Ruttenberg (2016), Distributed ledger technologies in securities post-trading. European Central Bank, Occasional Paper Series No.172/ April 2016.

Pizer, W. and D. Raimi (2012), Carbon markets: Past, present and future. Resources for the Future, Washington.

Schwartz, D., A. Britto, and N. Youngs (2014), The ripple protocol consensus algorithm. Ripple Labs Inc.

Swartz, J. (2016), China's national emissions trading system: Implications for carbon markets and trade; ICTSD Global Platform on Climate Change. Issue Paper No. 6.

Swan, M. (2015), *Blockchain: Blueprint for a New Economy*, 1st edition. Sebastopol, CA, USA: O'Reilly Media Inc.

Szabo, N. (1994), Smart Contracts. Available at: https://www.fon.hum.uva.nl/rob/Courses/InformationInSpeech/CDROM/Literature/LOTwinterschool2006/szabo.best.vwh.net/smart.contracts.html. Retrieved 2018-10-30.

Tang, Q. and L. Luo (2014), Carbon management system and carbon mitigation, *Australian Accounting Review* **24**(1), 84–98 (ABDC rank: B), doi:10.1111/auar.12010).

Tang, Q. (2016), Carbon management system studies: Contributions, limitations and future opportunities: A response to discussion comments (2016). *International Journal of Accounting*, doi:10.1016/j.intacc.2016.04.001.

Tang, Q. (2017), Framework for and the role of carbon accounting in corporate carbon management systems: A Holistic Approach. Working paper. Western Sydney University. SSRN. Available at: https://papers.ssrn.com/sol3/papers.cfm?abstract_id=2903366.

Tang, Q. (2018), Institutional influence, transition management, and the demand for carbon auditing: The Chinese experience, *Australian Accounting Review(B)*, March. doi:10.1111/auar.12224.

Tang, L. Ming, and Q. Tang (2019), Towards a distributed carbon ledger for the integration of carbon asset management and emissions trading, *Journal of Emerging Technologies in Accounting*. In-Press. Available at: https://doi.org/10.2308/jeta-52409.

United Nations Framework Convention on Climate Change (UNFCCC) (2015), *Adoption of the Paris Agreement*, draft decision, http://unfccc.int/resource/docs/2015/cop21/eng/l09r01.pdf; https://unfccc.int/sites/default/files/english_paris_agreement.pdf, last accessed December 28, 2015.

Victor, D. (2001), *The Collapse of the Kyoto Protocol and the Struggle to Slow Global Warming*. Princeton University Press.

Weyant, J. P. and J. Hill (1999), Introduction and overview, in the costs of the Kyoto protocol: A multi-model evaluation, special issue, *Energy Journal* **20**, 1–398.

Yu, T., S. Lin, and Q. Tang (2019), Blockchain: The introduction and its application in financial accounting, *Journal of Corporate Accounting and Finance*, Available at: https://onlinelibrary.wiley.com/doi/pdf/10.1002/jcaf.22365.

https://doi.org/10.1142/9789811220470_0015

Chapter 15

Usefulness of Corporate Carbon Information for Decision-Making

Rong He[*,§], Le Luo[†,¶] and Qingliang Tang[‡,‖]

[*] *University of Newcastle, Callaghan, NSW 2308, Australia*

[†] *Macquire University, Sydney, Australia*

[‡] *Western Sydney University, Penrith, Australia*

[§] *R.He@uon.edu.au*

[¶] *le.luo@mq.edu.au*

[‖] *q.tang@westernsydney.edu.au*

Abstract

There is a general consensus that climate change negatively affects the physical environment, our ecosystem, economy, and the society. Thus, corporate response to global warming is becoming one of the most important topics in business studies. Carbon information is increasingly relevant for various users for their decision-making. This chapter provides a review of previous studies regarding the usefulness, quality, and adequateness of climate change information disclosed. The chapter explains how carbon reports can be used to assess GHG reduction performance, monitor business climate risks, and assist the decision-making of investors. In addition, we discuss the incentives of managerial voluntary carbon disclosure. We highlight the role the emerging carbon accounting and reporting system can play for the measurement of carbon assets and liabilities, carbon strategy development, and carbon management toward a decarbonized future.

Keywords: Carbon disclosure; Carbon accounting; Climate change; Corporate voluntary GHG statement.

1. Introduction

Strong scientific consensus shows that global climate change is underway, with rising greenhouse gas (GHG) emissions caused by human activity being a major contributor. The increase of the global temperature is expected to cause a rise in the sea level, increased frequency and severity of extreme weather events, and a change in the amount and the pattern of precipitation (IPCC, 2007a). Efforts to reverse this trend are triggering new regulations in the world to reduce GHG emissions — efforts that will include explicit carbon emission limits that will encourage low-carbon technologies and discourage higher polluting technologies (CERES, 2010).[1] All of these trends will have far-reaching effects on numerous business sectors and the financial institutions that invest in them.

Businesses *per se* have gradually recognized that they suffer material risks related to climate change, either through direct physical impact[2] or via climate change policies or regulations, changes in consumption pattern (e.g., consumers switching to products with a lower effect on climate

[1] The earliest influential international regulation is the Kyoto Protocol. Initially established on December 11, 1997 and becoming effective on February 16, 2005, the aim of the Kyoto Protocol is to fight global warming. It is generally seen as an important first step towards a truly global emission reduction regime that will stabilize GHG emission concentrations in the atmosphere and provide the essential architecture for any future international agreements on climate change. Under the framework of the Kyoto Protocol, three market mechanisms are proposed to stimulate green investment and achieve their national targets in a cost-effective way, namely, the Emission Trading Scheme, the Clean Development Mechanism (CDM), and the Joint Implementation (JI).

[2] Direct physical impacts of climate change on a company's assets and processes include damage to production facilities or the availability of raw materials due to storms, floods, droughts, sea-level rise, and extreme weather, as well as an increased risk to human health (e.g., the potential spreading of tropical diseases) (Busch and Hoffmann, 2007). The visibility of these direct effects has increased steadily; e.g., the global economic losses due to natural catastrophes have increased seven-fold in the last 40 years (Munich Re, 2005).

change) and short-term adjustments of contract conditions (e.g., insurance carriers may request higher risk premiums due to high climate change exposure) (Busch and Hoffmann, 2007). For years, investors managing trillions of dollars have been pressing companies to disclose material information on these risks as well as on the carbon opportunities related to climate change (CERES, 2011). Information concerning carbon emissions, carbon governance, and carbon reduction activities should, therefore, be of interest to investors and other relevant stakeholders like consumers and regulators. Proper dissemination of carbon information on an individual company's efforts to reduce carbon emissions is critical to keep stakeholders informed about an individual company's strategies, risks, and actions on GHG emissions and in turn to monitor and aid their decision-making (Freedman and Jaggi, 2010). In view of the importance of carbon information for investment and other decisions, national mandatory carbon reporting legislation has increasingly been proposed or implemented throughout the world.[3] In 2007, the National Greenhouse and Energy Reporting Act (NGER) was introduced by the Australian government as a national framework for reporting and disseminating information about GHG emissions, GHG projects, and energy use and production. Similarly, effective in October 2013, all UK quoted companies are required to measure and report their yearly GHG emissions in their directors' report. In addition, the Securities and Exchange Commission (SEC) in the United States (US) has decided to require that companies disclose the impact of climate change on their businesses in their public filings.[4] Because of new carbon regulations or legislations, firms may face

---

[3]Mandatory reporting rules include the US Environmental Protection Agency's Mandatory Reporting Rules and the Australian National Greenhouse and Energy Reporting rules.

[4]The US SEC's Commission Guidance Regarding Disclosure Relating to Climate Change, released in February 2010, outlines public companies' obligations under securities laws and SEC regulations to disclose to investors material information concerning climate-related risks and opportunities. The Guidance follows longstanding efforts by major investors, state law enforcement officials and others to focus companies' attention on the quality of their climate-related disclosure, and its release coincides with important new regulatory developments, including the EPA's adoption of regulations for GHG emissions from motor vehicles and large sources such as power plants and factories under the Clean Air Act. The new Guidance serves as a reminder that climate risk disclosure is a matter of not only responsiveness to investors' demands but compliance with basic legal obligations (CERES, 2010).

significant changes in economic trends or physical risks, both domestically and abroad (Mounteer and Ranchod, 2010). Moreover, many industry associations have undertaken environmental initiatives that encourage their member firms to become more transparent with respect to their carbon management and carbon reduction performance. Nonetheless, carbon disclosure[5] is predominately optional in most of the countries in the world. Many companies have decided to voluntarily take proactive emission reduction and disclosure, while others are reluctant to take actions or communicate their carbon information with the outside world.

The chapter is organized into six sections as follows. Section 2 discusses the issues in financial accounting of carbon assets and liabilities, as well as the use of carbon information in management accounting. Section 3 outlines some theoretical frameworks to explain the incentives of voluntary carbon disclosure practices. Section 4 investigates the determinants and motivations of a firm to voluntarily disclose carbon information. Section 5 analyzes the quality and adequateness of voluntary carbon information. Section 6 addresses whether or not voluntarily disclosed information reliably reflects the underlying carbon performance so that the carbon information can be used by stakeholders for their decision-making. Section 7 provides a review of previous studies regarding the usefulness of carbon information by two critical investors: shareholders and debtholders. Section 8 introduces a voluntary carbon reporting program — CDP. The conclusions and discussions are brought together in Section 9.

2. Carbon Financial and Management Accounting

2.1. *Carbon financial accounting*

Carbon accounting provides financial and management information for both decision-making external users and internal managers. Carbon financial accounting deals with carbon-related assets (such as carbon allowances), liabilities, and carbon performance disclosure, etc. The debate on the accounting treatment of carbon allowances allocated or purchased in a cap-and-trade market has seen the withdrawal of International Financial Reporting Interpretations Committee (IFRIC) Interpretation 3: Emission Rights (IFRIC 3) in June 2005 (Bebbington and Larrinaga-González,

[5]Carbon disclosure can typically be thought of as comprising information relating to a corporation's activities, aspirations, and public image with regard to climate change issues.

2008). The accounting difficulties under existing standards are argued to be created by the conflict between the unique features of carbon markets and the need for consistency with other standards (Cook, 2009).

Currently, three different approaches are commonly adopted in accounting practices for emissions accounting: (1) a net liability approach that classifies allowances as intangible assets and only shows an emission liability when emissions exceed the free allocated allowances; (2) a gross liability approach that recognizes the free allocation at fair value and a corresponding gross liability under the emission trading scheme; and (3) an inventory approach with free allocations given at nil value (Black, 2013). The diversity in accounting treatments of emission allowances can impair the comparability of firms' financial statements (Griffin, 2013; Warwick and Ng, 2012) because firms have total discretion for the recognition and measurement of the carbon allowances as an asset, expense, or liability (Mete *et al.*, 2010). Therefore, some scholars call for a common approach to be set by accounting standard setters (Giner, 2014; Haupt and Ismer, 2013; Raibor and Massoud, 2010).

Regarding the recognition and measurement of carbon assets and liabilities, Ratnatunga *et al.* (2011) propose an analytical model for valuing an organization's assets that have carbon credit-producing capabilities. The authors define Environmental Capable Enhancing Asset (ECEA) as an intangible asset of an organization that is capable of generating or using carbon credits. Thus, the ECEAs reflect the capability of the organization to control or sequester CO_2 in the future. The authors also propose the method of recording ECEA for financial reporting purposes and integrating it into conventional financial statements.

2.2. *Carbon management accounting*

Carbon management accounting aims to provide managers with information that will assist their decision-making on carbon emission issues. The introduction of carbon market and other climate regulations brought various changes to firm management accounting practices. For example, firms had to "learn to account for carbon" to respond to the implementation of ETS through the use of external and internal expertise for emission trading (Engels, 2009). Firms collect past- and future-oriented, carbon-related information in both financial and non-financial terms for various purposes including regulatory reporting, performance measurement, and supporting management decisions related to costing, planning, and resource allocation (Burritt *et al.*, 2011). The carbon information can help capital investment decision and change the way an organization works (Vesty *et al.*, 2015).

Some new practices of carbon management are proposed to help companies transition to the low-carbon economy. For example, a multi-methodological approach is proposed to measure economic and environmental performances simultaneously to provide relevant information to promote green initiatives (Lee and Wu, 2014). Further, a combined carbon management accounting system focusing on both products and the organization is recommended to improve the efficiency in terms of both performance measurement and external communication (Gibassier and Schaltegger, 2015). In summary, a well-practiced strategic carbon management and accounting system will be useful in evaluating the "whole-of-life" costs of products and services in terms of carbon emissions and facilitate the development of business policy, human resource management, marketing, supply chain management, and finance strategies and the resultant evaluation of performance (Ratnatunga and Balachandran, 2009).

3. Theories of Voluntary Carbon Disclosure

The current literature offers various theories for the motivation of voluntary carbon disclosure: legitimacy theory, stakeholder theory, signalling theory, and institutional theory. Underlying by multiple theories, the propensity to disclose a firm's true position regarding carbon emission is hypothesized to be associated with social, financial, market, economic, and regulatory and institutional pressures, and these pressures can be transferred and become disclosure incentives. An understanding of how firms interpret and respond to pressures imposed by governments, communities, and external groups is essential to establish a regulatory framework to achieve a low-carbon environment.

Legitimacy theory argues that companies conduct extensive disclosure in response to social pressure in an attempt to legitimize their long-term operations and execute their "social contract" voluntarily (Cormier *et al.*, 2005; Gray *et al.*, 1995; Solomon and Lewis, 2002). More specifically, legitimacy theory posits that an organization is a member of society, which provides the organization with resources. So, it is expected to operate in a way to meet the demands of society and various stakeholders (Gray *et al.*, 1995). In the current context, as public expectations regarding environmental and carbon performance evolve, companies that do not meet these expectations have their legitimacy threatened. Thus, these firms have incentives to increase their carbon disclosures. Some researchers point out that the purpose of such disclosure may be to enhance legitimacy rather than to make actual changes to strategies, performance, and operations (e.g., Deegan and Rankin, 1996; Patten, 2002).

Stakeholder theory is another common theory that is often used interchangeably by social and environmental studies. However, Gray *et al.* (1995, p. 52) argued that although legitimacy theory and stakeholder theory can be seen as two overlapping perspectives, these two theories are different both literally and conceptually. Legitimacy theory often embraces issues of compliance with expectations of society as a whole. However, the society is made of various stakeholders who may have varying influences on firms. A stakeholder was defined by Freeman (1984, p. 25) as "any group or individual who can affect or is affected by the achievement of the organization's objectives" and by Clarkson (1995, p. 106) as "a person or group that has or claims ownership, rights or interests in a corporation and its activities, past, present, or future". Thus, the incentive of firms to voluntarily disclose carbon information is likely to be motivated by the information demands of different stakeholders, an argument which is underpinned by the stakeholder theory. A major objective of the firm was to attain the ability to balance the conflicting demands of various stakeholders in the firm, as opposed to shareholder theory, which argued that managers take care of the shareholders' interests exclusively. Stakeholder theory provides another perspective and explanation regarding the motivation of voluntary carbon disclosure from a stakeholder perspective.

Signalling theory posits that firms with "good news" in performance (financial or environmental) have incentives to signal their "type" to the market to avoid the adverse selection problem by making credible environmental disclosures that are difficult for poor performers to mimic (Dye, 1985; Verrecchia, 1983). Financial market pressures come from shareholders and debtholders, to whom management is directly accountable and who are considered as the most powerful stakeholders (Cormier *et al.*, 2005). Thus, failure to disclose decision-making relevant information could result in wider information asymmetry and increase the cost of capital (Healy and Palepu, 2001). Third, economic pressures are generated by the management's desire to reduce carbon charges, such as the costs imposed by carbon tax, under an ETS which in turn increases a company's propensity to voluntarily disclose carbon information (Pinkse and Kolk, 2009).

Coercive institutions (e.g., legislation or regulation) which are among the main impetuses of voluntary carbon disclosure are underpinning by institutional theory. The existing or proposed changes in legislation regarding carbon abatement create regulatory and institutional pressures for carbon disclosure (Solomon and Lewis, 2002). Such disclosures may mitigate or avoid compliance costs or regulatory risks especially for firms within carbon-sensitive sectors. It can also be argued that firms in a country with a culture with a high degree of corporate transparency are more likely to disclose carbon information (Cormier *et al.*, 2005). While this perspective may result in the same response pattern seen using the legitimacy or stakeholder perspective, the company's underlying motivation differs. From legitimacy or stakeholder perspectives, firms may make voluntary disclosures to satisfy a society's expectation or needs of various stakeholders, while the institutional theory views voluntary disclosures as being made by firms so as to reduce the possibility of serious punishment and disadvantages by existing regulations.

4. Determinants and Motivations of Voluntary Carbon Disclosure

This section will discuss the determinants and motivations of firms' voluntary carbon disclosure. Carbon reporting gives a greater degree of visibility to corporate carbon activities and consequences. An understanding of the determinants of voluntary carbon disclosure is important because global carbon reporting has been developed as a tool for analyzing and monitoring efficient business processes and measurement. External carbon transparency will in turn exert pressure on companies to tackle climate change, reduce carbon emissions, and achieve energy and operational savings as well as create brand building benefits (Kolk *et al.*, 2008). Policymakers also need an understanding of the motivation for companies' carbon disclosure in order to design more effective reporting policies so as to create incentives for them to reduce carbon emissions rather than just to manipulate perceptions of firms' true performance.

Many studies examine the determinants of companies' decision to make climate change-related disclosure, as well as the level of information they disclose. The extant literature identifies a number of country-level, sector-level, and firm-level factors that are related to firms' carbon disclosure decisions. To illustrate the findings on the determinants of corporate carbon disclosure, the determinant framework defined by

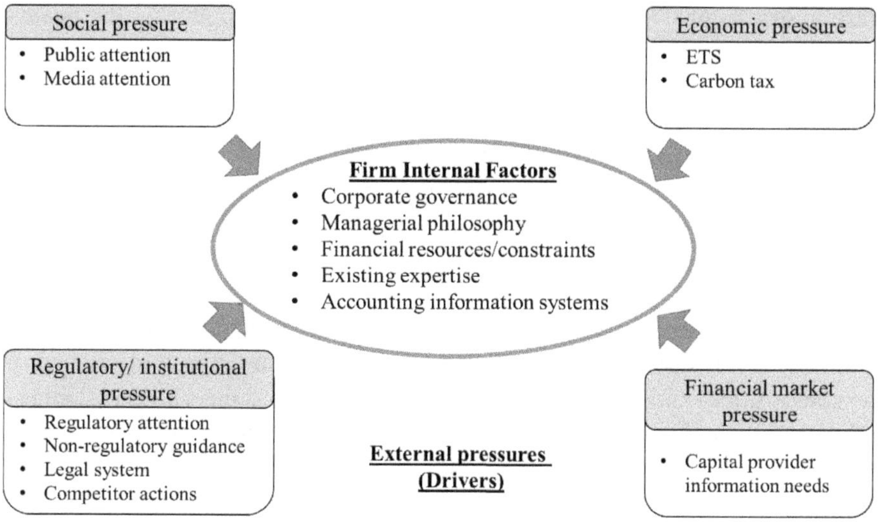

Figure 1: Corporate carbon disclosure determinants framework.
Source: Adopted from Luo *et al.* (2013).

Luo *et al.* (2013) is adopted and the factors are grouped into firm external pressures and firm internal considerations as illustrated in Figure 1. The firm internal considerations include firms' objectives and strategies, corporate governance characteristics and organizations' structures, managerial philosophies, as well as the availability of financial and non-financial resources. These factors work as drivers or constraints that affect managers' carbon disclosure decisions. Besides the firm internal factors, managers also have to consider the pressures from external stakeholders in making carbon disclosure decisions. With increased public awareness of climate change and various regulatory schemes to encourage carbon emission reduction, firms need to make decisions in carbon disclosures, either to satisfy stakeholders' information needs or to legitimize firms' business activities.

5. The Quality and Adequateness of Voluntary Carbon Information

This section aims to provide a snapshot of the quality, the level, and adequateness of voluntary carbon information provided by companies. Several researchers express their concerns over the quality of corporate carbon disclosure. For example, Kolk *et al.* (2008) comment on the development of carbon disclosure. Through an analysis of CDP responses from FT500 companies published 2007, they conclude that although the response rates of CDP survey are impressive and growing, the CDP reports do not provide information that is particularly valuable for stakeholders due to insufficient comparability and incompleteness of the disclosed information. Haque and Deegan (2010) investigate the climate change-related corporate governance disclosure practices of five major Australian energy-intensive companies over a 16-year period. They find an increasing trend in companies' climate change-related corporate governance disclosures over time. However, they suggest that in many instances the disclosures provide limited insights into the climate change-related risks and opportunities confronting the sample companies. Cotter *et al.* (2011) analyze the climate change-related disclosures of one large Australian company. Their results indicate an inadequate amount of disclosure in this company's reports about some aspects of climate change impacts and their management. Further, the disclosures that are made tend to lack technical detail and are somewhat skewed toward the more positive aspects of climate change impacts and management. Comyns and Figge (2015) examine the evolution of carbon disclosure practices by examining the sustainability reports of 45 oil and gas companies between 1998 and 2010. They develop a quality index based on seven disclosure quality principles: accuracy, completeness, consistency, credibility, relevance, timeliness, and transparency. They find that carbon disclosure quality has not significantly improved over the sample period and suggest that regulation is needed to improve the quality of information that is hard for users to verify.

The inadequacy of corporate carbon disclosure reflects the expectation gap between stakeholders and corporate managers regarding carbon disclosure. While green communities and environmental regulators are concerned about carbon pollution and climate change, corporations focus primarily on compliance costs and risks, firm financial performance and shareholders' interests (Haque *et al.*, 2016; Lodhia and Martin, 2012). In addition, a lack of proactive stakeholder engagement and a failure by managers to accept accountability are also the reasons of low level of carbon disclosure (Haque *et al.*, 2016). Further, the methodological diversity due to the voluntary nature of carbon disclosures may result in incomparable climate change-related data and undermine the usefulness of such information for investors' decision-making (Andrew and Cortese, 2011).

It suggests that there remains considerable scope for improvement in carbon reporting all over the world. The results in previous studies potentially signal a need for enhanced mandatory reporting requirements or standards to ensure more extensive and reliable carbon disclosures so that investors can make informed investment decisions. In this context, a uniform, standard, and mandatory carbon report is required and should preferably be independent from the annual report and subject to external verification or audit/assurance (IAASB, 2012). A mandatory carbon report has the benefit of reducing information asymmetry and enabling a true reflection of carbon performance by carbon disclosure for various stakeholders for their investment decision-making. The information reported in this mandatory carbon report should reflect the management's commitment to carbon mitigation and enable users in assessing the effect of carbon emissions on climate change. Since every entity, regardless of whether it is a commercial, public, or not-for-profit organization, emits GHGs, the mandatory carbon report might apply to the vast majority of organizations (even to entities not in the GHG-intensive sectors).

6. Does Voluntary Carbon Information Reflect Firms' Underlying Performance?

This section addresses to what extent the carbon information voluntarily disclosed by the companies is useful for stakeholders to make informed decisions. The concerns over the quality of voluntary carbon disclosure raise the question of whether, The carbon information voluntarily disclosed relate to their underlying carbon performance. If so, on what circumstances firms' carbon disclosure is useful to gauge their true carbon performance. For the disclosure to be useful, there should be a correspondence between carbon disclosure and the firm's actual carbon performance.

Empirical studies typically answer this research question by testing the relationship between the voluntary carbon disclosure and carbon performance. If there is a negative relationship between them, it indicates firms may use the voluntary carbon disclosure to change the perception of the stakeholders regarding their activities instead of addressing the need to reduce carbon emissions (Aerts and Cormier, 2009; Gray *et al.*, 1995; Neu *et al.*, 1998). A focus on perception management is generally consistent with the legitimacy theory. This legitimacy orientation raises concerns about the usefulness and reliability of voluntarily disclosed information. The association may be due to the lack of external monitoring of firms' carbon disclosure and the relevant carbon-reporting standards. Detailed carbon emission measurement and reporting system are advocated and required if perception management is the primary motivation. However, if there is a positive relationship between them, it suggests that voluntary carbon disclosure reflects the true commitment to carbon reduction and, thus, is relevant for potential users for decision-making. This underlying incentive could be explained by signalling theory (Spence, 1973; Verrecchia, 1983). Prior environmental studies (e.g., Clarkson *et al.*, 2008; Clarkson *et al.*, 2011) provided empirical support for signalling theory and argued that firms with good performance will disclose more information to differentiate them from firms with poor performance. If investors believe carbon emissions or performance information in relevant and reliable, the capital market will incorporate the information into the assessment of firms' valuations. The exploration on whether carbon information truly reflects firms' carbon performance has potential implications on investors and policymakers.

Focusing on US, UK, and Australian firms, Luo and Tang (2014b) find that the extensiveness of carbon disclosure is positively associated with firm carbon mitigation performance measured by carbon intensity, indicating firms that have good carbon performance disclose more to signal their effort to investors and other stakeholders. Ott *et al.* (2017) find that firm's carbon performance is positively associated with firms' decision of making CDP response publicly available, although it does not affect firms' response decision with a large international sample. The results of these two studies support the voluntary disclosure perspective and dominant legitimacy perspective.

However, other studies support the legitimacy perspective of voluntary carbon disclosure. For example, Alrazi *et al.* (2016) focus on 205 electricity generation firms from 35 countries and find that the comprehensiveness of carbon disclosure is not related to firm carbon performance measured by the level of GHG emissions. Moreover, Luo (2017) showed opposite results to Luo and Tang (2014b) by finding a negative association between carbon disclosure and carbon performance with international panel data, supporting that firms with worse carbon performance try to gain legitimacy by disclosing more. The author further finds that stringent carbon institutions — the presence of ETS, stakeholder orientation, and within carbon-intensive sectors (which attract more attention and regulation) — restrict firms' legitimation attempts and help better reflect the underlying performance, which may explain the discrepancy between the results of these two studies. The legitimacy perspective of carbon disclosure is also supported by studies that examine the linguistic strategy used in carbon disclosures. Hrasky (2011) confirms the results of Luo (2017) by finding that while carbon-intensive sectors disclose more behavioral information to signal their substantive action in coping with climate change, the less intensive sectors are relying more heavily on disclosing symbolic information. Ferguson *et al.* (2016) point out that the disclosures produced by participants in the UK ETS and Energy Efficiency Scheme were not only used to provide legitimacy to the organizational response to climate change but also served to displace their own responsibility to tackle climate change and shift responsibility/blame on to government or suppliers as barriers to progress.

7. Value Relevance of Carbon Information

As GHG emissions are an integral by-product of many industrial processes, the investing community has become increasingly concerned over how businesses will be able to handle new emissions constraints. Thus, it is expected that investors need information pertaining to the firm's GHG emissions and how well it is positioned to make the transition to a new regulatory environment. Quite a few studies have provided empirical evidence that investors tend to use carbon information for their decision-making. Shareholders and debtholders are deemed as the most prominent stakeholders in the traditional accounting concept (Cormier *et al.*, 2005). Thus, this section mainly discusses the usefulness of carbon information by shareholders and debtholders.

7.1. *The use of carbon information in the equity markets*

Quite a few prior studies have concluded that a firm's carbon emission information is value relevant for shareholders to make resource allocation decision. Two Australian studies, Chapple *et al.* (2013) and Luo and Tang (2014a) use event study method to examine the market effect of proposed ETS and carbon tax, respectively. Their results suggest that firms in carbon-intensive sectors suffer value reduction upon the release of news that report an increased probability of the carbon regulatory legislation passing through parliament. The results indicate the negative market value effect of carbon emissions. Some other studies directly examine the value effects of carbon emissions in UK, EU, US, and Japan by including carbon emissions in a market value model (Baboukardos, 2017; Clarkson *et al.*, 2015; Griffin *et al.*, 2017; Johnston *et al.*, 2008; Matsumura *et al.*, 2014; Saka and Oshika, 2014). Based on the rationale that existing and future compliance costs and carbon mitigation costs put an unbooked liability on firms, all these studies find that carbon emissions have a negative effect on firm market value. In addition, Clarkson *et al.* (2015) also provide evidence that firms' ability to pass on costs to customers mediate the value reduction effects of carbon emissions, and the emissions within EU zone have different valuation effects from emissions outside EU zone. Liesen *et al.* (2017) use Carhart four-factor model (Carhart, 1997) to examine the effects of emissions and carbon performance on risk-adjusted return with an EU sample. They suggest that after controlling for systematic risk, company size, book-to-market ratio, and the momentum effect, carbon efficiency is relevant to asset prices of European companies but the absolute GHG emission level is not.

Researchers also study the value relevance of carbon disclosure, and their results generally suggest a positive valuation effect of carbon disclosure (Baboukardos, 2017; Griffin and Sun, 2013; Liesen *et al.*, 2017; Matsumura *et al.*, 2014; Saka and Oshika, 2014). Specifically, Baboukardos (2017) find that the value reduction effects of carbon emissions are weaker after the UK mandatory carbon report regulation, indicating a better quality of disclosure. Liesen *et al.* (2017) suggest that financial markets were inefficient in pricing publicly available information on carbon disclosure and performance because investors could achieve abnormal risk-adjusted returns when simply investing in portfolios constructed from GHG emissions disclosure and good corporate carbon performance. These findings suggest that mandatory carbon disclosure would not only help increase the market efficiency but also result in better investment decisions in the real economy.

7.2. *The use of carbon information in the debt markets*

While most studies are conducted from the perspective of shareholders, only few studies take the perspective of another critical capital provider: debtholders, and banks in particular. Herbohn *et al.* (2017) test the capital market reaction to bank loan announcements of ASX listed companies during 2009–2015 and find positive and significant excess loan announcement returns for loan renewals for high-carbon-risk firms. They argue that a bank loan announcement for a firm with high-carbon risk conveys information to investors about the firm's carbon-risk exposure collected through a bank's pre-loan screening and ongoing monitoring. Thus, investors perceive that banks incorporate carbon-risk considerations into their lending decisions. In addition, Jung *et al.* (2016) and Maaloul (2018) find that firm carbon emissions level and carbon risk increase their cost of debt, which suggests that lenders incorporate a firm's exposure to carbon-related risk into lending decisions. Jung *et al.* (2016) further find that public disclosure of carbon-related information weakens the association between carbon risk and the cost of debt. This result suggests that firms can mitigate the penalty by demonstrating an awareness of their carbon risk. Moreover, Zhou *et al.* (2018) find that firms have a higher cost of debt if they receive a penalty such as fine or suspension of operation because of excessive carbon emissions. They further suggest that the relationship between carbon-related penalty and cost of debt can be mitigated by positive media reports that the firms are involved in carbon management, energy-saving, low-carbon production, low-carbon innovation, low-carbon investment, and other similar actions. Putting together, it appears that information about firm carbon emissions and carbon actions is useful for lenders in making lending decisions.

8. CDP

The CDP is an independent not-for-profit organization, which is committed to helping companies throughout the world to measure, manage, disclose, and ultimately reduce GHG emissions. Annually, the CDP sends the questionnaire to the largest companies[6] based on the capitalization listed on their national markets. The CDP questionnaire is designed and reported in a standard format (Kolk *et al.*, 2008), facilitating comparison across companies, industries, and regions. However, it has changed annually since it was launched in 2000, especially in the early years of its

[6]The number of targeted companies for each country is not the same. For example, the CDP targets the top 100 companies listed on the Johannesburg Stock Exchange (JSE 100) to prepare South African reports, while the top 500 companies (S&P 500) are required to respond the request for the US reports.

development. A range of carbon-related information is covered such as corporate carbon governance, climate change-related risks and opportunities, GHG emissions, carbon accounting methodology, carbon reduction initiatives, and public communication. The companies which received requests from the CDP need to decide whether or not to participate in it by answering the questionnaire. Their answers or responses are available on the CDP website for external users if they agree to publish publicly. After 10 years of development, the CDP holds the largest global database of primary corporate climate change information in the world.

The CDP operates in most major economies worldwide and channels information and progress through a few separate programs (e.g., climate change, water, supply change, city). The success of the CDP is underpinned by collaborative institutional investors (also called "signatories"). By 2019, the CDP comprised 525 signatory investors with more than US$96 trillion in assets including banks, investment managers, pension funds, insurers, foundations, endowments, private equity, and real estate investors.[7] This represents very rapid growth from just 35 signatory investors in 2003, with $4.5 trillion in assets (CDP, 2007). It should be noted that there are no costs or carbon commitments for being signatory investors. Thus, the CDP can be seen as a "secondary stakeholder" that has facilitated collaborative engagement by institutional investors to increase corporate accountability in relation to climate change (Arenas *et al.*, 2009). The research confirms that secondary stakeholders, such as NGOs of which the CDP is, are key players in the arena of CSR (Arenas *et al.*, 2009).

The CDP is so far the largest database for carbon information and is advantageous in the following ways. First, the CDP complements annual financial reports and provides information relevant to investors relating to the business risks and opportunities from climate change through voluntary effort and procedures (Kolk *et al.*, 2008). Guthrie *et al.* (2008) found that the companies tended to utilize corporate websites for their social and environmental reporting more than annual reports, indicating the need for researchers to consider alternative media. Unerman (2000) argued that an exclusive focus on annual report was likely to result in an incomplete picture of reporting practices. While many prior studies attempt to analyze environmental disclosures included in corporate annual reports,

[7]The information is obtained from the CDP website https://www.cdp.net/en/investor/request-environmental-information.

sustainability report or firm website, the CDP data have been used in several more recent carbon studies (Freedman and Jaggi, 2010; Kolk and Pinkse, 2008; Reid and Toffel, 2009). Second, the CDP stands out for its ongoing endeavor to provide comprehensive carbon information to the public. The quality and quantity of reporting on climate change have increased dramatically over time (CDP Global 500 report, 2010). The vast majority of large companies (e.g., those companies listed in the FT500) are now using the CDP as a mechanism for carbon disclosure (Kolk *et al.*, 2008; Pinkse and Kolk, 2009). To a large extent, the participation in CDP represents their willingness to communicate information about their internal carbon performance and carbon accounting to outside stakeholders. Prado-Lorenzo *et al.* (2009, p. 1134) argue that the information disclosed in the CDP can be used by outside users to appropriately assess the policy of GHG emissions control of a firm. In addition, it could generate competitive advantages for those companies that disclose it by allowing them to stand out from their competitors. Third, the CDP designs a universal uniform questionnaire for the potential participants and requests their response. These companies can either decide to report and reveal their carbon information publicly or turn it down or not provide any response at all. This context provides an "even treatment" that avoids selection issues because all companies in the sample received the same invitation at the same time (Reid and Toffel, 2009). The CDP also allows all responses of participants to be compared between companies, because it largely overcomes the individual selection of carbon disclosure made in annual reports and sustainability reports. Fourth, an increasing number of studies have utilized the CDP information in their research (Peters and Romi, 2009; Reid and Toffel, 2009; Stanny, 2013; Stanny and Ely, 2008; Tang and Luo, 2016), which contributes to the external validity of it as a data source.

The CDP report is a voluntary framework that encourages large companies in the world to manage their carbon activities and report the information to the public. Peer pressure and reputational consequences are likely to push firms to adopt such a framework. In the absence of a standard worldwide mandatory carbon report, the CDP acts as a self-regulatory code (or "soft law"), by constructing a common "bottom-up" framework, but leaving the decision on the adoption as voluntary (Baldwin and Cave, 1999). It provides a flexible bridge between individual companies' ununiform voluntary carbon disclosures and mandatory, legal, and uniform disclosures. On the one hand, the incentives and disincentives of voluntary action facing individual entities inevitably generate a variety of non-standard and inconsistent responses. On the other hand, the requirement for a common collective approach mandated by legal regulation may fail to reflect the particular situations facing individual companies. Thus, the CDP helps firms to systematically disclose their carbon information in a way which is likely to be understood by users and stakeholders.

However, based on previous findings, there are concerns that the information disclosed in the CDP is not indicative of firms' true carbon performance, and thus, the CDP disclosures are more likely to be a legitimizing tool instead of a self-regulating tool (Luo, 2017). It seems that the next step for the CDP is to encourage companies to provide more assured information. Based on this, both the wider scope and level of voluntary external assurance should be encouraged. In addition, some more information could be included in the CDP report, namely, more detailed carbon-sensitive information at the project level and segment level; details of sustainable production methods that are part of their integral market development; quantitative measures of carbon risks (such as a carbon tax); accounting for environmental assets and liabilities (e.g., emission permits). As there is a lack of an international accounting standard, a disclosure of the above valuation basis for environmental or carbon items is relevant for users. Another suggestion is that the CDP questionnaire should be tailored to fit the conditions of firms to reflect unique characteristics of the firms (such as size and industry membership), thus, firms in CISs and in less intensive sectors do not have to answer the same questions.

9. Conclusion

There is a general consensus in the literature that climate change affects the physical environment and will have a negative impact on our ecosystem and human health (IPCC, 2007b; Romilly, 2007; Stern, 2006). Thus, global warming is one of the most important topics on the business and public policy agenda over the last two decades or so. Carbon information is increasingly required by various stakeholders to monitor business risks associated with climate change and assist their decision-making. Nonetheless, carbon disclosure was predominately voluntary in most countries in the world. Thus, the chapter attempts to address the usefulness of carbon information by different stakeholders, factors, and motivations firms [voluntarily].

The concern for managing drivers of climate change is increasing as is interest in accounting for the effects of climate change. The response from the business community has been to gather and report more information about carbon-related activities to stakeholders. For instance, the CDP Global 500 reports indicate that the majority of the top global firms are now issuing carbon reports and that the number of the top 500 global firms issuing such reports within each country surveyed has increased since 2002. Although the content and quality of the reports vary widely, the CDP survey supports the view that carbon accounting and reporting is on the rise and is becoming an integral part of the information released to shareholders. In addition, the increasingly stringent forthcoming government regulations may have massive financial implications across the entire economy, which in turn would drive changes in how energy is generated, transported, priced, and ultimately consumed. The carbon mitigation initiatives and reporting that have been proposed and executed by large businesses open up many opportunities for accounting professionals to play a key role in GHG mitigation. With any paradigm shift in an economy comes the need for strategic policy development and execution. New ways of considering organizational cash flows and treasury risk are already being discussed across the accountancy profession (Clements-Hunt *et al.*, 2006; PriceWaterhouseCoopers, 2007). As polluting industries seek to abate liabilities, critical skills connected to carbon management are also emerging (Smith, 2013). Thus, accounting-based climate knowledge is highly valued by the industry. Therefore, it is urgent for accounting academics to develop course material regarding carbon accounting, carbon auditing, and carbon management to prepare accounting students to, first, comprehend the context of carbon legislation and, then, apply the new standards and reporting techniques in practice, and finally report the reliable and relevant carbon information for stakeholders' decision-making.

References

Aerts, W. and D. Cormier (2009), Media legitimacy and corporate environmental communication, *Accounting, Organizations and Society* **34**(1), 1–27.

Alrazi, B., C. de Villiers, and C. J. Van Staden (2016), The environmental disclosures of the electricity generation industry: A global perspective, *Accounting and Business Research* **46**(6), 665–701.

Andrew, J. and C. Cortese (2011), Accounting for climate change and the self-regulation of carbon disclosures, *Accounting Forum* **35**(3), 130–138.

Arenas, D., J. M. Lozano, and L. Albareda (2009), The role of NGOs in CSR: Mutual perceptions among stakeholders, *Journal of Business Ethics* **88**(1), 175–197.

Baboukardos, D. (2017), Market valuation of greenhouse gas emissions under a mandatory reporting regime: Evidence from the UK, *Accounting Forum* **41**(3), 221–233.

Baldwin, R. and M. Cave (1999), *Understanding Regulation: Theory, Strategy and Practice,* Vol. 182. Oxford, USA: Oxford University Press.

Bebbington, J. and C. Larrinaga-González (2008), Carbon trading: Accounting and reporting issues, *European Accounting Review* **17**(4), 697–717.

Black, C. M. (2013), Accounting for carbon emission allowances in the European Union: In search of consistency, *Accounting in Europe* **10**(2), 223–239.

Burritt, R. L., S. Schaltegger, and D. Zvezdov (2011), Carbon management accounting: Explaining practice in leading German companies, *Australian Accounting Review* **21**(1), 80–98.

Busch, T. and V. Hoffmann (2007), Emerging carbon constraints for corporate risk management, *Ecological Economics* **62**(3–4), 518–528.

CDP (2007). *Carbon Disclosure Project Report 2007 Global FT500*. Retrieved from https://www.rsc.org/images/CDP%20summary%20report_tcm18-100933.pdf.

CDP Global 500 report. 2010. *Carbon Disclosure Project 2010 Global 500 Report*. Retrieved from https://www.circleofblue.org/wp-content/uploads/2010/11/CDP-2010-G500.pdf.

CERES (2010), Investors analyze climate risks and opportunities: A survey of asset managers' practices. Retrieved from http://www.ceres.org/resources/reports/survey-of-asset-managers-practices-2010/view.

CERES (2011), *Disclosing climate risks & opportunities in SEC filings*. Retrieved from https://environblog.jenner.com/files/disclosing-climate-risks-and-opportunities-in-sec-filings.pdf.

Chapple, L., P. M. Clarkson, and D. L. Gold (2013), The cost of carbon: Capital market effects of the proposed emission trading scheme (ETS), *Abacus* **49**(1), 1–33.

Clarkson, M. B. E. (1995), A stakeholder framework for analyzing and evaluating corporate social performance, *The Academy of Management Review* **20**(1), 92–117.

Clarkson, P. M., Y. Li, M. Pinnuck, and G. D. Richardson (2015), The valuation relevance of greenhouse gas emissions under the European Union carbon emissions trading scheme, *European Accounting Review* **24**(3), 551–580.

Clarkson, P. M., Y. Li, G. D. Richardson, and F. P. Vasvari (2008), Revisiting the relation between environmental performance and environmental disclosure: An empirical analysis, *Accounting, Organizations and Society* **33**(4–5), 303–327.

Clarkson, P. M., M. B. Overell, and L. Chapple (2011), Environmental reporting and its relation to corporate environmental performance, *Abacus* **47**(1), 27–60.

Clements-Hunt, P., C. Fox, S. Pfeifer, and I. Woods (2006), Global framework for climate risk disclosure: A statement of investor expectations for comprehensive corporate disclosure. Retrieved from http://www.unepfi.org/fileadmin/documents/global_framework.pdf.

Comyns, B. and F. Figge (2015), Greenhouse gas reporting quality in the oil and gas industry: A longitudinal study using the typology of "search", "experience" and "credence" information, *Accounting, Auditing & Accountability Journal* **28**(3), 403–433.

Cook, A. (2009), Emission rights: From costless activity to market operations, *Accounting, Organizations and Society* **34**(3–4), 456–468.

Cormier, D., M. Magnan, and B. Van Velthoven (2005), Environmental disclosure quality in large German companies: Economic incentives, public pressures or institutional conditions?, *European Accounting Review* **14**(1), 3–39.

Cotter, J., M. Najah, and S. S. Wang (2011), Standardized reporting of climate change information in Australia, *Sustainability Accounting, Management and Policy Journal* **2**(2), 294–321.

Deegan, C. and M. Rankin (1996), Do Australian companies report environmental news objectively?, *Accounting, Auditing and Accountability Journal* **9**(2), 50–67.

Dye, R. (1985), Disclosure of nonproprietary information, *Journal of Accounting Research* **23**(1), 123–145.

Engels, A. (2009), The European emissions trading scheme: An exploratory study of how companies learn to account for carbon, *Accounting, Organizations and Society* **34**(3–4), 488–498.

Ferguson, J., T. R. Sales de Aguiar, and A. Fearfull (2016), Corporate response to climate change: Language, power and symbolic construction, *Accounting, Auditing & Accountability Journal* **29**(2), 278–304.

Freedman, M. and B. Jaggi (2010), Global warming and corporate disclosures: A comparative analysis of companies from the European Union, Japan and

Canada, *Advances in Environmental Accounting and Management* **4**, 129–160.

Freeman, R. E. (1984), *Strategic Management A stakeholder Approach.* Marshfield, Massachusetts: Pitman Publishing Inc.

Gibassier, D. and S. Schaltegger (2015), Carbon management accounting and reporting in practice: A case study on converging emergent approaches, *Sustainability Accounting, Management and Policy Journal* **6**(3), 340–365.

Giner, B. (2014), Accounting for emission trading schemes: A still open debate, *Social and Environmental Accountability Journal* **34**(1), 45–51.

Gray, R., R. Kouhy, and S. Lavers (1995), Corporate social and environmental reporting: A review of the literature and a longitudinal study of UK disclosure, *Accounting, Auditing & Accountability Journal* **8**(2), 47–77.

Griffin, P. A. (2013), Cap and trade emission allowances and US companies' balance sheets, *Sustainability Accounting, Management and Policy Journal* **4**(1), 7–31.

Griffin, P. A., D. H. Lont, and E. Y. Sun (2017), The relevance to investors of greenhouse gas emission disclosures, *Contemporary Accounting Research* **34**(2), 1265–1297.

Griffin, P. A. and Y. Sun (2013), Going green: Market reaction to CSRwire news releases, *Journal of Accounting and Public Policy* **32**(2), 93–113.

Guthrie, J., S. Cuganesan, and L. Ward (2008), Industry specific social and environmental reporting: The Australian Food and Beverage Industry, *Accounting Forum* **32**(1), 1–15.

Haque, S. and C. Deegan (2010), Corporate climate change-related governance practices and related disclosures: Evidence from Australia, *Australian Accounting Review* **20**(4), 317–333.

Haque, S., C. Deegan, and R. Inglis (2016), Demand for, and impediments to, the disclosure of information about climate change-related corporate governance practices, *Accounting and Business Research* **46**(6), 620–664.

Haupt, M. and R. Ismer (2013), The EU emissions trading system under IFRS — Towards a 'true and fair view', *Accounting in Europe* **10**(1), 71–97.

Healy, P. and K. Palepu (2001), Information asymmetry, corporate disclosure, and the capital markets: A review of the empirical disclosure literature, *Journal of Accounting and Economics* **31**(1–3), 405–440.

Herbohn, K., R. Gao, and P. Clarkson (2017), Evidence on whether banks consider carbon risk in their lending decisions, *Journal of Business Ethics.*

Hrasky, S. (2011), Carbon footprints and legitimation strategies: Symbolism or action?, *Accounting, Auditing & Accountability Journal* **25**(1), 174–198.

IAASB (2012), ISAE 3410, Assurance engagements on greenhouse gas statements. Retrieved from http://www.ifac.org/sites/default/files/publications/files/Basis%20for%20Conclusions%20-%20ISAE%203410%20Assurance%20Engagements%20on%20Greenhouse%20Gas%20Statements-final_0.pdf.

IPCC (2007a), Summary for policymakers, in *Climate Change 2007: Mitigation of Climate Change: Contribution of Working Group III to the Fourth Assessment Report of the Intergovernmental Panel on Climate Change*, B. Metz, O. R. Davidson, P. R. Bosch, R. Dave, and L. A. Meyer (eds.), Cambridge, United Kingdom, and New York, NY, USA.: Cambridge University Press.

IPCC (2007b), Summary for policymakers, in *Climate Change 2007: The Physical Science Basis: Contribution of Working Group I to the Fourth Assessment Report of the Intergovernmental Panel on Climate Change*, S. Solomon, M. M. D. Qin, M. M. Z. Chen, K. B. Averyt, M. Tignor, and H. L. Miller (eds.), United Kingdom and New York, NY, USA.: Cambridge University Press, Cambridge.

Johnston, D. M., S. E. Sefcik, and N. S. Soderstrom (2008), The value relevance of greenhouse gas emissions allowances: An exploratory study in the related United States SO2 Market, *European Accounting Review* **17**(4), 747–764.

Jung, J., K. Herbohn, and P. Clarkson (2016), Carbon risk, carbon risk awareness and the cost of debt financing, *Journal of Business Ethics*.

Kolk, A., D. Levy, and J. Pinkse (2008), Corporate responses in an emerging climate regime: The institutionalization and commensuration of carbon disclosure, *European Accounting Review* **17**(4), 719–745.

Kolk, A. and J. Pinkse (2008), Business and climate change: Emergent institutions in global governance, *Corporate Governance* **8**(4), 419–429.

Lee, K.-H. and Y. Wu (2014), Integrating sustainability performance measurement into logistics and supply networks: A multi-methodological approach, *The British Accounting Review* **46**(4), 361–378.

Liesen, A., F. Figge, A. Hoepner, and D. M. Patten (2017), Climate change and asset prices: Are corporate carbon disclosure and performance priced appropriately?, *Journal of Business Finance & Accounting* **44**(1–2), 35–62.

Lodhia, S. and N. Martin (2012), Stakeholder responses to the national greenhouse and energy reporting act: An agenda setting perspective, *Accounting, Auditing & Accountability Journal* **25**(1), 126–145.

Luo, L. (2019), The influence of institutional contexts on the relationship between voluntary carbon disclosure and carbon emission performance, *Accounting & Finance* **59**(2), 1235–1264.

Luo, L. and Q. Tang (2014a), Carbon tax, corporate carbon profile and financial return, *Pacific Accounting Review* **26**(3), 351–373.

Luo, L. and Q. Tang (2014b), Does voluntary carbon disclosure reflect underlying carbon performance?, *Journal of Contemporary Accounting & Economics* **10**(3), 191–205.

Luo, L., Q. Tang, and Y. C. Lan (2013), Comparison of propensity for carbon disclosure between developing and developed countries: A resource constraint perspective, *Accounting Research Journal* **26**(1), 6–34.

Maaloul, A. (2018), The effect of greenhouse gas emissions on cost of debt: Evidence from Canadian firms, *Corporate Social Responsibility and Environmental Management.*

Matsumura, E. M., R. Prakash, and S. C. Vera-Muñoz (2014), Firm-value effects of carbon emissions and carbon disclosures, *The Accounting Review* **89**(2), 695–724.

Mete, P., C. Dick, and L. Moerman (2010), Creating institutional meaning: Accounting and taxation law perspectives of carbon permits, *Critical Perspectives on Accounting* **21**(7), 619–630.

Mounteer, T. and S. Ranchod (2010), SEC issues guidance regarding disclosure of climate change risks. Retrieved from https://www.paulhastings.com/docs/default-source/PDFs/15065424df692334642881 1cff00004cbded.pdf.

Munich Re. (2005), Topics geo, annual review: Natural catastrophes 2004. Retrieved from

Neu, D., H. Warsame, and K. Pedwell (1998), Managing public impressions: Environmental disclosures in annual reports, *Accounting, Organizations and Society* **23**(3), 265–282.

Ott, C., F. Schiemann, and T. Günther (2017). Disentangling the determinants of the response and the publication decisions: The case of the Carbon Disclosure Project, *Journal of Accounting and Public Policy* **36**(1), 14–33.

Patten, D. (2002), The relation between environmental performance and environmental disclosure: A research note, *Accounting, Organizations and Society* **27**(8), 763–773.

Peters, G. and A. Romi (2009), *Carbon disclosure incentives in a global setting: An empirical investigation*. University of Arkansas.

Pinkse, J. and A. Kolk (2009), *International business and global climate change*, Taylor & Francis.

Prado-Lorenzo, J., L. Rodriguez-Dominguez, I. Gallego-Alvarez, and I. Garcia-Sanchez (2009), Factors influencing the disclosure of greenhouse gas emissions in companies worldwide, *Management Decision* **47**(7), 1133–1157.

PriceWaterhouseCoopers. (2007), Trouble-Entry Accounting — Revisited: London: PriceWaterhouse Coopers (PWC) and International Emissions Trading Association (IETA).

Raibor, C. and M. Massoud (2010), Emissions allowances: Accounting and public policy issues, *Accounting and the Public Interest* **10**(1), 105–121.

Ratnatunga, J., S. Jones, and K. R. Balachandran (2011), The valuation and reporting of organizational capability in carbon emissions management, *Accounting Horizons* **25**(1), 127–147.

Ratnatunga, J. T. D. and K. R. Balachandran (2009), Carbon business accounting: The impact of global warming on the cost and management accounting profession, *Journal of Accounting, Auditing & Finance* **24**(2), 333–355.

Reid, E. and M. Toffel (2009), Responding to public and private politics: Corporate disclosure of climate change strategies, *Strategic Management Journal* **30**(11), 1157–1178.

Romilly, P. (2007), Business and climate change risk: A regional time series analysis, *Journal of International Business Studies* **38**(3), 474–480.

Saka, C. and T. Oshika (2014), Disclosure effects, carbon emissions and corporate value, *Sustainability Accounting, Management and Policy Journal* **5**(1), 22–45.

Smith, M. (2013), *Assessing climate change risks and opportunities for investors: oil and gas sector*. Retrieved from https://igcc.org.au/wp-content/uploads/2016/04/Oil-and-Gas.pdf.

Solomon, A. and L. Lewis (2002), Incentives and disincentives for corporate environmental disclosure, *Business Strategy and the Environment* **11**(3), 154–169.

Spence, M. (1973), Job market signaling, *The Quarterly Journal of Economics* **87**(3), 355–374.

Stanny, E. (2013), Voluntary disclosures of emissions by US firms, *Business strategy and the Environment* **22**(3), 145–158.

Stanny, E. and K. Ely (2008), Corporate environmental disclosures about the effects of climate change, *Corporate Social Responsibility and Environmental Management* **15**(6), 338–348.

Stern, N. (2006), *The Stern Review on the Economics of Climate Change*, Cambridge: Cambridge University Press.

Tang, Q. and L. Luo (2016), Corporate ecological transparency: Theories and empirical evidence, *Asian Review of Accounting* **24**(4), 498–524.

Unerman, J. (2000), Methodological issues-Reflections on quantification in corporate social reporting content analysis, *Accounting, Auditing & Accountability Journal* **13**(5), 667–681.

Verrecchia, R. E. (1983), Discretionary disclosure, *Journal of Accounting and Economics* **5**, 179–194.

Vesty, G. M., A. Telgenkamp, and P. J. Roscoe (2015), Creating numbers: Carbon and capital investment, *Accounting, Auditing & Accountability Journal* **28**(3), 302–324.

Warwick, P. and C. Ng (2012), The 'cost' of climate change: How carbon emissions allowances are accounted for amongst European union companies, *Australian Accounting Review* **22**(1), 54–67.

Zhou, Z., T. Zhang, K. Wen, H. Zeng, and X. Chen (2018), Carbon risk, cost of debt financing and the moderation effect of media attention: Evidence from Chinese companies operating in high-carbon industries, *Business Strategy and the Environment* **27**(8), 1131–1144.

https://doi.org/10.1142/9789811220470_0016

Chapter 16

Motivating Innovation and Creativity: The Role of Management Controls

Shelley Xin Li* and Kenneth A. Merchant†

University of Southern California, CA, USA

**xli766@marshall.usc*

†*kmerchant@marshall.usc.edu*

Abstract

This chapter discusses the challenges of using performance metrics to stimulate creativity and innovations in organizations. Formal incentive systems have proven to be effective in motivating executional behavior. Using such systems to motivate creativity is more challenging because useful creativity and innovation are notoriously difficult to measure, and use of flawed systems can produce negative outcomes. Further an innovation's success is usually determined by the efforts of teams, not individual employees. But well-designed incentive systems, which use good measures and also allow for some slack and toleration of short-term failures, can be effective. Metrics can also serve an information role, by providing opportunities to exchange ideas, providing performance-related feedback, and enhancing individual and group accountability. The chapter concludes by discussing how the use of incentive systems in combination with other management controls can help make organizations ambidextrous; i.e., good at both execution and innovation.

Keywords: Innovation; Creativity; Management control; Performance metrics; Incentives; Ambidexterity.

1. Introduction

In today's fast-moving, competitive business landscape, innovation is an important driver of economic growth and organizational performance (Abramovitz, 1956; Solow, 1957; Acemoglu, 2008; Corrado *et al.*, 2009; Ahlstrom, 2010; Kogan *et al.*, 2017). An important, interesting, and controversial management issue related to innovation is regarding when, where, and how management controls can have positive, rather than negative, effects on employee creativity and, hence, organizational innovation. *Creativity* involves the use of imagination to develop things that are new, which are called *innovations*. But not all innovations are useful for the company. Lack of applicability — i.e., "creativity for creativity's sake" — can be a problem. Creative ideas have to be transformed into useful things, i.e., those that create value for the company.

In the business world, useful creative ideas might lead to innovations in the form of new products or services, new methods, new marketing programs, or the like. Companies spend a significant part of their revenue on Research and Development (R&D). However, companies vary in their abilities to turn R&D spending into good business outcomes, such as more sales or better efficiency. Cohen *et al.* (2013) examined all US firms that traded on major stock exchanges, who spent on average 17% of their revenue on R&D, and found that these firms exhibited very different yet persistent abilities of turning R&D into something that the firm values. Two firms that invest the same amount in R&D can have predictably divergent future paths given their skills of turning R&D input into successful innovation. This suggests that the way firms manage their creative efforts can lead to different innovation outcomes. Thus, it is essential that organizations learn how best to help their employees to be creative and how to be able to translate the good creative ideas into valuable innovations.

However, useful creativity and innovation are notoriously difficult to measure (e.g., Adams *et al.*, 2006, Davila *et al.*, 2009, Nelson *et al.*, 2014). Innovation projects are highly risky, tend to be idiosyncratic, and involve multiple stages spanning a long period of time (Holmstrom 1989). Furthermore, it is not clear *ex ante* what actions the innovators should take. Progress is often not linear. Some actions that lead to apparent failures might provide the learning that yields eventual success. Some seemingly valid early indicators of innovation (e.g., patents) might lead only to dead ends. So the eventual worth of some creative ideas is difficult to judge in the short term.

In this chapter, we provide a review of the management control literature related to stimulating creativity and innovation. We first review research related to motivating innovation with formal incentives. Then we look beyond the incentive role of performance metrics and examine how the information role of management controls can affect innovation. We also discuss how management controls can be set up to achieve *ambidexterity* (i.e., making organizations good at both execution and innovation). The chapter concludes with some practical implications of the research findings to date.

Let us first introduce some important definitions of terms used in this chapter. Schroeder *et al.* (1989, p. 6) defined *innovation* as "the application of new or different approaches or methods or technologies to meet organizational objectives". But innovations can vary dramatically in effect. In most of this chapter, we focus on a product/service-centric definition of innovation, i.e., "the development of any new products or services, or any new processes used to make or deliver existing products or services". *Incremental innovations* involve improvements to existing products (or services), technologies, or methods. They are designed to meet the needs of the existing customer or markets. More *radical innovations* involve the development of new products (or services), technologies, or methods to meet the needs of emerging customers or markets (Li *et al.*, 2019). At the extreme, radical innovations can disrupt entire industries and create considerable wealth for the inventors (Hage, 1980; Ettlie, 1983; Ettlie *et al.*, 1984; Dewar and Dutton, 1986; Nord and Tucker, 1987; Duchesneau *et al.*, 1979; Danneels, 2002; Benner and Tushman, 2003; Alexander and Knippenberg, 2014).

2. Motivate Innovation with Formal Incentives

Manso (2011) provided theoretical insights into the optimal incentive scheme for motivating innovation: Given the long-term, high-risk nature of innovation, the optimal incentive scheme exhibits substantial tolerance for early failure and substantial rewards for long-term success.

Among the implications of this theory are that a long-term compensation plan, job security, and timely feedback on performance are essential to motivate innovation.[1]

Consistent with Manso's theory, various empirical researchers have shown the beneficial effects of providing long-term incentives on innovation. Holthausen *et al.* (1995) found that the proportion of compensation for divisional CEOs tied to long-term components was associated with future innovation. Lerner and Wulf (2007), looking at firms with centralized R&D facilities, found that giving more long-term incentives to the head of corporate R&D was associated with more and better innovation outcomes, such as patents. These studies, however, employed a large "black box" because the processes induced by the incentives are not specifically identified. The managers themselves might not be doing the creative thinking themselves. They might just be creating the conditions necessary for those in their organizations to generate creative ideas and to develop those ideas into commercial successes.

Other research studies have collected data on practices and outcomes lower in the organization, where the innovation processes are likely to be different, to get inside the black box. Lower level employees often focus on just one aspect of innovation rather than the whole innovation process. They might have lower risk tolerance because their small portfolio of projects does not allow their failures to be covered up by their successes. And they face shorter time horizons and tend to work in teams. For these lower level employees, can formal incentives be effective in motivating creativity and innovation?

In practice, it has been shown that providing explicit creativity metrics-related incentives can induce creativity and innovation, especially in the early stage of innovation — idea generation. Many companies use

[1]The literature on formal incentives is mostly built upon agency theory which aims to explain the agency relationship observed in reality. As technologies advance (e.g., blockchain technologies), the nature of agency relationship (and agency cost) evolves overtime and could change the way in which companies are organized, governed, and managed. If a fundamental shift in the agency relationship does occur, all organizational activities, including innovation activities, could be impacted. It is beyond the scope of this chapter to predict the trajectory of these technological advances and their impact on production (and specifically, innovation). We acknowledge that it is important to follow the development in these technologies and refer you to another chapter in this book for a discussion of "blockchain solutions for agency problems in corporate governance".

variations of a "suggestion box" program to encourage employees to develop creative new ideas. For example, in 2008 IBM launched a collaborative corporate innovation program called ThinkPlace, which offered employees rewards for the best ideas in five categories — shareholder value, customer satisfaction, technical, teamwork, and people — on a quarterly and annual basis. The ThinkPlace web site served as an enabler, a repository where employees could contribute a new idea, provide input on existing ideas, or search for potential solutions. In just one 3-year period, the company gathered over 18,000 ideas with participation from half of the IBM employee population. More than 500 of those ideas were "wins" (i.e., implemented ideas) (Durmaz, 2014). Useful creative ideas can also come from individuals outside the corporation. Microsoft, SpaceX, and Amazon are among the companies that offer rewards for creative ideas open to anyone. The best ideas reap the reward. These explicit creativity metrics-based incentive programs are often effective.

Academic research has also shown that creativity-dependent firms can and do use performance-based pay to motivate their employees. Grabner (2014) used survey data collected from 457 European firms in creative industries to show that performance-based pay and subjective evaluations of non-task-related performance were complements in a creativity-dependent setting. Creative dependency constrains the ability to implement performance-based pay at the individual level, but it also creates a need for performance-based pay at the organizational level to direct creative activities toward achievement. The performance-based pay enhances accountability to organizational objectives and puts some constraints on employees being "creative just for creativity's sake". The subjectivity or managerial discretion in performance evaluation takes into account the "softer" aspect of creative jobs and helps to prevent the rigidity of extrinsic incentives from crowding out individuals' intrinsic motivations to create.

Several experiments have demonstrated more specifically how explicit incentives can be used to stimulate creative output. Kachelmeier *et al.* (2008) found that providing bonuses (based on quantity, creativity, or both) encouraged higher creativity-weighted productivity than a fixed wage did. However, a bonus linked to output creativity did not bring about a higher volume of high-creativity output as much as did a bonus linked to the output quantity. This suggests that the key to motivating idea generation is to reward the overall level of experimentation (i.e., reward for the total number of trials or ideas generated). That is because the more things people try, the more likely they will be to stumble upon great ideas. It is critical to first get the ideas flowing. A follow-up study (Kachelmeier and Williamson, 2010) showed that explicit incentives can affect innovation output through two mechanisms: inducing more creative effort and attracting more of the "creative" type of employees.

Firms face three main challenges in designing performance metrics that will avoid, or at least mitigate, negative effects on innovation. One challenge stems from the inherent difficulty in measuring the eventual commercial success of new ideas. There is almost inevitably a lag between the time the creative idea is first developed and the time when the idea provides returns to the organization. For smaller, incremental innovations, such as improvements to existing products or services, the lag is relatively small, perhaps only a few weeks or months. But for larger, more radical innovations, the lag can be quite significant. In the pharmaceutical industry, for example, the lag between the start of the R&D process and generation of the first revenues, even for a blockbuster drug, is typically more than a decade. In some other industries, such as space exploration or the development of fusion power sources, the lags can be even longer. In some cases, the creative individuals' rewards can mirror those of the organization, such as through licensing or royalty agreements that pay out if and when the organization reaps profits down the road. However, rewards that might be forthcoming a decade or more in the future are not highly motivating, so most organizations need to develop shorter term incentive agreements based on leading indicators of innovation success. They might base rewards on metrics that provide early indications of eventual commercial success, such as milestone achievements in the development of a product (e.g., success of a clinical trial), the granting of patents, or the first commercial sale. However, these metrics are not totally reliable. Achieving one milestone in an R&D process does not guarantee achievement of the next milestone. They can cause bonus payouts even in cases of eventual failure of the creative idea. Perhaps even worse, they can cause employees to focus on the measures, rather than on the eventual commercial success. Patent proliferation is one manifestation of this problem.

A second challenge in using metrics-based incentives to motivate the behaviors that lead to innovation is that most innovators are primarily driven by intrinsic, not extrinsic, motivation. Metrics-based incentive systems can crowd out intrinsic motivation, hinder explorative processes, reduce team collaboration, and/or distract employees from creative tasks (e.g., Amabile, 1983; Amabile, 1996; Shalley *et al.*, 2000). While positive links between the use of metrics-based formal incentives and creativity/innovation have been shown, as described above, negative links have also been demonstrated. Poorly designed performance metrics can obviously cause distraction and confusion, which can reduce innovation, and cause higher organizational costs. Even well-thought-out performance metrics, particularly when linked to extrinsic incentives, can decrease learning, reduce organizational flexibility and adaptation, and narrow employee focus, which can hinder innovation (Amabile, 1996; Elsbach and Hargadon, 2006; Wiley and Jarosz, 2012; Agrawal *et al.*, 2018; Grabner and Speckbacher, 2016). Innovators derive satisfaction from being innovative. But motivational orientation is not stable. It is influenced by the work environment, potentially both positively and negatively. Extrinsic motivation tends to drive out intrinsic motivation (Deci *et al.*, 1999; Frey and Jegen, 2001; Bénabou and Tirole, 2003; Grabner and Speckbacher, 2016).

A final challenge in providing innovation-related incentives is caused by the fact that modern innovation tends to occur in team settings. Chen *et al.* (2012) studied the challenge of designing reward systems to promote group creativity. They found that group tournament pay led to more creative group solutions than piece-rate pay. Group tournament pay increased the extent that group members built on other group member's ideas, whereas individual tournament pay increased the amount that people developed their own thoughts and built upon those ideas. To promote *team* creativity, it seems that it is beneficial to let teams compete with each other to stimulate the most creative team output, but it is detrimental to let the individuals on those teams compete.

3. The Information Role of Management Controls

Formal metric-based controls can be beneficial not only in motivating creative performance but also in providing useful information about it. All employee activities can benefit from more information. The performance metrics provide opportunities for employees to exchange creative ideas, provide feedback allowing the adjustment of actions, increase individual and group accountability, and enhance motivation (Chenhall *et al.*, 2011; Davila *et al.*, 2009).

Li *et al.* (2019) surveyed 290 small-to-medium enterprises (SMEs) in the United States and documented that the relationship between performance metrics and innovation depends on the type of innovation on which the organization relies. Firms that rely more on incremental innovation use greater metric intensity (i.e., the quantity and frequency with which performance metrics are tracked and used in an organization), while those that rely more on radical innovation have lower metric intensity. However, although incremental innovation is associated with greater metric intensity, the performance metrics used in those situations are less likely to be used for incentive purposes and more for information purposes such as strategy adjustment and organizational learning. Consistent with prior research on the fit between control systems and organizational context, metric intensity is associated with better organizational outcomes when the organization depends more on incremental innovation.

The information value of management control systems was also demonstrated in a field experiment conducted by Li and Sandino (2018). The experiment, conducted in a retail chain, was designed to test the effects of an information-sharing system recording employees' creative work — a control system often used to promote local experimentation — on the quality of creative work, job engagement, and financial performance. The mere introduction of the information-sharing system did not have a statistically significant effect on any of these outcomes, but the system had a significantly positive effect on the quality of creative work when it was more frequently accessed. It also had a positive effect on the quality of creative work in stores with fewer same-company stores nearby (i.e., with less natural exposure to peers' creative work) and on the value of creative work and the attendance of salespeople working for stores in divergent markets where customers had distinctive needs requiring customized service. The study also showed evidence that the system led to better financial results when salespeople had lower rather than higher creative talent prior to introducing the system. These findings shed light on when information-sharing systems can affect the quality and performance consequences of employees' creative work.

4. Setting Up Management Controls to Achieve Ambidexterity

At one time, Nokia and RIM (Research in Motion, the company that developed BlackBerry smartphones) were on all of the lists of the most innovative companies in the world. Their precipitous decline illustrates a central challenge companies face in the innovation game: it is often not enough to execute well on incremental innovation (especially in fast-changing markets). That works only in relatively stable markets. In fast-changing markets, companies that fail to keep up with disruptive technologies by developing radical innovations can find themselves in declines similar to those of Nokia or RIM. Davila and Epstein (2014) point out this innovation paradox: companies tend to do too well on one side of the equation and ignore the other. Too often, for well-established firms, this means excellent execution of existing strategy (incremental innovation) with little or ineffective focus on new strategy (radical innovation).

Organizations that are successful in both efficiently managing today's business and remaining adaptable for tomorrow's changing demands are called *ambidextrous organizations* (O'Reilly and Tushman, 2013). How can companies achieve ambidexterity? The short answer is that these different types of activities require different systems to manage. *Contextual ambidexterity* refers to the practice of requiring business units or employees to do both exploiting and exploring activities. Individuals have to make their own judgments about how to divide their time between these potentially conflicting demands. This type of ambidexterity is most suitable for settings with relatively more needs for incremental innovation, i.e., innovation not too far from its established business (e.g., traditional search/browser business in Google's case). In the case of contextual ambidexterity, a key challenge for managers is to provide employees with guidance as to how to balance existing tasks with innovation. Consistently high pressure for short-term performance does not allow time for creative thinking. Employees will inevitably gravitate toward the easier-to-measure routine tasks and will not allocate enough time to think about better ways of doing things. Employees from whom innovation is desired need some slack. Putting some boundary on routine tasks (e.g., providing both input and output targets) can also improve the performance on new tasks.

Some organizations (such as Google and 3M) are well known for "innovation time" policies that allow employees to devote 15% or 20% of their time to creative pursuits (putting clear time input limits on existing tasks). Some other organizations (e.g., Oracle) allow project teams to allocate the time of one or two people to "pet projects". A popular way to carve out time for innovation is corporate hackathons, which are widely adopted at almost all major technology companies now (e.g., Facebook, PayPal) and are quickly spreading to companies not traditionally viewed as tech firms (e.g., CapitalOne). In addition to the direct benefit to innovation, hackathons can facilitate team building, organizational learning, talent recognition and retention and satisfy employees' needs both for belonging and accomplishment.

There are risks as well: Employees can spend too much time on brainstorming new ideas and ignore their responsibilities for the routine tasks. This result is consistent with theory suggesting that individuals need guidance as to how much routine work to complete in order to achieve the cognitive closure necessary for them to think creatively (Latham and Locke, 1991; Kruglanski, 2004; Leroy, 2009). However, individuals also need guidance that encourages them to limit time on their relatively comfortable routine work and to spend time on more open-ended creative endeavors.

Bruggen *et al.* (2018) found that providing both an input and an output target on routine tasks led to greater creative task performance relative to providing either one or none of these targets. This result is consistent with theory suggesting that individuals need guidance as to how much routine work to complete in order to achieve the cognitive closure necessary for them to think creatively. It also suggests that individuals need guidance that encourages them to limit the time spent on their relatively comfortable routine work activities so that they can spend time on more open-ended creative endeavors. By setting expectations as to what employees need to achieve on their more routine day-to-day responsibilities, organizations can increase the efficacy of the growing practice of allowing employees to spend a portion of their workweek on creative endeavors.

Using detailed project- and employee-level data from a software company, Li (2018) showed that reduced strength of management control on execution tasks is significantly associated with a greater probability of self-initiated innovation. The effect was more pronounced for employees with high general ability (based on education or quality of past work) and in situations where employees were relatively sure that their superiors would not rigorously enforce time constraints on execution tasks. These findings suggest that in a multitasking environment, management control choices for non-innovation tasks can play an important role in enabling innovation.

Structural ambidexterity, on the contrary, requires the company to set up completely separate units to cope with innovation. This type of ambidexterity is most suitable when the needs for radical innovation are relatively high. For example, Google re-structured itself into Alphabet where radical innovation ("moonshots") is managed through structures (e.g. "Google X") that are from its main business ("Google"). Davila and Epstein (2014) introduced the concept of "Startup Corporation" and suggest that an ecosystem of strong soft foundations (leadership and culture) and strong hard foundations (incentives and management systems) need to be in place for a company to succeed in balancing exploiting and exploring activities.

5. Conclusion

Creativity and innovation are important for the vast majority of organizations. Research that has been done to date has a number of important implications for innovation-related management practice. Metrics-based management controls can play important roles in the development of creative ideas, but care must be taken to use them wisely because these controls can also produce negative outcomes. The issues are complex. The impacts of formal metric-based controls on creative performance depend on the type of innovation (Sorescu *et al.*, 2003; Li *et al.*, 2019), the stage of the innovation process (Amabile, 1997; Cooper, 1990; Davila and Wouters, 2006), the surrounding conditions (e.g., group vs. individual, slack), and, of course, the quality of the design of the metrics. However, some generalizable findings can be drawn from the research.

First, managers must recognize some necessary-but-not-sufficient conditions for the stimulation of successful creativity and innovation. These include having the right mix of employees, some organizational slack, and tolerance of both non-conformity and short-term failures. The research findings suggest that providing long-term incentives and some level of job security, which is consistent with tolerance of short-term failures, is important for motivating long-term innovation. People must feel free to experiment and fail. At managerial levels, that security can be implemented with a combination of stock options with long vesting periods, consideration of option repricing, and lucrative severance agreements ("golden parachutes"). These conclusions are consistent with what we observe in practice: Companies whose success depends on innovation tend to grant executives with a high proportion of long-term compensation (Ittner *et al.*, 2003; Lerner and Wulf, 2007; Francis *et al.*, 2009; Tian and Wang, 2010).

Second, if rewards are to be linked directly to specific performance measures, care must be taken to ensure that the measures are reliable indicators of future success, however defined. Poorly defined measures might cause employees' behaviors to be misdirected.

Third, in designing the incentive structures linked to the performance metrics, it is important to pay attention to whether innovation occurs in teams or at the individual level and adjust the incentive plan accordingly.

Fourth, in addition to results controls, indirect controls such as personnel and cultural controls also play very important roles in motivating innovation. CIMA (Chartered Institute of Management Accountants) published a survey study of 78 UK-based innovation companies which shows that metric-based results controls are intensively used in innovation companies with a positive overall impact. Furthermore, the study revealed that personnel controls (e.g., job design, training, and recruiting) and cultural controls (e.g., interaction, codes of conduct) were particularly effective in innovation settings (Luther *et al.*, 2018). This is generally consistent with the insights from the academic literature; metrics can be used for purposes other than deciding performance evaluations and incentive allocations. They can serve important informational roles and support indirect controls in innovative settings by facilitating social interactions and organizational learning. This is especially true as advanced technologies make available larger scale, more granular, and more timely (real-time) information. This information can be used for learning, for the pursuit of good ideas, or for decisions to cut off further investments in ideas with less promise. For example, many organizations use digital (or even gamified) scoreboards and enterprise social networks to encourage their employees to compete, collaborate, share knowledge, and innovate. Tools like Facebook Workplace and Yammer have been used by many organizations to capture, stimulate, share, improve, evaluate, and adopt new ideas across multiple stores or units around the world.

Last but not least, companies should carefully analyze their innovation strategy and, if appropriate, manage both efficiency and innovation (or both incremental innovation and radical innovation) to achieve structural or contextual ambidexterity. In achieving contextual ambidexterity (i.e., having the same employees engage in both exploiting and exploring activities), relaxing the control strength of the exploiting activities (routine tasks) can lead to more self-initiated innovation (at least for high-ability employees). Putting some boundaries on routine tasks (e.g., providing both input and output targets) can also improve the performance on innovative tasks.

References

Acemoglu, D. (2008), *Introduction to Modern Economic Growth*, Princeton, NJ: Princeton University Press.

Adams, R., J. Bessant, and R. Phelps (2006), Innovation management measurement: A review, *International Journal of Management Reviews* **8**(1), 21–47.

Agrawal, A., C. Catalini, A. Goldfarb, and H. Luo (2018), Slack time and innovation, *Organization Science* **29**(6), 1056–1073.

Ahlstrom, D. (2010), Innovation and growth: How business contributes to society, *Academy of Management Perspectives* **24**(3), 11–24.

Alexander, L. and D. Van Knippenberg (2014), Teams in pursuit of radical innovation: A goal orientation perspective, *Academy of Management Review* **39**(4), 423–438.

Amabile, T. M. (1996), *Creativity in Context*. Boulder, CO: Westview Press.

Amabile, T. M. (1983), The social psychology of creativity: A componential conceptualization, *Journal of Personality and Social Psychology* **45**(2), 357–376.

Amabile, T. M. (1997), Entrepreneurial creativity through motivational synergy, *The Journal of Creative Behavior* **31**(1), 18–26.

Bénabou, R. and J. Tirole (2003), Intrinsic and extrinsic motivation, *Review of Economic Studies* **70**, 489–520.

Benner, M. J. and M. L. Tushman (2003), Exploitation, exploration, and process management: The productivity dilemma revisited, *Academy of management Review* **28**(2), 238–256.

Brueggen, A., C. Feichter, and M. G. Williamson (2018), The effect of input and output targets for routine tasks on creative task performance, *The Accounting Review* **93**(1), 29–43.

Chen, C. X., M. G. Williamson, and F. H. Zhou (2012), Reward system design and group creativity: An experimental investigation, *The Accounting Review* **87**(6), 1885–1911.

Chenhall, R. H., J.-P. Kallunki, and H. Silvola (2011), Exploring the relationships between strategy, innovation, and management control systems: The roles of social networking, organic innovative culture, and formal controls, *Journal of Management Accounting Research* **23**(1), 99–128.

Cooper, R. G. (1990), Stage-gate systems: A new tool for managing new products, *Business Horizons* **33**(3), 44–54.

Corrado, C., C. Hulten, and D. Sichel (2009), Intangible capital and US economic growth, *Review of Income and Wealth* **55**(3), 661–685.

Danneels, E. (2002), The dynamics of product innovation and firm competences, *Strategic Management Journal* **23**(12), 1095–1121.

Davila, A., G. Foster, and M. Li (2009), Reasons for management control systems adoption: Insights from product development systems choice by early-stage entrepreneurial companies, *Accounting, Organizations and Society* **34**(3–4), 322–347.

Davila, A., G. Foster, and D. Oyon (2009), Accounting and control, entrepreneurship and innovation: Venturing into new research opportunities, *European Accounting Review* **18**, 281–311.

Davila, T. and M. Wouters (2006), Management accounting in the manufacturing sector: Managing costs at the design and production stages, *Handbooks of Management Accounting Research* **2**, 831–858.

Deci, E. L., R. Koestner, and R. M. Ryan (1999), A meta-analytic review of experiments examining the effects of extrinsic rewards on intrinsic motivation, *Psychological Bulletin* **125**(6), 627.

Dewar, R. D. and J. E. Dutton (1986), The adoption of radical and incremental innovations: An empirical analysis, *Management Science* **32**(11), 1422–1433.

Duchesneau, T. D., S. F. Cohn, and J. E. Dutton (1980), *A Study of Innovation in Manufacturing: Determinants, Processes, and Methodological Issues*, Vol. I and II, The Social Science Research Institute, University of Maine, Orono, 1979.

Durmaz, L. (2014), Lessons learned from successful employee suggestion programs, http://www.espninja.com/lessons-learned-successful-employee-suggestion-programs/.

Elsbach, K. D. and A. B. Hargadon (2006), Enhancing creativity through "mindless" work: A framework of workday design, *Organization Science* **17**(4), 470–483.

Ettlie, J. E. (1983), Organizational policy and innovation among suppliers to the food processing sector, *Academy of Management Journal* **26**(1), 27–44.

Ettlie, J. E., W. P. Bridges, and R. D. O'Keefe (1984), Organization strategy and structural differences for radical versus incremental innovation, *Management Science* **30**(6), 682–695.

Francis, B., I. Hasan, and Z. Sharma (2009), Do incentives create innovation? Evidence from CEO compensation contracts, Working paper, Rensselaer Polytechnic Institute.

Frey, B. S. and R. Jegen (2001), Motivation crowding theory, *Journal of Economic Surveys* **15**(5), 589–611.

Grabner, I. and G. Speckbacher (2016), The cost of creativity: A control perspective, *Accounting, Organizations and Society* **48**, 31–42.

Grabner, I. (2014), Incentive system design in creativity-dependent firms, *The Accounting Review* **89**(5), 1729–1750.

Hage, J. (1980), *Theories of Organizations: Form, Process, and Transformation.* Chichester, England: John Wiley & Sons.

Holmstrom, B. (1989), Agency costs and innovation, *Journal of Economic Behavior & Organization* **12**(3), 305–327.

Holthausen, R. W., D. F. Larcker, and R. G. Sloan (1995), Business unit innovation and the structure of executive compensation, *Journal of Accounting and Economics* **19**(2), 279–313.

Ittner, C. D., R. A. Lambert, and D. F. Larcker (2003), The structure and performance consequences of equity grants to employees of new economy firms, *Journal of Accounting and Economics* **34**(1–3), 89–127.

Kachelmeier, S. J. and M. G. Williamson (2010), Attracting creativity: The initial and aggregate effects of contract selection on creativity-weighted productivity, *The Accounting Review* **85**(5), 1669–1691.

Kachelmeier, S. J., B. E. Reichert, and M. G. Williamson (2008), Measuring and motivating quantity, creativity, or both, *Journal of Accounting Research* **46**(2), 341–373.

Kogan, L., D. Papanikolaou, A. Seru, and N. Stoffman (2017), Technological innovation, resource allocation, and growth, *The Quarterly Journal of Economics* **132**(2), 665–712.

Kruglanski, A. W. (2004), *The Psychology of Closed Mindedness.* Psychology Press.

Latham, G. P. and E. A. Locke (1991), Self-regulation through goal setting, *Organizational Behavior and Human Decision Processes* **50**(2), 212–247. doi:10.1016/0749-5978(91)90021-K.

Lerner, J. and J. Wulf (2007), Innovation and incentives: Evidence from corporate R&D, *The Review of Economics and Statistics* **89**(4), 634–644.

Leroy, S. (2009), Why is it so hard to do my work? The challenge of attention residue when switching between work tasks, *Organizational Behavior and Human Decision Processes* **109**(2), 168–181. doi:10.1016/j.obhdp.2009.04.002.

Li, S. X. (2018), Boss, cut me some slack: Control and innovation in a multitasking environment. Unpublished working Paper.

Li, S. X. and T. Sandino (2018), Effects of an information sharing system on employee creativity, engagement, and performance, *Journal of Accounting Research* **56**(2), 713–747.

Li, S. X., K. A. Merchant, and F. Y. Wang (2019), Performance metrics and innovation Dependency. Unpublished working paper.

Luther, R., E. Haustein, and G. Webber (2018), Management control in UK innovation companies, *CIMA Research Executive Summary* **14**(3), 1–24. Available from https://www.cimaglobal.com/Documents/Thought_leadership_docs/Academic-research/Management%20Control%20Academic%20Report.pdf

Manso, G. (2011), "Motivating innovation", *The Journal of Finance* **66**(5), 1823–1860.

Nelson, A., A. Earle, J. Howard-Grenville, J. Haack, and D. Young (2014), Do innovation measures actually measure innovation? Obliteration, symbolic adoption, and other finicky challenges in tracking innovation, *Research Policy* **43**(6), 927.

Nord, W. R and S. Tucker (1987), *Implementing Routine and Radical Innovations*. Lexington, MA: Lexington Books.

O'Reilly III, A. Charles, and M. L. Tushman (2013), Organizational ambidexterity: Past, present, and future, *Academy of Management Perspectives* **27**(4), 324–338.

Schroeder, R. G., A. H. Van de Ven, G. D. Scudder, and D. Polley (1989), The development of innovation ideas. In Van de Ven, A.H. H. L. Angle and M.S. Poole (eds.), *Research on the Management of Innovation: The Minnesota Studies*. New York: Ballinger/Harper and Row, pp. 107–134.

Shalley, C. E., L. L. Gilson, and T. C. Blum (2000), Matching creativity requirements and the work environment: Effects of satisfaction and intention to leave, *Academy of Management Journal* **43**(2), 215–223.

Solow, R. M. (1957), Technical change and the aggregate production function, *Review of Economics and Statistics* (August), 312–320.

Sorescu, A. B., R. K. Chandy, and J. C. Prabhu (2003), Sources and financial consequences of radical innovation: Insights from pharmaceuticals, *Journal of Marketing* **67**(4), 82–102.

Tian, X. and T.Y. Wang (2011), Tolerance for failure and corporate innovation, *The Review of Financial Studies* **27**(1), 211–255.

Wiley, J. and A. F. Jarosz (2012), Working memory capacity, attentional focus, and problem solving, *Current Directions in Psychological Science* **21**(4), 258–262.

https://doi.org/10.1142/9789811220470_0017

Chapter 17

Board Governance and Information Quality

Bin Srinidhi

College of Business, University of Texas Arlington, USA

bin.srinidhi@gmail.com

Abstract

In this chapter, I discuss how the information environment of a firm is affected by the functioning of the board. Independent opinion formation by directors, the richness of information that is brought to bear on board decisions, as well as inter-director communication, are essential for improving the information environment of a firm and the credibility that its disclosures instill in its investors. Specifically, I address board independence, gender and ethnic diversity among directors, and inter-director communication as factors that contribute to information quality. Because the incentives of directors are markedly different between family and diversified non-family firms, I discuss this aspect of ownership in the chapter. While board functioning is only one of the determinants of information quality, it is a critical one and therefore, an understanding of the board functioning and its links to information quality is of paramount importance.

Keywords: Information quality; Board independence; Board diversity; Inter-director communication; Family firms.

1. Introduction

In this chapter, I discuss the role of the corporate board in improving the quality of the information provided by publicly listed corporations to two of the stakeholders, namely the equity investors and lenders. I also discuss how the dynamics in the board could affect the quality of information used by the board in making their decisions.

The limited liability corporation in a capitalist setting is organized in a way that while investors provide the capital, the decision rights to use (or not use) the funds in a manner that benefits the investors are mostly delegated to the managers. The delegated rights are held mostly by the Chief Executive Officer (CEO), who is supported by a top management team. The managers not only are accountable for the use of the capital provided by the investors (and additional retained earnings from that capital) but are also responsible to periodically report to investors about how the funds have been deployed and how the corporation has performed. If the quality of reporting does not generate enough credibility among investors, they are likely to withhold investments or demand a higher return. A critical feature of the free market system is that the investors do not face serious impediments and constraints about trading in the capital market. This ability to trade freely allows investors who are skeptical of the firms with relatively low reporting quality to demand a higher cost of capital from them. More generally, if the information quality in an economy is poor, the investors face a higher uncertainty about their invested money (referred to as information risk) and are likely to lose trust in the reported information. They "exit" the market and the lack of investment in productive activities results in a slower or negative growth in the economy. The quality of reported information is, therefore, a critical factor in the growth of the economy. The quality of the information in this context refers to the quality of reporting by the managers to investors. The term "quality" refers to the usefulness of the reported information for investors in making decisions about investment/disinvestment.

An elaborate system of checks and balances has been developed to induce the managers to provide adequate information quality in their reports and disclosures. At the country level, the accounting system, typically enforced by a regulatory body with legislative authority from the government, mandates periodic reporting in financial statements and comprises standards that the managers need to comply with. In the US, the accounting standards are embodied in the US Generally Accepted

Accounting Principles (GAAP) and are enforced by the Securities Exchange Commission (SEC) that derives its authority from the securities laws enacted by the US Congress.[1] The incentives for compliance with accounting standards are provided by mandated auditing of the financial reports by registered and certified third-party auditors. The legal system ensures that the auditors face legal liability for giving unqualified reports to firms that have accounting failures. The associated legal and reputation costs incentivize auditors to be independent and devote enough effort to ensure compliance.[2]

Legislators and regulators, keenly aware of the impact of the law, regulations, and their enforcement on good governance and production of high quality information to sustain an effective capital market, have regulated both the composition (in terms of directors) and the committee structure of the corporate boards, as well as the functioning of the auditors. For example, the Sarbanes–Oxley Act of 2002 (SOX) requires all boards of publicly traded firms to have a majority of non-executive directors. It also mandates all such boards to constitute at least three committees (audit, nominating, and compensation) comprising only non-executive directors. SOX also requires every firm's audit committee to either have at least one designated financial expert or disclose the reason for not having one. To preserve the auditors' independence, SOX limits the non-audit services that external auditors can provide to the firm (the setting up of the accounting system is not allowed). Further, to ensure the integrity of the information produced by the firm, SOX requires every firm to set up an internal control system (if it did not have one) that needs to be attested by the external auditor regarding the absence/presence of material weaknesses. It also requires the top managers, namely the CEO and the CFO, to personally assure the veracity of the information that is disclosed in the financial statements.

---

[1] Although the standards themselves are developed by a semi-autonomous private board — the Financial Accounting Standards Board (FASB) — to which the SEC has delegated the authority to develop standards, the ultimate enforcement authority lies with the SEC. Outside of the United States, the primary body to develop standards is the International Accounting Standards Board (IASB) located in UK but the IASB does not have the authority to enforce the standards in any country.

[2] In several countries where the legal enforcement is weak and/or the political interference shields the corporations and auditors, the audit quality is weak and the resulting information quality is also weak (Haw *et al.*, 2004; Srinidhi *et al.*, 2009).

Maintaining transparency is essential for sustaining investors' trust (Shleifer and Vishny, 1997). Corporate governance is the process by which the regulators, policymakers, and investors seek to incentivize managers to provide the needed transparency. Hart (1995) views corporate governance as a "mechanism for making decisions that have not been specified in the initial contract". More specifically, corporate governance is the structure that allocates residual decision rights of control over the firm's non-human assets that are either not enumerated or cannot be practically enforced through contracts. He identifies both the agency problem and contract incompleteness as individually necessary and jointly sufficient for the existence of a corporate governance mechanism. An implication of this argument is that the demand for, and the impact from, the corporate governance mechanism increases with the severity of agency problems and the extent of contract incompleteness.

In a limited liability corporation, the agency problem arises from the separation of ownership from control wherein the several decision rights that are normally associated with ownership are transferred to managers. The owners — the equity financiers — hold only the residual rights.[3] Explicit and implicit enforceable contracts have only a limited ability to protect investors' rights. The unobservability (and non-contractibility) of managerial effort (moral hazard), the pre-contract information asymmetry about the skills and ability of managers (adverse selection), and post-contract information asymmetry that arises from the operational engagement (non-engagement) of managers (investors) limit the contracts from fully protecting the rights of the investors (even assuming that the legal enforceability is good and the cost of enforceability is low). Expanding on this idea, Shleifer and Vishny (1997) conceive of corporate governance as the set of all measures that the financiers of a business can take to assure

[3]We note that the US–UK model of a firm is the prevalence of a structure with a large number of small owners. In this setting of diffuse ownership, the owners have neither the incentive nor the resources to exercise their ownership rights directly. They need to delegate their rights to the managers (in fact, to the board of directors — which we will discuss shortly), creating the agency problem that we speak of. In closely held firms, the primary agency problem could arise because the powerful insider-owners (family) control most of the decision rights and could expropriate from the minority external shareholders who do not share the decision rights. This inter-principal agency problem is often referred to as the Type 2 agency problem and is more characteristic of concentrated ownership that is found in Asia and Eastern Europe (Shleifer and Vishny, 1997).

themselves of a return of their investment. These arguments suggest that the primary purpose of corporate governance mechanisms is to alleviate the adverse consequences of information asymmetry between managers and investors. Stated differently, the primary purpose of corporate governance is to ensure and sustain the quality of information flow from managers to investors such that it adequately protects investors' rights.

Regulators seek to ensure adequate information quality through mandated financial statements and other mandated disclosures.[4] At the level of the corporation, the primary institutional feature of the governance structure is the board of directors (BODs). The BOD exercises critical influence over the reporting information quality through management oversight. Specifically, it oversees the management in providing transparency about the operations and the disposition of the resources by the firm. The (equity) investors elect a slate of directors to the board to represent their interests. The directors are tasked with the responsibility to both monitor the management and advise them in their operating, strategic, and reporting decisions.

Proper monitoring and oversight of managers require non-executive directors to contest management viewpoints in the board and demand supporting information when needed. Therefore, proper monitoring requires the non-executive directors to get unbiased[5] information from independent sources. Further, it requires the non-executive directors to have the gravitas, the time, the confidence, and the inclination to assess the evidence and form independent viewpoints on management proposals as well as to propose alternatives.

In practice, the monitoring and oversight functions could be compromised by several factors. First, the CEO is always one of the directors on the board, and often, some other executives are also on the board. Clearly, they cannot be expected to oversee or scrutinize their own decisions. Further, they are often the sole providers of non-public information to the board. Self-interest is likely to drive the information that they choose to provide to other board members. Even when independent information sources might exist outside of the firm, getting information from those

---

[4]In the US, the mandate is for the corporation to file annual 10-K reports (annual reports) that are audited and filed with the SEC before 90 (75, 60) days after the end of the fiscal year for all listed (accelerated, large accelerated) filers.

[5]The information provided by the managers and executive directors could be biased to further the interests of the managers at the expense of the investors.

sources involves considerably higher effort than getting it from the management. It is therefore unrealistic to assume that the non-executive directors act on unbiased information. Second, the non-executive directors might have ties with the CEO and/or other executives and be obliged to them for their board position and status. They might lack both the independence and the gravitas to effectively oversee the CEO and other managers. Consequently, the monitoring of the managers by the board is imperfect at best and ineffective at its worst. Therefore, these incentives of the board directors and managers could compromise the quality of information that is made available to investors.

Every firm is characterized by an equilibrium that jointly determines the board's composition, structure, and the relative power in decision-making on the one hand and the quality of information on the other. Adams *et al.* (2010) point out that each firm solves a different optimization problem that depends on the distinguishing firm-specific characteristics, rendering a direct comparison of any governance attribute between two different firms open to multiple interpretations. On the one hand, the empirically observed differences across the firms could mostly be due to the differences in their optimum board compositions. On the other hand, these differences could be due to different levels of inefficiency resulting from differential agency costs and differential CEO influence. Unless all the observed and unobserved factors that result in different optimum board compositions are controlled for (impractical), it is not possible to say conclusively that these differences are due to differential agency costs and the differential bargaining powers between the board and the managers. I note this as a potential limitation of research in corporate governance and, thereby, of this chapter.

Another point of interest is the *mutual relationship* between governance and information quality. Good governance exemplified by effective BOD results in greater scrutiny of the management. In anticipation of this scrutiny, managers devote more effort to collect accurate, objective, and defensible information than when the board governance is weak. This argument, the one made in this chapter, suggests that higher information quality *is the result* of good governance and effective BODs. However, good governance requires unbiased high-quality information. Bushman and Smith (2001) identify three channels through which financial information is used in affecting management contracts — governance in general: to screen the bad projects from the good ones; in monitoring and disciplining managers to reduce both moral hazard and adverse selection.

Their paper shows that *informed managerial decisions and better governance are the results of higher information quality.* In effect, while the attributes of the board, its committees, and its directors, in conjunction with the personality and power of the CEO constitute significant determinants of the quality of the information, the quality of information also affects the effectiveness of the board. It is an equilibrium that is reached in the context of the firm's environment that includes the resource, product, labor and capital markets, the technology associated with each of the markets, and the information technology. The chapter does not directly deal with the environmental variables but draws upon studies that control for these factors. I note this as a second limitation of this study.

Within the context of the environmental and technological variables, the quality of firm-specific information is determined by the incentives faced by managers (particularly the CEO), the CEO's personality attributes, and the managers' interaction with the BOD. The scope of this chapter is limited mainly to the effect of board structure and composition and director attributes on information quality. The overall framework used in this chapter is presented in Figure 1.

In this chapter, I draw upon the current literature on the board composition in terms of the observable manifestations of the independence and diversity of its directors. From an *agency theory perspective*, a director who is not economically or socially connected to the firm's management has better incentives and ability to monitor managerial actions, question their decisions, and thereby improve the quality of information that is used in the board decisions as well as the quality of information that is released to the market. From *the resource dependency perspective* (Pfeffer and Salancik, 1978), the board's value to the firm derives from the resources that the directors have access to. Female and male directors have different socialization experiences and expectations and bring their diverse experiences and exposures to bear upon board decisions. Similarly, ethnically diverse directors have different exposures and experiences that they can bring to bear upon board decisions. Diversity of perspectives creates a synergy (referred to as board capital — Hillman and Dalziel, 2003) that increases the board's ability to monitor as well as advise the managers. Although this synergy creates a potential for improvement in transparency and information quality, the benefits might not be realized in the absence of effective communication and coordination between directors. In fact, acrimonious relationships could result in inefficient board working, sub-optimal board decisions, and degradation of information quality.

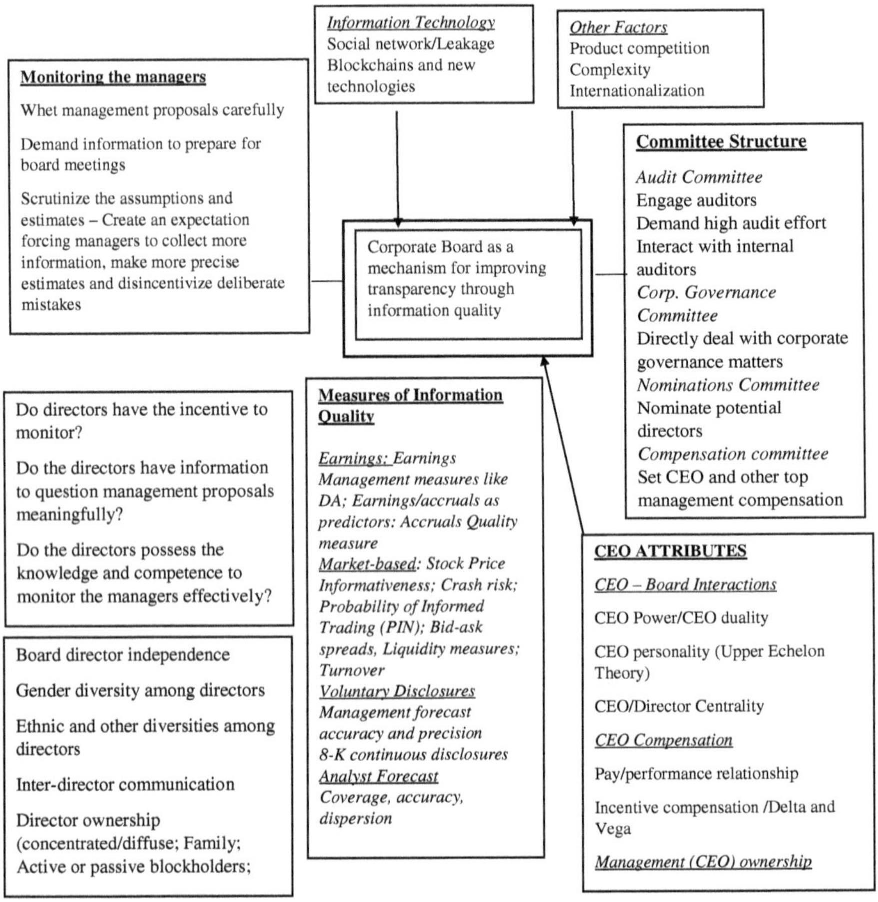

Figure 1: Board structure, director attributes and information quality: A conceptual framework.

A separate stream of literature examines the inter-director interactions on the board (Malenko, 2014). Van Peteghem *et al.* (2018) use the Group Faultline theory to integrate diversity literature with inter-director communication. In this study, I include the growing ideas about both the costs and benefits of diversity on information quality.

Section 2 focuses on board independence, how it is measured, and its effect on transparency and information quality. Section 3 deals with the effect of the gender composition of the board on information quality. Section 4 deals with inter-director communication, fault lines, and the ethnic composition of the board and their joint effect on information quality. In Section 5, I deal with family control of listed firms and the role of the board governance as a moderator of the relationship between family control and information quality. Section 6 refers to the emerging research on the effect of new information technologies on information quality. In Section 7, I point out the scope limitations of this chapter.

2. Board Independence and Information Quality

In the case of a corporate board, independence refers to the ability of non-executive directors to assess management proposals, and proposals by other directors and committees, in an unbiased manner. A director who is dependent on the CEO and management for information or legitimacy or has economic or social bonds or is obliged in some other way to the CEO or other executives in the firm is less likely to exercise oversight by critically assessing management proposals and confronting the managers during board meetings. In effect, this laxness in oversight could compromise the quality of information used in board decisions (leading to less informed strategic decisions) as well as on the quality of information reported in the firm's financial statements and other disclosures. When the number of such dependent directors crosses a threshold on the board, "groupthink" prevails because the other directors (those who are independent) are neither incentivized to devote the effort to critically assess the proposals nor would they be willing to openly confront the overwhelming sentiment, even if they have reservations. Conversely, if enough board directors are independent, the management proposals are likely to be subjected to greater scrutiny and their reports are likely to be met with more skepticism. The assessment of the proposals by the board is likely to benefit from the expertise and knowledge of different directors as well as from the additional effort devoted to their preparation by the managers who anticipate the scrutiny.

Several factors could impair independent opinion formation and the expression of those opinions by directors. The most glaring factor is the influence that the CEO, the other executive directors, and top managers have on the information received by the directors on the firm's operations and prospects. Another important factor is how obligated the director is to the CEO for his or her standing and status and how confident the director is in confronting or criticizing management proposals when needed. Conceptually, the degree of independence exhibited by a director in board and committee meetings is determined by several factors: (i) the private information that he or she receives from the management *vis-à-vis* other sources; (ii) the public information that is disclosed about the firm and the other firms in the industry; (iii) the effort that the director is able and willing to devote to assess the proposals that come before the board; (iv) the relationship that the director has with the CEO and other directors and managers; (v) the extent of pre-board exchange of ideas with other directors; and (vi) the personalities of the director and the CEO. One can view the board outcome and the information quality as equilibrium outcomes in a perpetual game between the CEO and other managers on the one side and the non-executive directors on the other side. However, the complete modeling of this system is very complex and impractical, not the least because most of these variables cannot be directly measured and the indirect measures are likely to have large measurement errors.

The most common measure used to measure the independence of the board is the proportion of independent directors on the board and on the committees of the board. A large body of academic literature — Houston *et al.* (2019) cite around 70 chapters in accounting and finance in their Appendix A — have used the proportion of independent directors as defined by either Institutional Shareholder Services (ISS — Risk Metrics) or Boardex databases to measure board independence and examine the effect of independence on various board outcomes including the quality of reporting and the richness of the firms' information environment. ISS classifies non-executive directors into two categories — affiliated outside directors and independent outsiders. The affiliated outside directors are those with previous employment with the company[6] or have transactional (payments or fees received by them or their family members) or professional relationships with the firm (investment banks, auditors, consultants, market research firms, etc.) or have family relationships. The overarching criterion used in defining an affiliated outsider is whether the director has private access to sensitive operational or strategic firm information.

The seminal chapter on board independence in accounting is that by Klein (2002), which shows that after controlling for most other factors, the board and audit committee independence are associated with lower abnormal accruals. She uses the proportion of outside directors as a

[6]NYSE and NASDAQ consider ex-employees as independent after a 3-year "cooling-off" period, before which they are considered affiliated outsiders. ISS uses a 5-year period in its classification. The exception is that no cooling-off period applies to an ex-CEO, who is always considered an affiliated outsider.

measure of independence, where an outside director is defined as a non-affiliated non-executive director. This paper laid the foundation for further research on the effect of board independence on the reporting quality. Complementing this result, Xie *et al.* (2003) show that earnings management is lower in firms with a higher proportion of independent directors. They find that the effect is higher in firms with a higher proportion of directors with a corporate background (financial sophistication) and that it is lower in firms with larger board sizes, suggesting that larger boards bring in more experienced directors. Jaggi *et al.* (2009) use a different international context — Hong Kong — and show that the proportion of independent directors is associated with lower abnormal accruals and higher accruals quality.[7]

Although these early studies show that there is an association between the proportion of independent board directors and information quality, it is not clear how the potential inadequacy of the measure could affect the result. The issue is to distinguish *independence in fact* from *apparent independence.* Larcker *et al.* (2007) develop comprehensive measures of board governance that include a total of 39 variables of which 21 are board-related variables. These variables are then aggregated into 14 governance factors. The authors test the effect of these 14 factors on eight different measures of earnings quality and find very weak, mixed, and often contradictory results. Even more surprisingly, they find that corporate governance variables have little influence on earnings restatements and operating performance. Garcia Meca and Sanchez-Ballesta (2009) conduct a meta-analysis of 35 chapters on the effect of board and ownership structure. They analyze the effect of several dimensions of governance on earnings management: (1) Boards of directors: Board independence, board size, CEO duality, and audit committee independence; and (2) Ownership structure: Insider ownership, concentration, and institutional ownership. They find that the board independence's effect on earnings quality is weak (stronger in Anglo-American countries), CEO duality does not seem to affect it much, board size is negatively associated with

[7]Accruals quality is defined as the association between working capital accruals and the cash flows of the preceding, current, and succeeding years. The idea is that a working capital accrual needs to be realized as cash in at least one of the 3 years. The extent to which it does not, the quality of accrual estimation is flawed and therefore the quality of accruals is lower. For a full definition and description of the accruals quality measure, see Dechow and Dichev (2002) and Francis *et al.* (2005).

earnings management, and independent audit committees improve earnings quality. Board ownership improves the quality of earnings, but management and block holder ownerships do not produce significant results.

From the results of these studies, it is not clear whether the variables in question merely capture the independence in appearance instead of independence in fact. There are two studies that address this issue. In a study of gender diversity on earnings quality, Srinidhi *et al.* (2019) show that only more *active independent directors* (measured by the positive changes in the boards with which they have been associated in the preceding 3 years) are associated with higher earnings quality. Hwang and Kim (2009) study the effect of independent directors' monitoring of the managers by examining the CEO's compensation. They find that while a "conventionally" independent board makes little difference to CEO compensation, a *conventionally and socially independent board* has a significant and material effect. A director is not considered socially independent if he or she has ties with the CEO in the form of mutual alma mater, military service, regional origin, academic discipline, or industry. A board is defined as conventionally and socially independent if and only if more than 50% of the directors on the board have neither conventional nor social ties with the firm and its management. These studies show that the proportion of independent directors is not an adequate measure of board independence.

Further, a board director, even if nominally independent, could be inhibited from expressing his or her views independently because of lower status (the other directors do not take him or her seriously and the director in question is aware of this) or if the CEO is very powerful. According to the traditional agency-theoretic view, the board of directors, acting on behalf of the investors, negotiate a "second-best" contract that optimizes the investors' payout subject to the CEO's participation and incentive compatibility constraints. This equilibrium reflects the compensation of the CEO, his effort, and his actions. However, it is unlikely that the CEO's payout is held to the "reservation level" and the surplus accrues to the investors. Moreover, the board consists of both executive and non-executive directors. Neither the executive directors nor the non-executive directors have the same preferences and face the same environment as the investors.[8] In other words, there is an agency conflict between the

[8]The investors are not homogeneous, either. Institutional and retail investors could face different incentives, have different preferences, and possess different resources. Among

non-executive directors and the investors. A CEO rationally exploits this disconnect between investors and the directors to increase his own compensation, decrease his effort, and change the disclosure and reporting strategies. Therefore, the traditional agency-theoretic equilibrium might not be descriptive of reality. Bebchuk and Fried (2002, 2003, 2004, 2005) are critical of the traditional view and argue that CEOs have a considerable bargaining power and often control the board. In effect, they set (or at the least, significantly influence) their own compensation and limit the critical scrutiny and opposition from the board. As a result, the equilibrium quality of information available about a firm could depend on the relative powers of the CEO and the board. Adams *et al.* (2005) argue that powerful CEOs could deviate from the board and make decisions on subjective and less debated information, thereby decreasing the quality of information that goes into board decisions.

A different strand of literature examines the personality and traits of the CEO and how it affects board outcomes. They draw on the Upper Echelon theory (Hambrick and Mason, 1984) which suggests that the personality characteristics of the CEOs influence the decisions and outcomes in the firms they lead. Gul *et al.* (2019) show that CEOs who are primarily motivated by promotional opportunities indulge in aggressive reporting, whereas CEOs who are motivated primarily by the need to reduce risk and instability choose conservative reporting. Ahmed and Duellman (2013) show that the financial statements of firms with overconfident CEOs exhibit low conservatism. Complementing their results, Hsieh *et al.* (2014) show that overconfident CEOs indulge in aggressive earnings management and thereby reduce the information quality. Francis *et al.* (2008) show an association between reputed CEOs and both poorer discretionary earnings quality and poorer total earnings quality but attribute it to the need for firms with poorer information quality to restore investor confidence by attracting CEOs with greater reputation. Ali and Zhang (2015) show that the firms exhibit earnings overstatement in the early years of a CEO's tenure and during the final year of tenure. Clearly, this demonstrates that the personal incentives of CEOs have an impact on the firm's information quality. Moreover, they show that the impact is lower with better monitoring — implying that a strong board that is engaged in intensive oversight of the firm's reporting practices can

---

the institutional investors, the hedge funds, mutual funds, and pension funds have different incentives and preferences.

mitigate the CEO's influence on information quality. The takeaway from all these studies is that information quality is an outcome not only of the board characteristics such as independence of directors but is the outcome of a confluence of interacting forces reflecting the incentives, preferences and relative powers of the directors and the CEO.

3. Board Gender Diversity and Information Quality

In pursuit of greater transparency and higher information quality for their investors, many countries have enacted laws and regulations that mandate the proportion of women directors on the boards of listed firms. Norway was the first country to legislate a mandatory 40% quota for female representation on corporate boards. Since then, other European nations have legislated similar quotas — Germany requires supervisory boards to have 30% female representation; Spain and Sweden have non-binding targets for their boards to have at least 40% and 25% female directors, respectively (Burke and Vinnicombe, 2008). On September 30, 2018, the State of California legislated gender quotas for all US-listed firms with their principal executive offices in the state. High-level committees in the United Kingdom and elsewhere have called for more female directors to be appointed to boards to improve corporate governance (Higgs, 2003; Tyson, 2003).

Academic research has, in general, supported the proposition that gender diversity among directors on the boards of listed firms results in better governance, greater transparency, and higher information quality. Adams and Ferreira (2009) document higher attendance for meetings when the boards are gender diverse and show that female directors are more likely than male directors to serve on audit committees and other monitoring committees. Srinidhi *et al.* (2011) show that board gender diversity translates to higher earnings quality. Using stock price informativeness as a measure of information quality, Gul *et al.* (2011) show that board gender diversity results in a richer information environment. Lai *et al.* (2017) show that both the auditor choice and audit quality are improved when boards become gender diverse.

The induction of female directors to the board and its committees could influence the resulting information quality in several ways. Typically, two strands of thought (not mutually exclusive) are presented in the literature. The first focuses on *the gender aspect* — that women bring qualities and traits that are different and often superior to those of men.

Viewed from this perspective, women directors contribute more to the board governance and information quality than male directors. The second strand of thought focuses on *the diversity aspect*. Women bring perspectives that are different from those of men and break the groupthink because they make different assumptions. The differences in assumptions and preferences also increase the skepticism in the board because the male and female directors often do not see eye-to-eye forcing the development of more objective evidence to satisfy the diverse board. These differences could also result in unresolved differences in opinions and dysfunctional board behavior that could adversely impact the quality of information.

The superiority of women directors arises from the following argument. Women constitute only 10% of board directorships (Gul *et al.*, 2011), although they hold 51.6% of managerial and professional positions[9]. If we assume that male and female managers and professionals possess similar leadership skill distributions, the bar that the women need to cross to become directors is evidently higher, creating a "glass ceiling" effect. In effect, the truncation of the leadership skill distribution for female directors is more severe than for male directors, creating an artificially higher average leadership skill among female directors compared to male directors. This could result in better oversight by female directors compared to male directors, and as a result, the information quality in firms with gender-diverse boards could be higher due to more stringent and competent oversight and scrutiny.

Other literature that focuses on gender pertains to observed differences in traits, preferences, and motivations between men and women. Prior literature has documented that women exhibit greater sensitivity to ethical issues than men (Cohen *et al.*, 1998; Bernardi and Arnold, 1997; Bruns and Merchant, 1990). The literature in management and psychology has also documented that women are more averse to risk and complexity (Brooks and Zank, 2005; Jianakoplos and Bernasek, 1998; Barber and Odean, 2001). Both these female qualities imply a greater focus on the accuracy and objectivity of information that is brought before the board for decisions as well as the information that is released to investors by the firm.

The second strand of thought that focuses on diversity is supported by the resource dependence hypothesis (Pfeffer and Selancik, 1978). Extending the concept of resource dependence to information, several

[9]The 2014 Bureau of Labor Statistics survey http://www.bls.gov/cps/cpsaat11.pdf.

papers (Srinidhi *et al.*, 2011; Gul *et al.*, 2011; Lai *et al.*, 2017) argue that female directors are socialized differently and have exposure to different segments of customers and other stakeholders compared to male directors and therefore, bring different perspectives based on their own experiences to the table in the discussion of board matters. Hillman *et al.* (2002) show that while male directors are predominantly business experts and bring a business perspective, female directors are more likely to be professionals (support specialists) who bring perspectives from the view of lawyers, bankers, public relation specialists, and marketers or are likely to be active in the community who bring up non-business perspectives on issues, problems, and ideas as well as expertise about and influence with powerful groups in the community. They also show that female directors are likely to have greater exposure to multiple boards, enabling them to bring in different business perspectives as well. Recent literature in psychology and brain science (Eagleman, 2011) shows that most of the human responses to stimuli are the result of the unconscious brain that is shaped by both the genes and experience of the responder. In effect, the reflexes and intuitions of women who are socialized differently are likely to be different from those of men. Even when the female directors are consciously trying to be like their male counterparts in their board functions, their reflexive responses to the proposals before the board could be systematically different from those of male directors. Together, these studies suggest that female directors are more likely to bring different perspectives and respond differently to the proposals discussed by the boards and their committees compared to male directors. *Ceteris paribus,* this perspective-broadening effect increases the demand for information. Moreover, because the perspectives are different, there could be greater skepticism among both the male and the female directors toward each other's opinions. Such skepticism further increases the demand for objective and persuasive evidence to convince the other directors in arriving at majority decisions.

There are many circumstances under which gender diversity might not result in superior information quality. First, if female directors are brought in only for improving legitimacy, they will be "token" directors and will not have the voice on the board to influence its decisions and procedures. However, Hillman *et al.* (2002) show that this is unlikely to be widely prevalent. Her conclusions are also supported by the tests of tokenism in Srinidhi *et al.* (2011), Gul *et al.* (2011), and Lai *et al.* (2017). Second, female directors are in a minority on almost all gender-diverse boards. If coalitions form among male directors, the votes of female directors might not be decisive.[10] Srinidhi *et al.* (2019) show that the mechanism through which the female directors influence board outcomes is through norm changes. Their findings complement those by Adams and Ferreira (2009), who show that the attendance in board meetings (a norm change) improves when boards include female directors. Third, a dividing line could develop between male and female directors precluding communication, and worse still, could result in acrimony. Extant studies are not consistent with this argument. To the best of our knowledge, no study on board gender diversity has shown a negative impact on monitoring and information quality. Fourth, if the tasks are well defined, then perspective broadening might have a limited effect. Both task autonomy and task complexity allow the benefits of prospective broadening to be realized (Man and Lam, 2003). Unlike most other tasks, the board is tasked with making decisions that are fairly complex and the board itself has considerable autonomy in making the decisions. Therefore, the limiting effects of task autonomy and complexity are not likely to limit the prospective-broadening effect on board decisions.

Overall, gender diversity on boards has a positive impact on information quality — both the information that the board considers in making all its decisions and the information that the firm discloses through its financial statements and other disclosures.

4. Inter-director Communication, Board Ethnic Diversity and Information Quality

4.1. *Inter-director communication*

In a board, as in any workgroup, the synergistic effects are realized only when the team members effectively communicate with each other. Effective communication implies not only that a director independently airs his or her opinion without fear of retribution but also that his opinion will be accorded respect and taken seriously by the other directors. In practice, inter-director communication is impeded because of several

[10]Anticipating this, the female directors are less likely to be active in board decision-making, and in effect, the perspective-broadening effect might not improve information quality.

factors. First, only a limited time is available for interaction during board meetings. If the management proposal is controversial, it is in the interest of the CEO and other executive directors to take more time in explaining the proposal (both because it calls for more explanation that requires more time and to willfully limit the time for dissensions), and at the same time, limit the time available to board directors to scrutinize the proposal. Second, the directors work with limited information. Often, the only source of relevant information for board decisions is provided by the CEO and the management team. Under those circumstances, the directors are not able to exhibit their independence even if they want to.

In addition to working with limited time and information (and partly because of it), individual directors could be inhibited from challenging managers. Most independent directors have considerable outside reputations and often work with a high self-image. The fear of being isolated in board meetings[11] while challenging management proposals could inhibit them from being forthright in expressing their views. Another factor is that many of the independent directors hold outside positions as professionals, community leaders, or top executives in other firms. As a result, they could be busy with their non-board workload, and this could prevent them from communicating with other directors prior to the board meeting and/or devoting the effort needed to assess and scrutinize the management proposals. Given that CEOs and other executive directors are also often quite powerful both in and out of their firms, directors could also fear potential retaliation from the CEO and other executive directors when they challenge their proposals and question their judgment. All these factors make it personally costly for directors to communicate openly and effectively (Malenko, 2014).

For every board decision, we could model each director as having some private information that is different from other directors. The board decision process takes place in two stages: (i) Communication stage where each director decides on whether to incur the cost of communicating the information prior to or during the board meeting; and (ii) Decision-making stage where directors vote based on their remaining

---

[11]Isolation in groups could lead to a "loss of face" and a blow to the self-image of the individual. The possibility of wrongly challenging a good proposal could also damage the reputation of the individual director.

individual private information as well as the shared common information. Their (different) preferences and the forums available for pre-board communication determine both whether (and how much) they communicate before the board meeting and how they vote during the board meeting. Decisions made without prior communication are based on a small subset of common information that is made available, mostly by the executives. These decisions tend to be (management intended) biased toward the management and smack of a lack of scrutiny. Therefore, when the pre-board communication is either absent or is highly limited, the information quality used for board decisions could be low because of biases and lack of scrutiny. This also reduces the pressure felt by the management to improve the quality of the information that is disclosed to the investors.

Malenko (2014) argues that out-of-board communication prior to the board meeting reduces the cost of effective board communication and improves the shared information for decision-making. Outside directors' meetings in the absence of the executive director (often lead by a lead director) and informal meetings between independent directors in affiliated communities (clubs, golf courses, alumni meetings, professional association meetings, conferences, etc.) reduce the cost of communication in several ways. Directors can gauge whether the others also feel the same way about the management proposals, and this could reduce their fear of isolation on the board. Exchange of ideas and the availability of informal quality time to discuss some aspects of the proposals can increase the understanding as well as the objectivity of the information about the pros and cons of the proposals. Harmonious pre-board communication (that is more likely in informal forums) between independent directors can increase the confidence level of the directors in challenging management proposals.

At the decision-making stage, the open ballot system is widely used in board meetings. Such a system increases the personal cost of uninformed voting for the directors and in effect encourages more communication and discussion prior to voting at the board meetings. Proposition 3 in Malenko (2014) says that when outside directors are less busy, are geographically closer to each other, and their social and professional connections are stronger, all else being equal, the board's decisions are more informed and better for firm value. The takeaway point from all this research is that pre-board inter-director communication leads to more informed decisions and higher information quality.

4.2. *Board ethnic diversity, fault lines, communication, and information quality*

While Malenko (2014) lists several factors that could impede inter-director communication on the board, these factors could be amplified if there is diversity on the board. An extensive literature in management deals with the development and consequences of fault lines developing in any team. Lau and Murnighan (1998) define fault lines as "hypothetical dividing lines that may split a group into subgroups based on one or more attributes" (p. 328). They attribute the development of these fault lines to social identity and self-categorization theories. Applied to the board, when a sub-group of directors socially identify themselves with each other but not with others, there is a potential of fault line. Directors in strong-fault line groups see high levels of similarity in their own subgroup and high levels of differences in the other subgroups.

The study by Van Peteghem *et al.* (2018) documents that board diversity results in fault lines and promotes the division of the board into subgroups separated by these fault lines. The fault lines impede communication and the study documents several adverse effects of diversity, particularly on the board's ability to govern. Ethno-cultural linguistic (CEL) diversity has been shown to create the strongest faultlines (Spolaore and Wacziarg, 2009 in economics; Markus and Kitayama, 1991; Li, 1999; Scollon *et al.*, 2012 in cultural psychology; McPherson *et al.*, 2001; Lynall *et al.*, 2003 in Homophily research) that result in strong communication within sub-groups and weak or no communication across sub-groups. Cheung *et al.* (2019) show that while CEL diversity on the boards has the potential to improve information quality, it also has the potential to impede communication and degrade information quality. Specifically, they show that while the CEL-diverse boards exhibit higher earnings quality on average, there are significant cross-sectional differences between boards with or without strong communication. When the communication is low, firms with a CEL-diverse board produce a lower information quality compared to all-Anglo boards, whereas when communication is good, the CEL-diverse board produces higher information quality compared to all-Anglo boards.

As in the case of gender diversity, several forces are at play when there is a cultural, ethnic, and linguistic diversity among the board directors. Similar to gender diversity, the glass ceiling affects non-Anglo directors. On average, a non-Anglo director needs to cross a higher bar to be selected as a board director. Therefore, a non-Anglo director is likely to possess higher leadership and other skills than an Anglo director (the human capital effect). The perspective-broadening effect arises from the different cultural and socialization experiences of non-Anglo directors compared to their Anglo counterparts. Task complexity and task autonomy — both of which are high for corporate boards — are likely to amplify the perspective-broadening benefits of diversity.

However, the factor that impedes the realization of the benefit of diversity, namely inter-director communication, is likely to be much stronger in ethnically diverse boards than in merely gender-diverse boards. Based on the studies cited above, ethnic sub-groups on the board are more likely to exhibit strong faultlines compared to gender-based sub-groups. Further, these faultlines not only prevent the benefits of perspective broadening from being realized but also introduce dysfunctionality in the functioning of the board, creating adverse effects on the board outcomes such as the quality of monitoring. As Cheung *et al.* (2019) show, unlike in the case of gender diversity, introducing ethnic diversity in the board could impair the quality of information that is reported by the firm.

5. Family Ownership, Board Governance, and Information Quality

Most of the discussion on independence and diversity of directors on the board is focused on the agency conflict and the allocation of decision rights between privately informed managers and investors whose ownership is too diffused to give them significant decision rights or the incentives to directly monitor and supervise the managers. However, a large part of the US corporate landscape and an even larger part of the global corporate landscape comprises family firms with concentrated ownership. Ali *et al.* (2007) document that family firms in the US constitute a third of the S&P 500 firms. Listed family firms in the US have a market capitalization of about $2 trillion, which is about 10% of the total market capitalization of all listed firms. Some of the most highly capitalized US firms such as WalMart, GAP, CBS, Thomson Reuters, Marriott International, and Nordstrom are family firms (Srinidhi *et al.*, 2014). In the international setting, the prevalence of family firms is much higher: 44% in 13 European countries with up to 60% of the firms in France, Italy, and

Germany (Faccio and Lang, 2002); and about half of the corporations in East Asia (Claessens *et al.*, 2000).

Unlike diffusely owned firms, family firms have less conflict between the family investors and the managers who either belong to the family or are affiliated or controlled by the family. Srinidhi *et al.* (2014) document that family members participate in senior management in 82% of the family firms in their sample. In 68% of the cases, the CEO is a family member, and in 79% of the cases, the chairman of the board is a family member. In effect, family participation at both the board and senior management levels makes them effective insiders. The separation of ownership and control, that is innate to diffusely owned firms, is no longer the main agency cost in a family firm where the family investors and the family of family-controlled managers are likely to have similar preferences. Moreover, the information asymmetry between family investors and managers is likely to be much lower than in diffusely owned firms, thus reducing the possibility of moral hazard. The intimate knowledge that family insiders have about the firm also reduces the possibility of opportunistic reporting of information by the managers, particularly if it is not in the interest of the family investors. This *alignment* of preferences, information, and incentives between family investors and managers is likely to result in a higher information quality even in the absence of active oversight by an independent board. Indeed, Ali *et al.* (2007) and Wang (2006) document that family firms have superior earnings quality compared to similar diffusely owned firms. The literature in this area establishes superior outcomes for family firms compared to similar diffusely owned firms: better performance using both market measures such as Tobin's Q and accounting measures like the return on investment (Anderson and Reeb, 2003) and lower cost of debt (Anderson *et al.*, 2003).

Even though family firms exhibit a lower agency cost between investors and managers, there is a potential for family entrenchment and expropriation of minority shareholder wealth by the family insiders arising from their ability to control and influence decisions. Specifically, the family insiders could influence the firm in making decisions that are in the interest of the family even if it is value reducing for the firm — in effect, for the minority shareholders. One could argue that anticipating this potential for expropriation (referred to as *entrenchment* or Type 2 agency problem), the minority shareholders become more skeptical about managerial (insider) intentions and could, therefore, force a lower market valuation compared to similar diffusely owned firms. Several papers address this issue. Liao and Srinidhi (2019) show that while on average, the family ownership reduces crash risk (a measure of information asymmetry and therefore, a measure of information quality), there is cross-sectional variation in the impact. First, consistent with the idea of minority investor skepticism about family ownership, family firms are consistently valued lower than similarly placed diffusely owned firms. Second, even after controlling for the valuation effect, the crash risk in family firms is lower than that of non-family firms. Third, family firms with good board governance exhibit lower crash risk compared to similar non-family firms but family firms with weak board governance do not exhibit lower crash risk compared to non-family firms. In effect, it seems that the positive effect of lower agency costs in family firms leading to higher information quality is moderated by the board governance strength. The positive effect can only be realized even in family firms only with good board governance.

It is an empirical question as to whether corporate boards have any effect on the adverse consequences of entrenchment in family firms. Corporate boards are constituted primarily to address the Type 1 agency cost between investors and managers. They are not constituted to address the Type 2 agency cost between two different classes of investors, namely the family investors and minority investors. The empirical evidence, however, shows that in fact, strong independent boards are associated with lower entrenchment and contribute to greater information quality even in family-controlled firms. Using US-listed family firms, Anderson and Reeb (2004) show that minority directors are better protected in family firms by independent directors. Family firms with more independent directors perform better than non-family firms (performance measured by Tobin's Q). In family firms with few independent directors, performance is worse than in non-family firms. However, they also show that families often seek to minimize the presence of independent directors on the board. Specifically, spline regression suggests that when family representation on the board is higher than 0.5*# of independent directors, performance starts declining. Till then, family directors add value to minority shareholders. An alternative explanation is that the families who do not expropriate are more likely to appoint independent directors to the board. The authors show that family presence in nominating committees reduces the fraction of independent directors. In other words, the presence of a high proportion of independent directors might signal non-expropriation by the family. In that case, it is not the presence of the independent board that results in higher information quality, but it is the non-expropriation by the family that drives both the independent board and higher information quality.

Srinidhi *et al.* (2014) show that strongly governed family firms are more likely to choose specialist auditors and exhibit higher earnings quality than non-family firms. Weakly governed family firms demand lower audit effort and exhibit earnings quality that is no different from that of non-family firms. Within family firms, we show that strongly governed family firms choose higher quality audits in the form of greater use of specialist auditors and higher audit efforts and exhibit higher earnings quality than other family firms. These findings provide consistent evidence that strong board governance can effectively mitigate the adverse consequences of the Type 2 agency problem on financial reporting and transparency in family firms. Fan and Wong (2005) use the "wedge" — the difference between cash flow rights and voting rights — to measure entrenchment in family firms in East Asian markets and show that family firms with a greater wedge are more likely to employ Big 5 (higher quality) auditors. They argue that while skeptical investors drive down the share value of firms with entrenched families, the higher quality auditors are used by the firms to signal non-expropriation to mitigate the adverse effect on firm's valuation in the market.

In summary, the above studies consistently show that family firms, on average, exhibit higher information quality but the relationship is moderated by the board governance. Better board governance limits entrenchment and allows the family firms to realize higher information quality from the alignment of interest. On the contrary, in firms with weak governance, the less constrained entrenchment effect prevents the realization of the potential improvement in earnings quality from alignment.

Recently, several studies have examined the effect of cross-sectional ownership and control differences within family firms. Villalonga and Amit (2006) show that the incremental value in family firms comes from the presence of founders. This incremental value disappears when founders are not present and the descendants, even though they are family members, take over. Miller *et al.* (2007) and Andres (2008) complement the findings of Villalonga and Amit and show that when the founder is active and is the CEO, the incremental valuation of the family firm is higher than when that is not the case. In a recent working paper, Hsu *et al.* (2019) show that the presence and the influence of the founder (the role that the founder plays in the firm) are both associated with greater transparency (higher information quality), better operating performance, and greater market value. Their findings also support the contention that once the founder exits or is deprived of decision rights in the firm, their heirs and other family members do not provide the incremental value or induce higher transparency. The authors further analyze the different mechanisms through which the founders with decision-making authority in their firms add value and find that they add value mainly through greater agility in responding to the environment and through increased transparency. Founders are incentivized to provide improved information quality to ensure that the otherwise-skeptical non-family investors get the confidence that they are not being expropriated.

The studies on founders within family firms confirm their primary role in improving information quality and delivering incremental value to investors. Specifically, the founders are closely engaged with all aspects of the firm, have a long-term interest in sustaining and growing the firm, dedicate more personal human and financial capital to their firm than an average outside investor would, react faster to changes in environment than the managers of non-family and non-founder family firms (an advantage of single-point decision-making), and have an incentive to credibly communicate their integrity (in not expropriating other investors) through financial disclosures.

6. Information Technology, Governance, and Information Quality

There has been very little extant academic research about the emerging information technology and how that might affect both the governance of organizations and the quality of information. There is, however, a strand of academic research that has examined the effect of news dispersion — the effect of media and press coverage on corporate governance and information quality (Dyck *et al.*, 2008). The free media in the US and other western nations have exposed scandals and corruption within corporations several times. A free press and investigative journalism constrain misappropriation and misrepresentation by managers and thereby have a positive effect on both the governance and the quality of information that is disclosed by the firm. WSJ opinion piece; 09/10/2019 details the (currently ongoing) case of an initial public offering by WE, a real estate office leasing firm. After an initial valuation of $47 billion, it was revealed that the name "We" was trademarked in a separate company owned by the

CEO and sold to WE for $6 million. The investor confidence in the governance of the firm dropped on this news, resulting in a revised valuation of the firm to less than $20 billion (more than 50% drop). Clearly, this information was not available to investors from the disclosures by the firm, but the press investigation extracted this information and made it available to the potential investors.

Improvements in communication technology and social media have increased the speed with which the press can get information about possible misdealing in corporations. Both the speed with which the news is spread and the scope of dissemination are significant factors that could affect governance, transparency, and information quality. Employees, customers, and outside observers can employ tweets, Facebook postings, WhatsApp messages, etc., to their friends and the spread of information (and misinformation) in today's world could be very fast. Because each individual can access a number of others, the scope of dissemination is also very high. Aula (2010) gives three instances of how the spread of information through social media resulted in responses from corporations. The first is the case of United Airlines that refused initially to compensate a professional musician for breaking his guitar. The second is the case of the clothing company H&M that was found throwing away unsold clothes in New York instead of giving it to the needy. The third is about a Finnish car dealership whose internal communications revealed that a customer was reviled by the employees. The takeaway point from these observations is that the increased speed and wider dissemination of news (and rumors) force the firm's hand in terms of disclosing information and make them much more sensitive to the societal environment than was necessary for the past. In the past, there was a greater ability for the firm and its managers to strategically withhold information selectively, but that ability has been eroded by the spread of social media. This could have two contrasting effects. On the one hand, the firm needs to be nimble and react/respond fast with credible information. This increases the information quality. On the other hand, the ability of the firm to withhold strategic and competitive information has decreased. This could hurt the operations and the strategy of the firm as well as the morale of the employees. A third possibility is that firms could strategically release unverified information in self-interest through social media, creating greater confusion and degrading the quality of information available about the firm. Recent research on strategic dissemination of information (refers to the use of specific channels of dissemination — not strategic disclosure which refers to managers' choice of whether and how much to disclose) has shown that the firms are strategically using the social media platforms such as twitter to selectively disclose more good news than bad news (Jung *et al.*, 2018). While these results indicate that the firms, as well as their employees and stakeholders, strategically use social media to exchange news about the firm, a broad consensus on how equilibrium is reached in this setting is not clear.

Another emerging technology is the use of blockchains in accounting. Blockchains obviate the need for a central authority such as the board for increasing the trust of the investors in the information that is produced and reported. The concept of distributed trust could disrupt the current workings of the board in monitoring the reporting function and improving information quality. However, at this early stage, in the absence of research in this area, these are at best speculative thoughts.

7. Limitations of Scope

It is important to note that this chapter does not provide comprehensive coverage of all aspects of governance that affect information quality. I have focused on the corporate board as the means of monitoring the reporting function in a listed corporation with a particular focus on the board structure in the United States. I have not dealt with the dual boards that are prevalent in countries such as Germany and China. Furthermore, I have not dealt with the effect of external governance mechanisms such as regulations, lawsuits, resource and product market structures, and competition. I have also not dealt with institutional ownership (though most of the studies cited in this chapter control for institutional ownership), block ownership, activist shareholder involvement, and management ownership (except the case of family ownership).

References

Adams, R. B., H. Almeida, and D. Ferreira (2005), Powerful CEOs and their impact on corporate performance, *The Review of Financial Studies* **18**(4), 1403–1432.

Adams, R. B., B. E. Hermalin, and M. S. Weisbach (2010), The role of boards of directors in corporate governance: A conceptual framework and survey, *Journal of Economic Literature* **48**(1), 58–107.

Ahmed, A. S. and S. Duellman (2013), Managerial overconfidence and accounting conservatism, *Journal of Accounting Research* **51**(1), 1–30.

Ali, A. and W. Zhang (2015), CEO tenure and earnings management, *Journal of Accounting and Economics* **59**, 60–79.

Ali, A., T.-Y. Chen, and S. Radhakrishnan (2007), Corporate disclosures by family firms, *Journal of Accounting and Economics* **44**(1), 238–286.

Anderson, R. C., A. Duru, and D. M. Reeb (2009), Founders, heirs, and corporate opacity in the United States, *Journal of Financial Economics* **92**(2), 205–221.

Anderson, R. C. and D. M. Reeb (2003a), Founding-family ownership and firm performance: Evidence from the S&P 500, *The Journal of Finance* **58**(3), 1301–1328.

Anderson, R. C. and D. M. Reeb (2003b), Founding-family ownership, corporate diversification, and firm leverage, *Journal of Law and Economics* **46**(2), 653–684.

Anderson, R. C. and D. M. Reeb (2004), Board composition: Balancing family influence in S&P 500 firms, *Administrative Science Quarterly* **49**(2), 209–237.

Anderson, R. C., S. A. Mansi, and D. M. Reeb (2003), Founding family ownership and the agency cost of debt, *Journal of Financial Economics* **68**(2), 263–285.

Andres, C. (2008), Large shareholders and firm performance — An empirical examination of founding-family ownership, *Journal of Corporate Finance* **14**, 431–445.

Aula, P. (2010), Social media, reputation risk, and ambient publicity management, *Strategy & Leadership* **38**(6), 43–49.

Barber, B. M. and T. Odean (2001), Boys will be boys: Gender, overconfidence, and common stock investment, *The Quarterly Journal of Economics* **116**(1), 261–92.

Bebchuk, L. A. and J. M. Fried (2003), Executive compensation as an agency problem, *Journal of Economic Perspectives* **17**(3), 71–92.

Bebchuk, L. A. and J. M. Fried (2004), *Pay Without Performance: The Unfulfilled Promise of Executive Compensation.* Cambridge and London: Harvard University Press.

Bebchuk, L. A. and J. M. Fried (2005), Pay without performance: Overview of the issues, *Journal of Corporation Law* **30**(4), 647–73.

Bebchuk, L. A., J. M. Fried, and D. I. Walker (2002), Managerial power and rent extraction in the design of executive compensation, *University of Chicago Law Review* **69**(3), 751–846.

Bernardi, R. A. and D. F. Arnold Sr. (1997), An examination of moral development within public accounting by gender, staff level, and firm, *Contemporary Accounting Research* **14** (4), 653–668.

Brooks, P. and H. Zank (2005), Loss averse behavior, *Journal of Risk and Uncertainty* **31**(3), 301–325.

Bruns Jr, W. J. and K. A. Merchant (1990), The dangerous morality of managing earnings, *Management Accounting* **72**(2), 22–25.

Burke, R. J. and S. Vinnicombe (2008), Women on corporate boards of directors: International issues and opportunities, in *Women on Corporate Boards*, S. Vinnicombe, V. Singh, R. J. Burke, D. Bilimoria, and M. Huse (eds.), Cheltenham, UK: Edward Elgar, pp. 1–11.

Bushman, R. and A. Smith (2001), Financial accounting information and corporate governance, *Journal of Accounting and Economics* **32,** 237–333.

Catalyst Group (2004), The bottom line: Connecting corporate performance and gender diversity. Research report sponsored by BMO Financial Group; Catalyst Publication Code D58; ISBN #0-89584-244-0.

Cheung, S., S. Fung, and B. Srinidhi (2019), Impact of board ethnic diversity and commonality on earnings quality, Working paper, Deakin University, Australia.

Claessens, S., S. Djankov, and L. Lang (2000), The separation of ownership and control in East Asian corporations, *Journal of Financial Economics* **58**(1), 81–112.

Cohen, J. R., L. W. Pant, and D. J. Sharp (1998), The effect of gender and academic discipline diversity on the ethical evaluations, ethical intentions and ethical orientation of potential public accounting recruits, *Accounting Horizons* **12**(3), 250–70.

Dechow, P. M. and I. D. Dichev (2002), The quality of accruals and earnings: The role of accrual estimation errors, *The Accounting Review* **77** (Supplement), 35–59.

Dyck, A., N. Volchkova, and L. Zingales (2008), The corporate governance role of the media: Evidence from Russia, *The Journal of Finance* **LXIII**(3), 1093–1135.

Eagleman, D. (2011), *Incognito: The secret lives of the brain*. Knopf Doubleday Publishing Group; ISBN: 9780307377333.

Faccio, M. and L. Lang (2002), The ultimate ownership of Western European corporations, *Journal of Financial Economics* **65**(3), 365–395.

Fan, J. P. H. and T. J. Wong (2005), Do external auditors perform a corporate governance role in emerging markets? Evidence from East Asia, *Journal of Accounting Research* **43**(1), 35–72.

Francis, J., R. LaFond, P. M. Olsson, and K. Schipper (2005), The market pricing of accruals quality, *Journal of Accounting and Economics* **39**(2), 295–327.

Francis, J., A. H. Huang, S. Rajgopal, and A. Y. Zang (2008), CEO Reputation and Earnings Quality, *Contemporary Accounting Research* **25**(1), 109–47.

García-Meca, E. and J. P. Sánchez-Ballesta (2009), Corporate governance and earnings management: A meta-analysis, *Corporate Governance: An International Review* **17**(5), 594–610.

Gul, F. A., B. Srinidhi, and A. Ng (2011), Does board gender diversity improve the informativeness of stock prices? *Journal of Accounting and Economics* **51**(3), 314–38.

Gul, F.A., J. Liang, and B. Srinidhi (2019), CEO's regulatory focus, organizational choices and audit fee. Working paper, Deakin University, Burwood, Vic. Australia.

Hambrick, D. C. and P. A. Mason (1984), Upper echelons: The organization as a reflection of its top managers, *Academy of Management Review* **9**(2), 193–206.

Hart, O. (1995), Corporate governance: Some theory and implications, *The Economic Journal* **105**(430), 678–689.

Haw, I.-M., B. Hu, L.-S. Hwang, and W. Wu (2004), Ultimate ownership, income management, and legal and extra-legal institutions, *Journal of Accounting Research* **42**(2), 423.

Higgs, D. (2003), Review of the role and effectiveness of non-executive directors. Available online at https://ecgi.global/sites/default/files/codes/documents/higgsreport.pdf retrieved July 23, 2020.

Hillman, A.J., A. A. Cannella Jr., and I. C. Harris (2002), Women and racial minorities in the boardroom: How do directors differ?, *Journal of Management* **28**(6), 747–763.

Hillman, A. J. and T. Dalziel (2003), Boards of directors and firm performance: Integrating agency and resource dependence perspectives, *The Academy of Management Review* **28**(3), 383–396.

Houston, J. F., J. Lee, and H. Shan (2019), In search of board independence: Former employees, shades of gray and director classification. Revisited https://ssrn.com/abstract=2824150.

Hsieh, T., J. C. Bedard, and K. M. Johnstone (2014), CEO overconfidence and earnings management during shifting regulatory regimes, *Journal of Business Finance & Accounting* **41**(9) & (10), 1243–1268.

Hsu, W., Y. Lee, N. Nagarajan, and B. Srinidhi (2019), Mechanisms for value creation in founder firms. Working paper, the University of Texas at Arlington, Arlington, Texas, USA.

Jaggi, B., S. Leung, and F. Gul (2009), Family control, board independence and earnings management: Evidence-based on Hong Kong firms, *Journal of Accounting and Public Policy* **28**, 281–300.

Jianakoplos, N. A. and A. Bernasek (1998), Are women more risk averse?, *Economic Inquiry* **36**(4), 620–630.

Jung, M. J., J. P. Naughton, A. Tahoun, and C. Wang (2018), Do firms strategically disseminate? Evidence from corporate use of social media, *The Accounting Review* **93**(4), 225–252.

Klein, A. (2002), Audit committee, board of director characteristics, and earnings management, *Journal of Accounting and Economics* **33**(3), 375–400.

Lai, K., B. Srinidhi, F. A. Gul, and J. S. L. Tsui (2017), Board gender diversity, auditor fees, and auditor choice, *Contemporary Accounting Research* **34**(3), 1681–1714.

Lau, D. C. and J. K. Murnighan (2005), Interactions within groups and subgroups: The effects of demographic faultlines, *Academy of Management Journal* **48**, 645–659.

Li, H. Z. (1999), Communicating information in conversations: A cross-cultural comparison, *International Journal of Intercultural Relations* **23**(3), 387–409.

Liao, Q. and B. Srinidhi (2019), What determines crash risk in family firms? Alignment, entrenchment or investor skepticism? Working Paper. Available at SSRN: https://ssrn.com/abstract=3048466.

Lynall, M. D., B. R. Golden, and A. J. Hillman (2003), Board composition from adolescence to maturity: A multitheoretic view, *The Academy of Management Review* **28**(3), 416.

Malenko, N. (2014), Communication and decision-making in corporate boards, *Review of Financial Studies* **27**(5), 1486–1532.

Man, D. C. and S. S. K. Lam (2003), The effects of job complexity and autonomy on cohesiveness in collectivistic and individualistic workgroups: A cross-cultural analysis, *Journal of Organizational Behavior* **24**, 979–1001.

Markus, H. R. and S. Kitayama (1991), Culture and the self: Implications for cognition, emotion, and motivation, *Psychological Review* **98**(2), 224–253.

McPherson, M., L. Smith-Lovin, and J. M. Cook (2001), Birds of a feather: Homophily in social networks, *Annual Review of Sociology* **27**, 415–444.

Miller, D., I. Le Breton-Miller, R. H. Lester, and A. A. Cannella (2007), Are family firms really superior performers? *Journal of Corporate Finance* **13**, 829–858.

Pfeffer, J. and G. R. Salancik (1978), *The External Control Of Organizations: A Resource Dependence Perspective*. New York: Harper & Row.

Scollon, R., S. W. Scollon, and R. H. Jones (2012) Intercultural Communication: A Discourse Approach. 3rd Edition. West Sussex, U.K.: Wiley-Blackwell, John Wiley & Sons.

Shleifer, A. and R. Vishny (1997), A survey of corporate governance, *Journal of Finance* **52**(2), 737–784.

Spolaore, E. and R. Wacziarg (2009), The diffusion of development, *The Quarterly Journal of Economics* **124**(2), 469.

Srinidhi, B., C. Y. Lim, and M. Hossain (2009), Effects of country-level legal, extra-legal and political institutions on auditing: A cross-country analysis of the auditor specialization premium, *Journal of Contemporary Accounting and Economics* (5), 34–46

Srinidhi, B., F. A. Gul, and J. S. L. Tsui (2011), Female directors and earnings quality, *Contemporary Accounting Research* **28**(5), 1610–1644.

Srinidhi, B. N., S. He, and M. Firth (2014), The effect of governance on specialist auditor choice and audit fees in U.S. family firms, *The Accounting Review* **89**(6), 2297–2329.

Srinidhi, B., Y. Sun, H. Zhang, and S. Chen (2019), How Do Female Directors Improve Board Governance? Mechanism-based on Norm Changes, Working paper, University of Texas at Arlington.

Tyson, L. (2003), The Tyson Report on the Recruitment and Development of Non-executive Directors. Available online at http://facultyresearch.london.edu/docs/TysonReport.pdf, retrieved July 23, 2020.

Van Peteghem, M., L. Bruynseels, and A. Gaeremynck (2018), Beyond diversity: A tale of fault lines and frictions in the board of directors, *The Accounting Review* **93**(2), 339–367.

Villalonga, B. and R. Amit (2006), How do family ownership, control, and management affect firm value?, *Journal of Financial Economics* **80**(2), 385–417.

Wall Street Journal, Opinion piece, September 10, 2019: WeWork's China Syndrome.

Wang, D. (2006), Founding family ownership and earnings quality, *Journal of Accounting Research* **44**(3), 619–656.

Xie, B., W. Davidson Ill, and P. Dadalt (2003), Earnings management and corporate governance: The role of the board and the audit committee, *Journal of Corporate Finance* **9**, 295–316.

https://doi.org/10.1142/9789811220470_0018

Chapter 18

Evolving Standards of Fair Value and Acquisition Accounting

Stephen Bryan[*,¶], Steven Lilien[†,‖], Bharat Sarath[‡,**] and Yan Yan[§,††]

[*] *Fordham University, New York, NY, USA*

[†] *Baruch College, City University of New York, NY, USA*

[‡] *Rutgers University, Piscataway, NJ, USA*

[§] *Fairleigh Dickinson University, Teaneck, NJ, USA*

[¶] *sbryan@fordham.edu*

[‖] *slilien@baruch.cuny.edu*

[**] *bsarath@andromeda.rutgers.edu*

[††] *yyan@fdu.edu*

Abstract

Many of the new accounting standards that have been enacted over the past two decades have not only impacted accounting on their own but also interacted with the existing standards in unanticipated ways, particularly since many of the new standards require managerial estimates to be incorporated into the financial statements. As an illustration, we focus on the interaction between the adoption of fair value assessments and the use of acquisition method accounting (formerly called purchase accounting). We highlight the unusual effects on goodwill measurement. After explaining why this combination is potentially problematic, we provide examples of how these standards are being implemented in practice.

Keywords: Fair value accounting; Goodwill; Managerial estimates; Statement of financial accounting standards 142.

1. Introduction

The last two decades have witnessed an increasing emphasis on the incorporation of managerial estimates into financial statements. The many new standards that have been adopted over this time period have not only impacted accounting on their own but also created unexpected consequences through their interactions with other standards. As an illustration, this chapter focuses on the interaction between the adoption of fair value assessments and the use of acquisition method accounting (formerly called purchase accounting). After explaining why this combination is potentially problematic, we provide a few examples of how these standards are being implemented in practice.

On its own, the use of fair value accounting is uncontroversial. After all, any asset bought in the market is recorded at full purchase price (fair value) and subsequently depreciated over its productive life. In the same way, when an entire firm is purchased, it is reasonable that the assets be recorded on the books using the aggregate value paid for the firm. While the purchase price is often objectively verifiable, the allocation of this price to the underlying assets and liabilities involves judgment, particularly if some of the assets are illiquid. If some of the purchase price is left unallocated, then this amount is recorded as goodwill. Since the amount recorded as goodwill is a residual, it varies significantly based on the allocation to the other assets and liabilities. Further, while its measurement at the time of acquisition is precise (i.e., an arithmetic residual calculation), any economic decrease (depreciation) in the value of goodwill is hard to quantify. These considerations were reflected in SFAS 141 and 142 (now codified as ASC 805) that transformed accounting for acquisitions, both at the time of purchase and in subsequent years.

SFAS 141 mandated the use of acquisition accounting for acquisitions of an entire firm, thereby aligning the accounting treatment with that used for partial acquisitions of assets. In both, the attribution to fair value of underlying net assets is required. Additionally, SFAS 142 revoked the systematic amortization of goodwill since such amortization could not be justified from an economic perspective. Instead, the standard required goodwill to be tested for impairment at a segment level. Since goodwill was a nebulous asset and testing it for impairment was complex, subsequent standards tried to separate potentially depreciable assets from the goodwill classification. An important development was the enactment of ASC 805 that required identifiable assets to be recorded separately from goodwill.

The below extract is from ASC 805:

> *An asset is identifiable if it meets either of the following criteria:*
> a. *It is separable, that is, capable of being separated or divided from the entity and sold, transferred, licensed, rented, or exchanged, either individually or together with a related contract, identifiable asset, or liability, regardless of whether the entity intends to do so.*
> b. *It arises from contractual or other legal rights, regardless of whether those rights are transferable or separable from the entity or from other rights and obligations.*

The above Clause b is particularly interesting since it applies to contractual or legal rights that may not be marketable in any normal sense but nevertheless must be assigned some fair value. The requirement of generating fair values for any identifiable asset is motivated by the fact that goodwill amortization is difficult to measure.

In July 2019, FASB issued a request for comments titled *Identifiable Intangible Assets and Subsequent Accounting for Goodwill.* The first paragraph (below) summarizes the difficulties that have been encountered in practice:

> *This Invitation to Comment (ITC) is being issued as part of the Financial Accounting Standards Board's (FASB) project on certain identifiable intangible assets acquired in a business combination and subsequent accounting for goodwill. In previous outreach, the staff received mixed feedback from users, preparers, and practitioners of financial reports on this topic. Consequently, it is presently unclear whether the benefits justify the costs for public business entities (PBEs). Because the Board has not received conclusive feedback about whether a change to*

financial reporting is warranted and, if so, whether cost-effective solutions that maintain or improve decision usefulness are feasible, the staff is issuing this ITC to solicit additional feedback. Your insight is requested at this time to gauge:

a. Whether changes to financial reporting should be addressed by the Board
b. Whether and how to proceed with simplifications and/or improvements to these topics, and
c. How optionality in the accounting for intangible assets and goodwill is viewed.

As outlined above, the primary motivation behind the identification of intangible assets is the difficulty in amortizing goodwill. As the acquisition cost is reflected in future revenues, matching (i.e., expense recognition) requires an amortization of the acquisition cost against these additional revenues. However, allocating a large proportion of the acquisition cost to goodwill makes it difficult to perform any systematic amortization. Therefore, allocating the acquisition cost to assets that can be amortized is more consistent with accounting principles. When these assets are intangibles, the valuation depends on managerial estimates, which may, however, be chosen strategically to further management's interests rather than shareholder interests. The benefit of this trade-off is difficult to determine *ex ante* and underlies the above ITC.

Before developing our examples pertinent to the ITC, it is worthwhile outlining the theoretical framework underlying fair value estimates. The use of fair values implies a shift toward the balance sheet and away from the income statement. While the application of the fair value principle to assets that are traded in active markets (Level 1 fair values) is commendable, the extension to Level 2 and Level 3 fair values is more controversial. Level 2 assets are not traded actively but can be valued using inputs from traded assets. Level 3 assets are valued using managerial estimates with unobservable inputs. Some researchers have concluded that Level 3 disclosures are particularly subject to intentional management bias. However, even Level 2 can be manipulated for opportunistic purposes. For instance, consider the example of the LIBOR index. In this instance, leading British Banks allegedly distorted the rates that they would expect to pay for borrowing from other banks, affecting the value of LIBOR in such a way as to increase their own trading profits. This and other such occurrences have led some researchers to conclude that the information content of fair value disclosures is severely eroded, perhaps even to the point of uselessness.

While accountants have been skeptical about the usefulness of fair values, the Securities and Exchanges Commission (SEC) has been consistently in favor of forward-looking estimates that are reflected in fair values. From the passage of the Private Securities Litigation Reform Act (PSLRA) in 1995 that included a safe-harbor provision for such estimates and their strong support of fair value disclosures, the SEC has taken a position that managerial estimates, although they may be subject to manipulation, provide valuable information to investors. Empirical studies have exhibited disagreement on the extent of market reaction to fair value or other forward-looking information that rely substantively on managerial estimates.

Under prior accounting, when the fair value of the net assets acquired exceeded the purchase price, this led to negative goodwill. Negative goodwill was first used to offset non-monetary assets and intangibles, reducing their value to at most zero. Any remaining negative goodwill was recognized through income and accounted for as an extraordinary item. Amounts reported as extraordinary items were expected to be small, since any acquired assets were first written-down (even to zero) on the acquirer's financial statements. Under ASC 805 Business Combinations, negative goodwill is reported as a bargain gain through the acquirer's income subsequent to the business acquisition. The bargain gain is the difference between the acquisition price and the fair value of the net assets of the acquired.

The requirement to identify intangible assets, coupled with the use of fair value accounting, had the unintended consequence that the (net) fair value of acquired assets and liabilities could exceed the consideration paid. In addition, this gain was allowed to flow through net income rather than, say, Other Comprehensive Income (OCI), creating an avenue for boosting net income through a judiciously valued acquisition. Such a possibility is acknowledged in ASC 805, but it is considered a rare and an unlikely outcome. However, we show that Bargain Purchase Gains (BPG) occur quite frequently (see Section 3). The rest of this chapter discusses various examples of fair value accounting, and it identifies the intangible assets (and their valuations) that resulted in income-boosting BPG. The next section provides a concrete example of a BPG acquisition and the later sections discuss market-wide consequences.

2. How an Unprofitable Acquisition Increased Reported Profits

BFC is a publicly traded bank holding company, one of whose principal holdings was a controlling interest in Bluegreen (BG), itself a publicly traded company. In November 2009, BFC increased its stake in BG from 29% to 52% by acquiring an additional 23% interest. The additional ownership in BG made BFC's stake a controlling interest. As a result, the assets of BG had to be remeasured on a fair value basis. The basic details of the acquisition are laid out in Table 1.

As seen in the above table, BFC reported a bargain gain of US$183 million in its 2009 year-end financial statements. Including this gain, BFC reported a net income of US$25 million. BFC reported US$113 million in shareholder's equity as of December 31, 2008; without the bargain purchase gain, BFC's losses during the year 2009 would have eliminated all opening balance sheet equity. With the gain from the acquisition of a controlling interest in BG and an additional US$95 million in gains from other merger transactions (not examined in this article), BFC attained US$245 million in shareholder's equity before non-controlling interests. To summarize, the entire equity value of BFC in 2009 derived from a BPG recognized on the acquisition of an entity in which they held 23% of the shares.

In essence, BFC bought out 29% of the shareholders in Bluegreen at a hugely discounted price. The same point is reflected in the fact that the loss attributable to non-controlling interests ($122,414) exceeds the total loss of BFC ($96,693) generating the positive net income for BFC. It is questionable whether shareholders would have surrendered their shares on such disadvantageous economic terms. More likely, the deal generated no real economic profits but was an exercise in questionable purchase price allocation. A further examination of the acquisition reveals the method through which these "book profits" were generated.

We begin our analysis by looking at a summary of the transaction at the level of equity that is provided in Table 2.

A major observation in Table 2 is the discrepancy between the valuation of the assets acquired using Level 3 values and the Level 1 values reflected in the stock price. Specifically, BFC increased their stake from 29% to 52% (an increase of 23%) leaving 48% in the hands of non-controlling shareholders, which was valued at $41,254,000 (Line 4 of Table 2) indicating a total value of about $86,000,000 for Bluegreen.

Table 1: Details of BFC acquisition of Bluegreen.

Item 6. Selected Financial Data	For the years ended December 31	
Dollars in thousands, except for per share data	2009 (in US$)	2008 (in US$)
Statement of operations data (e)		
Revenues		
Real estate and other	39,276	16,870
Financial services	354,087	449,571
Total revenues	393,813	466,441
Costs and expenses		
Real estate and other	206,892	76,470
Financial services	573,467	634,970
Total costs and expenses	780,359	711,440
Gain on bargain purchase of Bluegreen	183,138	—
Gain on settlement of investment in Woodbridge's subsidiary	29,679	—
Equity in earnings from unconsolidated affiliates	33,381	15,064
Impairment of unconsolidated affiliates	(31,181)	(96,579)
Investments gains (losses), interest, and other income	19,549	(5,722)
(Loss) income from continuing operations before income taxes	(151,980)	(332,236)
(Benefit) provision for income taxes	(67,218)	15,763
(Loss) income from continuing operations	(84,762)	(347,999)
Discontinued operations, net of income tax	(11,931)	19,388
Extraordinary gain, net of income tax	—	9,145
Net (loss) income	(96,693)	(319,466)
Less: Net (loss) income attributable to non-controlling interests	(122,414)	(260,567)
Net income (loss) attributable to BFC	25,721	(58,899)
Preferred stock dividends	(750)	(750)
Net income (loss) allocable to common stock	24,971	(59,649)

Based on this valuation, the 23% acquired was worth $20,000,000 and the cash payment of $22,939,000 indicates the payment of a 10% premium to induce some of the non-controlling shareholders to sell their stake. In addition, the equity holding of 29% by BFC prior to the merger is valued

Table 2: Acquisition of Bluegreen breakdown.

Net assets acquired	282,052	Levels 1, 2, and 3
Less: Cash consideration on acquisition of additional 23% interest	22,939	Level 1
Less: Fair value of previously held equity interest	25,126	Level 1
Less: Fair value of non-controlling interest	41,254	Level 1
Less: Loss on previously held equity interest	8,074	
Less: Loss on accumulated other comprehensive income attributable to previously held equity interest	1,521	Historical Cost
Bargain purchase gain	183,138	

Source: Lilien *et al.* (2013).

at $25,126,000, less a write-down of $8,074,000, resulting in a net value of $17,052,000, leading to an estimated value of $58,800,000 for the entire firm. In summary, the valuation of the net assets of Bluegreen based on the Level 1 criteria fall roughly between $60 million and $90 million. However, the fair value of assets acquired as recorded using Level 2 and Level 3 methodology results in a net value of $289 million — an inflation of approximately 300%.

How was this value inflation justified? The explanation provided by BFC is detailed in Table 3.

While it is difficult to identify which particular asset was inflated, it is clear that there is a prevalence of Level 3 valuations. Note that Level 3 valuation was even used for Accounts Payable, which we find particularly curious. One possible explanation is that these are longer term payables and have been discounted using an estimated (unobservable) discount factor. Also curious is the Level 3 valuation of the "management contracts" (intangible assets), which represents the present value of future payables on properties that are not owned by, but are managed by, Bluegreen. It is possible that these contracts may be canceled or otherwise amended. The adjustment of the Fair Value for such contingencies are in the hands of the management, as is also the choice of the discount rate. The discretion exercised by the manager may convey useful information to shareholders, for instance, that current Level 1 market values are unnaturally depressed. Alternatively, such discretion might mislead investors into a false optimism regarding the future value of the stock. In our next section, we discuss the banking industry during the same period, namely 2008–2009,

Table 3: BFC's allocation of purchase price.

Cash and cash equivalents	51,621	Level 1	
Restricted cash	25,079	Level 1	
Property and equipment	83,083	Level 3	
Management contracts	63,000	Level 3	
Real estate inventory	313,869	Level 3	
Notes receivable	285,000	Level 3	
Retained interests in notes receivable sold	29,250	Level 3	
Other assets	40,983	Level 3	
FV of total assets acquired			891,885
Accounts payable and other liabilities	50,764	Level 3	
Deferred income	10,996	Level 3	
Deferred income taxes	29,784	Level 3	
Lines of credit and notes payable	198,947	Level 2	
Junior subordinated debentures	56,783	Level 2	
Receivable-backed notes payable	236,359	Level 2	
FV of total liabilities			–583,663
Non-controlling interest (Big Cedar Joint Venture)	26,200	Level 3	–26,200
Net assets acquired			282,052

Source: Lilien *et al.* (2013).

when the stock market (Level 1 values) was extremely low and BPG acquisitions were frequent.

3. BPGs and Market Reaction during the Financial Crisis

BPG acquisitions occurred frequently in the financial services industry during and following the financial crisis of 2008. The main reason was that the market value of loans had fallen far below the carrying value. While there was some risk that borrowing entities would be unable to repay loans, there was also a risk that the lending entity would not survive long enough to collect the payments. For this reason, troubled banks that were likely to fail could be acquired at bargain purchases, but non-troubled banks who could technically have profited by acquiring failing banks at market prices were unwilling to do so. The acquiring bank would have assumed the responsibility owed to the depositors, but this would have been uneconomical if the entire loan portfolio of the troubled bank had to be written-off. On the contrary, if the troubled bank was allowed to fail, the burden would have fallen on the FDIC which insures all deposits up to a limit of $250,000. Any single failure can be very costly to the FDIC. For example, the failure of Florida's BankUnited was expected to cost the FDIC $4.9 billion.[1] However, as explained on the FDIC website,[2]

> *The FDIC works cooperatively with the applicable chartering authorities and Federal regulators to expeditiously resolve failing banks in a least costly manner. The FDIC does not negotiate the proposed transactions terms with each potential bidder. Rather, the FDIC conducts a sealed bid process based on standard transaction terms. Bids are submitted to the FDIC electronically via a separate secured website to ensure confidentiality, and all bids must be submitted on the FDIC's standard forms. Failing institutions are usually closed within a few weeks after bids are submitted. The whole resolution process usually occurs over a two- to three-month period. The FDIC provides limited indemnification designed to protect the acquirer against liabilities created by the institution prior to the sale date that are not assumed by the acquirer.*

Consequently, the FDIC had to devise a plan to encourage healthy banks to acquire failing banks in a way that would cost the FDIC less and ensure minimal disruption for depositors.[3]

The FDIC entered into loss-sharing agreements (hereafter, LSAs) with the acquirer whenever it was deemed necessary in order to facilitate the acquisition. Typically, the agency agreed to partially reimburse incurred losses on "covered loans" (typically, 80% of the incurred losses). During the acquisition, the LSA had to be fair-valued and reported as part of the acquired assets. A typical example is illustrated below:

---

[1] See https://www.theatlantic.com/business/archive/2009/05/the-backdoor-bailout-for-banks-and-the-fdic/18093/.

[2] https://www.fdic.gov/buying/FranchiseMarketing/marketing_process.html#processOverview.

[3] Ideally, a failing bank closes on a Friday and resumes under a new management the following Monday.

"On June 19, 2009, First Bancorp had entered into a purchase and assumption agreement with the FDIC, as a receiver for Cooperative Bank, Wilmington, North Carolina. According to the terms of the agreement, First Bank acquired all deposits (except certain brokered deposits) and borrowings, and substantially all the assets of Cooperative Bank and its subsidiary, Lumina Mortgage. The loans and foreclosed real estate purchased are covered by two loss share agreements. Under the[se] loss share agreements, the FDIC will cover 80% of covered loan and foreclosed real estate losses up to $303 million and 95% of losses in excess of that amount. The term for loss sharing on residential real estate loans is ten years, while the term for loss sharing on non-residential real estate loans is five years in respect to losses and eight years in respect to loss recoveries. The reimbursable losses from the FDIC are based on the book value of the relevant loan as determined by the FDIC at the date of the transaction" (First Bancorp 10-K, 2009).

The Business Combination Disclosure in First Bancorp (FBNC) 10-K Annual Report for the acquisition of Cooperative Bank Fiscal Year Ending December 31, 2009 ($ in thousands)

ASSETS	Cooperative Bank	Fair Value Adjustment	First Bancorp
Cash and cash equivalents	$66,096	—	66,096
Securities	40,189	—	40,189
Presold mortgages	3,249	—	3,249
Loans	828,958	(227,854)	601,104
Core deposit intangible	—	3,798	3,798
FDIC loss share receivable	—	185,112	185,112
Foreclosed properties	15,993	(3,534)	12,459
Other assets	4,178	(137)	4,041
Total	958,663	(42,615)	916,048

As a result of this acquisition, First Bancorp reports $916,048,000 in assets acquired and $873,913,000 in liabilities assumed at fair value. First Bancorp wrote down Cooperative Bank's book value of loans from $828,957,000 to the estimated fair value $601,104,000 and a fair value adjustment of $185,112,000 for the FDIC loss share receivable. First Bancorp reports that differences in interest rates paid on their deposits and the acquired loans also affected fair value calculations and that the application of acquisition accounting results in a bargain purchase gain of $67,894,000, which is included in the Consolidated Statement of Operations for the year ended December 31, 2009.

In order to examine whether FDIC assisted the transactions and consequently BPGs were involved in real value transfers to the acquirer, we examined all banking acquisitions, both FDIC assisted and unassisted, as well as BPG acquisitions (acquisition cost less than reported fair value) and goodwill transactions (acquisition cost more than fair value). Over the period 2008–2012, a total of 412 acquisitions resulted in day one gains as defined under SFAS 141R. Of these, 201 (roughly half) are in the financial industry. These 201 bargain purchase transactions constitute 12.15% of the 1,654 acquisitions reported on Compustat as being performed by public financial institutions over this time period. Out of this sample we selected 134 observations which had detailed financial information allowing for thorough statistical analysis. 109 of this sample of BPG transactions were FDIC assisted and 25 were not FDIC assisted. In addition, we selected 201 goodwill acquisitions which had financial characteristics most closely matching the BPG (negative goodwill) acquisitions. The cross-group comparisons revealed some interesting patterns.

A comparison of FDIC and non-FDIC transactions showed that the BPGs in the FDIC transactions were closely linked to the value of the FDIC LSAs (loss share arrangements). The value of the LSA was not factored into the transaction price resulting in the economic value being transferred to the acquiring establishment. As a consequence, the acquisition was indeed a "Bargain" and the acquiring shareholders profited from the transaction. In addition, these acquisitions resulted in long-term improvements in the performance of the acquiring institution. In the non-FDIC transactions, the BPG was related to the fair value of the loans acquired. In other words, the acquiring bank suggested that they had negotiated a price less than the (present) value of the money to be collected on the acquired loans. This was not, *prima facie*, an unlikely claim given that the market value of debt had fallen far below its corresponding carrying value. However, a more careful examination showed that the additional cash flows implied by the fair value were not realized, suggesting that the acquiring banks had used the reporting flexibility to boost their income through optimistic estimates in the year of acquisition.

An examination of the stock market reaction to BPG acquisitions also supported the conclusion that FDIC-assisted BPGs were real, whereas non-FDIC BPGs were illusory. At the announcement of the acquisition, FDIC-assisted acquisitions resulted in a stock price increase for the acquirer, whereas the stock price fell for non-FDIC BPG acquisitions. That is, investors viewed the FDIC-assisted transactions as increasing the acquirers' value, whereas they viewed non-FDIC transactions as reducing value, even though the acquirer claimed to have made a profit through the acquisition. The investor reaction suggested that they did not fully believe the fair values reported by the acquirer and did not bid up their stock price.

A comparison of goodwill and BPG transactions provided further evidence that investors generally valued FDIC assistance and believed the BPGs associated with these transactions. The stock price of both goodwill acquirers and BPG acquirers rose on the announcement of the acquisition for FDIC acquisitions with the average increase being greater for BPG acquisitions. In contrast, neither group displayed a positive stock price reaction for non-FDIC acquisitions. That is, investors were not convinced that these acquisitions generated any particular synergies.[4]

One final finding was also somewhat surprising. The acquiring banks in FDIC-assisted BPG transactions did not appear to be particularly profitable. Indeed, their ROA in the year preceding the merger decreased from prior years, suggesting that they might also have been heading for financial distress. The acquisition strengthened these banks, allowing them to survive the crisis. This is somewhat in contrast to the FDIC's claim that they were merging weak banks with strong banks. Instead, it appears that the FDIC merged a failing bank into a weak bank but offered LSA's that benefited only the acquiring bank. By this procedure, the FDIC ensured that the acquiring bank returned to profitability in the future.

The possibility of reporting gains at the time of acquisition (ASC 805) through inflated fair values could lead to misleading financial statements. We examined a number of BPG acquisitions during the financial crisis which may have been associated with overly optimistic reporting choices. However, the evidence suggests that the acquisitions assisted by the FDIC resulted in the creation of genuine economic value, using LSAs that benefited the acquirer. In contrast, non-FDIC acquisitions did not generate additional value even if they reported BPGs, implying a highly profitable acquisition. One positive point from our examination is that investors

[4]In general, the average stock price reaction across acquisitions is negative suggesting that investors are wary of the possibility that acquiring managers may have overpaid in their enthusiasm to grow the firm.

were not mislead by the optimistic reporting, at least in the financial services industry. The results are further elaborated in Lilien *et al.* (2019b).

4. Intangible Valuation and BPG's after the Crisis

Outside the crisis period, BPG acquisitions should be infrequent, particularly for non-financial firms where the markets are fairly competitive. However, reviewing the 10-K of Plures Technologies of December 31, 2011, where the acquisition of AMS is reported, there is a gain of $1.66 million largely attributable to recording on the acquirer's financial statement $1.88 million in intangibles and $1.92 million in property. Both these numbers are fair value estimates primarily from Level 3 judgments. The existence and valuation of intangibles is highly questionable, since the acquisition price was mainly a $1.7 million forgiveness of advances by Plures Technologies.

As indicated in Table 4, the gain related to the acquisition of AMS Inc. ($1,652,523) was recorded in other income in the statement of operations for the year ended December 31, 2011.

The past financial losses of AMS Inc. were a result of the declining legacy tape head business. During 2010 production began on magnetic sensors and sales from this product had grown each quarter since. Future revenue growth, and therefore AMS profitability, is based in part on this new market area. These assumptions were used in the valuation of the intangible assets (of approximately $1.9 million, per above), which did not exist on the balance sheet of AMS prior to the acquisition.

In arriving at the bargain gain, SFAS 141 and SFAS 142 require the measurement and reporting of identifiable intangible assets at acquisition date fair values. Intangible assets are distinguished between finite lived intangibles and indefinite lived intangibles. Finite lived are both amortized and tested for impairment. Indefinite lived are only tested for impairment. For non-financial firms, the bargain gain often arises from customer-related intangibles, which are highly unlikely to be sold or licensed independently of other assets of the acquired firm. Additionally, there is much judgment if Level 3 is used to estimate these customer related intangibles.

Similar to financial firms (discussed in the next section), it is not as uncommon as might have been expected for non-financial firms to have bargain gain acquisitions. For the years 2009–2012, Edgar Online I-metrix identifies 122 non-bank bargain acquisitions. Looking at the

Table 4: The allocation of the purchase price and acquisition method accounting is based on the fair value of the acquired assets and liabilities measured as of May 23, 2011, in accordance with ASC 805 (Business Combinations).

Fair value of shares of common stock issued to AMS	$385,000
Advances to AMS including interest (obligation to repay released at closing of merger)	1,707,326
Total consideration	2,092,326
Estimated Allocation of Purchase Price:	
Cash and cash equivalents	180,436
Accounts receivable	332,568
Inventories	414,038
Prepaid expenses and other	54,285
Equipment	1,923,650
Intangible assets	1,881,000
Accounts payable	(538,628)
Accrued expenses	(100,433)
Deferred rent and other	(402,067)
Gain on bargain purchase	(1,652,523)
Total	2,092,326

Source: Lilien *et al.* (2013).

ROA of these acquiring firms with and without the BPGs, the gain through income enables firms to avoid a sharp drop in income in the year of the acquisition. As in the case described above, the BPGs are largely driven by fair value estimates of both the acquisition price and the underlying net assets.

For non-financial firms, the key fair value estimate is for intangibles which are recognized on the books of the acquirer at acquisition date. Fair value estimates for intangibles require the acquiring management to estimate future cash flows and construct model-based estimations. Key steps require management to identify intangible assets, to estimate the discount rate, to select a valuation methodology, and to reconcile to the underlying acquisition price. A key question is: when one observes such a drop in reported earnings, when compared to earlier, is management using the flexibility in underlying critical estimates to avoid a decline in the coming year?

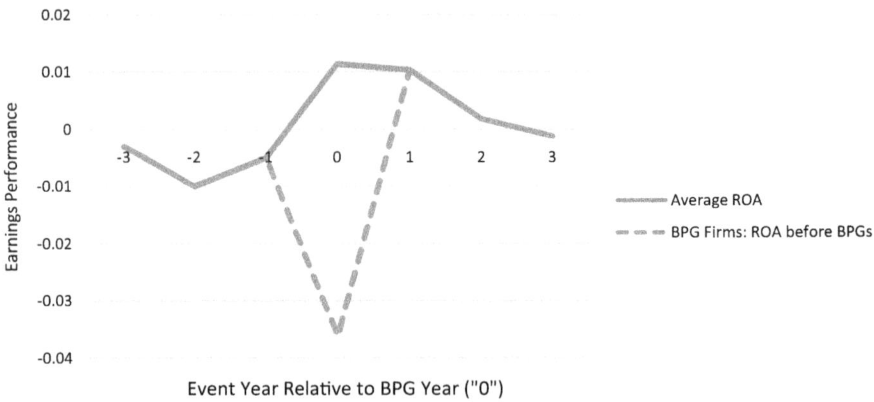

Figure 1: Time-series comparison in event-time of the average ROA vs. ROA before BPGs for acquiring firms in bargain purchase acquisitions.

As in Figure 1, ROA exhibits a transitory decrease in the transaction year when BPGs are excluded. ROA in the transaction year is much closer to earnings, 1 year prior and 1 year after, if BPGs are included (compared to when BPGs are excluded). The results are further elaborated in Lilien *et al.* (2019a).

5. The Curious Case of Kentucky Power — SEC Accounting and Auditing Enforcement Release No. 3344, 2011

Fair value computations are often complex, raising the concern that management might use the complexity to mislead investors. However, it is also possible that the complexity might mislead the management into making mistakes, even though there is no intention to improve the appearance of the financial statements. One such instance was described in an AAER (Accounting and Auditing Enforcement Release) in 2011.

These proceedings arose out of quarterly reviews of an audit performed by Kempisty & Company of their client, Kentucky Energy, Inc. ("Kentucky Energy"), for the year ended December 31, 2005. In these financial statements, Kentucky Energy improperly accounted for warrants and convertible notes it had issued to third parties. Kempisty & Company (the auditors) rendered an unqualified report stating that, in the firm's opinion, the financial statements presented fairly the financial position of the company in conformity with generally accepted accounting principles ("GAAP") However, as described below, Kempisty & Company were subsequently banned from practicing before the SEC.

Beginning in 2004 and continuing into 2005, Kentucky Energy obtained a series of loans from third parties evidenced by notes that were convertible into common stock. As an additional incentive to the lenders, Kentucky Energy issued warrants along with each note. The warrants were convertible to common stock at the request of the bondholder.

Bonds with complex provisions for convertibility to equity present difficult accounting problems. In recent years, there has been an attempt to separate such bonds into a pure debt component accounted for as a liability and a separate equity component. Such separation is required under international accounting rules. (There are some exceptions to this requirement under US accounting rules.) In the case of Kentucky energy, Rubino (the auditor in charge at Kentucky energy) had never previously dealt with the issue of how to account for warrants or a beneficial conversion feature of a convertible note, both of which are derivatives. Rubino told the consultant (who prepared the accounts for Kentucky Energy) that he would need to value the warrants using the Black–Scholes option pricing model.

Accordingly, the consultant found a Black-Scholes calculator on the internet. This calculator called for him to fill in variables for the warrants' "equity price", "strike price", "volatility", "riskless interest rate", and "time to maturity", and would then generate a Black–Scholes valuation. Using this calculator, the consultant valued the warrants at $16,000,000 and was faced with a dilemma — although the bonds together with the warrants generated $3,100,000 in cash when sold to investor, the warrants were valued at $16,000,000 which meant that the debt was worth –$12,900,000. This made no sense, so the consultant and he decided to create an asset account to balance out the entry as follows:

Debit	Credit	$	$
Cash		3,100,000	
Stock Warrant Asset		16,000,000	
	Bonds Payable		3,100,000
	Stockholders' Equity		16,000,000

However, assets must be depreciated or amortized. For the first quarter of 2005, using the same methodology established in 2004, the consultant arrived at a value of $15,694,422 for the warrants, and that amount less amortization of $1,881,139 (or $13,813,283) was recorded as an asset on the company's balance sheet. This improper warrant valuation amounted to over 60% of Kentucky Energy's total assets. Further, the amortization on the 2005 year-end statement of operations amounted to 70% of Kentucky Energy's net loss.

Surprised by this dramatic change in Kentucky Energy's profitability, the SEC asked for the documentation underlying the reported numbers. The calculations revealed the rather astounding error. The consultant did not know how the Black–Scholes model worked and had apparently used some sample numbers provided for illustrative purposes on the web site, but not the actual numbers associated with the warrant. The resulting calculations had clearly been unrealistic, but the auditor, nonetheless, did verify their accuracy and had signed off that they were fair and accurate. The SEC sanctioned the accountants Kempisty & Co. Indeed, model-based valuations can be problematic, to say the least.

6. Conclusion

Over the last decade, financial reporting has shifted increasingly from an income statement perspective to a balance sheet perspective. As a consequence, there is greater emphasis on the direct valuation of assets and liabilities. When reliable market values are available, there could be merit to using these "forward"-looking valuations rather than relying on historical information that may be obsolete. However, when market values are unavailable or unreliable, direct valuation of assets requires estimates from managers. The obvious problem is that these estimates may be overly optimistic, either as a conscious choice or as a sub-conscious bias. Under these circumstances, it is possible that investors may be misled, reducing the efficiency of the market. Our discussion shows that while the tendency to use valuations to present a rosy picture of the firm is not uncommon, forward-looking estimates can provide useful information to investors in other circumstances. In particular, we provide some evidence that day-one gains calculated based on fair-value estimates provided relatively accurate information to investors in FDIC-assisted acquisitions over the period of the financial crisis.

References

Lilien, S., B. Sarath, and R. Schrader (2013), Normal turbulence or perfect storm? Disparity in fair value estimates, *Journal of Accounting, Auditing, and Finance* **28**, 192–211.

Lilien, S., B. Sarath, and Y. Yan (2019a), Fair value accounting, earnings management, and the case of bargain purchase gain, *Asian Review of Accounting* **28**, 229–253.

Lilien, S., B. Sarath, and Y. Yan (2019b), Intended or unintended consequences of business regulations? The case of acquisitions in the financial services industry. Working Paper.

https://doi.org/10.1142/9789811220470_0019

Chapter 19

Evolving Blockchain Applications: Multiple Semantic Models and Distributed Databases for Blockchain Data Reuse*

Daniel E. O'Leary

University of Southern California, Los Angeles, CA, USA

oleary@usc.ecdu

Abstract

As blockchain-based applications continue to evolve, there are at least two emerging trends. First, increasingly, there are multiple semantically different models proposed for similar tasks. As an example, researchers and companies have either proposed or developed different models for supply chain and other concerns. As a result, unfortunately, it is increasing likely that firms will need to choose between those systems and/or interface their internal systems, such as their enterprise resource planning systems, with multiple blockchain-like systems. Second, the importance of database models underlying blockchain transaction information

*A shortened version of this chapter was presented at Rutgers University, November 9, 2019, at the 47th World Continuous Auditing and Reporting Symposium. The author would like to acknowledge the comments from the participants.

is becoming increasingly apparent. The blockchain provides a source for immutable data, but participants are interested in gathering information from the data. Unfortunately, blockchain data is not in an easy to use format. As a result, the data is likely to be taken "off of the blockchain" in order to be queried, etc. This paper examines these emerging trends and this paper develops a "blockchain-like" application with blockchain and distributed database capabilities for the case of a virtual organization.

Keywords: Blockchain; Distributed Database; Virtual Organization; Semantic Model; Off-Blockchain; Blockchain Data Reuse.

1. Introduction

Nakamoto (2008) generated two basic ideas that have had substantial impact. The first idea was capturing a chronological set of transactions, using an append-only approach, in the context of a public ledger in a distributed, peer-to-peer computing environment. This approach provides two controls that have garnered the attention of many commenters: immutability of the transaction set and peer voting on transactions provide a measure of trust. The second idea was to use this public ledger as the basis of a market for a cyber-currency, Bitcoin. Our concern is primarily with the first idea, the public ledger.

There has been substantial positive hype about blockchain and accounting and how blockchain could change the world. Deloitte (2016) called blockchain a "game changer". Ovenden (2017) and others have argued that blockchain will make accountants and auditors "irrelevant" because all transactions would be logged on the blockchain and the immutability would make changing information impossible. Patil (2017) and other commentators have suggested that accountants will "go away" because of the advent of blockchain in accounting. Roberts (2017) suggested that blockchain would fix the "broken" Internet.

However, there also has been substantial criticism of the potential use of blockchain and distributed ledgers for accounting and supply chain systems. Researchers have noted that there are technical limitations associated with blockchain, including throughput, latency, scalability and power requirements (e.g., McConaghy *et al.*, 2016 and others). Other researchers have questioned the extent of the contribution of putting accounting information on a blockchain. For example, as noted by Ovenden (2017), "All the blockchain does is verify that a transfer of funds has taken place. Like a bank reconciliation. At this point, it doesn't tell us anything else. And I doubt it ever will, since what company will want the details of every transaction available to the public?" Still other researchers and commentators have noted that there can be disclosure issues in accounting blockchains, for example, O'Leary (2018) noted the potential of "spoof", "wash" and "off-blockchain" transactions in public blockchain accounting systems.

1.1. *Multiple semantic models and distributed databases*

Despite the limitations, reportedly, a number of blockchain-based systems have been developed. In those applications there have been at least two emerging trends: multiple semantic models and integration with databases. The first purpose of this paper is to investigate those trends.

Since there are many types of transactions and many points of view for those transactions, there have been multiple models built to model the processes taking place, e.g., supply chains. In those multiple models the multiple semantic views of the different developers and consortiums are captured. Organizations may then be faced with choosing between different systems to accomplish particular tasks and they may need to develop program links between those different systems and their enterprise resource planning systems, each likely requiring a different application program interface.

Another critical aspect of virtually every accounting or supply chain system is the need to be able to perform a broad range of queries in order to gather information from the data. Unfortunately, since "pure" blockchain-based systems are focused on capturing and preserving transactions, they have virtually no processing and querying capabilities. Some have suggested that blockchains be integrated with databases, to the extent that some researchers (e.g., McConaghy *et al.*, 2016) refer to those systems as "NoQL", to describe a blockchain database with "no query abilities". In the case of accounting or supply chain systems, the inability to query numeric information would be quite a handicap. As a result, the data is taken "off of the blockchain" and put into databases and other tools so that it can be analyzed, queried and reported on.

Accordingly, emerging transaction-based systems that employ blockchains consistently appear to rely heavily on database models. This paper recognizes that although a system may be referred to as a "blockchain", unless it only captures and distributes encrypted transactions, the "blockchain" is likely only a small part of what the system does and much is done "off-blockchain".

An alternative to using a combined systems of blockchains and databases for accounting and supply chain systems is to use a system that integrates the best of databases and blockchain capabilities, *and* use it in an organizational and strategic setting where it "fits", i.e., where providing information broadly to a number of decentralized sources is desirable.

1.2. *Virtual organizations and blockchain-like applications*

Public blockchains that capture the transaction information of all comers could disclose too much information to too many people. Further, consistent with the above quote by Ovenden (2017) and previous research, this paper argues that few organizations are interested in sharing the accounting information with other agents. However, there are settings where organizations need to know what other organizations are doing at the transaction level. In particular, virtual organizations, put together to use underemployed assets to create multi-firm value, typically require members to meet certain resource contribution needs. Further, the distributed nature of virtual organizations requires a distributed solution that gets information out to the members of the virtual organization in real time. In addition, their accounting systems need the ability to query the data. As a result, the second purpose of this paper is to investigate the design of an accounting system for virtual organizations, based on a distributed database that includes key blockchain and database features, "BigchainDB". This investigation is done using a design science approach and sample artifacts are developed in the chapter.

1.3. *Organization of the chapter*

This chapter proceeds in the following fashion. Section 2 investigates some of the characteristics of blockchains, such as the different kinds of blockchains, blockchain architectures, limitations of blockchain, and an example of blockchain-based system. Section 3 provides a summary of distributed databases and drills down on a particular distributed database system. Section 4 provides background on virtual organizations and accounting for virtual organizations. Section 5 briefly reviews the design science approach used in this paper. Section 6 focuses on presenting the basic design of a BigchainDB for virtual organizations, based on design science requirements. Section 7 examines some potential and descriptive artifacts associated with such a distributed database system. Section 8 analyzes the relationship between data reuse and the type of blockchain application. Section 9 summarizes the chapter, examines its contributions and examines some extensions.

2. Blockchain and Accounting and Supply Chain Systems

Blockchain has been proposed for use in accounting and supply chain by a number of commenters in order to capture and preserve a set of transactions. However, researchers have suggested that there are a number of limitations associated with that notion. This section summarizes the different types of blockchains, basic blockchain architectures, blockchain in accounting, examines some limitations of those systems and analyzes an existing blockchain-based system.

2.1. *Different kinds of blockchains*

A key distinction among blockchains is whether the ledger is public or private. In a public setting, virtually anyone can use the blockchain, whereas in a private setting, user access can be limited (Jayachandran, 2017)). In a public blockchain, substantial information is visible to users. For example, assume that there is interest in using a public blockchain for supply chain provenance. In that case, in order to understand the origins of produce, users would need to be able to follow the information trail through each transaction, suggesting that substantial information would need to be available and that information would be "openly" available. That open information could be used to do business intelligence, but it also could be used to "fool" participants monitoring the information. For example, participants could perform exchanges with themselves to provide the blockchain with false signals. In contrast to public blockchains, by limiting access rights, private blockchains can control those who can participate in the blockchain and access the information.

Another distinction is whether the blockchain uses centralized or decentralized management. In a centralized setting, user permissions are determined centrally, and the blockchain is managed centrally. As seen in the discussion of TradeLens in the following section, one of the key concerns with potential participants is who will be that central manager of that blockchain system. This concern generally is not an issue with decentralized systems with decentralized system management.

Still another difference is the type of computing, peer-to-peer or cloud. Typically, cloud-based systems do not require participants to capture and reproduce information about transactions as in the case of peer-to-peer systems. Instead, such systems often have external parties review the transactions to establish trust. TradeLens discussed later in this section is a cloud-based system. The virtual organization example developed later in this paper is primarily concerned with peer-to-peer computing.

2.2. *Architecture of blockchains*

Blockchains gather and distribute information to networks of users. Because their design is based on capturing transaction information "forever" and distributing that information to a network of concerned participants, blockchain entries contain very limited amounts of information with each transaction. In addition, blockchains do nothing more than capture and preserve the original information about a transaction. This basic promulgated architecture is illustrated in Figure 1.

Because the network underlies the architecture, blockchains are associated with real-time systems (e.g., O'Leary, 2008; O'Leary, 1993). As a

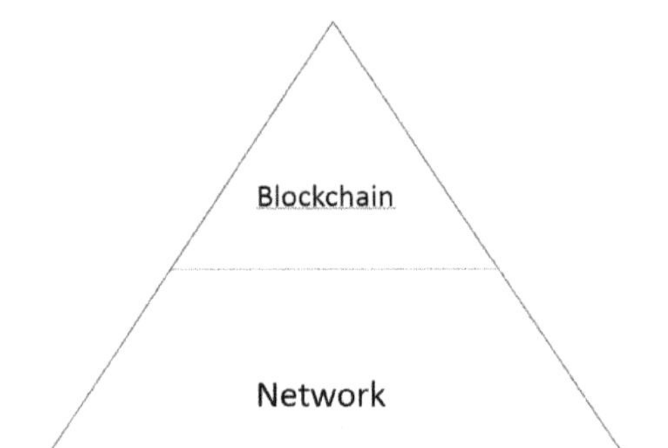

Figure 1: Basic blockchain architecture.

result, in some settings, blockchains are promulgated as not just information capture and preservation sources, but as distribution networks.

However, emerging applications are doing more than just capturing, preserving and distributing information. This raises the question "Is there more than just blockchain to blockchain applications?" It might also get us to ask, "if there is more than just blockchain to an application, why do we call it a blockchain application?" In response, some are likely to suggest that attaching blockchain to the name might affect the ability to generate interest by potential buyers because of the "hype" associated with such systems.

2.3. *Blockchain in accounting and supply chain systems*

As noted by researchers there are a number of concerns with applying a public Bitcoin-like blockchain approach to accounting and supply chains, both technically and from other perspectives. The technical problems include throughput limitations, latency, capacity and power requirements. Although companies such as Visa handle 2,000 transactions per second, Bitcoin is limited to seven transactions per second.[1] Bitcoin's transaction processing capacity also is limited by the average of 10 minutes to create a block and by the block size limits, resulting in a "bottleneck".[2] The current size of the blockchain database is roughly at 200 gigabytes and growing exponentially.[3] As noted by Lee (2018), Bitcoin currently consumes 2.6 GW of power, roughly the same as Ireland, and that figure could rise to 7.7 GW, or roughly 0.5% of the world's electricity consumption.

If the accounting or supply-chain transactions are done using an open public blockchain, then each of the transactions is captured by however many nodes are capturing the data (say N). This is in contrast to simple arms-length exchanges where the transaction would need to be captured by only the two parties to the transaction. As a result, power, computing, networking, etc. would need to track a transaction N times, rather than 2 times, resulting in substantially more computing and potentially people resources (O'Leary, 2017).

---

[1] https://en.bitcoin.it/wiki/Scalability.

[2] https://en.wikipedia.org/wiki/Bitcoin_scalability_problem.

[3] https://www.statista.com/statistics/647523/worldwide-bitcoin-blockchain-size/.

Further, depending on the design, configuration and controls of the blockchain, there can be additional difficulties. If there is no control over which participants can be party to transactions, then participants can transact with themselves in order to affect available information about resources, e.g., prices. As another example, in blockchains where information is broadcast in an open peer-to-peer setting, such an approach to accounting can lead to information being openly available to others on the blockchain. Unfortunately, "open information" when combined with "off-blockchain transactions" can result in so-called "spoof" and "wash" transactions (e.g., O'Leary, 2018).

In addition, a number of the proposed uses of blockchain are redundant with more efficient approaches. For example, as noted in O'Leary (2011), Sysco (and others) use data warehouses to capture all of their transactions and then make those transactions available to all of their customers. In contrast, depending on the configuration, information available on a blockchain is not easy to capture a database for analysis. As noted above, one set of researchers called the limited ability to query blockchain like settings, "NoQL" for no query.

Finally, many proposed uses of blockchain for accounting, are effectively copies of existing processes and do not leverage the capabilities of the technology. Those approaches are not reengineering but are simply automating existing processes (e.g., Hammer, 1990).

2.4. *Blockchain in accounting and supply chain: IBM Maersk "blockchain"*

Perhaps the best-known accounting and supply-chain application is the IBM Maersk blockchain system, called "TradeLens". The system originally was designed to be available to Maersk and non-Maersk clients and partners to facilitate trade in the supply chain. According to Castillo (2018) there are now over 90 participating organizations with over 150 million shipping events in different ports around the world, with a growth rate of over one million events per day. However, Castillo (2018) notes that at this point the effort largely includes Maersk and Maersk-related companies, such as Hamburg Sud but also along with numerous customs authorities, cargo owners and freight forwarders. Castillo (2018) argues that most carriers opt out of joining the system because of "competition". As noted by a rival of Maersk, CMA CGM, "Technically the solution (by

Maersk and IBM) could be a good platform, but it will require governance to make it an industry platform and not just a platform for Maersk and IBM. And this is the weakness we're currently seeing in many of these initiatives, as each individual project claims to offer an industry platform that they themselves control. This is self-contradictory". Further, as noted by Ometoruwa (2018) " … a private permission ledger may have many of the same characteristics as a public ledger (a distributed network of nodes, consensus protocols, etc.). However, it is still very much centrally controlled by the architects of the ledger. They decide who has permission to access the network, control the IP, and could potentially create backdoors to circumvent the rules of access". Thus, at one level, centralized parties' control over decentralized systems potentially is a primary impediment to enterprise blockchain adoption.

This discussion also suggests that there are multiple evolving semantic models as a range of companies generate alternative solutions. Each approach to using blockchain, can capture slightly different bits of information or process that information differently, potentially to the advantage of the developer. Unfortunately, the potential for multiple semantic models indicates that in some cases participants will be subject to those multiple models as the interact with participants on different solutions.

In addition, TradeLens illustrates the importance of the underlying database model in the development of so-called "blockchain models". Blockchains capture and preserve transaction information, but they do not make that information easy to use or query. As noted by Castillio (2018), TradeLens allows users to do a range of activities, including doing queries such as identifying the location of a shipping container. Such an activity cannot be done easily on the blockchain, but instead would be done by a database using information derived from blockchain transaction information. As another example, in the case of TradeLens, the system can "Track shipments in real time with greater precision via 120+ dynamic events published direct from the source - without the back and forth".[4] Again, this indicates the importance of a database system with a design centered on those events and the information around those events.

[4] https://www.tradelens.com/.

2.5. *On-blockchain vs. Off-blockchain*

Oftentimes so-called "blockchain applications" only involve blockchain as the "tip of the iceberg". This results from the basic nature of blockchains where only a small amount of encrypted information actually is captured about each transaction and stored "on the blockchain". Typically, only the original transaction is captured "on the blockchain". However, there also is the potential to capture changes in transaction state on the blockchain. Further, as noted above, because of its link to the underlying enterprise network, information also can be distributed by placing the information on a blockchain and using it as a distribution mechanism.

All processing and querying of the transaction information is done "off the blockchain". Information is captured from the blockchain and embedded in database solutions and other system processing capabilities so that the data can be queried and used to schedule, answer questions, generate reports, etc. In those settings, typically all additional processing and information about the transaction is off the blockchain. Further, information that is off of the blockchain typically is not stored in an encrypted form because off the blockchain, there is more focus on efficiency and the original transaction is still available on the blockchain if it were needed. However, that still opens that information up to vulnerabilities of not being encrypted.

2.6. *Blockchain benefits are more than what the blockchain provides*

In summary, in so-called accounting and supply chain blockchain systems,

- Blockchain captures initial transactions and may capture changes in the state of the transaction, depending on the system design.
- Blockchain encrypted transactions typically need to be un-encrypted and taken-off of the blockchain and put into a database, where they are stored in unencrypted form for database access and use.
- A database model is then used to process the information and answer queries about the information system.
- There generally is a user interface facilitating interaction with the database as an application.

As a result, this discussion suggests an alternative architecture and approach that actually includes the database as an integral part of the system from the beginning, resulting in the question, "Can we build the same capabilities using a distributed database?"

3. Databases and Distributed Systems

This section introduces the typical three-tier architecture captured in distributed database systems. In addition, it summarizes some of the characteristics of a specific distributed database system.

3.1. *Architecture and design*

Generally, systems design employs a three-tier architecture consisting of the network, a database and an application (see Fig. 2). (In some cases, "presentation" is included as another level in the system design.) However, with blockchain applications, as seen in Figure 2, there appears to be a mixing of architectural components. The blockchain may capture data but not in a typical database format, and the format limits the ability to query the data. Further, the role of a database in such systems is often ignored, and the focus is on "hyping" the blockchain portion of the system. In this chapter, we treat the database as separated from the applications and the network of participants.

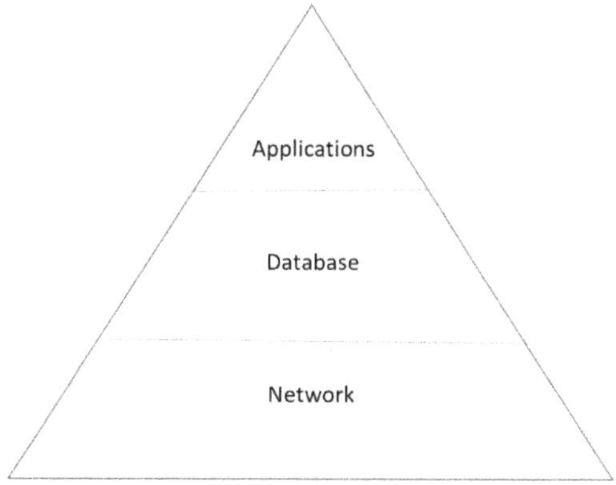

Figure 2: Promulgated three-tier system design (Tiwana, 2013).

3.2. *BigchainDB*

BigchainDB, is a private, peer-to-peer, distributed database system that was developed to mitigate many of the limitations of the blockchain public ledgers and yet leverage the capabilities suggested by blockchain. As noted by BigchainDB (2016, p. 1), "the original design started with a database and added some blockchain characteristics, such as decentralization, immutability and owner-controlled assets". The database design was developed to mitigate some of the technical limitations of blockchain associated with latency, capacity and throughput. A summary of some of these characteristics is given in Table 1.

BigchainDB was built on top of an open source database, Rethink (McConaghy *et al.*, 2016). (Although a Mongo database also can be used.) Rethink is a NoSQL database where all of the data is a "JavaScript Object Notation (JSON)" document.[5] JSON is an XML replacement that uses human readable text to transmit data objects and information. McConaghy *et al.* (2016) also indicate BigchainDB is designed to work well with other systems, suggesting that BigchainDB "... is complementary to decentralized processing platforms like Ethereum, and decentralized file systems like InterPlanetary File System (IPFS)".

Table 1: Blockchain and distributed database characteristics (McConaghy *et al.*, 2016).

Characteristic	Typical Blockchain	Typical Decentralized DB	Bigchain DB
Decentralization	X	X	X
Immutability	X		X
Owner-Controlled Assets	X		X
High Throughput		X	X
Low Latency		X	X
Indexing and Querying of Structured Data		X	X
Rich Permissioning		X	X

[5]"NoSQL systems are also sometimes called 'Not only SQL' to emphasize that they may support SQL-like query languages, or sit alongside SQL database in a polyglot persistence architecture". Wikipedia

As noted by BigchainDB (2016), each node in a BigchainDB 2.0 network has its own local database. That means that each node operator has access to the full power of the underlying database for indexing and querying the stored data (transactions, assets, metadata and blocks, all of which are JSON strings). In the case of accounting systems, the ability to query the data using NoSQL can be critical, particularly in an increasingly analytic and big data world. Further, each decentralized node operator has the ability to determine what capabilities they expose to their external users, providing local controls.

4. Collaboration and Virtual Organizations

Increasingly, firms are collaborating with other firms because of increases in product and service complexities (e.g., Westphal *et al.*, 2007; O'Leary, 2013). Collaboration helps overcome the limitations of single enterprises, particularly with small to medium sized enterprises. The virtual organization, which includes a confederation of different enterprises, integrates their processes in a non-hierarchical way, typically using technology.

Goldman *et al.* (1995) define a virtual organization as occurring when "... complementary resources existing in a number of cooperating companies are left in place, but are integrated to support a particular product effort for as long as it is viable to do so ... . Resources are selectively allocated to the virtual company if they are underutilized or if they can be profitably utilized there more than in the 'home' company".

Virtual organizations are designed to facilitate multiple types of capabilities, including:

- Create or assemble productive resources quickly.
- Create or assemble productive resources frequently and concurrently.
- Create or assemble a broad range of productive resources (such as research, manufacturing, and design).
- Provide resources to others in the form of partial or complete products.

Virtual organizations have been applied in a number of situations, ranging from manufacturing and supply chain, to white collar functions, such as accounting and supply chains. For a detailed example, see

Gunasekaran and Ngai (2004) who examined the use of virtual organizations in the supply chain.

Virtual organizations attempt to employ slack resources, such as machines, buildings and people, in order to create additional value. They assemble resources in conjunction with other enterprises in loosely configured confederations of firms. As a result, many of the actions of interest in a virtual organization relate to organizational use of assets, not just the production of goods. For example, in virtual organizations, firms' contributions can come from the amount of time that a facility, machine or personnel are involved in the confederation's project. Further, it can be important for participating firms to inform others in the confederation of the planned and actual use of assets to mitigate asymmetries of information.

Generally, those confederations have limited centralized control and hierarchy, and are heavily decentralized. Thus, to ensure coordination in virtual organizations there needs to be a communication of plan and actual production information. As a result, any system designed for virtual organizations likely is necessarily a distributed system designed to ensure that members get timely information from other participants.

Typically, the coordination between the confederation enterprises is done using a range of technologies. Most virtual organizations are developed to function over the Internet or other proprietary networks. As a result, Kurumluoglu *et al.* (2005) define a virtual organization "… as a set of co-operating (legally) independent organizations, which to outside world provide a set of services as if they were one organization, supported by a computer network". However, virtual organizations do not just use networks. In addition, a number of other technologies have been developed for them. For example, a number of artificial intelligence applications have been built to help coordinate projects in virtual organizations (e.g., O'Leary and Turban, 1987; O'Leary *et al.*, 1997; and others). Many intelligent agent applications have been built around the notion of virtual organizations (e.g., Corchado *et al.*, 2013).

4.1. *Trust for virtual organizations*

In a world where self-interest can be assumed of most agents, trust is particularly important in virtual organizations because there is limited centralized and formal hierarchy and control. As noted by Handy (1995) in a discussion of virtual organizations, the notion of trust in virtual organizations raises some concerns:

- "It is unwise to trust people whom you do not know well, whom you have not observed in action over time, and who are not committed to the same goals".
- "At its simplest, the managerial dilemma comes down to the question, How do you manage people whom you do not see?"

One approach to attaining trust in virtual organizations is to ensure transparency of asset use, by generating timely information flows between members of the virtual organization. As an example, Gunasekaran and Ngai (2004) analyze the importance of transparency in virtual organizations assembled for supply chain purposes. Another approach to generating trust is to ensure that members provide the resources promised and that tasks are done at the times they were promised. In this last setting, trust is attained because the members know what other members are doing and that they are doing their job for the project. A third approach to building trust is to provide each participating organization all of the accounting information, eliminating the asymmetries of information of a centralized accounting system. Thus, technologies designed to support virtual organizations must provide that transparency and capture information about member asset use, with information provided by a distributed, real-time accounting system.

4.2. *Accounting and resource information for virtual organizations*

Because enterprises in virtual organizations employ their own resources or make expenditures on behalf of the virtual organization, there is a need to capture and forecast information about that resource use. Unfortunately, it can be quite challenging to measure, evaluate and track the work done by the different component organizations within the virtual infrastructure. Further, organizations with such confederations are likely to have their own accounting systems and those systems are not likely to be compatible with each other. In addition, component organizations need to coordinate efforts in order to create the anticipated value, and mitigate potential coordination problems. Finally, this all needs to be done in real time so that the component organizations can meet the various project needs. As a result, virtual organizations require an accounting system that will integrate across each of the organizations in a timely manner. Unfortunately, as noted by Lee (2014) and others, such systems are a major challenge to virtual organizations.

4.3. *BigchainDB for virtual organizations*

BigchainDB can provide an important approach for modeling virtual organizations. Mohan (2017) notes that BigchainDB is modeled around assets. The two key mechanisms for asset control transfer are inputs and outputs, as is critical for a virtual organization accounting system. The amount of assets transferred or used are encoded in outputs of a transaction. Further, each output can be, but is not required to be "spent" separately. In order to spend an output, its conditions must be met by an input that provides corresponding fulfillments. In addition, there is a simple signature condition, where an asset given to an entity is controlled using a corresponding private key.

BigchainDB's focus on decentralized nodes and on assets is broadly aligned with use in virtual organizations, where each member would be a node and their virtual organization specific assets would be the focus of the system. Each node could interface their own accounting systems with the node's database, to import the data to their own systems.

Further, although it has been suggested that broadcasting open information in a peer-to-peer environment in accounting systems likely is a limitation in most accounting settings, as discussed above, it can be a *requirement* of a successful system for virtual organizations. All of those agents in a virtual organization need accounting and resource use information from the other organizations in the virtual organization and they need it in a timely manner. The decentralized peer-to-peer database can provide the information rapidly and trust can be facilitated by the transparent flow of resource information.

Finally, as a database, BigchainDB provides the ability to include roles, and other controls, such as limiting and identifying potential agents, through private keys. Although BigchainDB is a decentralized database, some of its functions would require central administration. Perhaps the most important aspect would be determination of partner organizations and establishing nodes for each such organization in the virtual organization. In addition, determination of "who" resource exchanges can occur with would also be critical to ensuring that transactions are legitimate.

5. Design Science

Design science is one of the primary paradigms in information systems research. In contrast to natural science that tries to understand reality, design science involves trying to create things aimed at serving human purposes and solving human problems (e.g., March and Smith, 1995). Design science typically is technology-oriented and it tries to create new systems or improve existing systems, often introducing new technologies into existing organizational, strategic and problem-solving settings. Thus, design science typically involves considering system architecture and artifact design. But, as noted by Simon (1981, p. 133), design science also involves "… devising artifacts to attain goals". Thus, there is a purpose to the system design.

As noted by March and Smith (1995, pp. 256–258) design science research artifact outputs include constructs, models, methods and instantiations, where

- Constructs are " … concepts form the vocabulary of a domain. They constitute a conceptualization used to describe problems within the domain and to specify their solutions. They form the specialized language and shared knowledge of a discipline or sub-discipline".
- Models are "… simply as a description, that is, as a representation of how things are".
- Methods are " a set of steps (an algorithm or guideline) used to perform a task. Methods are based on a set of underlying constructs (language) and a representation (model) of the solution space…."
- Instantiations are "… the realization of an artifact in its environment".

Our use of each of these types of outputs is discussed later in Section 6.

March and Storey (2008, p. 726) suggested that design science research can include six different aspects:

"(1) identification and clear description of a relevant organizational IT problem,
(2) demonstration that no adequate solutions exist in the extant IT knowledge-base,
(3) development and presentation of a novel IT artifact (constructs, models, methods or instantiations) that addresses the problem,

(4) rigorous evaluation of the IT artifact enabling the assessment of its utility,
(5) articulation of the value added to the IT knowledge-base and to practice, and
(6) explanation of the implications for IT management and practice".

This chapter drills down on each of these concerns in Sections 6 and 7.

Design science can be used to facilitate analysis of the interaction of organization designs, strategy and information technology. Specifically, Figure 3 illustrates the interaction between organization design and information systems design, with links between strategic alignment and infrastructure alignment. Unfortunately, as an emerging technology, blockchain and its hybrids have received limited analysis in terms of its impact on or relationship with different organizational forms, and with accounting systems.

Virtual organizations provide an organizational design with an application of a strategy to using resources (particularly spare resources), and this chapter proposes that rather than blockchain approaches, an alternative hybrid blockchain — distributed database approach be used. Although this chapter uses BigchainDB, alternative peer-to-peer databases also could be used. However, the choice of BigchainDB was made because of

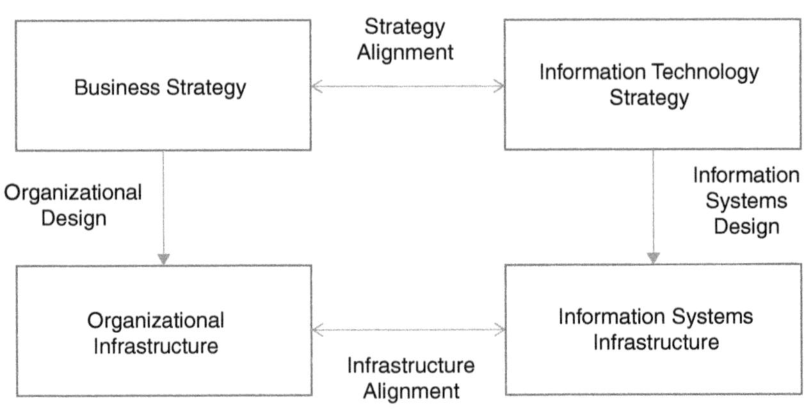

Figure 3: Organization and information systems design.

Source: Adopted from Henderson and Venkatraman (1993)

the unique "alignment" between the organizational requirements of a virtual organization, and the capabilities of that peer-to-peer database to provide real-time accounting information.

6. Design of an Accounting System for Virtual Organizations

The purpose of this section is to present some design science issues associated with the basic design of BigdataDB design for accounting system use for virtual organizations, using the criteria generated by March and Storey (2008).

6.1. *Identification and description of organizational IT problem*

Virtual organizations need to capture and distribute accounting and resource use information, in a timely manner. The systems need to provide open information, sharing resource exchanges and resource use with the other organizations in the virtual organization in order to facilitate projects and promote trust. The system needs to be decentralized since there will be limited centralized hierarchy and control in a virtual organization. However, there is a need to control user access and to be able to identify both partners, customers and vendors, to ensure that transactions are legitimate.

6.2. *Demonstration that no adequate solutions exist*

This chapter is based on the integration of three broad concepts: virtual organizations, accounting information systems, and blockchain. An analysis of the literature using Google Scholar found two papers at the intersection of those concepts, when the search terms were quoted. One of the papers was a crypto coin paper and the other had references that included each of the concepts, but was not about the nexus of the concepts. However, it is not just the absence of literature, but instead that the alignment between virtual organization accounting information system *requirements* and the BigchainDB, blockchain-based, decentralized database system *capabilities* that lead to the focus on this solution.

6.3. *Development and presentation of a novel IT artifact (constructs, models, methods or instantiations) that addresses the problem*

This research has used a number of constructs from both blockchain, distributed databases, and virtual organizations. The key models are the types of resource uses captured in virtual organizations discussed throughout this chapter and in the following.

In this research we have used existing vocabulary (constructs) as they relate to blockchain and distributed databases throughout the chapter. In addition, as part of our discussion, we create the following:

- A model of the interaction of the virtual organization and the platform BigchainDB, discussed above in Section 5.
- A model of a partial "asset use" database, in Table 2 in Section 7.
- Methods in the context of building messages for the BigchainDB (in Section 7).
- Instantiations that represent different messages in the context of some programs (in Section 7).

6.4. *Evaluation of the IT artifact*

Our perspective is that a complete design, implementation and validation of such a system is impractical for a single paper. In addition, even using this design in one virtual organization would only provide a single point of validation. As a result, consistent with much of the previous design science research in accounting information systems we call on the academic community to extend and validate the concepts here in multiple real world settings as has been done in previous accounting literature in the analysis of previous accounting artifacts (e.g., Geerts, 2011).

6.5. *Articulation of the value added to the IT knowledge-base and to practice*

Virtual organizations depend on different technologies to provide integration and information flow to the members of their confederation. A private integrated blockchain and distributed database system designed for particular virtual organizations can use the strengths of blockchain and the strengths of distributed database to provide capabilities to generate and distribute information about resource use in the virtual organization.

The distributed database systems provide query capabilities, which are essential for analyzing accounting information, but also providing timely information to participants. User identification is necessary for each firm in the confederation and agents involved in resource exchanges or uses. As a result, in our design, each user involved in a transaction requires a public and a private key. Further, each asset in the virtual organization would require a digital identification so its use and exchange can be captured in the system.

6.6. *Explanation of the implications for IT management and practice*

There are substantial implications for real-world virtual organizations. First, the capabilities of BigchainDB generate real time information to decentralized nodes for *virtual organizations*. In that system, participant organizations would have timely access to open information about the resource use and accounting transactions by participating organizations. Second, the information would be accessible to query which would seem to be a critical capability for accounting information. Third, the "append only" and broad-based distribution of information capabilities would help generate trust in a virtual organization environment by ensuring that information does not change and that there are limited asymmetries of information. Fourth, in order to limit the potential for spoof and wash transactions, all potential parties to transactions would need to be included in the database of users. Only these members would have a public and private key, and with open messages, potentially the network would have information every time a new partner is added.

7. Artifacts and Sample Instantiations

This section discusses some sample artifacts associated with a distributed, peer-to-peer accounting system in the context of the capture of events using BigchainDB.

7.1. *Asset use database*

Transparency of virtual organization member's efforts can also be integrated into the system design. In particular, since firms bring unused assets to virtual organizations, they can expect that they can received credit for freeing up facilities and people devoted to virtual organization projects. Accordingly, much of the design for a virtual organization would need to capture information about "asset use".

A classic resource-event-agent and location system could be used as part of the underlying database design. As part of that design, a key concern is that the organizations need to determine "what" events should be "shared" with the other members of the virtual organization. The events that need to be shared depends on the particular virtual organizations, however, that set of transactions can range from resource exchanges between different parties to use of facilities for virtual organization projects to assignment of particular people to the virtual organization.

The event set could also include "planned" events and the actual instantiation of those events, allowing comparison of the two. Planned and actual events would be structured as dual events, with the plan preceding the actual event in terms of its execution. Capturing planned events can be critical to the virtual organization and letting members know what is planned for when. Such information informs confederation members that other members are executing important aspects of plans.

Using a resource-event-agent-location approach provides a general structure that would likely provide sufficient information for most accounting systems interfacing with the node's database. Some of these sample issues are summarized in Table 2.

7.2. *Users*

Users need to be created before using BigchainDB. Users are represented as a pair of keys, one public and one private. Depending on the particular virtual organization, there can be one such pair representing each organization at the node level.

In our case, a key pair for each of the companies in the events will be created. The event will capture information as to the owner of the assets, and the owners will be the only ones able to make changes to the digital

Table 2: Sample types of "asset use" resources, events, agents and locations in virtual organization.

Resources	Events	Agents	Location
People	Use a warehouse	System Users at Firms	Participating Firm
Trucks	Use a manufacturing facility	Exchange participants	Facility locations
Warehouses	Truck materials to a location		People locations
Manufacturing facilities	Use a person		
	Plan to use a warehouse		
	Plan to use a manufacturing facility		
	Plan to use a person		

representation of the painting. Using the public key, anyone can also verify that the company is the owner of the building.

7.3. *Digital representations of assets*

Assets have a digital representation in BigchainDB. As a result, any asset brought to the virtual organization needs to be created in BigchainDB. Those digital representations can be an entry in a database, a certificate representing the asset, an RFID number, or some other form. Historically, in other organizations, this would be represented by the "paper trail", however, as things become more digital, those paper trails are disappearing. BigchainDB is designed to capture that information and act as a digital asset registration and tracking tool. As a result, all assets used in the virtual organization would require some sort of identification.

7.4. *Event/transaction messages*

The Appendix of this chapter summarizes sample instantiations of transactions in the context of programs designed to capture event information including the sale of an asset and the use of an asset. Each of the programs creates a transaction of interest to the virtual organization, captures data about that transaction, gathers information about the asset owner and then sends that transaction information to BigchainDB which then sends it out to all of the nodes. In the case of the sale, there is data about the date, the location and the value of the building. In the case of the use of an asset there is similar information, but also the time/date that the asset was used. The specific building is "warehouse1", it is located in Las Vegas, while the person "star" has control of the ownership of the building. In the second transaction, the use of the building is reported to the virtual organization.

7.5. *Roles, identities and permissions*

An identity is held by a person with a private key. Roles and identities can be granted permissions. BigchainDB has substantial ability to control user behavior as seen in Table 3. As an example, note that in this particular instantiation, the auditor can "read asset information" and "read certificate authenticity". As another example, note that there is a system administrator and that they are responsible for constructing initializing the network of nodes. However, once the network is live, the system administrator cannot act unilaterally. This also illustrates that even for a highly decentralized organization, such as a virtual organization, there likely would be some centralized decision making in the choice of the BigchainDB and the configuration to meet virtual organization requirements.

8. Blockchain Applications: Data Reuse and Multiple Semantic Models

The purpose of this section is to investigate emerging types of blockchain and blockchain-like applications and the extent of data reuse, as seen in Figure 4. As organizations move beyond simple blockchain document capture there can be increasing needs to analyze, query and report on the transactions captured. Generally, this requires either using a centralized database or a distributed database as in the above applications for TradeLens and virtual organizations.

First, classic uses of blockchain transaction capture are illustrated in the lower left-hand corner (1), where the primary concern is capturing and preserving the blockchain transactions. In this quadrant, there is not likely to be substantial data analysis of the information on the blockchain,

Table 3: Example actions, roles and permissions in bigchainDB*

Action	Requires Vote	Voting Node	Sys Admin	Issuer	Trader	Broker	Authenticator	Auditor
Vote on Admin & Asset Actions		Y						
Update Role or Permissions	Y	Y	Y					
Add/Remove Voting Node	Y	Y	Y					
Update Software	Y	Y	Y					
Issue Asset	Y			Y				
Transfer Asset	Y			O	O	P		
Receive Asset	Y			Y	Y	Y		
Grant Read Access on Asset	Y			O	O	P	P	
Consign Asset	Y			O	O			
Receive Asset Consignment	Y			Y	Y			
Add Asset Information	Y			O	O	P		
Add Authentication Information	Y			O	O		P	
Create Certificate of Authenticity				O	O	P		
Read Asset Information		Y	Y	O	Y	P	P	P
Read Certificate of Authenticity		Y	Y	O	Y	P	P	P

*Y — Identity can perform; O — Owner of asset can perform; P — can perform after owner has given permission; Based on McConaghy *et al.*, 2016, p. 38.

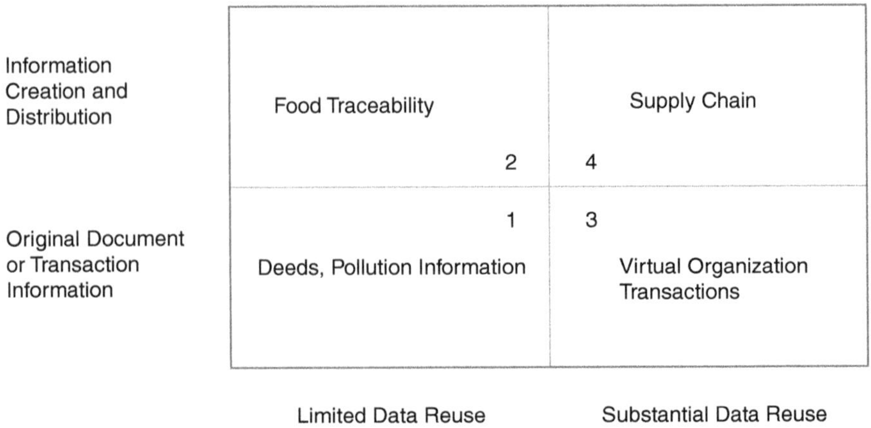

Figure 4: Blockchain application and data reuse.

instead the blockchain document transactions provide history. Second, in the upper left-hand corner (2) contains the food traceability application (e.g., Kim and Laskowksi, 2018). In this quadrant, there is likely to be a data need if there is a problem with the food that would require action, such as a recall. However, that quadrant differs from the lower left quadrant because of the potential need to trace food as it moves through the food supply chain.

Third, in the lower right-hand column (3), the virtual organization system created in this chapter is likely to need a distributed database. A distributed database would allow for local capture of all contributions to the virtual organization. This would allow the participants to access the transactions that directly affect them. In addition, the participants may be interested in information about the contributions that the other participants make to ensure that others are contributing their fair share to the virtual organization.

Fourth, in the upper right-hand quadrant (4), participants may be interested using the data for scheduling or resource balancing or a number of other purposes. Participants may also be interested in tracing or locating shipments. This quadrant is likely to have the most robust data reuse needs. Data needs here could be accommodated by a centralized cloud-based database or a distributed database.

Finally, each of the four quadrants is likely to experience the existence of multiple semantic models. In quadrant 1, different laws are likely to govern the information chosen for the document. In quadrant 2, different participants and different foods are likely to have different requirements. In both quadrants 3 and 4, different virtual organizations and supply chains are likely to have different processes and rules.

9. Summary, Contributions and Extensions

This chapter has argued that although there are definite limitations associated with embedding accounting systems in public blockchains for broad-based use, the unique and specific requirements of an accounting system for a virtual organization are accommodated by a distributed, peer-to-peer database system (BigchainDB) that is designed to include a number of characteristics from blockchain. The decentralized database gets participants rapid information and supports trust in other members. The database provides the ability to query the data, which aligns the messages with necessary accounting capabilities. The BigchainDB focus on assets is consistent with the basic notion of virtual organizations. The "append only" capability provides a control over the information and generate trust in the information and the organization.

9.1. *Contributions*

This chapter has a number of contributions. First, there has been both substantial hype about the potential use of blockchain distributed ledgers, and using them as the basis for accounting and supply chain systems. However, as noted by previous researchers there are a number of limitations to embedding a general purpose accounting system in a public blockchain, both technical and from an information disclosure perspective. This chapter summarizes a number of those limitations, and contrasts them to the hype. Second, this chapter also provides an analysis of the interaction between blockchain technologies and organization form, as illustrated in Figure 3, stressing the need to align organization form and technology.

Third, this chapter notes that although a number of systems are referred to as "blockchains", the blockchain typically plays a small role in the overall system, generally capturing, encrypting and distributing information across a network of participants. However, a database is required to actually analyze, query and report on that data and that database system is likely to be off blockchain. In a private cloud-based system, such as TradeLens, that database is likely to be a centralized database, whereas in a distributed system, such as the one for the virtual organization design in this paper, that database is likely to be a distributed database.

Fourth, this chapter has argued that there is a proliferation of blockchain systems to accomplish different accounting and supply chain activities. As part of that proliferation, there are multiple semantic models of those processes being generated. Although models allow choice, their existence suggests that there may need to be multiple links from those systems to other existing systems, such as the firms' enterprise resource planning system.

Finally, the primary contribution of this paper is to generate a hybrid distributed database system with both blockchain and distributed database capabilities in order to generate an accounting system for a virtual organization. The needs of an accounting system for virtual organizations and the capabilities of the hybrid software provide a close alignment between capabilities and requirements. The system design would provide timely and open information about transactions to the firms that need the information. Timely distribution of open information likely facilitates trust.

9.2. *Extensions*

The research in this chapter can be extended in a number of directions. First, the approach used here can be extended to a range of other accounting settings, such as asset management systems. Second, perhaps this discussion and the use of hybrid blockchain and database systems could be extended to additional organizational forms beyond virtual organizations. Third, perhaps data generated from the BigchainDB transactions can be used to help measure the extent of virtual organization collaboration (Westphal *et al.*, 2007). For example, as transactions are captured, networks of resource expenditures can be generated and analyzed for collaboration. Fourth, as virtual organizations make use of systems such as BigchainDB, additional hybrid characteristics can be generated and embedded in the software. Fifth, as seen with virtual organizations, decentralized systems are particularly useful in those settings where there is a loosely controlled confederation or where information needs to be sent to and monitored by many parties. As a result, this same approach could be used in a project setting where the system would provide project management information to different parties to the project. Sixth, alternative database systems beyond BigChainDB could be used. Alternative types of applications could be examined for the notion of data reuse as seen in Figure 4. Finally, the approach used here could employ a blockchain to capture the events and then allow participants to use either a decentralized or their own databases to process and query the information.

References

BigchainDB, May (2018), *BigchainDB 2.0: The Blockchain Database*, https://www.bigchaindb.com/whitepaper/bigchaindb-whitepaper.pdf.

Castillo, M. (2018), IBM-Maersk Blockchain Platform Adds 92 Clients As Part Of Global Launch, https://www.forbes.com/sites/michaeldelcastillo/2018/08/09/ibm-maersk-blockchain-platform-adds-92-clients-as-part-of-global-launch-1/#109f723368a4.

Corchado, J. M., G. Villarrubia, J. F. De Paz, S. Rodríguez, C. Zato, F. de la Prieta, and J. Bajo (2013), Practical applications of virtual organizations and agent technology. In *International Conference on Practical Applications of Agents and Multi-Agent Systems* (pp. 17–23). Springer, Berlin, Heidelberg.

Deloitte (2016), Blockchain technology: A game changer in accounting. Retrieved from https://www2.deloitte.com/content/dam/Deloitte/de/Documents/Innovation/Blockchain_A%20game-changer%20in%20accounting.pdf.

Geerts, G. L. (2011), A design science research methodology and its application to accounting information systems research, *International Journal of Accounting Information Systems* **12**(2), 142–151.

Goldman, S., R. Nagel, and K. Preiss (1995), *Agile Competitors and Virtual Organizations*. Van Nostrand Reinhold, New York.

Gunasekaran, A. and E. W. Ngai (2004), Virtual supply-chain management, *Production Planning & Control* **15**(6), 584–595.

Hammer, M. (1990), Reengineering work: don't automate, obliterate, *Harvard Business Review* **68**(4), 104–112.

Handy, C. (1995), Trust and the virtual organization, *Harvard Business Review* **73**(3), 40–50.

Henderson, J. and N. Venkatraman (1993), Strategic Alignment: Leveraging Information Technology for Transforming Organizations, *IBM Systems Journal* **32**(1), 472–484.

Hevner, A., S. T. March, J. Park, and S. Ram (2004), Design science in information systems research, *MIS Quarterly* **28**(1), 75–105.

Jayachandran, P. (2017), The difference between public and private blockchain. Retrieved from https://www.ibm.com/blogs/blockchain/2017/05/the-difference-between-public-and-private-blockchain/#:~:text=The%20sole%20distinction%20between%20public,and%20participate%20in%20the%20network.

Kim, H. and M. Laskowski (2018), Towards an ontology driven blockchain design for supply chain provenance, intelligent systems in accounting, *Finance and Management* **25**(1), 18–27.

Kürümlüoglu, M., R. Nøstdal, and I. Karvonen (2005), Base concepts. In Camarinha-Matos, L., Afsarmanesh, H. and Ollus, M. (Eds.). *Virtual Organizations. Systems and Practices*, Springer-Verlag.

Lee, M. (2014), *Leading Virtual Project Teams: Adapting Leadership Theories and Communications Techniques to 21st Century Organizations*. New York: CRC Press Taylor & Francis Group.

Lee, T. (2018), New Study Quantifies Bitcoin's Ludicrous Energy Consumption, https://arstechnica.com/tech-policy/2018/05/new-study-quantifies-bitcoins-ludicrous-energy-consumption/.

March, S. T. and G. F. Smith (1995), Design and natural science research on information technology, *Decision Support Systems* **15**(4), 251–266.

March, S. T. and V. C. Storey (2008), Design science in the information systems discipline: An introduction to the special issue on design science research, *MIS quarterly* **32**(4), 725–730.

McConaghy, T., R. Marques, M. Muller, D. De Jonghe, T. McConaghy, G. McMullen, R. Henderson, S. Bellemare and A. Granzotto (2018), *BigchainDB: A Scalable Blockchain Database*, https://mycourses.aalto.fi/pluginfile.php/378362/mod_resource/content/1/bigchaindb-whitepaper.pdf.

Mohan, C. (2017), Tutorial: Blockchains and Databases, *43rd International Conference on Very Large Databases*, Munich, Germany.

Nakamoto, S. (2008), Bitcoin: A peer-to-peer electronic cash system. https://bitcoin.org/bitcoin.pdf.

O'Leary, D. E. and E. Turban (1987), The organizational impact of expert systems, *Human Systems Management* **7**(1), 11–19.

O'Leary, D. E. (1993), Determining differences in expert judgment: Implications for knowledge acquisition and validation, *Decision Sciences* **24**(2), 395–408.

O'Leary, D. E., D. Kuokka, and R. Plant (1997), Artificial intelligence and virtual organizations, *Communications of the ACM* **40**(1), 52–60.

O'Leary, D. E. (2008), Supporting decisions in real-time enterprises: autonomic supply chain systems. In *Handbook on Decision Support Systems 2* (pp. 19–37). Springer, Berlin, Heidelberg.

O'Leary, D. E. (2011), Building and evolving data warehousing and business intelligence artefacts: The case of Sysco, *Intelligent Systems in Accounting, Finance and Management* **18**(4), 195–213.

O'Leary, D. E. (2013), Exploiting big data from mobile device sensor-based apps: Challenges and benefits, *MIS Quarterly Executive* **12**(4), 179–187.

O'Leary, D. E. (2017), Configuring blockchain architectures for transaction information in blockchain consortiums: The case of accounting and supply chain systems, *Intelligent Systems in Accounting, Finance and Management* **24**(4), 138–147.

O'Leary, D. E. (2018), Open Information Enterprise Transactions: Business Intelligence and Wash and Spoof Transactions in Blockchain and Social Commerce, *Intelligent Systems in Accounting, Finance and Management* **25**(3), 148–158.

Ometoruwa, T. (2019), IBM and Maersk's Struggles Cast a Shadow Over Private Blockchains, https://medium.com/hackernoon/ibm-and-maersks-struggles-cast-a-shadow-over-private-blockchains-1892cbc86a1b, accessed on 11/25/2019.

Ovenden, J. (2017), Will blockchain render accountants irrelevant? Retrieved from https://channels.theinnovationenterprise.com/articles/will-blockchain-render-accountants-irrelevant.

Patil, H. (2017), 22 ways that blockchain will change the accounting profession forever. CPA Trendlines. Retrieved from https://cpatrendlines.com/2017/07/03/22-ways-blockchain-will-impact-accounting-profession/.

Roberts, J. J. (2017), Blockchain offers hope for the broken internet. Retrieved from https://fortune.com/2017/05/27/blockchain-offers-hope-for-the-broken-internet/.

Simon, H. (1981), *The Sciences of the Artificial* (2nd Ed.), Cambridge, MA: MIT Press.

Westphal, I., K. D. Thoben, and M. Seifert (2007), Measuring collaboration performance in virtual organizations. In *Working Conference on Virtual Enterprises* (pp. 33–42). Springer, Boston, MA.

Appendix

A.1 Sale of an Asset[6]

```
function createAssetsale() {
  // Construct a transaction payload
  const txCreateAssetsale = BigchainDB.Transaction.
  makeCreateTransaction(
    // Asset field
    {
      warehouse1,
    },
    // Metadata field, contains information about the transaction itself
    {
      datetime: new Date().toString(),
      location: 'Las Vegas',
      value: {
        value_dol: '$2000000',
      }
    },
    // Output. Create Ed25519 condition
    [BigchainDB.Transaction.makeOutput(
      BigchainDB.Transaction.makeEd25519Condition(star.publicKey))],
    // Issuers
    star.publicKey
  )
  // The owner of the building signs the transaction
  const txSigned = BigchainDB.Transaction.signTransaction(txCreateA
  ssetsale,
    star.privateKey)
  // Send the transaction off to BigchainDB
  conn.postTransactionCommit(txSigned)
    .then(res => {
      document.body.innerHTML += '<h3>Transaction created</h3>';
      document.body.innerHTML += txSigned.id
      // txSigned.id corresponds to the asset id of the warehouse1
    })
}
```

[6] Based on www.bigchaindb.com. Ed25519 is a public key signature system.

A.2 Asset Use

```
function createAssetuse() {
  // Construct a transaction payload
  const txCreateAssetuse = BigchainDB.Transaction.
  makeCreateTransaction(
    // Asset field
    {
      warehouse1,
    },
    // Metadata field, contains information about the transaction itself
    {
      datetime: 'March 1, 2019, 800 hours to 1500 hours'
      location: 'Las Vegas',
     }
    },
    // Output. Create Ed25519 condition
    [BigchainDB.Transaction.makeOutput(
      BigchainDB.Transaction.makeEd25519Condition(star.publicKey))],
    // Issuers
    star.publicKey
  )
  // The owner of the building signs the transaction
  const txSigned = BigchainDB.Transaction.signTransaction(txCreateA
  ssetuse,
    star.privateKey)
  // Send the transaction off to BigchainDB
  conn.postTransactionCommit(txSigned)
    .then(res => {
      document.body.innerHTML += '<h3>Transaction created</h3>';
      document.body.innerHTML += txSigned.id
      // txSigned.id corresponds to the asset id of the warehouse1
    })
}
```

https://doi.org/10.1142/9789811220470_0020

Chapter 20

Have Accounting Reports Become Less Useful for Decision-Making?

Joshua Ronen

Stern School of Business, New York University, USA

jronen@stern.nyu

Abstract

Accounting reports have come under increasing criticism for being inadequate in the information age. The proliferation of big data combined with the increasing ability to extract knowledge and to detect patterns from the trillions of bits of information is argued by some to render accounting reports superfluous. Contrariwise, I argue these recent information age abilities can complement the systematic chronicling of the past history of an organization in creating a yet richer platform for making informed decisions. To make this possible, however, a remake of the financial reporting model would be helpful. This essay elaborates on what a better and more comprehensive accounting system would look like. It would combine the reporting of historical events with management forecasts and exit values to facilitate meaningful reporting on economic performance.

Keywords: Accounting reports; Machine learning; Big data; Forecasts; Exit values.

1. Introduction

Recently, exciting developments in the area of machine learning have raised questions about the role of accounting information in decision-making and valuation. The explosion of data and the inventive activity directed to extracting knowledge from available abundant data have greatly enhanced the ability of decision-makers — both internally within a firm and externally among investors, regulators, consumers, employees, and others — to discover knowledge about firms' activities. Does this proliferation of data, and the consequently hugely expanded possibilities of detecting patterns that facilitate decision-making render traditional financial reports less relevant? In this chapter, I argue this is not the case. Contrariwise, machine learning combined with big and deep data compliments accounting reports so as to produce a much richer platform for making informed decisions, especially in anticipating firms' prospects, an essential prerequisite to improving decisions both by managers and by investors.

Importantly however, to attain this synergistic effect between knowledge extracted from the abundant data generated outside the firm and the financial reports generated by the firm, I contend the accounting model must be extensively modified and reshuffled to deliver the synergy benefits. For too long, financial reports have provided a hodgepodge of facts and conjectures, of historical data and implied forecasts, of how assets and liabilities are measured: historical costs, adjusted historical costs, net realizable values, fair values (replacement values and/or exit values), and amortized historical costs, which in turn generate correspondingly opaque measures of revenue and expense. This is accompanied by equally confusing and occasionally inconsistent recognition and measurement rules. Some see indicia of decline in the utility of accounting reports following the transition of the economy from the industrial age to the information age (e.g., Beaver *et al.*, 2005, Chaudhry and Sam, 2018), although others offer an opposite view (Landsman and Maydew, 2002). What likely led accounting standard setters to give rise to this labyrinthine web of financial reports is the quest for a balance between relevance and reliability. Such a balance, however, detracts from the utility of the reports: the current accounting model perforce generates relevant data only by sacrificing reliability, and conversely, ensures reliability only at the expense of relevance. A better accounting model will not compromise either: accounting reports can be made to be both relevant *and* reliable.

The role of financial reporting is to describe the past and facilitate the formulation of expectations about the future. The objective is to enable the diverse users of the reports to predict a relevant future: specifically, the future return and risk associated with investment in the firm. Indeed, the objective of financial statements as spelled out in Financial Concepts 1 (FASB, 1978) is the provision of information that is helpful in predicting future cash flows, their timing, and uncertainty. These are the pieces of information that facilitate the prediction of risk and return, and hence the ability to make wise investments.

For example, Beaver *et al.* (2012) examined 40 years of financial data garnered from thousands of public corporations. They analyzed key financial ratios, such as return on assets and leverage, reported in filings to the US Securities and Exchange Commission and market-related data such as market capitalization and stock returns. Over the period they examined — from 1962 to 2002 — the data became significantly less useful in predicting bankruptcy. On the contrary, in their 2018 reconsideration of the role of accounting earnings, they find evidence that the information content of earnings increases over time with a dramatic increase from 2001 onward, a period that includes the implementation of the Sarbanes–Oxley (SOX) reforms, and that the information content of earnings announcements is positively associated with profitability, firm size, and analyst coverage. This seems to be somewhat surprising since, as mentioned above, any earnings figure is contingent on arbitrary choices concerning cost allocation, depreciation, accruals, deferrals, and so on. Moreover, the quality of the data may have declined — consider the failure to capture the value of intangible assets and the inability to capitalize intellectual property, a key driver of success in today's economy. Finally, and more pertinent to this essay, digital technology lowered the cost of disseminating information, and investors today have access to timelier insights from analysts, blogs, and statistical services, not to mention ongoing updates from the companies themselves. Paradoxically, the study finds that the informational value of earnings announcements has actually increased at a time when the Internet and internet-based business models were supposed to have made them less informative. These findings, however, are confounded by the possibility that none of the regulations under SOX increased public confidence in financial statements. Also, Dontoh *et al.* (2004) empirically confirm the hypothesis that the decline in the association between stock prices and accounting information as measured by *R*-squares is driven by an increase in noise trading. In sum, studies are inconclusive regarding the utility of accounting reports and whether the relevance of accounting declined over time.

Nonetheless, we witness an increasing academic interest in the role of artificial intelligence and machine learning in prediction. If machine learning algorithms can better predict revenues and costs of a business than reliance on information contained in financial reports alone, what does this bode for the relevance of accounting? Can we gradually wean ourselves from relying on the allegedly "stale" information contained in mostly historically based aggregations of transactions and events?

A budding literature in accounting and finance utilizes data that are external to information contained in financial reports to evaluate and predict a firm's performance (for example, Teoh, 2018). Such external data include population coverage, market penetration, and customer satisfaction (for example, Kaplan and Norton, 1996; Riley *et al.*, 2003); product reviews on Amazon.com (Huang, 2018); employee satisfaction (Hales, Moon, and Swenson, 2018); and mobile phone activity (Froot *et al.*, 2017). Allee *et al.* (2019) use external proprietary data to detect financial misrepresentation. They find that, among Korean firms, inconsistent growth patterns between accounting performance and electricity consumption presage financial misreporting. Chiu *et al.* (2018) use publicly available Google searches of firm products and compare the information derived from those searches to reported sales growth based on financial statements data to detect upward revenue manipulation. This emerging literature showcases the ability to exploit advances in computing processing speed and storage capacity to allow performance data to be recorded, transmitted, and processed rapidly. As a result, credible information that is correlated with firm transactions but generated outside the firm's financial reporting by such entities like Google can be easily used by investors, regulators, and others to learn about firm activities and fundamentals even before disclosure by the firm itself.

Are these alternative sources of information a substitute for traditional financial reporting, or do they complement the latter to achieve even better prediction than using either alone? I would argue these are complementary sources of information that can enhance the ability to predict relevant future metrics. In fact, it is not only individuals and entities outside the firm who can utilize these outside sources of information to enhance the utility derived from financial statements; rather, the management of the firm itself can utilize these outside sources to improve its ability to predict and hence to plan growth strategies based on a larger set of information and more accurate predictions of the environment.[1] Thus, managers, investors, and other users of information can benefit from the information technology innovations in the marketplace. However, further improvements can be made if the financial reporting model itself is overhauled in such a way as to further facilitate prediction and reduce information asymmetry by shining light on management's inside information, as well as by according the provided information both relevance and reliability, rather than being compelled to compromise both relevance and reliability by attempting to trade-off one against the other.

2. A Comprehensive Reporting Framework[2]

In this section, I present an alternative and expanded model of accounting that (1) facilitates the elicitation of management's inside information in a way that incentivizes truth telling, (2) provides information about historical events and transactions, current valuations, and future expectations in such a way as to afford both relevance and reliability, and (3) in combination with emerging big data and machine learning makes possible not only enhanced predictive ability but also the assessment of managerial skill and/or the honesty of management's expectations against realizations over time.

The informativeness objective — facilitating the prediction of future cash flows and their magnitude, timing, and uncertainty — is derived from investors' desire to predict future movements in market prices and identify situations in which there are discrepancies between actual prices and intrinsic or fundamental values. The latter are the risk-adjusted discounted value of prospective cash flows attributable to the firm. Such a calculation requires information about the future sequence of cash flows and the uncertainty surrounding them.

---

[1] In addition, as an example of how management can use emerging technologies, elsewhere in this handbook, Dr. Katrin Tin discusses the digital ledger technology's potential to make verification (nearly) costless. Thus, without the pressing issue of verification costs, it may become easier to design and offer to young firms a much wider menu of financing contracts: equity, convertible assets, "smart" contracts where the contractual terms adjust based on incoming and verifiably recorded data.

[2] This section and those that follow borrow heavily from Ronen (2008) and Ronen and Sorter (1972).

The present accounting model does not explicitly deal with expectations about future cash flows or their associated risk. Ideally, accounting should provide information that is useful for (a) prediction of cash flows, (b) assessing the risks of these flows, and (c) the realization of expectations. The last of these is important for assessing the reliability of expectations and the quality of managerial performance, as well as in facilitating the improvement of the forecasting process.

In a world of information asymmetry, the role of accounting is to convey information that the firm has a comparative advantage in providing (Ronen 1979). Although future cash flows are determined by market forces, industry forces, and the firm's own actions, the firm's management has current knowledge of its specific decisions and plans. Historically, the best source of information about future cash flows has been the firm itself. But this is changing in a world awash with increasing amounts of data emanating from sensors of human and business activity.

Accounting would serve its role if management *honestly* communicated its own estimate of prospective cash flows through the accounting reports (see, e.g., Lorie and Niederhoffer, 1968; Jaffe, 1974; Givoly and Palmon, 1985; Seyhun, 1986; Rozeff and Zaman, 1988; Lakonishok and Lee, 2001)[3] based on its plans and market knowledge. How forecasts of cash flows should be communicated is of course a serious question. Management can legitimately protest that providing detailed forecasts may put the firm at a competitive disadvantage. Hence, a period of experimentation is required. As a first step, however, it is clear that no competitive advantage is compromised by summarizing the expected cash flows in the form of a single number — the present value of the expected cash flows — reflecting management's subjective valuation of the firm. Even such a single measure would make reports more relevant to investors so long as it is unbiased; random forecasting errors of course cannot be avoided as a source of risk. A variety of risk measures are provided currently in financial statements, and the degree of uncertainty associated with these forecasts can also be required as part of the supplementary disclosures. Similar disclosures and the construction of diversified portfolios could mitigate and diversify away the risk associated with random forecasting errors. Biased forecasts present a far greater problem, but this

---

[3]The qualifier "honestly" may well seem wishful thinking at this point. See Ronen (2008) for mechanisms that incentivize truth telling.

can be dealt with by appropriate corporate governance mechanisms that induce honest reporting (Ronen, 2008).[4]

To make financial reports comparable, management's forecasts should be discounted by a rate that is constant across firms and not by the firm's specific cost of capital. A reasonable candidate is a market rate of return, such as the composite equity rate of return of all stocks available. In a sense, this market rate of return reflects the universal opportunity cost of providing capital to firms. Such a rate makes it possible to communicate the magnitude and timing of future cash flows with no consideration given to the specific risks, other than market risks, associated with cash flows.[5] Risk considerations could of course be reflected by using a risk-adjusted discount rate. High-risk flows would then be discounted at a higher rate and low-risk flows at the lower rate. The problem with this procedure is manifold: first, the elements that determine risk are many and diverse and to a great degree subjective; hence, a single measure reflecting both the amount and the risk of expected cash flows would not be useful, since it is difficult to capture all the determinants of risk through a single modification of the discount rate. Second, any such modification would inevitably be affected by management's attitudes toward risk, and these may well differ from those held by investors. Third, if a single risk-adjusted rate is used, the financial statement user would have no readily available mechanism for disassociating the amount of expected flows from their associated risks. Hence, discounting expected cash flows by a single universal rate of return is superior to discounting by a risk-adjusted discount rate that would deprive users of financial statements of the ability to separate the amount of expected flows from their associated risks. Because a market rate is used to discount the flows, the resulting present value can be described as the market risk-determined (MRD) value of the firm.

---

[4]Ideally, management could provide the probability distribution of cash flows. This, however, would be too radical a departure from the present model, albeit certain supplementary disclosures (e.g., the risk disclosure requirements imposed on financial institutions) already mark a rudimentary beginning in that direction.

[5]It would also be possible to present the estimates of cash flows by presenting a schedule of expectations for each year and not aggregating these expectations through discounting. However, if an aggregate measure is desirable, some discount rates must be used, since the expected cash flows cover different periods.

2.1. *Specific advantage and specific residual*

While the MRD value of the firm summarizes the magnitude and timing of future cash flows, it does not by itself communicate the risk associated with these cash flows. An important dimension of risk can be communicated through the exit values of assets and liabilities. The exit value of an asset is defined as the net proceeds (after transaction costs) that can be realized by severing the assets from the firm. The exit value for liability and of the stock equity is the amount necessary to redeem these. This is where the FAS 157 (ASC 820) exit value measures come into play. Useful insights into some aspects of risk can be gained by comparing the MRD value with the exit value of the net assets (the difference between the exit values of assets and those of liabilities). This excess of MRD value over the exit value of the net assets is referred to as the *specific advantage* of the firm. On the contrary, the difference between the firm's MRD value and the exit (market) value of its equity is defined as the *specific residual.*

2.2. *The specific advantage*

The specific advantage reflects the expected cash flows that cannot be realized unless the firm continues its specific operations and assumes the risks associated with them. The exit value of net assets represents cash flows that could be realized if the firm does not continue its specific operations and is largely independent of the risks associated with the specific operations.

The specific residual, on the contrary, reflects that portion of the expected flows that have not yet been captured by the market value of the firm's equity (a) because the market assigns a risk factor to the firm's expectations that is higher than the risk embedded in the market return or (b) because the market does not accept the magnitude of the cash flows as reflected in the MRD value, or (c) through a combination of these two.

Significant elements of risks can be assessed using these two differences. The larger the specific advantage, the higher the risk of realizing the expectations. For example, two firms with equal MRD value, where one firm has zero exit values (the specific-advantage firm) and the other has an exit value that equals the MRD value (the exit value firm), are significantly different in their potential losses upon a failure of expectations to materialize. A total loss would ensue for the specific-advantage firm, but the latter's individual assets could be sold separately. And although exit values could also decline, this decline is likely to be smaller than the potential decline in the firm's MRD value, since positive exit values imply the existence of other uses for the firm's assets. Other users may demand the assets not only to replicate the firm's own business model but also to provide other products and services. Thus, the higher the proportion of specific advantage to MRD value, the greater the firm's exposure to a potential decline in its value.

A specific-advantage firm is exposed to more risk since it is restricted in its alternatives: its assets have zero exit values. Moreover, the specific-advantage firm's expectations may not be shared by anybody else, and their realization is less under the firm's control than is the case for exit value firms. If the firm's expectations are not accompanied by exit values of its assets, the expectations apparently are held only by the firm itself. That is, although the MRD value may reflect only one firm's expectation, the assets' exit values represent the mean expectation of more than one entity. The variance associated with exit values (mean of expectations) is presumably smaller than that associated with expectations held by only one entity. Thus, even if the demand for a firm's specific product declines, it is less likely that a similar decline will occur in the assets' exit values, which may be derived from other users and other products and services. If a decline in exit values comparable with the decline in MRD value is to occur, it is necessary not only that the demand for the output of the particular firm declines but also that the demand for the output of other like firms also decline; further, if the assets can be used for other services, a decline of the demand for these other services must occur as well. Hence, the higher the proportion of specific advantage to the firm's MRD value, the higher the firm's exposure to potential decline in its value. More of its future will depend on the market's acceptance of the firm's particular service or products. The larger an asset's exit value, the more flexible is the firm in employing its resources and the less dependent it is on its specific plans and operations. The specific-advantage firm is restricted in its alternatives since its assets have zero exit values. Stated differently, to realize the portion of the firm's value that is not reflected in the exit value of the assets requires the existence of a future market for which no evidence may yet exist and which will be determined by factors that are not under the firm's control. For all these reasons, the larger the specific advantage of the firm, the larger is the risk that can be associated with that firm's cash flows.

2.3. *The specific residual*

The exit value of equity reflects the capital market's evaluation of both the magnitude and the risks attached to the firm's expected cash flows. If investors accept management's forecasts and feel that the risk associated with the flows is correctly expressed through discounting by a market discount rate, then the exit value of the equity will equal the MRD value; if it is less, either the market does not fully accept the firm's expectations or it attaches a greater-than-market risk to these expectations. Thus, the larger the specific residual, the larger the risk that attaches to the firm's cash flows, regardless of which of these factors produce a divergence between the MRD value and the equity's exit value.

The specific residual and the specific advantage are incrementally informative. For example, a firm with a large specific advantage could at the same time have a small specific residual (both relative to the MRD value). An innovative, high-tech company such as Google may be such a firm. If demand for Google's services slackens, the options are few — it has a large specific advantage. On the contrary, the small specific residual implies that the market shares Google's forecasts and has validated them, as reflected in the prices of its securities.

2.4. *Past transactions and events*

Prospective cash flows and exit values alone would not fully satisfy the needs of either investors or management. To evaluate, audit, and improve predictions of prospective cash flows, it is also necessary to communicate events that have occurred. This would allow users to evaluate management's performance and predictions, as well as to better predict and control future management performance, actions, and policy. Unlike the manner in which past events are recorded, under the current accounting model, however, data regarding past transactions should be separated into expected and unexpected components. This would help users evaluate the forecasts embedded in the MRD value of the firm in earlier periods, as well as the effectiveness of management. In addition, past events must be described not only in terms of historical cost but also in terms of their effect on exit values.

It is necessary to communicate both the expectations of the firm as reflected in the MRD value and the exit values of its assets and equities. Ideally, both values should be communicated in the form of probability distributions. Both exit values and discounted expectations cover a range of values and cannot be adequately reflected through a single number. Probabilistic measures, however, represent a dramatic departure from current practice. More research on both the behavioral and other implications of probabilistic measures should be conducted before their adoption is advocated.

2.5. *Retrospective data*

Prospective cash flows and exit values alone are not sufficient. To evaluate, audit, and improve predictions of prospective cash flows, firms must also communicate events that have occurred. Communication of past events is necessary to allow users to evaluate management's performance and predictions, as well as to better predict future management performance, actions, and policy. Of course, accounting reports have always included retrospective data. In the proposed system, however, the reporting of past events differs from current practice. Specifically, past transaction data should be separated into expected and unexpected components. Only then would the provided data be useful for validating and evaluating the forecasts that have been reported in earlier periods, as well as for evaluating the effectiveness of management. In addition, past events must be described not solely in terms of historical cost but also through their effect on exit values. Changes in exit values should be communicated when they occur.

2.6. *The reports*

The accounting reports under this framework would consist of a Balance Sheet and a Costs and Benefits Statement that is supported by two detailed statements: an Income Statement, which reports changes in the MRD value, and a Change in Asset Composition Statement, which reflects changes in the composition of assets and liabilities — an indication of risk.[6]

2.7. *The balance sheet*

The Balance Sheet would report historical cost, exit values, specific advantage, and Total Economic Value. It would distinguish among major

---

[6]See Ronen and Sorter (1972) for details, where the Change in Asset Composition Statement is referred to as the Realization and De-Realization Statement.

groups of assets. Even though the specific advantage results from the joint operation of assets, it might be possible to attribute incremental specific advantages (albeit non-additive) to individual assets and liabilities. Table 1[7] illustrates these components of the balance sheet. The proposed balance sheet contains three columns for assets, liabilities, and equities. The columns reflect historical costs, the specific advantage, and the exit value of the assets and liabilities and the specific residual of the firm. Three major groups of assets are presented: cash assets (cash, marketable securities, and accounts receivable), other current assets (inventories and supplies), and fixed assets. The specific-advantage column does not present individual values for specific assets or liabilities, since it results from the joint operations of all assets. It may be possible to attribute incremental specific advantages to individual assets and liabilities, but this would be subject to measurement problems and the incremental specific advantages would not be additive. To suggest that the desegregation problem for exit values may be less difficult than for specific advantage, exit values for each group of specific assets are shown in the table.

As indicated, in addition to historical costs, exit value would be shown for individual assets. In the case of jointly operated assets, the exit value theoretically should be the amount for which the assets are sold in combinations that maximize proceeds from the sale.[8] Exit values that are lower than historical costs result from the particularization of purchased assets (putting the asset to a specific use rather than selling it). For example, work in process may have a historical cost in excess of its exit value. The particularization of a fixed asset will typically produce exit values that are below the historical cost as of the date of purchase, but this may be offset later by fluctuations in exit values. The more unstable the environment and the older the assets, the more difficult it is to predict the relationship between exit values and historical costs. This is illustrated in the balance sheet by reporting exit values for fixed assets that are slightly higher in the first year and equal to the historical costs in the second year.

For cash assets, the exit values closely approximate historical cost. Any different evaluation is attributable to the difference between historical cost and exit value of marketable securities and accounts receivable. The latter difference is attributable to uncollectibility. The market value of equity, its exit value, reflect both contributed capital and retained

[7]This and all future tables are copied from Ronen and Sorter (1972).

[8]This is consistent with the approach adopted in FAS 157 (ASC 820).

Table 1: Comparative balance sheet as of 12/31/00 and 12/31/01: Liabilities and equity.

	Historical cost		Exit Values		Specific Advantage[a]		Total Economic Value	
Assets	12/31/00	12/31/01	12/31/00	12/31/01	12/31/00	12/31/01	12/31/00	12/31/01
Cash assets:								
Cash	2,100	2,600	2,100	2,600				
Marketable securities	150	150	200	200				
Accounts receivable (net)	3,320	2,820	3,320	2,820				
	5,570	5,570	5,600	5,600			5,600	5,600
Other current assets:								
Raw materials	700	1,000	650	1,130				
Work in process	800	2,250	300	3,050				
Finished goods	1,000	0	1,200	0				
Supplies	150	100	50	30				
	2,650	3,350	2,200	4,210			2,200	4,210
Fixed (net):								
Building	10,000	9,700	9,950	10,050				
Machinery and equipment	20,000	24,100	20,250	23,750				
	30,000	33,800	30,200	33,800			30,200	33,800
Firm's specific advantage					11,000	12,875	11,000	12,875
Total	38,220	42,720					49,000	56,485

(Continued)

Table 1: (*Continued*).

	Historical cost		Exit Values		Specific Advantage[a]		Total Economic Value	
Assets	12/31/00	12/31/01	12/31/00	12/31/01	12/31/00	12/31/01	12/31/00	12/31/01
Liabilities:								
Current:								
Accounts payable	1,500	5,580	1,500	5,580				
Short term	300	300	300	300				
Other	150	150	150	150				
	1,950	6,030	1,950	6,030				
Long term:								
Bonds	17,000	17,000	18,000	18,000				
Other	7,000	7,000	7,000	7,000				
	24,000	24,000	25,000	25,000				
Total liabilities	25,950	30,030	26,950	31,030			26,950	31,030
Equity:								
Stock:								
Contributed capital	10,000	10,000	13,050	15,000				
Retained earnings	2,270	2,690						
	12,270	12,690	13,050	15,000			13,050	15,000
Specific residual					9,000	10,455	9,000	10,455
Total	38,220	42,720					49,000	56,485

Note: [a] Incremental specific advantages associated with individual assets and liabilities are not provided (see text).

earnings; no separation between these two is possible in the exit value. The specific residual reflects that portion of the firm's MRD value that has not been validated by market consensus.

2.8. *The costs and benefits statement*

The two major determinants of a firm's value are the return (or magnitude of expected cash flows) and the risk associated with it. Thus, the benefits accruing to a firm should reflect both these dimensions. The benefits may accrue to a firm either through an increase in the size of expectations (due to the passage of time or the revision of expectations) or through a reduction in the risk or uncertainty associated with the expectations. Similarly, the cost to a firm represents either a reduction of the magnitude of expectations or an increasing risk, or both. This dual nature of benefits and costs is not adequately described through either economic income (the difference in wealth between two points in time) or accounting income under the current historical cost model. Economic income does reflect changes in the magnitude and in the timing of expected cash flows, the present value of which is wealth. It reflects changes in risk only through changes in the discount rate used. Moreover, it aggregates expectations and risk into one measure. That is, changes in risk are not reflected explicitly. Furthermore, economic income does not explicitly differentiate among the varying uncertainties associated with the composition of assets: it makes no difference whether the cash flows are expected to result from assets not yet acquired, from inventory that has not yet been manufactured, or from accounts receivable that have not yet been collected. Yet, the certainty of realizing cash flows from these different assets differs. By contrast, accounting income is affected only to a minor degree by expectations and changes in expectations; it is concerned almost exclusively with realizations. Thus, both economic income and accounting income describe different aspects of the benefits that accrue to the firm. Neither fully describes all benefits. A more complete description should reflect both expectations and changes in expectations as well as the pattern of realization and changes in this pattern. In the Costs and Benefits Statement, the benefits would be described as (a) the change in expectations (the MRD value, which consists of two elements — the passage of time, quantified by the imputed interest on the MRD value, and the revision of expectations as of the end of the period, based on information obtained during the year, most notably the unexpected events shown in the detailed supporting statements) and (b) changes in realizations: change in the composition of assets from more specific and therefore more risky assets to relatively less specific and therefore less risky assets (benefits) or vice versa (costs). Consider, for example, the conversion of inputs to outputs. If these conversions were expected, the MRD value would remain unchanged. Nonetheless, the conversion is likely a benefit to the firm: the exit value of finished goods, for instance, would generally be larger than the sum of the exit values of the inputs; it would be reported in the Costs and Benefits Statement as an increase in exit values. The risk inherent in selling output already manufactured is less than the risk surrounding expectations that require both manufacturing and selling.[9] If changes in exit values are unexpected, they may also lead to a change in the MRD value, which would be shown as a revision of expectations in item 7 of the Costs and Benefits Statement (see Table 2). Increases in exit values would be broken down into purchase gains (excess of exit value

Table 2: Statement of costs and benefits.

Costs:		
1. Decline in exit values	$1,800	
2. Purchase loss	120	$1,920
3. Imputed interest on exit values (net)		1,105
Benefits:		
4. Increase in exit values		
a. Appreciation of exit values		1,250
b. Value added (excluding depreciation)		2,200
		3,450
5. Purchase gain		0
		3,450
6. Time growth of expectations: imputed interest on total net assets (including specific advantage)		2,205
7. Revision of expectations		1,200

[9]The final stage of realization of course is the conversion of output to cash. Hence, it is important to report exit values of cash assets and other assets separately in the Change in Assets Composition Statement.

over purchase cost), which in this case are zero; into value added, which reflects an increase in exit values resulting from operating activities; and into the increase in the exit value of assets that appreciated, which does not result from operating activities. These three elements are added to produce the gross increase in exit values of assets of $3450. Both declines and increases in exit value are measured at their gross amount. Items 6 and 7 represent benefits attributable to the size of expected cash flows. Item 6 quantifies the time growth of expectations, that is, the change in expectations due to the passage of time, which is quantified by the imputed interest on the MRD value of the firm. Item 7 quantifies the net revision of expectations as of the year end. A major source of information for this revision would very likely be the unexpected events shown in the detailed statements discussed below.

Under costs would be shown decreases in the exit value of assets that declined in value, reflecting an increase in risk[10] and the purchase loss (excess of purchase price over exit value at the time of purchase). The increase in exit value of assets whose value appreciated is shown under benefits. This decline may or may not be associated with a decline in the total value of the firm. Whether or not it is, it always represents a cost in the sense of the increasing uncertainty associated with the cash flows. If the decline in exit values was expected, that implies the total value of the firm remained unchanged; that is, the decline in exit values is offset by an equal increase in the specific advantage. Since more uncertainty attaches to specific advantage than to exit values, this represents an increased risk. If a decline in exit values was unexpected, it may lead to a revision of expectations of future cash flows and therefore to changes in the value of the firm which would affect item 7 of the Cost and Benefit Statement. The purchase loss also reflects a decline in exit values but is separately reported to reflect the increasing uncertainty directly caused by the purchasing activities of the firm. Thus, items 1 and 2 together present declines in exit values that can be added to yield the gross total decline of $1920.

---

[10]This may or may not be associated with a decline in the MRD value of the firm. Indirectly, it may cause a revision of expectations to the extent it is unexpected. Such a revision would be reflected, as discussed, as part of the economic income in the Costs and Benefits Statement. If the decline was expected, the MRD value of the firm remains unchanged, in which case the decline in exit values is offset by an equal increase in the specific advantage.

Another cost item is the imputed interest on the exit value of net assets; this amount of $1105 represents opportunity costs — the returns forgone as a result of having held the assets, and it cannot be meaningfully added to the other costs.

To summarize, we have three non-additive elements of cost: (1) the decline in exit values, representing increased uncertainty; (2) possible unfavorable revision of expectations (item 7); and (3) forgone benefits.

Two subsidiary statements would furnish additional details in support of the benefits and costs presented in the Costs and Benefits Statement: the Income Statement and the Change in Assets Composition Statement. The Income Statement describes events affecting the MRD value of the firm, while the Change in Assets Decomposition describes events affecting the composition of the firm's assets and liabilities, which in turn reflect the uncertainty facing the firm.

2.9. *The income statement*

The Income Statement (Table 3) would provide historical cost data and economic income, showing changes in the MRD value. Both would be broken down into expected and unexpected components. Historical income would essentially be communicated in the same manner as is done currently: a record of market transactions.

The economic income column shows the change in the MRD value of the firm. Historical income would be communicated in the same manner as reported today, with the exception that expected and unexpected components are identified and separately reported. Historical cost income would reflect market transactions useful for discharging part of the traditional stewardship function of accounting.

In contrast, in the economic income columns, operating income — income realized by sales — is zero, since output would be quantified at its exit value (selling price less than transaction costs incurred in the selling process). These transaction costs are incurred on the date of sale and are shown as a part of the outflow. Thus, sales inflow and outflow would equal each other, although they would be presented separately. Despite this equality, the outflows and inflows are separately reported in order to provide insights into the operations of the firm. The sales outflow would be composed of two components: the exit value of the output recognized at the time of conversion and an increment in the exit value up to the

Table 3: Income statement (changes in the value of the firm).

	Historical Income		Economic	Income
Sales	Expected	Unexpected	Expected	Unexpected
Inflows	5,000	200	5,000	200
Outflows:				
Values of goods sold:				
On conversion:				
Inputs	3,000	100	2,000	200
Value added			1,800	
On sales:				
Additional inputs	700		800	
Value added			400	
	(3,700)	(100)	(5,000)	(200)
	1,300	100	0	0
Interest revenue	20		4,900	
Interest expense	(1,000)		(2,695)	
	(980)		2,205	0
Revision of expectations				1,200
Total	320	100	2,205	1,200
Interest appropriation			2,205	

time of the sale. For each of these components, a distinction would be made between an increase in the value of the inputs and the value added. Value added represents that portion of the exit value of the output that is attributable to the specific operations of the firm.

For historical cost income, interest revenue would be interest earned on interest-bearing assets, and interest expenses would be the interest accrued on interest-bearing obligations. For economic income, interest revenue would represent the market rate of return imputed on the total assets of the firm (including its specific advantage); the interest expense would represent the market rate of return imputed to the firm's liabilities. The net interest of $2205 would represent the market rate of return imputed to the firm's MRD value: firm-value growth as a result of the passage of time. Finally, the revision of expectations would be a component of economic income.

2.10. *The change in assets composition statement: Statement of realizations and derealizations*

As discussed above, benefits and costs associated with a firm consist of the magnitude of flows and the uncertainty associated with these flows. The Income Statement presents costs and benefits related to the magnitude of the flows. Table 4 details events causing changes in the assets composition that reflect changes in uncertainty. This statement reports the "realization events": events that result in conversion from more risky assets to less risky assets. These are conversions from specific advantage to exit values and from exit values of non-cash assets to exit values of cash assets. Derealization events, on the contrary, are those that cause shifts from less risky assets to more risky assets. They include conversion from exit value of cash assets to exit values of non-cash assets and from non-cash assets to specific advantage. Conversions from exit values of non-cash assets to exit value of cash assets represent sales of facets and services, while conversion from exit value of cash assets to exit value of non-cash assets represents purchases of facets and services.

Conversions of specific advantage to exit values may be due to three factors: (1) change in exit value due to the fulfillment of a firm's function: value added, (2) change in exit values resulting from holding assets, i.e. holding gains, which could be broken down to reflect the growth in exit value due to the passage of time, and changes due to general or specific price-level changes, (3) potential purchase gains. All three of these factors are reported separately in this statement.

These activities may or may not be associated with a decline in the MRD value of the firm. They may indirectly cause a revision of expectations to the extent that they are unexpected. Such a revision would be reflected, as discussed, as part of the economic income in the Costs and Benefits Statement. If the decline was expected, the MRD value of the firm remains unchanged, in which case the decline in exit values is offset by an equal increase in the specific advantage.

Derealization events are conversions from less risky assets to more risky assets. These events include conversion from exit values of cash assets to exit

Table 4: Statement of realizations and derealizations.

	Net Cash Assets		Other (Net)		Specific Advantage	
	Expected	Unexpected	Expected	Unexpected	Expected	Unexpected
Realizations:						
From exit values — non-cash to exit values — cash:						
Sales	5,000	200	(5,000)	(200)		
Interest revenue	20		(20)			
	5,020	200	(5,020)	(200)		
From specific advantage to exit values:						
Value added			2,200	(2,200)		
Changes in exit values of net current assets:						
On conversion			300	(300)		
At year end			150	(150)		
			2,650	(2,650)		
Derealizations:						
From net cash assets to exit values:						
Purchases:						
Current assets	(3,200)	(400)	3,200	400		
Fixed assets	(5,000)	300	5,000	(300)		
Interest expense	(1,000)		1,000			
	(9,200)	(100)	9,200	100		
From exit values to specific advantage:						
Purchase loss			(100)	(20)	100	200
Changes in exit value of fixed assets (net)			(1,000)		1,000	
			(1,100)	(20)	1,100	20
Total realizations	5,020	200	(2,370)	(200)	(2,650)	
Total derealizations	(9,200)	(100)	8,100	80	1,100	20
Net	(4,180)	100	5,730	(120)	(1,550)	20
Net change in assets	(4,080)		5,610		(1,530)	
From the income statement:						
Imputed interest					2,205	
Revisions of expectations					1,200	
Net change in specific advantage					1,875	

values of noncash assets and from exit values of non-cash assets to specific advantage. Here again, if unexpected, these events may affect the value only through the revision of expectations, which is separately reported.[11]

The last two items in the statement, the imputed interest and the revision of expectations, are also shown in the Income Statement. Although they are not realization and derealization events, they are added to the specific advantage so that all changes in assets' composition during the accounting are reflected in the statement. Therefore, the statement articulates with the comparative balance sheets presented in Table 1.[12]

3. Discussion

The communication of both expectations (MRD value) and exit values provides information useful to the assessment of risk and affords the means for highlighting the opportunity costs of both the entity and the investors. At any given time, the exit value of the assets represents a universal opportunity cost (i.e., an opportunity cost that is independent of a particular manager's decision alternatives and hence is independently quantifiable). The exit value of the equity represents the opportunity cost to investors holding their securities. By communicating the MRD value, the firm makes possible the comparison of these opportunity costs with the expected benefits, that is, the level of expectations. The opportunity costs of continuing to operate the firm's assets over a period of time are measured as (a) the interest, or the alternative return, that could have been earned on the assets if separated from the firm, and (b) the decline in exit values of the assets over the period. Had the assets been sold initially, the imputed interest on the exit values could have been earned; further, the decline in exit values that occurred would have been avoided. These unavoidable opportunity costs can be compared with the benefits of having operated the firm, which consist of both realization benefits and increments in value. The statement below illustrates these comparisons.

---

[11]The level of desegregation of events reflected in this statement is of course not the only possible level of disaggregation. The events may be shown in more or less detail depending on the informational needs of the users.

[12]Had the firm experienced capital contributions or distributions, these would not have been reflected in any of the statements except the Balance Sheet. These would have to be added to obtain complete articulation with the Balance Sheet.

Statement of Avoidable Opportunity Costs and Unique Benefits	
Avoidable opportunity costs	
Decline in exit values	$1,800
Less: increase in exit values	1,250
Net decline in exit values	550
Add: foregone interest on exit values (net)	1,105
Net avoidable costs of having held the assets and continued as a firm	$1,655
Unique benefits of having operated as a firm	
1. Realization benefits:	
Purchase gain	$ —
Less: purchase loss	120
	(120)
Add: value added (excluding depreciation)	2,200
	$2,080
2. Increments in value:	
a. Time growth	2,205
b. Revision of expectations	1,200
	$3,405

It is also possible to focus on the economic benefits and costs alone without considering risk. Thus, the economic income can be compared with the alternative returns. The economic income would consist of imputed interest on the total net assets (including the firm's specific advantage) plus the revision of expectations. The alternative returns — the benchmark against which economic income is compared —would be the imputed interest on the exit value of net assets.

Statement of Increase in the Value of the Firm and Alternative Returns	
Economic income	
Imputed interest on total net assets (including specific advantage)	$2,205
Revision of expectations	1,200
	$3,405
Alternative returns	
Imputed interest on exit value (net)	$1,105

In the above comparison, the risk change is not included among the benefits or costs. The economic income is merely the increase in the MRD value of the firm. It consists of the interest imputed on the MRD value plus a revision of expectations, totaling $3405. This is contrasted with the alternative return, which is imputed interest computed on the net exit value of the firm's assets and is taken from the cost and benefit statement.

Also, meaningful comparisons can be made with alternatives available to the stockholders, as shown in the next statement.

Avoidable Opportunity Costs for Stockholders

1. Imputed interest on stock	$1,305
2. Decrease in exit value of stocks	0
	$1,305

Specific Benefits of Having Continued to Invest in the Firm — Appropriation of the Increase in the Firm's Value[20]

Economic income	
1. Increase in exit value of stocks	$1,950
2. Increases in specific residual	1,455
	$3,405

This shows the avoidable opportunity cost of the stockholders continuing to be associated with the firm. This cost consists of the market rate of interest computed on the beginning stock value plus the decline in the value of the stock during the period, if any. This is compared with the specific benefits of continuing to invest in the firm. These benefits are the economic income other than change in the MRD value of the firm, which must be reflected as an increase in the exit value of stock and/or an increase of the specific residual.

The specific residual describes the portion of the MRD value that has so far not been captured by the market value of a firm that has so far not been captured by the market value of the security. Therefore, the higher the proportion of the specific residual to the MRD value, the larger the uncertainty of stockholders realizing their cash flows. Hence, other things equal, an increase in the exit value of the stock with an equal decrease in the specific residual represents an increasing acceptance of the firm's expected cash flows and the assessment of the risks associated with them, and a greater degree of reliability can be attached to these forecasts.

The comparison of expected events with past events generates information that improves the ability of investors and managers to assess the reliability of future forecasts, as well as to evaluate past performance (thus fulfilling the stewardship objective) and predict future performance (thus fulfilling the informativeness objective). Comparison between forecasts and actual occurrences for one firm over time will make it possible to judge the reliability of these forecasts. Reporting the differences between forecasts and actual occurrences for all firms makes it possible to judge the comparative forecasting ability of different firms. These comparisons would indicate to investors the extent to which they could rely on different firms' forecasts and would provide managers with valuable feedback for improving their future forecasts. Furthermore, if forecasts and the achievement of forecasts are communicated for all firms, investors would be able to contrast the variability and measure the co-variability of a given firm's flows and expectations with the flows and expectations of other firms. The extent of such variability is an important input into efficient investment strategies.

The information provided by the proposed system would be more nuanced, more multidimensional, and therefore initially more difficult for investors to use. However, one should keep in mind that it is far more difficult for investors to evaluate a company without the richer information set proposed. Furthermore, under this proposal, forecasts (MRD value), exit values, and historical costs are provided separately such that the juxtaposition of the three makes it simpler to evaluate the prospects and the risk of the company.[13] In contrast, current financial statements mix together historical and implicit future values as well as fair values, thus making it difficult to assess the overall reliability of the statements. By decomposing accounting reports into measures of value (return) and measures of risk, users of financial statements can make more informed decisions that accommodate their attitudes to risk. Also, one of the objections to exit values as proposed by FAS 157 is that they are measured in the context of hypothetical markets where selling the assets is an alternative seldom used. This objection is valid if only exit values are to be

---

[13]Making forecasts part of the mandatory accounting systems proffers the advantage that forecasts would be available for all companies so as to facilitate comparability. Moreover, systematic periodic mandatory reporting of forecasts along with actual realizations allows *ex post* monitoring of the forecasts' reliability. Also, note that FAS 157 (ASC 820) sanctions forecasts as implicit in Level 3 fair-value measurements.

communicated. Under the proposed framework, however, although the exit values would reflect a value, it would not be the only value. Moreover, exit values would be communicated not for valuation purposes but also to provide a standard of comparison to facilitate the evaluation of risk and alternative returns. That is, exit values would serve as surrogates for many attributes relevant to information users.

3.1. *Is the proposed system incentive compatible?*

Objections to discounted cash flow values typically center on the necessarily subjective nature and hence lack of reliability of the estimates. Yet, these problems are mitigated by also providing objective data that place the expectations in proper perspective. The proposed framework provides this context by communicating the MRD value of a firm only in conjunction with exit values and historical measures.

Nonetheless, moral hazard and hazards of misrepresentation may compromise the credibility of the expectations that form the MRD value. This is an especially serious problem in the early stages of implementation, when the sequence of forecasts and their realizations is not long enough to allow for reasonable evaluation of management's truthfulness. Corporate governance mechanisms now in place are not sufficient to elicit truthful reporting from managers.[14] And although incentives for truthful reporting can be fine-tuned in a properly designed compensation package, the institutions responsible for creating such packages may not find it in their interest to do so. For example, one possible linear compensation scheme that could elicit truthful reporting would reward managers for higher magnitudes of expected cash flows as reflected in the MRD value of the firm, but penalize them for deviations from the forecasts embedded in the MRD value, as reflected in the unexpected components of the Income Statement and the Changes in Assets Composition Statement. However, boards of directors, acting as surrogates for shareholders, especially shareholders with short horizons, would lack incentives to design and enforce such a compensation scheme: short-horizon shareholders

[14]Witness the accounting scandals during the early years of this decade and the vast literature addressing the failures of corporate governance (Baber *et al.*, 1995; Levitt, 1998; Bratton, 2002; Chaney and Philpich, 2002; Gordon, 2002; Brickey, 2003; Cunningham, 2003, 2004a, 2004b; Coffee, 2004a, 2004b) and cooking the books. These perceived failures ultimately gave birth to the Sarbanes–Oxley Act of 2002.

would be interested in exiting the firm at a profit (selling their stock) and hence would prefer managers to paint a falsely rosy picture of the firm's future prospects rather than tell the truth (Ronen and Yaari, 2002).

The system proposed is principle-based, and similar moral hazard concerns will plague any principle-based accounting model, even when it is restricted to the current framework. Specifically, so long as a principle-based system of accounting requires the reporting of particular items and accords managers and their auditors a significant degree of judgment in meeting those objectives, the flexibility so accorded will be abused, triggering costly litigation. A historical cost system is not free of judgments and estimations, and it would be especially vulnerable to abuse under principle-based or objective-oriented standards. However, a principle-based system can function effectively if the hazard of misrepresentation is eliminated. In other words, once the incentives of managers and auditors are aligned with those of investors, principle-based accounting standards can become effective and indeed superior to the bright-line rules that some claim have produced perverse incentives to structure transactions so as to obfuscate. In Ronen (2008), I describe corporate governance mechanisms that could encourage truth-telling and, as a result, facilitate principle-based accounting such as the system just proposed.

3.2. *Data requirements*

While the proposed financial accounting model may seem onerous and require significant data requirements, I contend that the proliferation of Internet and social media platforms such as Google, Amazon, and Twitter makes increasingly more data available.

Cash flow forecasts have been and continue to be made by firms, since they are required for managerial plans and daily decisions. But these forecasts are communicated only in an *ad hoc* fashion through press releases and presentations before financial analysts and other investors. Such forecasts are essential inputs into users' decision-making, assuming incentives are in place to ensure honesty. With the increasing use of machine learning in combination with big data, managers can make these forecasts with ever-increasing accuracy by utilizing external sources of information to complement their inside information stemming from the fact that they create the plans and budgets internally within the business. Once these forecasts are made, they should be communicated within the framework of systematic accounting reports and thus be made available for systematic validation by comparing them with *ex post* factual events. This would provide a realistic measure that could be used by investors and other interested parties to evaluate subsequent forecasts. While not auditable or verifiable when made, forecasts can be evaluated *ex post* as subsequent events materialize. Moreover, when these forecasts are made, they may be leaked to a subset of market participants; incorporating them systematically into the financial statements would make them available to all interested parties, hence reducing the possibility of unfair gains from insider information. No firm should be required to make forecasts. However, all firms would be required to communicate forecasts if they were made. The MRD value of a firm that did not make forecasts would consist only of exit values, identifying the firm either as a conservative firm or as a conservatively reporting firm; such a firm would pay the price of reporting only the exit values of its assets. If the specific advantage were informative for investors, the market would penalize firms that did not make and report forecasts. Competitive pressures would be created to induce firms that have not either made or reported forecasts to start doing so in order to provide more relevant information. Indirectly, the firms would benefit through the improved decision-making made possible by explicitly considering forecasts. Furthermore, to avoid revealing proprietary information, forecasts can be communicated at various levels of aggregation. In the system described above, forecasts are aggregated into a single MRD value. Detailed forecasts are only reported retrospectively, once the actual events have occurred and when they are separately reported as expected or unexpected. At that point, forecasts are past history. Requiring detailed forecasts to be reported prospectively might be desirable but subject to the cost of benefit of doing so.

Exit values are now already provided for financial assets and liabilities. For the proposed model, if the distinction between expected and unexpected changes in exit values is to be made, exit values as of the accounting period will have to be forecasted. There would also have to be estimates as of the end of the forecast horizon, if that horizon does not coincide with the termination of the firm. This is necessary because terminal values must be provided whenever the forecast horizon ends. As with the forecast of cash flows, these should not be mandatory. However, investor pressure may induce firms to provide such forecasts and thus allow expectations to become a part of the accounting system. As indicated, exit values of financial assets and liabilities are already provided. As to other assets and liabilities, it is likely that an established market will provide satisfactory evidence such as wholesale prices for inventory. Also, with the proliferation of data services, information aggregators, etc., increasingly more information is becoming available to attach exit values for fixed assets, services, and intangibles. Where second-hand markets do not exist, indirect methods may be employed to estimate exit values by relating them to available surrogates. Many intangibles and services have zero exit value. This is not to say that they do not have use value; they simply do not have a separable value.

4. Conclusion

The advances in machine learning technology make possible, more than ever before, the utilization of data from multiple sources to make predictions of value-relevant metrics. Such predictions, however — while reliant on objective data such as searches of products on websites, indications of sentiment (likes or dislikes), observations of how many cars are parked next to retail stores, job postings, willingness to invest in crowd-funded products, etc. — do not include vital information possessed only by corporate insiders (CEOs, CFOs, and others) acquired naturally because of the necessity to make plans, to strategize, and to create budgets. In this essay, I contend that the enhanced ability to predict based on machine learning can be utilized by both insiders (within the firm) and outsiders, in conjunction with an overhauled model of financial reporting, such as to improve significantly the ability to predict cash flows and hence to value firms.

The proposed reporting model provides information separately about risk and return, hence avoiding a combined measure as reflected in the current accounting reports, which does not afford investors the possibility of assessing these measures separately so as to bring to bear their own risk preferences to their decision-making. Moreover, the proposed model provides separate information on facts (past events and transactions), current values (exit values), and future expectations. This separation enables the use of the objective data to assess the reliability of past subjective data (forecasts). By doing so, the ability of management to forecast accurately, and/or their honesty in doing so, can be assessed over time.

While the proposed accounting system may seem complicated, it is interesting to observe that the Financial Accounting Standards Board has been requiring substantial additional disclosures and forecasts to be made, including exit values. With the advances in technology, it should not be too difficult to implement a more comprehensive accounting model such as the one described above.

References

Allee, K. D., B. Baik, and Y. Roh (2019), Detecting financial misreporting with real production activity, *SSRN Electronic Journal*. 10.2139/ssrn.2856472.

Baber, W. R., K. R. Kumar, and T. Verghese (1995), Client security price reactions to the Laventhol and Horwath bankruptcy, *Journal of Accounting Research* **33**(2), 385–395.

Beaver, W. H., M. Correia, and M. F. McNichols (2012), Do differences in financial reporting attributes impair the predictive ability of financial ratios for bankruptcy? *Review of Accounting Studies* **17**(4), 969–1010.

Beaver, W. H., M. F. McNichols, and J. W. Rhie (2005), Have financial statements become less informative? Evidence from the ability of financial ratios to predict bankruptcy, *Review of Accounting Studies* **10**(1), 93–122.

Bratton, W. W. (2002), Enron and the dark side of shareholder value', *Tulane Law Review* **76**(5/6), 1275–1361.

Brickey, K. F. (2003), Andersen's fall from grace, *Washington University Law Quarterly* **81**(4), 917–959.

Chaney, P. K. and P. L. Philpich (2002), Shredded reputation: The cost of audit failure, *Journal of Accounting Research* **40**(4), 1221–1245.

Chaudhry, M. I. and A. G. Sam (2018), Herding behaviour and the declining value relevance of accounting information: Evidence from an emerging stock market, *Applied Economics* **50**(49), 5335–5353.

Chiu, P., S. H. Teoh, Y. Zhang, and X. Huang (2018), Using google searches of firm products to assess revenue quality and detect revenue management. Available at SSRN: https://ssrn.com/abstract=3252314.

Coffee, J. C. (2004a), Gatekeeper failure and reform: The challenge of fashioning relevant reforms', *Boston University Law Review* **84**(2), 301–364.

Coffee, J. C. (2004b), What caused Enron? A capsule social and economic history of the 1990's, *Cornell Law Review* **89**(2), 269–309.

Cox, J. D. (2003), Reforming the culture of financial reporting: The PCAOB and the metrics for accounting measurements, *Washington University Law Quarterly* **81**(2), 301–327.

Cunningham, L. A. (2003), The Sarbanes–Oxley yawn: Heavy rhetoric, light reform (and it might just work), *University of Connecticut Law Review* **36**(3), 1–47.

Cunningham, L. A. (2004a), A model financial statement insurance act, *Connecticut Insurance Law Journal* **11**(1), 69–106.

Cunningham, L. A. (2004b), Choosing gatekeepers: The financial statement insurance alternative to auditor liability, *UCLA Law Review* **52**(2), 413–475.

Dontoh, A., S. Radhakrishnan, and J. Ronen (2004), The declining value relevance of accounting information and non-information-based trading: An empirical analysis, *Contemporary Accounting Research* **21**(4), 795–812.

Financial Accounting Standards Board (FASB) (1978), *Statement of Financial Accounting Concepts No. 1: Objectives of Financial Reporting by Business Enterprises*. Norwalk, CT: FASB.

Financial Accounting Standards Board (FASB) (2006), *Accounting Standards Codification 820 (Financial Accounting Standards 157). Fair Value Measurements*. Norwalk, CT: FASB.

Froot, K., N. Kang, G. Ozik, and R. Sadka (2017), What do measures of real-time corporate sales say about earnings surprises and post-announcement returns? *Journal of Financial Economics* **125**(1), 143–162.

Givoly, D. and D. Palmon (1985), Insider trading and the exploitation of inside information: Some empirical evidence, *Journal of Business* **58**(1), 69–87.

Gordon, J. N. (2002), What Enron means for the management and control of the modern business corporation: Some initial reflections, *University of Chicago Law Review* **69**(3), 1233–1250.

Hales, J., J. Moon, and L. Swenson (2018), A new era of voluntary disclosure? Empirical evidence on how employee postings on social media relate to future corporate disclosures, *Accounting, Organizations and Society* **68–69**, 88–108.

Huang, J. (2018), The customer knows best: the investment value of consumer opinions, *Journal of Financial Economics* **128**(1), 164–182.

Jaffe, F. (1974), Special information and insider trading, *Journal of Business* **47**(3), 410–428.

Kaplan, R. S. and D. Norton (1996), Using the balanced scorecard as a strategic management system, *Harvard Business Review* **74**(1), 75–85.

Lakonishok, J. and I. Lee (2001), Are insider trades informative? *Review of Financial Studies* **14**(1), 79–111.

Landsman, W. and E. Maydew (2002), Has the information content of annual earnings announcements declined in the past three decades? *Journal of Accounting Research* **40**(3), 797–808.

Levitt, A. (1998), *The Numbers Game*. Speech delivered at New York University, Center for Law and Business, September 28.

Lorie, J. and V. Niederhoffer (1968), Predictive and statistical properties of insider trading, *Journal of Law and Economics* **11**(1), 35–53.

Riley, R., T. Pearson, and G. Trompeter (2003), The value relevance of non-financial performance variables and accounting information: The case of the airline industry, *Journal of Accounting and Public Policy* **22**(3), 231–254.

Ronen, J. (1979), The dual role of accounting: A financial economics perspective, in *Handbook of Financial Economics*, J. L. Bicksler (ed.), New York, NY: North-Holland Publishing Company.

Ronen, J. (2008), To fair value or not to fair value: A broader perspective. *ABACUS* **44**(2), 181–208.

Ronen, J. and G. H. Sorter (1972), Relevant accounting, *Journal of Business* **45**(2), 258–282.

Ronen, J. and V. Yaari (2002), Incentives for voluntary disclosure, *Journal of Financial Markets* **5**(3), 349–390.

Rozeff, F. and M. Zaman (1988), Market efficiency and insider trading: New evidence, *Journal of Business* **61**(1), 25–44.

Seyhun, H. N. (1986), Insiders' profits, costs of trading, and market efficiency, *Journal of Financial Economics* **16**(2), 189–212.

Teoh, S. H. (2018), The promise and challenges of new datasets for accounting research, *Accounting, Organizations, and Society* **68–69**, 109–117.

Tin, Katrin. In this Handbook.

Trompeter, G. (1994), The effect of partner compensation schemes and generally accepted accounting principles on auditor judgment, *Auditing: A Journal of Practice and Theory* **13**(2), 56–68.

https://doi.org/10.1142/9789811220470_0021

Chapter 21

Value of Fixed Asset Usage Information for Efficient Operation: A Nontraditional View

Kashi R. Balachandran

Stern School of Business, New York University, USA

kbalacha@stern.nyu.edu

Abstract

Firms build excess capacities in fixed cost resources for two purposes — to accommodate uncertainty and to plan for potential growth. Fluctuating demand and internal processing times result in uncertainty, while lead times in building fixed resources result in excess capacities being built to meet future growth in demand. Dropping a product from the production line also creates unused capacity that needs to be replanned into production or disposed. An example is presented in this chapter for a classic keep or drop a product situation where product line shows negative income. The usual advice is to look at only the variable costs related to the product and see the contribution to common costs. The fixed costs, in this approach, are termed irrelevant information. However, this chapter argues that the fixed costs that stay with the company are the really relevant costs and shows that dropping the product decision can be made considering the fixed costs only and ignoring the variable costs as irrelevant.

Keywords: Drop a product decision; Unused capacity; Fixed cost; Relevance.

1. Introduction

Information to aid decision-making, particularly, in businesses is expected to be given by accounting reports through the financial statements whose forms are regulated. Customarily, however, businesses depend on other routes to obtain further information that, though not regulated, can be trusted to be truthful, relevant, and reliable. Numerous academic studies are conducted to determine the relevance of such information to outcomes such as stock prices, sales levels, and fluctuations in these. With the increasing capacity of computers, the source for such additional information has multiplied. Yet, the importance of financial statements put out by companies cannot be undermined in its value to decision-makers. The management, however, rely on using the inside information on all aspects of the business to make efficient decisions. With the added information, available publicly and provided through the use of big data and blockchain, the efficiency of all decisions pertaining to the operation of the firms is expected to increase. The increase in efficiency of decisions can be obtained only if the enormous amount of information is processed and distilled to be useful to make the decision. Data overload can be counterproductive as it will likely change the necessary focus. At the same time using the wrong data to make a decision may lead to bad decisions or even if correct, to delaying the delivery.

This chapter will deal with the fixed asset cost data along with unused capacities in various assets in their root measurements such as square feet, gallons, pounds, man-hours, etc., along with their costs in a chosen currency. It is traditional in management accounting to ignore costs spent on fixed assets for making anything but basic product cost determination, terming them "sunk costs" and thus irrelevant to making decisions to be made at hand. We show this, apparently sunk cost notion is erroneous. Let us illustrate the importance of unused fixed cost assets with a popular example.

2. Keep or Drop a Product Decision

Suppose a manager is faced with a dilemma whether to continue producing a specific product C or discontinue it. The issue comes up if the product line income statement for C works out a negative income before taxes. This statement is prepared in the conventional format as per the generally accepted accounting principles.

So, the statement goes:

Net operating income for product C = sales-cost of goods sold expense – selling and administrative expense.

Both the expense items have variable and fixed cost components. The fixed costs are typically allocated to all the products, say A, B, and C. The traditional approach to help the decision-maker is to separate out the variable and fixed cost components and redo the income statement for product C as follows:

Sales

— Variable production costs for C
— Variable selling and administrative costs for C
= contribution margin by product C
— Fixed manufacturing and selling costs that can be reduced or avoided if the product C is not made
= segment margin for product C
— Allocated common costs to product C
= Product operating income of C

One is supposed to look at segment margin, ignoring all the fixed costs, and if it is negative to discontinue the product.

The problem with this approach is several.

It is difficult to differentiate variable and fixed costs in cost of goods sold and selling and administrative costs.

There are a large number of variable expenses' categories for any firm to be assigned to the products.

It is quite cumbersome, time consuming, and error prone to assign each indirect variable expense to every product using suitable cost drivers, whether they are under study for drop or not.

Elaborately, ascertain each fixed cost to determine whether it is direct and avoidable if the product is dropped.

It may necessitate to undertake creating the income statement in a totally variable costing format that may be time and cost consuming. Essentially, an Activity-Based Costing approach needs to be installed.

The issue is why should one undertake a study of each variable cost, the specific suitable cost driver, and assign to all products though the other products are not under scrutiny for being dropped. The traditional view of calling all indirect or unavoidable fixed costs as irrelevant costs and ignoring them is at the root of this inefficient manner of decision-making that may also lead to errors. After all, the so-called irrelevant costs do stay with the company if the product is dropped. Should one not worry about what stays with the company and ignore the variable costs and avoidable costs that do not stay with the company if the product is discontinued?

What is useful is to know the fixed cost capacities that remain with the company if the product is dropped. That is, the incremental unused capacities created by dropping the product. The manager has to contend with how to utilize the newly created unused asset capacities.

3. An Illustrative Example

The concept is best illustrated with a simple example.

A company manufactures and sells three products A, B, and C. Product C gives a negative operating income figure and the question facing the manager is whether to continue making this product C. The statement, as per generally accepted accounting principles and then reconstructed in a variable format is given below.

Product	A	B	C	Total
Sales revenue	3600	3200	420	7220
Less: variable costs	2700	2000	280	4980
Contribution margin	900	1200	140	2240
Less: direct fixed costs	300	600	160	1060
Segment margin	600	600	(20)	1180
Less: common allocated costs	340	300	40	680
Operating income	260	300	(60)	500

Suppose there are some direct fixed expenses that cannot be avoided (for example, machinery depreciation costs where the machines cannot be gotten rid of or increased idle time in machines or factory supervisory):

For A: $60; for B: $240; for C: $50.

Then rewrite the statement as follows:

Product	A	B	C	Total
Sales revenue	3600	3200	420	7220
Less: variable costs	2700	2000	280	4980
Contribution margin	900	1200	140	2240
Less: avoidable direct fixed costs	240	360	110	710
Contribution to common and unavoidable costs	660	840	30	1530
Unavoidable or sticky direct fixed costs	60	240	50	350
Less: common costs	340	300	40	680
Operating income	260	300	(60)	500

The solution will be to not drop product C.

The reasons are: Product C contributes $30 toward common and unavoidable costs and dropping it will reduce operating income by $30.

Going through starting with sales revenue and subtracting variable costs is not only time consuming and costly processwise but we lose important information on unused fixed capacity costs.

So, let us look at going backward from the bottom line of product C net income of negative (60).

3.1. *Fixed unused capacity cost analysis approach*

The main features of this approach are the following:

- Study only product C under consideration for dropping.
- Do not need to analyze how all variable costs are allocated — they are too many
- Study common fixed costs allocated to Product C and add them back to operating income of Product C. If some common fixed cost resources can be reduced or diverted to another product line, take the net value to add. This is simple procedurally and error free.
- Add back direct fixed unavoidable costs that are sticky and stay with the firm even if the product is dropped. This is done by going through the actual production process with the help of the supervisor.
- If the number is positive, do not drop.
- Study only product C under consideration for dropping.

Traditional variable costing approach maintains that fixed costs that are unavoidable are sunk and should not be considered as relevant for incremental decision-making.

However, they are important because they will still remain even after dropping the product.

This solution procedure is less error prone and much quicker. It is much easier to identify the common allocated costs and go to a list of direct fixed costs in both manufacturing and selling functions to identify those that will still stay as unused if the product is dropped. It will also identify the extent of unused capacity created in fixed cost resources.

The irrelevant information is as follows:

- Data on products that are not under consideration of discontinuation are not considered. So, no need to consider assignment of any of the variable costs.
- Revenue and costs of the selected product that will vanish with dropping the product need not be considered.

The relevant costs are sticky costs that are allocated to the product C that will remain even if product C is dropped. That is, only the fixed cost resources.

To summarize, what are considered relevant in traditional analysis are irrelevant costs. What are considered as irrelevant and sunk costs in traditional analysis are, indeed, the relevant costs.

To fine-tune this analysis, one should look at the newly created unused capacities if the product is dropped to see whether they can be used fruitfully in other activities.

Further planning may be needed to utilize such unused capacities. It is necessary to identify these unused capacities not as just costs but in their original root dimensions as gallons, pounds, board feet, etc.

Suppose, the Contribution to common and unavoidable costs for product C is 100 (instead of 30 as in the table), then the operating income for product C will be positive 10. It will still be worthwhile to look at this product with a low return to analyze whether the freed unused capacities can be utilized elsewhere by dropping product C. If they can be utilized to realize an increase in return of more than 10, the decision will be to drop the product. This observation can be useful in make or buy decision situations.

The main point is take cognizance of the importance of fixed asset capacities that are unused in improving the profit of the firm.

Let us see the broader picture of the recordkeeping for unused capacities.

4. Unused Capacity Account Keeping

Unused capacities are created for many reasons. It is good to systematically keep track of them in a report to have them useful for decision-making.

4.1. *Categories of utilizations that lead to unused capacities of fixed cost assets*

Key issues in cost management are as follows:

To determine the costs of unused capacity in various categories; to ascertain the responsible party for the existence of unused capacity; and to plan for the reduction of unused capacity to maintain market competitiveness.

Practical or normal capacity is considered in many textbooks on management accounting to determine an application rate to products. The unit cost determined this way may be too large if the resource capacity is planned for long-term growth. Also, this approach has built in allowance for inefficiency. We suggest an alternate capacity for allocating the fixed cost to products.

The total unused capacity costs of each asset can be divided into two main components:

- Planned unused capacity = Maximum capacity – budgeted capacity
- Unplanned unused capacity = budgeted capacity – actual capacity used

The following discussion relies heavily on Balachandran, Li, and Radhakrishnan (2007). The planned unused capacity can be subdivided into several categories to increase the focus on them for reduction.

We classify resource capacity into five categories: theoretical capacity, maximum capacity, efficient capacity, bottleneck (practical/normal) capacity, and budgeted capacity. We add a sixth category for the actual capacity utilized.

- **Theoretical capacity:** Theoretical capacity is the theoretical maximum output that is possible if the resource is utilized to its fullest possible extent. With time as the common measurement unit, for equipment, this implies 24 hours a day for 365 days a year, while for employees it would be 8 hours a day for 365 days a year. Similarly, for other unit measurements.
- **Maximum capacity:** Maximum capacity is maximum output that is possible with the current technology and environment. In essence, this allows for normal maintenance and breaks. For instance, in an 8-hour day, employees might be able to work effectively for only 6 hours, because of fatigue factors; an equipment might need to undergo regular maintenance, etc. Essentially, the difference between the theoretical and maximum capacity provides a measure of a potential increase in output with innovation in business processes and/or technology. However, it is essential to note that with the present technology the theoretical capacity is a mere "unattainable" benchmark. Maximum capacity can be viewed as the best utilization by the most efficient firm that experiences no or minimal uncertainty.
- **Efficient capacity:** Efficient capacity is the optimal utilization of capacity allowing for randomness in demand and production process. Uncertainties in demand and process times in production preclude utilization of capacity to its fullest possible extent. Efficient capacity is thus the maximum expected capacity utilization that can be attained given the current uncertainties in demand and production/service technologies. The difference between maximum capacity and efficient capacity is entirely due to random factors and provides a measure of a potential increase in output by reducing randomness in demand by adopting innovative scheduling strategies, etc., and reducing randomness in processing times by reducing uncertain breakdowns in process, lower quality parts entering the process, etc.

To see the intuition behind this excess capacity notion, consider a service setting. The distinguishing feature in a service setting is that demands cannot be inventoried or backlogged. Hence, wait appears to arise because demand is greater than the capacity of service resource. Simply, making the service capacity equal to demand capacity will not solve the utilization problem. There is no guarantee of zero or no unused capacity even if demand is lesser than process times. Consider a scenario in which a checkout clerk can service one customer every 5 minutes, and there are two checkout clerks (the capacity) who can serve two customers in 5 minutes. Suppose, there can be zero, one, two, three, or four customers who can potentially demand service in each 5-minute block with equal probability. Thus, on average there are two customers in each 5-minute block. There will be 5-minute blocks when only one customer demands service, at least 20% of the time (in the long run); 20% of the time no one will demand; at that time one or both the checkout clerks will be idle — and this idle time cannot be utilized later. On the contrary, 40% of the time there will be three or four customers demanding to check out, which will make the customers wait. If this continues, the waits will become infinitely longer. This is because in equilibrium the number of customers coming to check out (the input flow) is set equal to the number of customers leaving the checkout counter (the output flow). Because of periods of idle capacity, the capacity needs to be larger than the expected demand to keep the balance of input and output flows. This creates a demand for excess capacity that arises due to uncertainty of demand. The uncertainty in production (service) time works in a similar fashion. Thus, efficient capacity is strictly lesser than the maximum capacity.

- **Bottleneck capacity:** Bottleneck capacity is the efficient capacity that can be employed in the short run, due to imbalance across resources. This is directly related to the concept of practical/normal capacity that is discussed in management accounting textbooks. In general, this is the capacity that would normally get utilized in the present environment, given the technology and uncertainty. The difference between this and the efficient capacity provides a measure of the potential future growth that the management expects, and should, in general, be planned. Note that for at least one of the resources the difference between the efficient and bottleneck capacities will be zero. If the difference between efficient and bottleneck capacities is not zero, then the management can take actions to sublet/lease or look for alternative output markets to utilize the capacity.
- **Budgeted capacity:** Budgeted capacity reflects the short-term plan and the difference between bottleneck and budgeted capacity. It reflects the management's expectation of future growth potential, perhaps through continuous improvement.
- **Actual capacity:** The actual capacity utilization shows the extent of under utilization below the budget that may be due to inefficiencies. These have the importance of signifying inefficiencies in the process

that may need corrective action. The actual capacity utilization may exceed the budgeted capacity. However, it cannot exceed the maximum capacity.

The overall unused capacity is the difference between the maximum utilization capacity and the actual capacity utilized. The six capacity definitions enable desegregation of unused capacity cost into various categories that provide relevant information for appropriate managers. Given the above capacity definitions, several unused capacity costs or effects can be derived. The rate per unit is computed as the fixed cost of the asset divided by the maximum capacity for each asset. The usual practice of dividing by normal or practical capacity is not useful.

Definitions of unused capacities are as follows:

(a) The Uncertainty Effect is the rate per unit times the difference between maximum and efficient capacities.
(b) The Bottleneck Effect (or lumpiness effect) is the rate per unit times the difference between efficient and bottleneck capacities.
(c) The Practical Effect is the rate per unit times the difference between bottleneck and practical capacities (provided they differ).
(d) The Budget Effect (or stickiness effect) is the rate per unit times the difference between practical and budget capacities.
(e) The Adjustment Cost Effect is the total of the Bottleneck Effect, Practical Effect, and the Budget Effect.
(f) The Planned Unused Capacity is the total of the Uncertainty Effect and the Adjustment Cost Effect.
(g) Unplanned Unused Capacity is the rate per unit times the difference between budget and the actual utilization capacities.
(h) Total Unused Capacity is the sum of Planned and Unplanned Unused Capacities.

Assigning a cost to these unused capacities can help to highlight their relative importance.

Any make or buy a product or expansion of product lines should take into consideration all the unused capacities for the assets. Strategic decisions can be made as to which fixed assets to invest for expansion. Ignoring fixed cost assets as sunk in all these determinations will be erroneous.

With increased capacity of data gathering through big data or blockchain, major efforts need to be undertaken to develop analytics and algorithms to effectively aggregate the data to enable its usage in decisions. Providing the big data in its raw form is useless. Blockchain has tremendous potential because of its positive characteristics. The advantages should be reined in with intelligent modeling and analytics.

Bibliography

Balachandran, K. R., S.-H. Li, and S. Radhakrishnan (2007), A framework for unused capacity: Theory and empirical analysis, *Journal of Applied Management Accounting Research* **5**(1), 21–38.

Balachandran, K. R. and B. N. Srinidhi (1987), A rationale for fixed charge application, *Journal of Accounting, Auditing and Finance*, spring 1987.

Balakrishnan, R. and G. B. Sprinkle (2002), Integrating profit variance analysis and capacity costing to provide better managerial information, *Issues in Accounting Education* **17**(2), 149–162.

Balakrishnan, R., K. Sivaramakrishnan, and S. Sunder (2001), Is the Opportunity Cost of Idle Capacity Zero? Coase (1938) versus managerial accounting circa 2000, Working Paper, Yale University, CN.

Berman, D. K. (2002), Global crossing seeks to sell unused capacity, *Wall Street Journal* May 22.

Brierley, J. A., C. J. Cowton, and C. Drury (2006), Reasons for adopting different capacity levels in the denominator of overhead rates: A research note, *Journal of Applied Management Accounting Research* **4**(2), 53–62.

Cooper, R. and R. S. Kaplan (1992), Activity-based systems: Measuring the cost of resource usage, *Accounting Horizons* **6** (September), 1–13.

Ng, I. C. L., J. Wirtz, and K. S. Lee (1999), The strategic role of unused capacity, *International Journal of Service Industry Management*, Bradford, **10**(2), 211–235.

Radhakrishnan, S. and K. R. Balachandran (1995), Delay costs and incentive schemes for multiple users, *Management Science* **41**(4), 646–652.

Radhakrishnan, S. and K. R. Balachandran (2004), Service capacity decisions and incentive compatible cost allocation for reporting usage forecasts, *European Journal of Operational Research* **157**, 180–195.

https://doi.org/10.1142/9789811220470_0022

Chapter 22

Role of Blockchain, AI and Big Data in Healthcare Industry

Prashant Sharma[*,§], Shikha Mehra[†,¶] and Pankaj Gupta[‡,||]

[*]*Associate Professor, IIHMR University Jaipur (India)*

[†]*Co-founder, MainChain Research and Consulting New Delhi (India)*

[‡]*President, IIHMR University Jaipur (India)*

[§]*prashantsharma1989@gmail.com*

[¶]*shikhamehraster@gmail.com*

[||]*prof.pankaj@gmail.com*

Abstract

This chapter focuses on the role that Blockchain in combination with AI/Big Data can play in addressing the healthcare industry's severest pain points. The aim is to develop thought leadership on this subject to enable governments, corporates, and developers gain insight and start building out the future. The study found that blockchain in electronic healthcare can avoid adding another layer of organization between the patient and the records and addresses the four major issues such as fragmented slow access to medical data; system interoperability; patient agency; and improved data quality and quantity for medical research.

Keywords: Blockchain; Bigdata; National Health Mission; Healthcare industry; Healthcare analytics.

1. Introduction

Healthcare industry is a trillion-dollar industry with stakeholders such as doctors, hospitals, medical equipment vendors, clinical trial researchers, pharmaceutical providers, insurers, governments, and most importantly patients/common people.

We have come a long way from the times where getting treatment for diseases was impossible to being on the verge of finding cures for cancer, HIV, etc. Yet, a quick look through facts and figures of global healthcare shows that less than 35% of the people have access to proper healthcare facilities. Four major conditions — cancer, heart disease, stroke, and respiratory conditions — were responsible for majority of deaths with obesity, hypertension, sedentary behaviors, tobacco use, and poor nutrition being the major drivers. These are behaviors that can only be changed through proactive involvement of the patient. But unfortunately, patients have taken a very passive position in their own health due to payer and provider dominance and siloed clinical behavioral data. Of course, each country has its own take on how the ecosystem is maintained with a single payer government-backed healthcare system in Australia, the UK, and Canada while the Public–Private Partnership model is taken up in most of the developing countries. Even though healthy people are a prerequisite and proportional to the economic development of a country, no country spends more than 5–8% of their GDP on healthcare.[1]

2. Contemporary Concerns of Healthcare Industry

Some of the concerns about the current healthcare ecosystem infrastructure are listed as follows:

(a) The Electronic Healthcare (EHR) systems being used by healthcare organizations such as hospitals, community clinics, general practitioners, specialists, diagnostic clinics, etc. to keep track of patients are not interoperable. Each hospital has its own format of maintaining the

[1] Lancet, Global Burden of Disease 2015.

patient records, thereby forcing the patients to go through the same series of examinations again if they want to move out of the silos thus making it next to impossible to have aggregated records.

(b) The credibility of the drugs available at the stores has been a concern for decades now with studies showing that more than 25% of the drugs available are counterfeit.[2]

(c) The equipment being used at hospitals cannot be verified for authenticity.

(d) There is a heavy reliance on humans manually attempting to reconcile medical data among these clinics, hospitals, labs, etc.

(e) The certificates of the doctors have been brought into question with more than half of them being proclaimed to be fake.

(f) The medical claim process is tedious as well as opaque and health insurance coverage is a pain due to the private players' cherry picking the premium levels and how it can be claimed.

(g) The patient healthcare records, which are sold at approximately $50 on the dark web,[2] are kept in silos by hospital chains and doctors with the patient being least aware of what his/her records are being used for.

(h) Even with all the advancements, approximately 5–6% of patients are misdiagnosed due to lack of proper medical history.[3]

(i) The system in place to track the success of several initiatives being undertaken by the government is not credible enough due to multiple levels of manual interventions at various levels.

3. Activities Undertaken

It is not that no one is aware of these pain points or that initiatives have not been taken up to improve the system. Artificial intelligence in fitness wearables have been a major breakthrough for patients to keep track of their vitals. But, since this data collected are not used as a part of patient medical history, it defeats the purpose of complete implementation of artificial intelligence. We don't have deep data, which should include clinical and contextual information. Medical imaging is another perfect example. We are still burning images onto CDs and DVDs to transfer them by hand.

---

[2] https://www.ncbi.nlm.nih.gov/pmc/articles/PMC4355878/.

[3] https://www.washingtonpost.com/national/health-science/20-percent-of-patients-with-serious-conditions-are-first-misdiagnosed-study-says/2017/04/03/e386982a-189f-11e7-9887-1a5314b56a08_story.html.

Medicare has released a number of chronic care management codes in recent years that have shown that payers, when they incentivize providers to charge the right fee for services, and encourage proper services for managing patients between office visits, see improved population health and lower medical costs. The one person that we are missing was incentivizing the patient to seek only proper care. Such patient incentives are seen in self-insured corporations. And that is one important piece that we have to tie together in order to really align the whole system. And this is what blockchain and digital assets can enable.

There have been attempts to implement blockchain in the healthcare ecosystem in multiple silo structures by the insurers, hospitals, and end users. The major issues observed with all these attempts have been:

(a) Attempt to tokenize the projects without actual use of physical tokens.
(b) The on-chain–off-chain data storage conundrum.
(c) Scalability issues.
(d) Specific blockchain-dependent solutions.
(e) Not enough incentivization for all the stakeholders in the ecosystem envisioned.

4. Current State of Deployment of Blockchain Technology

From the multiple interactions with leaders in the healthcare and blockchain fields, we were able to compile a list of use cases that have been undertaken or are being considered:

(a) Medical Record Management: Giving patients the control of their healthcare records.
(b) Clinical Trials: For a new drug to be approved, it takes between 10 and 20 years which can be shortened by implementing the record keeping on the blockchain and making the data readily available to the concerned stakeholders.
(c) Mediclaim & Health Insurance: The time to get reimbursed for mediclaim ranges between 45 and 60 days with most of the time being wasted in interdepartmental work and accounting for lack of documents.

(d) Emergency Support: Wearables on the patient, which have medical history records attached to them, will be helpful for the correct diagnosis.
(e) Drug Anti-counterfeiting: IoT and blockchain-based solution will be helpful.
(f) Inventory Management.
(g) Wellness Management.
(h) Hospital Administration.
(i) Doctor ID Management: Certificate and license verification.
(j) Provenance tracking of healthcare initiatives.

5. Synergies Between Blockchain, Big Data and AI

Healthcare needs better audit trails, secure private data sharing, improved algorithm development to focus on relevant data, and patient-friendly incentive systems that correlate to financial incentives based on performance. To accomplish this, we need to combine blockchain-based tools with other advancements in cryptography, analytics, and governance.

6. Big Data in Healthcare

In the healthcare industry, large volume of data is being generated and collected in various fields such as personal medical records, radiology images, clinical trial data, data genomic sequences, 3D imaging, genomics and biometric sensor readings, and others. To present this voluminous data in a decision-enabling format, it is important for the industry to make optimum use of the big data techniques. The application of efficient algorithms using big data is highly relevant in the healthcare as it enables the industry to make data-driven decision-making to minimize the costs and risks, support clinical decisions and precision in choice of medicines, faster drug discovery, and provides relevant and timely information for the effective management of chronic diseases. In 2016, the global big data market in healthcare industry was valued at $11.45 billion and is expected to be $68.75 billion by 2025 (BIS Research, 2018). There are three segments of big data in healthcare such as hardware, software, and analytics services. Out of the three, the analytics services are expected to grow at higher compound annual growth rate (CAGR) of 22.25% till 2025 (BIS Research, 2020) (see Figure 1).

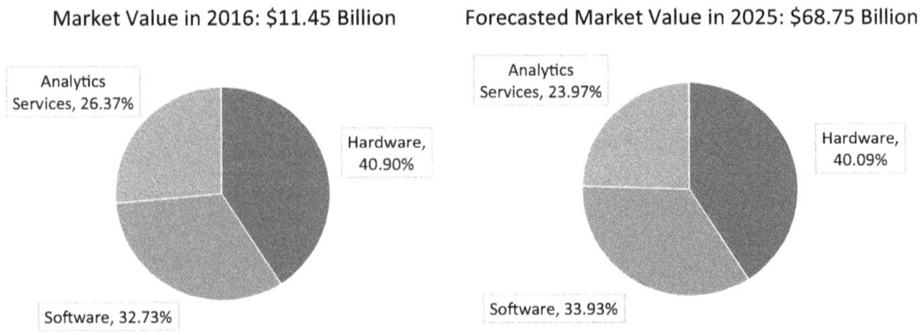

Figure 1: Market value of different segments of big data in healthcare.
Source: BIS Research, 2020.

From the geographical point of view, the penetration of big data in health care is highest in North America with revenue generation of $6.44 billion in 2016 reaching a target of $31.12 billion by 2025. US took the lead to create favorable technological and regulatory environment and encouraged the healthcare industry for early adoption of advanced health IT infrastructure and big data in the region. The hospitals and health organizations were encouraged to invest significantly not only in the clinical processes but also in the big data analytics market. The emergence of cloud-based services and subscription models has further reduced the up-front investment and infrastructure development required for managing big data and could be a key driver for the market. It is expected that increasing number of players could migrate towards cloud analytics (see Figures 2 and 3).

6.1. *Application of big data in healthcare organizations and hospitals*

The application of big data is varied in the market as follows (see Figure 4) (BIS Research, 2020):

(1) Financial analytics helps healthcare organizations to understand the cost and the profitability of the healthcare services provided. The key providers of financial analytics solutions are Cerner Corporation, GE Healthcare, McKesson Corporation, Optum Health, and Xerox. Financial analytics was the largest application segment in 2016 with the revenue generation of $1.65 billion in 2016 and is expected to

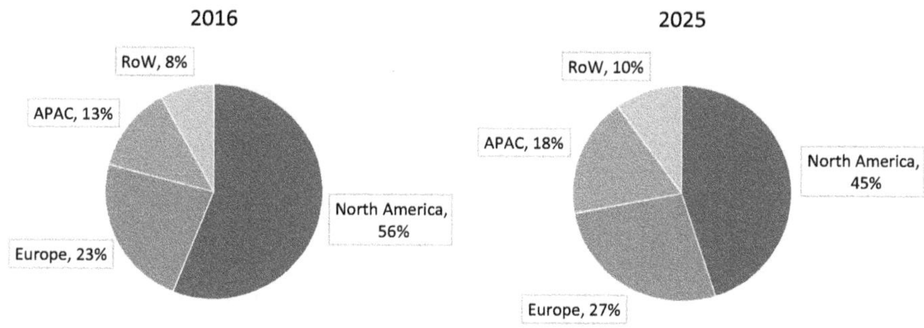

Figure 2: Market value of big data in healthcare across geographic regions.
Source: BIS Research, 2020.

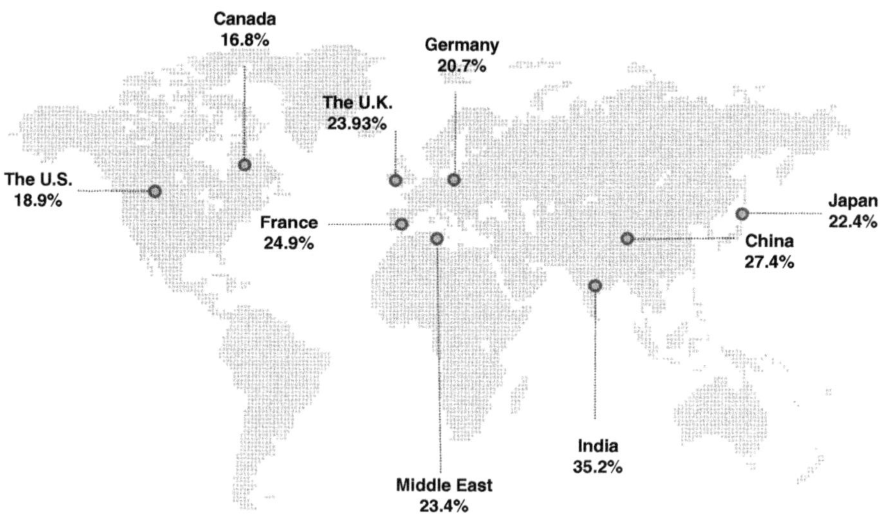

Figure 3: Geographical distribution of big data market.
Source: BIS Research, 2018.

grow at the CAGR of 20.7% from 2016 to 2025. Financial analytics applications such as revenue cycle management, insurance claims handling, and fraud detection were the first to be adopted by most healthcare providers.

(2) Clinical data analytics extracts data from EHRs and health information exchange to analyze patient populations and proactively provide

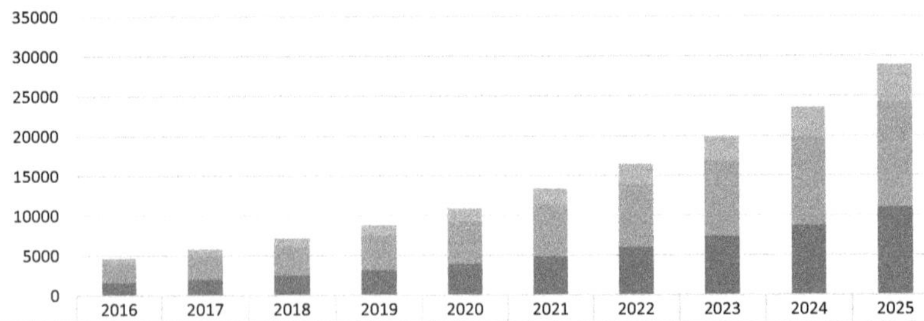

	2016	2017	2018	2019	2020	2021	2022	2023	2024	2025
Operational Analytics	645.8	815.5	1027.1	1289.2	1622.9	2013.1	2493.4	3064.3	3656.0	4688.8
Financial Analytics	2384.3	2923	3571	4354.5	5328.7	6469.9	7862.1	9462.6	11116.7	13273.4
Clinical Analytics	1652	2061.3	2564.5	3184.5	3970.1	4896.4	6037.2	7381.2	8788.4	10976.2

Figure 4: Global big data in healthcare market by application.

Source: BIS Research, 2020.

quality of care to them. Clinical analytics helps to ameliorate patient outcomes and minimize avoidable readmissions in hospitals. The continued "digitization" of healthcare provides the data toolsets needed to direct care to the right setting. Clinical analytics should be a priority investment for many companies and will thus witness the highest CAGR of 23.77% from 2017 to 2025, to reach the value of $11.35 billion by 2025. Clinical intelligence is being used to improve patient outcomes, reduce readmissions, and for population health and disease management.

(3) Operational analytics focuses on the improvement of the existing operations in the organizations. Some of the key players providing analytics solutions are Cerner Corporation, GE Healthcare, McKesson Corporation, IBM Corporation, Xerox, and Kronos. The operational analytics market is expected to grow from $645.8 million to $4.69 billion in 2025, due to the growing deployment of analytics to smoothen administrative processes and improve workforce management in hospitals and organizations.

6.2. *Application of big data in healthcare analytics*

Healthcare analytics targets to enhance patient outcomes by assisting healthcare practitioners with the use of medical knowledge that has been memorized and analyzed by computer-enabled robotic systems, and that results in an effective medical solution. These systems provide researchers and physicians with real-time, clinically relevant, and quality information sourced from EHR.

Analytics in healthcare can help identify patterns among people who suffer from similar illnesses. For instance, the medical history of a 45-year-old man, 5" 7' tall, weighing 80 kgs, who leads a sedentary lifestyle and consumes 120 ml of alcohol daily will give insights into others like him who lead similar lifestyles. When data about lakhs of such people are collated, it grants insights into what kinds of illnesses they are susceptible to, what medication they are likely to respond to/or are responding to, and how lifestyle and treatment behavior are impacting their health progress.

6.2.1. *Types of healthcare analytics* (*Brinkmann, 2019*)

(1) Descriptive analytics: Differing healthcare decisions and their implications on various services such as hospital service performance, clinical outcomes of patients, and results are studied using descriptive analytics The results obtained by using descriptive analytics like data related to hospital occupancy rates, patient discharges, and the average length of stay of patients are represented in the form of simple graphs and tables. Descriptive analytics mainly uses a lot of data visualization to answer specific questions or identify patterns of care, which in turn provides a broader view for evidence-based clinical practice.
(2) Predictive analytics: It is more complex in nature than simple descriptive analytics as it focuses on the use of information rather than simple data. It is used to examine existing past readings and indicators to predict future performance. Predictive analytics is used by medical practitioners to suggest actions and provide insights in a predictive manner.
(3) Prescriptive analytics: Prescriptive analytics offers suggestions on possible treatments based on diagnosis. Prescriptive analytics does not only predict what is likely to happen, but actively suggests how organizations can take appropriate actions to avoid or mitigate any negative circumstances. It requires a seamless and completely integrated data analytics infrastructure.

6.2.2. *Why health care data security is important?*

For example, the U.S. Health Insurance and Portability Act always asks for additional security levels on military grade, because patient records are sensitive data and prone to be used by terrorists (TRG Datacenters, 2019). The stakes are high because the government has punitive sanctions if cyber defenses fail. Various governments globally have following concerns with respect to privacy:

(1) Operator is required to perform a risk assessment and conduct a security check and report if any problems arise.
(2) Healthcare provider must implement physical, appropriate administrative and technical safeguards.
(3) The availability of protected health information with integrity and confidentiality must be secured and should not be shared with outside parties.
(4) The *Health Insurance Portability And Accountability Act* (HIPAA) Journal reports that the Department of Health and Human Services' Office for Civil Rights has taken an effort to increase security due to rise of threats in the US. A continuous audit is done for all offices to maintain security and compliance.

6.3. *Trends of adoption of big data in India and other countries*

(A) Adoption of Telehealth Solutions: Telehealth Solutions or Telemedicine involves the provision of care to patients when the patient and healthcare provider are in different places. On a visit basis, telemedicine is materially cheaper than a visit to a face-to-face primary care unit, walk-in urgent-care center, or emergency department. For example, Content Management Report (CMS) 2020 report it is estimated that US healthcare spending reached $3.81 trillion in 2019 and would increase to $4.01 trillion in 2020. CMS projected that by 2028, healthcare spending would reach $6.19 trillion, and would account for 19.7% of GDP, up from 17.7% in 2018 (see Figures 5 and 6).

(B) With the **growing prevalence of chronic diseases** such as diabetes and blood pressure, kidney disorders, etc., the global market for IT healthcare is likely to increase. On the other hand, acceptance among the medical professionals and falling cost deployment is supportive

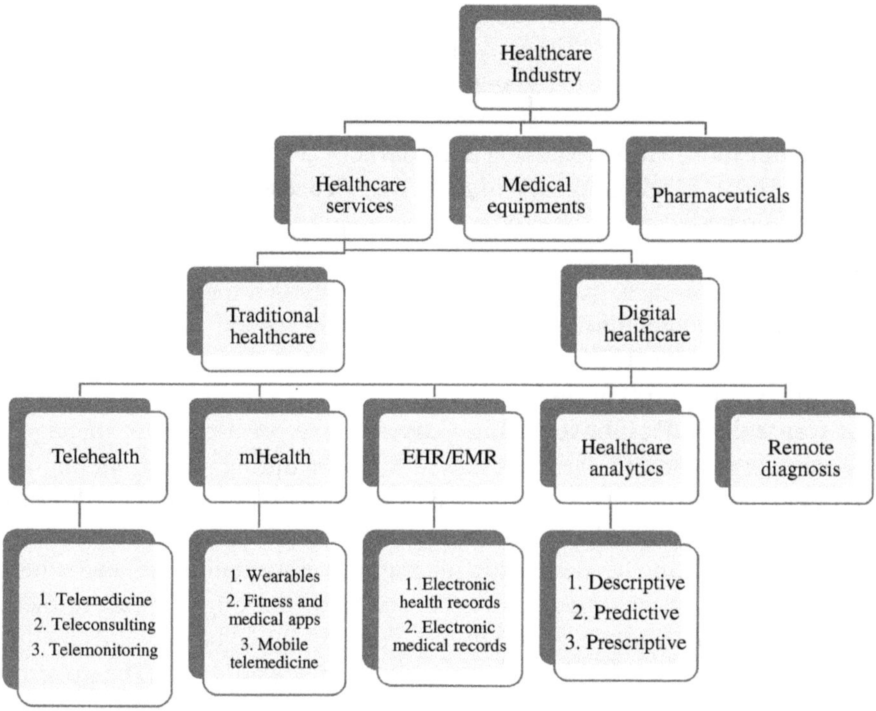

Figure 5: Healthcare industry in India.

Source: Netscribes, 2020.

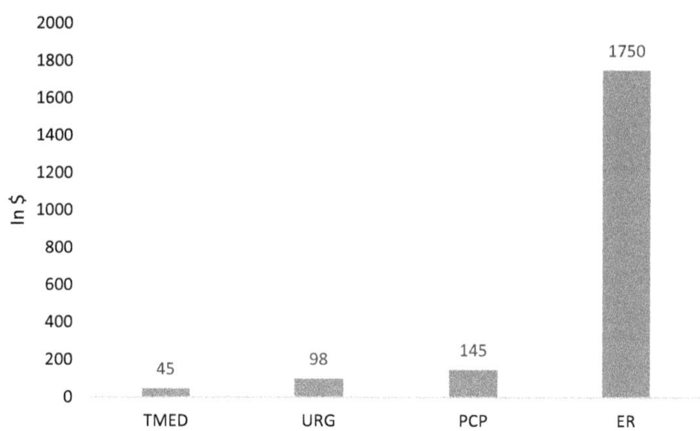

Figure 6: Average cost of doctor visit by location (2018).

Source: Berenberg Corporate report, 2018.

for overall market in the coming years. The strong demand for healthcare IT solutions is driven by the growing need to reduce healthcare costs while adhering to the regulatory requirements set by government organizations for ensuring safety, security, and confidentiality of patient information (Markets and Markets, 2020a, b).

(C) **Artificial Intelligence Bridging the Processing Gap:** The most significant barrier to healthcare innovation in the past was awareness, and the pandemic has all but eliminated that barrier. Now that many patients have used the platform, it is unlikely that they will go back to exclusively encountering doctors through in-person visits. McKinsey says data-crunching algorithms could slash medical and pharmaceutical costs by $100 billion annually.

(D) **Centralized Database on the Cards:** In the private sector, managed care organizations have increased support during the pandemic as well. The latest trend in patient care centers is electronic health records in 2020 which contain all medical information of patients. This will help the doctors to access the information as and when required for a better diagnosis. They will have a single access to their records. For example, recent introduction of digital health cards by the Prime Minister Modi in India is such a step towards this. The governments and R&D organizations can also access that information to identify the disease and illness trends.

These digital health cards are also called electrical medical records technology globally that will rely on more automation using AI and deep learning. And with supporting informatics tools, its decision support systems will allow clinicians to access their patient's information and help them make better decisions. Figure 7 is market size information of such electrical health records (EHR).

6.4. *Application of big data in epidemic/pandemic management*

Data and analytics are critical to enabling the transition to value-based care, which requires robust data collection, documentation, benchmarking, patient risk stratification, care gap identification, and quality and safety reporting, among other capabilities. Moreover, the pandemic has highlighted the need for robust data and analytics capabilities to support

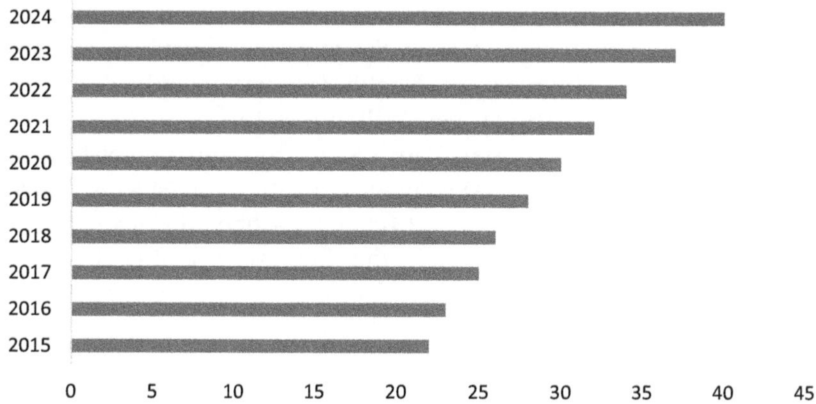

Figure 7: Market size of EHR 2014–2024 (in $ billion).
Source: chinadaily.com.

key operational areas such as patient safety, capacity planning, staff and resource management, and supply chain management — all of which are critically important to hospital operations during the pandemic. For example, the Healthcare Prognosis, 2020 report by Venrock found that 39% of providers indicated they either already have or are very/somewhat likely to incorporate predictive analytics (which requires robust data aggregation tools) or AI into their operations (HealthITSecurity, 2019). In addition, younger generations of providers seem to be more receptive to analytics utilization, suggesting a long tail of demand over time. More specifically, 50% of providers with 15 years of experience or less responded that they are very/somewhat likely to incorporate predictive analytics or AI, compared with 35% of those with more than 15 years of experience. The pandemic has significantly affected the financial positions of many provider organizations (both acute-care operators and physician practices of all sizes) too.

While many of the trends such as the ongoing shift in the point of healthcare delivery to more retail locations and virtual care, as well as increasing momentum for value-based reimbursement models by both payers and providers were in place before the pandemic, but the pandemic can help in accelerating the adoption of these trends in the years to come.

At William Blair's 40th Annual Growth Stock Conference on 10th June 2020, Dan Burton (CEO of Health Catalyst) mentioned that Health

Catalyst has seen a "massive uptick" in use of its data and analytics platform with existing customers. Use of the company's platform has never been higher, and deployment of Health Catalyst's applications suite increased by more than 20% of late (William, 2020).

Recent Example: Memorial Care Health System, (a not-for-profit health system with six hospitals) leveraged Health Catalyst's data operating system (DOS) and ACO risk stratification dashboard. This helped the organization identify patients with the highest mortality risk from COVID-19 (including subcategories for patients over the age of 70, patients under 70 with high-risk underlying conditions such as asthma, and pregnant women). Using this toolset, care management staff from Memorial Care were able to proactively engage 66% of the individuals considered to be extremely high risk (Ryan, 2020).

Healthcare providers made a sharp change to invest in telehealth infrastructure early on in the pandemic to offset declines in traditional visits. Moreover, one of the leading telehealth vendors in the public markets, Teladoc, reported sharp increases in utilization of its platform when stay-at-home orders began (Teladoc Investor Presentation, 2020). In a press release issued on March 13, Teladoc reported a 50% week-over-week uptick in visit volume, with more than 15,000 visits conducted per day, highlighting the speed at which patients pivoted to virtual care. Lastly, Intermountain Healthcare, which has supported telehealth since 2012, hosted 63,000 virtual patient visits in April 2020, up from only 7,000 the month prior (Harrison, 2020).

In a nutshell, we agree with Health Catalyst CEO Dan Burton, who noted in the company's first quarter 2020 earnings conference call: "we cannot think of any event in recent history that has galvanized the awareness and importance of data and analytics more than COVID-19 not only at the healthcare provider level, but also at the state and national healthcare infrastructure levels. As such, we believe that we have reached an inflection point in our healthcare delivery model, which is likely to serve as a medium- to long-term tailwind in the industry's adoption of data and analytics".

7. National Health Mission: Indian Approach

In July 2019, the Ministry of Health and Family Welfare released the National Digital Health Blueprint in the public domain. This National

Digital Health Blueprint is an extension of the National Health Policy of 2017 (NHP, 2017) that was formulated to provide universal healthcare to all citizens of India based on digital technologies. In 2018, the NITI Aayog introduced the National Health Stack (NHS), which is a digital arrangement aimed at developing a clearer and sturdier health insurance system.[4]

The NHS covers multiple mechanisms:

- an electronic national health registry that would function as a single foundation of health data for the nation.
- a coverage and claims platform to function as the building block for robust health protection schemes, allowing for the horizontal and vertical expansion of schemes such as Ayushman Bharat by the states, and further allowing a robust system of fraud detection.
- a Federated Personal Health Records (PHR) system to provide the citizens with access to their health data, and further facilitating the accessibility of the health data for medical research, which is crucial for evolving the understanding of human health.
- introduction of National Health Analytics (NHA). The NHA provides an inclusive data-sharing platform covering various health schemes, and sustaining this platform for smart policymaking and regulation by way of improved techniques, such as, for example, by enhanced projecting analytics.
- introduction of supplementary horizontal systems with a unique digital health ID, health data language, and supply chain control via health programs.

The underlying idea is to make a national digital health ecosystem that supports universal health coverage in a competent, available, comprehensive, reasonable, opportune, and safe manner, through the provision of an extensive collection of data, information, and infrastructure services.

The key features of this blueprint include a unified architecture, a set of architectural elements, a five-layered structure of architectural institutional blocks, a Unique Health ID (UHID), privacy and consent control,

---

[4] https://www.expresshealthcare.in/blogs/guest-blogs-healthcare/national-digital-health-blueprint-an-overview-opportunities-and-legal-challenges/422168/.

national portability, electronic health records, appropriate principles and guidelines, and health analytics. But the concerns are the following:

(1) This National Blueprint illustrates yet another example of *the Centrer moving forward with a major digitization program involving the data of millions of citizens without a data protection law in place*.
(2) Data security is a prerequisite for any data movement. Currently, data privacy in health is a questionable area.
(3) Blueprint proposes *a health data set-up on a foundation of India Stack* — a bouquet of privately-owned proprietary software applications.[5]

Herein lies the imperative of considering blockchain tech as a publicly owned and controlled backbone for data management powering the software applications mentioned above. In this way, consumer protections and privacy, data security and integrity, interoperability and patient-consented accessibility across the spectrum of stakeholders are guaranteed *By Design* and not laws and sanctions and monitoring/enforcement activities, etc.

8. Technical Underpinning of Blockchain-Based Databases

Applications running on the World Wide Web (web 2.0) most often use a client-server network architecture. By changing the "master copy" on the server, whenever a user accesses a database using their computer, they will get the updated version of the database entry. Control of the database remains with administrators, allowing for access and permissions to be maintained by a central authority. For a blockchain database, each participant maintains, calculates, and updates new entries into the database. All participant nodes work collaboratively to co-create a database through open source software that ensure they are all coming to the same conclusions independently, thereby providing in-built cyber security and data

[5] https://www.expresshealthcare.in/blogs/guest-blogs-healthcare/national-digital-health-blueprint-an-overview-opportunities-and-legal-challenges/422168/.

integrity for the entire network of users and relevant stakeholders. In this way, databases can be managed autonomously. There's no need for an administrator; the users are the administrator.

The nice thing about medical records is there is no Facebook for medical records.

Web 2.0 is when a central authority essentially tracks you, uses that data to help you — and also monetizes that data for themselves by essentially renting the algorithms/code (customer is the product, selling our data to advertisers) that result from it to advertisers — UK declared FB as digital gangsters recently. So Web 3.0 (blockchain-based backbone for data management) is where we own our data, we have agency over it, and we need *permission* for others to see it — Maybe a knee specialist doesn't need access to your dental health history. Blockchain could allow for this level of personal control.

9. Envisioning Healthcare Ecosystem: Ensuring Trust, Transparency, Privacy, Scalability, and Interoperability

9.1. *Incentivization*

Most of the healthcare solutions on blockchain have tried the easy way, followed by majority of projects to raise capital as well as incentivize the end users, by creating tokens to be used in the ecosystem. On deeper dive, the use of the tokens is no more than raising funds for development of projects or getting them redeemed to avail services only at specific partner institutions, creating small closed silos rather than an open system — which is the main purpose of using blockchain.

Tokenizing projects is a major challenge along with how to incentivize each stakeholder in the ecosystem to use the services; these are the two things needing further research and investigation on how to align healthcare service providers' interests along patient-centric values. Some attempts have been made but still are in nascent stages:

(a) Incentivize patient/customer behavior by reducing insurance premiums.
(b) Incentivize doctors and hospitals for lower readmission rates.

At a time when trust and confidence in reputation-based governance is at an all-time low, blockchain tech offers an algorithmic, ledger-based governance system that uses cryptography in combination with distributed computing standards.

Blockchain offers an unprecedented data "storage & transfer" standard for security, privacy, verifiability, and accessibility that can be managed via smart contracts, controlled by patients/data subjects. It is estimated that health data breaches across the world cost approximately $6.2 billion each year.[6]

- NHS data hack 2018 notes more than a million patient records were compromised.
- Recently, the US government rolled out a $4.3 billion medical records system to help care for the military.
- Because of the military's stringent cybersecurity, physicians were regularly kicked out of the system, causing delays and frustrations for patients and physicians alike. Referrals and orders were lost, and essential health information were sent to the wrong hospitals.
- Since forming the partnership with Cerner two years ago, the EHR project to allow for interoperability and data sharing to enable better care has not yet been deployed.[7]

10. Blockchain Application in Healthcare

A vexing problem facing healthcare systems throughout the world is how to share significant medical data with diverse stakeholders to be used for many purposes, yet ensuring data integrity and protecting patient privacy.

Traditionally, the interoperability of medical data among institutions has followed three models: push, pull, and view. FHIR (Fast Healthcare Interoperability Resources) is supposed to be the savior of healthcare interoperability to allow universal access to patient data across various

[6] https://www.beckershospitalreview.com/healthcare-information-technology/healthcare-breaches-cost-6-2b-annually.html#:~:text=Breaches%20in%20the%20U.S.%20healthcare, from%20IBM%20and%20Ponemon%20Institute.

[7] https://www.beckershospitalreview.com/ehrs/former-va-secretary-decision-to-delay-cerner-ehr-go-live-is-a-sign-the-process-is-working.html.

healthcare ecosystems. Despite increasing levels of electronic availability of patient medical records from outside sources, most hospitals still use physical methods such as mail and fax to share patient health information, according to Office of the National Coordinator (ONC) data.[8]

The rationale for considering a blockchain in electronic healthcare records is twofold. First, it avoids adding another organization between the patient and the records while addressing the four major issues such as fragmented slow access to medical data; system interoperability; patient agency; and improved data quality and quantity for medical research.

Imagine in the near-future where patients have the ability to view, access, and update their medical records in collaboration with their physician in real time.

Imagine that every EHR sends updates about medications, problems, and allergy lists to an open-source, community-wide trusted ledger, so additions and subtractions to the medical record were well understood and auditable across organizations. Instead of just displaying data from a single database, the EHR could display data from every database referenced in the ledger. The result would be perfectly reconciled community-wide information about the patient, with guaranteed integrity from the point of data generation to the point of use, without manual human intervention. What happens to the patient lab reports from Pathlabs? Where do prescriptions and over-the-counter medicines from say Religare end up? How does medical information become integrated for the patient and doctor to utilize?

The blockchain implies a decentralized control mechanism in which all have an interest, but no one exclusively owns it. For example, MedRec does not store health records or require a change in practice. It stores only a signature of the record on a blockchain and notifies the patient, who is ultimately in control of where that record can travel. The signature assures that an unaltered copy of the record is obtained. It also shifts the locus of control from the institution to the patient, and in return burdens and enables the patient to take charge of management.

It has been noted that in the US alone 40 million of the 56 million deaths that occurred in 2012 were from essentially four major conditions: cancer, heart disease, stroke, and respiratory conditions. The main causes for these diseases are obesity, hypertension, sedentary behaviors, tobacco

[8]https://www.beckershospitalreview.com/ehrs/hospitals-use-mail-fax-the-most-to-share-patient-records-onc-report.html.

use, and poor nutrition. Fortunately or unfortunately, these are behaviors that can only be changed through proactive involvement of the patient.

But unfortunately, patients have taken a very passive position in their own health due to payer and provider dominance and siloed clinical behavioral data. And blockchain technology can break down those silos, can enable self-sovereign health record, a global unique identifier, and allow for the secure and seamless transfer of clinical and behavioral data among patient-authorized stakeholders. The patient could add a layer on top of it … This is what may even be the most unique aspect, an incentive model through digital tokens that can reward positive and proactive behaviors. And so, one can start to build an ecosystem that's driven by the patient.

Blockchain tech allows people to take back control, agency, and ownership of their own health data and consequently take charge of their own health. At present, we have frustrated patients and frustrated doctors because patients have data stored in multiple EHRs across multiple primary care physicians or specialists. They may have their behavioral data in an app stored in MyFitnessPal. Perhaps their steps are in HealthKit or a Fitbit app. Demographic info in one place, socioeconomic info in another, pain, stress, sleep, etc. are not even recorded. Hence, all these valuable contextual data are spread over all these different silos. Scattered. Even the promise of artificial intelligence and machine learning have not been realized because we cannot really get all this data in one place. We have broad, shallow data. We do not have deep data, which includes clinical information.

Medical imaging is another perfect example. We are still burning images onto CDs and DVDs to transfer them by hand.

The basic idea is to use blockchain technology to get all the data in a personal cloud storage that can be protected by a distributed ledger technology and controlled by the patient by giving permissions. Eventually, the process is to bring together health apps, wearables, implants, mobile health solutions, handheld med tech, and various EHR data, as well as medical imaging data, into a single, blockchain-protected, personal cloud storage tied to a global unique identifier mapped to individuals that can transcend across state and national boundaries, that can be shared through this open source network. All these things are essential to maximizing patient's health over long periods of time, without individually tracking them at various locations.

This enables a person traveling anywhere in the world to access their complete medical history at the click of a button from any medical doctor's office.

So how would this work? Mary might go to Dr. Jones's office. She has an app with a QR code on it, that's her public cryptographic key. Dr. Jones will scan that public cryptographic key, and he or she has their own cryptographic key, and that will allow for the transfer of clinical data, medical imaging data, into Mary's personal cloud storage. Subsequently, suppose she goes to Dr. Smith, who might be a cardiologist or might be another specialist who wants to study her records of care with another provider. At the same time, the patient is compiling this data into her own personal cloud storage. And in addition to that, she's also compiling information over weeks and months of behavioral data, geographic data, sleep, blood pressure, weight. Thus, there is contextual information with clinical data that can really facilitate AI, machine learning, and predictive analytics, allowing us to identify the true predictors of health and disease.

And so what this does is, it allows a patient to truly be empowered, because they have access. They have control of a growing information set that they can then share based on permissions built into the blockchain.

Blockchains in healthcare can also improve coordination challenges and incentive systems. Blockchain enabled contracts make money "programmable" by predefining the rules and agreements between parties. For example,

- In the complicated and often fragmented hospital setting, where efficient tracking of pharmacy orders, medical devices, surgical tools, and critical resources is essential, blockchain is already showing itself to be a new approach worth exploring. Say a hospital's inventory of blood pressure cuffs or insulin decreases to a certain level. A smart contract can automatically reorder the product, pay for the shipment, and record the transaction in a distributed ledger which multiple parties can review. Before a physician can officially join an office, network, or hospital, the organization must confirm credentials like education, licensing, and more. As it stands, it takes 120 days[9] to transfer physician data on average. Blockchain could change that. A PwC report[10] states that blockchain-enabled system would permit data relevant to the provider and payer credentialing process to be shared and updated in real time. Processes that take weeks or months could be accomplished in days. Back-office functions and payments

[9] https://www.namss.org/Portals/0/Regulatory/NAMSS%20Roundtable%20Credentialing%20Best%20Practice%20Criteria%20White%20Paper.pdf.

[10] https://www.pwc.com/us/blockchainhealthcare.

could be managed similarly. Contracts and payments checked manually in a long linear process, but blockchain transactions could be coded into smart contracts, with information stored on blockchain. This would lead to reduction of the time it takes to make and audit payments and cut back on contract fulfillment time and fraud.

Blockchain-based products are being launched by tech companies such as IBM's *trust your supplier* to adapt existing blockchain supply chain products for hospitals to use during the Covid crisis. Hospitals facing shortages need to expand their supply chain quickly.

Blockchain allows companies to share data without fear it will fall into the wrong hands. Vetting new suppliers takes time, usually one to two months, even if other hospitals have worked with the companies, asking the same questions, and verifying the same information. Blockchain tech can allow those suppliers to create a verifiable digital identity; The company that first works with the supplier puts them through the usual vetting process, and subsequent companies in the network are able to rely on that validation process and substantially shorten their own time for due diligence, saving time and money.

- Programmable money also makes it possible to create powerful, real-time incentive systems that extend well beyond the supply chain. Some of these can influence behavior. For example, a company could set up a smart contract to release funds as soon as an employee walks a certain number of miles per week, passively tracked via a wearable.
- A smart contract could also speed up outcome-based reimbursement by releasing bonuses to hospitals that lower their readmissions by a predetermined percentage.
- Blockchain also enables data confidentiality and integrity and thus addresses issues within medical insurance and fake drugs.
- Chronicle is an example from the Industry building an electronic system that would meet the requirements of the "Drug Supply Chain Security" Act to identify and trace prescription drugs distributed in the United States. This blockchain-based project would help companies comply with "track and trace" regulations, making the transfer of custody from a pharmaceutical company to a lab, hospital, and patient more secure. Using a decentralized blockchain that makes permanent, time-stamped records removes the risk of having a rogue central system administrator edit, modify, delete, or alter records.

India is importing illegal cancer drugs worth ₹300 crore from Bangladesh. The exorbitant price of cancer drugs has turned India into a thriving market for spurious drugs. This racket is being run by smugglers who are sourcing them from Bangladesh and other neighboring countries.

A few pharma companies from Bangladesh are targeting patients and doctors across the border via chemists located near cancer hospitals, suggested *Journal of Medical Sciences*. As it stands, almost every party involved in the shipping process of a given drug struggles to know exactly where a specific shipment comes from. They trust that the party in the chain one level before them performed all their duties appropriately, and the products were not switched or mishandled before they reached the distributor. In the 1980s, patients who tested HIV-positive needed blood and hospitals held blood drives, the bags were quickly marked and shipped off, and even though they were re-tested in a lab before being administered to patients, there was still a lot of room for error.[11]

Today, we are seeing this happen with more specialized treatments such as gene therapy. Patients must provide samples of their DNA (or stem cells are withdrawn) and then the drug is created specifically for that individual patient. But throughout that entire process, samples have to move from the patient to the drug manufacturing facility, and then from the facility back to the hospital, where it is stored and finally administered.

Elaborating on the blockchain solution: The samples from the lab are noted with a cryptographic identity similar to the chip in your credit card and a destructible tamperproof form factor that prevents moving a chip and seal from one vial to another. The mobile App is used to register the identity in the CryptoSeal to the blockchain and then, the same mobile app can be used at the other end of the chain to verify the shipment that has been received by the lab or the patient or the doctor. The record keeping on blockchain is permanent in case there is ever a need to prove the record keeping. The advantage of blockchain over a central database is that a central database has a systems administrator who can edit, modify, delete, or alter records if the stakes are high enough — which is not the case with a blockchain. With the blockchain the records are permanent and cannot ever be changed. This is what is meant by blockchain-enabled "secure transfer of custody"

[11] https://www.ncbi.nlm.nih.gov/books/NBK232419/.

- Another notable example is the case where the Estonian government partnered with Guardtime, an enterprise blockchain system, to implement a verifiable tracker any time someone accesses a healthcare record or makes a change in it. This means recording and reporting whenever an insurance broker — or anyone else — looks at an individual's secure data online. As the *New Yorker* reported, in Estonia "peeping at another person's secure data for no reason is a criminal offense", and blockchains create a mechanism to track those violations.
- Addressing issues of data accessibility for medical research and clinical trials, OpenMined is developing artificial intelligence algorithms that can be trained on data it never has full access to. This is a revolutionary breakthrough: the ability to perform calculations on encrypted information without decrypting it first. Put in practice, something like this could mean that a patient who wants to participate in research or a clinical trial would never have to share a decrypted copy of his or her personal information.

Therefore, blockchain tech provides not only an optimal infrastructure or mechanism for secure and privacy preserving data exchange but can also be designed to incentivize participation by creating a health data marketplace.

In this way, it presents a solution to both: to the problem of interoperability in healthcare and the generation of an entirely new community led economy — facilitating new connections, collaborations and innovations, and creating significant business opportunities, while widening access to healthcare, and ultimately lowering the cost of its delivery.

Let us take the example of a specific project called Grapevine. The Grapevine Token (GVINE) is used on its platform to incentivize and provide a mechanism of data sharing. From hospitals to local doctors and specialized medical care units, all systems will be able to communicate with each other seamlessly upon the patients' approval to share their personal medical history. From an institutional point of view, Grapevine blockchain will offer an open environment where data and information can be made available to other players in the industry such as universities, pharma, technology companies, medical device manufacturers, and Healthcare Provider Organizations (HPOs). Their costs in order to acquire this information will drop significantly thanks to Grapevine.

Currently, this process is very costly, there is a lot of litigation involved and, consequently, a lot of research is just halted. According to a Cutting-Edge information report published in 2013, the most significant factor for increased clinical trial costs *is patient recruitment* where per patient costs topped $40. According to the WHO's (World Health Organization) report in 2017, lack of empirical data is one of the major obstacles for formulating the necessary policy to ensure healthy lives and promote well-being for all ages.

Blockchain technology can create a win–win situation as opposed to most current solutions for interoperable health data exchange that are driven by corporate interests, necessarily adopting a "winner-takes-all" attitude. The blockchain implies a decentralized control mechanism in which all have an interest, but no one exclusively owns it.

Research institutes or medical facilities will be able to purchase GVINE and use them on the platform to pay patients to access their anonymized data. Patients will then be able to use their GVINEs for different products and services in the medical sector, such as apps, gadgets, and medical advice and care. Grapevine will not only give patients control of their privacy about their medical data but also help in preventing mistakes in diagnosis and prescriptions. Essentially saving more than 400,000 lives each year, which are lost due to medical errors resulting from absence of an interoperable healthcare.

References

BIS Research (2018), *Global Big Data in Healthcare Market to Reach $68.75 Billion by 2025*, Available at https://www.prnewswire.com/news-releases/global-big-data-in-healthcare-market-to-reach-6875-billion-by-2025-reports-bis-research-678151823.html.

BIS Research (2020), *Global Big Data in Healthcare Market: Analysis and Forecast, 2017–2025*. Available at https://bisresearch.com/industry-report/global-big-data-in-healthcare-market-research-report-forecast-614.html.

Brinkmann, B. (2019), *Comparing Descriptive, Predictive, Prescriptive, and Diagnostic Analytics*. Logistic Analytics, Available at https://www.logianalytics.com/predictive-analytics/comparing-descriptive-predictive-prescriptive-and-diagnostic-analytics/#:~:text=Descriptive%20Analytics%20tells%20you%20what.

CMS (2020), *US Health Care Spending Will Reach $4T in 2020.* Available at https://www.advisory.com/daily-briefing/2020/04/03/health-spending#:~:text=CMS%20in%20the%20report%20estimated,up%20from%2017.7%25%20in%202018.

Harrison, M. (2020), *What One Health Care CEO Is Learning from the Pandemic.* Harvard Business Review, Available at https://hbr.org/2020/07/what-one-health-care-ceo-is-learning-from-the-pandemic.

HealthITSecurity (2019), *As Artificial Intelligence Matures, Healthcare Eyes Data Aggregation.* Available at healthitanalytics.com/features/as-artificial-intelligence-matures-healthcare-eyes-data-aggregation.

Markets and Markets (2020a), *Healthcare IT Market Worth $390.7 Billion by 2024,* Available at https://www.marketsandmarkets.com/PressReleases/healthcare-it-market.asp.

Markets and Markets (2020b), *IoT in Healthcare Market. 2020*, Available at https:// www.marketsandmarkets.com/Market-Reports/iot-healthcare-market-160082804.html.

Netscribes (2020), Healthcare analytics market in India, Available at https://www.netscribes.com/industries/healthcare/.

Ryan, D. (2020), *Healthcare Mosaic Preparing for a Post-Pandemic World; Top Five Expectations for the Post-COVID Marketplace.*

TRG Datacenters (2019), *6 Healthcare Technology Trends and Their Impact on IT Infrastructure.* Available at https://www.trgdatacenters.com/6-healthcare-technology-trends-and-their-impact-on-it-infrastructure/#:~:text=McKinsey%20says%20data%2Dcrunching%20algorithms.

William, B. (2020), *William Blair Hosts 40th Annual Growth Stock Conference | William Blair.* Available at https://www.williamblair.com/en/News-Items/2020/June/09/William-Blair-Hosts-40th-Annual-Growth-Stock-Conference.aspx.

https://doi.org/10.1142/9789811220470_bmatter

Index

D

I

K

L

M

O

P

Lightning Source UK Ltd.
Milton Keynes UK
UKHW021831231120
373954UK00004B/311

9 789811 220463